EARLY ISLAM

EARLY ISLAM

A Critical Reconstruction Based on Contemporary Sources

Edited by KARL-HEINZ OHLIG

Prometheus Books
59 John Glenn Drive
Amherst, New York 14228–2119

Published 2013 by Prometheus Books

Cover design by Jacqueline Nasso Cooke
Cover image © javarman/Shutterstock.com

Inquiries should be addressed to
Prometheus Books
59 John Glenn Drive
Amherst, New York 14228–2119
VOICE: 716–691–0133
FAX: 716–691–0137
WWW.PROMETHEUSBOOKS.COM

17 16 15 14 13   5 4 3 2 1

Library of Congress Cataloging-in-Publication Data

Frühe Islam. English
Early Islam : a critical reconstruction based on contemporary sources / [edited by] Karl-Heinz Ohlig.
pages cm
Includes bibliographical references.
ISBN 978-1-61614-825-6 (hardback)
ISBN 978-1-61614-826-3 (ebook)
1. Islam—History. I. Ohlig, Karl-Heinz, 1938- II. Title.

BP55.D4713 2013
297.09'021—dc23

2013030228

Printed in the United States of America

Early Islam – Contents

ENDNOTES

Foreword to the English Edition

Comparative religious and cultural studies, historical linguistics and philology, especially when the object of one's study are ancient manuscripts, are generally perceived as disciplines of semi-autistic quixotic bookworms, who volunteer to be buried alive in an ivory-tower, where they can avoid contact with living beings and instead plunge into the assiduous study of yellowed manuscripts and dusty old books with incomprehensible contents.

A short look at the history of modern Western civilization, the roots of the Era of Enlightenment and the development of scholarly standards, however, teaches us that it was precisely this often ridiculed brand of humans that prompted a development bound to change the world.

Until the mid 17th century the Bible was considered the "word of God", and especially the Pentateuch was universally acknowledged as a series of books written by Moses himself. It was the philological studies of people like the philosophers Baruch Spinoza (1632-1677), Thomas Hobbes, Isaac de la Peyrère and the French scholar Jean Astruc, who started to question the authorship of this legendary figure for the whole Pentateuch, one of their arguments being the use of the two forms "Yahwe" and "Elohim" to designate God.

The doubt they cast on the divine nature of the Bible led to the spiritual revolution commonly called the *Age of Enlightenment*, replacing the primacy of legends, superstitions and alleged revelation by reason, science and rationality.

This process, however, did not take place without backlashes – the human mind often favoring the comfortable way of *believing* over the more demanding one of *thinking* – and the struggle between rationalists and fundamentalists, in some cases rationalist and fundamentalist civilizations, is now more violent than ever.

"Enlightenment" – in Arabic "Inārah", – was chosen as the name of an interdisciplinary group of researchers, originally a Germany-based research society, albeit with members from many countries, which has taken the first steps to rewriting the Islamic history of the first two centuries as it can be reconstructed from material evidence and by strictly applying the historical-critical method.

If one consults any European or American encyclopedia and looks up the entry "Islam", one will find the same legendary story about the beginning of Islam, of the prophet Muḥammad who was born in Mecca around 570 CE, received his first revelation at about the age of forty, founded the religion of Islam and started a new Empire, which just one generation after his death had become a superpower. The same applies for introductory books on religions, Middle Eastern history, documentaries, news programs etc.

Although the first doubts as to the veracity of these reports were already uttered almost forty years ago, – people like Günter Lüling, John Wansbrough and Patricia Crone/ Michael Cook have to be mentioned here –, their opinions and research results have deliberately been ignored and left out of standard works concerning Islamic Studies. At best they were mentioned as mavericks outside the accepted scholarly community.

Unlike Buddhist studies, Iranian Studies, Sinology, Indology and Egyptology – well-established disciplines in our universities –, it is only representatives of Islamic Studies who refuse to question the dogmata, tenets and axioms of the civilization they purport to study. In order not to be reproached with what Edward Said called "orientalism", Western Islamicists keep treating the Muslim tradition as sacrosanct, no matter how thin and questionable the material evidence, and even the myths of the origin of the Qur'ān are taken as a basis for all further study.

INÂRAH wants nothing short of a *paradigm shift*. In Germany, so far six anthologies have appeared (the seventh is in preparation, see below) of an average size of about 600 pages. Moreover, two of our members, Christoph Luxenberg and Karl-Heinz Ohlig, have written monographs about their studies. The reactions to our publications have been mixed so far. While some Islamologists were very open-minded, others did not even deign to consider our arguments. Only two of our publications have been translated into English so far:

Christoph Luxenberg, The Syro-Aramaic Reading of the Koran: A Contribution to the Decoding of the Language of the Koran, Berlin 2007.

Karl-Heinz Ohlig / Gerd-R Puin (eds.), The Hidden Origins of Islam: New Research into Its Early History, Prometheus Books 2009.

In the English-speaking world, the reactions were equally mixed as they were in Germany, with one major difference: Only the two publications that had been translated into English appear in bibliographies. Although Christoph Luxenberg's monograph has been widely discussed in printed and digital form, one of his best articles – the one about the mysterious letters in the Qur'ān – has been entirely ignored as it was published only in German in our third anthology.

The plan to have all of our books translated into English is not new, but considering that INÂRAH is a private society entirely dependent on the donations of members and supporters, this plan had to be postponed.

The present translation of the second anthology would not have been possible without the donation of a private supporter and the kind help we have received from Ibn Warraq.

The translations were made by myself and a small team of translators/ proof-readers. In some cases the authors of the single contributions also checked the English version and in many cases suggested additions and some minor changes, which, however, never affect the core results.

In the German version most of the Qur'ānic quotations had been taken from Paret's prestigious translation with copious commentary. If not otherwise indicated, the English "default" translation is Pickthall's well-known version. For Bible quotations the "New American Standard" was chosen. The transliteration of Qur'ānic passages is from Hans Zirker's version, which is downloadable as a pdf-file:

http://www.eslam.de/begriffe/t/transliteration_des_quran.htm

We hope that this publication will help foster debate on the emergence of Islam, on scientific standards and on history in the sense of "what really happened" and not "what we would like to have happened".

Markus Gross,
Editor of the English edition
Co-editor (together with K.-H. Ohlig) of INÂRAH anthologies 3-6

Other anthologies of the "Inârah Institute for Research on Early Islamic History and the Koran":

Markus Gross / Karl-Heinz Ohlig (eds.), Schlaglichter. Die beiden ersten islamischen Jahrhunderte (Inârah. Schriften zur frühen Islamgeschichte und zum Koran, Vol. 3), publisher: Verlag Hans Schiler: Berlin 2008, 617 pages.

Markus Gross / Karl-Heinz Ohlig (eds.), Vom Koran zum Islam (Inârah. Schriften zur frühen Islamgeschichte und zum Koran, Vol. 4), Verlag Hans Schiler: Berlin 2009, 721 pages.

Markus Gross / Karl-Heinz Ohlig (eds.), Die Entstehung einer Weltreligion I. (Inârah. Schriften zur frühen Islamgeschichte und zum Koran, Vol. 5), Verlag Hans Schiler: Berlin 2010, 490 pages.

Markus Gross / Karl-Heinz Ohlig (eds.), Die Entstehung einer Weltreligion II. (Inârah. Schriften zur frühen Islamgeschichte und zum Koran, Vol. 6), Verlag Hans Schiler: Berlin 2012, 820 pages.

in preparation:
Markus Gross / Karl-Heinz Ohlig (eds.), Die Entstehung einer Weltreligion III. (Inârah. Schriften zur frühen Islamgeschichte und zum Koran, Vol. 7), Verlag Hans Schiler: Berlin.

Shedding Light on the Beginnings of Islam

Karl-Heinz Ohlig

Ignaz Goldziher, one of the "fathers" of Islamic Studies, started off a lecture, which he held in 1900 at the Sorbonne, with the sentence,

> "For a long time we have been content with the simple assertion: All of a sudden Islam came into existence and immediately sprung up *into broad daylight.* (My emphasis, in the original: "au plein jour")."[1]

He warned against drawing on "*the abundant materials*" of Muslim tradition as the source for clarification of "*the early years of Islam*".

> "Modern historical criticism protects us from such an antediluvian method of approach."

Historical criticism may still have been modern around 1900, but no longer after that. Goldziher's warning against the easy way was not heeded and early history of Islam was and still is interpreted back from the Sīrah and Ṭabarī, despite all those reservations expressed incidentally and despite critical publications, which were not widely received.

However, the apparent *broad daylight* did not exist for the first two Muslim centuries, because the sources used are not conclusive. In the anthology "The Hidden Origins",[2] a number of Western researchers of Islam have had a go at working on different aspects of this early history by means of historic criticism. The way was cleared to further analysis.

The present volume is continuing along this path. Since not only contemporary Muslim literary sources – apart from the Qur'ān – are missing, regarding the first two centuries, but also the Christian sources at the time report of *Arabs, Saracens, Ismaelites* and so forth, but not, however, of a *new religion* and a succession of events according to later Muslim historiography,[3] a reconstruction of the actual development can only be achieved by falling back on the only dateable and locatable evidence: coins and inscriptions; this history is analyzed and illustrated by Volker Popp.[4] Due to the scantiness of the symbols and texts documented in this fashion, obviously some statements concerning the question of detail remain hypothetical. However, it is still possible to identify the fundamentals of historical and theological development in the history of early Islam.

Coins make it clear that for a long time *muḥammad* was not a name, but a motto which puts the value of the Messiah Jesus, son of Mary – as in the inscription on the Dome of the Rock –, right at the center of this both religious and political concept.

'Abd al-Malik brought this concept from the regions of eastern Mesopotamia and it spread as far as West Syria. The motto *muḥammad* was first historicized and considered to be a name during the 8th century and supported by a biography in the 9th century.[5]

Qur'ānic Material, which retains a theology and a Christology of a pre-Nicean kind in its countries of origin, also came from the East to the West with 'Abd al-Malik, and has developed further in isolation – in a sect-like manner.

In the time of 'Abd al-Malik these originally Aramaic (and possibly Middle Persian) texts were transcribed into a kind of Arabic originating from Syria – a Syro-Aramaic mixed language.[6] This "original Qur'ān", of which the exact scope is unknown, was expanded during the 8th (and possibly also the 9th) centuries.

The Qur'ānic material does not only have a history of the spoken word in Syriac, but had evidently been secured in written form before its transcription into Arabic.

By looking at errors which occurred during transcription, Christoph Luxenberg – in an 'empirical' manner – proves the existence of texts written in Syriac.[7]

More than a hundred years ago, Ignaz Goldziher already illustrated instances of the adoption of Persian concepts and notions into Islam.[8] This trail has hardly been followed up at all. Here there is a definite deficit both in Christian historiography, in which there is no mention of inculturation of (Syrian and Arabian) Christianity into Persian culture to be found, and in Islamic Studies, which did not take up the idea of I. Goldziher. Volker Popp analyzes these influences using several illustrative examples.[9]

Previous analyses of the language of the Qur'ān will be reinforced by a comparative linguistic analysis by Markus Groß of records of both spoken and written texts from numerous cultures and religions and will therefore be put into a broader context.[10]

As a whole the political and religious development in the 7th and 8th centuries is quite complex. Many aspects have to be considered: the history of the Ancient Near East, the political and military conflicts between the Byzantines, the Sassanians, and the Arabs, the role of the peoples living in these realms, history of religions and missions, the varied cultural traditions and their influences beyond their original peoples and so forth. Thus many questions not only concerning details but also very central aspects cannot (yet) be answered.

However, there is a fundamental prospect of finding answers that are justifiable based on the historical-critical method, provided that research can avoid getting in the way of itself. This self-limitation essentially comes down to *not questioning* the fundamental theories of Islamic literature of the 3rd century AH (Islamic year), i.e., the 9th century CE, despite all reservations about its historic and religious validity. These tenets are the following:

(1) The Qur'ān is attributed to the proclamation of the Prophet of the Arabs Muḥammed, who lived and preached from 570 to 632;
(2) All of this took place on the Arabian peninsula, in Mecca and Medina;
(3) The final version of the Qur'ān already existed soon after the death of the prophet;
(4) Islam was already a complete new religion in the early 7th century;
(5) The language of the Qur'ān is pure Arabic.

A scientific approach to these theories calls for them to be treated at least once with *systematic scepticism* and to check whether they can be verified using *contemporary* historical documents and the literary characteristics of the texts. If so, there would be a definite starting point; if not, research must endeavor to document, analyze, and interpret the source material still available.

This is what the present volume attempts to do. The whole work demonstrates how the beginnings of a Qur'ānic movement originated from a specific form of Christianity and came from regions much further east of Mesopotamia and not from the Arabian Peninsula. Basically after the victory of Heraclius in 622, and factually after the collapse of Sassanid rule, which happened soon after, this peculiar tradition was able to find its way from the East to the West, to Jerusalem and to Damascus, and was documented there in an Arabian-Syrian mixed language. Further complex, though to a certain extent understandable developments led to the formation of the *Šīʿa* (Shi'ah), which initially was still characterized by Christian motives, and shortly afterwards to an independent religion (towards the end of the 8th and in the first decades of the 9th century). Traditional literature, which was shaped following Persian conceptual patterns, later on composed a splendid re-interpretation of these first two centuries of Islam from the perspective of the putative "knowledge" of its own time about the alleged origins of the religion.

Theological, and in this case Islamological analysis, only makes sense if methods are used which stand the test of historical criticism. Of course, mistakes may be made in the process which have to be corrected during one of the subsequent academic discussions. The authors of this volume are aware of this and do not consider their theories to be unalterable and the last word. They are, however, convinced that the contemporary sources available up to the present day provide the only (in the historical-critical sense) sound access to the earliest stages of the religious and political history of the 7th and 8th centuries in the Ancient Near East and adjacent territories, its peculiarities and motives.

It must be mentioned that already in the 19th century there had been a series of valuable detailed analyses, which, however, often failed to understand the relevance of their own findings. If the authors of these studies themselves frequently did not draw the obvious conclusions, it is not surprising that their colleagues did so even less.

Self-limitation and the refusal to take into consideration what neighboring disciplines have found was and is another major obstacle in Islamic Studies. Only if History of Theology, Church History, Islamic Studies, Iranian Studies and philological and linguistic disciplines cooperate, can the phenomena to be analyzed be properly investigated, as the objects of research can hardly be assigned to only one field of research and thus have to be looked at from different angles. Interdisciplinary cooperation in terms of research is imperative for such questions.

The objective must be to understand historical phenomena as they originally were. Research is at no time concerned with damaging any religion, which, in this case, would be Islam. In comparative religious studies, all religions are analyzed theologically in this way, from religions of the past to religions of the present and those which have potential for the future. The Age of Enlightenment – after an initial phase of antagonism and disruptions – has not harmed Christianity, indeed, quite the opposite, it has facilitated its modernization; difficulties only occur with incidents of regression behind the critical level of knowledge already reached.

Understanding the historic beginnings – for Islamic Studies a given postulate from the start – will not harm Islam and its theology –, but could serve to bring it forward into a modern and pluralistic world.

From Ugarit to Sāmarrā’

An Archeological Journey on the Trail of Ernst Herzfeld[1]

Volker Popp

Preliminary Remarks

On the following pages, the history of a religious movement later to be known as *Islam* will be retold, – not as it can be found in all encyclopedias, history books and TV documentaries, – but as it can be inferred from the material evidence if investigated in an unbiased fashion. "Unbiased" here means that all we know – or rather only seemingly know – from the Islamic historiographic literature (the "Traditional Account/ Report") will be ignored: First as it stems from an era several centuries after the alleged events it describes, secondly as it is mostly legendary and follows a "theological program", and thirdly as in many cases it flatly contradicts the material evidence we have on coins, inscriptions etc. The re-interpreted history will be presented in the form of the account of a journey. In some cases, words everyone would expect in a history of "early Islam" will not appear, and for good reason. The term *"muslim"*, for example, appears only very late on in non-Islamic sources, in fact only several generations after the alleged founding of the new religion. Other words appear with different meanings, e.g. "*Islām*" originally does not designate a new religion, "*ʿArabī*" does not designate an ethnic group and other examples.

1. A few remarks on the Prehistory of the Qur’ān and of Islām

1.1 Where *muḥammad* and *ṣamad* originally came from and what the term "Arabia" originally designated

The archeological journey commences with an etymological and a historical reminiscence. Ugarit, a town in Canaan, which had already been destroyed in the 13th century BC, was significant with reference to expressions which have remained in Ancient Near East culture since then and have been reused later. The reference to Ḥaṭrā makes it clear that *Arabia* originally had nothing to do with the Arabian Peninsula, but was in Mesopotamia (and in the region dominated by the Nabateans).

1.2 About Ugarit

In 1928 the ruins of a city-state, circa 0.25 square miles, were discovered by accident on the Syrian coast of the Mediterranean Sea. Comprehensive archives have been found in the three palaces excavated so far. These also contained texts in cuneiform consonant script, the language being Ugaritic, a Semitic language. It contained mythical and cultic poetry of a Canaanite people with parallels to the Bible.

In these texts the term "*M(u)Ḥ(a)M(ma)D*" is also to be found. It is connected to gold and refers to the best, selected quality of gold at its highest level of purity. The word appears in a text which is analyzed in Segert's[2] standard grammar:

> "15. tblk. ǵrm. mid. ksp. (The mountains will bring you much silver)
> 16. gbʿm. *mḥmd.* ḫrṣ (and the hills *desirable* gold)." (my emphasis)

Segert's translation of the form, "desirable, precious (thing)", together with Gordon's[3] rendering, "the best/choicest of gold", show that the literal sense of the word *mḥmd* in Ugaritic was "best, select(ed)" or "choicest of, chosen", a meaning which remained until the time of early "Islām". Even the fathers of Islamic tradition still take *muḥammad(un)* to mean *selected* or *chosen one.*

In this respect we might consider what Alois Sprenger said about the dawn of Islam:

> "If the name Mohammed had been commonplace amongst the heathen Arabs, then the fact that their prophet had that name could have been regarded as incidental. Let us, however, hear what Muslim theologists have to say on this matter, which – after the way that he came to this name had been forgotten, – well and truly exploited these circumstances when discussing with Jews and Christians.
>
> Ibn Mosayyib (who died AH 90 at the age of 80) says, 'The Arabs had heard from the proprietors of scripts and their own prophesiers that a prophet would emerge from amongst them and his name would be Mohammed. Some fathers then called their sons Mohammad in the hope that they would be chosen to take on this responsibility.'"[4]

Another expression is found in Ugarit texts – "Ṣ(a)M(a)Ḏ" – which only crops up again after almost two millennia in connection with a Qur'ānic text. In surah 112 of the Qur'ān God is described as "al- Ṣ(a)M(a)D(u)".[5]

Around 1210 BC the storm of the so-called "Sea peoples", an alliance of seafaring raiders probably from the Aegean Sea, devastated Ugarit.[6] Nobody settled in the ruins again. The existence of Ugarit only came to the knowledge of the ensuing ages in the 20th century when the texts written in cuneiform script in the Ugarit language were deciphered and read. Only now did it become possible to gain access to the "archeology" of some religious *topoi* which had been passed on by tradition for millennia.

1.3 Concerning Ḥaṭrā

The ruins of Ḥaṭrā (Ḥaṭrā), which are still impressive today, lie in the region of Gazaratâ, the area of Upper Mesopotamia separated by the Tigris and Euphrates rivers, in the so-called *Jazīra* (*Ǧazīra*; secondary meaning in Arabic: "island", "peninsula"), the land between the Tigris and the Euphrates. The town itself is connected to the Tigris by the Wādī Ṯarṯār. These links between Ḥaṭrā and the deep rivers (*al-baḥr*) made fishing and sea transport possible. The town was also connected to the Roman road system. Ḥaṭrā's heyday was in the 2nd century when the Romans were in Mesopotamia, but could not overcome Ḥaṭrā's walls.

The town was surrounded by an almost perfectly circular wall. In the centre of the circle was the temple of the Sun God.[7] The construction of Ḥaṭrā as a round town with a sacred area at the centre was the archetype for the conception of Baġdād being a round town later on. We have no inscriptions which refer to the Name "Baġdād" from the days of the Abbasid caliphs. The earliest epigraphic testimony of the use of this term as a place-name is a coin inscription on an issue of the Mongol conquerors after the destruction of the caliphate in 1258 CE, dated (AH) 656.[8] Once the Abbasid caliphate was defunct, the Middle Persian reading "Baġdād (God's Grace/Gratia Dei)" of the ideogram "Heleka Yahweh" was used as a place-name for the location, where "God's Grace", the caliph, had acted by the *Grace of God* as leader "Dei Gratia (Ḫalqat Allah)" until the demise of the Caliphate in the year AH 653.

However, the idea of an ideal and typical round town lived on and was finally realized by the brother of the Abbasid caliph, al-Ma'mūn, the misunderstood al-Mu'tasim, when he built Sāmarrā', his residence, in the 9th century.

Contemporary inscriptions make reference to the rulers of Ḥaṭrā as *"mlk hdr"* and to the whole of the *(a)ʿR(a)B*.

In the language of Ḥaṭrā, *(a)ʿR(a)B* simply means: *West*. Today a flight from Israel to Europe is therefore a flight to "*eʿR(e)B*" (מערב – *(m)ʿrb* means "west" in Hebrew). From the Israeli perspective Europe is "*(a)ʿR(a)B*".

According to these inscriptions the king of Ḥaṭrā reigned over a town and the surrounding land. This corresponds to the idea of rulers having their domicile in one town and simply incorporating the surrounding land, common also in later times. For the 7th century, in the case of Syria, it is known that there was an issue of coinage for the town of Tiberias on the Sea of Galilee and, at the same time, there was a separate issue for the surrounding land. Therefore QTRĪ (phonetic: *qutrā*) was added, an Arabization of the Persian term *kūrā* (district), which is derived from the Greek expression *chôra* for "environs". In Arabic there is a plural form: *kuwar*.[9] The "environs of" or "land surrounding" Ḥaṭrā is called "*(a)ʿR(a)B*", as it lies to the West when seen from the Tigris. Thus "*Arabia on the island*" is in Mesopotamia. This is also confirmed by Xenophanes, whereas the Romans referred to the Nabataean region as a "Province of Arabia".[10]

The inhabitants of this "Arabia on the island" (Arabic: *Ǧazīra*) between the Tigris and Euphrates, were not *Arabic-speaking Arabs*, but "*(A)ʿr(a)bī*", i.e., inhabitants of the "West". That is why they did not speak *Arabic* (*lisān al-ʿArab*), but "*(A)ʿr(a)bī*", the *language of the province of Ḥaṭrā*.

The only definite thing we can say about this language is that it was neither Greek nor Latin; as this would have been perceived by contemporary writers and passed on to ensuing generations. Just what is to be understood by "*(A)ʿr(a)bī*", the language of the *(A)ʿr(a)b* region, remains undetermined in tradition. Even in the Qur'ān it is unclear as to which language *Aʿr(a)bī* refers to. According to the common view *lisān(un) ʿarabī(yun) mubīn(un)* (surah 16:103) refers to the (clear) Arabic language (R. Paret). At a different point (surah 9:90), however, R. Paret translates *al-(A)ʿr(a)b* as "Bedouin". If, then, according to Paret, "(A)ʿr(a)bī" means *Bedouin* and also designates the *language of the nomadic people of the desert* (following the tradition of a romantic orientalism), then it is still unknown as to how the *(A)ʿr(a)bī* living in Arabia, i.e. in the Jazīra between the Tigris and Euphrates, could have adopted the language later known as *Arabic*.[11]

Only knowledge of historical developments in the region leads to any results. Philology fails to achieve anything as an essential tool is missing: an etymological dictionary of Arabic. With the aid of such a dictionary it would be possible to check if there are any links – and if there are, then which ones – between *(A)ʿr(a)bī* and *Arabic*, and how these can be explained with the help of historical linguistics.

Clarifying the historic sequence of events in the region can illustrate just to what degree the resident population were the victims of war and disaster. In the case we are discussing the original speakers of the language of the Qur'ān (a language not identical to Classical Arabic) were later replaced or superseded by populations who then, during the Islamic era, can be considered as *Arabic-speaking Arabs*, whose language R. Paret believes was already to be found in the Qur'ān. Before Arabic-speaking Arabs could emerge in this region (in the 9th century CE), it was to take many historic upheavals. Only then could the Persian Sībawayh from Basra write his famous grammar of their Arabic language.

1.4 The Appearance of the Sassanians (appr. 224–651 CE) and the downfall of Ḥaṭrā (241 CE)

The Sassanians, like the Achaemenids, had their official homelands in the Persis (Southern Iran). The history of this dynasty shows that the Sassanians were anxious to re-establish Iran as ruler of the Ancient Near East following the example set by the Achaemenids (approx. 7th century BCE - 330 BCE). The historical myth that surrounds the Sassanian dynasty includes elements which are to be seen as constants in Iran and on the Arabian Peninsula up until the present: the link between cult and rule.

A part of the beginnings of the dynasty is said to go back to the marriage of Sāsān (Sāsān x^wadāy), the custodian of the "Fire Temple of Anāhid" at Istakhr (Eṣṭakr), who married a princess of the Bāzarangid family, the vassal dynasty of Fārs (Ṭabari, I, pp. 813-14)[12]. The son from this marriage, Pāpak, procured the office of "Castellan (*argbed*) of Dārābjird (Dārābgerd) for his youngest son Ardašir. That is as far as the account of the Ardašir story goes. This work recounts the foundation of the realm in poetic form.[13]

The systematization of the legendary early years of Islam was conducted in the Sassanian period. Among the Sassanians this literature was regarded as part of Iranian historiography. In later years, further parts of "Iran's history" were recorded in poetic form: the story of the "Arabian" successors of the Sassanians (i.e., the historiographic Arabic literature of the 9th century). A lot of this allegedly *Arabic* historiography is actually *Persian*, and little is actually historiography in terms of the European and American historiographic tradition.

The link between the occupancy of Dārābjird and the rule in Iran was to turn out to be a long-lasting constant. Even the Arabian successors of the Sassanians had first to claim occupancy of Dārābjird before they could reckon with any recognition from the Iranian emirs.

Šāpur I. (241–272 CE) conquered Ḥaṭrā. The ruins of the town were never inhabited again. The fate of the population is not known, however, it is assumed there was a mass deportation of people. It was only in the 20th century that excavation work was started.

1.5 Systematic Deportation as a Part of the Sassanian Rule

The history of Sassanian victories in the Roman Orient and later in the Byzantine Orient is linked to constant deportation of the subjugated to the East, the inner regions of the realm. Amongst those deported from Ḥaṭrā were Christians. These Christians probably took Tatian's Diatessaron, the Gospel Harmony which originated in this region, with them.

Besides Ḥaṭrā and Durā-Europos on the Euphrates, Šāpur I also conquered Antioch in Syria. The Bishop of Antioch together with all his religious community were incorporated into the newly founded Gundeshapur (Gund-ī

Shāh Pūr) in Khûzistân. It was in this way that Gundeshapur became the new home of Antiochian theology.

Thus the participation of Antiochian and Syrian Christians in the inner Iranian religious discourse is pinpointed from the middle of the 3rd century CE; there was, therefore, an inculturation of Syrian Christians into the Persian way of thinking. Consequently it is not surprising to find traces of Iranian religious thought models (Dīn Ibrahīm and the problematics of doubt) and the casuistic treatment of questions of religious practice in the Qur'ān, as is also still to be found in Zoroastrian literature of the 9th century CE.[14]

Roman soldiers, who had been captured, had to build the Caesar's Dam nearby (not far from the town of Šūštar) which is still in use today.

The captives taken by Šāpur in the three great wars against Rome and her allies in the Orient between 241-260 CE settled in the Persis, Parthia, Khūzistān and elsewhere. Šāpur I refers to this in the Parthian version of his inscription on the so-called *Kaʿba-ye Zardošt* in Persepolis (line 16, Parthian).[15]

The culmination of this practice was the second deportation of the whole of the Antiochian population. Around 540 CE Ḵosrow I (alternative English spellings: Chosroes, Khosrau; 531–579 CE) deported the whole of the captive population of Antiochia to Mesopotamia where he made them build up a new Antiochia. The town was called Vēh-āz-Antiok-Ḵosrow (the improved Antiochia of Khosrau). It was known as "Rūmīya" after the establishment of Islam. The great reception hall in the Sassanian residence in Ctesiphon, of which the ruins are known as *Tāq-e Kisrā* today, is said to be decorated with an illustration of these deportation events.[16]

Parts of the town-dwelling population of Syria were, however, deliberately settled along the old military roads from Babylon to Bactria where some of the towns founded by Alexander the Great still existed. The Sassanian rulers Ardašīr (224 – 241 CE) and Šāpur I eagerly followed Alexander's example. They were great planners and refounders of towns and in those places where they did not actually found the towns they had towns renamed after them.

Therefore it comes as no surprise that non-Iranian terms, which originate from the homelands of the deported Syrians, replaced the name of the *Šāhinšāh* ("King of Kings"; Middle Persian: šāhān-šāh) on coinage when the rule of the Sassanians was coming to an end: around 651 CE in the East, more accurately speaking in Sīstān, the decorative epithet: *m(u)ḥ(a)mm(a)d* emerged in the field of coinage and replaced the name of the Sassanian ruler.[17]

2. The Byzantine-Sassanian Conflict 590-630

2.1 The flight of the Sassanian ruler, Ḵosrow II (590-628) to the Byzantine Empire

In the course of long-lasting confusion as to who should be on the throne after the death of the Sassanian, Hormozd (Hormizd) IV (579-590 CE) his successor Ḵosrow II had to flee to the Byzantine Empire.

In this context there is said to have been an episode which was later used by the propaganda of Emperor Heraclius and traces of which can be found in the Qur'ān: Ḵosrow was accepted at the court of Emperor Maurice (582-602 CE) and gained his support for his plan to win back the throne. Maurice grasped the opportunity to his best advantage to put an end to the war with Persia, which had been going on for twenty years, and was the most recent in a series of conflicts, by securing Ḵosrow's return to the Persian throne using a Byzantine army. In return the Persians were willing to commit to permanent peace and surrender a large part of eastern Armenia.

Thereafter Ḵosrow II was presumed to be a personal friend and protégé of the Byzantine emperor who had also bestowed upon him a Byzantine princess as his wife. According to a message from the Byzantine Panegyric Theophylaktos Simokates (Theophylact[us] Simocatta), historian and secretary to Emperor Heraclius (610-641 CE), he is said to have pronounced the following prophesy: "The Babylonian tribe" will rule the Byzantine State for a period of three "cycle hebdomads" (*"year-weeks")*. In the 5th cycle hebdomad, however, the Romans will beat the Persians into submission. (...) The anonymous author of this prophesy, which presumes the successful conquests of Ḵosrow II, evidently intended to predict the future, absolute victory of Heraclius and to justify this using the biblical and apocalyptic scheme of "year-weeks" (i.e., seven years in a row; cf. the "seven fat and seven lean years" predicted by Joseph in the Bible). Although Theophylact dismissed this prediction remarking that it was based on the "stupidity of the stars of the Chaldeans", the very same *auctor intellectualis* was, without doubt, of the opinion that it had a particular persuasive power coming from the mouth of the Persian king. It may be presumed that this Ḵosrow prophesy appeared in order to persuade people who were in favour of the Persian king to change favor to the Byzantine emperor.[18]

Further information on this prophecy can be found in a publication by Gerrit J. Reinink[19]. So in the eyes of the Byzantines just who were these people who needed to be otherwise persuaded? Who should be advised that in the long term it would be wise to gamble on a Byzantine victory in the eternal Iran/Byzantium conflict? Who else but the Christians under Persian rule, who were not natural allies of the Byzantines, as profound theological differences caused conflict between them? The prophesy does put stress on the fact that the "katechon" would hold and save the Byzantines, called "*Rūm*", by the Fathers of the Qur'ānic materials. The term "katechon" goes back to a passage from the epistles: 2 Thess, 2:6-7:

> "6. And you know what restrains him now (τὸ κατέχον), so that in his time he will be revealed. 7. For the mystery of lawlessness is already at work; only he who now restrains (ὁ κατέχων) will do so until he is taken out of the way."

It designates "that which withholds" (in Greek: τὸ κατέχον [neuter, verse 6]), as well as "the withholder" (ὁ κατέχων [masculine]). According to an eschatological interpretation, the end of the world cannot come before the Antichrist and the force (neuter) or person (masculine) "that restrains him", – *the katechon*, – have appeared.

They recognized that this "hindrance" was impeding the progress of the apocalyptic era ushered in by John the Baptist. Therefore we have to understand the first verses of the *surat al-Rūm* ("The Romans have been defeated in the nearer land, and they, after their defeat will be victorious") not only as a reference to historic events, but also as an acknowledgment of the theological raison d'etre of the Byzantine Empire. By making Paul's teaching (2 Tess. 2:1-12) concerning the "hindrance", which stands between the *Believers* and the *Second Coming* into an ideology justifying the permanence of the Roman Empire in its Byzantine setting in the eyes of he fathers of the Qur'ānic materials, Byzantium as a manifestation of the "katechon" stood in the way of an orderly progress of apocalyptic dynamics.

Here it is especially the "Old Believers" among the Syrian Christians who should primarily be considered, those who had managed to keep their pre-Nicean tradition and now lived as Iranianized *'Arabī* in the towns of Iran (as people who had been deported in the 3rd century; one constant can be assumed: once adopted, the creed was kept in the same form). Thus it is not surprising that this pro-Byzantine prophecy had found its way into the Qur'ānic material of this *'Arabī* community. It is also possible that it served as the foundation for the cooperation with the Trinitarians because this was the most opportune thing to do at that particular moment. Thus, just as Heraclius had to justify his rational peace agreement in Byzantium, the leaders of the *'Arabī* community had to justify their partisanship for Byzantium to their community, since it was going to be a long journey before it would generally be found opportune to become one of the confederates (*foederati*) of the Rūm ("Romans", i.e., Byzantines). According to Christoph Luxenberg,[20] *foederati* is the Latin equivalent of *qurayš*, a term probably going back to Syriac "*q-r-š* – to collect, to gather".[21] In surah 30 ("al-Rūm – the Romans/ Byzantines") we read:

> "2 The Romans have been defeated. 3 In the nearer land, and they, after their defeat, will be victorious. 4 Within ten years Allah's is the command in the former case and in the latter and in that day believers will rejoice. 5 In Allah's help to victory."

R. Paret's German translation is closer to the Arabic original (nothing is said about "10 years") and clearer:

> "2 The Byzantines are defeated 3 in the closest region (*fī 'adnā l-'arḍi*). But, after they have been defeated, they will conquer again (*ba'di ġalabihim sa-yaġlibūna*), 4 in a number of years (*fī biḍ'i sinīna*). God stands by the decision, in the past and in the future. On that day the believers will rejoice (*wa-yawma'iḏin yafraḥu l-mu'minūn^a^*), 5 that God helped. (...)."[22]

2.2 The Murder of the Emperor's Family in Byzantium and Ḵosrow's Revenge

Ḵosrow's promoter to the Persian throne, Maurice (Maurikios), had faced the Sassanian enemy in the East for many years as a military commander and had also fought on Iranian soil. It was this experience that formed the basis of a strategy handbook which was composed under Maurice's reign and reveals insights into the fighting methods of the Byzantines.[23] Maurice did not give up on the idea of the universal Roman Empire,[24] although this meant that he had to consolidate Byzantine possessions in the West and could only feel safe from attack by Ḵosrow II in the East, at least for the time being, because of the fortunate stroke of fate of Ḵosrow II's flight to his court and the resulting peace.

The Byzantines must have found the events of the subsequent years up until 630 all the more agitating. At the end of this development Byzantium was totally different with a *basileus* (king) who considered himself a *servus christi*.

The precarious situation of Byzantium grew conspicuous when another burden occurred to shake the system: a ten-year-long, confusing and ultimately lost war with the Slavs of the Balkans at the Lower Danube. The apparent hopelessness of the fighting against the Slavs led to revolts in the army. In 602 CE the rebellion came to a head and Maurice was deposed in Constantinople and his whole family was killed.

Ḵosrow II appointed himself as avenger of the murdered Maurice and went on the attack. In 605 CE the stronghold of Dara fell and with it Byzantine Mesopotamia was lost. The Persians advanced to Chalcedon which is located on the Asian side opposite Constantinople.

Phokas, Maurice's murderer and successor to the throne of Byzantium, fell victim to a plot which put Heraclius, son of the exarch of Carthage, on the throne in 610 CE.

2.3 The Reign of a New Alexander (Heraclius)

Heraclius spent some two years fighting against the remaining partisans of his predecessor. In his first year of rule he was even granted success against the Persians who were driven from Cappadocia. Then the fortunes of war turned again and a decade of military disasters followed, which culminated in the Persian occupation of Jerusalem 614 CE[25] and the conquest of Egypt, the bread basket of the realm, from 618 CE onwards.

Ḵosrow II, four-year-long guest at the court of Byzantium as a political refugee and under the protection of Emperor Maurice, familiar as he was with the Byzantine ideology of state, did not only conduct a military operation, but did all that he could to make the emperor appear to be devoid of legitimation in the eyes of his subjects. Thus he usurped the symbols of rule and took them away from the emperor. This story of the removal of the True Cross and its recovery is the blueprint for the camel-raider camp-fire story of the removal and recovery of the *Black Stone* in Islamic tradition.

Ḵosrow II was already proceeding as the Qarmatians (Qarāmiṭa) allegedly did in the 9th century CE in Mecca from where they took the *Black Stone* in order to deprive the Abbasid caliphs of the legitimation of a protector of sanctuary. If we can regard this story to be more than a topos, then it can help to explain to an Islamic audience how and why the Black Stone came to pieces. In earlier days it had been sufficient to point to the Messianic belief that the cornerstone would be the stone discarded by the craftsmen (Psalm 118:22). The recovery of the Black Stone was made possible by a cooperation of arch-rivals, the Abbasids and the Fatimids. Such a cooperation of arch-rivals had led to the recovery of the True Cross. At that time it was the cooperation of the Byzantines with the Christian heretics in the Sassanian domain. In an act of symbolic politics the Sassanian ruler took the reliquary of the *True Cross* and destroyed the Church of the Holy Sepulchre, the pivotal sanctuary of Christian Orthodoxy. Ḵosrow II must have been aware of the significance of the Cross and of the sepulchre of Jesus to the Church of Byzantinium thanks to the Christians in his vicinity, his Christian wives, Shīrīn and Maria, his Christian minister Yazdīn and Yazdīn's son Shamtā, his doctor Gabriel of Sinjār, who had converted to the Monophysites, and owing to the experience gathered from his time at the court of Byzantium. The desired outcome came about.[26] In 618 CE, Heraclius decided to give up rule over the Byzantine Orient.

The Eastern Roman territories with Constantinople as their capital were to be surrendered in 618 CE., the capital was to be shifted to Sicily, and Byzantium was to be reorganized with the remaining territories in Italy, Spain and North Africa in the spirit of a Christian *Magna Graecia*. In the end it was the mass protests on the part of the population living in the capital that hindered Heraclius from implementing this plan. This intention reveals an indication that Heraclius no longer believed in a survival of the Empire in the shape and size that Maurice had still dreamed of in his testament.

The plan to reorganize territories in the form of a *Magna Graecia* had to be abandoned, but not the plan for a complete revision of the Roman imperial ideology. In 635 CE, Heraclius' action or lack of action in the Byzantine Orient was consistent with the behaviour of the Byzantines in Northern Italy or in Spain at the time. Accordingly, a local Praetorian was left in the Byzantine Orient as *magister militum*, who referred to himself as *amīr al-mu'minīn*. His task is described in a Spanish chronicle as *omnia prospere gerens* ("someone ruling everything in a propitious manner") dated 794 CE. Such Arabic governors, namely the Ghassanides (*al-Ġasāsina*), had governed Syria and the Western part of the Arabian Peninsula for Byzantium in the sixth century, adorned with the title of a *patricius*.

2.4 What is New with the New Alexander (Heraclius)?

Historians are of differing opinions concerning the evaluation of the way Heraclius ruled. On the one hand there is Georg Ostrogorsky, who puts forward a picture of a military innovator and who, after much indecision and manoeuvring, finally acted resolute (asymmetric warfare), and who strove for long-term solutions to religious conflicts by means of simultaneous negotiations over compromises in questions of Christology, on the other hand all changes are comprised in a "long history" of structural modifications, which provided for the formation of future structures of the Byzantine state even without direct interventions by the ruler (Haldon, Brandes).

Following the arguments of the latter, the image of Heraclius being that of a new Alexander shines even more brightly, as he is now no longer a man only of duty and a representative of national interest, but a historic character, whose motives remain, to a large extent, concealed. What is generally considered to be known about Heraclius does not explain how he came to be victorious in Jerusalem in 630 CE. After a struggle that was largely seen as eschatological, he contented himself with a rational peace agreement and gave up his title of *Emperor* ("autokrator") in the year that followed. As bearer of the vassal title *pistos en Christô Basileus*[27] he went to Jerusalem, and there, united with the oriental heretics, he celebrated the "Restitutio Crucis", the return of the relic of the True Cross from the hands of the "fire worshippers" (Zoroastrians).[28]

The homecoming of the relic of the True Cross is reminiscent of David's bringing the ark of the covenant back to Jerusalem (2 Samuel 6). Heraclius named a son born to him at this time "David". George Pisida (Georgios Pisidês), historian, cleric and court poet of Heraclius, recorded this act in a poem he wrote on the occasion of the return of the True Cross to Jerusalem, evoking the event: The arrival of Heraclius in Jerusalem is compared to that of Christ on Palm Sunday; he is, however, also Jason, who returned the golden fleece to its homeland; the retrieval of the Cross by Constantine is outclassed by its recovery by Heraclius, his "child", who had rescued it from the "Persian fire".[29]

Five years later the reconstructed Church of the Holy Sepulchre was consecrated without the emperor, the relic of the True Cross was taken to Constantinople and otherwise the affairs of the Byzantine Orient were left to develop freely. Just as he had scorned victorious peace over the Sassanians, Heraclius now scorned the reign over peoples[30] for whom there was no room in his plans to start anew and build a new Byzantium.[31] The heretical Christians were excluded from the realm. They could wander about in their spiritual deserts like the Sons of Hagar. Excluded from the Byzantine Church they were homeless "Tayyāye" and "Mhaggrāye", children of Abraham, kicked out from his tent.

2.5 The Church Organizes Resistance

The plan to give up Constantinople and risk a new beginning in the West obviously had to affect the Byzantine Church. The Church reacted and was forced to render its means available to the emperor. Sergios I of Constantinople, the Ecumenical Patriarch and a Patrician took over the regency for the underaged son of Heraclius in his absence. The war is said to have started in an atmosphere of religious tension as had not been known before in those early times.[32]

Contemporary Byzantine sources call Heraclius "God's campaigner" and his army "Philochristos" (the elect of Christ), and refer to his war as a fight with "Ḵosrow the fire-worshipper". The icons of Christ "not made by human hand" constituted the holy banner of the crusades against the Persians. This war was portrayed as a holy war and what other circumstance could Heraclius' glorious victory be attributed to than the protection that God had provided for the emperor and his army.[33]

By using the treasury of the Church, Heraclius was able to call together the troops and make haste to Armenia where he appeared behind the enemy who was at that point in Asia Minor. The Persians retreated from Asia Minor and were defeated during their retreat into Armenian territory.

This happened in 622 CE. The victory on Armenian territory was the turning point in this struggle. The psychological effect of this victory is still evident today; as two decades later the Arabs also recognized Heraclius' victory to be the beginning of the turning point in their fortune, the day of their return to renewed dominance in Syria and Mesopotamia: 622 became the *year of the Arabs*.

Around 620 CE the Empire of the Sassanians in the West had again expanded to the extent the Achaemenid Empire had achieved a good millennium previously. From this peak in the spread of power, it took less than a decade for it all to collapse and the cause of this were the actions of Heraclius, a Byzantine ruler, who only four years prior to the victory of 622 CE had planned to surrender large parts of his empire.

2.6 Heraclius' Troops

There is information that in 615 CE a *magister militum* fought against the Persians in Eastern and Central Anatolia. At this time the *magister militum per Orientem* was involved in battle at the Cilician Gates. There was still a certain solidarity within the Byzantine troops.[34]

Frank R. Trombley tried to find out whether the armies of Maurice were still at the command of Heraclius. Starting from the time of Gallienus and up until the seventh century he found 169 inscriptions on military graves which he analyzed for his study. From this he was able to deduce that the life expectancy of those ranked as officers was 38.4 years with an average military service period of 20.9 years. This, however, is only relevant for those few fortunate men who had an inscription on their gravestones. It is quite probable that a half of all those remaining nameless had to be replaced every ten years. Frank R. Trombley goes on to conclude that Emperor Maurice's troops – who were experienced in battle – and who, just like Heraclius, had personally led his troops against the Avars, no longer existed when Heraclius acceded to the throne. He comes to the conclusion that Heraclius' troops must have been made up of a large number of "ethnic fighters".[35]

For what reason would people living in the Caucasus and in Iran partake in the fighting on the side of Heraclius? One reason could be the fact that Heraclius disposed of the Church silver, another, more profound reason on the long term, was the discontentment amongst parts of the Iranian population concerning the way the Sassanians ruled. In order to take advantage of this discontentment Heraclius implemented the same type of symbolic policy as Ḳosrow II had demonstrated in the conquering of Jerusalem in 614 CE. Ḳosrow II had destroyed the Church of the Holy Sepulchre and turned the town over to the Jews.

In 623 CE Heraclius continued his militant activities with an attack on Ganjak. This was the location of the residence of Ardašīr, the first Sassanian king, and his Fire Temple. Heraclius had it destroyed.[36]

Apart from the Caucasian tribes such as the Laz, the Abkhaz and Iberians, Heraclius also involved the Khazars from north of the Caspian Sea in his strategical plans. The fact that he was constantly present in the border territories of the Sassanian realm was in all probability a great help to him in getting information even from the very court of the Sassanians. This behaviour, against all traditions of warfare, which could only be effective in terms of short campaigns, had to make the enemy troops nervous. Heraclius's presence as an uninvited permanent resident was like a plague which would not go away and grew to be a menace.

To the Christians in Iran Heraclius appeared to be a young Alexander. The psychological warfare of the Byzantines made sure of that. However, his adversary, Ḵosrow II, had been on the throne for 37 years. It was time for a change.

In the autumn of 627 CE, when Heraclius moved down the Tigris towards Ctesiphon, he was no longer in need of assistance from the Khazars. Their behaviour during the campaign led to them having a secure position in the later apocalyptic beliefs of the Muslims.[37]

In Mesopotamia there were other allies: the Christian Arabs offered their services as *foederati* (Arabic *qurayš*). Ḵosrow II had done away with their realm and its capital Ḥīra. On his return from Byzantium in 595 CE, after withstanding a coup in 590 CE, he could hardly trust any of his petty kings any more. After the execution of the Lakhmid dynasty of Ḥīra in 602 CE, the Arabs of Mesopotamia no longer considered themselves obedient allies of the Sassanians.

At the beginning of December in 627 CE there was a great battle at Nineveh which ended favourably for the Byzantines. Ḵosrow II, however, was still not ready to make peace. Thus the fighting continued right up to the plundering of his residence in Dastgerd.

Soon after, Ḵosrow II was deposed, ostracised and killed. In 628 CE the son of Ḵosrow II concluded a peace treaty. It was a matter of reason. Heraclius demanded and achieved the restoration of the status quo ante, i.e., as it had been before Ḵosrow II attacked Byzantium.

3 The Reflection of Contemporary Contexts in the Qu'rān

3.1 Where are there References to Heraclius in the Qu'rān?

Byzantine warfare was accompanied by a political and religious publicity, of which the obvious aim was to win over the support of the Iranian Christians for Heraclius. This was not an easy feat as, generally speaking, the Sassanian rulers in Iran had given preferential treatment to those Christian groups who had been subjected to persecution in the Byzantine Empire. The emperor only tolerated as his Christians in Iran the ones who had their theological and Christological differences with the Church of the Byzantine Empire. The Christians in Iran showed him their gratitude for this by conforming totally to the Sassanian rule.

Ḵosrow II, however, had completely surrounded himself with Monophysites. These were pursued gorily by the Byzantine emperor in Syria.

The ruler of the Sassanians intervened in the choice of the patriarch of the Syrian Church of Seleucia-Ctesphion and left the see vacant in order to benefit the Monophysites. These were the people closest to Ḵosrow II. His wife, Šīrīn, his doctor, Gabriel of Sinjār, his minister, Yāzdīn und the latter's son, Shamtā, were Monophysites.

Heraclius used this situation by having himself depicted in political and religious writings as the protector of the Syrian Christians, the Christian majority in Iran. Since the beginning of the deportation under Šāpur I in 241 CE the doctrine of the see in Antiochia had had priority over the Monophysites in Iran, who had only later advanced from Syria to Mesopotamia. Gabriel of Sindjâr had defected to them and promoted their cause at the court. That is how the followers of the older Christological doctrine came to be adulated by Heraclius. Amongst these followers were the Arabs and the *ʿArabī* of Iran. The *ʿArabī*, as well as the Arabs who had been converted to Christianity in the third, fourth and fifth centuries, were "old believers" and as such had had to reject the course of the Syrian Church in Iran since the Council of Seleucia-Ctesiphon in 410 CE. On this synod the theological doctrines that had been valid in the Byzantine Empire since Nicaea (325 CE) were adopted in the domain of the Syrian Church in Iran as well. In 630 CE, when the Syrian patriarch of Seleucia-Ctesiphon celebrated mass in Jerusalem in the presence of Emperor Heraclius at the return of the True Cross, he was right to presume that no more Christological differences stood between himself and the emperor.[38]

The *ʿArabī* and the Christian Arabs of Iran saw this differently because of their pre-Nicean theology, but did not give up hope of one day returning to a common understanding of the scripture; for otherwise their demanding a concord (Arabic: *islām*) would have made no sense. In light of the dogmatic developments in the Syrian Church after 410 CE they stood outside the church community of the patriarch of Seleucia-Ctesiphon, therefore the term "old believers" seems appropriate; as possessors of Qur'ānic material, however, they saw themselves as the real believers, as *Ḥanīfs* (originally: pagans; also used for Abraham, who believed even as a "pagan") and followers of *Dīn Ibrahīm* (the uncontaminated original creed/view of Abraham according to the teachings of Paul, Letter to the Romans, 4. Here the concept of Abraham as the "Father of All that Believe" is developed.)

The *Dīn Ibrahīm* of the Qur'ān has nothing to do with the "religion of Abraham" or even the "Abrahamic religions" heralded so much in many places today and which is supposed to be the foundation of a dialogue of the monotheistic religions. This sort of fashionable interpretation is only possible if the understanding of *Dīn* follows the semantics as given by the Encyclopedia of Islam.[39]

The *Dīn* in the Qur'ān, however, is not to be taken in the sense of Islamic semantics, but in the sense of the Iranian semantics of the 7th century. The Christians living in the Iranian domain did not use their terminology according to the understanding of modern Islamology, but according to the traditional use of terms in the inner Iranian religious discourse. Therefore *Dīn* has nothing to do with the relatively modern expression of "religion", but is concerned with Abraham's *attitude to questions of faith*. The *Dīn Ibrahīm* is the *faith of Abraham*.[40] This faith is characterised by its inflexibility and the absence of doubt. This is also an Iranian feature of pure faith.

How does Heraclius want to go about winning over the hearts of the Syrian Christians in Iran? – By using a Syrian legend to portray himself as an "Alexander *neós*", who single-mindedly, stubbornly and unrelentingly, like Moses, took on the fight against the (new) *Pharaoh* Ḵosrow, who had not allowed the *ʿArabī* (the "new" people of Israel) to go to the Promised Land. His struggle against Ḵosrow II repeats the battles of Alexander the Great against the Achaemenid King of kings.

This *Syrian legend of Alexander the Great* is then once again processed further in a piece of epic poetry about Alexander written by an *anonymous* from Northern Mesopotamia in approx. 630 CE. Both the *Syrian legend of Alexander the Great* and the later Syrian Alexander poem are concerned with the disappointing peace agreement at the end of the struggle of two world empires in Late Antiquity. The Alexander poem sees the peace of 628 CE as the restoration of the original border from the times of the Macedonian Alexander the Great. The *new Alexander* acknowledges this border after receiving exact and detailed instructions from the Angel of the Lord. The division of the Middle Eastern empires should continue to exist as it goes back to God's will in the formation of the original empire of Alexander.[41]

Where are these permanent borders between the empires to be found according to the Alexander poem? – Predominantly in the Middle Eastern parts of the Byzantine Empire. The list of provinces is long: *Aegyptus* (Egypt), the land of the *Jebusites* (=Palestine I), *Palaestina* (= Palestine II), *Arabia, Syria, Mesopotamia, Phoenicia, Cilicia, Cappadocia, Galatia, Phrygia, Asia, Hellespontus* and *Seleucia*, i.e., the list comprises regions where the Sassanians had spread war after 604 CE.[42]

How does the mention of Heraclius as *Ḏū-l-Qarnayn* (surah 18:82) in the Qur'ān come about?

Under the entry "*Dhu-'l-Ḳarnayn*" the Encyclopaedia of Islam, Vol. II, p. 241 we read: [see "Iskandar"]; *Iskander* is the Arabic name form of *Alexander the Great*. A reason why *Ḏū-l-Qarnayn* (the one with the two horns) is supposed to be Alexander is not given. Murad W. Hofmann made the following remark:

> "The one with two horns or 'the one from the two epochs' is an incorrect reference to Alexander the Great, because he was portrayed on coins as Jupiter Ammon with two horns."

Of course Murad W. Hofmann is right to refuse to see a heathen being in the two-horned creature mentioned in the Qur'ān. The religious group possessing Qur'ānic material saw this in a similar light. As a basis they were using the *Syrian legend of Alexander the Great*. In that narrative Heraclius is the new Alexander. His horns are no longer horns of the god Ammon from the Shiva oasis in Egypt, they rather go back to images from the prophecies of Daniel.

In a prayer at the beginning of the legend *Ḏū-l-Qarnayn/ Alexander/ Heraclius* speaks of the core motive for his actions: the foundation of the *Christian Empire*. Alexander is aware of his pious task to make God's name known to all peoples and refers to the prophecies of Daniel[43] when he asks for God's help. Here the *fourth creature* of Dan 7:7-8 and the ram of chapter 8 (chapter 7 is in Aramaic, chapter 8 in Hebrew) has horns, which were later interpreted as belonging to Alexander:[44]

> "7:7. After this I saw [...] a fourth beast, terrible and powerful, and strong exceedingly; [...] and it had ten horns (וְקַרְנַיִן עֲשַׂר לַהּ: *wə-qarnayin* ʿ*ᵃśar lah*). 8. I considered the horns, and, behold, there came up among them another horn, a little one, before which three of the first horns were plucked up by the roots: and, behold, in this horn were eyes like the eyes of a man (עַיְנִין כְּעַיְנֵי אֲנָשָׁא בְּקַרְנָא־דָא – *ʿaynīn kə-ʿaynē ʾᵃnāšā bə-qarnā-ḏā*), and a mouth speaking great things."

The Aramaic word for "horn", *qarn-ā* (the *–ā* being the emphatic article), is the same as the one in Arabic[45]. It is interesting to note that in the quoted expression "*qarnayin ʿaśar lah* – it had ten horns" the dual is used,[46] which is identical to the Arabic one. The *ram* appears in chapter 8:

> "8:3. Then I lifted up mine eyes, and saw, and, behold, there stood before the river a ram which had two horns (וְלוֹ קְרָנָיִם – *wə lō qərānāyim*): and the two horns were high; but one was higher than the other, and the higher came up last."

In his literal translation of the Old Testament with copious linguistic commentary E. Kautzsch interprets the fourth animal as representing "the Greek Empire" and comments about the ten horns in verse 7:7-8:

> "= ten kings which represent the succession in the Syrian Empire from Alexander the Great up to Antiochus Epiphanes [...]"[47]

The connection to Moses, who was later depicted *with two horns*, e.g. by Michelangelo, is an incorrect interpretation of Ex 34:30. In the modern NAS we read:

> "So when Aaron and all the sons of Israel saw Moses, behold, *the skin of his face shone*, and they were afraid to come near him."

That "the skin of his face shone" was translated more or less correctly in the Septuagint:

> "ἦν δεδοξασμένη ἡ ὄψις τοῦ χρώματος τοῦ προσώπου αὐτοῦ"

So it is quite surprising that we find the following rendering in the Latin Vulgate:

> "Videntes autem Aaron et filii Israël *cornutam Moysi faciem*, timuerunt prope accedere. – But when Aaron and the sons of Israel saw *the horned face of Moses*, they became afraid to approach him."

The misunderstanding goes back to the Hebrew original:

> "וַיַּרְא אַהֲרֹן וְכָל־בְּנֵי יִשְׂרָאֵל אֶת־מֹשֶׁה וְהִנֵּה קָרַן עוֹר פָּנָיו וַיִּירְאוּ מִגֶּשֶׁת אֵלָיו׃
> *wə-yarə' 'Ahᵃrōn wə-ḵol bənē yiśra'ēl äṯ-mōšäh wə-hinnēh qāran 'ōr pānāw wa-yyīrə'ū miggäšäṯ 'ēlāw.*"

The verb "to shine: *qāran* – קָרַן" used here is derived from the same radicals "q-r-n" as the noun "horn: קֶרֶן – *qärän*, before a suffix: *qarn-* ".

Thus Heraclius is the *one with two horns* from the prophecies of Daniel: the Alexander in the legend of the year 630. Geritt Reinink remarks:

> "In the last few months of the year 629 Heraclius stayed in Edessa. At this time, here in 'The blessed City' or maybe in Amida – either way in these regions of northern Mesopotamia – there lived an anonymous person who appointed himself as the spearhead of Heraclius' church policies. However, he did not write a panegyric on the emperor's final victory over Chosrau as his Byzantine contemporary, Georgios Pisides, had done. He created a story about Alexander the Great, in whose brilliant persona and through whose laudable achievements the victorious Heraclius, the perfect religious ruler, could be identified. He created his Alexander-Heraclius typology so that when his

> readers came to retell the story of Alexander in their own time, they would become aware of the oneness/ unity of the salvation history of God, in which Byzantium had an unparalleled position, and would therefore become convinced that this unity on Earth should lead to a political and religious unity in the Byzantine empire. Both Alexander and Heraclius took objects symbolising this unity to Jerusalem; Alexander took the silver throne bestowed to Christ and Heraclius took the Sacred Cross of Christ."[48]

3.2 The Account of the Syrian Legend of Alexander in the Qur'ān

There follows a comparison of an outline of the contents of the Syrian legend of Alexander the Great and the text of the Qur'ān, which reflects the way it was understood by the *'Arabī*. In short the contents are as follows:

In his second or seventh year of rule Alexander summons the greatest men of the realm and his generals and informs them that he wishes to delve into the secrets of heaven and earth. Despite the negative advice from his barons – that the foul-smelling and deadly ocean of Oceanus, which flowed around the entire world, was impossible to cross – Alexander decides to leave with his army (255:4–257:10). After a long prayer, in which he prays for God's assistance and takes an oath (257:11–238:9), Alexander travels to Egypt where the Egyptian King Sanargos gives him 7000 blacksmiths who are to accompany him on his journey (258:9–259:3). Alexander travels to the Oceanus. The lethal effect makes crossing the sea impossible so Alexander cannot reach the place where heaven ends (259:3–260:1).

From there they undertake to travel to where the sun goes down. A description of the sun's path then follows (260:1–15). After that Alexander travels to the headwaters of the Euphrates and the Tigris and from there he goes North through Armenia to the large mountains. Alexander's army sets up camp at the pass of the mountain (260:15–261:13). Alexander sends out peace messengers to bring him the 300 elders of the country. These elders tell Alexander about the Persian King who rules the land, about the geographical location of the great mountains, about the external appearance and the barbaric customs of the Huns and their expeditions to Roman and Persian regions and finally about the peoples who live beyond the Huns, about the location of paradise and the rivers of paradise (261:13–267:1).

Then Alexander builds a gate at the mountain pass with the help of the Egyptian blacksmiths to prevent the Huns from escaping. (...) At the end of time God will destroy Alexander's gate so that the kings and realms of the Huns will overwhelm the world. This will result in a great battle between the peoples. The Byzantine Empire will emerge as a vast Christian empire.[49]

In the tradition of the *'Arabī* the Alexander legend sounds as follows (Qur'ān 18: 83-97):

"They will ask thee of Dhul-Qarneyn. Say: I shall recite unto you a remembrance of him. (*wa-yas'alūnaka ʿan ḏī l-qarnayni qul sa-'atlū ʿalaykum minhu ḏikra*ⁿ) 84. Lo! We made him strong in the land and gave unto every thing a road. 85. And he followed a road. (*fa-'atbaʿa sababa*ⁿ) 86. Till, when he reached the setting place of the sun, he found it setting in a muddy spring, and found a people thereabout: We said: O Dhul-Qarneyn! Either punish or show them kindness. 87. He said: As for him who doeth wrong, we shall punish him, and then he will be brought back unto his Lord, who will punish him with awful punishment! 88. But as for him who believeth and doeth right, good will be his reward, and We shall speak unto him a mild command. 89. Then he followed a road. (*ṯumma 'atbaʿa sababa*ⁿ) 90. Till, when he reached the rising place of the sun, he found it rising on a people for whom We had appointed no helper therefrom. 91. So (it was). And We knew all concerning him. 92. Then he followed a road. (*ṯumma 'atbaʿa sababan)* 93. Till, when he came between the two mountains, he found upon their hither side a folk that scarce could understand a saying. 94. They said: O Dhul-Qarneyn! Lo! Gog and Magog are spoiling the land. (*'inna ya'ǧūǧa wa-ma'ǧūǧa mufsidūna fī l-'arḍi*) So may we pay thee tribute on condition that thou set a barrier between us and them?"

The narration is not very elaborate. Verses 89 and 92 are identical, verse 85 nearly identical. Moreover, in the meantime the narrator has forgotten that the Egyptian king had given Alexander-Heraclius 7000 blacksmiths who, according to the Syrian legend, build the iron gate. Thus he lets the *one with two horns* build the gate himself in the manner of giants, that fill whole valleys with iron, which is then brought to smolder using bellows and is subsequently sealed with molten tar:

"95. He said: That wherein my Lord hath established me better (than your tribute). (*qāla mā makkannī fīhi rabbī ḫayrun;* Paret: *He said: 'What my Lord has given me, is better.*) Do but help me with strength (of men) (*fa-'aʿīnūnī bi-quwwatin;* Paret: But help me to strength), I will set between you and them a bank. 96. Give me pieces of iron till, when he had levelled up (the gap) between the cliffs (*'iḏā sāwā bayna ṣ-ṣadafayni;* Paret: *And when he had filled the gap between the two (mountain slopes*), he said: Blow! till, when he had made it a fire, he said: Bring me molten copper to pour thereon. *('ātūnī 'ufriġ ʿalayhi qiṭran;* Paret: *Bring me molten tar ...)* 97. And (Gog and Magog) were not able to surmount, nor could they pierce (it) (*wa-mā staṭāʿū lahū naqban;* Paret: *neither were they able to go through it*)."

The text is not entirely clear, as we can see from the differing translations. The Syrian legend continues at another place (surah 21:96-97). As predicted, one day God will open the gate and the great battle will commence from which Byzantine will emerge as the Universal Christian Empire:

> "96. Until, when Gog and Magog are let loose (*ḥattā 'iḏā futiḥat ya'ǧūǧu wa-ma'ǧūǧu;* Paret: *Until Gog and Magog is opened*), and they hasten out of every mound (*wa-hum min kulli ḥadabin yansilūna;* Paret: *and they come running from every hill*). 97. And the True Promise draweth nigh; then behold them, staring wide (in terror), the eyes of those who disbelieve! (They say): Alas for us! We (lived) in forgetfulness of this. Ah, but we were wrong doers!"[50]

Paret's translation for "*futiḥat*", – they were opened, – is literal, although he assumes that *Gog and Magog* are people. In his commentary he admits the difficulties with the translation of the text and quotes diverging interpretations.

3.3 Putting a Date on the Syriac Legend of Alexander in the Qur'ān

As the Syriac Legend of Alexander acknowledges the peace of 628 CE between the Byzantine Empire and the Persians, Gerrit J. Reinink is right in assuming that it can only have come to exist in 629 CE at the earliest. The legend contains eschatological notions current in the Byzantine Empire.

In the Qur'ān, however, the eschatology of the *'Arabī* has replaced this typically Byzantine eschatology. This topic serves to demonstrate to those possessing Qur'ānic material that they are players in a cataclysmic event. They adopt beliefs of the end of all time, which originally accompanied the coming of the *Universal Christian Empire of Byzantium*, and attribute this to the fate of their community. Such a process of reinterpretation cannot have taken place overnight.

The transformation of the Alexander legend in Qur'ānic material is effected via a theological reevaluation as defined by the apocalyptic beliefs of the *'Arabī*. Apparently, in the 9th century it was still generally known that *Ḏū-l-Qarnayn* did not refer to the Macedonian Alexander, but to the Byzantine Alexander-Heraclius. Wilferd Madelung cites a *Ḥadīṯ* in this sense. It is about a story from the life of the Prophet of the Arabs. This prophet is said to have mentioned Syria in conversation, obviously with the intention of seizing this country. Thereupon he was asked: How can we have anything to do with Syria, oh messenger of God, as there are the Romans, who bear horns (*ar-Rūm ḏāt al-qurūn*). The *al-Rūm* mentioned at this time evidently no longer refer to Romans, but to Eastern Romans, i.e., Byzantines.[51]

3.4 Who is the Pharaoh in the Qur'ān?

The Pharaoh is the Persian king. The portrayal of the unreasonable despot in the Old Testament is applied to the enemy of the early Christians.[52] The equivalence of *Šāh = Pharaoh* becomes clear through changes made to the content if compared to the depiction in the Old Testament.

Instead of the rescuing of the Jewish first born, here the general slaughtering of sons is reported.:

> "And (remember) when We did deliver you from Pharaoh's folk (*min 'āli fir'awna*), who were afflicting you with dreadful torment, slaying your sons and sparing your women: That was a tremendous trial from your Lord." (surah 2:49).[53]

The procedure described here is in accordance with the general practice of deportation in the Near and Middle East as it has been for thousands of years. Even in the first quarter of the 20th century Islamologists would have been able to study the occurrences of such events locally on the Jazîra. During this period, too, there were trains filled with deported Christians rolling east. Women were allowed to live if they found a new home.

In the Old Testament the Jews in Egypt are spared this trial. Therefore the fate of the *'Arabī* is even more tragic than that of the children of Israel in Egypt. This fate can only be accepted if it is understood to be a divine trial. He who passes the exam can hope for a change of fate. Moses is the personification of this hope. However, who is the Moses of the Qur'ān? Who leads the children of Israel to the Holy Land?

The same thing happens to the Persians as had once happened to the Egyptians. They are an army to be drowned (surah 44:24). However, the divine vengeance continues. They, too, lose their homeland (Sure 44):

> "25. How many were the gardens and the water springs that they left behind,
> 26. And the cornlands and the goodly sites
> 27. And pleasant things wherein they took delight! (*wa-na'matin kānū fīhā fākihīna;* Paret: *And how good was the life they had been happy to live!*)
> 28. Even so (it was), and We made it an inheritance for other folk; (*ka-ḏālika wa-'awraṯnāhā qawman 'āḫarīna* Paret: *Thus it came to be that we allowed all this to be inherited by another people.*)"

Today the beginning of this inheritance is generally taken to be the period of Islamic conquest of Iran. However, historically speaking, it signifies the start of the rule of the Christian Arabs after the end of Sassanian rule, so the victims of the Pharaoh (= Šāh) turned out to be his heirs.

It is generally known that it was not the ancient Egyptians of the Old Testament who lived in gardens with springs, but the gardeners of the garden of paradise, the Persians. To the Jews, the life in the enclosed garden, given the name Paradise (*Paradaêza*) by the Persians, was so remarkable that they linked the story of Adam and Eve to it: for it was in the Garden of Paradise that man finally had solid ground beneath his feet at the time of the Creation.

In the shady gardens one enjoyed the amusement provided by Luqmān ("the clever one, the trickster"). He came from a collection of Indian pieces of wisdom and ended up in the text of the Qurʾān. From the beginning, the *sunnah* has no boundary. He heeds the advice he had been given:

> "Be modest in thy bearing and subdue thy voice. Lo! in harshest of all voices is the voice of the ass. (*wa-qṣid fī mašyika wa-ġḍuḍ min ṣawtika ʾinna ʾankara l-ʾaṣwāti la-ṣawtu l-ḥamīri;* Paret: *And go at a moderate pace and lower your voice; for indeed the most disagreeable of all sounds is the braying of a donkey.*" (surah 31:19)

Even as the reception clerk he knew to protect the dignity of the place for he followed the advice:

> "Turn not thy cheek in scorn toward folk, nor walk with pertness the land. Lo! Allah loveth not each braggart boaster. (*wa-lā tuṣaʿʿir ḫaddaka li-n-nāsi wa-lā tamši fī l-ʾarḍi maraḥan ʾinna llāha lā yuḥibbu kulla muḫtālin faḫūrin,* Paret: *And do not disparagingly act proud and do not walk in joviality on Earth, for Allāh does not love those who are arrogant and boast.*" (surah 31:18).

He bore the moods of the guests with composure, for so it was written in his little book:

> "Paret: O my dear son! Establish worship and enjoin kindness and forbid iniquity, and persevere whatever may befall thee. Lo! That is of the steadfast heart of things. (*yā-bunayya ʾaqimi ṣ-ṣalāta wa-ʾmur bi-l-maʿrūfi wa-nha ʿani l-munkari wa-ṣbir ʿalā mā ʾaṣābaka ʾinna ḏālika min ʿazmi l-ʾumūri,* Paret: *Oh my son, say your prayer and do good and forbid evil and bear whatever befalls you with patience. That truly shows strength in all things*)."[54] (Q 31:17)

A few words of this verse deserve closer inspection: First, "*bunayya*" is a diminutive ("my little son"), so it sounds like an address of affection. Secondly, "*ʾaqimi ṣ-ṣalāta*" is the normal expression designating the performance of prayer, Pickthall's translation "establish worship" sounding too much like the act of a lawmaker. Thirdly, "*wa-ʾmur bi-l-maʿrūfi wa-nha ʿani l-munkari* – enjoin kindness and forbid iniquity" refers to the pair of words "*maʿrūf* ("the known") and *munkar*", which obviously refers to "permitted" and "forbidden" things. It is interesting to note that the verbs used in connection with these words are "*ʾamara* – to order; originally: to say" and "*anhā* – to finish; cause to end". So this advice is given to someone who has got the power to give orders!

4 The Establishment of Arab Rule in Syria and Mesopotamia

4.1 After the retreat the Arab auxiliary forces remain

After the peace treaty between the Byzantines and the Sassanians in 628 CE there were further negotiations between Heraclius and the successors of Ḵosrow II to the throne, Kavād (II), Šahrvarāz (the "Boar [i.e., the hero] of the empire") and Queen Bōrān (628–31 CE). It was with Šahrvarāz, who made an agreement with Heraclius, to return the True Cross and to withdraw the Persian troops from the Byzantine Orient.

What was to be understood by this retreat of the Persian troops? No doubt it comprised only the Iranian contingent of heavy cataphracts and other components of the regular Sassanian army. The notion that the allies hardly adhered to this kind of agreement is shown by the history of Byzantine-Sassanian relations. Clauses always had to be included in the peace treaties between these two empires which pertained to the peoples on the border, as these were mostly involved in proxy wars on behalf of their lords and also escaped their control whenever there was an opportunity for raids and plundering.[55]

The verses of praise about the Persian manoeuvres of Heraclius and the victory of 622 CE show reference to the dominant alliance relations.[56] An Arab general fighting on the side of the Persians is mentioned as well as a Persian defector.

Accordingly, in the eyes of the writer, it was the Arabs who were the natural allies of Byzantium and exceptions are portrayed as such. The Arab general fighting on the side of the enemy is graciously accepted by Heraclius. This is a sign for the procrastinative monophysitic Arabs of the Byzantine Orient, who, for almost half a century, had undergone persecution as heretics from the base in Constantinople, to hope for a change to their situation under Heraclius. The Persian defector undoubtedly stands for the internal tension on the part of the Persians which became evident through his actions. In the poem these are attributed to the masterful tactics of Heraclius.

Who were the Arabs whom Heraclius had to thank for his victory over the Persians? In the first place they were the Mesopotamian Arabs, followed by the Syrian Arabs.

4.2 The Lakhmids

Historical evidence for the appearance of Arab tribes outside the Arabian Peninsula can be found in Mesopotamia. To the Northwest of the Shatt al-Arab was the region where the Lakhm (Laḫm) tribe had settled. After the destruction of the city states of Palmyra, Edessa und Ḥaṭrā by the Great

Powers in the 3rd century CE, Ḥīra became the leading urban centre of non-Iranian Mesopotamians in the region of the Lakhm.

Interestingly the traditional Islamic historiography also assumes an ethnogenesis in the area of Mesopotamia. It portrays the first king of the local dynasty in the role of a conqueror in Arabia who organizes his war moves from Ḥīra. His son and successor, Imru l-Qays, continues with these conquests in Arabia. Imru al-Qays came into conflict with his Sassanian lords. The reason for this is not known. However, it is possible to draw some conclusions from the existing information. One reason may be the conversion of Imru al-Qays to Christianity. In his time the town of Ḥīra was already a center of the Christianization of Arabia. There were connections to Bosra (Buṣrā) in Syria and the see of those deported from Antiochia in Gundeshapur (Gund-ī Shāh Pūr) in Khūzistān. Imru al-Qays might only have converted to Christianity after entering Byzantine territory, because of political deliberations, but still he must have had a reputation for being friendly towards Christians in his home country. The Persian King of kings realized the potential for conflict: A vassal appoints himself protector of the Christians and thus protects the new religion in Iran, the religion of the Roman enemy. This was an attack on the cult of the Zoroastrian state religion and therefore also an attack on the ideology of the Sassanian rule.

The father of Imru l-Qays had also been accredited with the role of protector of another religion, in his case the Manichaeans. This kind of behavior is a matter of course for a vassal king: as the protector of a religious minority he can come forward with claims that encompass the whole kingdom. What we see here are activities in the sense of an *umma as it is understood by the Islamologists.* The legendary first king of Ḥīra appointed himself speaker (*kalphā*, Aramaic: representative) for the Manichaeans in Iran, and his son speaker (*kalphā*) for the Christians.

At some point, however, the patience of the "King of kings" ran out and Imru l-Qays, along with his tribe, had to take flight. He entered Roman territory in Syria. It was at this time at the latest that conversion to Christianity had become inevitable, as this was demanded by Rome for anyone wishing to remain on Roman territory. This decision was facilitated by means of payments from the Romans as a kind of "compliance assistance". Imru l-Qays died in 328 CE as a vassal of the Romans. His people found a new home in Syria. The epitaph on the grave of Imru l-Qays calls him: King of all *(a)ʿR(a)B.*

Ḥīra and Ḥaṭrā had their western location in common. Ḥaṭrā is located to the west of the Tigris and Ḥīra west of the lower Euphrates, on the edge of the desert at the outer west of Mesopotamia. Both the King of Ḥaṭrā and the King of Ḥīra dominated the regions to the west of Mesopotamia.

It was only in the 5th century that a new dynasty of local rulers in Ḥīra came about. They were recruited from followers of the previous rulers and took on the name of the land they came to live in. They had arrived in the country as a tribe, now they had become rulers of the land, something like the royal families of Prussia or Austria, who had previously been the Houses of *Hohenzollern* and *Habsburg*, before they migrated into the countries they occupied and took their names from them.

These followers of the kings of Ḥīra who had taken to flight, accepted the inheritance. Their home was the *Arabia Deserta*, one of a number of regions Ptolemaeus labeled *Arabia*.

4.3 An Attempt to Reconstruct the Form of Government of the Arab Kings of Ḥīra

When considering the ancient Phoenician model of long-distance trading, maritime aspects come to the fore. The network of maritime links between Tyrus, Sidon and Carthage, between Sardinia, Sicily and Spain is generally known. The Phoenicians traded on their own account with raw materials of each surrounding area and luxury goods they manufactured themselves like glass and Tyrian purple.

This was not the case in Ḥīra. The economic model of Ḥīra was similar to that of Ugarit. In Ugarit there were districts of Egyptians and Akkadians in the town. The harbour served as a storage yard. The Egyptians in Ugarit traded with and for Egypt; the Akkadians in Ugarit traded between Mesopotamia and the Mediterranean Sea. Ugarit lived from its harbour, it was an emporium.

Whoever ruled in Ḥīra was therefore interested in keeping the movement of goods running smoothly. He had to make sure the routes to and from Ḥīra were safe. Just how this worked was demonstrated by the Nabateans: They were only interested in the safety of the transit routes through the areas which they controlled and thus made possible the overland trade of frankincense from the Ḥiǧāz of today to Damascus. The gains from securing this trade made it possible for them to give up their nomadic way of life and move into urban palaces which proved they had a rich material culture.

However, the inhabitants of these impressive urban buildings did not change the way they led their lives. They kept only a few slaves, did no farming, the king served himself at the table and offered his guests the best food, and the consumption of wine was forbidden. There were communal meetings in which the king explained his political actions and had to answer questions. The Nabataean population in the area between the Ḥiǧāz and Damascus hardly reached ten thousand. It was therefore a matter of a network of economic subjects motivated by material interest, overlying the local structures on hand over a large area.[57]

Regarding Ḥīra this means: After the flight of the Lakhmids their customers took over the businesses. The Arab business providers in Arabia became the business leaders in Ḥīra. The title "*Amīr al-mu'minīn* – the leader (the one who speaks/ gives orders) of those who guarantee safety (participle of the causative stem of *'-m-n* (be safe)" was appropriate for the "safety business". The head person of those who granted this aplomb bears the title.

The history of the period between the first and second dynasties in Ḥīra, which is still largely unclear, gives us hints in this direction. At this time Ḥīra was conquered and burnt down by the Ghassanids (al-Ġasāsina), who were active in the West. The reason probably was to eliminate Ḥīra as a competitor for Bosrā.

The second dynasty, for which we have historical evidence, may well constitute a secondary formation which derived its legitimacy from the continuation of Lakhmid history. In short, the Arabic speaking Arabs from the North of the Arabian Peninsula had taken the place of their former Chaldaic masters. The second dynasty existed until 602 CE. Then it was destroyed by Ḵosrow II, as he had recognized the danger for his own rule which could arise from a Christian Arabian vassal kingdom. The consequence was that Ḵosrow II also made sure that the chair of the Syrian patriarchs of Seleucia-Ctesiphon remained vacant. It was the monophysites surrounding Ḵosrow II who were expected to represent the Christians at court.

Thus in Iran, an alienation grew between the orthodox *'Arabī* on the one hand and the followers of the Eastern Syrian church of Seleucia-Ctesiphon and the Persian *King of kings* on the other. The latter only tolerated Christians around him who were being persecuted in the Byzantine Empire at the time – the Monophysites. Their base was Takrīt, to the north of Seleucia-Ctesiphon.[58]

During the Byzantine-Sassanian war Heraclius used the alienation between the Iranian groups for his own purposes. By means of his propaganda he was able to get the Christians, who were estranged from the King of Kings, on his side. The Alexander Legend was to serve this purpose, traces of which are still to be found in the Qur'ān.

4.4 The Ghassanids

The Ghassanids had their settlement far away from the Arabian Peninsula in the old Nabataean town of Bosra (Buṣrā), known today as Eski-Shâm, not far from Damascus.

Irfan Shahid[59] traces their ancestry back to the great southern Arabian confederation of tribes, the Azd. In his view they wandered around the Arabian Peninsula until they settled down in the "Limes arabicus" in 490 CE. The Romans had allowed them in after the Ghassanids had declared themselves willing to convert to Christianity and pay tribute.

Here, once more, a popular myth about descent: The parentage of the Southern Arabs. However, the question of where their *northern* Arabian dialect could have come from, – Old South Arabian is a distinct Semitic language, – is not clarified, or even expounded.

The topos of the asserted aristocratic or noble descent of immigrants is such widespread common knowledge that it is surprising how Islamic Studies can fall for such. It does not take a trip to Arabia to track down this sort of phenomenon of enhancement of some obscure past. Well paid genealogists provided for Ottoman forefathers, who were contemporaries of Moses and Jesus. The Habsburg and Hohenzollern families managed to come up with family in Troy and Rome, patricians, caesars, the Merowingians and Charlemagne.

It has to be assumed that it is not known where the Arabs came from that stood at the Roman *Limes Arabicus* around 490 CE and demanded to be admitted. The story of a South Arabian background may as well be a pious invention. Wanderings in the desert were biblical themes.

In 1976, archeological investigations showed that the Romans had already relinquished the southern border fortifications during the fourth and fifth centuries. After the forts of Fityan, Yasir and possibly Bsir had been relinquished the complex of Lajun was abandoned after the earthquake of 551 CE. At the end of the reign of Justinian (565 CE) the two camps of legions stationed there – sixteen of the existing twenty-four *castella* and twelve of the investigated watch towers – were deserted. A further part of the border with Arabia, a sixty-mile-long strip from Wadi Hasa to Edom, was no longer fortified either. There were no military camps or watch towers. Furthermore, the Byzantine Empire had apparently not carried out any administrative activity for a long time, for there are no public buildings from the sixth century to be found and likewise no traces of imperial inscriptions on buildings. Judging by archeological findings, Byzantium had already retreated from Syria some one hundred years before the start of the Sassanian attacks in 604 CE, leaving behind several military garrisons. It was only the Arab Praetorian Guard of Rome, the Ghassanid Arabs, who displayed any construction activity. The inscriptions on buildings they left can be used as evidence. There is a Greek inscription on the tower of the monastery of Qasr al-Ḥayr al-Ġarbī. This is dated 559 CE and names the builder of the monastery as the Arab ruler al-Ḥāriṯ bn Ğabala, the Ghassanid. The Byzantine emperor is not mentioned in the inscription.[60] The name of the Ghassanid is a variation of the theme "Elagabal", the Roman emperor of Syrian descent. Elagabal was the son of a priestess at Emesa (Ḥimṣ) and a Roman emperor. His Semitic Name was "elā(ha) + ğabal – God (Aramaic) + mountain (Arabic)". Elagabal brought his sacred Rock with him to Rome and made the senators dance around. *Ḥāriṯ* ("ploughman") might be considered an Arabic translation of the title "Shah". This word form goes back to the Old Persian *xšāyaθiya-*, a derivation of the verbal root *xšā(y)* – "to rule". The equivalent in the closely related, but much better attested Sanskrit is *kṣatriya* ("member of the warrior [and royal] caste"). The root is derived from the word for "earth" (Sanskrit: *kṣām*), to which the word for "field" (Sanskrit: *kṣetra*) goes back as well. Until today, the Thai king has been called "mahā-kṣatriya" (a Sanskrit loan-word in Thai) and performs a "Royal Ploughing Ceremony" once a year. So *Ḥāriṯ bn Ǧabala*, could be transposed into a mixed Aramaic-Arabic-Persian form "Šāh min/bin al-Ǧabalā" – *Lord of the mountain*. This may help to explain the prominence of Emesa in the days of Early Islam. Old Syrian elites, in an Old Testament setting, carried on.

It is said that the Ghassanids, after a period of existence as followers of the Ṣāliḥ – a confederation of tribes, which had already been in the service of the Romans – overcame them and succeeded to them.[61] This just about represents the pattern of historic events that is associated with the appearance of the second Lakhmid dynasty in Ḥīra. It is a recurrent pattern in the narrative of the kerygmatic history of Early Islam. It can be found in the Sīra of Ibn Hišām as well, where the Qurayš supplant an earlier "tribe" in Mecca.

Around 502/3 CE the Ghassanids were counted as the new allies of Rome. The relationship between the two was laid down in a contract. On the basis of this *foedus* they received annual subsidies, euphemistically called *annonae foederatica*.

The regional leaders of the confederation of the Ghassanids were involved in the Byzantine hierarchy. They were given the title of a *phylarch* and the rank of a *clarissimus*; the leader of the confederation of tribes based in the Roman province of Arabia was given the title of *patricius* with the lauding epithet *gloriosissimus*. In addition he was allowed to wear the crown of a vassal and was therefore also a *basileus*. Apart from him, the only other person bearing this title was the king of Axum in Ethiopia who was also an ally of the Byzantines.[62]

The relationship between the emperor in Constantinople and the Arab vassal in Syria and in the west of the Arabian Peninsula suffered from structural problems, just as did the relationship of the *King of kings* in Ctesiphon and his Arab vassals in Ḥīra and in the east of the Arabian Peninsula, which led to the end of the Arab vassal rule both in the west and in the east: as representatives of a deviant religion or religious denomination, even as leaders of parallel societies, the vassals were increasingly considered domestic religious competitors.

The Ghassanids remained followers of Monophysitism, the form of Christianity which they had taken on when they transgressed to Roman territory, even after the council of Chalcedon in 451 CE. They became a symbol of resistance in the Byzantine Orient. Their status documented the conflict of the realm with regard to Christology.

4.5 The Christians in the East and in the West

After 501 CE, while Ḵosrow II was absent, the Lakhmid ruler of Ḥīra had himself christened at the Byzantine court. This move made him the natural leader of the Syrian Christians in the Sassanian territory and, in view of the advancing Christianization, a threat to the King of kings, the representative of Zoroastrianism. One short-term reaction of the King of kings was that he surrounded himself with the Monophysites from Northern Mesopotamia, who were only a minority in Iran, and took away the power of the ruling Syrian-Christian majority by leaving the see of the Patriarchs of Seleucia-Ctesiphon vacant and getting rid of the Lakhmids in 602 CE. The rivalry the King of kings had fostered among the Christians in the Iranian domain did not lead to a regaining of lost territory for the state religion, which was Zoroastrianism, but to an increase in its erosion. Christianity was the living religion, and Iran was on the way to a complete Christianization. The success of the attack on the Byzantine Empire in 604 CE and the expansion of Iran right up to Egypt immediately afterwards, only concealed the progressive disintegration at the centre of Iranian power for a short time.

During the course of the Great War Heraclius was able to get the Christians from Syria and Iran to join him by constantly looking for possibilities to find agreements concerning the questions of Christology. Existing differences and antagonisms were subordinated to his goal to gain complete victory over his religious adversary. In this situation, in a quasi "eschatological" struggle between Christianity and Zoroastrianism, the conflicting views among the Christian parties seem to fade from time to time.

It was only after Heraclius died in 641 CE, in the twentieth year of the great victory of 622 CE, that the pendulum swung back the other way. As long as the war continued, thanks to the demonization of the Persian *Šāhan-šāh* as the new Pharaoh, Heraclius was, in the eyes of the Syrian Christians, the *one with two horns*, – *Ḏū-l-Qarnayn*, – who, when following the apocalyptic prophesy, would destroy entire empires. Thus the victory of the Byzantines over the Sassanians took on the significance of a victory of Christianity over paganism. As participants in the great victory over the common enemy, the Arabian princes in Syria, Mesopotamia and Iran won back some influence, which they had lost in previous internal conflicts as regional powers under Byzantine and Sassanian suzerainty.[63]

5 The Beginning of a New Era

5.1 When did the Arabs Gain Sovereignty?

As a consequence of the implosion of Sassanian rule after the peace agreement achieved in 628 CE, Heraclius had the chance to free himself from the burdens of imperial tradition once and for all. His attempt in 618 CE to free himself from Constantinople had been a foretaste of things to come. His Christian "End Times Empire"[64] owed its position not to his dominance over territories, but to his victory over his religious adversary. From then on Heraclius no longer ruled as *imperator, caesar, augustus* of a thousand-year-old empire, but as a *dominatus*, who saw Christ as his Lord and who acted as Christ's vassal (*basileus*).

Heraclius relied on his Church. The Church is wherever the emperor is. Wherever the Church is not present the emperor cannot rule in terms of his imperial ideology. Heraclius' self-portrayal as founder of a new Davidic dynasty and as the saviour of the relict of the original True Cross, cannot convince those who, since the days of their fathers, had wrapped their theology in pictures of the Old Testament and saw the crucifixion as only a consequence of Christian living, but associated their hope with the birth of Jesus, the resurrection and the Day of Reckoning

Fig. 1: Above the symbol for the face value, a capital letter M on the reverse, instead of a cross a palm tree is depicted. It is a symbol for Jesus. He was born under a palm-tree (surah 19:23). This action of replacing the cross on the Byzantine type with a palm-tree on the Arab issue clearly shows the influence of the Qur'ānic materials in the days before 'Abd al-Malik's reign and "Monetary Reform". These materials are concerned with the life of Jesus. The circumstances of his death are not relevant. On the obverse John the Baptist is depicted with the reliquary containing his chopped off head. This was kept in al-Walīd's Umayyad mosque in Damascus. The coin imagery depicts the theme of surah Mariam, the background of John the Baptist as a forerunner (prodromos) and the birth of Jesus.

Therefore Heraclius allowed the Christians of the previously Byzantine Orient and of Iran, where at that time he ruled indirectly, to do something they had been denied by the Persian Pharaoh: he allowed them to move away.

One last attempt at unification failed. The "ekthesis" ("exposition (of faith; creed)" of 638 CE, – a compromise formula to reunite the quarreling factions, which was attached in the narthex of the Hagia Sophia, – was a fiasco. It was rejected by both the Orthodox and the Monophysites. Thus Syria and Egypt were lost for good.

Heraclius led a comprehensive military retreat from Mesopotamia, Syria and Egypt. This was secured by means of treaties with local Pretorians. The treaty with Egypt only came into effect after the death of Heraclius, as his widow Martina, his successor de facto, was temporarily refused allegiance in this matter.[65]

The occupation of Syria and afterwards of Egypt by the Persians from 613 to 629 CE had led to changes which had made it impossible to re-establish Byzantine rule, however rudimentary it may have ever been before. Generally, the region was ruled by Church dignitaries, who took advantage of stragglers and condottieri from the Great War, to prevent the reconstruction of the circumstances as they had been before 613 CE. The battles among the rest of the Arab auxiliary forces of the Sassanians and the former Ghassanid proprietors returning from the Byzantine Empire in 634 CE at Ġazza and Ağnādayn and 636 CE near the Yarmouk valley (Yarmūk; anyway a topos, not a historic event. The Arabs had a habit of gaining victory at rivers and bridges. This followed the example of Constantine's victory at the Milvean bridge), are evidence of the unsettled situation after the end of the Great War between Byzantium and Iran.

The later Islamic historiography fills this black hole of history with the alleged acts of the Prophet of the Arabs. The Persian occupation and destruction of the Byzantine Orient for a quarter of a century has not been appropriately perceived by European and American historians. The circumstances in Syria at the time Heraclius died are the result of the upheaval after this period of occupation and not the result of a tempest of peoples pouring into Syria and Egypt from the Arabian Peninsula in the name of the Prophet of the Arabs. On the stage of historic world events of the year 622 CE, Islamic historiographers build a theatrical set depicting a Meccan leader taking flight. The great military victory at the beginning of the religious war between Byzantium and Iran is turned into the flight of the Prophet of the Arabs from his enemies in the form of a *new exodus*.

Historical facts and probability, however, prove that the beginning of the new era is not marked by the emergence of new religion in Mecca and Medina, but by the autonomy of Christian Arabs and *'Arabī* after the victory of Heraclius over the Persians in 622 CE.

5.2 The Events of the year 20 according to the Arabs

In the 20th year of his surprise victory over the Persians Heraclius died. His death meant the end of the relationship which he had personally built up with the Arab and *'arabī*-emirs of Iran. With his death the loyalty of the allies from the time of the Great War also died. As a sign of their newly won independence the emirs of Iran started striking Iranian coins in the style of the last Sassanians, dated from the year 20 onward. The 20th year of victory falls on 641 CE, the year Heraclius died.

It is interesting to note that this movement towards independence manifested itself predominantly in the East of Iran, in Khorāsān (Merv, al-Marwā) and Sīstān.[66]

The Arabian Pretorians of the Byzantines in the former Byzantine Orient and the Arabian auxiliary troops in Iran also struck imitations of imitations of Byzantine coins.

The year 20 saw the introduction of regular and consecutively dated issues of silver coinage of the Arabian emirs in Iran.

It is only after the year 20 that documented written records of the new masters of the former Byzantine Orient are to be found. In the text of the oldest Arabic document the signatures of those involved show how far they were still adhering to Aramaic writing habits: the final N is still written as in Aramaic. This wonderful "document" was purchased in the last decades of the nineteenth century by an Austrian Archduke during his sojourn in the Orient. Those travails in the Orient had replaced the Italian voyages of young nobility from Northern Europe. Instead of going on a buying spree for Italian master paintings, Orientalia and Islamica were acquired. This led to the discovery of the unique handwriting of al-Ṭabarī, an undated manuscript, and other "uniques" and rarities.

The topic of the text of the unique papyrus from the year 22 (sic!) is provisions for the troops. Istephan, a caliph, receives acknowledgment that he has handed over a number of sheep. After stating the year there is no mention of the era. The year stated stands completely alone: the year 22.

Fig. 2: Iranian copper coins depicting Byzantine rulers as evidence for the Byzantine occupation of Iranian territories.

Fig. 3: In the 20th year after the victory of the Byzantines over the Persian army in the year 622 CE (the "Year of the Arabs"), i.e., the year of Heraclius' death (641 CE), the ʿArabī/Arabs start striking coins as sovereigns. The first words constitute the formula: "bi-sm(i) llāh(i) r-rahmān(i) r-raḥīm" (in the name of the gracious and merciful God). There are no clues as to the origins and to the creed of the signatories to be found that go further than this formula, today known as the "basmallah".

The document can be dated precisely on the basis of the Greek text, which contains the tax year of Byzantium. According to this text, the date in question is 25 April, 643. This is the 22nd year after the victory of Heraclius over the Persians.

In the Greek part of the text of the document the origins of the recipient are recorded. According to this, it was one *Amir Abdellas* (*'Abdallāh*) of the *magar*(*i*)*t*(*ais*). As the person in charge of the unique papyrus was not able to make head or tail of this word, he "appointed" the Amīr to be a *muhāğir* and his troops to be *muhāğirūn ("emigrants, escapers")*. Today this term is understood as designating those who "*emigrated*" with Muḥammad from Mecca to Medina, but in this document it probably designates those who betook themselves to the great camp in order to take part in the military campaigns.[67]

Now the question remains what this term "*magar(i)t(ais)*" meant. The solution lies in the difficulties the Greek have when transcribing Arabic terms. This term will hardly designate "relatives of Magaret", but it is relatives of "Hagar", – *m[uh]âgaritais,* – who are meant. The Greek form goes back to the Aramaic form "*mhaggraye – Hagarenes*", i.e., descendants of *Hagar,* Abraham's concubine and mother of Ishmael, the term often found in Syriac documents designating "Arabs". Already in the Bible, the descendants of Ishmael and Hagar are identified with the nomads between Egypt and Assyria:

> "So Hagar bore Abram a son; and Abram called the name of his son, whom Hagar (הָגָר *Hāgār*) bore, Ishmael. (Gen 16:15) [...]These are the years of the life of Ishmael, one hundred and thirty-seven years; and he breathed his last and died, and was gathered to his people. They (*i.e., the descendants of Ishmael*) settled from Havilah to Shur *which is east of Egypt as one goes toward Assyria*; he settled in defiance of all his relatives (Gen 25:17-18)."

So here we have a case of *popular etymology*: The original name *mhaggraye* is no longer understood, neither by the Greeks, who turned it into "*magaritai*", nor by the Arabs, who interpreted the consonants *m-h-g-r-* as the participle "*muhāğir* – emigrant". Cases of popular etymology are quite frequent, even among the designations for ethnic groups. The "Tatars" were often spelt "Tartars", as if the name was derived from "*tartaros* – hell". In this particular text, it even made sense: the troops designated by the term had in fact "emigrated" to the military camps to take part in campaigns. Only much later was the story of the emigration from Mecca to Medina built around this newly fangled name.

5.3 Why there are no Coins and Documents from the Independent Emirs before the Year 641 CE that can be Dated

There is an imitative issue of a coin with a problematic inscription[68] which demonstrates the situation very well: the year on the coin is 17, and on the reverse the letter "M" for the denomination is inscribed; Islamologists, who uncritically follow Islamic historiography, consider it to refer to Damascus, as this town was supposedly conquered by the Muslims in the year *17* of the *hiğra*. The letter "M" is understood as meaning "40 Nummia", i.e., the face value. This is where Islamologists are confronted with problems they would prefer to ignore:

1. How can the Islamic conquest of Damascus be dated as of the year "17 of the *hiğra*", – the beginning of the *Islamic* numbering of years, – in the light of the fact that the term "*Islām*" is mentioned in inscriptions for the first time only in the year 72?
2. How can an alleged number on a coin be connected with an era after the *hiğra* of the Prophet of the Arabs from Mecca to Medina when the title which is taken to be the name of the prophet is only mentioned in inscriptions for the first time in the year 32? It is written in Aramaic lettering „*M(a)ḤM(a)T*", i.e., this is the Middle Persian ideogram pronounced "Mehmet" by the Turks. Such coins originate from Zaranj, the capital of Sīstān, in Southeast Iran.[69]
3. Above the letter "M" is the monogram of Heraclius, who was still emperor in the year 622+17 = 639!

When historicizing the title „*M(u)H(a)M(ma)D*" the historiographers had not considered that one day the evaluation of archeological findings would make it possible to reconstruct a historical account of events. This is one reason why archeology has no friends amongst the pious.

Up to now there has never been any significant indication that the numbers on the coins, which were regarded as dates, show any clues pertaining to an era. There is merely a number on the coins and no clue as to which era this number can be attributed.

The omission of any indication of an era in the manner of "Anno Domini" or of the Byzantine indiction (a cycle of 15 years) or of the era of a town made all sorts of interpretation of these numbers possible within the framework of the totally unchallenged Islamic historiography. However, despite this prestidigitation, Islamology has not been able to dispel the discrepancies between the numbers specified and historiographers' accounts. Consequently, in 1941, J. Walker came to the conclusion that in many cases the evidence to be inferred from coins cannot be reconciled with information from traditional Islamic historiography.[70]

Three inscriptions have been preserved from the time of the rule of Muʿāwiya, the first ruler of the Arabs after the death of Heraclius:

1. These are to be found on the coins struck on the occasion of his promotion to *Amīr al-mu'minīn* in Dārābjird in the year 41. In the space next to the portrayal of the Sassanian ruler they bear the following inscription in Middle Persian, in Aramaic script: MAAWIA AMĪR-i WURROYISHNIGĀN.

Here Muʿāwiya's name is written in the tradition of Aramaic names. This is also the case for the next inscription:

.+ ЄΠΙΑΒΔΑΛΛΑΜΛΑΝΙΑΛΜΗΡΑ
ΛΛΜΥΜЄΝΝΑΠЄΛΥΘΗΚϹΑΝЄ
ΝЄΩΘΗΟΚΛΙΒΑΝΟϹΤΩΝЄΝΤΑΥ
ΘΑΔΙΑΛΑΒΔΑΛΛΑΝΙΟΑΒΟΑϹЄΜΥ
ϹΥΜΒΥΛΥЄΝΜΗΝΗΔЄΚЄΜΒΡΙΩ
ΠЄΜΠΤΗΗΜЄΡΑΔЄΥΤЄΡΑΙΝΑϹ
ЄΤΟϹΤΗϹΚΟΛΩΝϹΚΥΚΑΤΑΑΡΑΒΑ
ЄΤΟϹΜΒЄΙϹΙΑϹΗΝΤΩΝΝΟϹΥΝ
ΤΩΝϹΠΟΔΗΙΩΑΝΝΥΜΓΑΔΑΡΗΝΥ

+Ἐπὶ Ἀβδάλλα Μαάυια ἀμῆρα
ἀλμουμενὴν ἀπελύθη κ(αὶ) ἀνε-
ναώθη ὁ κλίβανος τῶν ἐνταῦ-
θα διὰ Ἀβδάλλα υἱοῦ Ἀβουασέμου
συμβούλου ἐν μηνὴ δεκεμβρίῳ
πέμπτη ἡμέρᾳ δευτέρᾳ ἰνδ(ικτιῶνος)ς
ἔτους τῆς κολων(ίας) ςκψ κατὰ Ἄραβα(ς)
ἔτους μβ εἰς ἴασην τῶν νοσούν-
των σπουδῇ Ἰωάννου μ(αγιστριανοῦ?) Γαδαρηνοῦ

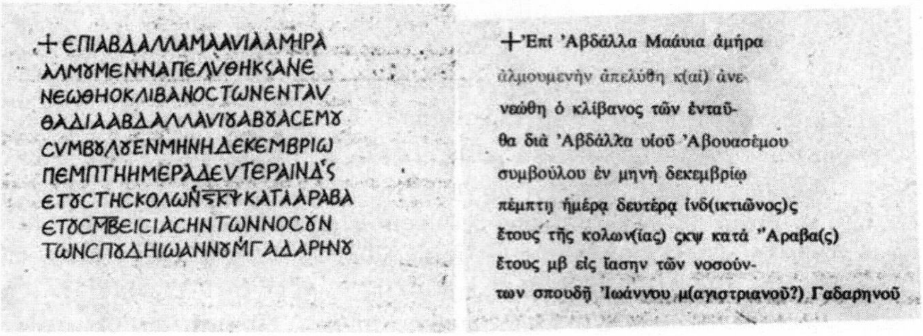

Fig. 4: *The inscription of Muʿāwiya in the baths of Gadara from the year 42 "kata Arabas – according to the Arabs". Israel Exploration Journal, vol. 32 (1982), p. 94.*

2. The inscription in the baths of Gadara from the year 42. This is where the first ruler of all Arabs is named in the Greek inscription: MAAVIA AMIRA AL-MOMENIN. Here again the Aramaic spelling of the name is conspicuous. This inscription alone indicates an era which can be attributed to Muʿāwiya's rule: It is dated according to the regional tradition of the Decapolis in the Roman *Provincia Arabia*. This means that the imperial indiction of Constans II was on top. The local era then followed. After that came the era of the Pretorian/regional ruler, Muʿāwiya. The time indication according to the imperial indiction of Byzantium is found in the text of the inscription: 6th year of the indiction, 2nd weekday, 5th day of December. This falls on the end of the year 663 CE.

The dating according to the "era of the *colonia*", i.e., from the time the town was founded, can also be verified. Gadara belonged to Decapolis, the *Federation of Ten Cities*. The coins of Gadara were dated. In the collection of the Franciscan monastery in Jerusalem there is one example from the first year of the Roman occupation. Year 1 of Rome is 64/63 BCE. In the inscription of Muʿāwiya, the year 726 is stated as the year according to the *era of the colonia*. This falls on 662/663 CE.

The era of Muʿāwiya, the regional ruler, is stated as the year 42 *according to the Arabs* (KATA ARABA[S]). This is the 42nd year of the victory of Heraclius over his Persian adversaries. The 42nd year after the victory of 622 CE is 663 CE. This goes to prove that the counting used according to the imperial indiction, the *era of the colonia* and the era of the regional ruler, Muʿāwiya, was done according to the *solar year*.[71]

3. The inscriptions on a dam in Ṭā'if are dated the year 58. They refer to Mu'āwiya as *Amīr al-mu'minīn,* a term translated by a Spanish chronicle of 754 as: *omnia prospere gerens*[72] (the one who rules everything in a propitious manner). The text of the inscription is written in Arabic script.[73]

The three inscriptions lend valuable clues to the rule of Mu'āwiya, as he is known to the Islamic tradition. Also, as the commander of all those responsible for security *(Amīr al-mu'minīn)* he appeared in Iran, according to local tradition, and had himself appointed ruler over Iran at the location of the Sassanian palace in Dārābjird in the old Persis.

In Syria he continued to follow the tradition of dating official documents according to the imperial indiction, maintaining the local tradition by respecting a pre-Christian *era of the colonia* and only naming his era in third place. This era was given a name. It is the era known as "of the Arabs" (KATA ARABA[S]). The era is synchronous to the lunar years of the era according to the indiction and to the era of Gadara. It should be mentioned that in the *Syrian History of the World* by Johannan bar Penkaye it is stated that the work was finished in the 67th year of Arab rule. There is no reference to the life of the Prophet of the Arabs whatsoever.

On the Arabian Peninsula, in the region of the former Ghassanid rule in Western Arabia, the inscription from Ṭā'if shows respectful treatment of the local tradition.

The later, historiographic overlap of one historic incident can be clarified using these three inscriptions:

All numbers stated are dates without naming an era. Only the inscriptions of Gadara make it clear that Mu'āwiya's numbers refer to dating "of the Arabs" (KATA ARABA[S]).

Thus it was not difficult some 150 years later, at a time which was understood to be the era of the caliphs Harūn al-Rašīd and of his son, Ma'mūn, to replace this era "of the Arabs" with an era after the *hiğra* of the Prophet of the Arabs. This step from the counting after the battle of 622 as the symbolic beginning of the liberation of the Christian Arabs of Iran from their heathen oppressors, to the counting after the *hiğra* of a Prophet of the Arabs, can only be comprehended since the discovery of the inscription of Gadara[74].

6 The Time of Mu'āwiya

6.1 The Rise and fall of Mu'āwiya.

Mu'āwiya had realised that a unity of the western and eastern Arabs could only take place if an imperial project could satisfy regional ambitions and overcome differences. This was a lesson learnt from the experience gained in the Great War between the Christians and the Persian Zoroastrianists when internal differences were pushed into the background for the duration of the conflict.

As, in the meantime, Byzantium had redefined itself and freed itself from the burdens of its imperial inheritance, it was now time for the Arabs to redefine the imperial legacy they had inherited from the Sassanians. From this, the idea arose to finally establish the Iranian claim to leadership in the form of an Arabian Empire. This meant a shift of power to the western domains of Iranshahr and western religious concepts. The powerhouse of the Sassanians had been the East of Iranshahr, were the Zoroastrian revival had gained influence. The riches of the Sassanians came from their China-trade along the Silk Road. The notion of taking over leadership in the field of theology together with the conquest of Constantinople was, naturally enough, linked to this. The struggle between Byzantine Christianity and the Iranian state-religion was replaced by a struggle between Byzantine Orthodoxy and Eastern Christianity in an Iranian mold.

In 648 CE Constans II, the Byzantine emperor, had made an attempt to distance himself from the theological mistakes of the past. He had the ekthesis of Heraclius removed from the Narthex of the Hagia Sophia. This is how one point of conflict was eliminated which had led to protests in North Africa in 646 CE. This is where Maximus Confessor, the most important theologian of his time, had held synods, in which the teachings of monotheletism and monoenergism, compromise doctrines fostered by the power center in Constantinople, were attacked as heresy. In order to put an end to the permanent Christological conflict between Constantinople and the previous Byzantine Orient, Constans II issued his decreed *Type of Constans* in 648 CE, in which he forbade any discussion about the topic of Christ possessing either one or two wills, or one or two energies.[75]

Muʿāwiya may well have been successful in joining together the western and eastern Arabs with the help of this sort of projection. His originating from the East, from Mesopotamia – his Aramaic name gives it away – may well have helped. It is unknown just as to how his rise in the West took place. It is possible that he became ruler of Syria as an ally of the Byzantines (as a "Qurayš"). Nothing is known about his career before the year 28 of the Arabs. In 647 CE Muʿāwiya advanced to Cappadocia. He is said to have been militarily active in Armenia beforehand. However, all this comes from unreliable sources.

These reports are supported by Theophanes, the Byzantine historian. However, it should be taken into consideration that Theophanes' accounts about the Arabs could possibly be "Trojan horses" that stem from an Arab tradition. The chronicles of Theophanes, which are the most important source for the Arab-Byzantine relations of this period, first emerged between

810 and 814 CE, when the reinterpretation of early Islamic history had already been completed at the court of the caliph known as Hārūn al-Rašīd. Therefore it is important to pay regard to the Byzantine documents, recorded by Dölger, which mention ceasefires, peace agreements, divisions of power (Cyprus) and payment of tribute, which makes it possible to paint a more differentiated picture of the former relationships between the court in Damascus and Byzantium.

In 659 CE Muʿāwiya sought an agreement with Byzantium and declared he was willing to pay tribute.[76] From the viewpoint of an uninvolved observer, Muʿāwiya had been able to follow how the dictatorial attempt of Constans II to put an end to Christological debate had failed.

One year after the announcement of the emperor's *Type*, Martin, the new Pope, held a great council in the Lateran Palace. The synod denounced both the ekthesis and the *Type*. Consequently, the emperor then had the Pope brought to Constantinople in 653 CE where he was charged with high treason and first sentenced to death, then banned to the Crimea. That is where the Pope died in 656 CE, sick, distressed and suffering from hunger. Soon after, Maximus Confessor was also brought to court. He was not treated as badly as the Pope, as he was seen as the spiritual leader of the Orthodox Greeks. He died in exile in West Georgia in 662 CE, after years of negotiations and maltreatment.

It was in this year that Constans II had finally had enough of wearing himself out with religious conflicts. He left for new shores. He gave up the capital city of Constantinople. His destination was the Byzantine West, the homeland of his family.

Muʿāwiya made use of the calm that had resulted from peace with Byzantium, to forge an alliance. The Syrian and Egyptian Monophysites still had a score to settle with Byzantium. The Iranian Arabs might possibly have been ill-disposed to Byzantium in as far as they originated from *ʿArabī*-clans or belonged to the Arabs from the East of the Arabian Peninsula, who had been converted early on and who were bearers of the pre-Nicean, Antiochian theology.

In the same year that the emperor turned away from his capital city, Muʿāwiya had himself appointed to the first *Amīr al-mu'minīn*. The assembly of the emirs took place in Dārābjird in the 41st year of the Arabs (662 CE).[77]

He had given rise to the impression that an opportunistic conquest of Constantinople could be possible under his leadership. It was believed they could build on the experience they had gathered previously in Syria and Egypt. Constans II travelled west. The East seemed ready for assimilation into the Arabian Empire.[78]

Emperor Constans II travelled to Rome via Thessalonica. After a twelve-day-long stay he continued to travel and, via Naples, reached Syracuse where he set up his new residence on 17th June in 663 CE.

At about the same time Muʿāwiya reappeared. He arrived in Asia Minor with his army. From 663 CE on, the troops of Muʿāwiya appeared every year. A nice topos describing traditional warfaring of those days of summer campaigns. The Ottomans had a saying for this type of making war: "Yazın kızlara, kışın oğlanlara" ("Going after the girls during the summer [campaigns] and after the boys in winter [at the barracks]"). The country was devastated, the population deported to the East. The troops advanced as far as Chalcedon, just as the Sassanian army had done before them. This recurrent pattern is not seen by the Islamic hagiography, which represents a world view that is based on the assumption that the start button of history relevant for mankind was pushed in the desert somewhere in the year 622 CE.

Muʿāwiya got himself into a more advantageous starting position than the Sassanians had done. In the Byzantine-Sassanian conflicts the Persians had always been able to bring their superiority in regard to land-forces to bear, but had always lost out in the end due to their maritime inferiority. Whenever they managed to reach Chalcedon, which was located opposite Constantinople, they had to rely on local allies who supported them with a fleet in the Bosporus and in the Sea of Marmara. At first these were the Avars, later the Slavs had a role to play. However, each attack on Constantinople failed in the end due to the superiority of the Byzantines at sea and to the inability of their adversaries to cut off the capital city from the corn provision from the Crimean peninsula. Here we seem to encounter more topoi from Classical history and Pompeus' adventures with the pirates.

As ruler over Syria and Egypt Muʿāwiya was able to use the fleets of the region for his own purposes. In the course of an operation of island hopping and of furtively inching his way forward to the Cyprus-Rhodes-Kos line, he reached the peninsula of Kyzikos near Constantinople. In 672 CE the mainland city Smyrna was occupied and the coastline was secured: a nice mixture of staff-officers' dreaming and history teachers' standard of reporting.

Despite this apparent success, what the Arabs had planned was threatened by the changes going on in Byzantium. In 668 CE Emperor Constans II was murdered in Syracuse. Thus the attempt of the emperor to initiate a change in orientation of the Empire towards the West had failed. This attempt at a change of orientation was the natural consequence of the failure of the emperor's role as mediator in the religious conflicts in the East. His son, Constantine IV, (668-85 CE), took over rule in Constantinople. Muʿāwiya could no longer reckon with finding a palace abandoned by the emperor, which would have been easy prey.

When the attack on Constantinople finally came, the unexpected happened: Muʿāwiya came to grief before Constantinople. Greek fire devastated his fleet, – another topos for divine intervention. The fighting beneath the walls of the strongest forts in the world at the time had to be abandoned in the autumn. While retreating, the fleet of the Arabs was dispersed by a storm and the territorial army in Asia Minor was completely beaten: a disaster of biblical dimensions, a show of hybris and a well-deserved outcome. Apocalyptic events happen when the timing is right. This explains the Sultans' fancy for watches and clock towers. Arabs of today love watches and clocktowers, they are keen to know the "Hour".

Muʿāwiya pledged to pay an annual tribute in gold, horses and slaves.[79]

Fig. 5: Coins from the time of Emperor Constantine IV. Solidus of an imperial mint and two Arabic imitations.

After the failure of this test of the "katechon" before Constantinople, the bond between the western and the eastern Arabs was dissolved. It was a double failure: Apart from the failing of the optimised Sassanian plan of attack, the continuation of the existence of imperial theological dominance weighed heavily and had long-term effects. It had become impossible for Muʿāwiya to legitimate his rule by means of founding a new, Eastern state religion. The Christians in his realm were not united under his spiritual leadership. They were at odds with each other or still leaning towards Constantinople when it came to questions of theology.

6.2 Muʿāwiya's Adversaries

The eastern Arabs now began to separate from Muʿāwiya and elected a new *Amīr al-mu'minīn* in Dārābjird in the year after the defeat before Constantinople. The defeat in 674 CE falls in the 53rd year of the Arabs. The earliest coins of ʿAbdallāh bn al-Zubayr from Dārābjird have this date. He is referred to as *ʿAbdallāh Amīr-i-Wurroyishnigān* on the coins in Pahlavi script, which is derived from the Aramaic script. Coins with a reference to ʿAbdallāh from Dārābjird are extant from year 53 of the Arabs to year 60 of the Arabs.[80]

It is striking that it is only on the coins from Dārābjird that the title of *Amīr al-mu'minīn* is referred to in its Pahlavi-form. This also occurs later with ʿAbd al-Malik's coins after year 60 of the Arabs. On the coins from the years 60 and 61 of the Arabs there is the inscription: "APDLMLIK AMĪR-i-Wurroyishnikān." On all coins from Dārābjird, those from Muʿāwiya, ʿAbdallāh bn Zubayr and ʿAbd al-Malik, no reference to the family of the respective ruler is to be found. These inscriptions thus follow the Sassanian tradition.

We only possess the coins of Muʿāwiya from Dārābjird and his inscriptions from Gadara and Ṭā'if, where he is referred to as Maavia or Muʿāwiya respectively, so we cannot determine his ancestry from the inscriptions. It cannot be clarified whether he was an Arabic speaking Arab or an Aramaic speaking Arab, although his Aramaic name ("the weeper, the pleureur") hints at an Aramaic background, nor can we know from the inscriptions whether he was a Ṣufyānī or not.

The provincial coins of ʿAbdallāh bn Zubayr from outside Dārābjird, state that he descended from the tribe of the *Zupirān* (or more exact: "*Znpylan*").[81] ZNPYL is an Aramaic word for "consigliere, counselor, advisor". The Greek rendering of this expression is "soumboulos". We can translate the name as: "The Servant of God descended from the Advisors". The question as to whether God has an advisor, was raised in the Old Testament (Is 40:13). It was negated by Paul (Romans 19:23). So we are confronted here with a problem concerning the understanding of the scriptures, not with tribal lore from an Arabia Deserta. It is a matter of which kind of prophethood: a custodian according to Isaiah (1:26, in the Septuaginta) to build up Zion, or a messianic one like the Servant of the King of the Day of Judgment. We have a continuous radicalization of a Messianic concept before us.

This Iranian name form of the Zubayrids corresponds to the one used on provincial coins of 'Abd al-Malik. There the tribe is referred to as the "MRW'n+ān". It is significant that the name of this lineage is found on the coin from Merv.[82] This old cultural center in Khorasan is the home of 'Abd al-Malik. His family is referred to as Marwānids, derived from their home town MRW (Merv/ Marw). This is a historic coincidence: The names *Marwān* and *Marw* (Merv) have a common Aramaic background. Merv is a well-watered oasis. The pure water comes from the rock al-Ṣafā, when Moses' stick hits the rock. This water from the Rock streams into a tank, a basin, that overflows with directions and revelations. The unadulterated word of God comes forth from the Rock, it is collected in the *marwa* and overflows into a stream to supply men with the pure word of God and water to the creation.[83] ʿAbd al Malik is the "Servant of the King" in the opening words of the Qur'ān, the Lord of the Day of Jugement, the Messiah. He is not only a Messianic figure, but as a "Marwān" a kind of paraclete, a vessel for the word of God from the Rock.

In the case of Muʿāwiya and his two successors it can be assumed that they took office in Dārābjird and are referred to on coinage according to the tradition of the Sassanian rulers.[84] The regional rulers of Iran, however, have their spiritual lineage mentioned in the coin inscriptions, but do not include a mentioning of a title.

'Abd al-Malik's home town was Merv. Thus it is understandable that in the inscription on the coin from Merv of the year 75 of the Arabs, he does not carry the title of *Amīr al-mu'minīn,* – that he only did on the coins from Dārābjird and not as the ruler of his homeland province, – yet he does display his spiritual lineage. Thus it is also understandable why coins are struck for *Ziyād bn Abī Sufyān* in Dārābjird in the year 41 of the Arabs. The inscription on this coin refers to him as *Ziyāt-i-Abusfiyān*. There is no reference to any title.[85]

In the year 41 of the Arabs Ziyād bn Abī Sufyān was the local ruler of the province, the capital of which was Dārābjird. As the old ancestral seat of the Sassanians, Dārābjird also served as the location for choosing the *Amīr-i-wurroyišnigān*. Therefore it is not surprising that coins of Muʿāwiya, 'Abd-allāh bn Zubayr and 'Abd al-Malik from the respective first year of their rule, are found with the official title from Dārābjird.

6.3 An End in Arabia?

The dating of Muʿāwiya's inscription on a reservoir at Ṭā'if as the year *58 of the Arabs* possibly allows conclusions to be drawn as to the end of Muʿāwiya.

As ruler in Damascus he had accepted the inheritance of the Ghassanids. After the disaster before Constantinople, the outrageous peace agreement with Byzantium, the loss of the East and the transfer of his Iranian title of *Amīr-i-wurroyišnigān* to Ibn Zubayr, the only thing he was left with was the Ghassanid legacy. This also comprised parts of the Arabian Peninsula. There the dam of a reservoir in the style of a *marwa* served as a reminder of Muʿāwiya's charitable act in the year 58 of the Arabs (669 CE). His popularity in Syria even beyond his death is referred to in many places in the historiographical literature of the Arabs.

Nothing is known about Muʿāwiya's end. The biographies of the sons that followed him are probably products of religious literature. According to them, Muʿāwiya, always level-headed, frugal and irreligious in a typically Bedouin manner, was punished by the heavens in the form of the son who succeeded him and who did not keep within the bounds of known customs and morals. After the heavenly punishment had put Muʿāwiya's life and achievements into perspective to such an extent, the final obliteration of the disbelieving lineage followed. The second son was doomed. He lapsed into illness and came to an early end. A biblical treatment of a fantasy with Neronic ingredients and an end of Romulus Augustulus.

The story progresses in this biblical style. The report of great outrages gives the listener an idea of what is to come. The lineage of Muʿāwiya's successor also fell victim to the punishment of the heavens. The beginnings of the Umayyads are linked with an attack on Mecca, where the pious ʿAbdallāh bn Zubayr was hoping for the end of the usurpers. The latter, however, sent the arch heretic and Crypto-Manichaean al-Ḥaǧǧāǧ to Mecca. The former school teacher apparently knew his way around there well, as tradition credits him with Ṭā'if as his place of birth. He used the most powerful weapons of the time against the Kaʿba. He had the Kaʿba shot at by catapult in order to test whose stone was hardest. The Kaʿba burnt and fell apart.[86]

He who does such things, does not end well. And so it was indeed. In the year 134 of the Arabs in the Wadī l-Awǧā' close to Antipatris everything was over. Many Christians were massacred there as relatives of the Umayyads.[87] After that the story of the Umayyads goes on in al-(W)Andalus. This was far away from the Kaʿba, and thus only good things are reported about the time of the Umayyads in al-(W)Andalus.

The amount of material accumulated by Islamologists about this epoch and subject matter could fill libraries. The end of production of such scientific literature on this topic is not in sight, particularly as the history of the Umayyads in Spain seems to have an exemplary character for the successful integration of the modern religion of Islam into Europe. However, the fact that the "Islām" of the Umayyads referred to the right *understanding of the (biblical) scriptures*, is not taken into consideration. They had written down their own understanding of the scriptures in the Qur'ānic texts, against the background of the internal Iranian religious discourse. There was constant work on the composition of this material as the *Islām* of the 9th century CE demanded an extended textual basis. It is also thanks to the 9th century that many colorful, kerygmatic and pious stories depicting the alleged proceedings in Mecca have been passed down to us.

If these colorful depictions of the battles of caliphs are seen as what they are, – later concoctions, not the description of reality, – then reality will get a chance to return to the history books, a reality of realia, material evidence in the midst of scrappy numbers and meagre inscriptions that document a historic course of historic events. As it stands now, we can conclude that the narrators were only interested in the *esprit* of a narrative, but got the numbers wrong. Dates of the chronology were manipulated to fit into a pattern of kerygmatic literature. At the end of this process there is an unbroken line of transmitters, be they Caliphs or Popes.

From the evidence of the coins struck in the name of ʿAbdallāh bn Zubayr, we can infer that his appointment as *emir of those who grant safety/who led the faith* came to an end in Dārābjird in the year 60 of the Arabs.[88] Immediately afterwards he was mentioned as a provincial ruler, but with no title, in Ardašīr-Khurra from the years 65–67 of the Arabs.[89] In Kirmān his name is found on coins from the years 62–69 of the Arabs.[90] Coins from the years 63 and 66 of the Arabs are known for the mint of Istakhr in the Persis.[91] This shows that he had been sidelined and the leadership had been taken over by the more radical, messianic "Servant of the Lord of the Day of Judgement (ʿAbd al-Malik)".

By looking at the names on coins it is possible to determine that he lost his title and his function as "*Amīr al-mu'minīn (Arabic)/ Amīr-i-wurroyiš-nigān (Persian)/ emir of those who grant safety*" in the year 60 of the Arabs (681 CE). However, he still ruled for almost another decade as ruler of the central provinces of the Arab-Sassanian Emirates. For the title "Caliph" we have no epigraphic evidence from the days of the Umayyads.

The horrific transformations of the conflicts the historiographers refer to as *fitna* (secession, upheaval) can only be presented in a short scenario: The conflicts between the western Arabs and the eastern Arabs in the last years of Muʿāwiya's life and after his death are described in the historiography of the 9th century using all personalities and stage props that could be availed of in Mesopotamia at the time. This means that caliphs emerge whose caliphates were not yet created in the 1st century of the Arabs, and that heroes (*ʿAlī*) became martyrs, whose roles as "companions" of *muḥammad*, at that time, i.e., in the 1st century of the Arabs, still a Christological title, had not even been casted. In the beginning, what was expected was the return of Jesus, the Messiah, the *muḥammad* (originally: "the desired one" [*desideratus*; Aramaic meaning], later understood as the "praised one" or "the one to be praised" [*benedictus*; Arabic meaning]) and not the incarnation of a Christological title (the historicized figure in Mecca and Medina). The inevitable conclusion is that the texts recited by modern Muslims, that they consider to be the unaltered Qur'ān, transmitted to Muḥammad in Mecca and Medina, were actually composed over a long period which only ended in the 9th century.

Of course, the setback before Constantinople, the failed attempt to overcome the "katechon" protecting the Rūm, must have had unmissable repercussions. The traces left are visible in the changing of the actors in this drama of biblical proportions. It is not difficult to imagine just what hope Mu'āwiya's great project must have aroused. When this great project failed, which connected the former Byzantine Orient with the Post-Sassanians in Iran, old rivalries were rekindled, and the unresolved problems arisen due to Sassanian policy since the expansion of Ḵosrow II into Syria and Egypt, again became a matter of urgency.

7 The Time of 'Abd al-Malik and his Sons

7.1 The Alleged Battle for Mecca, the Rivalry of the Opposing Caliphs and the Emergence of 'Abd al-Malik.

Just as in other parts of world history, this is also a case when the failure of great ambitions led to further radical events. It is the actions and rule of 'Abd al-Malik from Khorasan that stand for this radicalization. He made sure that there was always something left to do tomorrow. His clan, the *MRW'nān*, originated from Merv in what is now Turkmenistan. The mint mark of the mint of Merv: MRW,[92] can already be found on Sassanian coins.

The great oasis of Merv at the lower reaches of the Murghab river in the Northeast of the Iranian territories had already had diocese status since 553 CE.[93] According to Islamic historiography, it was there that Elias, the metropolitan of the city, provided for the burial of Yazdegerd III, the last of the Sassanians. The latter was supposed to have fled from the conquering Arabs as far as Merv where he was said to have been struck dead by the Marzbān (provincial governor) Māhōy Suri of Merv in a mill, in which he had taken refuge in 651 CE. This cannot be proven in historical terms and it is difficult to comprehend. It seems rather to be the case that the legend legitimizes the transfer of power in Iran to the iranianized Christian *'Arabī*. A "ruler of the border" (*marzbān*) would only kill his master if the latter had been ostracized beforehand by the fire priests (mobads). However, according to Zoroastrian tradition the last Sassanian is still honoured today. To the Zoroastrians his death is still considered a national tragedy.

Therefore this report can be seen as a sanction from God for the actions of the Muslim contemporaries of Ṭabarī and as an attack on the contemporary Zoroastrians in Iran. According to this, their downfall is due to a betrayal of their own tradition. He who kills his own master, will be punished by God. He who kills the living God of the Iranians, can no longer legitimately rule in Iran.

'Abd al-Malik's connection with Merv is documented by a coin from the year 75 of the Arabs (696 CE). The inscription on this coin from Merv names 'Abd al-Malik as APD'LMLIK-i-MRWānān without the title of *Amīr-i-wurroyišnigān*. This is how a ruler of a province is named on Arab-Sassanian coinage. As a paramount ruler in the former Sassanian East he bears the title *Amīr-i-wurroyišnigān*, yet is only referred to by his name. The name of his "clan", the *MRWānān*, is not mentioned on the coinage of the paramount ruler, but on the coins struck in his own domain as the lord of a province. The name of 'Abd al-Malik's "clan" or "tribe", according to the biblical understanding, is composed of several elements: MRW (the town and oasis of Merv) + the genitive ending *-ān* + the plural ending *-ān*, i.e., "the people who belong to the *Marwa*/the people of the *Marwa*". The "Marwa" or Murgh-Ab stream is the "Water of Life" for the oasis and 'Abd al-Malik's followers.[94] It is a fitting coincidence that the home town's name already stands for a program of spiritual irrigation and sustenance with "Water of Life" collected in the Marwa, coming from the Rock of the Hindu-Kush.

This Iranian form of the name was later arabized to *Marwān*. At first the name was taken to be the Iranian form in the West since the Iranian plural ending *-ān* in *MRWān<u>ān</u>* was abandoned when it was arabized, thus the form (*bn*) *Marwān* was established.

The reason for striking this provincial coin of the year 75 of the Arabs was probably a power struggle in the former Sassanian Iran. 'Abd al-Malik's apocalyptic movement was no longer supported by the Christian fundamentalists in Iran. 'Abd al-Malik's leadership was no longer recognized. There was call for a different form of rule. In the year 75 of the Arabs, in the mint at Ardašīr-hurra, coins were minted with a *motto* instead of the "name of the governor". Those "names" are often "motti" made into names by pious traditionalists. For European history this would mean that we encounter Roman heroes in our textbooks like: "Inhocsignovinesgetorix" ("in hoc signo vinces – "in this sign you will conquer", Constantine's motto; "-getorix" is part of the Celtic (Gaulish) name "Vercingetorix", the morpheme "rīx" corresponding to Latin "rēx" = "king").

Next to the bust of the ruler on the obverse of the coin there is the inscription in Pehlevi (Middle Persian): LWYTW ḎATWBR BLA YYZTW (There is no ruler [legislator] apart from God). This legend was already explained by Carl Salemann in 1879.[95]

This reading also explains the Arabic rendering of the Pahlevi text on the rim of the coin: *lā ḥukma illa li-llāh*. Other translations to that of Saleman are misleading and only make sense if seen within the framework of traditional historiography.[96]

There is yet another reason to assume Merv in the valley of the Murghab to be the home of ʿAbd al-Malik's family: stubborn adherence to the family of ʿAbd al-Malik even after their apparent end in Palestine. In the valley of the Murghab, followers of this family were still to be found in the year 137 of the Arabs (758 CE). There is evidence of this in the coinage struck in the style of the Umayyads from the year 137 in Gharshistân at the upper reaches of the Murghab river.[97]

7.2 ʿAbd al-Malik's Move into the Promised Land and the Evidence of his Religious Agenda

According to the inscription in the Dome of the Rock, ʿAbd al-Malik's Jesus is *ʿAbdallāh* (servant of God) and *muḥammad^{un}* (the praised one, [God's] chosen one). In 1903 excavations led by M. Macalister near Jaffa in Palestine unearthed a group of lead sealings.[98]

This kind of lead seal was used for sealing enclosures in shipments by post (barīd), in order to make it possible for the recipient to positively identify the sender of a courier package. Evidently excavations had revealed a courier mailroom or an archive from the time of ʿAbd al-Malik. The papyruses had rotted in the earth but the seals of the courier sacks had been preserved.

Fig. 6: Lead sealings mentioning ʿAbd al-Malik. Idealized Depiction of the Promised Land "Filasṭīn". The obverse with capital "A" set in circle of Omega.

The lead sealing bears a religious inscription around the rim of the obverse: *lā illāh(a) illā llāh(a) waḥdah(u) lā šarīk(a)la-h(ū) muḥammad(un) rasūl Allāh*

(There is no deity other than God alone, he has no companion, the messenger of God is the chosen one). This text can also be found in the Dome of the Rock in Jerusalem as part of 'Abd al-Malik's programmatic inscription.

The field of the obverse is divided into segments by the Greek capital letter Alpha. In the segments of this area to the right and to the left of the sides of the letter Alpha, there is a cartouche naming 'Abd al-Malik: *li-'abdallāh / 'Abd al-malik / amīr al-mu'/ minīn* (from the "servant of God" (ruler's title) 'Abd al-Malik / *Master of the Protectors/ emir of those who grant safety*). The title: *Amīr al-mu'minīn* is translated in a Latin Spanish chronicle of 754 – preserved in a manuscript of the 9th century – as "*omnia prospere gerens* – someone ruling everything in a propitious manner"), i.e., governor.[99] Beneath the top part of the capital Alpha, which looks like a roof, two birds (peacocks?) are looking at one another. This brings to mind the meal in the Paradise of the Qur'ān: poultry meat.

The area on the reverse is struck with *incus* and gives the impression of a capital letter Omega. There are two animals portrayed in this area: on the left there is a predator, on the right an animal lying on its back either asleep or in a humble pose, and between the two the emblem of an eagle. Above the two illustrations of animals there is a frieze bearing the inscription: *Filasṭīn* (Palestine). This is surrounded by a decorative edging depicting luscious grapes hanging on vines.[100]

Fig. 7: Early Christian oil lamp depicting the return of scouts with grapes of the Promised Land.

So much for the portrayal of the notion "Palestine" as the Promised Land on a lead sealing naming 'Abd al-Malik and possibly connected to the letters Alpha and Omega, i.e., The Second Coming of Jesus.

For the first time the mentioning of Filasṭīn (Palestine) is also encountered in inscriptions on coins of this period. The mentioning of *Zion* on imitative coins of Byzantine originals from the time of Constans II is replaced by the mention of *Jerusalem* in the form of *Iliya Filasṭīn*. It is here that the Roman name Aelia

(Capitolina) is taken up again. This is obviously an anti-Jewish statement. And it is to Jerusalem, the town on the height, that 'Abd al-Malik is drawn.

Not only in the historiographical literature of the Arabs is there some mystery about just what significance Jerusalem might have had for 'Abd al-Malik, but his Messianic name betrays his program. His utopia was the imminent parousia and his role as a servant to the "King", sitting on his throne at the End of Time. He is accused by the authors of the undated kerygmatic Islamic literature of having wanted to divert the pilgrimage to Jerusalem to the detriment of Mecca. Mecca represents the utopia of Ezekiel 47:1-12. When the seasonal rains hit the town, flooding causes water to come out from under the door of the *Bayt*. Mecca is an Old Testament utopia having come to life like a mirage.

It is certain that 'Abd al-Malik had the road from Damascus to Jerusalem improved. Milestones with dates and references to his building activities have been found.[101] Furthermore, it is certain that it was 'Abd al-Malik who had the Dome of the Rock built and that it was modelled on the Sassanian architecture of the fire temples. The four pillar construction of the Chahār Tāq was used here as well. Twelve columns distributed between the four pillars in groups of three, support a rotunda. On top of this is the wooden dome.

Twelve years had gone by since the beginning of his rule in the year 60 of the Arabs before the inscription was created, which has the date "72". It shows what was proposed to the Byzantine rivals – according to 'Abd al-Malik's interpretation of the imperial eschatology – to clarify their differences concerning the understanding of the scripture.

The long Christological part of the inscription also refers to 'Abd al-Malik's concept of a triad, bonded together. As *ṣ*(*a*)*mad*(*u*) God is joined with the spirit (*rūḥ*). From the latter Mary conceives. Furthermore, she receives the Word whose bearer is Jesus in the function of *'Abdallāh*(*i*) (servant of God; 'Ebed-Yahwe according to Isaiah 40 ff.). Here the expression: *ṣ*(*a*)*mad*(*u*), already known from Ugarit, crops up again. Originally, it only occurs in Ugaritic and in the inscription on the Dome of the Rock as an epithet of God. Then this text from the Dome of the Rock found its place in the Qur'ān.[102]

The triadic bond of God, Spirit (*rūḥ*) and the servant of God (*'Abdallāh*) as the bearer of the *Logos* (Middle Persian PTGAMbl Y YAZT [bearer of the Logos of God]) referred to on coinage from the time of 'Abd al-Malik,[103] is not understood by mainstream Western Islamic Studies. The inscription of the Dome of the Rock would appear to be an anti-Trinitarian text, as Trinity could only be envisaged according to the definition decided on by the council of Nicaea in 325 CE.

The notion of the ʿArabī, who came from the area influenced by the diocese of Antiochia, of a triadic bond as defined in the Dome of the Rock, is pre-Nicean, because the ʿArabī had already been deported from Šāpur to the East of the Sassanian Empire before the Council of Nicaea.

Whoever came from Antiochia knew all about triadic notions as they had dominated the pantheon of the home shores for over a thousand years. What was never expressed in the theology of the Antiochian Church written in Greek, was nevertheless a prevalent idea in the vernacular of the descendants of the Phoenicians on the coast of Syria. The Semitic vocabulary of this vernacular, which was certainly influenced by Ugaritic, was more familiar to the common people than the Greek of theologians.

The crux lies in the Islamic interpretation of the expression *šarīk* (translated as "*partaker; partner; associate*"). This Islamic interpretation of a seemingly anti-Trinitarian terminology clouds the sense of the word. It should be understood in the sense of the Iranian religious discourse which the deported *ʿArabī* had taken part in for hundreds of years before their march to Jerusalem under the leadership of ʿAbd al-Malik. Here it means: "*mingled, blended (one); one added to the mixture*". According to Iranian religious thinking the worst thing was to amalgamate. To mingle would lead to corruption of thought and to heresy. This is represented by the two demons / gods *Âz* and *Varan* (desire / doubt, *logos of evil*).[104] When God declares his bond with Jesus and the Spirit *ṣ(a)mad(u),* this means that the bond that links them is to be understood in the Persian sense, i.e., without mingling or any division of power according to Syrian understanding. In any case God is a single entity; the triadic bond is located on a level beneath God's sphere.

Thus ʿAbd al-Malik's God is *al- ṣ(a)mad(u) Allāh*, a trinity connected with the *spirit* and the *servant of God* as bearer of the *Logos*. However, the *servant of God* is not the *son of God*. This also becomes clear in the Latin rendering of this concept in the West. On coins we find the Latin inscription: NON EST DEUS NISI UNUS CUI NON EST ALIUS SIMILIS and NON EST DEUS NISI UNUS CUI NON EST SOCIUS ALIUS SIMILIS.[105]

The son of God of the Greeks, as seen by the Arab Christians, is understood to be a *socius*; the *servant of God* is not. This becomes clear in the emphasis of the question pertaining to the birth of Jesus. Who was actually born here? In no case was this a "physical" son of God or a son of god adopted by the Father. The Qur'ān calls him "*ġulāman*" (Q 19:19: "He said: I am only a messenger of thy Lord, that I may bestow on thee a *faultless son*."), Aramaic for "incomplete". The very idea of an adoptive son, a "blend", is alien to the ancient Iranians. If God had wanted a son, then he would have said: *Be it so*.

The background to this is a rejection of any kind of *blend*, which could conceivably blemish the purity of the concept, thus falsifying it and rendering it a lie, which, – according to Iranian thinking – is the absolute sin.[106]

Should there be a warning against naming the three in the inscription on the Dome of the Rock, then this could be a matter of rejecting the "admixture" of the Logos (identified with Jesus as his incarnation) and the Spirit, or alternatively of a triad "Father, Mother (*theotókos*, i.e., birth-giver to God), Son of God", which the ʿArabī encountered under ʿAbd al-Malik in Syria. At this point it should not be forgotten that the Church of the emperor at this time still had many followers, but as little as these followers of the Byzantine Church could comprehend the concept of Jesus being the *muḥammad*, the descendants of the ʿArabī, who had returned to the promised land of Palestine from Iranian territory, were willing to understand the orthodoxy of Byzantium.

Where can archeological traces of the concept of Jesus being the *servant of God* be found in the 7th century?

The answer is: on Iranian territories. It is here that names of rulers can be found in inscriptions on coins without mentioning the name, as was normal for the inscriptions on the coins of the late Sassanians. Should names be mentioned that cannot be allocated to any of the latter Sassanians, then it can be assumed that these are imitative issues of coins and that the purported name appearing on the coin is actually an epithet. Nothing is known of a Sassanian ʿAbdallāh-Šāh. Thus the name in Pehlevi script: *pdwl* (*ʿAbdallāh*) is not the name of a ruler, but a characteristic that can be attributed to that person: *ʿAbdallāh* = God's servant. On coinage of the Arab emirs in Iran the name always has the patronym with it. They then read e.g.: "Abdallāh bn ʿAmīr."[107] This "name" could be read "the Servant of God from the Speaker". Jesus, while wandering about in this world, was the "Amīr" (speaker, spokesman), the one who was in charge to speak for the *amr*. Carl Salemann from St. Petersburg found out that researchers as Mordtmann and Thomas had read "motti" as names. They proceeded like finders of a Maya-inscription looking up parts of the text as "names" in the Yucatan telephone directory. This also happened to the school of al-Ṭabarī. That way al-Ṭabarī created many heroes from misunderstood motti. It is like teaching the history of German Jews from Hitler's book "My Struggle". The translation of "Abdallāh bn ʿAmīr" reveals this as a motto: "The Servant of God descended from the one who is acting for the *amr*", meaning: a messianic follower of Jesus. A closer look at the inscription reveals that the Aramaic *rasm* of the Pehlevi inscription cannot be read in the light of hermeneutics of the present religion of Islam. The "*ʿEbed-Yahwe/ʿAbdallāh*" is not the royal title of present day rulers of Islamic monarchies. What has been read as *"amīr"* is written "amorā", the Preacher. The inscription tells of a "Servant of God who is descended from the Preachers". This is a messianic reference to Jesus as a preacher". This motto could be used to circumscribe the Christological point of view of a faction that was marching under this banner: Jesus, as a messianic figure, according to the *'Ebed-Yahweh* ("servant of God") concept of Isaiah. His role in his lifetime, his preaching, is the message and is the way of salvation. That is why J. Walker has already categorized coins with the inscription: *'Abdallāh* (from "*'Ebed-Yahweh*" according to Is 40 f.) [108]

To cut it short: We are dealing with problems of hermeneutics. The findings from material relics in the Middle East dated post 622 CE are regarded as being witnesses to an Islamic past in the light of today's religion of Islam. So what is to be done with remnants and leftovers from religious people who were, in their day, not aware of the fact that later generations would see them as a part of an Islamic heritage. It is the good fortune of those who were the heroes of their days, that they are dead and forgotten and an army of heroes is marching on in their place, who are the creatures of the theological harmonizers of history, the gholems of the Islamologists. Here are the specimens which J. Walker assigned without any doubt:

> "Zaranj, capital of Sīstān, year 41 of the Arabs;
> Al-Shîrajân, to the East of Dārābjird in Kirmân, year 50 of the Arabs;
> Dārābjird, former residence of the Sassanians in the Persis, year 41 of the Arabs;
> Bischâpûr in the Persis, years 42 (?) and 44 of the Arabs;
> Nahr-Tirâ in Khuzistân, years 20 (?) and 48 of the Arabs;
> Nihâvand (Mâh al-Basra) in the Jibal, year 41 of the Arabs."

Where are the first traces of inscriptions to be found of the mentioning of Jesus as MḤMT/ *muḥammad* (the desired one, the chosen one) in regions of Iranshahr? – Whatever has been said in regard to coin inscriptions displaying *'Abdallāh*, also applies to the epithet MḤMT or *muḥammad* respectively in inscriptions on Arab-Sassanian coinage.

John Walker (1941) knew just one specimen with the inscription: MḤMT on the obverse of an Arab-Sassanian coin. This refers to the well known specimen in the Berlin Collection, published by Heinrich Nützel in his catalogue issued in 1898.[109] Heinz Gaube wrote the following about this coin:

> "Walker (124) reads the mint-mark ZR for no apparent reason. The inscription on the rim of coin Nos. 2.3.6.16 is only on this one coin. [The part of text referring to Nos. 2.3.6.16 is not in Gaube's book. The description of inscriptions on the rim of coins and abbreviations on coins ends with Nos. 2.3.5.3. pp. 56-7. On p. 58 the heading of the chapter reads: The Issuing Authorities ("die Prägeherren"). The text starts at Nos. 3.1.] The name of Muhammad (M.H.M.T.) cannot be clearly connected to any historic person

due to the date, which can be read as 40, but of which the era cannot be identified. The archaic character of the coin would point to an eastern mint location."[110]

H. Gaube made further references to silver coins with the title *muḥammad*:

"3.2.2.5.4. Muhammad. The name of a person owning the sovereign right of coinage ("eines Prägeherrn") "Muhammad" is found on a series of coins from a mint which cannot be identified (mint-mark 4.2.1.). According to the present state of the material it is impossible to come to any sort of conclusion about the person responsible for the striking of coins in this name."[111]

On another occasion Gaube is satisfied with the quality of the material evidence, which leads him to the following conclusion:

"12. (...) The name of the prophet Muhammad is found on coinage of the Xusrô type from Shîrajân (abbreviation 4.2.35., year 38) and Ray (abbreviation 4.2.32., year 52)."[112]

R. Gyselen understood that these purported names are, in fact, attributes. So we can conclude that what was used in the years 38, 40 and 52 of the Arabs was the Christological title MḤMT / *muḥammad*.

All of the silver coins displaying the forms *'Abdallāh* and MḤMT/ *muḥammad* were struck at locations on the roads from Khûzistân to Khorasan.

Fig. 8: Iranian Bronze coin with the motto "MḤMD" to the right side of the bust on the obverse/ Image of MḤMD as eschatological figure in the centre of flames, Ryka Gyselen, Arab-Sasanian Copper Coinage, p. 179.

Fig. 9: Arab-Sassanian drachm mentioning MḤMD (muḥammad) on the obverse, at the side of the bust; inscription on the rim: "wafin" (in Arabic): on the reverse Zoroastrian fire-altar.

Fig. 10: Arab-Sassanian drachm mentioning MḤMT in Pehlevi-script in the field to the right of the bust on the obverse; inscription on the rim in Arabic letters: muḥammad; on the reverse image of fire-altar with two attendants.

Fig. 11: Obverse of a coin with the 'muḥammad'-motto. 'Ammān; to the left of an image of a ruler in frontal position; to the right of the figure long-cross, from the top down: bi-'Ammān; on the reverse in the center capital "M". M stands for 40 as a Roman number; 40 copper coins were equal to one silver drachm. Cross above the letter M, in the exergue "MḤMD" in Arabic letters.

The discovery of copper coins naming Jesus as *muḥammad* in Palestine caused great confusion. In 1947 Sir Alexander S. Kirkbridge, the excavator from Gerasa/ Jerash, made public the first specimen of a square-shaped copper coin showing a Christian ruler (?) with a long cross on the obverse of the coin and the inscription: *muḥammad*, the reverse displaying the value M (=40 Nummia).[113]

Due to the low grade of the coin, no one has even attempted to connect this coinage with the "name" of prophet of the Arabs.[114] A mint is named on the coin. The inscription downwards on the obverse in the style of the Sassanians reads: *'Ammān.*[115] Thus this could be an early indication of the distribution of the notion of Jesus being the *muḥammad* from the East of Iran to Transjordanian regions. The distribution of coinage naming the *chosen one (muḥammad)* is proof of 'Abd al-Malik's movement from the East to the West.

When considering the appearance of the epithets 'Abdallāh and *MḤMT/ muḥammad* as titles in the inscriptions on coinage of the Arab-Sassanians, it becomes obvious that the distribution of the coins follows the road from Khūzistān to Khorasan, whether on the North West route via Nihāvand and Rāy, or the South East route via Arrajān, Bišāpur, Ardashīr-Khurra, Shīrajān, Kirmān and Zaranj. Muḥammad, as the name of a historic person, first occurs in Harat in the year 67 of the Arabs as the name of an Arab emir.[116] This mint is also on the Khūzistān-Sīstān-Khorasan route.

There is no record of any inscription of *Muḥammad* being used as the name of a person at an earlier date. Also on this route was the mint of GRM-KRMAN (Kirmān*):*

Fig. 12: Arab-Sassanian drachm dated year 70 of the Arabs. On the obverse Middle Persian inscription: MHMT PTGAMIY ḎAT; on the rim in Arabic letters the "translation". On the reverse fire-altar with the purifying fire and two attendants.

In the year 70 of the Arabs the silver coin of fig. 12 with the Middle Persian inscription: MHMT PGTAMI Y ḎAT ("chosen is the bearer of the word of God") was struck. On the rim of the obverse of the coin there is an additional inscription in Arabic letters: *bi-sm(i)llāh(i) walī l-'amr* (in the name of God; he is the representative of the *amr*. The *amr* is the *memra/ logos*, here the equivalent of the "*word*".[117]

The representative of God, *walī (A)llāh*, also appears on coins of the same year from this mint. On one variation of this coin[118] the inscription on the rim reads: *bi-sm(i)llāh(i) walī llāh* (In the name of God he is the representative of God).

The epithet *walī Allāh* (representative of God) for the MḤMT (chosen one) would appear to contradict the understanding of the chosen one as *Ḫal(ī)fat Allāh* (spokesman for God). This contradiction became stronger in the year 75 of the Arabs. It resulted in a conflict, which, although successfully resolved by 'Abd al-Malik for the time being, in the end led to the demise of his descendants half a century later.

The idea of a representative with the title *walī Allāh* is still encountered today in the Shiite concept of Islam. This *walī Allāh* bears a different title: *'Alī* ("the sublime one; exalted one"), which is also quite possibly Christological.

The combination of two historic and Christological titles in a Moses-Aaron constellation leads to the son-in-law of the prophet of the Arabs, combining two epithets of Christological nature: *'Alī, walī Allāh* and the concept of Jesus being the *muḥammad* leads to the emergence of *'Ali* as an *aspect* of Jesus. This, together with the idea of Jesus being the 'Abdallāh of the Old Testament, are combined as aspects of the son-in-law of the prophet of the Arabs. The Zoroastrian concept of the genealogical tree and the

Manichaean teaching of aspects of a person help to create a Holy Family from the stock of Christological titles, like: Muḥammad bn ʿAbdallāh.

In the inscriptions from Kirmān an idea surfaces which defines the interaction between God and his MḤMT (chosen one). This is a concept of the MḤMT playing the role of the *representative of God* or of the *commander in God's stead* respectively.

But where does this concept come from? This, too, can be taken from the inscriptions in Kirmān. From: *allāh rabb al-ḥukm* ("God, Lord of the law [rule]").[119] The notion of the chosen one being the representative of God and representative in God's stead seems to go together with a view of God which portrays him as the Lord of the law. Thus the chosen one is subject of divine law. We are faced with the concept of a messianic figure in its own right and as the alternative direct rule of the lawgiver.

Fig. 13: Obverse: Depiction of the eschatological Jesus with flame mandorla and flame sword; inscription on the left: 'muḥammad', mint: Ḥarrān; reverse: in the center depiction of the 'stone' (יְגַר שָׂהֲדוּתָא Yəḡar Sāḥ^{a}ḏūṯā); inscription on the right: 'muḥammad', on the left cippus with rhomboid-shaped betyl within the naos.

Just who is referred to by MḤMT (the chosen one) in the Iranian inscriptions can be learnt from the text of inscriptions of the year 66 of the Arabs (687 CE).[120] Here we have the earliest known mention of MḤMT in the form of *muḥammad* as *rasūl* (messenger/apostle).[121] On the rim of the obverse of a silver coin of the year 66 of the Arabs from the Bišāpūr mint there is the Arabic inscription: *bi-sm(i)llāh muḥammad rasūl(u)llāh.*[122] Just who this messenger (apostle) is, is explained by ʿAbd al-Malik in the inscription in the Dome of the Rock built in Jerusalem: *ʿĪsa bn Maryam* (Jesus, son of Mary).

Who ordered the striking of this coin from the year 66 of the Arabs in Bišāpūr? It is ʿAbd al-Malik bn ʿAbdallāh (Middle Persian: APDLMLIK-i-APDULAanan). Only this unique specimen is known of him naming the chosen one as a messenger/apostle in Arabic script.

The Islamic chronicles of the 9th century report of an *ʿAbd al-Malik bn ʿAbdallāh* in the context of the year 64 of the *hiǧra*:

> "In this year the inhabitants of Baṣra elected him as governor after the flight of ʿUbaidallāh b. Ziyād (...). He only stayed in office for one month (Ṭabarī II, 462)."[123]

This is how al-Ṭabarī rearranged the chronological sequence and synchronized it with his kerygmatic chronology. The historic ʿAbd al-Malik has, according to al-Ṭabarī's work, a role to play only as an adversary of ʿAbdallāh bn al-Zubayr in the fight over the supremacy of the Places of Pilgrimage, Mecca or Jerusalem. Therefore the historic ʿAbd al Malik was set to remain in the limelight of history in the years 60 onward. As ʿAbdallah bn al-Zubayr is the pillar of the kerygmatic history of the first 127 years, he has to reach the apogee of his importance in half this time span, at nimrah, around the year 63 of the kerygmatic history of al-Ṭabarī. Al-Ṭabarī portrays al-Zubayr as a staunch defender of a kerygmatic temple at Mecca. This construction of history has two settings: ʿAbd al-Malik stands for Jerusalem as a centre of messianic ideas and doomsday fantasy, ʿAbdallah bn al-Zubayr represents the prophetic, non-messianic version: the Temple utopia of Ezekiel, built up by Muḥammad, the Prophet of the Arabs. The Arabs had inherited this concept from the ʿArabī, the dwellers of an Old Testament landscape, the Araba. This treatment of literature could, as well, reflect events from the days of the crusades. It could be a propaganda piece for the Ayyubids. Salaḥ al-Dīn had restarted the hajj to Mecca, before he was able to conquer Jerusalem. Al-Kāmil gave away Jerusalem again. Why could he do this? It was possible, since Mecca had been re-established as the paramount place of pilgrimage. Had the Muslims kept better written records, archives like the Vatican, and recalled old coins under strict control, the exchange of a kerygmatic narrative for a historic history may have worked. Today the discrepancies between what the material relics and the sources on paper tell us create job opportunities for Islamologists harmonizing the story. The pious work of al-Ṭabarī, an author who had dedicated all his life to writing a manuscript which grew by 40 pages day by day, was a titanic achievement.

Here it should be made certain whether it is not the ephemeral ʿAbd al-Malik bn ʿAbdallāh of the chronicles who is being referred to, but the ruler of Fārs, the heartland of the empire. As the example of the inscription on the afore-mentioned coin from Merv of the year 75 of the Arabs shows, in the year 60 of the Arabs the *Amīr al-muʾminīn* calls himself *M.P. APDULMLIK-i-MRWānān* on his coins. This shows that the "two" ʿAbd al-Maliks mentioned under different dates and at different mints are one and the same person. It was the author of the kerygmatic history who had to create two actors for his Mecca drama from one historic person.

According to this epigraphic attestation he, ʿAbd al-Malik, is naming the "spiritual parentage" of his "biblical tribe", but not the "name of his father". The *MRWānān* are the "people from the *Marwa*, as Merv is a *Marwa*. They compare themselves to a Marwa, but they are not always *Marwazī*. Marw*azī* are just ordinary inhabitants of Merv, a Marw*ān* is like a fountain of the "Water of Life" that comes from the Rock, a basin filled with water streaming downhill from underneath the Door of the Temple. When the Aramaic name

"Marwānān" was arabized it became: "*bn Marwān*". This description of a spiritual quality was taken for a proper name. That is how it came about that Islamic historiography reports about a certain *'Abd al-Malik bn M(a)RWān*. This *M(a)RWān*, whose origin is not understood to be more than a Persian title detailing the quality of his bearer as a Marwa-like spiritual character, that because of its arabization in the historical literature of the 9th century, is historicized as the forefather of the *Marwānids*, a family branch of the so-called dynasty of the Umayyads, which, of course, is not historic either, as their family's origin is shrouded in the mist of the forty-year prehistory of Islam in the desert.

Thus 'Abd al-Malik's name and his "real parentage" from a "spiritual tribe" in a Biblical tradition from Merv, the Marwa irrigating the oasis which was regarded as an earthly paradise, can be inferred from the inscriptions. His father's name is missing in the inscription on the provincial issue, since a Marwān has a Heavenly Father, sitting in the Rock, may it be the rock of Zion, the Rock of Ēl-al-Ǧabal or the rock of Dhusares. What could be more logical than to see one and the same person in the *'Abd al-Malik bn 'Abdallāh* from Bišāpūr and the *Amīr al-mu'minīn* 'Abd al-Malik bn M(a)RWān, particularly as the ruler of Bišāpūr shows a propaganda inscription as a motto on his coins equating *muḥammad* with the *rasūl*. But what if he had changed his "spiritual" tribe? He could have moved from the Ebed-Yahwe to those who regard themselves as a "Marwa". The Marwa comes downhill as a stream, called Murgh-Ab today. The Marwa is the stream flowing through the earthly Paradise of Merv. In Merv his eyes could behold a Biblical landscape, a vision of the prophet become true.

The *Amīr al-mu'minīn* must have had his power base somewhere. It is natural to assume that this was in the Persis. According to Sassanian tradition, whoever exercised rule in the Persis held power over Iran. Therefore the striking of coins in Bišāpūr could demonstrate confirmation of the occupation of the Persis. That is why 'Abd al-Malik is also named in the manner of a provincial governor: the "programmatic name" and "name of tribe" both appear in the inscription. His origins from Merv, his spiritual role as a Marwa, have just as little relevance as his title as *'Amīr al-mu'minīn*.

In the West, in Syria, the name of 'Abd al-Malik's "father" Marwān, and his origin do not appear in the inscriptions. On the mark of his seal on a lead sealing he called himself *(li-)'abdallāh* 'Abd al-Malik ("[from the] servant of God [= 'Ebed-Yahwe according to Isaiah] 'Abd al-Malik). His name on the Dome of the Rock was replaced by the name al-Ma'mūn in 217 after the *hiǧra*. We have dated copper coins marking the occasion of the visit of al-Ma'mūn. He left the "date" intact.

Therefore it would make sense to assume that the mint authority responsible for minting in Bišāpūr, where from the year 66 of the Arabs (687 CE) for the first time the Arabic notion of the "chosen one" as apostle of Allah (*bi-*

sm[i]llāh muḥammad rasūl[u] llāh) is found, was the *'Amīr al-mu'minīn*. The full name would then be *'Abd al-Malik bn 'Abdallāh Āl (or bn) M(a)RWān.*

Thus the construct of a "dynasty of the Umayyads" would also be obsolete. After all, the legendary ancestor of the dynasty was conceived in the genealogical constructions of Ṭabarī from the 9th century CE, which links historical persons (like e.g. Maavia) with protagonists of a sacred era in Mecca and Medina, which lasted forty years (from the *hiǧra* of the prophet of the Arabs until the death of his son-in-law *'Alī*). The doubtlessly historic figure Maavia established the "rule of his family", which ended in the year 60 of the Arabs. In the year 60 of the Arabs 'Abd al-Malik established the rule of his house which ended with the death of his "spiritual" son, al-Walīd. The line of these "Marwas", filled with the Water of Live, ended with the messianic Hišām (as for Persian ears "h" and "ḥ" sound alike and "s" and "š" have the same rasm, this could be considered an anagram of "Mašīḥ – Messiah") in the year 125 of the Arabs. His "nephew", Marwān bn Muḥammad, who was not his legitimate successor (in terms of "tribal law", as we are told by the hagiographers), usurped this rule and called this usurped position: *caliphate*. They probably ruled as governors did. However, the afore-mentioned Marwān bn Muḥammad can hardly be considered a historic figure. Here again we are facing a historical construct. He ended drowning in the Nile as did Antinoos before him.

The choice of 'Abd al-Malik's own name was certainly just as little a matter of coincidence as 'Abdallāh, the name of his father, was. It was with this *programmatic* name, – the way Octavian chose the programmatic name "Augustus" ("the revered one, the elevated one"), – that he was able to publicize his understanding of a monarchianistic conception of God. In the further course of history it can be seen that two diverging theological concepts developed among the 'Arabī / Arabs of Iran. Those adherents of 'Abd al-Malik from Khorasan represent followers of the monarchianistic idea.[124]

In conclusion it can be said that the idea of an *'Abdallāh* (servant of God) and a programmatic MḤMT (chosen one) has been apparent in Iran since the years 40 to 49 of the Arabs (after 660 CE). The notion of the chosen one being an "apostle" (*rasūl*) of Allāh can be first found, phrased in Arabic, in an inscription on a coin struck under 'Abd al-Malik bn 'Abdallāh in Bišāpūr in the Persis in the year 66 of the Arabs (687 CE).

At this time in Kirmān God was regarded as the *rabb al-ḥukm* (Lord of the law). The idea of the MḤMT (chosen one) is connected to this. The chosen one is seen in the role of the *walī l-'amr* (representative of the word = the "Logos") and *walī Allāh* (representative of God). 'Abd al-Malik, as the ruler exercising the mint authority, replaced this notion from Kirmān of a *representative of the Logos* with his own interpretation of the chosen MḤMT/

muḥammad as the *Ḫalfat Allāh* (not: "Ḫalīfa" – "caliph", in the sense of *successor of the prophet*, as is commonly understood!; the rasm also allows the reading "Ḫalqat Allāh – *creature of God*", a problem which will be discussed in detail in a later anthology).

A note on ʻAbd al-Malik's imperial eschatology: ʻAbd al-Malik sees in the chosen one (MḤMT/ *muḥammad*) the *Ḫalfat Allāh*. This is proven by the coins of the *Amīr al-mu'minīn* from the year 75 of the Arabs (696 CE).[125]

On the obverse there are religious inscriptions all around the rim. In the centre there is a depiction of Ḳosrow II(?) and to the left and right downward, there is the date in Arabic: year 75 (of the Arabs) written in Sassanian style. On the reverse, in the centre, the MḤMT/ *muḥammad* is depicted standing in an apocalyptical portrayal as judge of the world.

Fig. 14: Dirham struck in the year 75 of the Arabs (696 CE). In the center of the reverse depiction of the eschatological Jesus with his flame-sword; on the left: title of the ruler: amīr al-mu'minīn; on the right: designation for the eschatological Jesus: ḫalfat Allāh.

To the left of the depiction of the *chosen one* with his flame-sword there is the wording, *Amīr al-mu'minīn*, downward. To the right of the depiction there is the wording, *Ḫalfat Allāh* (in Aramaic: **ḥlpā d-Alāhā*), from top to bottom.[126] There is no letter corresponding to the long "ī" that one would expect to find in the designation of a caliph (*ḫalifa)* on the coin.

The mistake that led to the understanding of the term *Amīr al-mu'minīn* as *"ruler of those who believed in God"* and *Ḫalīfat Allāh* as the *"representative of God"* (i.e., representative with God's approval, I. Goldziher) is based on a misreading of two titles as one. As is shown by the Spanish chronicle of 754 and a philological analysis of the term *Amīr al-mu'minīn,* this is an official title of a person, whose task was described in Latin as *omnia prospere gerens* (lit.: the one who makes everything flourish/ prosper), a task which Luther referred to as "Landpfleger / governor". According to the *communis opinio* of scholars of Islamic studies, of course, the title *Amīr al-mu'minīn* innately implies the dignity of a caliph, the Latin equivalent, however, shows that this is an innovative understanding from much later.[127]

Should the title *Ḫalfat Allāh* (God's caliph) appear in the inscriptions in the field of the coin, as is here the case, then it should be read as: N.N., *Caliph* and *Ruler of the Believers ("caliph"* not having the modern meaning of the term*).*

At the same time titles and predicates should not be amalgamated or "composed" if they do not originally belong together: the depiction of the Messiah returning with his flame-sword is placed between the inscriptions that run parallel to the figure of the sword-bearer, so they are not to be read as if they belong together. Therefore the interpretation can only be determined by a "parallel reading": The "*Representative of God*" (*Ḫalfat Allāh*, i.e., Jesus) and the "*Governor*" (*Amīr al-mu'minīn*, i.e., 'Abd al-Malik) have one project in common: 'Abd al-Malik sees himself as the last emperor of the Syrian Apocalypse and will pass rule over to the Messiah.[128] This is a coin in the name of *two protagonists* and not of one ruler with *two functions*: worldly rule (*Amīr al-mu'minīn*) and spiritual rule (*Ḫalfat Allāh*). The iconography of the coin also shows indications of later design peculiarities: The aniconic coins have a similar layout concerning the field. In the place of a figure or a fire-altar between two lines of script there are three parallel lines of inscription. When the matrix is turned by 45 degrees and the depiction of the Messiah is replaced by a line of writing, the design of the coin then resembles those of the Arabian Empire with a three-line-long inscription in the field of the coin.

A direct clue that apocalyptical conflicts were expected can be seen in the fact that neither date nor mint location appear on the coin. The design on the reverse side is new, it follows the Sassanian pattern of the depiction of the fire altar, framed by two guarding figures. Instead of the two guards there is an arch supported by two columns. Under the arch there is a lance standing upright. This is the traditional description of this image. To the right and to the left of the lance there is an inscription: *naṣṣārahu/Allāh* (May God grant him victory), from top to bottom. To the left of the two overarched columns there is the title: *Amīr al-mu'minīn*, and on the right Jesus is mentioned: *Ḫalfat Allāh* (God's caliph, Representative of God).[129]

Fig. 15: Reverse of a drachm from the time of 'Abd al-Malik. Depiction of a spear and a naos for prayer (mihrāb), according to the tradition of the Islamologists. It shows a polished shaft in a quiver, according to Isaiah 49:2. This is the biblical definition of the 'Ebed-Yahwe, 'Abdallāh; on the shaft: nṣr 'llh; nṣr mn 'llh; Naṣar min Allāh (Help from God, protection from God) on the left: title of 'Abd al-Malik: Amīr al-mu'minīn; on the right: title of the eschatological Jesus: Ḫalfat Allāh.

Further indications of the apocalyptical conflicts can be found in the Persian legends of copper coins and in the writing on the rims of coins of al-Ḥaǧǧāǧ. On these coins Jesus is referred to as M.N.Ṣ.W.R. (Manṣūr, victor).

Fig. 16: Arab-Sassanian bronze coin from the Persis. On the obverse in the field on the right side of the portrait the epithet of the eschatological Jesus: manṣūr. Complete inscription: manṣūr bi-l-'abdallāh/Victorious with the "Servant of God", the messianic 'Ebed-Yahweh.

7.3 An Attempt to Reconstruct the Trail of 'Abd al-Malik's movements from Khorasan to Jerusalem

From the evidence of the material culture of the 7th century shown so far the following picture can be reconstructed: a move to Palestine as the Promised Land and an imperial eschatology of the Arabian Empire at the time of 'Abd al-Malik, which had Jerusalem as its point of reference.

The appearance of the terms *'Abdallāh* and MḤMT/*muḥammad* in Iranian territory along the roads from Khuzistân to Khorasan should be regarded in connection with the Syrian Christians, who had been deported there and who had settled there under the rule of the Sassanians. The notion of a chosen servant of God can only have been preserved by these people. They were followers of an Early Christianity in a Hebrew mould.

They benefitted from the disintegration of the Sassanian Empire. After a period of provisional order under the former allies of the Byzantine Emperor Heraclius (*foederati*, Arabic: Qurayš) there was another collapse in the balance of power between the Arabs of Syria and Iran. The reason for this was Mu'āwiya's defeat in the course of the combined military effort against Constantinople. After the defeat Mu'āwiya, the ruler of Syria and suzerain of the Arab Empire, was no longer accepted in the Orient and was replaced by 'Abdallāh bn al-Zubayr in the year 53 of the Arabs. Mu'āwiya, then marginalized, left his last traces behind him in Ṭā'if on the Arabian Peninsula in the year 58 of the Arabs.

In the year 60 of the Arabs 'Abd al-Malik bn 'Abdallāh from Merv was elected as the new suzerain of the Arabs of the East. His power base was in the Persis. His predecessor in the East, 'Abdallāh bn al-Zubayr, retreated to Kirmān.

'Abd al-Malik and his followers made their way westwards and reached Palestine. This is the country referred to by the symbols on his lead sealing: this was where everything began and where everything will end when it comes to messianism. On the obverse there are two peacocks. On the reverse of the sealing, grape vines can be seen, typical of the promised land. Wild animals are resting, tame and humble in the space under the inscription: "*Filasṭīn*" (Palestine). The depiction of the eagle may be a part of a Christian iconography, but is also found in Nabatean iconography. Sculptures of the eagle are found in tombs of Madā'in Sāliḥ in Saudi-Arabia.

What can be learnt from the language of iconic imagery in this material evidence from the time of 'Abd al-Malik, is not just about Joshua and whatever the scouts found out about the Promised Land. Messages about *Iescho* (Jesus) can also be found in coin images from the time of 'Abd al-Malik. One copper coin, found in Baisan (Galilee), shows a fish in a square surrounded by the inscription: *muḥammad rasūl Allāh*. Here the metaphorical language of 'Abd al-Malik's iconographic theology provides for the interpretation of the set phrase: *muḥammad rasūl Allāh*. The religious community that had chosen the fish as a symbol of Christ, is imparting that the one addressed here is an apostle and chosen by God.[130]

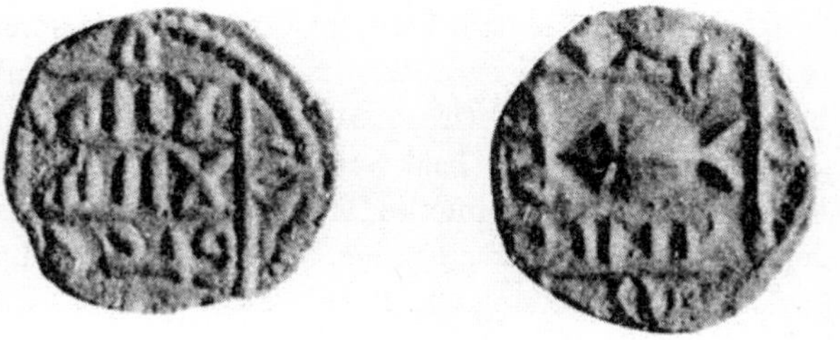

Fig. 17: Bronze coin from Baisan; obverse: religious inscription; reverse: depiction of a fish inside a square. Inscription around the square: the "muḥammad" is the apostle of Allāh; Walker, Cat II. No. 686.

In Jerusalem, 'Abd al-Malik restored the temple. Within the framework of his eschatological ideas he saw the place at the Rock as the location of the last judgment.[131] Before Judgment Day comes, the unity of all Christians is to be restored. The Messiah should find a community which has no quarrel (*mā (i)ḫtalaf*). That is why 'Abd al-Malik called for unity among all Christians in the Dome of the Rock. This is where 'Abd al-Malik's Christological understanding becomes evident. The *muḥammad* (chosen one) is Jesus, son of Mary. He is the Messiah (*al-masīḥ*). He is the servant of God (*'Abdallāh*) on the Iranian coin inscriptions from the year 40 to 49 of the Arabs.[132]

'Abd al-Malik lived in anticipation of the Messiah's appearance. This expectation is reflected in a coin mirroring the expectation of the awaited

Messiah. In its pictorial theology this coin mirrors ‘Abd al-Malik’s understanding of the beginning and end of history.

7.4 The Yəḡar Sāḥaḏūṯā as a Symbol of the Foundation of Israel

The series of copper coins in Syria and Palestine that mirror the iconographic program of the apocalyptical concept of the *muḥammad*, show on the reverse a program of commemoration of the beginning and on the obverse a program of expectation of the end that is nigh. The coin is something like a time machine. If you look at the reverse, you are reminded of the beginnings of Israel. A glance at the obverse will show you what will happen in the future, i.e., the end of the period from the foundation of Israel to the return of the Messiah as recorded in the iconographic program. The reverse depicts a mysterious cross at the top of some steps.[133]

Philip Grierson explains the symbol as a “*pillar-on-steps*”.[134] He recognizes a pillar on a base of steps, but cannot attach any function or meaning to the object at the time of ‘Abd al-Malik. Therefore it is necessary to look out for comparable historic monuments of this sort in order to learn more about their significance. It is possible that in this way the right trail will be found.

A black vertical column is known from Roman history. It was taken to Rome by the Priest of Baal from Emesa (Ḥimṣ). In Rome it was assigned to a temple on Palatine Hill. This black stone, which was believed to be the residence of a Baal, had accompanied his priest and the Roman Emperor Elagabal Ammudates (from 218-222 CE) to Rome. During his rule the originally Semitic god Baal was raised to the rank of supreme God of the Roman Empire. In Rome the “stone” exercised the same protective function guarding the town, which he had already fulfilled in his homeland as sun god of a sidereal mountain cult.[135]

As we have already come across a kind of Old Testamental pictorial theology on objects from the time of ‘Abd al-Malik, the search should start here. There is certainly no direct connection between the pillar of Elagabal and the theological program represented by ‘Abd al-Malik.

In the text of the Bible, however, there are still reminders of the Baetylia (a meteoric stone with magical qualities) and the time of adoration of aniconic stone idols. In the context of the Old Testament a stone pillar plays a role in the story of Jacob. The story of Jacob’s dream is generally known: after Jacob had woken from his dream he took

> “the stone that he had put under his head and set it up as a pillar and poured oil on its top. He called the name of that place Bethel.” (Gen 28, 18-19).[136]

The *baethylus* (sacred stone) also appears with this function in the depiction of ‘Abd al-Malik’s coin in anticipation of the Messiah. The *baethylus* is the guardian of the covenant and the guarantor of the promise. As guardian of the covenant such an aniconic pillar stone functioned as the foundation of Israel: the covenant between Jacob and his father-in-law, Laban.[137]

The depiction of Jacob's covenant stone on the coins of 'Abd al-Malik stands for the notion of *salvation history,* the beginning of which is marked by the covenant between God and the People of Israel at the time of the patriarchs and prophets. *Salvation history* begins with God's act of first choosing and then segregating his people. Therefore, there is no space on the coins of 'Abd al-Malik for a symbol of Christology of the Church, like the cross, a notion he himself must have considered hellenistic, but there is ample room for the commemoration of the beginnings of Israel.

After the end of Muʿāwiya the symbol of the cross had already disappeared from "imitative" coins struck by the 'Arabī. Muʿāwiya, a former ally of the Byzantines and also their confident in Syria early on, had minted coins the Byzantine way. At first there was even a Byzantine inscription on his coins.[138]

The normal symbols on early Arabic coins were either the cross on the letter "M", which designates the value, or the monogram of the emperor Heraclius. After the end of Muʿāwiya the cross is replaced by the symbol of a palm. The palm symbol stands for the event of the birth of Jesus under a palm (cf. Qur'ān 19:23-25):

> "23. And the pangs of childbirth drove her unto the trunk of the palm tree (*'ilā ğiḏʿi n-naḫlati*). She said: Oh, would that I had died ere this and had become a thing of naught, forgotten! 24. Then (one) cried unto her from below her, saying: Grieve not! Thy Lord hath placed a rivulet beneath thee, 25. And shake the trunk of the palm tree toward thee, thou wilt cause ripe dates to fall upon thee (*wa-huzzī 'ilayki bi-ğiḏʿi n-naḫlati tusāqiṭ ʿalayki ruṭaban ğaniyyan*)."

For 'Abd al-Malik the *birth* of Jesus under a date palm is significant, not his *death* on the cross.[139]

The earliest depictions of Jesus as the *muḥammad* on the copper coins found in Syria show him in the form of a Christian ruler.[140] The mint of the earliest mention of *muḥammad*, 'Ammān in East Jordan, is a hint that the notion of Jesus being the *muḥammad* was made public in the western domain by the Eastern Arabs.

The depiction of the chosen one changes with the development of these coins. As in the case of the coin from 'Ammân, the designation of the value – M = 40 Nummia – is found on the reverse with no mention of the location. The obverse shows the frontal view of the *chosen one* without the sign of a cross, but with a gigantic sword portrayed in larger-than-life style.[141] It has long been a matter of controversial discussion as to how the portrayed person, the *chosen one,* is dressed on this portrait.[142] George C. Miles pointed to the similarity to Byzantine depictions of Christ. This also applies to the portrait on the coin from Edessa. Here the person pictured has no headdress of Arab style, but long hair like a traditional Jesus-icon:[143]

Fig. 18: Obverse of a bronze coin from Edessa (Syriac: ܐܘܪܗܝ Ūrhay). Depiction of the eschatological Jesus with coins placed on his eyes, hitherto erroneously interpreted as depiction of a "caliph".

Whoever looks at this coin portrait through the eyes of a modern mainstream Arabist or Islamologist is more likely to come to the conclusion that this is the picture of a "standing caliph" wearing a *kūfiya* (Arab headdress) in the style of the Bedouins. If this picture, however, is interpreted from the perspective of the contemporary Syrian eschatology and the apocalyptical notions linked to it, then one is more likely to see a *halo* above the *Messiah*'s head.[144] In fact, the renowned numismatist John Walker, was convinced he saw a halo above the person depicted on a coin from *Īliyā* (Jerusalem) in *Filasṭīn* (Palästina).[145]

Fig. 19: Bronze coin from Yubna in Palestine, depicting the eschatological Jesus with a halo or flame mandorla. Hitherto erroneously interpreted as depiction of an Arab caliph with a kūfiya (Arabic headdress); reverse: value (M = 40 nummia).

The value indicator M on the reverse, which had been common in Syria, disappears completely. The value of M (= 40 nummia) had become obsolete. It was only seen one last time on a coin of 'Abd al-Malik from 'Ammān. The same applies to coins for Jerusalem.[146]

All later copper coins showing the Messiah with his flame-sword have got the *Yəğar Sāhadūtā* (Jacob's pillar stone of the covenant) on the reverse. Thus 'Abd al-Malik is here able to demonstrate his eschatological program: from the very beginning of the history of Israel onwards history has run a course heading for an eschatological anticipation of the Messiah. The approaching apocalyptical end led to the construction of the Dome of the Rock and to the demand for a peaceful *agreement* (i.e., *"islām"*) with reference to the scripture, the original meaning of *islām* thus not being *"submission"*, but *"concord"*). For ʻAbd al-Malik the place where the world would end was certain: Jerusalem. The time of the event was also certain: the 77th year of Arab rule. The 7th century since the birth of Jesus was coming to an end.

The motto *Filasṭīn* ("Palestine", in the sense of "Promised Land") is found on coins for Jerusalem.[147] The motto *Filasṭīn* has already been mentioned as a conspicuous element on ʻAbd al-Malik's lead sealing.[148]

ʻAbd al-Malik's notion of history is a matter of adaptation and repetition of Israel's history by his *ʻArabī* / Arabs. He perceived himself to be a second *Joshua* (יְהוֹשֻׁעַ yəhōšuaʻ: the originally Hebrew name which in Greek was transcribed as Ἰησοῦς – Jesus), who was to lead his people, the *ʻArabī* / Arabs, who were wandering lost in the desert, to the Promised Land. The *Yəğar Sāhaḏūṭā* in Beth-El, which stands for Jacob's (and therefore their own) dream, is also of significance to the (still Christian) *"Arabs"*, whom contemporary sources never call "*Muslims*", but the "sons of (Abraham's minor wife) Hagar" (הָגָר *Hāğār;* Arabic form: هاجر *Hāğar)*: in Greek: *ma<u>hagar</u>itai;* Aramaic: *M<u>haggr</u>āyē;* later Arabic vocalization: *mu<u>hāğir</u>ūn*). The later understanding of "muhāğirūn" as "those who escaped" is secondary.

Previously, the new Moses in the Qur'ān had freed the *ʻArabī*/Arabs from the oppression of the Persian pharaoh. Forty years in the desert follow this liberation, a period which runs from the battle of 622 CE to ʻAbd al-Malik's appointment to *amir al-mu'minīn.* The latter plays a messianic role in the restoration of the temple. As did Heraclius before him, he saw himself as a founder of a Davidic dynasty: This concept was also followed by their sons, David's son *Solomon* and ʻAbd al-Malik's "son" *Sulaymān* (715-717 CE), who, as ruler of the Promised Land, built Ramla and started the mission for the *muḥammad* in the West.

It was not without reason that Constantinople looked to Jerusalem in admiration. Whereas Byzantium saw itself as a Christendom surrounded by enemies, ʻAbd al-Malik implemented Byzantine imperial eschatology, based on Syrian notions, testing the "katechon" in Jerusalem. He completed the octagon, which Heraclius may well have intended to construct above the Rock when he demonstrated his Davidic idea in 630 CE in Jerusalem.[149] To make the competition with Byzantium even clearer, ʻAbd al-Malik had gold and silver coins struck in the former Byzantine East.

Now ʻAbd al-Malik also assumes the succession of the Roman Empire in the West. In the East he was the successor of the Sassanians, the conqueror of the Persis and elected there as the *Amīr al-mu'minīn.* In the West, up to this date, he had only been the successor of Muʻāwiya. The latter's relationship with Byzantium is not clear. For a long time, the Byzantines probably saw him as a *magister militum*, a Pretorian much like Theoderic (the Great) in Italy, who – like Mu'āwiya – was a Christian (an adherent of Arianism), but of a different denomination. Mu'āwiya may have carried out a dual role: one as the leader of the Iranian 'Arabī/Arabs and one as the headman of the Qurayš. As a Qurayšī, – according to the coin inscriptions already mentioned, not the member of the fictitious clan of the Qurayš, but a "*foederatus*" (ally) – he was officially an ally of the Byzantines up until his betrayal of Byzantium. However, even as a traitor he never had any coin struck in his own name on Byzantine territory. Until today no coin of Maavia from a mint in previously Byzantine territory has been discovered. The pious Christian sources see him as an issuer of his own gold coinage. But these coins are extant on paper only.

In addition to the copper coins struck with 'Abd al-Malik's title and name, there are silver coins in the style of the 'Arabī/Arabs from Iran. Like on his silver coin from Bišāpūr of the year 66 (of the Arabs) the inscription here is also written in Arabic. So it must have seemed that the alien 'Arabī/Arabs, who were completely unknown to the contemporary Syrian Christians, were proclaiming an entirely new message clad in the new Arabic language and script.

It was certainly not known to the Syrians in Jerusalem that the Antiochian notion of Jesus as a MḤMT/*muḥammad* in the East, along the roads to China, had lasted for hundreds of years in its Syriac style, and that it had been continually discussed and re-defined there, still in Syro-Aramaic, both spoken and written, according to the Middle Persian script tradition. It was certainly just as little known to them that the implications of the term *muḥammad* – "monarchianism" – were also discussed in the West in Latin and made public by the followers of 'Abd al-Malik in Carthage: Jesus is not the Son of God, consequentially God is a single entity without a second (*alius*) or a companion (*socius*).

Gold coins from North Africa depicting the *Yəḡar Sāḥaḏūṯā* in a manner typical of 'Abd al-Malik's rule, bear the inscription:

on the obverse: NONESTDSNISIPSESOLCISN –
Non EST Deus NISI IPSE SOLus CuI Socius Non est –
"there is no god except for him alone to whom there is no companion";
on the reverse: DEDNVBTMETOMNNINMANO –
DEus Dominus Noster Unus Benignus eT Misericors ETernus OMNia Noscens INgenitus Magnus Alius NOn est –
"God our Lord the one, (he is) merciful and compassionate, eternal, all-knowing, uncreated (unbegotten), great and there is no other".[150]

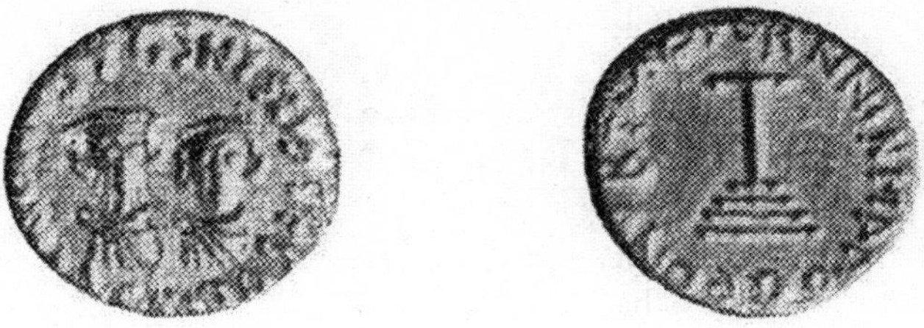

Fig. 20: Obverse and reverse of an Arabic coin from North Africa, apparently from the time of ʿAbd al-Malik, as can be seen in the depiction of the Yəḡar Sāhaḏūṯā on the reverse. Such a symbol is extant on Tory Island off Western Ireland as well.

In Jerusalem and Damascus alone ʿAbd al-Malik's rule and his teachings appeared as monolithic. It was only at these locations that they could be seen in purely Arabic guise. And it was this impression which led the Christian Church Fathers to their judgments about them. This passed-on interpretation of a new religion of the Arabs and of the Prophet of the Arabs with the name MḤMT (the original pronunciation being *Meḥmet* or *Maḥmat*) is based purely on contacts in Syria/Palestine and the experience made there with heresy and false prophets.

To begin with, ʿAbd al-Malik made it clear with his silver coins in Damascus and Ḥimṣ that he had been influenced by Sassanian tradition. Thanks to the great number of Sassanian silver coins they were the prevalent silver currency, however, it was not compulsory to keep to the Sassanian type of coin. From the year 72 of the Arabs onwards, at the same time as the dating of his inscription on the Dome of the Rock, he began to mint Sassanian drachms with inscriptions in Arabic in Damascus and Ḥimṣ.[151]

Here, too, the competition with Constantinople must have been an important factor. During his campaign to the East in 626 CE, the Byzantine emperor Heraclius had had silver coins struck with the sign of the cross and the Byzantine war cry: DEUS ADIUTA ROMANIS ("God, help the Romans!").[152]

There is evidence of this competitive behaviour again in later times. The Byzantines reacted to the minting of Arabic drachmas with the introduction of a silver coin at the time of the rule of Leo III. (after 717 CE).[153] There are examples of Byzantine coins as overstrikes of Arabic silver issues.[154]

Fig. 21: Latin inscription with the "Yəḡar Sāhaḏūṯā". Missionary work for the "muḥammad" was done in Middle Persian, Arabic and Latin.

The decisive challenge to the Byzantine Empire, however, was the minting of gold coins of a new type with captions in Arabic and the weight of a Byzantine solidus.

In the Byzantine Empire a synod was held in the year 682 in the so called "Trullo", a domed hall in the emperor's palace in Constantinople, diversely referred to as the "Quinisext Council", the "Council in Trullo" or the "Penthekte Synod". Just how far the texts that 'Abd al-Malik had ordered to write on the walls of the Dome of the Rock in the year 72 of the Arabs (693 CE) provided an answer to the outcome of the Council in the Trullo, still has to be explored. Questions regarding the iconography and the way Jesus was to be portrayed were also discussed and decided there. The portrayal of Jesus as God's lamb was forbidden. Instead Christ was to be portrayed in human form. This led to corresponding changes in coin design. The portrait of the emperor moved to the reverse of the coin. The portrayal of Christ took pride of place on the obverse. The iconography of the depiction was specified as well. Accordingly, in the design of Byzantine coins after 692 CE, Christ was depicted with long hair and a beard and with eyes open, as a Jesus who was alive, and not like someone coming back from the dead with coins on his eyes, see Fig.18.

Fig. 22: Solidus of Emperor Justinian II. After 695 CE Christ was depicted with long hair and a beard on the obverse. On the reverse a portrait of the emperor as "servant of Christ".[155]

In the year 695 CE there was a revolt in Constantinople against Emperor Justinian II from the Heraclian dynasty. The history of Arab rule was closely linked to the fate of this dynasty. The emperor Heraclius had liberated the ʿArabī/Arab Christians of Iran from the repression by the Persian pharaoh. As his allies (Qurayš) they had done their share to contribute to the victory of Heraclius and had benefitted from the defeat of Sassanian rule. Only when the dream of imperial greatness drove the deluded Muʿāwiya to betrayal, did the protégé of Heraclius become a post-Sassanian, Iranian adversary.

The events of the year 695 CE in Constantinople suggested that the time for the Heraclian dynasty had come. The victory of the year 622 CE could be taken as a sign of divine endorsement of the rule of Heraclius and his house.[156]

ʿAbd al-Malik tried to fill the void, which had developed after the fall of the legitimate ruler of the Empire, at the forefront of Christendom, with his claim to leadership. This was demonstrated by striking gold coinage of his own. Only the emperor was entitled to mint gold coins which represented an independent type with a leitmotif.[157]

ʿAbd al-Malik's coin from the year 695 CE, the 74th year of the Arabs, showed the Syrian-Oriental depiction of the apocalyptic concept of Jesus with his flame-sword on the obverse and the *Yəḡar Sāḥaḏūṯā* on the reverse. This was a programmatic coin without mention of the ruler's name or the mint. Only the year of the issue is evident. Nothing else but the dating of the coin, fixing the period, appears important to ʿAbd al-Malik, only the way time passes seems to count.[158]

7.5 The Great Schism after the Catastrophe of the Year 75 of the Arabs. (696 CE)

Whatever ʿAbd al-Malik might have planned or expected, in the year 75 of the Arabs he had to learn that his position no longer went unchallenged. While the events in Constantinople appeared to help him to gain status in the West, in the East, behind his back, a revolt broke out against a theology which sanctioned his rule and especially his Christological ideas. The conflict must have been smoldering for a long time, and even after the suppression of the revolt it kept on smoldering until after the death of Hišām, the last of ʿAbd al-Malik's "sons", which led to a complete reversal of the situation after the year 125 of the Arabs.

ʿAbd al-Malik's Messianic character, his self-perception as the "New Joshua" and the implications linked to the restoration of the temple (i.e., the Dome of the Rock in Jerusalem) must have led to such alienation in the East that there was an election of a new *Amīr al-mu'minīn*. ʿAbd al-Malik had achieved his aim, but found himself alone in Jerusalem – with the prospects of moving towards an apocalypse certain to happen in the year 77 of the Arabs.

The crisis would seem to have been looming for a long time. Already in the year 56 of the Arabs an inscription appeared on coins in the valley of the Murghab, the home of ᶜAbd al-Malik's kin, which named Allāh the *rabb al-ḥukm* (Lord of all law, legislator, rule).[159] Clarification that this term should be understood in this way can be achieved by means of a bilingual, Middle Persian/ʿArabī/Arabic inscription.

The inscription in Pehlevi: "LWYTW DARWBR / BLA YYZTW", which was first read and consequently translated by Carl Salemann as: "There is no ruler (legislator) apart from God", also plays on the idea of law and rule (both *ḥukm* in ʿArabī / Arabic).[160] On the rim of the coin, there is the ʿArabī/Arabic depiction of this motto with the wording: "La ḥukm(a) illā li-llāh – there is no *ḥukm* apart from Allāh". It is translated by Heinz Gaube as: "God alone is entitled to arbitrate (Gott allein steht der Schiedsspruch zu)."[161]

Heinz Gaube came to this "Islamological" interpretation due to his confidence in Islamic historiography. And this, although he himself mentions Carl Salemann's translation:

> "These concerns cannot call Salemann's interpretation of the caption as 'There is no ruler (legislator) apart from God' into question."[162]

The point is whether the term *ḥukm* refers to "arbitration" (the interpretation of Gaube and later Islam) or to the "legitimation of rule", as the Middle Persian parallel text seems to insinuate? In other words, is it a matter of "law as divine law" and of "rule as theocracy"?

The Middle Persian word *DARWBAR*, however, is ambiguous as it refers to the sphere of rule, of law and of passing judgement. This also applies to the ʿArabī / Arabic term *ḥukm*. Thus it was possible to read this motto in such a way – as "arbitration/verdict" –, that it made sense in the context of Islamic literature. But is this the original meaning? On closer inspection, this understanding is playing around with semantics and obscures the historic context. When the expression "DARWBAR" cropped up in the inscriptions of the first century of Islam, it was a question of how the community was to be constituted under the direct rule of divine law or under the rule of a representative of divine law. It was a matter of theocracy as a direct rule or by an indirect rule via a representative or a representative body.

7.6 EXCURSUS

How the Foundation Charter for a Religious Movement was Created from a Motto Directed against ʿAbd al-Malik in Islamic Traditional Literature

The Traditional Islamic Literature dedicates many chapters to ʿAlī, both relative and son-in-law of the Prophet of the Arabs, who had married the latter's daughter and thus became heir to the claims of the family of the Prophet of the Arabs. This is the Iranian pattern when a new dynasty gets started: A strong man with the sword marries the daughter of a priest, see the beginning of the Sassanians. But ʿAlī is depicted as a real "Man of Sorrows".

When the biography of the Prophet of the Arabs became more and more elaborate, the first problem was the creation of his lineage. He obviously could not be a "bn Āmina", bearing the name of his mother, as with Jesus, who was called ʿĪsa bn Maryam (Jesse, son of Mary). So in addition to his "given name", the originally Christological title "MḤMT" (the chosen one, praised one), another Christological title, *ʿAbdallāh* (servant of God), was added as the name of his father.

Thus, a proper patrilinear lineage not only according to the notions of Arab traditional law: Muḥammad bn ʿAbdallāh – (originally: the chosen one, [the son of] God's servant – to be understood as: Muḥammad, the son of ʿAbdallāh.

This "chosen one, son of God's servant" (Muḥammad bn ʿAbdallāh) has, in his son-in-law, an *alter ego*. According to the Persians' interpretation of Arab inheritance law, the daughter of the "chosen one, son of God's servant" cannot inherit the claim of the family of the Prophet to rule the community in the future, (the *umma* as a society of pious persons is a creation of the 9th century). Therefore this claim falls to the son-in-law (and relative), who has to publicly claim the rule.

ʿAlī, the son-in-law, continued the tradition of his father-in-law. The status accredited to "*M(u)Ḥ(a)M(ma)T*" (Jesus) by the ʿArabī / Arabs of the 7th century and the function of a "*Walī Allāh*" (representative of God) were transferred to ʿAlī, the son-in-law. His end on earth is as bloody as that of "*M(u)Ḥ(a)M(ma)T*" (Jesus). The quasi deification after his death as a martyr can be put down to the significance of his name. Here the proverb "nomen est omen" applies; because ʿAlī, the son-in-law of the "chosen one, son of God's servant", is not only a "sublime one" (the original meaning of *ʿalī*), his name also sounds similar (at least to Persian ears, who could not distinguish an Alif [ʾ] from a ʿAin [ʿ]), to the Semitic term "El", which is probably the oldest designation of God, still to be found as part of many names such as: *Beth-el* (house of God), *Dani-el* (judge of God, or: my judge is God), *Isra-el* (he wrestles with God), *El-i-jah* (my God is Ja[hwe]).[163]

Islamic religious literature allows the son-in-law of the prophet of the Arabs to negotiate with Muʿāwiya, the governor of Syria in the year 37 of the *hiğra*. These events all took place in the period of the first forty years after the *hiğra* of the Prophet of the Arabs. The story goes that followers of ʿAlī, who did not want to bow to arbitration, left the camp crying: *lā ḥukm(a) illā li-llāh*. This phrase, that we have already encountered as a coin inscription, is translated as "*No decision save God's*".[164] Several thousands of these dissidents, however, regretted their behavior and they remained in the village of Harūrā' near Kufa. Thus they are called *Harurites*. Later some of them thought again and decided to leave the camp and to carry on the protest. These are called *Ḫawāriǧ* ("those who went out", singular: *Ḫāriǧī*; English form: *Kharijites*).[165]

Julius Wellhausen commented on this situation and presented the facts thus:

> "the lamentations of the bereaved of those killed touched Ali's heart, the open mockery of those supporting Uthman wounded him: the insincere were happy and the sincere were despondent. Twelve thousand men separated themselves from Ali and did not move to Kufa with him. They seceded to the location of Harura, with the rallying cry of the Tahkim: the Hukm (i.e., the Arbitrium) only appertains to God! They were named after the Muhakkimun. Often they were called the Harurites or generally the Chavârig."[166]

These turbulent events, as they have been reported by Islamic historiographers, are certainly not historic in the sense of the European-American tradition of historiography. In the spirit of "respect for religious feelings", appeasement of fanatics and tolerance towards the narrators of a "special history", a tacit agreement seems to be in force amongst Western historians, who refrain from applying the usual standard procedures when it comes to the history of the Middle East after the year 622 CE, commonly and erroneously labeled "Islamic" history (the term "muslim" appears very late!). In this field, academic requirements and scientific scepticism have apparently been replaced by the uncritical adoption of narratives comparable to those of "Arabian nights". The small escapes of the "West-eastern Divan" and the fantastic stories of the Traditional Account seem too precious to give up. The more the original history – "history" in the sense of "what really happened" – is deconstructed, the more affectionately a story about the Prophet of the Arabs is constructed. It is easy to believe in him, even for *us*, as it is also *our* own ink that runs in his veins. In the meantime, the facts have flourished and multiplied to such an extent that any day in the life of the Prophet of the Arabs could be turned into a documentary and his whole life fills massive and comprehensive biographies.[167]

7.7 The Events of the Year 75 of the Arabs (696 CE)

"The question" of the legitimacy of the rule of the 'Arabī/Arabs in Iran is the question of on which principles it is founded? Only genuine Iranian politico-religious theories can be considered. Irānšahr does not allow herself to be ruled by Bedouin traditional law. The intelligent Iranians spruced up their politico-religious ideas in an "Arabic" manner so that these kept their significance in an "Arabic" society. Being an 'Arabī was just one side of the coin, the other was Iranian traditions. The Persians had behaved as ʻArabī for centuries. They had financed Esra's temple project. Their party, the Pharisees, were present in Jerusalem.

Coins have a long history as a medium for propaganda, also in Iran. The fire altar on the reverse of the coins of the ʻArabī/Arabic emirs no longer represented the state cult of the Sassanians, but the notion of continuity of the Iranian tradition of rule.

Just as the coins of the Sassanians occasionally carried a message in form of a motto to illustrate a political turnaround, in the year 75 of the Arabs coins were struck with the slogan: LWYTW ḎATWBR BLA YYZTW – "There is no ruler unless from God" in the place of the name of the ruler. These coins from the Persis raised the question, according to which justice, according to whose law and on what foundation did ʻAbd al-Malik lead the ʻArabī / Arabs?

In order to legitimize rule in the times of the Sassanians it had been sufficient to claim descent from the ancient gods. The moment when all rulers became Christian servants of God (*ʻabdallāh*), this fundamental basis, –being living gods –, disappeared. From that time onwards the cosmic order was a function of the Dēn.

Whoever wanted to rule as "Dadwar" ("bearer of the law"), had to rely on God alone, and not on his representative. Therefore, in inscriptions by Iranian traditionalists the indication "MḤMT" (i.e., Jesus) is (only) a representative of Allah and (only) a representative of the *amr* (logos), appeared.

ʻAbd al-Malik's mistake in the eyes of these Iranian traditionalists was the attachment to the *Ḫalfat (wrongly vocalized: Ḫalīfat) Allāh* ("representative" (= caliph) of God). The inscriptions on ʻAbd al-Malik's coins suggest a symbiotic relationship between Jesus as the representative of God, and ʻAbd al-Malik, as his *Amīr al-muʼminīn*, who slipped into the role of a Joshua in order to be able to receive the Messiah befittingly in front of the restored temple in Jerusalem.

There must have been ample doubt as to whether this was God's or ʻAbd al-Malik's plan. A spiritual link with the representative of God is no substitute for divine legitimacy.

Therefore it is a matter of conflict regarding the legitimacy of rule. Is it sufficient legitimization for someone to represent the "MḤMT" (= Jesus), in other words: to be the "representative of the representative", or is a direct legitimization as "ḎATWBR YYZTW" necessary, for only then do the fortunate ones shine in God's glory, whilst it is merely his reflection that falls on the followers of the representative.

The ideas of the traditionalists from Sīstān, Kirmān and Fārs persisted in the long run. This explains the damnation of 'Abd al-Malik and his house by Islamic historiography. 'Abd al-Malik's attempt to found a Davidic dynasty had to be regarded with suspicion by all those who followed the old Iranian notion, that the *x^{v}arrah* (lat. *fortuna*), i.e., the *sign of divine election* might appear on any of the brave, on whose horse "the ram" as the bearer of glory could leap and thus render him capable of rule. Therefore, according to Iranian notions, legitimate rule can only be exercised by succeeding dynasties that rule in the spirit of Iranian theocracy. The complete restoration of the Iranian model of rule in the times of the Sassanians was finally accomplished by the Imām during the caliphate of al-Ma'mūn (= Maimonides) in the third Islamic century.

In the year 75 of the Arabs a new *Amīr al-mu'minīn* "appeared", the "Ḫāriğite" Qaṭarī bn al-Fuğā'a. The Encyclopedia of Islam has the following to say about him:

> "(...) the last chief of the Azraḳī Kharidjīs [see AZĀRIḲA], celebrated both as poet and as orator. (...)He must have reached a fairly mature age when, in 69/689, he was acclaimed 'Caliph' of the Azraḳīs when the latter, defeated by al-Muhallab and his lieutenants, were passing through a very serious crisis. Finally al-Hadjdjadi b. Yusuf, appointed governor of 'Irāḳ, decided to reappoint al-Muhallab to the command against the Azraḳīs, in which he had been replaced without success by other chiefs. Al-Muhallab soon drove the rebels across the Dudjayl and assuming the offensive, pursued them into the very centre of their power, Kirmān. Ḳaṭarī nevertheless was able to hold out for a long time in his lines (it is to this period that a silver coin with a legend in Pahlavi and Arabic of the year 75/694 struck in the name of Ḳaṭarī as Amīr al-Mu'minīn, refers [see ZDMG, xii (1858), 52, no. 303])."[168]

The coins of this "new caliph" have an interesting inscription on the obverse: It is the 'Arabī / Arabic translation of the Middle Persian motto from Ardašīr-Khurra: "LWYTW ḎATWBR BLA YYAZTW" = *lā ḥukm(a) illā li-llāh.*[169] Revolt broke out in the year 75 of the Arabs. From the year 76 of the Arabs there is a coin in the name of the *Amīr al-mu'minīn* Qaṭarī bn al-Fuğā'a of Dārābjird. The last indication of his rule is a coin from Kirmān from the year 77 of the Arabs. The end of Qaṭarī was violent, as the EI tells us:

> "(...)The Azraḳīs, surprised by Sufyan's troops in a defile in the mountains, suffered a decisive defeat. Ḳaṭarī, who fell under his horse and was abandoned by his followers, was discovered and killed by a local inhabitant. His head was cut off and borne in triumph to Kufa and then to Damascus to be presented to the caliph."

A nice arrangement of topoi from the Classics and another "head relic" for the Herod in Damascus: But just how unreliable all this information is, is indicated as well:

> "The chronology of these events is far from certain: the sources which say that Ḳaṭarī was in command for 13 or even 20 years are of no value. According to Wellhausen (see Bibl.), the election of Ḳaṭarī as caliph probably took place at the end of 69 A.H. and his death in 78 or 79."

In the year 75 of the Arabs coins were struck for ʿAbd al-Malik in the style of a provincial ruler. This means that his Iranian title: *amīr-i wurroyishnigān* is not mentioned on the coin. This is consistent with the style of later coins of ʿAbdallāh b. Zubayr. After the latter had had to give up the title of *amīr-i wurroyishnigān* to ʿAbd al-Malik in the year 60 of the Arabs (681 CE), his name, even if with no title, appeared until the year 67 of the Arabs in Kirmān and in the year 69 of the Arabs in Zaranj, an outlying district of Sīstān. Until 1993 inscriptions naming ʿAbd al-Malik from the year 75 of the Arabs had not been known.

What can be inferred from these scanty and shaky data? These alternative possibilities are conceivable based on numismatic evidence:

First possibility: ʿAbd al-Malik was first in the East of Iran to quell the revolt and reinforced his status in Merv. Having the province in his possession coins were struck for him in the style befitting a provincial ruler without the title.

Second possibility: Qaṭarī bn al-Fuǧā'a retreated to the East. ʿAbd al-Malik secured his base in Merv. Both adversaries were deposed.

Third possibility: ʿAbd al-Malik returned to Jerusalem in the year 76 of the Arabs or had indeed never left.

The third possibility seems to be the most probable one. This is proven by a coin/medal which only had an inscription and no mention of a mint dated the year 81 of the Arabs, and which mentions ʿAbd al-Malik and his son, al-Walīd, in the text of the inscription.[170]

In traditional literature Muʿāwiya, the first *Amīr al-mu'minīn*, who had become known from inscriptions, was accused of perceiving himself to be the founder of a dynasty since he had regulated succession in the way it was done in the Byzantine Empire. Whether or not this is historic is not known as there is no evidence in the way of inscriptions mentioning Muʿāwiya's sons in traditional literature.

In this regard ʿAbd al-Malik was successful. Inscriptions on the unique bronze medal of the year 81 of the Arabs confirm the status of al-Walīd as successor. As the *muḥammad*, Jesus is no longer mentioned. It is the "son" al-Walīd who takes his place as an emanation. We have no *end*, but a new *beginning*, a new period. A neoplatonic solution as "ersatz"-parousia – a way of saving the Davidian dynasty.[171]

Fig. 23: Obverse and reverse of the medal from the year 81 of the Arabs mentioning al-Walīd as the successor to ʿAbd al-Malik. In the year 82 a special commemorative gold coin was struck.

The text of the inscription on this medal, however, also confirms that a linking of ʻAbd al-Malik as *Amīr al-muʾminīn* and the *ḫal(ī)fat Allāh,* i.e., Jesus, was no longer up-to-date in the year 81 of the Arabs (702 CE). There was another reference to the apocalyptical Messiah on coins of ʻAbd al-Malik. On a copper coin from Sarmīn (northwestern Syria) the standing figure of the Messiah with his flame-sword is referred to as *ʻabd al-Raḥmān.* On either side, parallel to the right and to the left of the depiction of the Messiah and running from top to bottom, there is the inscription: *ʻabd al-Raḥmān*. Thus the *ʻabd al-Raḥmān* is identical to the *ḫal(ī)fat Allāh*, as this reference does not appear on this coin with the portrayal of the apocalyptical Messiah from Sarmīn. *ʻAbd al-Raḥmān* (servant of the merciful) is a Christological title, as is also *ḫal(ī)fat Allāh* (representative of God).[172]

7.8 The Events of the Year 77 of the Arabs (698 CE)

After the end of the revolt in the Persis and the East of Iran, ʻAbd al-Malik had to find a compromise with those powers which had supported the constitutional status of Qaṭarī bn al-Fuǧāʼa. This compromise did not keep the adversaries in the East satisfied on the long run, but did secure rule for ʻAbd al-Malik and his "sons". When the messianic input as a driving force weakened, it was replaced by the concept of the millesimal temple.

ʻAbd al-Malik abandoned the program of the near expectation and imminent parousia. The depiction of an apocalyptical Jesus with a flame-sword was erased; these depictions disappeared from coins. ʻĪsa bn Maryam, the Messiah, was never again mentioned in the form that had been the case in the restored temple in Jerusalem, the Dome of the Rock. There was a return to his being referred to as MḤMT/MḤMD (*muḥammad* = chosen, selected). 'Abd al-Malik's entire theological history program and its portrayal in pictorial theology fell victim to the settlement with the legitimist fundamentalists of the East in order to guarantee survival of the dynasty.

All dialogue with Byzantium was over. The new orientation within the land was directed at correctly interpreting the "Dēn" (Arabic: Dīn). In the future it was significant to have the right belief ("Dēn/Dīn") which made it easy to understand things correctly. Then it was simple to differentiate between the right and the wrong way.[173]

Here I intentionally use the old Persian form of the later Islamicized terminology, for which the modern interpretation as "religion", – in fact a concept stemming from the era of enlightenment, – is now to be found in Islamological literature. Because the reaction to 'Abd al-Malik's Messianic movement and his new version of the history of Israel as the history of the 'Arabī/Arabs led to a counter reaction on the part of Iranians, which is reflected in the inscriptions of al-Walīd from the years 86 and 87 of the Arabs in Damascus. The inscriptions have not survived *in situ* but we have reports from pious people confirming their existence even after the days of the crusaders.

The new, anonymous gold coins with no depictions from the year 77 of the Arabs were struck according to the Persian weight standard of the *Miṯqāl*. Three lines of writing replaced the depiction of the apocalyptical Messiah with his flame-sword and the explanatory inscription. From the year 78 of the Arabs onwards the minting of a new type of silver drachma was begun. These were also anonymous and only with inscriptions. Three lines of writing replaced the depiction of the fire altar and the two guarding figures on the reverse of the coin and three lines of writing also replaced the portrait of the Sassanian ruler with the two parallel lines of writing in Middle Persian on the obverse.

Sassanian traditions still continued to influence the lifestyle of the 'Arabī/-Arab rulers in Syria. Mshatta became conspicuous among the so-called "desert castles" of this dynasty due to the Sassanian origins of the extravagant relief décor on the walls.[174]

This new program with Iranian demands determined the tenor of al-Walīd's inscriptions from Damascus. The core message/statement now referred to the "Dēn/Dīn" and no longer to the Messiah, Jesus, son of Mary, as was still the case in the year 72 of the Arabs in the inscription on the Dome of the Rock. He who has the correct belief, wants harmony/concord (*islām*) and not conflict among Christians.

In order to make this about-turn possible, al-Walīd was appointed crown prince in the year 81 of the Arabs. It is possible that he had already been the "de facto" ruler. Although 'Abd al-Malik had had to sacrifice his theological program, he had, however, been able to secure survival of his new Davidic dynasty by means of a possible retreat from the politics of the day. The surrender of Jerusalem as a spiritual centre was also part of the politics of the time.

The historic legacy of Damascus was raised to a new line of tradition. A part of this legacy was the Nabatean tradition of aniconic depictions and stone idols; a further part was the Ghassanid tradition of using Arabic as the language of rule.[175]

An additional building block of the new ideology of rule is the role of John the Baptist as a prophet and patron of Damascus. John the Baptist replaced 'Abd al-Malik's Messiah from Jerusalem, who, as a mere "servant of God" had a much weaker position than in Western Christianity, as the saint of the dynasty. There was a shift from the Messiah in the inscription on the Dome of the Rock to a view of Jesus as "Seal of the Prophets".[176]

The basilica of St. John (known today as the Umayyad Mosque) became the new *Ḥarām* (sacred place) of the dynasty and not Mecca as is insinuated by the Islamic traditional literature. This illustrates a supposed "battle of sanctuaries": Jerusalem versus Mecca (as 'Abd al-Malik's fall from grace), Mecca's sanctuary versus the temple in Jerusalem, i.e., the annual covering of the Ka'ba on Yom Kippur) as the Arab renewal of the Solomonic temple tradition.

Islamic traditional literature refers to the finding of the relic of the head of the Baptist during the construction of al-Walīd's sanctuary in Damascus:

> "In 874 Yaqubi, the historian, wrote that a cave had been found in the foundations while the mosque was being built:
> 'In the night the caliph climbed down and behold, it was a beautiful chapel, (...) and in it there was a chest and in that was a basket on which was written: This is the head of John, the son of Zacharias.'

Yaqubi finishes:

> 'At the time when the head was put there, Zaid (the custodian) declared (...) that the hair and the flesh on the head was in no way decayed.'"[177]

Fig. 24: Depiction of John the Baptist on the obverse. Below, on the right, the relics of his head. The portrait displays the saint of Damascus. On the reverse the palm as symbol of Jesus' birth under a palm tree. The

iconography of this coin refers to surah Maryam and is an indicator for the early date of this surah, in the days when the legends on coins were not yet written in Arabic

Fig. 25: On this coin from Damascus (?) John the Baptist is depicted as a preacher. His unusual clothes, as mentioned in the gospels, are conspicuous.

It is interesting that, in view of the monetary turmoil, which accompanied the reform of the minting of coinage, there were effects similar to those that are associated with the effects of globalization today. Philip Grierson put this very impressively.[178]

Fig. 26: John the Baptist baptizes Jesus in the Jordan river. Above on the right: dove as symbol of the Holy Spirit. Bronze from the time of Muʿāwiya in Damascus.

The advance of Sassanian silver coins in the form of Arab drachmas struck in the region of the Mediterranean led to a five-century-long development of a purely silver currency in the area of Western Christianity. The significance of Persian silver as a metal used for coins can be determined from the archeological finds in Gotland. For years and years this Swedish island could pay its taxes to the Crown with silver coins which farmers found in the fields. They were regular finds and random finds from Viking graves. It is thanks to these Viking treasures that coins have been preserved which describe ʿAbd al-Malik's interpretation of the Moses of the Qur'ān long after his rule (766 CE). These Arab coins are to be found in Swedish museums. They bear the inscription: *Mūsā rasūl Allāh* (Moses is the apostle of God).[179]

To ʿAbd al-Malik this Moses is the prophet in his Qur'ān. In the theology of the ʿArabī/Arabs, the Moses of the Qur'ān is an illustration of the role of

Jesus from the Old Testament. The deported Christians from Mesopotamian Arabia put their hopes on *Jesus* as their savior, who – like *Moses* – would rescue them from the might of the *Persian pharaoh*, the *Joshua* (the Hebrew name form of "*Jesus*", Moses' successor, who "finishes the job"), who led them over the Jordan (Yarmūk) to the Promised Land, and the *Messiah* who would return to Jerusalem to be with them when the world would end. 'Abd al-Malik, however, is a *David* who reinstates the rite. He is the father of a new *Solomon/Sulaymān* (the name of his son). It is known that, when Heraclius brought the Cross home to Jerusalem in 630 CE, he saw himself as a "new David".

7.9 The Rule of 'Abd al-Malik's Sons and the Failure of Succession

After al-Walīd had distanced himself from the apocalyptical ideas of his father, it had become possible to regard the movement of the 'Arabī/Arabs in Syria in greater historical depth by falling back on the story of the Baptist in Damascus. In the place of a Messiah with a flame-sword, which indicated the end of the world was nigh, there was now a preacher, in the form of St. John the Baptist, who already centuries before had *called for change*. This was now interpreted as a *call for change* in the sense of a correct interpretation of the "Dēn/Dīn". This demand is in the opening part at the beginning of the text of al-Walīd's inscription from the year 87 of the Arabs (708 CE) in his *ḥarām* (sanctuary), the so-called Umayyad Mosque in Damascus: *lā ikrāha fī d-dīni* (Qur'ān 2:256). Both Pickthall and Rudi Paret translate this as: "There is no compulsion in religion."[180]

Apart from the fact that the "Dēn/Dīn" cannot be translated as "*religion*", Pickthall and Rudi Paret did not understand the construction of the sentence either. It deals with a rhetoric figure, a *speech of antitheses*. Just as 'Abd al-Malik had defined *islām* as the *absence of conflict* in his inscription on the Dome of the Rock, here the "Dēn/Dīn" is described as the *absence of toil and duress*. An apt translation for "*lā ikrāha fī d-dīni*" would thus be:

> "If the spirit of belief (Dēn/Dīn) is within you, then there is no further effort needed for understanding."

You do not have to force yourself to have the right attitude and to know how to differentiate between the right and the wrong.[181]

After their return to the Promised Land and after the disappointment of the anticipation of the Parousia (second coming of Christ) from the year 77 of the Arabs, it was now time for the 'Arabī/Arabs to demonstrate their "rightful faith/belief" (*dīn al-ḥaqq*). This had been regarded as a specific quality of the teaching of Jesus. Not only had he sealed and confirmed the teaching of his forerunners, he had preached his specific faith *(dīn al-ḥaqq)* as well. There was a change from the belief in the claims of the Messiah to the belief in and the protection of the "Dēn/ Dīn". This was consistent with the Iranian tradition of rule.

Despite the crisis in the year 75 of the Arabs, it had been possible to conserve the claim to have founded a new Davidic dynasty. Al-Walīd's succession was the key milestone on the way to the foundation of a dynasty. What Heraclius may have had in mind in Jerusalem in 630 CE, was realized by ʿAbd al-Malik's "family":

1. The Temple Mount was the location of the new temple.
2. ʿAbd al-Malik's family had replaced the family of Heraclius. When the last offspring of the Heraclides was banished (695 CE), it was ʿAbd al-Malik in his stead who continued the imperial gold coinage with a depiction of Christ.
3. When the last Heraclide disappeared from Constantinople, al-Walīd's succession made it possible to found a new Davidic dynasty according to the notion already conceived by Heraclius.

Al-Walīd's brother, *Sulaymān* (Solomon), built himself a new *Ramla*, a new town in Palestine. He thus followed an Iranian tradition whereby every ruler builds himself a new town or palace. This was the time when the mission to accept Jesus as the *muḥammad* was starting in North Africa. He is also the first to be considered a *Mahdī* ("guided one") in traditional literature. Here the function of the Messiah is reduced to the re-establishment of the *Dēn* in the sense of *"guidance"*. This may well have to do with the time of Sulaymān's rule at the end of the first century after the epoch-making victory of 622 CE. In later traditional literature the *Mahdī* was expected to appear at the turn of the century.[182]

The naming of the *muḥammad* first took place in North Africa at the time of Sulaymān's rule and then later in Spain.[183]

Here we have an indication of another change within the group which was based on the representation of theology and Christology of the Iranian ʿArabī/Arabs. The mission to regard Jesus as the *muḥammad* in North Africa, which was formerly part of the Byzantine Empire, and then subsequently also in "Spania", indicates that the exclusive representation of this idea was abandoned by a narrowly defined group that acted like a sect. The number of people from Khorasan around ʿAbd al-Malik and their notion of the representation of the "Halpat/ḫal(ī)fat Allāh" (Jesus as God's representative on earth) and the group of people from Kirmān and their notion of direct dependency of the ruler and his rule on divine law, were too small to satisfy the demands on the manpower necessary for an imperial administration.

Up until that point Islamology has solved this problem by accusing the conquered Christians of running the administration of an Arab realm in the name of the Arab victor.

The Islamological approach, which explains the events as a conquest of this cultural homeland of age-old civilisations by Bedouins, who came forth from "spiritual desert" under the leadership of a militant prophet from Mecca, is a mere legend based on literature written centuries after the alleged events and contradicting the material evidence and should be considered obsolete. The information from archeological sources and inscriptions shows that in reality, we are dealing with the establishment of rule of a (non-Trinitarian) Christian group in post-Sassanian Iran and its thirst for truth being stilled by the "Water of Life" streaming down from the Rock like a "marwa". In Merv the *marwa* Murgh-Ab, coming down like a stream from the mountain, had transformed the desert at the foot of the rock into an earthly paradise. There the river is lined with trees on both sides. The leaves of the trees are used as food by the silk-worm. Dried leaves are natural drugs for healing the sick. The *marwa* is full of fish, some of them as big as fish from the open sea. Fishermen abound and net in the fish on both sides of the river. Where the fresh water of the *marwa* meets the salty marshes, the black soil is "healed" from the detrimental effect of the salt. The water in the marches is also "healed", the salty load reduced. At the end the Murgh-Ab is swallowed up by a dead sea in the desert of today's Turkmenistan.

First and foremost the rule of the Iranian Christians has to be interpreted as a replacement of elites. Non-Iranian urbane elites replace the Iranian feudal nobility.

The Syrians were just as unfamiliar with the Byzantine officials as they were now with the rulers of the Arab Empire.

This animosity was reinforced further by the drive of the new lords from the Iranian East to openly propagate their theological and Christological concepts and to publicly name the areas of conflict: the representation of the idea of believing in one God only versus the Zurvanist cosmology in the Iranian East, in Jerusalem the representation of the idea of harmony (*islām*) versus the permanent conflict (*iḫtliāf*) of Christian doctrines, and in the Latin West the opposition towards the concept of the *Son of God* as propagated by the Councils from Nicaea until Chalcedon.

The Arab conquest, which allegedly took place in the 7th century CE, can not be proven archeologically, – neither buttons from Byzantine uniforms nor weaponry or coins from the war chest have been found by Palestinian merchants along the river Yarmouk (Yarmūk) or in the Yarmouk valley, where the Byzantine army was allegedly annihilated by the Muslim conquerors in the year 636 CE. This, however, is not surprising, as some of these "conquered" countries, Syria and the southern parts of Iraq, were already ruled by Arabs in the 6th century CE. Therefore, the real locations of the battles and conquests are more likely to be found in the literary transformation of biblical and apocalyptical concepts. Well educated urban elites and erudite monks created an Arab Antique Renaissance style as a background for the rehearsal of antique drama. All this was presented in the matrix of the Book of Daniel and the letters of Paul.

This also happened with the collection of Qur'ānic material. Following the Iranian example of the collection of the texts of the Avesta and of the Zand, all sorts of things from Oriental and Indian books of wisdom were taken on into the corpus in order to do justice to the claim that the Qur'ān, as a sacred scripture, is equal in value to the Avesta and the Zand, as it includes a comprehensive knowledge regarding the "Dēn" (Modern Persian: "Dīn").[184] This "inclusiveness" is typical for the way Iranian books were traditionally compiled.

In Egypt the leaders of the ʿArabī/Arabs would appear to have exercised particular reservation when propagating the idea of Jesus as the *muḥammad.* Due to its critical attitude towards Byzantium, the Egyptian Church was a natural ally with respect to political power. After the death of Heraclius it made peace with its "ma-hāgāritic" voluntary helpers (the Qurayš). The administration had continued to function thanks to the respective experience of the Egyptian Christians (Copts). There are indications of a large extent of autonomy on the part of the native elites. In Egypt a few copper coins are reminiscent of the activities of the administration of the Arab Empire, apart from a few glass weights bearing the names of tax officials.

7.10 The Caliphate as the Result of the Usurpation of Power by Marwān II.

Copper coinage was first struck in four locations in Egypt at the time of the caliphate of Marwān bn Muḥammad (after 127 of the Arabs [748 CE]). They bore no religious captions. There is even no mention of Jesus as a *muḥammad.* The first caliph along with the title of the ruler and his function is mentioned in the inscription: "ʿAbdallāh (*title*) Marwān (*name*) Amīr al-mu'minīn (*function*)".[185] It could be regarded as an anonymous issue from an inter-regnum as well when read: "The servant of God who is like a stream of 'Water of Life' and a Speaker of those who lead to the Faith."

Marwān was the first caliph (representative), since his rule was not legitimized by inheritance. As the son of a father, who had himself never held power, he was not entitled to succeed. His father, Muḥammad, was allegedly a brother of ʿAbd al-Malik. According to traditional literature Marwān had made sure that those princes, who were entitled to succession, had been disposed of. Historically speaking, whenever he used the term *caliphate,* he did so to define the legitimation of his rule.[186] This could be the case, as long as we are kind enough to listen to this pious lore, without disturbing the narrator in the course of this Arabian night. When it comes to these genealogies we should remember that the true Arab takes interest only in the lineage of his horse. He will tell you that his *birdawn* is a symbol of the heritage of the Arabs from the time they spent in the desert. The Ottoman family of Sultans could present a forefather who was a friend of Jesus.

Marwān could be regarded as a kind of imperial governor. The usurpation of power by Marwān ([MaRWān], meaning: "the man being like a *marwa* from MRW; as a Marwān he was likened to a stream of the "Water of Life") led to the end of rule by ʻAbd al-Malik's "Holy Family". The lack of legitimation of Marwān's rule led to violent protests. Marwān's caliphate (rule by proxy) was not accepted as the legitimate succession to the rule of ʻAbd al-Malik's "sons". Again the question was asked that had already caused a stir in the year 75 of the Arabs: can rule be exercised on the foundation of a "representation" (God's representative or that of his prophets), or is it to come directly from God for it to be validated as legitimate?

In Egypt the lack of programmatic inscriptions in the sense of an imperial tradition, as are to be found in Syria, is striking.

ʻAbd al-Malik's brother, ʻAbd al-Azīz, as governor in Egypt, abstained from mentioning the "muḥammad" in the text of an inscription for a bridge near Fusṭāṭ (Old Cairo). From the beginning of the striking of silver coins with inscriptions only, i.e., from the year 78 of the Arabs (699 CE), until the end of the rule of ʻAbd al-Malik's dynasty, no silver coin was struck bearing the name of an Egyptian mint.

It is remarkable that up until the end of the rule of ʻAbd al-Malik's family, there are no inscriptions to be found in Egypt that can be considered "Islamic" in the sense of traditional Islamology. Not only did the mint authorities refrain from mentioning the *muḥammad*, but inscriptions, which in any way deviated from the Christian ideas of the Egyptians, were also avoided.

This practice contradicts the Islamic theory of the *sikka*.[187] According to this, coins had to be struck with the name of the ruler and bearing the name of the territory which was ruled over as a symbol of the rule exercised, as only he, who had coinage struck in his name, could rule. This practice was already prevalent among the Romans and the Persians. The coins of the time after the year 77 of the Arabs up until the years 30 to 39 of the 2nd century of the Arabs, which were, to a great extent, anonymous, could hardly be reconciled with the Islamic idea of exercising the right of coinage as a criterion of rule. Silver coins from Egypt are only known from the time of the dynasties of the late 2nd century of the Arabs.[188]

North Africa and Spain would appear to have been regarded as fertile ground for a mission to suggest that Jesus was the *muḥammad*, the chosen one, as the Christology of Arianism, – "Christ was created and is therefore distinct from God the Father" – still had adherents in these regions, which were once ruled by the *Arian* Vandals and later also by the *Arian* Visigoths.[189]

The opponents of the conversion of the Visigothic king to Catholicism in 584 CE were numerous. That is for certain. The Visigothic nobility felt they had been done out of their privileges, as conversion to Catholicism meant the end of the Gothic elective monarchy. In 588 CE a faction of the nobility under Witteric revolted with the aim of reinstating the Arian faith. Witteric rebelled again in 603 CE and ruled until 609 CE. He was murdered by a group of Catholic members of the nobility.

As former vassals of the Byzantine emperor, the lords of the Arab Empire had good reasons to regard the South of Spain as their own dominium, as the region had been a part of the Byzantine Empire before. Here, too, a succession to Byzantium seemed possible and natural.

The Catholic Franks intervened in Spain on the side of the Catholic Visigothic dynasty. This was a thorn in the side of the Visigothic nobility which was still Arian-minded. Thus, when the Berber allies of the Visigothic nobility were reinforced by the ʿArabī/Arabs, a rather opportunistic conquest of Spain, – totally different from the legends to be found in all history books about the "conquista", – took place. The common aim was already achieved in the first battle: the death of the Catholic king and the end of his Catholic dynasty. Thus any interference on the part of the Franks was stopped. There was an amicable distribution of the spoils. The lords of the Arab Empire took on the Byzantine legacy in the South of Spain and the Visigothic nobility contented themselves with the North of Spain.

In order to prevent any further Frankish interference in favor of the Catholic party in Spain, military campaigns were undertaken which reached into the heart of the Merovingian realm. Karl Martell's victory near Poitiers in 732 CE and near Narbonne in 737 CE "saved the Occident".

Contemporaries could not have been aware of what the Occident was being rescued from. They could only see that Karl Martell saved the Franks from having to pay for their interference in Spanish affairs.

Later on, in Spain, it was deemed necessary to find a way to reconcile the conviction of the lords of the Arab Empire that Jesus was a *Servant of God* and not a *Son of God*.

Without any knowledge of the inscription on the Dome of the Rock, where the idea of adoptionism is rejected, the Bishop of Toledo and the Bishop of Urgell taught that Jesus' *human nature* was *adopted* as *divine*. This aroused resentment from all sides and Charlemagne had this Christological concept condemned immediately.[190]

7.11 The Fiction of a Caliph called 'Umar – The *Mahdī* as Successor to the Concept of Jesus Being the *Manṣūr* (victor)

The end of Sulaymān's rule was the end of the first century of 'Arabī/Arab absolute rule. This is how traditional literature would have it believed. Islamic tradition regards Sulaymān as a ruler who fattened his own belly and allowed his sexual desire to run wild.[191] This shows us that he was a Neronic clone of the biblical Solomon.

The *Mahdī* was expected at the beginning of the new century. The good caliph 'Umar II. (allegedly ruled AH 99-101) was not a suitable candidate for this role. Thus, after successful transition into the new century, – the end of the world had not yet come, – he was buried next to his father. Abū Hamza, the rebel, also said of him:

> "So curse them, may God curse them! Except that 'Umar b. 'Abd al-'Azīz was from [among] them: he had good intentions and did not act [upon them]; he fell short of what he intended."[192]

Following the narrative patterns of traditional literature, it becomes clear that now was the time for a new Umayyad caliphate. It is completely irrelevant whether or not the historic Sulaymān still reigned for a few years on. The insertion of a Messianic figure into the religious history to overcome the problem of the "turn of the century" ('Umar II), was an apocalyptic solution. The good caliph 'Umar and his Mahdī-like ("guided") nature had been able to avert the worst. Now, however, the sacrilege of 'Abd al-Malik – in religious history he had built up Jerusalem to oppose Mecca and encouraged pilgrimage to Jerusalem – now had to avenge itself down to his last family member.[193]

For this reason, in the traditional portrayal of history by historiographs, – which narrates what "should have happened" rather than "what really happened" – there cannot have been a second period of rule for Sulaymān. Furthermore, there was only a disposable period totalling 60 years for all protagonists of this dynasty. After that, the time of this outrageous dynasty had run out.

It is interesting to note that, according to the dating of traditional religious history, the time span between the year 65 of the *hiğra* of the prophet of the Arabs, i.e., 686 CE, the year when 'Abd al-Malik's rule began, and the end of the rule of the last of his ruling sons in the year 125 of the hiğra (747 CE), is exactly 60 years and thus corresponds to the *Sexagenary Cycle* of such prominent importance e.g. in the Chinese culture (六十花甲 – liùshí huājiǎ). There are several differing interpretations for the choice of a period of 60 years. The number is the result of multiplying the prime number 5 (also the number of fingers on hand) with the highly popular "symbolic" number 12: the 12 disciples, the 12 tribes of Israel etc.

But even for a mathematician, 12 is a special number: the duodecimal system (12 is used as a division factor) was used for many ancient and medieval weights and measures. That is why we still have clocks with 12 hours and buy a "dozen", not ten (or a "score of") apples: (12 can be divided among 2, 3, 4 or 6 people, 10 only among 2 or 5). The system probably originates from Mesopotamia. Whether it was 60 years or 60 minutes, after 60 cycles of religious history, time had done its bit. There were seven years left before the downfall. Only the seven plagues of the bible were left out. Traditional literature places this at the year 132 of the hiğra of the Prophet of the Arabs (753 CE).

Here it is not necessary to be concerned about the significance of the result of multiplying the prime number 11 (the next prime number after 5 and 7) with the symbolic number 12. It is another piece of evidence that the concoction of traditional history follows ancient traditions, that those who cooked up this highly symbolic and more than *semi*-fictitious "*salvation history*" had taken on from their Babylonian ancestors. In addition to this there was the Iranian idea of *time* that crushes everything: *Zurvān* as the God of infinite time, somewhat comparable to the *Norns* in Norse mythology, who could prophesy even the destiny of the Gods, or the Moirai in Greek mythology. Verses in best Zurvanist tradition can be found in the *Kitāb al-Aġānī*. Gernot Rotter quotes one bit which refers to the demise of the *Kalb*:

> "Oh Kalb, time (*zamân*) has thrown itself upon you and you have suffered specific punishments from me (...)."[194]

Thus, as in the Sassanian translation offices of Esra, ancient dynasties of secretaries, as representatives of ancient tribes, created history, thus making sure that lexical material originally stemming from the Akkadian language, then adopted into the Aramaic *lingua franca* of the ʿArabī, finally made its way into the Arabic grammar of the Abbasid caliphs. When modern Islamologists read the giant history of Ṭabarī ("the one from Ṭabaristān"), believing every word to reflect historical truth, then they are ignoring the tried and tested "recipes" of history creation current in Ancient Iran. Moreover, the possibility or rather probability should be taken into consideration that the *Tārīḫ al-rusul wa-l-mulūk*, also called *Tārīḫ al-Ṭabarī*, the famous "Chronicles of Ṭabarī (allegedly lived from 838 to 923 CE)", much like his equally gigantic commentary of the Qur'ān (*Ğāmiʿu l-Bayān*), are more likely the output of a team (a kind of "Ṭabaristani Society" for the assessment of useful archive material) than the books written by a single man.

The story of the fictitious relative of ʿAbd al-Malik, the caliph ʿUmar, as Mahdī ("the guided one") is a Trojan horse in the depiction of history of the 3rd century of the *hiğra*.[195]

At this moment, the notion was already established that the arrival of a *Mahdī,* who, according to widespread views, restored the "Dēn/Dīn" before the end of the world and thus also provided for justice, could be linked with each upcoming new century. The basis of the concept the *Mahdī,* the resurrection of the "true religion" ("Dīn al-Haqq" in the Qur'ān), is also of Iranian origin. The call for justice is first found in the inscriptions on the coins of Rāy (Tehran today) from the year 101 of the Arabs (722 CE).[196]

This later conception of the appearance of a *Mahdī* at the turn of the century was retrospectively projected into the history of the 1st and 2nd centuries of the Arabs. Just how uncertain this terrain is, can be attested by the deliverance of a *ḥadīt* by al-Šāfiʿī (allegedly died in the year 204 of the *hiǧra* of the Prophet of the Arabs, at the time of the caliph al-Ma'mūn), according to which the *Mahdī* is no other than *ʿĪsa bn Maryam* (Jesus, son of Mary).[197]

The concepts of the arrival of the Mahdī are historically later than recorded in traditional literature. In the texts of inscriptions of the 1st century of the Arabs, the only concept that is referred to in ʿArabī/Arabic is "*manṣūr*". It is striking that the term *manṣūr* (victorious, the one who is given victory) also occurs in Middle Persian spelling, as is the case with "MḤMT" (*muḥammad*). Neither of the expressions is Iranian and they are both treated as ideograms in the context of Pehlevi spelling. "Ideograms" or "heterograms" here designates words spelt in Aramaic (or in this case Arabic), but pronounced in Middle Persian, of which there were around a thousand common. It is a bit comparable to English abbreviations like "e.g.", which are not pronounced or spoken as "exempli gratia", – as they should be, – but "for example". Here, too, there is discussion in Islamological literature as to who could be meant by the alleged name form *manṣūr*. However, it is once more a matter of an *epithet*, a Christological *title* and *not* a proper name. This had already been considered by Rika Ghyselen.[198] She had even grown to be convinced that the form *muḥammad* in inscriptions on coinage is not to be interpreted as the personal name of an Arab emir, but as an honorific title.[199]

The mention of the Christological title *manṣūr* is an indicator that apocalyptical notions, as propagated by ʿAbd al-Malik until the year 77 of the Arabs (699 CE) in Jerusalem, lived on. Half a century later the title *manṣūr* was included into a series of Messianic names which later rulers used as self-decoration.[200]

This means that the influence of the Syrian apocalyptical scenarios of the end of the world continued to have effect in the East, particularly under the rule of al-Ḥaǧǧāǧ bn Yūsuf, described as viceroy of ʿAbd al-Malik in traditional history.

The apocalyptical scenarios, which are portrayed in ʿAbd al-Malik's pictorial theology, were also found in the Syriac Apocalypse of Daniel from Elam and Persia. There we read:

"Then Christ the King will come in all his glory, his name is before the sun [*author's note:* Therefore he is pre-existent, like an Iranian *fravahr*], and before the moon, his rule and his kingdom. The honest and righteous will accompany him. They will appear in holy clouds at the beginning of the apparition of his arrival, like a fighter and like a warrior, a powerful force in battle. A fire will consume everything before him and flames will flare around him."[201]

Fig. 27: Frontal depiction of the eschatological Jesus with flame mandorla; bronze from Yavne/Palestine from the time of 'Abd al-Malik.

The description corresponds to the iconography on the coins from Palestine at the time of 'Abd al-Malik. The so-called "standing caliph" of Islamic numismatics is a Syrian depiction of the apocalyptical Jesus.

If the portrayal of the "standing caliphs" in the design of 'Abd al-Malik's copper and gold coinage, where the depiction is accompanied by the words "*Ḫal(ī)fat Allāh*" ("representative of God", i.e., the Messiah), is interpreted as referring to the apocalyptical Jesus posing as a warrior, a powerful force in the battle against evil, – just as he is described in the Syriac Apocalypse of Daniel, – then further text of this Apocalypse of Daniel should also render a better understanding of 'Abd al-Malik's construction program in Jerusalem.

To adduce an example, in the Apocalypse of Daniel it is claimed that:

"Then the God of all gods, Lord of all lords and King of all kings, Adonai Zebaoth, the almighty Lord, will appear on Zion in his entirety. On Zion he will establish the holy cherubim (the cherub serves as God's throne) and the throne of righteousness on the hills of Jerusalem. Besides … of Christ the King will appear from heaven on earth."[202]

Fig. 28: Depiction of the apocalyptic Jesus with his flaming sword.

Where might the Arab-Byzantine coins with the mint "Zion" have been struck other than in a region which had been influenced by such apocalyptic expectations?

Whether the reference to "CION" was referring to Jerusalem, or, to be more precise, to the location of *the Rock*, is not known. In any case, the reference to the mint of "CION" reflects an apocalyptical expectation in the region of Jerusalem which is understood to be the location of the Theophany.

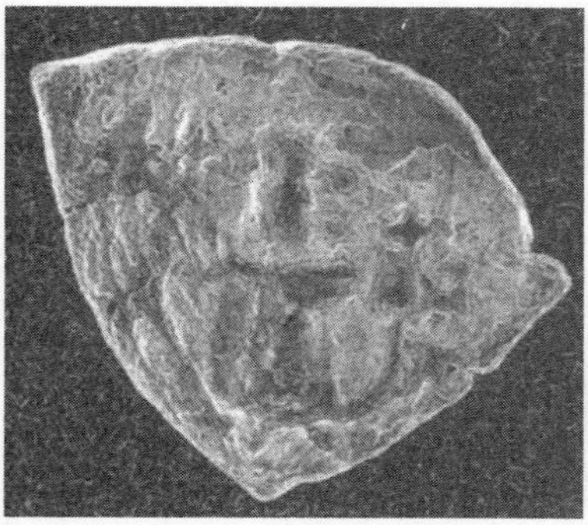

Figs. 29 (left) and 30 (right): Obverse of a bronze from Palestine with the depiction of the Byzantine emperor Constans II; reverse of the bronze with the depiction of Constans II; indication of value: M; below: mint: 'CION' (Zion). Whether Zion means Jerusalem in this context must remain undecided. See also Isaiah 1:26. From a German private collection.

The time when this Syriac Apocalypse of Daniel was written is also significant. In the Qur'ān the account of *Ḏū-l-Qarnayn*/Alexander's "Gate in the Caucasus" and its construction in connection with the fear of Gog and Magog can only date from after Pseudo-Ephraem's "Sermon at the end of the World". Only there can motives of Alexander's Gate in the Caucasus and Gog and Magog be found together.[203]

This apocalyptical material was developed further in the late Pseudo-Methodius. The point in time when motives from this apocalypse were included into Qur'ānic material therefore corresponds well to the idea of an early collection of Qur'ānic material at the time of al-Walīd, around the end of the first century of Arab absolute rule. At this time the apocalyptical material was on the market in the constellation as it is found in the Qur'ān.

However, the Syriac Apocalypse of Daniel is older. The peculiarities that can be found in 'Abd al-Malik's apocalyptical notions date into the fourth and fifth centuries CE.[204]

The last "son" of 'Abd al-Malik to rule, Hišām (723 – 743 CE), is said to have resided in Ruṣāfa. Ruṣāfa is located not far from the Euphrates in Northern Syria. This is recorded in traditional literature. Traditional literature also refers to him keeping court the Persian way. In addition to this, there is a tradition which refers to Hišām as "lord of a great treasury". He is said to have been eager to make it even bigger. This, too, rendered him similar to his Sassanian predecessors. One of his successors, the first Abbasid caliph Abū l-'Abbās, who had the Messianic name "*al-Saffāḥ*" ("the generous one", lit.: "the one who pours out", 749–754 CE), was able to bring this treasure to the people. All of this is purely allegorical; the Saffāḥ being the Rock "in action", the process of overflowing with water, watering the desert, pouring it out to the believers, quenching the "spiritual" thirst of the believers.

8 Political and Religious Motives and Developments in the Context of 'Abd al-Malik's Dynasty

8.1 Byzantium and Damascus

The dinar, which had been struck since the year 77 of the Arabs (698 CE), was based on the tradition of Iranian metrology and was therefore struck according to an Iranian coin standard. It was only 'Abd al-Malik's gold coinage, with the depiction of the Messiah surrounded by a fire mandorla and with his flame-sword, from the year 74 of the Arabs (695 CE) until the year 77 of the Arabs, that was struck according to Roman or Byzantine standards respectively.

From the year 74 of the Arabs (695 CE) onwards, 'Abd al-Malik was able to feel he was the rightful successor to the Heraclian dynasty in Constantinople. As Justinian II was banished and mutilated in this year, the epoch of the Davidic dynasty seemed to be over and 'Abd al-Malik could rightly assume that his Christian family had a vocation to succession. Amidst apocalyptical concepts of a "last emperor", this idea seemed to affect the future of his family, because Constantinople was in the hands of rebels. These ephemeral figures on the emperor's throne hastened to remove the depiction of the *Pantocrator* (Byzantine emperor) from the design of Byzantine coinage.

Leontius, the strategist elevated to the throne by the people of Constantinople, made sure that the dominating depiction of Christ on the obverse of coins was removed and indeed all portrayals of Christ on the coinage. The obverse was once more decorated with the portrait of the emperor. Leontius (695-698 CE) had himself portrayed in imperial mantle along with a cross-bearing orb and akakia.

Thus it comes as no surprise that the lords of the Arab Empire claimed their legitimate rights in North Africa just two years after the upheaval in Constantinople. They now considered their family to be legitimately entitled to succession of rule as former allies of Heraclius, since Byzantium had disposed of her legitimate ruler. It was the Diadochi of Heraclius who were entitled to succession, not a military commander of an army of the rebels.

As the "Princes" of a diarchy, both in the former Byzantine provinces and in their previously Sassanian homeland, 'Abd al-Malik's family pursued dynastic claims which resulted from the succession in parts of both of the former Empires. It is completely inconceivable that these claims went uncontested as Islamic traditional literature would portray it. In reality it was about claiming legitimate rights, while the traditional Islamic literature talks about a jihad. According to the Traditional account all claims to rule are based on intermarriage and social contacts among the entourage of the Prophet of the Arabs in a mythical eon in Mecca. This is not history, but pious narration. Nor does it correspond to the way of wielding power in the 7th century CE.

The dynastic entanglement of interests of the empires tells a different story. Here a Persian ruler was avenging a Byzantine emperor when it came to sustaining the legitimacy of rule for the dynasties. The general state of affairs after the murder of Maurice was similar to the conditions in Constantinople after the murder of Justinian II and that of his heir apparent. 'Abd al-Malik's family had to avenge their benefactors, the family of Heraclius just as Ḵosrow II had avenged the death of his benefactor, Maurice, and his family. Families ruling an Empire lived in a special sphere, they were cousins, since they had the "Dei gratia".

The homeland of Heraclius therefore fell (697 CE) to his Christian successor and "relatives", the Davidic family of 'Abd al-Malik, which reinstated the dream of Heraclius for a new beginning in Jerusalem in 630 CE. The dynasty of Heraclius had ruled for almost 90 years until the banishment of Justinian II, not only in Constantinople, but also, in the beginning, in parts of the conquered Sassanian Empire. Heraclius saw the natural heirs to his rule in the East in his 'Arabī/Arab allies and did not pose any resistance towards their seizing of power after his retreat from the East.

Now 'Abd al-Malik's family could emerge as avengers of the Heraclians of Byzantium, just as once Ḵosrow II had acted as avenger of his imperial benefactor, Maurice, when he prepared to conquer the Byzantine Orient.

In order to succeed the former emperor's family as legitimate rulers, 'Abd al-Malik's dynasty needed a justification. This was felt to be of such great significance that he had a coin-like medal struck in commemoration. The inscription begins with a short opening phrase, which at first glance looks Islamic, but in fact does not contain anything which is not perfectly Christian: *bi-sm(i)llāh)i r-raḥmān(i) r-rahīm* ("in the name of God, the merciful and compassionate"). This coin-like medal from the year 81 of the Arabs (702 CE) commemorated only the succession and mentioned only the fact that al-Walīd had been appointed successor.[205]

It is not surprising that Islamic traditional literature rants to such an extent about the foundation of a dynasty by Muʿāwiya in the nature of the Byzantines; however, the foundation of a Davidic dynasty succeeding the Byzantine imperial family by 'Abd al-Malik must be regarded as the real aim of these attacks.

The mutilation of Justinian II, – his nose had been cut off and was later replaced by a gold replica, – that came before his banishment, had desecrated him forever in the eyes of his contemporaries and had rendered him incapable of carrying out a sacral function. The sacral aspect of rule demands a physically perfect ruler. An emperor could only stick his nose into state affairs as long as he had one. It was precisely this that Justinian II had lost after the official act of his mutilation, which preceded his banishment.

When the news of the mutilation of the emperor in Constantinople and his banishment and replacement by a high-ranking officer of the army was received in Damascus, people must have assumed that it was the end of the dynasty of Heraclius.

Seven years later the foundation of their own dynasty was celebrated in Damascus. Thereby 'Abd al-Malik pursued two aims: The conflict concerning the legitimation of his personal rule and his Messianic program was ended. Iran received a succeeding dynasty; the post-Sassanian period of new orientation could be brought to a close.

The foundation of a new dynasty, which was to be in a position to govern over both East and West, could only be effected on the basis of divine confirmation thanks to the pursuance of messianic ideas. The legitimation of the Sassanians had been based on their descent from the gods. As long as divine glory shone down on them, their rule was assured. When the priesthood came to the conclusion that divine glory no longer shone down on Ḳosrow II, he was ostracised and murdered.

In Iranian inscriptions Jesus is referred to as "*Farrox-zād*" (offspring of divine glory, Middle Persian: *x^varrah*).[206]

After the end of the ancient gods it was therefore appropriate to use messianic concepts, or at the least messianic titles, to legitimize rule. Just how far

ʿAbd al-Malik went towards this cannot be verified. It can no longer be determined to what extent he perceived himself to be a new Moses or a new Joshua, when he moved to Jerusalem – or whether he, from an Iranian perspective, saw the eschatological Jesus as his *royal fravashi*, his "higher self". The later successors of his family were, however, only able to rule in Iran thanks to the personification of messianic concepts alone. The names of the Messiah: *al-Saffāḥ, al-Manṣūr, Muḥammad* and *al-Mahdī* were not considered to be remainders of a past messianism of the ʿArabī/Arabs and the family of ʿAbd al-Malik, but as a *program* which authenticated his partaking in divine glory (*xᵛarrah*).

ʿAbd al-Malik's family, as a new dynasty, however, also declared their claim to the succession to the throne in Byzantium. The claim resulted from the relationships of allegiance with Heraclius during the war against Ḵosrow II (as *foederati*/Qurayš).

ʿAbd al-Malik also had reason to assume he could rightly portray himself as an *Alexander neos* as Heraclius had done. It was not without reason that the story of Alexander, the iron gate and Gog and Magog were taken up in the Qurʾān. Whatever should be the case for the Byzantine "last emperor", could just as well be the case for a "last emperor" of the ʿArabī/Arabs. It might as well be an offspring of the new Davidic dynasty of ʿAbd al-Malik to be designated to deliver rule to the Messiah when the time is ripe.[207]

Neither Leontius nor Tiberius II, his successor (698-705 CE), could foresee that Justinian II, after his ten-year-long banishment, would turn up again outside Constantinople with a Bulgarian-Slav army, and rule for another five years as emperor Ῥινότμητος (Rhinótmetos) "(the one) with the cut-off nose/the slit-nosed" and would take revenge for the horror he had suffered. Tiberius II had had himself portrayed on gold coins struck in his name in a warlike outfit according to old custom: helmet, armour, spear and shield decorated the depiction of his bust.

With the renewed rule of Justinian II after 705 CE, the depiction of Christ reappeared on the obverse of his coinage. The emperor, however, no longer presented himself as a "servus Christi" ("slave/servant of Christ"), as he had done in the inscriptions on his coins from the year 695 CE, but celebrated himself as: "D N IYUS-TINIAN-YS MYLTYS AN(nos)", wishing himself many years to come. The news of the exile of the emperor and the apparent end of the Heraclian dynasty had cost Byzantium her dominion in North Africa.

As soon as an effort is made to found historical suppositions on archeological finds and their competent interpretation, and priority is given to material evidence over written records composed centuries after the purported events they describe, then a completely new view of the complexity of the relationship between Damascus and Constantinople emerges. As soon as it is assumed that claims pertaining to the throne of the Roman Empire, or as

Heraclius had done, to the Eastern Roman Empire camouflaged as Alexander territory, are intertwined and interdependent, then the context of attacks from the former Byzantine Orient and its 'Arabī/Arab rulers on Constantinople or on Byzantine territories in North Africa and Spain becomes clear.

The first great attack on Constantinople was triggered by the impression left by Emperor Constans II when he departed for Sicily, that the capital city and Asia Minor had been surrendered. The crucial attack on Carthage took place when people heard the news of the banishment and mutilation of Justinian II and got the impression that the Heraclian dynasty had come to an end.

In 702 CE it was publicly announced that al-Walīd should be 'Abd al-Malik's successor. As there is no documentation to verify the end of 'Abd al-Malik, we must content ourselves with the information of traditional history that 'Abd al-Malik had still ruled until the year 85 of the Arabs (706 CE). The mere existence of the inscription may be a topos: Augustus has his "Monumentum Ancyranum", so al-Walīd has his inscription in his *kanīsa*. It may also follow the tradition of the ekthesis and the inscription in the Dome of the Rock. This may well be the case as we have an inscription of al-Walīd in Damascus, which is dated the year 86 (of the Arabs). This means that in the year 81 of the Arabs (702 CE), al-Walīd had been appointed to co-regent/co-ruler in the manner of the late Romans and late Byzantines. This practice had been exercised by Heraclius and his sons.

Justinian II, who had made an adventuresome homecoming from his banishment, was murdered in 711, as was Tiberius, his young son and heir apparent. Thus a dynasty, which had founded Byzantium anew, had come to a definite end. After a century of rule on the part of Heraclius and his descendants there was now the question of legitimation of succession.

However, the ruling of the de-facto successor demonstrates the balance of power: Leon, the Northern Syrian, as a strategist for the Theme of the Anatolics (*thema anatolikòn*; a military province in Asia Minor), teamed up with Artabasdos, as a strategist for the Armenian "Theme", and then entered into negotiations with Damascus. An agreement with the rulers of the Arab Empire lent him support and made it possible for him to usurp the throne of Byzantium as man of the 'Arabī/Arabs. The confusion surrounding the throne after the murder of Justinian II was thus brought to a close in 717.[208]

In Damascus Leon was probably considered as just another usurper of the throne of Rūm (lit.: "Rome", meaning "Constantinople", the New Rome), which the protégé of Heraclius, represented by the house of 'Abd al-Malik, was now entitled to. However, Leon, the clever Syrian, and his Armenian ally, did not give up the spoils.

This was the trigger for the second great attack on Constantinople by the powers of the Arab Empire. 'Abd al-Malik's kin stood before the decision as to whether they should continue the succession of Heraclius in Constantinople or that of the King of kings in Iran. Ever since the victory of the benefactor of the 'Arabī/Arabs in 622 CE, their aim had been to take over the legacy of Constantine. After the victory of Heraclius and the peace of 628 CE, the 'Arabī/Arabs, as keepers of their Antiochian heritage, were once again a part of Christian Syria and no longer isolated in the Iranian diaspora.

The inscription in the Dome of the Rock bears reference to their participation in the dialogue within the church and documents their will to rule.

Now the decision was pending. After the end of the legitimate dynasty of the emperor in Constantinople, 'Abd al-Malik's house was the only dynasty in the former Byzantine Orient. Their rise to rule was closely connected to the fate of the Heraclians. As loyal vassals, why should they not succeed to their lord? There were historic examples of Diadoch Wars. Just as Alexander had been succeeded by his generals, it should be possible for his followers to succeed the *new Alexander* – Heraclius.

It was a matter of either becoming Byzantine emperor and taking on the succession of Constantine or turning to the East and pursuing the succession of the Sassanians. Dual rule could not last in the long term. Being in second place in the Byzantine province and elected regent in Iran did not mean double power, but twofold powerlessness. In order to avoid being paralyzed in one's decisions, it was necessary to claim omnipotence. If the highest level of power in the West was not attainable, then it had to be achieved in the East. The attempt to succeed the emperors in Constantinople in the West, in particular in their function as heads of the Church, had put the family of 'Abd al-Malik, which had been supported by parts of Iran, in a precarious situation which ultimately led to their demise. One reason was the religious legacy from Syria. It led to a split between the affiliation to a church, the head of which was the emperor in Byzantium and his following the teaching of Paul in regard to the "katechon", and the exercising of power as successors of the Sassanians. What managed to re-establish absolute rule in Iran was the clear separation from the church on the one hand and the total integration of the Syrian legacy into the religious tradition of Iran on the other. This absolute rule in Iran was based on religious foundations, not being part of an established church, but of heretical movements which preserved very old traditions in a Christian guise. At the heart of it was the effort to read the writing on the wall with Zurvanite spectacles in order to find out whether a messianic or a millesimal path was leading to the temple. This question was of importance until after the caliphate of the Ḫalīfat Allāh al-Ma'mūn in the 9th century CE.

The turning point was the attack on Constantinople. Leo had to hurry to prepare his defence.

> "Half a year after he had come to the throne the Arabs were waiting with army and navy outside Constantinople. As in the days of Constantine IV a bitter conflict began again which was to decide over the existence or non-existence of the Byzantine Empire."[209]

Sulaymān (Solomon) was the ruler in Damascus at this time. His name was to be just as programmatic as the name that Heraclius had given to his son after his victory over the Persians: David.

Only six months after Leo's rise to the throne, which must have seemed like a usurpation from the point of view of the ruler in Damascus, the troops of the Arab Empire were at the walls of Constantinople. The war plan was similar to the pincer attack once used by Mu'āwiya, a combination of an Iranian army and a Syrian fleet. Thus he combined the land forces of Iran with the naval forces of the former Byzantine Orient. Again, an attempt was made to take Constantinople in this way. The undertaking took a similar course to Mu'āwiya's attack on the capital of the Byzantine Empire. It was once again possible for the Byzantines to burn down the Arab fleet with Greek fire. This is a nice topos never missed out in the description of Byzantine warfare at that time. The attack on land failed due to the insurmountable walls of the strongest fortress in the world at that time. Byzantine sources again describe the event as an ordeal rather than a military conflict. The Arab adversary was defeated three times: first Greek fire burnt their ships, then an unusual cold wave in the winter affected the army and, in the end, they became victims of a plague. These elements were obviously inclined towards the Byzantine cause.

In the end, the Bulgars, the enemy of the Empire, joined the war on the side of the Byzantines and caused serious losses to the troops of the Arab Empire. In the middle of August 718 CE, the blockade was lifted. Whether or not the fleet was damaged and fully destroyed by a storm on its way home is not known. The chronicler at the time of Mu'āwiya had not wanted to renounce on this topos of a fleet sunk by a heaven-sent storm, when he described the previous siege.[210] Now, however, the final remark about the storm that destroyed the fleet on its way home is missing.

War on land, however, was soon resumed. Since 726 CE the armies of the Arab Empire had initiated their military campaigns in Asia Minor. Cappadocia was occupied and Nicaea was seized. It was not before the victory of the Byzantines on the South coast of Asia Minor in 740 CE, the year 118 of the Arabs, that the conflicts ended.

During this time of military disputes with the Arab Empire the Byzantines found support from the Khazars. Just as at the time of Heraclius a century before, the Khazars supported the Byzantines by running a series of relief attacks against Persarmenia and the regions of the Caucasus.[211]

The beginning of the siege of Constantinople in 717 CE was still in the time of al-Walīd's rule. The Diadochs of Heraclius saw the only means of continuing the Davidic dynasty was to be bestowed imperial honors. The history of the Arabs in Syria during the 6th century CE had taught them that only rule over the Church could guarantee the Arab Empire permanence. The ruins of the palaces of the Ghassanids in Buṣrā served as warning signs for the precarious situation of a Pretorian rule by Arabs in Syria who were not supported by the church of the emperor, but were fought because of their opposition to the decision of the Council of Chalcedon. Their reign had suffered the same fate as the Pretorian rule of the Ostrogoths in Italy. The Ghassanid Pretorians had not represented the Christology of the Byzantine ruler in Constantinople either.

The extent to which the apocalyptical expectations in Byzantium and in the former Byzantine East show similarities and led to a unified apocalyptical view of the world, can also be observed in other areas as well.[212] 'Abd al-Malik's messianic movement represented hopes that Heraclius had already linked to his new beginning in 630 CE.

Here, it is important to consider to what extent 'Abd al-Malik did not only see himself as a representative of the "Ḫal(ī)fat Allāh" and of the "'Abd al-Raḥmān", but considered himself a new Moses, the Joshua and the Jesus of his movement. In view of the imminent return of Christ in the year 77 of the Arabs, it can certainly be assumed that one of his motivating factors was the hope that he would be given the chair of his father, David (Lk. 1, 32).

His title "'Abdallāh" identified him as a "servant of God". This idea from the Old Testament indicates a complete turnaround of the Iranian concept of a ruler being godlike. Even Ḵosrow II had had himself addressed as *bāgī* (godlike). Against the background of the Iranian view of the ruler, it is conceivable that 'Abd al-Malik, the man from Khorasan, perceived himself as a protagonist on the stage of the apocalyptical drama. His role in restoring Solomon's Temple would point to this, likewise his acting as a "Prince of Peace". Further evidence for this can be found in what he publicly demanded in his inscription on the renewed Temple of Solomon, the Dome of the Rock: harmony (*islām*) as a function of the holy faith (*d-Dīn[a] 'ind[a] llāh[i]*) and the renunciation of conflict among those "possessing the script".

The events in Byzantium, which followed the mutilation and banishment of Justinian II, had to arouse the impression that the era of legitimate rule in Byzantium was over. The successors of Justinian II were insurgents who were responsible for the end of the dynasty of Alexander-Heraclius. Alexander-Heraclius had conquered the Persian Antichrist in 622 CE. The demise of his legitimate dynasty seemed to mean the end of Rome had come. That is why 'Abd al-Malik began striking his gold coins to the Byzantine standard with the depiction of the apocalyptical Jesus of the Syriac Apocalypse of Daniel in 695 CE (the year 74 of the Arabs). Therefore the conditions in Constantinople in 695 CE can be seen as the trigger for the events in Jerusalem from the year 74 to the year 77 of the Arabs. ʻAbd al-Malik had had a messianic project with a screenplay according to the Syriac Apocalypse of Daniel. However, the temporal course of the apocalyptical drama had not been determined from the very beginning, but was also oriented towards the political catastrophes in the Byzantine Empire. This means that history was regarded and interpreted according to apocalyptical aspects. Thus, in 695 CE, ʻAbd al-Malik was able to assume that "Rome" was the "*katechon*". He interpreted the Persian King of kings as the *Antichrist* and the Byzantine Empire, "Rome", as the *katechon*. After the Antichrist, – the Sassanians, – had been defeated by the surprise success of the Byzantine victory on Armenian territory in 622 CE and completely beaten in the war that followed, the *katechon* "Rome" had served its purpose to pave the way for the second coming of Christ and no longer existed.[213]

The dual rule in the former Byzantine and former Sassanian regions suffered from the fact that two different concepts of legitimation of rule existed. Both concepts had a common denominator: the rule had to be ordained by God. In Byzantium, ʻAbd al-Malik's counterpart saw himself as the "servus Christi" (servant of Christ). The apocalyptical Jesus in the depiction on the copper coin of Sarmīn is "ʻabd al-Raḥmān" (servant of the merciful God). In Byzantium the identification of a servant of Christ with the role of the emperor was sufficient as legitimation of rule. This may also have applied in the former Byzantine Orient as well. The imperial rule was sufficiently based on both the Old and the New Testament, so that the actions of the emperor as a vassal of Christ (*basileus*) or servant of Christ (*servus Christi*) were legitimized enough not to be questioned.

In post-Sassanian Iran this did not apply. Here the ruler himself had to be a Messiah. As a consequence, the de-facto ruler could meet this requirement in the second century of the Arabs by giving himself a Messianic name. The glory of God had to shine on him directly (see the Christological title: *farrox-zād*), just a reflection of that glory would not suffice. Thus only the "glorified one", whose return was anticipated, could be the de-facto ruler. All rule was in his name.

It was not enough to be a representative of a "Ḫal(ī)fat Allāh" (representative of God) in the form of a "servus Christi" (servant of Christ), because, as such, the ruler was not the direct bearer of divine glory.

After the disappointment concerning the Parousia of the year 77 of the Arabs (698), – the end of the world had failed to come, – the difficulty in coping with both interpretations of the legitimation of rule led to the search for an unambiguous solution. Had 'Abd al-Malik been the emperor in Byzantium, head of the church and successor to the Alexander-Heraclius in Iran, then he would have had a chance to meet these twofold requirements for the legitimation of rule. His own community of orthodox, Antiochian Christians with their Iranian historical background would have become part of the church of the emperor and as such would have risen or fallen with it.

8.2 The Emergence of the Idea of a Hiğra

'Abd al- Malik's minting activity is conspicuous in many sacred areas of Syria and Palestine. He struck coins in Īliyā-Filasṭīn (Jerusalem-Palestine), Ba'la-bakk (Baalbek, Heliopolis), Bayt Ğibrīn (Bait Jibrin, Baitogabra), al-Ruhā (Edessa), Ḥarrān (Carrhae), Ḥalab (Aleppo), Ḥimṣ (Emesa), Damascus, Sarmīn, 'Ammān, Qinnasrīn (Chalcis), Qūrus (Cyrrus in Syria), Manbiğ (Bambyke) and Ma'arrat Miṣrīn. All coins depict the Messiah with his flaming sword.[214]

Islamic historiographers accuse 'Abd al-Malik of having diverted the Ḥağğ from Mecca to Jerusalem in order to boost the status of Syria and to devalue the Ḥiğāz.[215]

There, Zubayr, his adversary according to the pious literature, had allegedly barricaded himself in the Ka'ba. Of course, in the meantime, thanks to Zubayr's coins struck in Kirmān, it is known that he spent his twilight years there in the province, quietly as a seigneur, and was not buried underneath the Ka'ba, which was allegedly set ablaze.

For 'Abd al-Malik Palestine was the aim of the *hiğra*. With the defeat of the Iranian despot, the "Antichrist" Ḵosrow, who was described in the Qur'ān as having the role of the pharaoh to a tee, the moment had come that made the return possible; the "exodus" (*hiğra*) out of Egypt/Iran commenced. The scenario for the restaging of the history of Israel as the history of the 'Arabī/Arabs made it compellingly clear that the destination of the exodus had to be the Promised Land. The destination, Filasṭīn, was known as it had been announced in the Syriac Apocalypse of Daniel. The way was open, since the victory of Heraclius in 622 CE meant the rule of the Persian Antichrist in Jerusalem was over.

As a symbol of the completion of the conquest of Canaan the depiction of the "Yəğar Sāḥaḏūṯā" appeared on 'Abd al-Malik's coins; the symbol that goes back to the separation of Jacob from his father-in-law, Laban. By defining the borders of their territories with a "Yəğar Sāḥaḏūṯā", Laban and Jacob could reinforce their claim to possession. Thus the "Yəğar Sāḥaḏūṯā" documented Jacob's successful seizure. On 'Abd al-Malik's coins it appears as a reference to this successful conquest. The conquest and Jacob's dream, his ascent up the heavenly ladder, the erection of the Beth-El and the reminder of the promise made to him, documented the foundation of Israel. Thus the exodus from the lands of the new pharaoh is also connected with a new conquest, the re-appropriation of Palestine by the ʿArabī. These were not sons of Abraham's illegitimate wife Hagār, they were not Ismailites. Therefore they were entitled to this inheritance. According to the model conquest of Canaan in the Old Testament, some collateral damage must have been incurred.[216]

The word *hiğra* as a noun does not occur in the Qur'ān. The Qur'ān is only concerned with the fate of the deported ʿArabī. The relationship of the Qur'ān to the emigration is ambivalent. It is a divine test. Therefore the emigration is portrayed as a rather positive event, as it served the purpose of avoiding their downfall (Qur'ān 16:109-111):

> "109. Assuredly in the Hereafter they are the losers. 110. Then lo! thy Lord for those who become fugitives *(li-llaḏīna hāğarū)* after they had been persecuted, and then fought and were steadfast lo! thy Lord afterward is (for them) indeed Forgiving, Merciful 111. On the Day when every soul will come pleading for itself, and every soul will be repaid what it did, and they will not be wronged."

He who complains from among the repressed on this earth, will be asked by the angels why he did not migrate (Qur'ān 4: 97):

> "(...)They will say : We were oppressed in the land. (The angels) will say: Was not Allah's earth spacious that ye could have migrated therein? *(qālū 'a-lam takun 'arḍu llāhi wāsiʿatan fa-tuhāğirū fīhā)*"

It is essential to avoid destruction. Therefore the faithful are ordered to emigrate in case of persecution and not to resist deportation so as not to have to live in misery or fall victim to annihilation. The model this is based on is Jesus' flight into Egypt. The birth of Jesus under a palm tree, which replaces the cross, is depicted on coins in Syria after 622 CE. This is a reference to the fact that the time to prove one's worth starts at birth. Emigration is a further test of personal value. In order to avoid a mixture of bloods, marriage regulations for the exile are defined. This is a typical Iranian train of thought (Qur'ān 33:50):

> "(...)We have made lawful unto thee thy wives unto whom thou hast paid their dowries, and those whom thy right hand possesseth of those whom Allah hath given thee as spoils of war, and the daughters of thine uncle on the father's side and the daughters of thine aunts on the father's side, and the daughters of thine uncles on the mother's side emigrated with thee (*wa-banāti ḫālātika llātī hāğarna maʿaka*), and a believing woman if she give herself unto the Prophet (*'in wahabat nafsahā li-n-nabiyyi*) and the Prophet desire to ask her in marriage, a privilege for thee only, not for the (rest of) believers. (...)"

For the community of the deported, the Qur'ān here makes up for what the Iranian sacred books stipulate for the Mazdayasnis. No community can hold together without regulations on marriage. This verse makes it possible to follow how a problem of the exiled community is regarded concerning Iranian issues (what choice of partner is allowed under the conditions of exile?) and later, when reinterpreting this – the Iranian exile of the 'Arabī had long been forgotten – it is brought in connection with a prophet, who, it goes without saying, is regarded as the prophet of the Arabs, *Muḥammad bn 'Abdallāh* ("the chosen one, son of the servant of God"). When here "prophet" (*nabī*) is found in the text and "we have allowed you this and that", then this is not to be taken literally! First the meaning of the word "*nabī*" in this text must be ascertained. From an Iranian perspective, this might first of all just be a heterogram, a word spelt in a Semitic language (normally Aramaic; in this case common Semitic) to be read in Persian and corresponding to the Iranian way of thinking. It might have stood for *Zarathustra, Manī, John* or *Jesus*. It is a fact that for all of them marriage regulations were important. The marriage policy declared in this surah is sanctioned accordingly. The prophet says: "So be it!" and thus it is valid as divine law.

However, not only the emigration can be necessary and compulsory, the return should also always be envisaged. The return to the Promised Land, the place where God and his Apostle (Jesus) are near the faithful, should not be forgotten. Whoever should die on the way back belongs to the Lord (Qur'ān 4:100):

> "Whoso migrateth for the cause of Allah (*wa-man yuhāğir fī sabīli llāhi*) will find much refuge and abundance in the earth, and whoso forsaketh his home, a fugitive unto Allah and His messenger, and death overtaketh him, his reward is then incumbent on Allah."

The centre of 'Abd al-Malik's messianic movement was the Dome of the Rock, as this was a part of the apocalyptical plan. Of course, the pilgrimage (*hağğ*) led to Jerusalem. This was part of the apocalyptical event. For 'Abd al-Malik the objective of his movements was the return to the Promised Land and the anticipation of the end of the world in Jerusalem, where the time left was used to rebuild the temple. 'Abd al-Malik's actions were aimed at the achievement of peace among Christians so that the community was prepared for the end and would not be caught out still in conflict within one another.

This also involved the introduction of a calendar of Christian festivals as "sacred time", which, besides the secular calendar according to the year of the Arabs, was valid for the concept of an all-encompassing recognition of the radical change, with which the notion of the exodus was identified. A religious calendar was necessary for the messianic movement. Like the secular calendar KAT' ARABAS ("according to the Arabs") the point of reference was the year 622 CE, but unlike the secular one it followed the lunar year. This exodus ended with the death of Hišām, the last of 'Abd al-Malik's sons. The revolts that followed the year 125 of the Arabs and the foundation of the caliphate of the Choresmians under the titular name "Marwān" allowed 'Abd al-Malik's messianism of his movement to become history.

These ideas were taken up again at the time of the caliphate of al-Ma'mūn. Just as the expression "*Ḫalīfat Allāh*" was redefined, so was the idea of the exodus; in this way the establishment of a religious calendar was re-projected into a legendary eon in Mecca.

Thus, as 'Abd al-Malik had staged the history of the 'Arabī/Arabs as a new version of the history of Israel, a century later the alleged early history of what was later to become the religion of Islam was located in the desert of the Arabian Peninsula. The story told contained fragments of 'Abd al-Malik's real past, biblical elements from an eschatological world view and a considerable number of pieces taken from the civilization of Iran. Thus the representative of the Ma'mūn (*ḫalīfat al-Ma'mūn*) stood in an Iranian tradition. His Iranian prophet undertook his exodus from Mecca, just as Zarathustra had once had to flee from his homeland until he found asylum with sensible people in Sakastan, who were willing to take up their swords to spread his message.

However, the disappointment when the expected Parousia in the year 77 of the Arabs (698 CE) failed to happen did not mean the end of the *hiğra*. The expectation that the world would come to an end still existed and the appearance of the Messiah was merely postponed. As long as 'Abd al-Malik and his sons ruled, the messianic movement of the Khorasanians continued to exist in the Promised Land and received further influx from Christian centres which shared a common Syrian-Christian prehistory. Among these were the great Christian centres in Armenia and on the Arabian Peninsula and in Ethiopia (Axum). Axum lived in a dream-world CION-style as well with an arc recovered by David. The Davidic dynasty and the house of Solomon came to an end with the arrival of another sect of bloody dreamers from the Lumumba-University/Moscow.

8.3 The Failure to Regulate the Succession after Hišām's Death, the Foundation of the Caliphate and the Anonymous Caliph as Imperial Regent

The only material evidence for the historicity of Hišām is an inscription mentioning his name on the Qaṣr al-Ḫayr. Since anonymous gold coins were introduced in the year 77 of the Arabs (698 CE), followed by anonymous silver coins in the year after, the only coins where the rulers' names can be found are occasional copper coins. Al-Walīd is mentioned on a copper coin struck for Damascus from the year 87 of the Arabs. The second of his inscriptions on his sanctuary in Damascus, today known as the Umayyad Mosque, dates from the same year (708 CE).[217] The name "Sulaymān bn 'Abd al-Malik" does not appear on any coins. This is in contrast to the Islamic idea of mint authority called *sikka.*[218] Sulaymān is, however, mentioned in the inscription of a lead sealing.[219]

There is no evidence of the name 'Umar, the "caliph" with a *mahdī*-like nature, neither in inscriptions on buildings, nor on lead sealings or coins. There is evidence for the existence of Yazīd, who followed 'Umar, in the form of inscriptions on official weights.[220] An amīr Yazīd bn 'Umar is mentioned in an inscription on a coin struck in Rayy from the year 130 of the Arabs (751 CE).[221]

Four rulers are said to have followed Hišām between the year 125 and 127 of the Arabs: al-Walīd II, Yazīd III, Ibrahīm and Marwān II. The existence of Walīd II is only indirectly documented by epigraphic evidence.[222] The same cannot be said for Yazīd III. His successor, Ibrahīm, did not leave any traces outside of traditional literature.

Marwān II might be linked to Marwān I due to conceptional similarities. It is a matter of the concept of the "Khorasanian". 'Abd al-Malik originally came from Merv (MRW) in Khorasan. Therefore he indicates his lineage with "MRW'n'n (Marwān-ān)" (originating from the "tribe" from the *marwa*). Traditional literature assigns him a father called *Marwān*, since it no longer recognizes the Persian form "MRW'n'n" as such and therefore tries to read it as Arabic, which means that a father called "MRW'n" (*Marwān*) is assumed.

This is how the reading of "Marwān" came about in the case of the assumed last ruler from the family of 'Abd al-Malik. If there had been a historic *Marwān bn Muḥammad*, – the spiritual meaning of a motto no longer understood in later days: "Like a stream of Paradise coming from the Chosen One", – then he would have been a usurper; as he was not entitled to succession. His fictitious father, Muḥammad in Harrān, never ruled. Therefore a legitimate successor was created by turning him into the avenger of family members who had been entitled to succession. Thus he did not rule in his own right, but according to the secondary right he could claim as an avenger. Vengeance had already served as justification for the attack of Ḳosrow II on Syria and Palestine, when he acted as avenger of Maurice, his Byzantine protector. The way the right of avengers is regarded here says a lot about the Iranian understanding of "family" (*ahl al-bayt*). The term "family" is stretched to include benefactors and minions, much in the manner of a patronage system.

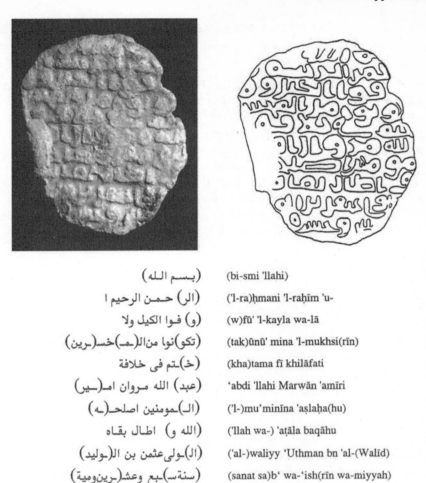

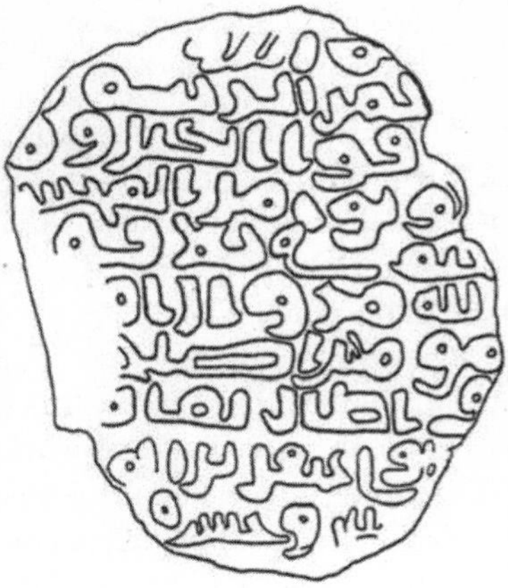

(بسم الله)	(bi-smi 'llahi)
(الر) حمن الرحيم ا	('l-ra)ḥmani 'l-raḥīm 'u-
(و) فوا الكيل ولا	(w)fū' 'l-kayla wa-lā
(تكو)نوا من ال(مـ)خسـ(ـرين)	(tak)ūnū' mina 'l-mukhsi(rīn)
(خـ)تم فى خلافة	(kha)tama fī khilāfati
(عبد) الله مروان امـ(ـير)	ʻabdi 'llahi Marwān 'amīri
(الـ)مومنين اصلحـ(ـه)	('l-)mu'minīna 'aṣlaḥa(hu)
(الله و) اطال بقاه	('llah wa-) 'aṭāla baqāhu
(ال)ولى عثمن بن ال(وليد)	('al-)waliyy ʻUthman bn 'al-(Walīd)
(سنة سـ)بع وعشـ(ـرين ومية)	(sanat sa)bʻ wa-ʻish(rīn wa-miyyah)

Fig. 31: Lead seal mentioning the caliphate of Marwān from the year 127 of the Arabs.

The "Marwān" construct is mentioned in inscriptions on lead sealings from the year 127 of the Arabs.[223] They read:

> "fī ḫilāfat(i) ʻabd(i) ʼllāh(i) M(a)RW(-)ĀN ʼamīr(i) [ʼal-]muʼminīn(a) ..."

The Persian suffix *-ān* designating origin is rendered phonetically in Arabic as *-ʼn* (M(a)RW-*ʼn* / Marwān – "the one like the Marwa (Merv)". Therefore the translation of the inscription should read as follows:

> "During the representation (*ḫilāfa*) of the servant of God (*'Abd-allāh*; title of the ruler) of the man from the Marwa/ Merv (*Marw-ān*), head of the protectors (*amīr al-mu'minīn*)."

In the inscription of Medina from the year 135 of the Arabs, the reference to the "man of Merv", the Khorasanian, is missing. The only things mentioned there are the title of the ruler (*'Abdallāh*) and his Pretorian capacity as head of police (*Amīr al-mu'minīn*). Unfortunately, the inscription has been seen by pious people only. There is no photograph or archeological report extant.

The way the man of Merv is referred to is not unusual. When traditional literature calls the Persian ruler of the time of the Sassanians "Kisrā" (Ḳosrow), then it is not clear whether the reference is to the name of a person or his office, much like the Romans called the Celtic king who conquered most of their city "*Brennos*" (Celtic for "*king*"), regarding it a name. Similarly, when the Qur'ān refers to the pharaoh (*fir'awn*), it is not clear whether this refers to a person or an office. The traditional Islamic historiography mentions a monk (in Syriac: ܒܚܝܪܐ *baḥīra*) who discovers the signs of prophethood between the shoulders of the young boy Muḥammad and calls him *Baḥīra,* considering it a proper name. If translated back into Syriac the meaning would be "the monk called Monk".

The lead sealing mentioning the "Marwān" is also revealing for other reasons. In the inscription on the lead sealing dated from the year 127 the name: *'Uṯmān bn al-Walīd II* crops up, who was believed dead. According to what was related by Ṭabarī, the historiograph, (Ta'rīḫ II, 1890–2), this 'Uṯmān bn al-Walīd had already been killed in a dungeon. This is supposed to have been the reason for the revenge of the fictitious Marwān II.[224]

In contrast to what is related in traditional literature, however, the Amīr 'Uṯmān bn al-Walīd affixed a lead sealing in the year 127 of the Arabs. The alleged name of the ruler, "Marwān – the one of Merv", is no longer used to observe the claims of the Khorasanians ("those from Khorasan, an area including Merv"). The inscriptions on the lead sealing also provide information pertaining to current affairs of the time. A piece of Qur'ānic material is quoted that makes it possible to draw conclusions about a widespread discontentment. It refers to a quote from the Punishment Stories ("Straflegenden") of the Qur'ān:

> "Give full measure, and be not of those who give less (than the due). (*'awfū l-kayla wa-lā takūnū mina l-muḫsirīn[a]*)"(Q 26:181).

The Qur'ānic text continues with further reprimands:

> "182. And weigh with the true balance. 183. Wring not mankind in their goods, and do not evil, making mischief, in the earth."

The demand for "justice" (*'adāla*) had already been raised in the inscriptions on coins from Rayy and Kūfa after the year 100 of the Arabs.[225]

A man called 'Abd al-Malik bn Marwān ("servant of the 'King' of the fātiḥa and the gospels, being from one who is like a stream of 'Water of Life'") was allegedly the financial director of Egypt from 127 to 132 of the Arabs.[226] His "name" is also nothing but the enumeration of predicates legitimizing his rule.

The trend towards a largely anonymous rule had already started in the year 77 of the Arabs (698) in connection with the disappointment of the Parousia. When the caliphate was established after Hišām's death, the ruler became nameless. As a kind of "imperial regency", headed by emanations of the expected One, the caliphate served to preserve the power of one group, in this case the Khorasanians of 'Abd al-Malik's former messianic, now chiliastic movement.

This insistence on an administrative role, however, could not resolve the legitimation crisis of the dual rule. A violent end to the dynasty was inevitable. It stood in the way of a new order. A choice had to be made between a model of rule that would satisfy the former Byzantine Orient, and one that would meet the Iranian requirement, that unless it was directly from God, no reign would last. To be acceptable in the former Byzantine Orient, the rule had to consider a specific Christology, whilst in Iranian territory, a specific understanding of the "Dēn" legitimized the rule.[227]

Hence a ruler could reign in the former Byzantine Orient as a *servant of Christ*. According to the Iranian model of rule, the "divine grace (fortuna)" had to directly shine on the ruler, with no deviation via a representative of God.[228]

'Abd al-Malik had attempted to find a way to reconcile the two concepts of rule by means of a messianic role and had failed. The descendants of his family radicalized his concept in the spirit of Iranian tradition. By appearing to represent messianic titles, divine grace was shining on them.

Both Islamology and Islamic tradition interpret the unrest after the death of Hišām as civil war. This is assuming the existence of citizens of an Arab Empire. This is questionable. The Arab Empire must have been an extremely amorphous structure. The only solid political structures were to be found in Merv, Jerusalem and Damascus, the centres of the religious movement of the 'Arabī/Arabs. These still existed thanks to the continuance of the Sassanian administration and the government of the former Byzantine Orient. Within this web of outdated stability, the protagonists of religious movements acted according to Iranian concepts.

Apart from the anticipation of the second coming of the Messiah there was a movement of Iranian fundamentalists who demanded the inclusion of messianic notions into the Iranian model of rule. Here divine law had priority, and Jesus is merely the "*walī Allāh*" (representative of God) and the "*walī al-'amr*" (representative of the logos, the Demiurg, the word, today the title of the Iranian religious leader Ayatollah Ali Khamenei). Thus, once again the demand that there can be no rule (no law) unless it comes (directly) from God, crops up, just as it did in the year 75 of the Arabs.

Here traditional historiography and Islamological adaptation present a scenario with a protagonist called "Abū Muslim". The latter is supposed to have contributed to the fall of the rule of the sons of 'Abd al-Malik, the alleged Umayyads.[229]

If we continue to read the epigraphic material "microscopically", then a different picture emerges. On a copper coin dated the year 131 of the Arabs (752) the inscription reads: "Abū Muslim, amīr 'āl-Muḥammad".[230]

Abū Muslim is therefore commander of the "family of Muḥammad" *(āl Muḥammad)*. The "family" here designates the *followers* of "Muḥammad". This "Muḥammad" has been known since he was mentioned in the inscription on the Dome of the Rock in the year 72 of the Arabs. Like many Christians prefer to say "our savior" instead of "Jesus" or "the Lord" instead of "God", this term is an epithet of 'Īsa bn Maryam (Jesus), which had gradually replaced the primary term.[231]

But is Abū Muslim a *person ("father of Muslim")* or a program ("abū" being an emphatic prefix, the whole thus meaning: *"arch Muslim", "inveterate Muslim"*)? Therefore we might prefer to call him "Primal Muslim"?[232]

Should this *nom de guerre* be taken as a program, then this would appear to be an adherent of *harmony* (*islām*) among the Syrian Christians, the leader of the followers of the idea of Jesus being the "Muḥammad".

The same program that is to be found in inscriptions on coins from the year 131 of the Arabs can be found on coins from the year 132.[233]

In the following year, the programmatic statement contained in the name of the minting authority is defined even more precisely. Now he calls himself *'Abd al-Raḥmān bn Muslim.*[234] The term "'Abd al-Raḥmān" (*servant of the merciful*) had already been found as an inscription on a coin from the time of 'Abd al-Malik. This term could be found next to the depiction of the Messiah with his flaming sword. 'Abd al-Raḥmān is a variation of the theme of Jesus as the *Ḫal(ī)fat Allāh*. Raḥmān (the merciful) is only one of the epithets for God. An 'Arabī background can be clearly seen.[235]

According to this, the "emir" ('amīr = spokesman; from Semitic "'-m-r" – to speak; later in Classical Arabic: "to order") "Servant of the merciful (God) *('abd allāh)*, descending from *(bn)* the advocators of harmony (*islām*) among Christians ("advocator of islām/harmony" = *muslim*)" led a movement, which, – according to traditional literature, – was supported by the Shiites, and which holds them responsible for the establishment of the Abbasid dynasty. None of this, not even anything like it, is backed historically. Instead, here we have the Khorasanians, the supporters of the messianic movement of 'Abd al-Malik. This is where they fight their last battles. This emission came to an end in the year 136 of the Arabs (757 CE). At this point the interregnum was over. Rule in the form of a caliphate (in the sense of "representation") continued to exist.

8.4 Excursus

The Warrior Saint, Sergius, as the Archetype for the Creation of an Iranian Ideal of a Heroic Saint, as a Starting Point to Understand the Typology of Saints in the Second Century of the Arabs: 'Alī, Hassan and Hussain.

The failure to conquer Constantinople and the inglorious end of the war of succession, which had gone on for decades, delayed the establishment of the legitimation of rule for 'Abd al-Malik's family, which had already been widely accepted, until the reign of the last of his sons, Hišām, who found a small-scale solution according to an old Iranian model. He returned to Ruṣāfa to specifically honor Sergius, the warrior saint, and thus trod in the footsteps of Ḵosrow II, his Sassanian predecessor.[236] Traditional literature appropriately refers to his court as following Iranian models.[237]

Traditional literature is inconclusive when it comes to the reasons for Hišām's return to Ruṣāfa. Trivial reasons have been cited, which only go to show that at the time of Ṭabarī, the actual reasons for the choice of this residency were either no longer known or had to be concealed. Ruṣāfa was allegedly spared from the plague of flies, which occurred in the regions of the Euphrates, because of its remote location in the semi-desert. Ruṣāfa's water supply was provided by extensive constructions from the late Roman period. The Ghassanids are also said to have completed similar projects of this kind.

The deciding factor for the identification of Hišām with Ruṣāfa are the pilgrimage sites that had existed there for hundreds of years. The explanation that this was referring to Hišām's *badīya*, an area of semi-desert, which remained spared from the plague of flies of the nearby Euphrates valley, derives from the view that the ruler is the highest ranking Bedouin of the tribe. Instead an entirely different structure of rule can be detected here. The ruler is not a high-ranking Bedouin residing in a falconry region, but a "high priest". He can only exercise rule by controling a cult site. The sources from the time of Muʿāwiya speak of his time in Jerusalem as marking the beginnings of the Arab Empire. Just what role Buṣrā and the old Ghassanid residency at Damascus played in his era is not clear. He was the guardian of the shrine of John the Baptist.

Hišām, the last ruling son of 'Abd al-Malik, left an inscription on the Qasr al-Ḫayr near Ḥimṣ, dated the year 110 of the Arabs.[238] He is also said to be the constructor of the mosque of Ruṣāfa. This is, however, nothing more than an extension built onto the late Roman church with the tomb of Sergius, the saint.

Concerning the role of the Sergius cult in the Sassanian Empire at the time around 600 CE, Gernot Wiessner ascertains:

> "We would still like to draw attention to several religious and historical facts, which could perhaps make the far-reaching spread of the Sergius cult in the Sassanian State appear in a different light, and could largely free it from its original roots in the Byzantine Empire. The Sergius cult in the Sassanian Empire is obviously closely connected to the creation of religious traditions in Eastern (...) Christianity, where genuine Persian and Christian religious traditions entered into a close symbiotic relationship with each other. This creation and the absorption of vernacular Persian traditions into the Christian faith may have had an effect on the king's court, perhaps making the acceptance of female Christian rulers alongside the king and the inclination of the King of kings to resort to particular Christian saints and promote their cults, appear in a different light.
>
> The loss of Mazdayasnist religious substance in the king's house would then not be the renunciation of essential elements of the New Persian State, nor would they be the renunciation of essential elements of this tradition by the house of the ruler, but should be understood as the revival of these elements due to the link which had been created between them and Christianity. [author's note: In the sense of the Iranian understanding of "Dēn/Dīn", this perception is an extension of the "āsn-xrad – innate human wisdom".] Understandably, this revival would be understandable within the process hinted at by Widengren of a slow but sure advance of Christianity in the Iranian sphere of power due to the missionary vitality of this religion, which manifested itself in its ability to adopt Persian elements into their worldview at strategic points."[239]

This transformation is demonstrated by the roles of the two saints, Sergius and Qardag. The Christian saint becomes the incorporation of the Iranian depiction of a hero, who acts correctly in terms of ethics and who – even as a Christian – need not deny his being Iranian. He dies the death of a martyr, because he stood up to the unrighteous ruler and did not falter from his faith, that is to say he did not allow himself to be corrupted. These thoughts by Gernot Wiessner point to a possible understanding of the Mesopotamian saint of the 2nd century of the Arabs. According to this, ʿAlī is the Iranian elaboration of the "El". The Iranian saints of the 2nd century of the Arabs follow the example of ʿAlī. They, together with "Iranianized" saints from the period of the transformation between the rule of Ḳosrow II and the end of the family of ʿAbd al-Malik were seen to be emulations of Christ.

"The epoch when the Sassanian Empire was coming to an end was the time when a new type of saint in Christian tradition became apparent inside Iran. Around the turn from the 6th to the 7th century aristocratic saints penetrated the Christian cult in the Sassanian State. An excellent example of this process is the creation of the legend confirming the existence of Qardag, the saint in Adiabene and the surrounding provinces. The Qardag novel, written in Syriac, can serve as an example representing several other legends."[240]

At the core of this story there is an aristocratic adherent of Mazdayanism. He is brought up according to the religious tradition of the Sassanians. After successfully passing the tests as a warrior, he is appointed governor of Adiabene by Šāpur II. He then converts to Christianity after being influenced by a Christian hermit, a Baḥīra. He then transforms his realm into a peaceful Christian region. This cannot be tolerated by the power-hungry shah (for the understanding of traditional historiographers the title "caliph in Damascus" can be inserted). After the unsuccessful siege of his residence, Mār (=Lord) Qardag realizes the hopelessness of his situation. In order to save the people, he surrenders to this cruel despot and accepts his fate to die as a martyr of his own free will.

"Mar Qardag, however, is only one example of a number of other saints who populated the realm of human imagination of Christians in the New Persian Empire at the time. Other references that can be compared to him are those of the "princes charmantes" (Fiey), Behnam of Ator, Gufrnasp of Adiabene, Abbai of Qullet, but also of Pethion, all of whom embody the same kind of hero and may have been directly based on Mar Qardag's person and his literary fixation. Unfortunately, this new type of saint has not been thoroughly investigated yet. The material available on the names of people from the few legends that have survived, still shows their spiritual connection and would seem to make it plausible to explain this link to be derived from the same spiritual tradition and behaviour as is documented in the story of Qardag's martyrdom. As already mentioned above, in the following we will focus on this exemplary martyrdom.

In a different context it has been indicated that the figure of a saint like that of Mar Qardagh can in fact only be comprehended when that figure is regarded as the reflection of those Iranian circles, who, even after their conversion to Christianity, came to terms with heathen tradition and in doing so incorporated an essential element of this genuine Persian heroic ideal into their Christian self-conception. [*author's note:* This ideal figure of a hero is still represented by the failing heroes of traditional literature: ʿAlī, Ḥassan and Ḥussayn. It is not without reason that the Iranians regard these protagonists as heroes according to their own tradition.]

Thus they were able to both be Christians and remain Iranians. The preservation of this Persian ideal of a hero in this new type of hero and saint allowed to keep the feudal "structure" of the Sassanian empire alive and thus to persist in the social status, which the Mazdayanist religion had assigned to the noble heroes for their lives as warriors within their decision between good and evil. (...)

The significance of this new formation of tradition for Iranian religious history in the final years of the Sassanian realm cannot be overestimated. It combines the heroic elements of Iranian nationhood, which cannot be separated from the feudal structure of the Sassanian state, and which basically were the conditions forming the state, with a thriving Christian religion within this state. In its broadest sense here Iranian 'life' is establishing a symbiotic relationship with a non-Iranian religion (...). According to the few literary records that still exist, during this process a Christian Iranian nationhood came into being, which was able to continue to exist due to its social connection to the given polity of the empire and which, unlike Mazdayasnism with its close linkage to nationhood, could remain open to spiritual influences from different cultures and spheres and thus to continual development. [*author's note:* This is where the road to the formation of the Islamic *umma* is predetermined. The *umma* is tantamount to the overcoming of the connection of the Prophet of the Arabs to Bedouin cultural identity. The idea of the *umma* overcomes tribal borders and those of national identities. Here again, by camouflaging early Islam as purely "Arabian", its real development on Iranian territory was disguised. This aim could be achieved by portraying it as seemingly "Arabian" in the traditional literature of al-Ṭabarī].

The depiction of the hero in the story of Qardag and the literary parallels in the accounts of lives and fates of other saints, however, does not only go to prove that a genuine Iranian Christianity existed and brought with it the complete preservation of prospering Iranian traditions, supportive to the state. Several more aspects of the Qardag story would appear to supply arguments for the fact that the formation of this Christian Iranian heroic figure did not come about independently from the cult wave that flowed from Rusāfa to the Sassanian realm in the form of the veneration of saint Sergius. According to the novel, Qardagh becomes a Christian hero, because Saint Sergius continuously intervenes in his life, rendering it completely perfect until reaching final martyrdom. (...)

It might be appropriate to consider the appearance of Saint Sergius in Qardag's life only from the point of view of legend creation in traditional literature. It is known to be the style of legends that the development process of the hero is steered from "above" in a variety of ways. The intention to show the life of the hero to be exemplary is underlined by his development, which is portrayed as being supervised by divine powers. [*author's note:* The survival of this kind of vocational revelation can be confirmed in Iranian regions as well.].

According to this interpretation it is well possible that the supervisory and helper functions in the Qardag story were assigned to Sergius, the saint from Ruṣāfa, by mere coincidence, as this saint was generally known and venerated at the time when the Qardag legend became fixed in its final literary form, and could thus become generally binding as a model for the correct Christian way of life [*author's note:* the Qurʾānic expression for this is: *rušd*].

However, this interpretation of the figure of Sergius in the Qardag novel mainly from the perspective of history of literature need not be the only explanation for the close connection that exists between the two saints in the legend we are dealing with. Sergius is not just Qardag's patron saint and guide. There is a close affiliation between himself and his protégé in terms of character and profession; both are Christian warriors. [*author's note:* Here the influence becomes obvious which would lead to the development of concepts regarding the way in which ʿAlī, Hassan and Hussayn would be considered]. In the passage mentioned above, Sergius is specifically described as a warrior, a horseman armed with a lance for battle. He was venerated in this form in Greek territories as well. (...)

It was the warrior saint Sergius, and not one of the other, non-violent saints that took on contacting the noble Iranians in the Qardag story. The warrior saint offered his assistance to one similar to himself and was the mediator of revelations between Christ and the future martyr.

We believe it would not be right to ignore this affinity. It would seem safe to assume that when the saint Sergius of Ruṣāfa was chosen as the patron saint of the saint Qardag, this reflects the intention of those circles which were responsible for the creation of the Qardag legend. The Christian Iranians saw in Sergius, the Byzantine warrior and patron saint someone similar to themselves. By linking this saint with the national saint Qardag, a connection was established with the thriving piety of Christianity outside Iran. At the same time, this combination of the figures of Sergius and Qardag also served to glorify the Iranian Christian tradition, and to justify the preservation of its particular form, the Iranian idealized heroic figure. The Qardag story proves that Saint Sergius, most certainly because of his warlike activities, enjoyed a particular popularity even in those Christian circles of the Sassanian empire that did not want to give up their national Persian heroic tradition, but who at the same time, – and this also seems to be made evident by the role of Sergius in the Qardag story – remained open to the Christian traditions outside of Iran, and by means of this open-mindedness documented an essential and vital characteristic of their very being."[241]

It is in these traditions, which Hišām started to adopt after turning to Ruṣāfa, that we find the beginnings of the later tales of 'Alī, which tell of a noble fighter who, in the end, dies the death of a martyr.

8.5 Similarities of the Renunciation of Pictorial Theology in the West of the Arab Kingdom and in Byzantium

After the disappointment in the anticipation of the Parousia in Jerusalem in the year 77 of the Arabs (698 CE), pictures with religious content disappeared from coinage of regional copper coins in Syria. Apart from that, the striking of gold coins depicting the Messiah and following the Byzantine weight-standard was discontinued. Instead a new issue of aniconic gold coinage started according to Iranian weight-standards. This development was characteristic of Syria-Palestine. The pictorial tradition of Iran continued to survive in the East. Only in Damascus does a return to the aniconic concepts of the old Syrian and Nabataean tradition seem to have taken place. The closeness to the Nabataean tradition is also evident in the adoption of traditions from Nabataean/Ghassanid Western Arabia into the central texts of the Qur'ānic material (the so-called "punishment stories – Straflegenden").

The Christians in the towns of Palestine demolished the mosaics of their church and destroyed religious icons.[242]

In the year 79 of the Arabs (711 CE), a new attempt was made in Constantinople to adapt to circumstances in Syria. Bardanes, the Armenian, had taken the throne in the capital of the Byzantine Empire. He got rid of the regulations of the VI Ecumenical Council by means of an imperial edict and declared *Monotheletism* ("Christ has two natures, but only one will"), which had already been favored by Heraclius, to be the only valid church doctrine. As an Armenian he must certainly have been a secret follower of the Monophysite Christology of his Armenian Church, but could not openly advocate these teachings as emperor. The return to the Monotheletism of Heraclius seemed to be a way to come to an arrangement with the Jacobites of Syria and the Copts of Egypt. Apart from this, the proposal was certainly directed to the former Byzantine Orient as well. The iconic illustration of the VIth Ecumenical Council was removed from the Emperor's palace. The depiction of Christ was also banned. Instead, the depiction of the emperor reappeared on coinage, the role of the emperor as a "servant of Christ", however, was not mentioned.

The question should be asked as to whether there is a connection between the disappearance of the pictures in Damascus and the disappearance of the depiction of Christ on gold coinage after the year 711 CE in Byzantium, and if so, what that connection is. In 695 CE, after the banishment of Justinian II, the depiction of Christ was removed from Byzantine coinage for the first time. In 605 CE, after the adventurous return to the throne of Justinian II, the depiction of Christ was put back onto coinage. After Justinian II was murdered in 711 CE, it was removed again. Did the type of illustration and the fact that Christ was depicted on coinage have anything to do with the messianic ideas of the emperor?[243]

Some years later the conflict concerning the permissibility of pictorial representations intensified.

The family of Emperor Leo III (717-741 CE) originally came from Northern Syria, but had been deported to Thrace amidst the resettlement measures of Justinian II. It can only be speculated as to the reasons why the family fell victim to such a compulsory measure.

Leo's behavior can only be compared to the way traditional literature depicts ʿAbd al-Malik and his cult at the Dome of the Rock: "As he later wrote to the Pope, he considered himself not only to be emperor, but also to be a high priest."[244]

Leo began striking new silver coins modelled on the drachms of the Arab Empire. They no longer portrayed the emperor. On the reverse was a cross potent on three steps, an aniconic illustration.[245]

Fig. 32: Sketch with remnants of Arabic writing (Leuthold). Evidence of Arabic silver drachmas overstruck by Byzantine, aniconic silver coins.

Theophanes, the Byzantine chronicler, reported that Yazīd, a ruler from the house of ʿAbd al-Malik, ordered that all pictures be removed from Christian churches in his realm in the year 723 CE. In the year 726 Leo III publicly and for the first time spoke against image worship in Byzantium. It might appear at first glance that these two events are dependent on one another, on closer inspection, however, this idea seems without doubt contrived.[246]

Theophanes wrote his work between 810 and 814 CE. Thus, the revision of history by the successors of the family of 'Abd al-Malik had already started to have an impact on the account written by him. Theophanes should be regarded as a source for the existence of a revision and not as a Byzantine source for the history of the movements of 'Abd al-Malik in Syria after 680 CE.

The disappearance of pictorial illustrations on coinage of the Arab Empire has to do with the sudden end to all hope of a messianic movement in Jerusalem in the year 77 of the Arabs. The reasons, which provide arguments for the disappearance of the images, the internal conflict concerning a messianic movement and its place in Iranian state law, may have been just as understandable in Byzantium, albeit for different reasons, as the Byzantine Church suffered from internal conflicts. During the iconoclastic period in Byzantium, monasticism was attacked. The heads of the church in Syria were inclined to join the ban on images.

> "A special kind of martyrdom was allocated to the brothers Theodoros and Theophanes from Palestine, whose verses against iconic representation were written on their foreheads with glowing iron rods and who afterwards received the epithet Graptoi. For Theophanes was a poet, known for his poetic appraisal of images of saints (...)."[247]

'Abd al-Malik's iconographic theology was replaced by the inscription in Damascus from the year 87 of the Arabs, which declared that the "Dēn/Dīn" makes it possible to recognize the right path (Persian: *razišta*, Arab: *rušd*), i.e., innate wisdom makes it possible to know right from wrong. Where there had once been images and metaphors referring to the Promised Land (Filasṭīn), Joshua and the spies (vines with grapes) and the Messiah with his flaming sword as the "Ḫal(ī)fat Allāh", the situation now was programmatically described in the inscription: all difficulties can be mastered with the help of the "Dēn/ Dīn". If we believe, that the inscriptions had ever existed.

Now the Messiah disappears amidst the general demands of the "Dēn/ Dīn". Only the "Dēn/Dīn" is of any core significance. The message of the prophet is no more and no less than an integral part of the whole "Dēn/Dīn". His name is unimportant. In the inscription in Damascus, the Messiah, *'Īsa bn Maryam*, is no longer referred to by name. He is *muḥammad* (the praised/ chosen one): this has to suffice. The messianic character of 'Abd al-Malik's movement is only accepted to the extent that it is consistent with the "Dīn/Dēn". The Messiah/Mahdī components have no central significance for the religious doctrine of later, Sunnite Islam. Opinions differ greatly when it comes to the concept of the Mahdī.[248]

9 Anonymous Regency after the Death of ʿAbd al-Malik's Sons

9.1 The Protest of the Law-Abiding People

The end of copper coinage of the Āl-Muḥammad in the year 136 of the Arabs (757 CE) coincides with the end of anonymous silver coinage struck in the style of the Arab Empire. In the year 137 of the Arabs (758 CE),[249] only the mints of Carthage in the West and Gharshistān in the East still issued coinage.

A coin of the movement, which bore the same motto as the coins of Abū Muslīm, the "Arch-Muslim", is attested for the year 138 of the Arabs. The friendship between relatives maintained this unity:[250]

"I demand no wage from you other than the friendship among relatives." This was the Qurʾānic motto which kept the movement of the Khorasanians from the region around Merv together and made them join in the battle for succession of ʿAbd al-Malik's family. The relatives mentioned here are the followers of the concept of Jesus as the "Muḥammad".[251]

This idea of a "(spiritual) relationship" may possibly come from the Iranian belief that a ruler is accompanied by a "Frawahr/Fravaši". The Encyclopaedia Iranica (see bibliography) defines it as:

> "FRAVAŠI (O[ld] P[ersian] *fravarti, Pahl. fraward, frawahr, frōhar, frawaš, frawaxš), the Avestan word for a powerful supernatural being whose concept at an early stage in Zoroastrianism became blended with that of the urvan. (...) Harold Bailey (Zoroastrian Problems, p. 109) saw the basic element in the concept to be the fravašis' warlike activities, and suggested that the term was originally used in a hero-cult, 'fravaši' meaning 'protective valor (vərəti),' from √var- 'cover, protect,' with fra- 'ward off.' The fravaši would thus be the spirit of a valiant warrior, (...) Bernfried Schlerath accepted the hero-cult as basic, but suggested deriving 'fravaši' from √var- 'choose,' with *fravarti being the public acclamation – a 'choosing forth' – in this life of an outstanding warrior whose spirit was venerated thereafter. (...)
>
> At the beginning of this century (Moulton, 1913a, p. 268), the prevailing opinion was, like Schlerath's, that the term fravaši came from √var- 'choose,' but stress was laid on the fact that in Avestan fravar- means 'choose/profess a faith.' Hence the fravaši was seen as the spirit of confessional faith. This interpretation was put forward again decades later by Karl Hoffmann (p. 91).

> Meanwhile the same derivation had been used by Herman Lommel (pp. 102-5) to yield the meaning 'decisive choice.'"

This spirit of a "decisive choice" is put out into the world to support mankind. The pre-existing eschatological Jesus, as portrayed in the Syriac Apocalypse of Daniel, can be interpreted as the *Frawahr* of the ruler from 'Abd al-Malik's family. The despatch of the *Frawahr* is described in an Iranian text:

> "He [Ahuramazda] took counsel with the consciousness and Frawahr of man and infused omniscient wisdom into man, saying, 'Which seemeth more profitable to you, whether I should fashion you forth in material form and that you should strive incarnate with the Lie and destroy it and that we should resurrect you at the end, whole and immortal, unageing, without enemies; or that you should eternally be preserved from the Aggressor? And the Frawahrs of men saw by that omniscient wisdom that they should suffer evil from the lie and Ahriman in the world; but because at the end (which is) the Final Body, they would be resurrected free from the enmity of the Adversary, whole and immortal for ever and ever, they agreed to go into the material world."[252]

Mithra (Avestan *Miθra-/Miθrō*, Pehlevi *Mihr*) is regarded as the Frawahr of the Sassanian rulers.

The disruption which had to do with the unsettled succession, which began after the death of Hišām in the year 125 of the Arabs, had led to a regency during the interregnum (*ḫalīfat*) in the year 127. Since the year 127 of the Arabs, all parties of the Arab Empire, with their differing messianic or legalistic programs, had made demands, which were either met or rejected under Hišām's rule.

On the assumption that exercising the right to strike coins is a documentation of a sovereign's right to rule – whether or not the Islamic institution of the *sikka* (striking of coinage) had already come into being –, then the succession of dates and the mentioning of mints on coins can help us to reconstruct a scenario of change in ownership of domains. If, in addition, the dates and names of mints are combined with the mentioning of a motto, under which the political and religious demands are made public, then it is also possible to reconstruct ideological differences. If the Islamic law of the *sikka* should not have already been in existence in the regions ruled over, then coinage was struck on the basis of old laws. This means that Sassanian and Roman common law was still in vigor. These legal traditions regulated the right to strike coins in the same way as was later the case in the Islamic concept of the *sikka*.

If we follow the trail of coinage struck with inscriptions, then we can see that a movement started in the Iranian regions, which, as *Āl-Muḥammad* ("family/relatives of the chosen one"), called for loyalty to the idea of Jesus as the *muḥammad* (chosen one), being the successor to 'Abd al-Malik's family.

What was going on in Syria, the usurpation of power, embodied in one of those from Merv, evidently met with resistance in the Iranian areas of the Arab Empire. The protests encompassed areas of the Iranian highlands which had not been the focus of conflicts between the Kirmanians and Khorasanians before. A conflict could only be initiated if the legitimation of the ruler was questioned. The rule of the "Marwān", the man of the *marwa*, was apparently contested by those who demanded the loyalty of subjects as remuneration for those ruling. The troubles of ruling were thus compensated by the loyalty and the obedience of those ruled over.

The protests began in the area of Isfahān (Jayy) in the year 127 of the Arabs. In the year 128 of the Arabs it had already spread to other towns in the Iranian highlands and to Khūzistān (al-Taymara, al-Rayy, Rāmhurmuz and Istakhr).

In the year 128 of the Arabs the Kirmanians attacked the town of Merv and occupied it. In Merv they struck silver coins bearing the name of their party, the *Āl Kirmānī bn ʿAlī*.[253] Thus, just as the Khorasanians had regarded themselves as "*Āl-Muḥammad*" (i.e., relatives of an eschatological Jesus), who was understood to be the *muḥammad* (chosen one), the Kirmanians regarded themselves to be the followers of *ʿAlī* (bn ʿAlī), i.e., followers of a concept of Jesus who is understood to be *ʿalī* (elevated, sublime). It is no more than a matter of two differing concepts occupying the place that the eschatological and non-eschatological Jesus could be assigned in the Iranian view of the world.

According to the concepts of fundamentalist legalists, the eschatological Jesus was an "El" (in the Hebrew sense, i.e.: divine); he could not simply be a "chosen one". This position was already taken. It was taken by the ruler, who was understood to be *bāghī* (divine). He was the one chosen by God; for God's glory (*x*^{v}*arrah* [lat. fortuna], i.e., the sign of divine election) shone upon him, and he stood out due to his *fortuna*.

A solution to this problem was found. The divine ruler henceforth ruled in the name of messianic titles. He regarded the "Muḥammad" as his "Frawahr", his counselor when a decision had to be made. Thus the latter was connected to him.

The systematization of the models aiming at assigning the right place for Jesus in the Iranian ideology of rule can be traced by the succession of Kirmanian silver coinage. Already from the year 54 of the Arabs on, the inscription around the rim of Kirmanian coins was: "Allāh rabb al-ḥukm" (Allāh is Lord of all law/command).[254]

This motto: "Allāh is Lord of all law/command" corresponds to how Jesus is placed in the hierarchy in inscriptions on coins of the same province:

"Bismi-llāh walī al-amr" ("In the name of God, he is the representative of the *amr* [Arabic] /*memra* [Aramaic] /*logos* [Greek]").[255]

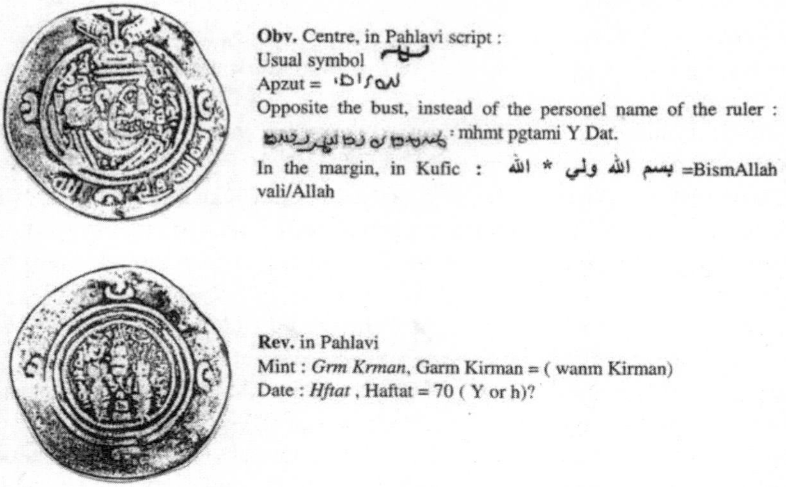
Obv. Centre, in Pahlavi script :
Usual symbol
Apzut =
Opposite the bust, instead of the personel name of the ruler :
: mhmt pgtami Y Dat.
In the margin, in Kufic : بسم الله ولي * الله =BismAllah vali/Allah
Rev. in Pahlavi
Mint : Grm Krman, Garm Kirman = (wanm Kirman)
Date : Hftat , Haftat = 70 (Y or h)?

Fig. 33: Drachm from Kirman, discovered by Shams-Eshrag, Isfahan. In the inscription MḤMT is called 'walī Allāh', the word PTGM (rasūl) is rendered as 'walī' here. In Islamic tradition this attribute is linked to 'Alī.

Fig. 34: Arab-Sassanian Drachma from Kirmān mentioning the 'MḤMT' as representative of the memra/logos (walī al-amr).

God is the Lord of all law and Jesus is the representative of the *memra/logos* for some weeks of the year 70 of the Arabs.

This statement was consolidated and modified in the same year. The die stating on the rim of the coin that Jesus was the *walī al-amr* (representative in command), was changed. This modified die now served to strike coins with the motto: *bismi-llāh walī Allāh* (In God's name [he is the] representative of God/the one appointed by God/in God's name he is the representative in command).[256] Apparently this motto: *bismi-llāh walī Allāh* was felt to be inappropriate as it clashed with the idea of: "*Allāh rabb al-ḥukm*" (God is the Lord of all law/command). Decisions were to rest with God and God alone, also in the future; the position of Jesus was limited to the function of the *walī allāh* (representative/appointee [later: friend] of God).[257]

The concept of Jesus as the *walī allāh* appeared in the Kirmān region in the year 70 of the Arabs. At this time the concept of an eschatological Jesus as the "*ḫal(ī)fat Allāh*" (representative of God) became known. Gold coins with this designation are dated to the year 74 of the Arabs. They were struck by the Khorasanians under ʿAbd al-Malik, whose Jesus is an eschatological figure who appears with fire and sword in line with apocalyptical concepts. The Jesus of the Kirmanians is the Jesus who *fails* and is tried at court of the High Priest. The court comprises the elders of the Jews. They have to recognize Jesus, only then can he fight. This recognition is not granted (Mt. 26:57-66). ʿAlī calls to battle. He is referred to the elders of the tribes, who are to accept his demand. Only after this requirement has been met does ʿAlī take command of the troops. But like the Jews in Jesus' case the elders refuse to accept his legitimate demand to fight against the Roman from Syria. Therefore he is unable to fight against Muʿāwiya, the new Roman, the favorite of the Byzantines. The re-orchestration here of the trial of Jesus also ends in death. ʿAlī has to bow to the verdict of the elders. They do not allow ʿAlī the possibility to assert his demand in battle. ʿAlī fails like Jesus had failed. The verdict of the elders at Siffīn is his death sentence. He is killed. In the year 128 of the Arabs there was talk of relatives of ʿAlī. This mentioning has to be seen in context with the naming of the party of the Kirmanians: "Āl-Kirmānī (*relatives of the one from Kirmān*)".

What evidence do we have that the purported name "ʿAlī" is nothing but an honorific name for Jesus? The inscription in the Dome of the Rock points to the connection between Jesus and the epithet *muḥammad* ("praised/chosen one") and *ʿAbdallāh(i)* ("servant of God"). In inscriptions on coins from Kirmān dated to the year 70 of the Arabs, Jesus is mentioned in Pehlevi script and language as "MḤMT PGTAMI Y ḌAT" (praised/chosen is the apostle of God). The writing on the rim of the coin interprets the explanation in the field and defines it more precisely as: *walī allāh* ([he is] God's friend).[258]

In later times, the phrase around the rim: *walī allāh* (God's friend) was used solely and exclusively as a reference to ʿAlī, the alleged son-in-law of the prophet of the Arabs. If it is also used here for "MḤMT PTGMI Y ḌAT" (chosen is the apostle of God), then an interpretation of Jesus is addressed, which, in later Islamic times, was embodied by ʿAlī bn Abī Ṭālib (the Abī Ṭālib being his community, his disciples, of whom Jesus had 12). It should be noted that the motto *walī allāh* ("God's friend"), which is directly connected to the idea of an "ʿAlī", occurs for the first time on the rim of a coin struck in Kirmania in the year 70 of the Arabs, which represented a program. The name ʿAlī also crops up in connection with incidents in Kirmania.[259]

The later son-in-law of the Prophet of the Arabs embodies the notion of the failing Jesus. He stands for the Iranian mythologization of the image of a Jesus-like figure called "ʿAlī", who stands trial before the elders, who do not support the legitimacy of his claims in his struggle against Muʿāwiya. Whoever wants to understand the process of *inculturation of Christian notions into Iranian religious thought* should consider how the son-in-law of the Prophet of the Arabs was depicted.

A third party was involved in the struggle for a new order after Hišām's death: those responsible for the schism in the year 75 of the Arabs, who were regaining influence. The motto from the year 75 of the Arabs, according to which there should be no rule unless it comes (directly) from God, was made public once again. We have evidence for coinage bearing this motto struck in Kūfa in the year 128 of the Arabs and from a mint read as Tanbuk(?) of the year 133 of the Arabs.[260]

The course of the rebellion against the caliphate of the "Marwān" in Syria can be retraced using the dates and locations in the coin inscriptions:

The rebellion started in the region around Isfahān. According to the traditional historiographical literature, the leader of this insurgence is said to have been a man called ʿAbd-Allāh bn Muʿāwiya. This name does not appear in inscriptions on coins of drachmas. In the place of the name there is a part of a verse from the Qur'ān which does not appear on the hitherto anonymous Dirham coins. This verse of the Qur'ān (42:23) is the guiding principle for the activities of the Āl-Muḥammad. The protest spread in the western part of the Iranian highlands, among others in the regions of Jayy and al-Taymara (area of Isfahān), Rayy (Ragae) and Hamadān. Then the Persis was triggered off. From the year 128 of the Arabs onwards, Istakhr, Darabjird and Ardašīr-Khurra all struck silver coins bearing the motto of the rebels. In the year 130 of the Arabs these coins were found in Balkh, Merv and Gurgān.

Information as to the names of those involved can be found in the inscriptions on copper coins struck by the rebels. The name of "ʿAbd Allāh bn Muʿāwiya" ("the servant of God related to the Weeper, the Humble, a reference to Jesus in the Garden of Gethsemane) appears on a *fals* (a copper coin), which was struck for Rayy (Ragae) in the year 127 of the Arabs. Even here the "name" might be a programmatic *motto*. In Egypt, evidence can be found that the rebellion must have achieved its aim.

Paul Balog has secured evidence for the influence of the Āl-Muḥammad in Egypt for posterity with his unique collection of Islamic glass weights for goods and for coinage, which are now in the Israel Museum in Jerusalem. Many of the glass weights in Balog's collection are undated. This is nothing out of the ordinary. The glass weights for goods and coins, which have survived in Balog's collection and which show the name of the "Āl-Muḥammad" as the state authority responsible for the issue of coinage ("amār(a) Āl-Muḥammad"), prove that the rebellion against the caliphate of the "Marwān" had spread as far as Egypt. Now follows a topos from the days of Hadrian: His entertainer Antinous is embraced by the jealous "Father Nilus" and now shares the river's bed. In traditional literature this caliph flees to Egypt. There he meets his death on the Nile River. The description of events is similar to the account of the end of Yazdegerd III, the last Sassanian king.[261] He met his death on the Murghab river near Merv. It is a nice topos, the treatment of this change of power seen as an act of the Marwa, leading to the rule of the Marwāns. The Marwans are the believers in the stream of water coming forth from the Rock. The Marwāns are Westerners, while Yazdegerd is on the path to the East, where there is the land of Moab and Zarathustra. The evidence concerning the name of the successors of the Āl-Muḥammad also comes from Egypt. In traditional literature these are referred to as *ʿAbbasids*. Their contemporaries knew them by the name "*banū Hāšim*" ("followers of Hāšim").[262] As the name *Hišām* is an anagram of the rasm of the title "*Masīḥ*", we can assume that the Hāšim were a messianic movement as well.

9.2 The Followers of Hāšim as Representatives of the True Belief (Dīn al-ḥaqq, Middle Persian "wēh-Dēn")

While the Khorasanians as Āl-Muḥammad and the Kirmanians as followers of ʿAlī were fighting against each other – a third group being the representatives of the fundamentalist opposition and their concept of rule coming directly from God, – it was now a fourth group that gained control, the "banū Hāšim".

Considering the religious environment of Iran around this period, traces of consolidation of Christian life cannot be ignored. Since the time of Ḳosrow II the Jacobites had pushed forward from Syria into northern Mesopotamia. At the same time the Iranian Church normally referred to as "Nestorian" was on the rise.[263]

After Heraclius had reconquered northern Mesopotamia, there had been an attempt to restore unity with the eastern Syrians. The Catholicos ʿIšōyahb II also took part in the peace negotiations at the court of the Sassanians. He met Heraclius in Syria in 630 CE and they agreed on a common creed as defined by the monenergetic formula (a precursor of monotheletism) propagated by Heraclius of the existence of *one* will and one active force (energy) in Christ. This common creed was the trigger for a discussion which led to the development of the "Nestorian identity".[264]

The "Nestorian" identity of the eastern Syrians first appeared openly around the end of the 7th century CE. It was based on the conflict with the Monophysites. During a visit of the eastern Syrians to Jerusalem to celebrate the return of the Relic of the True Cross in the presence of Emperor Heraclius in 630 CE, an argument ensued in the delegation of the Christians from the Iranian territories. One member of the delegation, Sahdona, defected to the Monophysites and attacked the followers of Theodore of Mopsuestia (al-Maṣīṣī) in the presence of Emperor Heraclius.

The new group of eastern Syrians, who opposed the Monophysites, were called "Nestorians". The Nestorians regarded the conflict between Cyrill and Nestorius, which had taken place in the 5th century CE, to be parallel to the conflict with the Monophysites at the beginning of the 7th century.[265]

The following trend can be discerned: the eastern Syrian Christians of Mesopotamia and Iran can be differentiated into two main groups after the downfall of the Sassanian Empire. Thanks to the contact to the western Syrians the influence of Monophysitism became stronger. This reinforced other Syrian Christians in their adherence to their belief in the two natures of Christ (Diphysitism). It was again a *Christological* conflict which led to religious factionalism.

So where did those Christian Syrians, who eluded further theological development because of their lack of contact to western Christianity, now stand? After Iran had opened towards Byzantium and Syria, after the advance of the western Syrian Monophysites to the East, the formation of a "Nestorian" identity under Syrian Christians of the East, groups remained, which could be referred to as "Old Believers"; a term normally used for a group of Orthodox Christians in Russia (старовéры), who separated from the Russian Orthodox Church in 1666, as they rejected certain reforms. Something similar must have happened here, the "main body" of the Christian Church(es) establishing reforms that the "Old Believers", – the forerunners of the later Muslims (in the modern sense), – rejected. This "Old Believer" attitude is obvious in many pieces of Qur'ānic material. They turn against the "modernizing Christians"[266] who get their impulse for further development of their theology from the contemporary West. They regard their Christianity as the "True Faith" (Dīn al-Ḥaqq) which can only be understood within an Iranian context. Just as the Mazdayasnians assumed they were representatives of the Wēh-Dēn (the "good and proper Dēn"), these Iranized Christians believed they could consider their Christianity to be the "True Faith" (Dīn al-Ḥaqq).[267]

The Āl-Muḥammad and the Banū ʿAlī also belonged to these as representatives of an earlier Syrian Christianity. The fundamentalists, who preach theocracy, are one step ahead. They come closest to the Iranian legacy. The Banū Hāšim now undertook a further step towards the interculturation of the Christian Iranian legacy into Iranian tradition. Whoever this "Hāšim – ancestor/progenitor" is, will be discussed in a later study.[268]

As all of the hitherto mentioned groups avail of an Iranian-Christian basis, it can also be presumed that the Banū Hāšim go back to a chiliastic movement based on an Iranian-Christian principle. Their motto is:

> "He it is who hath sent His messenger with the guidance (*al-hudā*) and the Religion of Truth (*Dīn al-ḥaqqi*), that He may cause it to prevail over all religion, (...)" (surah 9:33).

The aim was to restore the *true religion*, a task which in former times had been connected to the acts of Zarathustra. This at a time, when due to the development of Islamic hermeneutics, the Syrian beginnings were more and more replaced by an Iranian reading of the texts. In the Dome of the Rock we read: "wa asā la-hu bi-l hudā wa dīn al-ḥaqq". An Iranian reading of the sentence would be: "And he came forth with confirmation (guidance) and his *own* revelation." (ḥaqq – "one's own"; in Yemenite dialects "bayt ḥaqq-ī" means "my house" and corresponds to the particle "šel" in Hebrew and "mta'" in other Arabic dialects).

The central statements pertaining to this motto can only be understood against an Iranian background:

9.3 Concerning al-Hudā (the Guidance)

The indication that the apostle (Muḥammad, i.e., Jesus) had made public a message that contained a "guiding principle", was opposed to Zurvanism, a branch of Zoroastrianism which was widespread in the Iranian upper classes at the time of the emergence of Qur'ānic texts. Traces of Zurvanism are still evident in many areas of Islamic tradition. The *maǧūs* of the Qur'ān are Zurvanite "explorers", not "fire priests". They do research in the field of astronomy, since they need to know where the star will lead them. *Zurvān*, the god, and his pantheon are the lords of *time* (Arabic: *zamān*). *Zurvān* is the personal name of the god; Zamān (Modern Persian: *zamān*) is the name of his appearance. *Zurvān* is an equivalent to the Greek god *Chrónos* (Greek: *time*). They bear the same name. The ancient god from the family of the Titans had already had a long career before he found a new home with the mythological Sabians of Ḥarrān.[269] The "guiding principle" showed a way out of the subordination of mankind to the power of the stars.

The autonomy of mankind is opposed by astral fatalism. The statements in the Qur'ān with regard to the omnipotence of God, his providence and the limited control of man over his actions are an answer to the Zurvanists' total belief in fate. As representatives of the Iranian upper classes, the latter were also pious adherents of royal absolutism. For them the great question mark: *qadar?* (whatever is fixed or ordained by God) hung over everything. This idea of apportioning fate is also present in the Arabic *qadar*. In an Islamic context this brings forth the concept of preordination. "Baghdad" might etymologically be an answer to the question, as it is composed of "Baġ – God" + "dād – he gave", i.e., "God gave (it); gift of God".

9.4 Concerning Dīn al-Ḥaqq (the True Dēn/Dīn, the True Faith)

Up until this day there is no real clarity in Islamic literature as to the interpretation of this term. It is assumed that there are three differing stems to the word "Dīn". However, the assumption that three different cultures well and truly stretches the assumptions of probability theory. It is difficult to explain why the expression for one notion should go back to three different roots from three different cultures. However, this apparent complexity is clarified if the route from Ugarit to Sāmarrā' is followed to this point. It starts with an Aramaic-Hebrew primary root which means "justice". He who believes, also believes that he will have to stand trial. One alternative is supposed to be a genuine Arabic word which means "convention, custom". This can be understood by whoever can explain just what is to be understood by "genuinely Arabic". The third offering is supposed to be a completely different Persian word which refers to *daēnā,* the Iranian "religious spirit". It was Th. Nöldecke who came up with this idea as to the origins of the expression. Vollers endorsed this to some extent. This is where the discussion could have ended, had the modern term of "religion" not been linked to the terminology of "Dēn/Dīn".[270] If the attested forms and the current rules of sound change are closely inspected, we arrive at the following picture:[271] There is an Avestan form: *daēnā- < dāy* – "to see, look at" (Modern Persian "dīdan – to see"), the original meaning thus being "the right view/way of seeing things". The Middle Persian form of this noun is *dēn*. Moreover, there is a truly Semitic root *d-y-n* "right, justice" as well as "tribunal, court", e.g. attested in Biblical Aramaic: Dan. 4:37: "וְאֹרְחָתֵהּ דִּין - *wə-'ōrḥāṯēh dīn* – and His ways (are) just". In Syriac, "judgment day" is *yawmā ḏə-ḏīnā* ("day of the tribunal"), which is the root of the Arabic *yawmu d-dīn* in the first surah. It was probably the case that two different roots, Semitic *d-y-n* (right, just[ice], judgment) and Iranian *dēn* (orig. "the right view", later: "religion") merged into a new term, which preserved both original meanings and a later derived meaning. In the case of "*dīn al-Ḥaqq*", however, the only meaning that makes sense is the originally Iranian one, the translation of *dīn* as "religion" often to be found confuses a European notion from the Age of Enlightenment with a concept of Ancient Iran.

This led to blunders like the search for the "religion of Abraham" (*Dīn Ibrāhīm*). Y. Nevo reckons he found this religion in the Negev. Others have not even started to search for Abraham's religion, because they believe they know it already. They are now looking for the "Abrahamic religions" and think they have found them.

From an Iranian perspective, "Dēn" should rather be translated as the "*divine wisdom*" and its personification as innate human wisdom (*sophia*). It comprises the innate knowledge of the first man and prophet as well as the philosophy of the Greeks and the philosophical teachings from India. That is the reason for the Luqmān tales in the text of the Qur'ān (surah 31), which go back to the Indian book of Aḫikar (book of wisdom) via an Aramaic version found on the Elephantine island in Egypt. The Qur'ān collects the proclamation of divine and human wisdom. Therefore it does not refer to the Scriptures themselves – for their *Dēn* is dubious –, but to contemporary Jewish, Indian and Iranian writings: It discusses and makes use of these and of a set of early Christian authors from North Africa. This is another example of the model of merging Eastern and Western traditions in Late Antiquity. The Qur'ān is a compilation which follows earlier compilations about the *Dēn/Dīn*; the Avesta and the Bible (Torah) are amongst these. This becomes clear when we consider the casuistic style of debate in the Qur'ān. Nothing negative is said about the Iranian priests, the *maǧūs* (Aramaic: *magoša*), since they are the ones who know the hour of the second coming of Christ. Moreover, their participation in the *Dēn* is to be respected as well. Only he who does not understand the *Dēn* correctly, is attacked in the Qur'ān. The reason for the attack is always the suspicion of blending (*širk*). Whoever mixes the *Dēn* with a lie is a *mušrik*, mostly translated as "associator", originally more likely to mean "blender". A blend of any kind is not welcome as this would lead to a corrosion/corruption of the *Dēn*. The *Dēn* must be kept pure. Only then is it what is called "Wēh-Dēn" in Middle Persian, the good faith ('Arabī/Arabic: "Dīn al-Ḥaqq"). The Qur'ānic motto, which here sanctions the rule, communicates a perspective:

> "*Pickthall:* He it is who hath sent His messenger with the guidance *(bi-l-hudā)* and the Religion of Truth *(wa-dīni l-ḥaqqi)*, that He may cause it to prevail over all religion (*'alā d-dīni kullihī*), however much the idolaters (*al-mušrikūna*) may be averse.
>
> *Paret:* It is he who has sent his messenger with the guidance (Rechtleitung) and the true religion (der wahren Religion), in order to help it to victory over everything, that (else) exists as religion – even if the heathens (i.e., [those] who associate [partners to the one God]) abominate it."[272] (Q 9:33)

The verse of the Qur'ān puts expressions like *al-Hudā* (guidance) and *Dīn al-Ḥaqq* (True Faith) in antithesis to the *Dīn* "made common" (al-Dīn *kull*[*i*]-*h*[*i*]) and the *mušrikūn* (blenders).[273] On the right side are the followers of the apostle with the guidance (*al-Hudā*) and the true faith (Dīn al-Ḥaqq); on the wrong side are the "blenders" with a faith that has been "made common". The prophet announces a message, which contains *guidance*, in order to enable mankind to exist autonomously alternating between the power of fate and self-determination, between acting righteously and misconduct (harming oneself). This proclamation is linked to the restoration and the future maintenance of the True Faith (*Dīn al-Ḥaqq*). True Faith triumphs over the corrupted belief of blenders (*mušrīkūn*). These are not understood to be godless. Therefore R. Paret's translation of *mušrīkūn* as "heathens" is not appropriate. Their problem is just that their *Dīn* (faith; worldview) is not the *Dīn al-Ḥaqq* (the True Faith).

Where did the Banū Hāšim, the successors to the Āl-Muḥammad, rule? They allegedly lived in their paradise called "al-Hāšimīya". This term appears as the name of a mint in the inscription on anonymous silver drachmas with the above-mentioned Qurʾānic motto (Qurʾān 9:33).[274]

The historical *al-Hāšimiya*, however, could never be located.[275] Evidently the ruler and his royal suite moved around in the manner of a Germanic itinerant king. Previous Iranian rulers had also moved between their summer palace in the Iranian highlands and their winter palace in Babylon. Maybe that is just an abstract idea of living with a Messianic emanation, Hāšimīya being the place where the cloud with the messianic Jesus had landed, at the River of Paradise.

The capital of Baghdad was allegedly rebuilt as a "round city" in the year 146 of the Arabs.[276] This is reminiscent of the site of Ḥaṭrā, which at that time was already in ruins. A "round city" that was still populated at this time was Ḥarrān. There the temple of the moon god Sin still forms the center of the town. Darabjird, the palace of the Sassanians in the Persis, was designed as a round city as well, as was Ktesiphon, the predecessor of Baghdad as seat of a court. Baghdad had not been built as Baghdad, but as Madīnat al-Salām, the new Jerusalem. The name Baghdad was used by the Mongols for this site, after the fall of the Caliphate in 1258 CE.

Prior to the alleged "new construction" of a "round city", which Islamic studies acclaim as a unique innovation, what was later Baghdad was originally just Persian palace gardens ("gifts from God", "what God had bestowed on them"), a Sassanian palace, Christian monasteries and cemeteries. The alleged "new construction" only means that, after a long time of wanderings, a place had been reached where the Sassanian rulers had been accustomed to spending their winters, where Seleucus, the Diadoch, had founded cities, and where in villas in the country and courts in Persian palace gardens on the territory of Babylon, discussions were held about a new formation of rule in Iran and the founding of a new state religion.

An anonymous golden coin with the motto from Qurʾān 9:33 is attested for the year 132 of the Arabs (753 CE). Anonymous silver coinage from Damascus from the same year exists with the same motto Qurʾān 9:33,[277] similarly coins from al-Kūfa. In the year 133 of the Arabs the new, anonymous type of silver coinage with the Qur'ānic motto 9:33 was struck in al-Baṣra.[278]

Slowly the new kind of coinage came into circulation. The effects of post-Sassanian bureaucracy must have been connected to this, as it also increased its activities around the old core regions in Mesopotamia. Damascus lost its status as center and mint. In the year 134 of the Arabs a coin had already been struck in Ardhashīr-Khurra in the Persis.[279]

The new system of rule became stable early on in Khūzistān. In the year 134 of the Arabs silver coinage of the new type with the motto Qur'ān 9:33 can be found in Rām-Hurmuz.[280] In the year 135 of the Arabs the new type of drachma was struck in Surraq,[281] Junday Sabūr[282] and Sūq al-Ahwāz.[283] The very distribution of the new silver coinage demonstrates that the new rulers met with approval and could establish their rule in the region of the old Ḥīra (al-Kūfa), in the estuary region of the land of the two rivers (al-Baṣra), in Khūzistān and in the Persis. The near-collapse in the days of the revolt led to a redressment and a re-invention of the state. New cities were founded. Baṣra on the Gulf was a substitute for a Buṣra lost, Nağaf replaced the Negev, Samarrā' replaced Samaria and Madīnat al-Salām replaced Jerusalem. The messianic tribe of the 'Arabī left the Promised Land for the Land of the Paradise rivers.

9.5 The Fictitious Ruler al-Saffāḥ as an Eschatological Representative of Anonymous Rule

The first ruler of this new era was allegedly called al-Saffāḥ. According to references in traditional literature his mother came from Nağrān. At this time Nağrān was a significant pilgrimage site. It is located several days' march to the South of Mecca. The pilgrims' destination was the *Ka'bat Nağrān*, the great Martyrion (sacred place dedicated to a martyr), to which the pilgrimage was made. Nağrān was the Sacred City of the Christian Arabs. Along with Axum in Ethiopia, Edessa in Mesopotamia and Etchmiadzin in Armenia, it belonged to the Sacred Cities of the Christian Orient.[284] In the year 142 of the Arabs anonymous silver coins were struck with the new Qur'ānic motto (9:33) in Armenia.[285]

> "In his investigation into Messianic beliefs in early Islam, van Vloten had stressed that the first Abbasid caliph Saffāḥ had referred to himself as Mahdī. (...) Let us take a look at the reports about the circumstances surrounding this homage. 'On Friday Abū l-'Abbās went for a ride on a black and white spotted pack horse (*birdaun*) and prayed with the people.'(...) In a different version it is specifically mentioned that a certain (…) or someone else had brought

Saffāḥ a spotted pack horse, so that – as can be concluded from the rest of the story – the people could recognize just who would be the future caliph."[286]

Only members of the Persian nobility were allowed to ride the horse (called "*bardonā*" in Aramaic) of the heavily armored Persian horseman (cataphract). Saint Sergius, for example, would have been eligible to ride such a quadruped. The founder of the Jacobite Church in Syria was later called "Jacobus Baradaeus" since he had enjoyed the privilege of traveling on a *bardonā*-horse. The *birdaun* would have found a place appropriate for its rank in his life history as a fervent *warhorse*. In post 1945 German Islamic Studies the *birdaun* is merely left with the role of a "*pack horse*". With Bertold Brecht's "Saint Joan of the Stockyards" in mind, we might now talk about the "Messiah of the Pack Horses".[287]

Whoever mounted a *birdaun*, also wore golden ankle chains. Whoever wore trousers (Middle Persian *šalwār*, Arabic *sarāwīl*), wore scent and rode a *birdaun*, was considered a *diqhān*, a member of the Iranian nobility.[288]

"Now it has been shown that in the eschatological expectations of differing Ancient Near East religions, the promised ruler is depicted riding off towards the end of time on a horse, a concept which can be found again in the Islamic tradition e.g. in several traits of the Zanj rebellion (255-270). Although here there is reference to a horse without reins, it can still be assumed that the spotted pack horse of our version is likewise the mount of this ruler heading towards the end of time. (...).
It is said of Abū Muslim's contemporary, Bihāfrīd, that he rode up into Heaven on a pack horse and that when he would come down again, he would take revenge on his enemies. Here 'Birdaun' is quite clearly the mount of a religious leader and warrior. In this context, two hadiths from the middle of the second century should be mentioned, in which it is said that the Angel Gabriel came to the Prophet on a pack horse [or rather a 'birdaun', a fiery steed as otherwise only mounted by Iranian aristocrats]."[289]

This completely overlooks the fact that ʿAlī, the son-in-law of the Prophet, is generally portrayed riding his white horse, like the disciple St. James in Santiago de Compostela or Prince Charming. When he is not riding his white horse, he is sitting on the hide of a ram which has leapt onto the croup of his *baradonā*-horse. Another example is Muḥammad's "Night Journey" *(al-ʾisrāʾ wa l-miʿrāǧ)* from Mecca to Jerusalem. The prophet travels on a mount called *Burāq*, a name derived from the root "barq – lightning", a horse with a human, probably a woman's, head.

The name of al-Saffāḥ points to the Iranian concept of the ruler's person. The ruler is seen as the bearer of the divine glory. Thus he has to move into Kūfa riding on horseback. A man on foot cannot have the vocation to rule, because the ram with the golden fleece only jumps onto the croup of the chosen one's horse. This was how the divine glory was transferred to the person of the deified ruler. Therefore, Sassanian rulers were mostly depicted as horsemen on reliefs on rocks, and not on foot leading pack horses by the reins. The Iranian elected king appears as a *Tyche* on horseback. This appearance manifested itself as an eternal current of currency flowing from a ruler for those ruled over, a distribution from top to bottom. The fortune of the ruler was apparent in his power to create the impression that he was able to mobilize a constant flow of gold and silver and distribute it fairly. That is why the report of the enthronement of al-Saffāḥ in traditional literature ends accordingly:

> "I raise your income by 100 Dirhams! Be you then prepared (to fight for me?)!" and continues: "For I am the generous one, who allows the spoils of war to be shared freely among the soldiers; I am the avenger and the annihilator! (...)"

The epithet Saffāḥ already seems to have existed in pre-Islamic times. Unfortunately, its meaning is not known; in a later interpretation it is understood as "pourer of water".[290]

In the course of the "Arabization" of the image of a *Tyche*, who distributes her gifts like Santa Claus from his sack, the receptacle for money and gifts was transformed into a water-bag, a utensil of the ruling Bedouin Muslims from Mecca, who saw their salvation coming from a "pourer of water".

With regard to the eschatological concept that is connected to the name al-Saffāḥ, we learn:

> "In order to analyze the meaning of the name of the ruler, Saffāḥ, the only Ḥadīṯ known to me mentioning this name that was received into the canonical collections was consulted. We read: 'When some time will have passed and disturbances arise, a man will appear with the name al-Saffāḥ; he will give away money, quasi dispersing it.'"[291]

Wilfred Madelung also makes reference to the eschatological character of the name *al-Saffāḥ*.[292]

All this fumbling in the dark can be cut short when we return to the ʿArabī in the desert. Moses hits the Rock with his stick. The rock al-Ṣafā (the Pure) will provide the "Water of Life". The water purifies the ʿArabī and heals them. The Saffāḥ is the one who baptizes with the "Water of Life". He is the great Purifier who heals the world from the spiritual disorder created by the Umayyads.

In traditional Islamic historiography, Muʿāwiya already corresponds to this ideal of a ruler being a money-spinner. As a Praetorian in Syria he had an appropriate income at his disposal.[293] During the mythical eon of the Mecca of the Arabs even 'Umar, the fictitious caliph, allegedly dreamt of the riches of Syria and other countries. He had to keep his people happy, moreover, he had to be in a position to distribute large amounts of money. 'Umar said:

> "As soon as more money is available, then I will certainly assign an amount of 4000 Dirham to each man. (...)."[294]

The biography of the Prophet of the Arabs also reflects a number of Iranian traditions. The messianic rulers of the first half of the 2nd century of the Arabs can point out their humble (Greek: tapainos) origins from poor families, as was normal among the disciples of Jesus.

Just like the elected kings of Iran, in due course they are mounted on horses, not donkeys or mules, and can then play their role as distributors of the divine blessing in monetary form. The Prophet of the Arabs himself is described as having endured the hardships of poverty, like Jesus, the "son of a carpenter". His penury would end when he was chosen by a rich woman to be her husband. With the help of this *Tyche* he, himself, later becomes a great redistributor.

> "Did Mohammed distribute money? (...) Such an event is actually reported also after Mecca was taken: Muḥammed is said to have given each of the needy 50 Dirham after he had taken credit from the generously treated wealthy people of Mecca."[295]

Al-Manṣūr, the victorious Jesus of the eschatology, represented the royal *frawahr/fravaši* of the messianic ruler. After the decline of 'Abd al-Malik's family, the notion of rulers with messianic character did continue, but the protagonists preferred to remain anonymous. The incarnation of messianic rule had exposed the members of 'Abd al-Malik's family to the irreconcilable hatred of Iranian fundamentalists. The ruler was no longer understood to be a messianic personality, but rather a person whose *fravaši* is messianic. The *Royal Fravaši* here is the eschatological Jesus. He took over this office from Mithra, the *Royal Fravaši* of a previous era.

According to Iranian teachings of the late Sassanian period, humans are creations which consist of five components: *body* (Av[estan]: tanu), *breath of life* (Av. uštana), *soul* (Av. urvari), *prototype image* (Av. kehrpa), and *guardian spirit* (Av. fravaši). The *body* comprises the material existence; the *breath of life* is connected to the wind, to breathing in and out; the *soul*, together with the consciousness of the body, hears, sees, speaks and knows; the *prototype image* is situated in a position of the sun. The *fravaši* is the part which is in God's (Ahuramazda's) presence.

Mankind was created in this form. But when the enemy of Ahuramazda, Aŋra Mainiuu (the Evil Spirit) attacked, people died and their *bodies* became one with the earth, their *breath of life* one with the wind, their *prototype image* one with the sun and their *souls* go to their *fravaši* so that the demons cannot destroy them.[296]

The *fravaši* of the ruler, his higher self, is the eschatological Jesus. As a *fravaši* he is pre-existing and lives in the presence of God. It is to him that the soul of the ruler returns on his death. The concept of a higher self in the form of a *fravaši* is also to be found in the Gospel according to Matthew. To conclude this excursus a small example from the New Testament will be considered, which (to my knowledge) was ignored in biblical exegesis and which proves the closeness of Zoroastrian and New Testament angelology:

> "See that you do not despise one of these little ones, for I say to you that their angels in heaven continually see the face of My Father who is in heaven." (Mt. 18:10)

The connection between an angel and the human being this angel is assigned to is apparently seen to be much closer than is assumed in the commonly accepted understanding of a *guardian angel*: An offence suffered by a man living on Earth, hurts his angel to such an extent that this very fact is used as the justification for the need to avoid such offences. On the other hand, the angel beholding the face of the Father bestows such dignity on every single human being, that it would be sinful to offend. In my view such a notion is incomprehensible if one does not take into consideration the Zoroastrian doctrine of the *daēnā-fravaši* as its intellectual and historical background.

The thrilling story of the capture and release of Saint Peter (Acts 12:1-19) points in the same direction: When Peter, presumed to be bound in heavy chains, suddenly stood at the door of the house, "they kept saying: 'It is his angel.'" However, such a passage can only be considered as evidence regarding the view suggested here if it is considered together with other, by far more explicit, indications like in Mt. 18:10:

> "When they had passed the first and second guard, they came to the iron gate that leads into the city, which opened for them by itself; and they went out and went along one street, and immediately the angel departed from him."[297]

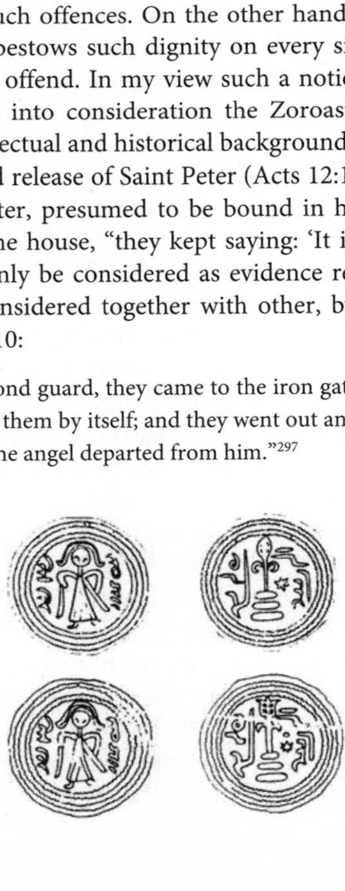

Fig. 35: Ryka Ghyselen noticed that the model for the depiction of the so-called "standing caliph" can be found in Iran. As the "caliph" is in fact the eschatological Jesus, it should come as no surprise that the model was Iranian depictions of angels and that this "standing caliph" is winged like a cherub. On the reverse, the fire altar has been replaced by a plant.

An earlier mention of the messianic term *manṣūr* (the victor, designation of the eschatological Jesus of the Syriac Apocalypse of Daniel with his flaming sword) in an inscription can be found on coins of al-Ḥaǧǧāǧ dated year 81 of the Arabs. Furthermore, a bilingual inscription in ʿArabī/Pehlevi can be found on copper coinage from the Persis.[298] Islamic traditional literature also acknowledges the messianic character of the name *Manṣūr*.[299] A ruler named "*Manṣūr*" is not attested on coins, or on glass weights, or on seals.

Fig. 36: Mention of the Messianic name "Manṣūr" on an Arab-Sassanian copper coin from the Persis.

As has already been explained, a name "bn Hāšim" was mentioned in Egypt. The name *Hāšimiya* is found as the name of a mint on coinage. Around the year 150 of the Arabs (771 CE) a mint called *ʿAbbāsīya* can be found on silver coins.[300]

Now, if we assume that the Iranian tradition lived on when towns were given a name, – be they newly founded or re-founded –, then this means that the towns would be named after their founders. This, in turn, would mean that the name of the mint *Hāšimīya*, which cannot be localized, is a town founded by a man called *Hāšim* or descendants of a *Hāšim*. Similarly, the existence of a place called *ʿAbbāsīya* around 150 of the Arabs would be an indication of the existence of a founder or name-giver of the town called *ʿAbbās*. This might be the case, as Berlin may have had a founder by that name. More probable, however, is the existence of religious factions propagating *Hašimīya* and *ʿAbbāsīya* as political-religious programs, like Philadelphia does not mean that a man called "Philadelphus" was the founder of the city, but is a programmatic name meaning "brotherly love".

The messianic rulers of the *banū Hāšim* or the already mentioned *ʿAbbās* act as founders of cities in the tradition of their Sassanian predecessors. Their names, however, do not appear in inscriptions on coinage, as the *de facto* ruler is the hidden eschatological Jesus. Nor are they connected with the cult of a saint or a cult site. This changes with their successors, who develop a new program to legitimize their rule by means of names from the Old Testament, which makes the ruler the guardian of a sacred site; thus the term of the *Harūn/Aaron* can be explained. Such a symbolic use of names and their meanings or origins has already been discussed with the successors of ʿAbd al-Malik.

Fig. 37: Bronze from Shiraz of the year 137 of the Arabs. The constancy of Iranian depictions is remarkable. An anonymous picture of the ruler in the style of the Sassanians appears instead of the aniconic image on earlier coins.

The fact that these names live on in traditional literature does not mean that the incidents or events connected to them are historic.

Since the death of Hišām bn ʿAbd al-Malik in 125 of the Arabs the exertion of power would thus have been in the hands of a regent appointed by the family of ʿAbd al-Malik from Merv. This Syrian group of members of the messianic movement from Merv was replaced by a subsequent influx from the East, the "Āl-Muḥammad" from Merv, Khorasan and Soghdia. There are still traces of them in Egypt. The "Āl-Muḥammad" is a messianic movement from Khorasan that fights against the anonymous representative rule in the West.

After the collapse of the anonymous rule by members of ʿAbd al-Malik's family after 132 of the Arabs, a restructuring took place towards a chiliastic rule. For the period until approx. 150 of the Arabs the names of rulers *Hāšim* and *ʿAbbās* are documented, but not *al-Saffāḥ* and *al-Manṣūr*. This will not change before the era of the al-Mahdī Muḥammad.

9.7 The Rule of the "Guided (?) Chosen One" and Paradise on Earth

The successor to *al-Saffāḥ* and *al-Manṣūr*, who are only known in traditional literature, but never mentioned in inscriptions, is "*al-Mahdī Muḥammad bn Amīr al-mu'minīn*"[301] who is named on coin inscriptions.

The name and the title constitute a program.

The messianic name of "*al-Mahdī*"[302] is connected to the term *muḥammad* (chosen one). According to this, *al-Mahdī* would designate the chosen one. What we are dealing with, however, is probably not a double name, as has so far been assumed,[303] but a motto composed of two terms. The inscription should be understood as follows:

> "The Mahdī is chosen (*muḥammad*) and is represented by the descendants of governors (*bn Amīr al-mu'minīn*) who were Protectors of Faith."

In inscriptions on weights from Egypt the name of the issuer is given as: "al-Mahdī".[304] This could be read as "Āl-Mahdi" as well.

The *fravaši* of the messianic ruler, who acts as a representative of the *Mahdī*, is *'Īsa bn Maryam* (Jesus, son of Mary), the eschatological Jesus. There is a Ḥadīṯ which refers to this interpretation. According to this Ḥadīṯ the *Mahdī* is none other than *'Īsa bn Maryam*.[305]

9.8 The Caliphate (i.e., the Representation) of the Mahdī

The indication on the inscription that *al-Mahdī* is the "chosen one" ("al-*Mahdī muḥammad*") is followed by the designation "*al-ḫalīfat al-Mahdī*" ("the representation of the guided one"). At the time of 'Abd al-Malik, "*halpat/ḫal(ī)fat Allāh*" was the title given to the eschatological Jesus, whose second coming was expected according to the account of the Syriac Apocalypse of Daniel. Jesus was seen as "*ḫalīfat Allāh*" ("representative of God"). In this case, however, we are dealing with the representation of the *Mahdī*, whose *fravaši* has to be regarded as the eschatological Jesus.[306]

From this period there is a coin from Baṣra, dated the year 160 of the Arabs, which bears the inscription: "'Alī(–) Muḥammad – ṭayyib" ("'Alī – Muḥammad – good!")[307] instead of mentioning the representation of the Mahdī.

How should this be interpreted? Can it mean that power is exerted in the name of the one who is known as both *'Alī* and *Muḥammad*? Maybe in the following way: No matter whether the Mahdī is to be seen as the *failing* Jesus (the 'Alī) of the Kirmāni, or the *eschatological* Jesus of the Khorasanians: in view of his imminent second coming, a debate about his nature is pointless.

The creation of a paradise on earth is connected to messianic or chiliastic rule. The Iranian paradise is characterized by the absence of conflict among people residing together, and the never-ending allotment of rewards, "manna from heaven" or "Baġ-dād". 'Abd al-Malik's apocalyptic visions had already demanded the creation of a paradisiac world. *Islām* in the sense of "concord, unity, harmony" was the call to end conflict (*iḫtlāf*) amongst the People of the Book (*ahl-kitāb*) in the inscription in the Dome of the Rock. The demand for *Islām* was opposed to conflict in typically Iranian fashion. *Islām*, as the "absence of conflict", is one step on the path to accomplishing paradisiac circumstances. The complex of motives "conflict *(iḫtilāf)*" as opposed to "concord (*islām*)" is paralleled with the complex "hell – paradise".[308]

The daily allowances in paradise are also a piece of Iranian tradition. As a popular etymology, the Arabic (possibly Aramaic) term *rizq* is equated with the Middle Persian word for "ration" or "pay": *roziq*,[309] itself a derivation of the word for "day". It is a kind of daily allowance of "manna", like rain from heaven. The expression of "daily bread", in the form of a daily allowance (*rizq*), appears in 55 places in the Qur'ānic text, the Arabic verb derived from this Iranian root is even more frequent (68 attestations). The frequent reference to God as the guarantor of the preservation of his creatures and as the source of their livelihood (*rizq*), can be interpreted as an anti-Zurvanist trend in the Qur'ānic text. This also goes for the notion of destiny, which is connected to God in the Qur'ānic text. From an Iranian perspective, *preservation* and *destiny* could not be seen as both being in God's hand. In many places belief in the Zurvanist pantheon with its *gods of fate* was predominant. These are the gods that the Qur'ānic text turns on. Just how biased the later Zurvanist and fate-believing interpretations of the Qur'ān are, can be demonstrated with a part of the chronicle of Bar Hebraeus from appr. 1286 CE. There we read that the Muslims are divided amongst themselves: Some of them acknowledge the existence of *free will*, others, however, do not even admit the question as to whether there *is* a free will.[310]

The funding of paradisiac circumstances seemed feasible by means of a recourse to the Sassanian tradition of the domination of the Arabian Peninsula and the exploitation of the mineral resources available there. The re-established presence in Northern Africa made it possible to gain access to the gold from West Sudan.[311] The well attested presence in Egypt by the name of "*al-Mahdī muḥammad*" suggests an interest in Egypt as the destination of African and Ethiopian gold.

However, the appropriation of the Arabian Peninsula was of particular importance for the flow of money in the paradise on earth. As an inscription of Mu'āwiya's near Ṭā'if and the inscription of Medina dated the year 135 of the Arabs suggest, the influence of the Arab Empire was at first limited to the former region of the Ghassanids.

Renewed interest in the Arabian Peninsula can be inferred from coins struck for the representative of the Mahdī. The penetration of the Peninsula evidently took place from the Northeast to the Southwest, which is the course of the old Sassanian silver road from Nağrān to al-Ḥīra. Evidence for this is coinage naming the representative of the Mahdī in al-Yamāma, the name of a region in central Arabia, the modern center of which is al-Riyāḍ (Arabic: "the gardens"), the capital of modern Saudi Arabia.[312] Riyāḍ is the Aramaic word for a "villa".

The Sassanians had already exploited the silver mines in the *Nağd* of today. The presence of the Sassanians in Central Arabia led to an invasion of South Arabia by the allies of the Byzantines in the region, the kings of Axum in Ethiopia, in around 525 CE. This course of action provoked the Sassanians into seizing the Yemen. The post-Sassanian administration of Mesopotamia followed the pattern of their predecessors and retook control of the silver mines of Arabia once again.[313]

At the time of the representation of the Mahdī, Bar Hebraeus referred to the use of the collected treasures in the spirit of the Iranian kingship as follows:

> "This Ḫalīfah opened his father's treasures, and scattered the riches of his father as with a fan."[314]

The Encyclopaedia of Islam has the following to say about the author of these lines:

> "Ibn al-'Ibrī's writings are not distinguished by great ability or by originality of thought or style; his contribution to literature commands respect rather by its sheer bulk and the fidelity with which he reproduces earlier writers."[315]

He does, however, have one advantage over all the other chroniclers of Islamic traditional literature: His grave is known. His grave in the monastery of Saint Mattai in Mosul is decorated with a detailed inscription. From his interpretations it can be assumed that in his time the rewriting of the history of the former Sassanian Empire in post-Sassanian times, first into a salvation history of Late Antiquity and then into an Islamic history with pseudo-historic protagonists (whose alleged names are mostly *programs* and *mottos*) had already been concluded.

9.9 Is Moses the Savior (*Greek:* Sotēr)?

According to Islamic traditional literature it was a caliph who was said to have taken on the succession of the representation of the Mahdī, and who called himself *Mūsā al-Hādī* (Moses the redeemer/savior/*sotēr*). He is supposed to have been the son and successor of the caliph al-Mahdī. Here a messianic name, which legitimizes the rule, is personalized and changed to mean "ruler". Traditional literature refers to the rule of a representative (caliph), appointed immediately after the death of the Prophet of the Arabs, who, after our re-evaluation of material evidence, is himself nothing but the personalization of a Christological title. This fictitious representative (caliph) is confused with the ruler as a representative of a messianic concept.[316] In a new type of inscriptions, a person called "Moses (Mūsā)" is mentioned. At this point, inscriptions on coinage from Baṣra might be adduced as an example. There we can read:

> "In representation of the Mahdī, only the command of Moses, the crown prince of the muslims (? – *walī 'ahd*), is valid."[317]

Whether the expression *walī 'ahd* (generally accepted as a defective spelling of *walī al-'ahd*) was already to be understood as "crown prince" in the sense of the Islamic tradition at this time, cannot be clarified here. However, as we are evidently not dealing with dynastic forms of rule, such an explanation does not make sense. It might also be considered a programmatic expression in connection with a system name. The system name of Moses would have to be interpreted allegorically. The inscription calls for a "Moses" who is *walī ʿahd al-muslimīn.*

Thus, the inscription should be understood as a documentation of rule in representation of the Mahdī, but under the command of an allegorically interpreted Moses. His function is not the one of the crown prince of a non-existent dynasty, but should be understood as the one of a *walī ʿahd* in the original sense of the word. The term "*walī* (appointee, authorized representative)" was well established. It is worth recalling the designation of the *muḥammad* (Jesus) as "*walī Allāh*" (God's representative). Here the term *ʿahd* means "covenant, i.e., duty, promise, guideline, charter". The Old and New Testaments are both *ʿahd.*[318]

The term *walī ʿahd* in the inscriptions of the years 164-168 of the Arabs (787-791 CE) in Baṣra is therefore not the defective spelling of the title of the successor to the throne, but rather stands for "the representative of the covenant", "the representation of the charter, the duty and the guidelines". As *walī ʿahd al-muslimīn* he is the "representative of the covenant, the rules with their duties and promises and with those who are peaceful (*muslimīn*)".

Instead of the caliph Moses, the savior and redeemer (*Mūsā al-Hādī*) from traditional literature, in inscriptions we come across the representative of the messianic rule of the Mahdī: He who – like a Moses – provides protection of the covenant and the charter of those who are peaceful (*muslimīn),* should be in command.

This representative of the rules of the *muslimīn* ("peaceful" in the sense that they reject *conflict* amongst the People of the Book [*ahl-kitāb*], as conflict does not belong in an Iranian Paradise) then becomes the representative of the Moses as "*ḫalīfat Mūsā*".[319]

Just how it happens that the "*ḫalīfat al-Hādī*" (representative of the Savior, Sotēr, Redeemer) and the "*ḫalīfat Mūsā*" (representative of the Moses) can be found at the same *time,* but in different *places,* must be due to rivalry between the different concepts.

This also applies to another "authorized representative" of the charter of the Muslims: *Hārūn* (Aaron). He is also mentioned at the time of the representation of the rule of the Mahdī.[320]

The introduction of the title *walī ʿahd* and the reinterpretation of the term as "rule as representative" constitutes a revolution. It leads away from the messianic concept of rule and back to the Iranian notion of the ruler as a "*dādbar* (upholder of the law)". As such he is to be seen as a *Moses,* like an *Aaron.* It is a view of the old idea of Iranian rule from an Old Testament perspective – a rule which, at that time, required a *Moses* and *Aaron*. Mentioning a *new Aaron* was tantamount to the dissolution of the Christian community and demonstrated the will to create a new community, defined by cult and rites. Mentioning the representative of Moses in inscriptions can be considered the last evocation of a common history, from which the new community, led by the new Aaron, distances itself. This is also the reason for the wording of early inscriptions in stone in the Negev in Israel: *rabb Mūsā wa Hārūn* (the Lord of Moses and Aaron).[321]

For the year 171 of the Arabs two mentions of the representative of Hārūn (Aaron) are of interest: In one residence called "Hārūnīya" silver coins are struck with two differing wordings. The inscription on the first of the two refers to a rule in representation of the "Marḍī" ("the well pleasing"), thus is still influenced by messianic concepts. The second one refers to a rule in the name of the "Rašīd" (the guided one who follows the right path; Iranian: *razišta*). Here the transition from the use of messianic names to concepts of law and justice inspired by Iranian models, in the sense of "following the proper path" (*razišta*) can be observed.[322]

10 The Way to al-Ma'mūn

10.1 The End of the Rule in Representation of a Messianic Anticipation and the Change to a Rule in the Name of Guidance: from Moses to Aaron, from Amīn to Ma'mūn

For the year 171 of the Arabs there is a confirmation of the rule of this Hārūn (Aaron) in an inscription on a gold coin without mint. It reads: "'abd-Allāh Hārūn (Aaron) amīr al-mu'minīn". The wording is a sequence of the ruler's titles: "Servant of God", the allegorical name: "Aaron" and the title already known from the first century of the Arab Empire: "*amīr al-mu'minīn* (head/spokesman of those imparting security; i.e., governor/protector of faith)".[323]

This is where the transition from an exertion of power in the name of a Hidden one (Saffāḥ, Manṣūr, Mahdī) to the exertion of power by one particularly named person takes place. In retrospect and in terms of present Islamic practice, this could be seen as the transition from a proto-shiite to a proto-sunnite exertion of rule.

In the year 172 of the Arabs, the system of rule was still a representative one, but representative of the "guided one" (*al-ḫalīfat al-rašīd*), i.e., the Iranian ruler, the "*dādbar*" ("the one who maintains law, justice").[324] The ruler Aaron (*ḫalīfat Hārūn amīr al-mu'minīn*)[325] emerges from the ruler in Aaron's representation (*ḫalīfat Hārūn*). The role of the ruler becomes clear in the inscription from Harat of the year 193: "(...) *'abd allāh Hārūn amīr al-mu'minīn.*"[326]

This is the record of the ruler as was normal in the days of Muʿāwiya after the year 42 of the Arabs. This inscription on a Dirham from Harat about the end of Hārūn's rule is in accordance with the tenor of the inscription already mentioned on the gold coin from the year 171 of the Arabs in the collection in Istanbul. There, too, we can find: "*ʿabd allāh Hārūn amīr al-mu'minīn* (God's servant Aaron, governor)".

The representation (*ḫalīfat*) of the Hidden One, in whose name power is exerted, becomes a motto of rule: *ḫalīfat rašīd* (the representation of the guided one); *ḫalīfat al-amīn* (the representation of the faithful); *ḫalīfat al-ma'mūn* (the representation of the one who can be trusted, "Maimonides").

Should the exercise of the minting right (*sikka*) be considered the prerogative of the ruler, then it becomes conspicuous that in many places anonymous coins were struck, which can only be accounted for as a part of the governing activities of a post-Sassanian Empire thanks to the canonical inscription in existence since the year 132 of the Arabs. These coins all bear the same inscription: Qur'ān 9:33. Moreover, they date from the year 132 of the Arabs. What should we therefore think of these anonymous administrative activities? For the period of messianic rule in representation of the *Saffāḥ*, the *Manṣūr* and the *Mahdī*, one can accept that the Hidden One, whose second coming was anticipated, is only mentioned as the *muḥammad* in the inscriptions of contemporary coinage.[327]

But how can it be explained that coins were still being struck without mentioning a concept of rule or a ruler at the times of *ʿabd allāh Hārūn amīr al-mu'minīn*, who saw himself as the representative of the *mardī* (well pleasing one) and of the *rašīd* (guided one)? Such specimens can be found on the Caspian Sea, e.g. in Ṭabaristān dated the year 190 of the Arabs[328] and on the Euphrates in Rafīqa dated the year 193 of the Arabs.[329] Many further examples of anonymous administrative activities could be listed. Moreover, it should be mentioned that coins with the name "Hārūn" and "Rašīd" on it are attested, but not a single one with the combination: "Hārūn al-Rašīd"

Another piece of evidence for the active bureaucracy of this post-Sassanian Empire is the fact that regions already dominated by the Sassanians are returned to the influence of the central administration in Mesopotamia. Silver coins of the "Arab" rule are struck in Egypt for the first time.[330]

In Yemen it becomes particularly clear that former Sassanian territories were won back. For the region of ʿUman, neighboring Yemen, the influence of the Arab Empire can be proved for an even earlier period. The coast of the Gulf would seem to always have been under the influence of the Arab Empire.[331]

In the Southwest of the Arabian Peninsula, the region formerly controlled by the Sassanians together with its significant silver mines, was already won back at the time of the messianic rule in representation of the *Mahdī*. The minting activity of the administration started in al-Yaman, Central Arabia, at the time of the messianic rule in representation of the *Mahdī*.[332]

Considering that according to Islamic constitutional law the ruler is legitimized by mentioning his name in Friday prayers and by his right to exercise the *sikka* ("minting right"; from an Aramaic verb meaning "to pour", referring to the production of planchets), then one has to assume that at least on the occasion of the appropriation of territory or of a change at the top of the community, the right to strike and issue coinage had to be effected. Even if one prefers to assume that the Islamic version of this practice had only come into existence in the period of the Islamic states ("Dawlat") since the fourth century of the Islamic calendar, it has to be acknowledged that this habit, in part, goes back to older ideals stemming from the time of the successors of Alexander and of the Roman Empire. So we must assume that whenever the exercise of rule over a territory began, the striking of coins must have started there as well.

In short, the evidence we expect to find for the exertion of rule in a territory is the coinage struck by the new ruler. As this evidence is absent, it is often simply claimed that, at the time of the Prophet of the Arabs, on the Arabian Peninsula, the *normal case* were non-statal activities, which did not leave any detectable traces. This is then adduced as an explanation since no coins or inscriptions are found from the time of the Prophet of the Arabs. Such an explanation would never be accepted by historians dealing with any other discipline but Islamic Studies.

If this highly improbable explanation should ever be dropped by Islamologists, then another fictitious claim would have to be dismissed as well: Islamic studies should no longer assume the historicity of the so-called "Constitution of Medina". But even if the classical claims of Islamology should be accepted, then this only shifts the necessity for an explanation: If at the beginning non-governmental activities were the order of the day, what was it then that drove the Bedouins to found a state in the end? If the Prophet of the Arabs did not act for the *state* (or the Constitution of Medina), but rather for a loose confederation of amorphous tribal structures, then some explanation is needed as to how some seventy years after the sandbox games of Mecca, extremely powerful Islamic states could develop from these tribal structures, which claim the existence of the Prophet on their coat of arms.

The right to strike and issue coinage makes it possible to determine the point in time at which land was seized and rule over it started to be exerted. Thus by looking at the dates provided by coins it can be ascertained that silver coins were struck at the time of al-Ma'mūn in San'ā'.[333]

Therefore it comes as no surprise that after the conquest of the Arabian Peninsula, coins were also struck in the Ḥiğāz. The earliest copper coin is dated the year 185 of the Arabs and is in the collection at the University of Tübingen.[334]

Last, but not least, there are coins from Mecca. The scientific consensus is that the year 201 of the Arabs is the earliest known date for the striking of coins at this location. A silver coin is known to exist mentioning the *Ḫalīfat* of the *Ma'mūn* dated the year 203.[335]

The ideology of rule is developed further: al-Ma'mūn becomes Imām.[336] For the year 196 of the Arabs a gold coin is known to exist which shows, besides its standard inscription, an additional inscription: *li-l-ḫalīfat/al-Ma'mūn*. In the same year a gold coin was struck with the additional inscription: *li-l-ḫalīfat/al-Imām*.[337]

After the introduction of the notion of a Moses and Aaron as "guardians of the covenant (testament) of the peaceful" (*wālī 'ahd al-muslimīn*), we now have to find a new, contemporary function for their representatives. It is the function of the *Imām*. This person leads the community at prayer. How this development was understood can be inferred from the apocalyptical prophecies from Ḥimṣ. Those who passed them on explained these traditions as belonging to the first century of rule of the Arab Empire. The terminology they use (e.g. the occurrence of *muhāǧirūn*), however, makes it clear that if anything they belong to the second and third Islamic centuries.

In this case we are still dealing with eschatological expectations. If, at the time of 'Abd al-Malik, the second coming of the eschatological Jesus as *ḫalīfat Allāh* was considered imminent, then this expectation was upheld after the end of the rule of 'Abd al-Malik's sons by means of a *de facto* rule in representation of the "hidden bearer" of the messianic names *Saffāḥ, Manṣūr* and *Mahdī*.

This diffuse expectation gave way to a call, which demanded the return to a legal system in the manner of Moses, the legislator, and his brother, the herald of this message. These diffuse expectations of the second coming of someone hidden in the clouds was replaced by the concrete expectation of a contemporary Moses and Aaron, who should be regarded as "guardians of the covenant of the peaceful (muslimīn)". This is probably the idea of a New or a *Renewed Covenant/Testament*.

The one that is trusted (*ma'mūn*), now takes on the leadership of the community via the newly created office of the Imām. Had this office existed before, it would have been documented in inscriptions. However, it is first referred to in the year 196 of the Arabs.

There cannot have been any reason to create such an office before the emergence of the notion that the community should be led by an "authorized representative of the covenant of the peaceful"; for the Hidden One still counted as leader of his community. Representation by an Imām was not yet necessary, as the eschatological expectation was still the basis of rule. Only when this was pushed into the background, when the rule of the *Saffāḥ*, the *Manṣūr* and the *Mahdī* was over, had the time come for the appointment of an Imām.

The apocalyptic prediction of the Ka'b al-Aḥbār in Emesa (Ḥimṣ) provides the legitimizing legend:

> "The Messiah, 'Īsa bn Maryam, will descend at the white bridge at the East gate of Damascus towards the tree standing there. A cloud will carry him and he will place his hands on the shoulders of two angels. He will be clad in two white cloths. He will be wearing one around his loins, the other as a loose cloak. As soon as he bows his head, drops will fall like pearls. The Jews will come to him and say: 'We are your companions.' And he will say: 'You lie.' Then the Christians will come to him and say: 'We are your companions', but he will say: 'You are lying, because my companions are the Muhāǧirūn, the survivors among the participants on Malḥama (the greatest possible catastrophe of apocalyptic scale).' Then he comes to the meeting of the Muslims, wherever that may be. There he finds their caliph (to be understood here as representative of a religious community, as leaders of a *millet*), as he prays is praying with them. The Messiah will stand behind him until he notices him and the caliph will say: 'O you Messiah of God. Lead us in prayer'. But he will say: 'It is up to you to lead your companions in prayer, for God is pleased by you. I was sent as an assistant (*wazīr*), I was not sent to command (*amīr*)'. Thus the caliph of the Muhāǧirūn will lead the prayer during two *rak'as,* while the son of Mary stays/stands among them. Then the Messiah will conclude / bring the prayers to an end (...)."[338]

The Qur'ān commented on the role of the caliph: Qur'ān 38:26:

> "O David! Lo! We have set thee as a viceroy (*ḫalīfatan*) in the earth; therefore judge aright between mankind, and follow not desire that it beguile thee from the way of Allah. Lo! those who wander from the way of Allah have an awful doom, forasmuch as they forgot the Day of Reckoning (*yawma l-ḥisābi*)."

The following can be said about the term Imām:

> "In the Qur'ān this expression is used seven times in the singular form and five times in its plural form, where it means: 'Characteristic, pattern, model, leader' etc."[339]

With the appointment of the Imām the concept of the community also begins to take concrete shape. The leading role in *Christianity*, that 'Abd al-Malik aspired to, is swapped with the leadership of the *new religious community*.

10.2 Al-Ma'mūn Becomes the Representative of God (Ḫalīfat Allāh)

In connection with one complete change in the religious-political scene described in traditional literature, al-Ma'mūn is said to have referred to himself as the representative of God (*Ḫalīfat Allāh*). Here, it must be clearly pointed out that the idea of a caliph being the representative of God with God's (silent) approval, which was set as a standard by Islamic studies, – *ḫalīfat Allāh*, God's Caliph – is depicted in traditional literature as the result of a "coup from above". The incontrovertible fact that al-Ma'mūn had declared himself to be the representative of God – even if only for a short time – is questionable due to the way it is portrayed in traditional literature.

Traditional literature assumes that there had already been a *Shiite* Imām at this time, who would thus have to be understood as a spiritual enemy of al-Ma'mūn, should it be assumed that he had taken on a proto-*Sunni* attitude. The Imām and the caliph would therefore have been leaders of conflicting religious communities. Just what kind of religious community al-Ma'mūn led is not clear. Obviously, his followers must have been non-Shiite believers. Whether or not there were such religious barriers at the time of al-Ma'mūn, however, is dubious. This would presuppose that *Sunni* Muslims already existed. These, however, cannot be detected at all before the establishment of the *Schools of Islamic Law (maḏhab [sg.])*. It is therefore more probable that we are dealing with the conflict between a Khorasanian tradition of the *muḥammad/Muḥammad* and a Kirmanian tradition of the *'alī/'Alī*.

The criticism of traditional literature concerning these issues is theological. In the end all of the protagonists except for al-Ma'mūn are dead. Heaven destroys the vizier al-Faḍl bn Sahl and the Shiite Imām 'Alī bn al-Riḍā.

The coup is said to have been as follows: In the course of solemn ceremonies the caliph al-Ma'mūn appointed the opposing Imām of the Alid party as his heir and successor. Thus the continuous conflict between the holders of different traditions should be brought to an end. The establishment in Baghdad rebelled against this "pro-Persian" decision by al-Ma'mūn. A relative called Manṣūr bn al-Mahdī ("[Jesus the] victor, from the family of the guided one") assumed power in Baghdad.[340]

The vizier was regarded as a "friend of the Persians" and was allegedly killed by the enemies of al-Ma'mūn in the year 202 of the *hiğra*. The delegated heir, 'Alī al-Riḍā, is also said to have been killed in the year 203 of the *hiğra*. In the year 204 of the *hiğra* of the Prophet of the Arabs, al-Ma'mūn was then reported to have returned from Persia (sic) to Baghdad, afflicted and cleansed by these strokes of fate. He was reconciled with his family, which steered straight towards the establishment of the Sunni orientation of Islam. The

Alids, and with them all the Shiites, were removed from power and forever banished from politics.[341]

What is historic and what is ideology in this story? The evidence on dated coins, which is expected to confirm this alleged course of events, contradicts the claims of traditional literature. The information found there on the coins even makes it appear dubious that the events depicted in traditional literature took place at all.

The portrayal of events at the time of al-Ma'mūn almost bears the characteristics of a justification for the later action against the Shiites. Barhebraeus describes this under the 'Year of the Arabs' 231. In this year, by order of the caliph, the tomb of Ḥusayn bn 'Alī was destroyed along with all the buildings around it. The area of these ruins was ploughed over and seeded. The caliph allegedly said: "The location of this tomb is to be effaced forever."[342]

When checking whether the events described are historic or not, on the basis of inscriptions on coinage, it becomes conspicuous that the vizier al-Faḍl bn Sahl, who, according to traditional literature, was killed in the year 202 after the *hiğra* of the Prophet of the Arabs in Baghdad, had coins struck bearing his title: "Ḏū l-riyāsatayn".[343] For the year 204 of the Arabs he is mentioned on coins of al-Muḥammadīya (Rayy).[344] For the year 205 of the Arabs the name of the vizier is even found on coins from Isfahān.[345]

Just what a glorious protagonist al-Faḍl bn Sahl must have been for the expansion of Islam is shown in the coins bearing his title from Khwarezm. After the defeat of the Khwarezm-Shāh, he had coins struck that only bore his name. The image of the ruler on the obverse remained unchanged, on the reverse side of the coin a Muslim is riding to victory, surrounded by an Aramaic (sic) legend. In the field of the coin we read "*Ḏū l-riyāsatayn*" ("the one with two commands", i.e., the civilian and the military). Where, however, do we find a profession of faith? Where is the mention of Allāh's apostle? Were the Aramaic traditional legends respected so much that it was not desired that the East Iranians should be bothered with the indication of a *muḥammad*? The East Iranian Khwarezmians might well have been wavering between the fire temple and the stupa. Apparently there was no rush to involve them in the religious conflicts of the rulers in Mesopotamia.

Fig. 38: Silver coin from Khwarezm. Depiction of a ruler with an Aramaic legend. Naming of the Arabic vizier in Baghdad. Where is the religious motto?

The Alid Imām is said to have died in the year 203 after the *hiǧra* of the Prophet of the Arabs. Still, he is also mentioned in the inscription of the above-mentioned coins. Thus it can also be assumed that the Imām was alive until the year 205 of the Arabs and fulfilled the role of "heir to the throne". According to later Islamic traditionalists, he was able to carry out this role, because they, too, had misunderstood the expression *walī 'ahd al-muslimīn* and interpreted is as referring to a "successor" instead of the "appointed representative of the covenant of the peaceful".

After the death of the Imām 'Alī al-Riḍā in Ṭūs (today the pilgrimage site Mašhad), according to Ṭabarī, al-Ma'mūn is said to have written a letter to the Abbasid family, their clients and followers in Baghdad, in which he justified the appointment of the Imām 'Alī Riḍā as the "appointed representative of the covenant of the peaceful" and made reference to the apocalyptical predictions of al-Rašīd regarding the duration of the rule of the Abbasid family. This letter is, of course, entirely preserved *in traditional literature.*

There it is said that in the seventh generation after al-'Abbās no pillar of the rule of the Banū 'Abbās would stand upright. The downfall would come by the sword! The Ḥasanī, the avenger and destroyer, would come and slay all of them. The same goes for the Ṣufyānī (the old phantom of the claims of Mu'āwiya's family). General bloodshed could only be prevented if the Qā'im, the Mahdī, would come. Then blood would only be shed where warranted.[346]

In order to avoid this apocalyptical scenario, in the year 200 of the *hiǧra*, al-Ma'mūn allegedly fetched 'Alī bn al-Riḍā from Medina and appointed him as his successor. He was necessary for the ruling family to cross the threshold into the new century safe and sound, i.e., he was installed as a scapegoat to deflect the ire of the gods of the Abbasids. They allowed themselves to regard the new century as a new, *Sacred Era* with a new year-numbering system, starting with the *hiǧra* of the Prophet of the Arabs. A century before, the fictitious 'Umar had skipped over the boundary of the New Era for the benefit of the family then in power – at least that is how it was seen by posterity.

Appointing 'Alī bn al-Riḍā as his successor was considered a compensation for the family of 'Alī, intended to prevent the downfall of the 'Abbasids at the turn of the century.

Whatever apocalyptical notions posterity assumed as being the reason for al-Ma'mūn's action, they cannot have been his real motivation at the time it happened. Later references to apocalyptic notions are nothing more than a new theological assessment of a situation which could no longer be interpreted historically. This discrepancy demonstrates once again just how historically late Islamic traditional literature must be.

The reason for appointing 'Alī al-Riḍā may lie in the lack of legitimacy of al-Ma'mūn's rule. The idea of ruling in representation of the *al-Saffāḥ*, the

Manṣūr and the *Mahdī* more likely comes from a worldview that also knows the concept of the failing Jesus as *'Alī*, than one of *Mūsā* and *Hārūn*, *Amīn* and *Ma'mūn*. Is it not rather the case that the Imām 'Alī al-Riḍā represented the followers of messianic rule, whereas al-Ma'mūn stood for the usurpers, who used the new office "appointed representative for the covenant of the peaceful" in order to create a new order in terms of Iranian tradition? He who appoints himself the protector of a tradition, more often than not intends to change it. Should we not rather assume that al-Ma'mūn tried to merge two threads of tradition into one, namely the concept of *messianic rule* and the *Iranian concept of rule of a legislator*? For himself, the position of "God's representative" emerges. The inscriptions of the years 202-205 of the *hiǧra* refer to a new organisation of the hierarchy in Iranian territory:

1) *Muḥammad rasūl Allāh* (Muḥammad is the messenger of Allāh);
2) *Al-Ma'mūn ḫalīfat Allāh* (al-Ma'mūn is the representative of God);
3) The command of the *Amīr* (not Imām) *al-Riḍā* alone applies;
4) *Walī 'ahd al-muslimīn* (appointed representative of the covenant of the peaceful)
5) *'Alī bn Mūsā / bn 'Alī bn Abī Ṭālib;*
6) *Ḏū al-riyāsatayn* ("the one with both commands", epithet of the vizier al-Faḍl bn Sahl).

Coins with these inscriptions are known only to exist from Iranian territory: Fārs, Isfahān, al-Muḥammadīya (Rayy); Samarqand. It is a fact that the wording "*ḫalīfat Allāh*", which appeared at the time of 'Abd al-Malik and during the years 202-209 AH of the rule of al-Ma'mūn, has sufficed for Islamologists to speak of a "caliphate" in the sense of a *theocracy* since the times of a Prophet of the Arabs in the town of Mecca on the Arabian Peninsula. As if words – especially when religion and politics come into play – cannot change their meaning radically within a relatively short period of time: The term "Republican" in the United States does not designate the same thing as one in a country with a monarchy, and a "senator" in the US and in the Roman Empire are quite different offices, not to mention the drastically different notions behind words like "God", "freedom", "scripture", "prophet" or "justice" etc.

Al-Ma'mūn's appropriation of this formula, which in the meantime has become historic, of an initially apocalyptic movement of the first century is understandable. He regarded himself as "*ḫalīfat Allāh*" in the role of the Iranian *dādbar* (legislator); because, just as the *Law* comes from *God* (the spelling of "God" and "law" are identical in Middle Persian!), so too do the power and the rule. As executor of divine law, he is God's representative. This Iranian, or in a broader sense, Ancient Near Eastern approach, reveals the reason why a new Moses and Aaron had to be called for. Only in this way could the replacement of messianic rule be accomplished by representation.

Moses and Aaron stand for a breaking point, which – in the spirit of a backward-looking reform – made a new development to already historic concepts possible.

The inscriptions on coinage of the years 202-205 after the *hiğra* provide information about the descent of Alī al-Riḍā: "'Alī bn Mūsā bn 'Alī bn Abī Ṭālib."[347]

The presence of a genealogy of the descendants of 'Ali demonstrates that a genealogy of the family of Muḥammad had already existed at this time. The personification of Christological concepts was accomplished. In order to legitimize rule, Christological concepts were used which ultimately led to the historicization of Christological titles. When messianic rule in representation of the Mahdī ended – the Mahdī was the de facto ruler, albeit incognito –, the legitimacy of rule became the most important issue.[348]

Thus it comes as no surprise that, in a period when a new role for the descendants of 'Alī was sought, the first Islamic coins were struck in Mecca. Whoever knows the genealogy of the family of 'Ali, also knows the genealogy of the family of Muḥammad in the sense of a new "House of David".

10.3 From Bakka to Makka

Thanks to the two coins struck in Mecca in the years 201, 203 of the Arabs, and to the coins which were struck during the tenure of 'Alī al-Riḍā in the years 202-205 of the Arabs, it can be determined that there was another attempt to redefine legitimacy of rule at this time. It is significant that mint activity in Mecca is only of any consequence after the turn of century, for the end of which doom had been prophecised for the Abbasids. It is also the first time that the location of Mecca seems to be of any importance. Mentioning the mint of Mecca provides the first clue of the town's significance concerning rule. Coins were not struck at locations that were politically insignificant unless their occupation had to be documented. How then did it come about that this location suddenly emerged from out of nowhere?

One explanation can be provided by a remark about Mānī from the book of heresies of the 'Abd al-Ǧabbār. The following is said about Mānī, the heretic:

> "He also praised Zoroaster, the prophet of the Mages. Mānī said: 'The light (al-nūr) chose him and sent him to the East whereas it sent Christ to the West.'"[349]

From an Iranian perspective it is perfectly reasonable to regard Zoroaster as the prophet of the East. He is reported to have originated from the eastern regions of Iran. Similarly, from an Iranian point of view, Christ is the prophet of the West as he originated from the western parts of the Iranian cultural sphere. Therefore it is only natural that he finds his final resting place in the extreme West.

The expectation of the second coming ends, once there is indication of a final resting place. The moment definite information pertaining to the end of a worldly career is available and a tomb is there to stand witness, the end of all aspirations has come. The designation of graves is an act of expulsion of the ghost of messianism. Jesus found his grave as the *Muḥammad* in the western sphere of the Iranian domains: He is buried in Medina. We know of many similar sights: Noah's tomb is in the Ǧazīra, the tomb of Jonah in Ninive, the tomb of ʿAlī Riḍā in Mašhad in Khorasan, that of ʿAlī in Mazār-i-Šarīf, not to mention the tombs of Ḥasan and Ḥusayn in Naǧaf and Karbala. With the beginning of orthodoxy holy men were laid to rest.

The following example makes it clear that the *Muḥammad* buried in Medina is the one named in the inscription in the Dome of the Rock in Jerusalem as *ʿĪsa bn Maryam*: Jeremy Johns complains that the inscription in the Dome of the Rock shows Muḥammad in a role that was not intended for him in the Qur'ān. It is the role of the intercessor on the Day of Judgment. According to Jeremy Johns there is a direct link between the Qur'ān and the teachings of the Prophet of the Arabs. He considers the *muḥammad* mentioned in the inscription of the Dome of the Rock to be the Prophet of the Arabs who found his final resting place in Medina. However, the role of the intercessor as it appears in the inscription in the Dome of the Rock, is inappropriate. In Jeremy Johns' opinion, Muḥammad obtained the role of intercessor for his community only 150 years later.

Of course, Jeremy Johns is right: His Muḥammad only pleads for his community on Judgment Day 150 years later. Then this happens by virtue of tradition; for, in the meantime, the *muḥammad* (chosen one, i.e., Jesus) has been transformed into the Meccan *Muḥammad*. In the inscription in the Dome of the Rock it is Jesus who is still spoken of as the intercessor on Judgment Day. This requires no Qur'ānic authority, reference to the Bible suffices. After the personification of the Christological title, *muḥammad* took the place of Jesus, now it must also take on the role of intercessor. In the end, everything remains the same: The role of intercessor formerly played by Jesus is now played by *Muḥammad*.[350]

It is not known what significance Mecca had prior to the establishment of the Sacred Site by the ʿAbbāsids. It is assumed that Mecca is the "Macoraba" of the geographer Ptolemy, although Macoraba is probably just the Greek transcription of *maġrib* (West). It is possible that the later location of the Kaʿba originally served as an Ethiopian Church, partly cut out of the rock. In the sixth century it is generally known that the Byzantines and their allies, the kings of Axum, fought the Himyarites in the area. The Axumites had trading colonies in the area south of Mecca, which is demonstrated by the existence of rock churches of Ethiopean style in ʿAṣīr. Mecca may well have gained in significance, when in the days of al-Ma'mūn, a new understanding of the Qur'ān set in. As the Syrian-Christian background of the Qur'ānic tradition of the Iranized *'Arabī* was no longer understood, a reinterpretation was attempted. So where could the Qur'ānic location of Bakka (Qur'ān 3:96) have been, if not in Mecca? Mecca did fit into the picture of a location in the desert in Old Testament style, an ideal place for creating a temple in an Old Testament setting. The Dome of the Rock represents a temple for a messianic movement; the temple to be built was needed for a chiliastic movement. In Jerusalem, Ma'mūn had his name inscribed in the inscription in the Dome of the Rock in place of 'Abd al-Malik's name. The inscription, however, remained unchanged.[351] This is an argument in favour of a reinterpretation of the role of the church in Mecca in a sacred site of the "representatives of the covenant of the peaceful", the new Moses and the new Aaron.

This would lead us to believe that Ma'mūn had understood the text in the same way as 'Abd al-Malik had done. This was probably not the case. Here Ma'mūn proceeds as he was taught to by Iranian tradition. The text of the Avesta was not always understood by everyone in Iran either, but had to be given a reading. Therefore the *rasm* of the text in the Dome of the Rock did not have to be changed to allow an Iranian reading. Amongst other things this led to the reading of "Muḥammad (bn) 'Abdallāh rasūluh(u)" (Muḥammad, offspring of 'Abdallāh, is his messenger), whereas at the time of 'Abd al-Malik, *muḥammad 'abd(u) llāhi wa rasūluh(u)* meant: "the chosen one is God's servant and apostle".

The establishment of the sacred site in connection with the tradition of a Meccan Prophet of the Arabs probably went along with the introduction of a fixed lunar calendar. As long as the *story* was still considered *history*, they could get by with a secular era according to local tradition. But when history started to be interpreted theologically, it became necessary to provide a sacred era. According to that, the Prophet lived in a holy place at a holy time.

Thus in Baghdad the way had been cleared for the rule of the Abbasids as sole mediators of salvation with their entourage of lawyers, Qur'ān readers and finders of tradition.

Later an Islamic eschatology formed on the basis of Syrian-Christian traditions. Syrian-Christian tradition was developed and flourished amazingly. A traditional report, attributed to 'Alī, who in the meantime had been accepted as a relative of Muḥammad, reads as follows:

> "After the swallowing up (of the Ṣufyānī's army) a caller will call out from heaven: 'Verily, the right is with the family of Muḥammad' at the beginning of the day. Then a caller will call out at the end of the day: 'Verily, the right is with the descendants (walad) of 'Īsa'."[352]

The decision is made by Heaven. Day and night form one unit, just like the rights of the descendants of Muḥammad and the rights of the descendants of Jesus (in the sense of the "House of David") do.

Just as the extent to which al-Ma'mūn had provided his rule with a theological foundation, his worldly power also declined. The caliph, as a mediator of salvation and priest of his *umma*, was ousted in the east of his domain. Up until the year 209 of the *hiğra* he was still named as the "Imām" in the inscriptions on coinage struck in East Iran. Then new rulers took his place. In Samarkand Ma'mūn is still referred to as "ḫalīfat Allāh" in the year 210 of the *hiğra* of the Prophet of the Arabs. In the same year he is no longer mentioned in the inscriptions on coins from Abarshahr. Instead the name found there is that of the new ruler of the Iranian East, the Ṭāḥirid Ṭalḥa. The Dirham for the year 217 in Samarkand is anonymous, as is the coin for Merv.[353]

Local governors in the West, the Aġlabids, had already pursued the replacement of the rule of the Abbasids decades earlier. In Yemen, for the year 217 of the *hiğra* of the Prophet of the Arabs, there is also an anonymous coin no longer mentioning Ma'mūn.[354]

One cannot avoid getting the impression that after the year 215 after the *hiğra* of the Prophet of the Arabs, Ma'mūn was possibly only known in Egypt, for in that year his name appeared there once more in the coin inscription of a Dirham.[355]

The copper coin from al-Quds (Jerusalem) of the year 217 after the *hiğra* of the Prophet of the Arabs bears no mention of his name, although it is said to have been issued in connection with a visit of Ma'mūn to Jerusalem.[356] During this visit, his name was allegedly set in the inscription in the Dome of the Rock instead of that of 'Abd al-Malik.

Afterwards Ma'mūn is reported to have travelled to the jihad on the border of the Byzantine Empire. He is said to have died in Tarsus in Cilicia. The location of his grave is not known. He died were St. Paul was born and in the manner of a Christian fighter as described in Paul's epistles.

This end during a campaign in the context of a jihad, is a nice topos of the traditional history of the 10th century CE. Since the last news of Ma'mūn exercising any power came from Egypt, the death he apparently met there would seem to be similar to the death of the last caliph of the alleged dynasty of the Umayyads: Marwān, who, as the last of his family, met his death in Egypt. It is worth noting that a river played an important role in bringing about the end of such personalities as Yazdegerd III (died on the Murghab river), Marwān II (drowned in the Nile) and the last king of the Visigoths (lost his life in the Guadalete river). They all met the same end as did the enemy of Constantine, the first Christian emperor, who lost his life in the river during the battle at the Milvian bridge in Rome. So it is obvious that the water of life always sides with the believers.

The removal of the mention of the Imām Ma'mūn in the coin inscriptions in Baghdad since the year 204 of the *hiğra* of the Prophet of the Arabs, may be related to a reform, which had led to a final break with the traditions of the first and second Islamic centuries. In the year 218 after the *hiğra* of the Prophet of the Arabs, the mention of the ruler's name in coin inscriptions followed a period of anonymous inscriptions with standard religious captions. Titles like "Imām" and "ḫal(ī)fat Allāh" were no longer to be found. Only the title "Amīr al-mu'minīn" was revived and reappeared in inscriptions, which named the ruler, around 870 CE.[357] So the "caliphate" before and after cannot have been a comparable institution as is constantly insisted upon by classical Islamology.

The meaning that Islamology attaches to the titles "caliph" and "amīr al-mu'minīn – commander of the faithful" is not older than the 10th century. This is reminiscent of the process of *translatio imperii*, which took place in Western Europe at approximately the same time. Therefore, just as the Germanic barbarians purported to be "new Romans" in a Roman Empire, the Iranian/Aramaic contemporaries of Ma'mūn felt at home as "new Arabs" in a caliphate, which had just as much or just as little in common with the previous government as was the case with Ancient Rome and the "Holy Roman Empire of the German Nation" of the 16th century.

It is interesting to note that there was no direct continuation of the coinage of Ma'mūn for Mecca in the year 203 of the *hiğra* of the Prophet of the Arabs. For the year 249 of the *hiğra* the earliest gold coinage is known in Mecca. The minting of silver coins was resumed in the year 253 of the *hiğra* and continued at irregular intervals over a period of several decades. Therefore it can be assumed that Mecca was now recognized for the first time as a new kind of religious center.[358] Equating Mecca/Makka with the Qur'ānic Bakka was evidently not generally accepted. Therefore the search for the place where Abraham had built his house was continued.

Ma'mūn's successor, al-Mu'taṣim-billāh, constructed a new residency, Samarrā'. This round town to the North of Baghdad, represents the realization of the plans for Baghdad to be a round city.

Samarrā' is the real successor to Ḥaṭrā. At the site of the temple there is now a mosque. Today it is still known for its minaret. It is constructed in the style of an ancient Mesopotamian *ziggurat*. The archaic style of the building could be an indication that, when it was constructed, it was intended to be linked to a Samaritan and Abrahamic past as the protagonist of a concept of antiquity.

Fig. 39: Minaret of the mosque of Samarrā'. It is in an archaizing Mesopotamian style. Is this a reminiscence of Samaria and the days of Abraham?

The Spanish *Chronica* of 741 still assumes that "Macca", which was considered to be the house of Abraham, was located "between Ur in Chaldaea and Harran in Mesopotamia". [359] Samarrā' is halfway between the two locations.

Apparently there was no agreement about the meaning of the name "Samarrā'". A new interpretation, based on popular etymology, was procured. Thus all doubt was removed. Samarrā' could be read as "Sāmarīya". It would also appear to have been understood as such for a long time. The court had been placed away from the "gift from God" (Baghdad), into a biblical location, Sāmarīya. When they no longer wanted to be Samaritans in Sāmarīya, a new reading came about. Instead of Samarrā', it was now read as *Surra man ra'a* ("pleased is the one who has seen it").

The new language rules after approximately 850 CE led to a new reading. This is symptomatic of a departure from early Islamic semantics and a shift to Islamic innovation in the sense of a state religion for the caliphate. The new dynasty and successor of the house of Sāsān was the "house of Muḥammad". Here again the Iranian view of the Prophet was linked to followers who were prepared to turn to their swords in order to put their message across. Thus, just as Zarathustra had once married his daughter to the heroic king, who granted him protection and shelter, his successor, Muḥammad, married his daughter, Faṭima, to the heroic 'Alī, famed for his intolerance of apostates and his mastery of the double-edged sword Ḏū l-fiqār (probably a reminiscence of the flaming sword of the caliphs).

11 New Beginning after al-Ma'mūn

With the death of al-Ma'mūn, traditional Islamic numismatics also regards the first period of the Abbasids to be over; after this a second phase followed. However, this is to be regarded as a completely fresh start.

The first epoch of the "Arab" religious development, which lasted until al-Ma'mūn's death, is characterized by Christian, or rather Christological concepts of a Syrian and Iranian kind. Only now does the basis of a new religion, Islam, begin to form: Law schools provided a turn to orthodoxy.

When Goethe's "apprentice wizard (Zauberlehrling)" had tried his piece and failed, he had to return his broom to his old master. Accordingly, care for the "Dēn" was handed back to experienced savants: the Islamic Law Schools. What was the Middle Persian Catechism of the Zoroastrians called again? "Thītag andarz ī pōryotkēschān"" ("collected advice of the old teachers"). The old teachers were aware of the dangers which threatened the Dīn. First and foremost: doubt. This was personified as the evil spirits Āz and Varan. The beginning of the Qur'ānic text (2:2) states the recipe old teachers use against doubt:

"This is the Scripture whereof there is no doubt."

Bibliography

Standard Works

*EI*²= The Encyclopaedia of Islam. New Edition, Leiden 1960.

Handwörterbuch des Islam. (corresponds to the EI), Leiden 1941.

A Catalogue of the Muḥammadan Coins in the British Museum.

Walker, Catalogue I=John Walker, A Catalogue of the Arab-Sassanian Coins, London 1941.

Walker, Catalogue II= John Walker, A Catalogue of the Arab-Byzantine and Post -Reform Umaiyad Coins, London 1956.

Sylloge of Islamic Coins in the Ashmolean.

Vol. I., The Pre-Reform Coinage of the Early Islamic Period, Oxford 2002.

Vol. X., Arabia and East Africa, Oxford 1999.

Encyclopaedia Iranica. http://www.iranicaonline.org

Journals

INS 10= Israel Numismatic Journal, Published by the Israel Numismatic Society, vol. 10, Jerusalem, 1988-89.

INS 13= Israel Numismatic Journal, Published by the Israel Numismatic Society, vol. 13, Jerusalem 1994-99.

Monographs and Articles

Paul Balog, Umayyad. 'Abbasid and Tulunid Glass Weights and Vessel Stamps, New York 1976.

Clifford Edmund Bosworth, The New Islamic Dynasties, Edinburgh 1996.

Patricia Crone & Martin Hinds, God's Caliph, Cambridge 1986.

Patricia Crone, Meccan Trade and the Rise of Islam, Oxford 1987.

Festgabe deutscher Iranisten zur 2500 Jahrfeier Irans, Stuttgart 1971.

Heinz Gaube, Arabosasanidische Numismatik, Braunschweig 1973.

Tony Goodwin, Arab-Byzantine Coinage, London 2005.

Matthias Henze, Syrische Danielapokalypse, München 2006.

Ryka Gyselen, Arab-Sasanian Copper Coinage, Wien 2000.

Der Koran. Übersetzung R. Paret, Stuttgart 1979.

Henri Lavoix, Catalogue des Monnaies Musulmanes de la Bibliothèque Nationale, Vol. I., Khalifes Orientaux, Paris 1887.

Christoph Luxenberg, Die Syro-Aramäische Lesart des Koran, Berlin 2004; English translation: The Syro-Aramaic Reading of the Koran - A Contribution to the Decoding of the Koran, Berlin 2007.

Wilferd Madelung, Religious and Ethnic Movements in Medieval Islam, Aldershot 1992.

Michael G. Morony, Iraq after the Muslim Conquest, Princeton 1984.

Tilman Nagel, Untersuchungen zur Entstehung des Abbasidischen Kalifates, Bonn 1972.

Georg Ostrogorsky, Geschichte des byzantinischen Staates. München 1952.

Gerd-Rüdiger Puin, Der Diwan von 'Umar ibn al-Hattab, Bonn 1970.

Gerrit J. Reinink & Bernhard H. Stolte (eds.), The Reign of Heraclius (610-641), Leuven 2002.

Gerrit J. Reinink, Syriac Christianity under Late Sasanian and Early Islamic Rule, Aldershot 2005.

Gustav Rothstein, Die Dynastie der Lahmiden in al-Ḥīra. Berlin 1899.

Gernot Rotter, Die Umayyaden und der Zweite Bürgerkrieg (680-692). Wiesbaden 1982.

Rüdiger Schmitt, Studia Grammatica Iranica, München 1986.

Augustus Spijkerman, The Coins of the Decapolis and Provincia Arabia, Jerusalem 1978.

Michael Stausberg, Die Religion Zarathushtras, Stuttgart 2002.

Muḥammad Abu-l-Faraj Al'Ush. Arab Islamic Coins preserved in the National Museum of Qatar, Doha 1984.

Julius Wellhausen, Die religiös-politischen Oppositionsparteien im alten Islam, Berlin 1901.

Julius Wellhausen, Das Arabische Reich und sein Sturz. Berlin 1902.

Evidence of a New Religion in Christian Literature "Under Islamic Rule"?

Karl-Heinz Ohlig

1 Methodical Preface

Apart from the Qur'ān, the allegedly "Islamic" empires did not leave behind any literary evidence in the first two centuries of their existence. The extensive religious-biographical and historiographical literature did not come into being before the 9th century (3rd century AH). Neither is there any evidence of a *new religion* current among the rulers of the Arabs in the Byzantine sources of this time; the Arabs were considered *vassals ("confoederati"*, the Arabic equivalent possibly "*Qurayš*") or *opponents*, without a new religion being mentioned. At that time, i.e., before the second half of the 7th century, many Christian regions had already lived under Arabic (and only putatively "*Islamic*") rule.

The Christians in this area left behind an abundance of literature, which reflects the flourishing intellectual life within their communities; by the end of the 8th century, they were even able to develop far-reaching missionary activities.[1] The status of Christianity under "Islamic rule" is not mentioned in this literature. This might be explained by the genres of the respective scriptures: theological tractates, sermons, letters, chronologies, lives of the saints, reports about the establishment of monasteries or philosophical publications and the like. However, one observation should make us suspicious from the very start: the contemporary state of affairs, which ought to be somehow reflected in such writings, is hardly touched upon, if we understand the "state of affairs" as referring to "Islamic rule". It is very difficult to explain why the monks and bishops of this time, some of whom had travelled extensively, should have wasted all their theological passion discussing "internal" Christian debates about doctrines like Monotheletism, Monenergism and others, when at the same time Christianity as a whole was being threatened by a totally new religion propagated by the new rulers.

Nevertheless, there are a number of texts which – according to the most frequent interpretation – present information on Islamic invasions, the religion of Islam and on Muḥammad. A few years ago, Robert G. Hoyland compiled them in such a way that they seemed to corroborate the

"Traditional Account", i.e., the information transmitted by the Islamic historiography of the 9th/10th century.[2] Moreover, for more than one hundred years, observations of this kind have been confirmed by experts on contemporary Syriac literature. Even today, this position is represented especially by Harald Suermann and also, at least to a certain degree, by researchers like H. J. W. Drijvers and G. N. Reinink. To date, the only historical-critical analysis of the material can be found in Yehuda D. Nevo and Judith Koren's monograph.[3]

Many questions arise when reading the commentaries about the literature examined. The first and most important problem is the interpretation of passages in literature on the basis of the Traditional Account, as Islamic historiography is generally considered to be objective. So whenever ships are mentioned, this is interpreted as referring to a *particular* sea battle, when "unrest" is spoken of, then it therefore must be about the first Arab civil war and so forth. *None of this is written in the original documents.* Even the term "*Muslim*" often found in the translations of Syriac texts is not present in the original, where the term used for the purported Muslims is *mhaggrāyē* ("Hagarenes") or *ṭayyāyē* (to be translated as "Arabs").

The literary genres of the texts were also disregarded: It is not easy to underlay the predicted eschatological battles in the apocalypses with historical facts, particularly not if they must be seen in literary continuity with "pre-Islamic" apocalypses.

The fact that the great chronological distance between the oldest manuscripts and the assumed time of composition of a document is often not critically investigated, is even more important, in many cases the problem is not even mentioned. However, every historian knows that in the process of every new copy, often spanning many centuries, amendments and corrections are made which correspond to the "standard of knowledge" of the respective scribes. The works of Josephus Flavius, for example, can definitely be traced back to him as their author, but it is also obvious that later Christian interpolations were inserted into his texts, e.g. about the figure of Jesus. This is also the case in the text this article is about. In each case we must examine individually if passages that clearly reflect the "level of knowledge" of the 9th century can belong to the original constituents of the text. The approach of many interpreters is often simply naïve and would not be accepted by any historian who, for example, analyzes texts of the Middle Ages. Unfortunately, even modern translators often get carried away and occasionally change the wording of the text, interpreting it in accordance with their seemingly higher "knowledge". If, for example, a text speaks of the Saracens or Ismaelites, the terms are simply translated as "Muslims".

R.G. Hoyland's book alone covers 872 pages, but so much space is not available here. Only the most important texts which come into question could be introduced and analyzed, and even they cannot be treated comprehensively. In a short contribution of less than a hundred pages, the focus will be on a few central issues relevant when investigating the sources in question:

(1) To begin with, and as a matter of course, the text to be investigated has to be taken seriously in its wording and may not be prematurely re-interpreted using the "knowledge" that the traditional literature of the 9th century appears to have, until it matches what exists.

(2) Furthermore, we have to find out what exactly is said about Arabs, Saracens, Ismaelites, Hagarenes/Agarenes, and which geographical evidence exists.

(3) The sparse evidence of the religious convictions of the Arabs should be documented and investigated with the question in mind as to whether they are to be interpreted as evidence for a new religion – Islam.

(4) Finally, it should be asked if and from which moment on there is knowledge of a Prophet of the Arabs.

2 The Designations "*Arabs, Saracens, Ismaelites* and *Hagarenes*" before the 7th Century

The terms stated here have a long "pre-Islamic" tradition which ought to be presented briefly. For this reason their usage in the literature of the 7th and 8th centuries must be justified if they are equated to the term "Muslims" by the translators. It is also important to find geographical assignations which were linked to the Arabs.

2.1 Arabs – Arabia

The etymological origin of the term Arab ("ʿ*arab*"; e.g. "those from the West" as seen from the Tigris;[4] Syriac: nomad; ʿ*erḇā:* Syriac: sheep; ʿ*ārāḇā* – "the low desert tract of the Jordan and the Dead Sea") should not be discussed further. The word was already used quite early on in the Middle East (e.g. in the inscriptions of Assyrian kings since the 9th century BCE) and in the Old Testament, firstly in Isaiah 13:20:

> "It will never be inhabited or lived in from generation to generation; nor will the Arab (Hebrew: עֲרָבִי – ʿᵃ*raḇī*; Greek: ἄραβες) pitch his tent there, nor will shepherds make their flocks lie down there."

ʿ*Araḇī* here obviously means "inhabitant of the steppe", from the Hebrew ʿᵃ*rāḇāh* – "steppe, desert". The text was probably written in the late 8th century BCE. Later, the word appears again in a series of passages up to the First Book of the Maccabees (5:39). At the end of the 1st or 2nd century BCE, the term "Arabs" always designates the non-Jewish tribes neighboring Israel in the south. Likewise the term "Arabia" can be found in the Old Testament, e.g. in Ez. 27:21:

> "Arabia (עֲרַב - *ʿarab̲*; ἀραβία) and all the princes of Kedar, they were your customers for lambs, rams and goats; for these they were your customers."

Here it is said of their inhabitants that they are traders (Ez. 27:21) or steppe inhabitants (Is. 13:20b, Jer. 3:2). Occasionally, they also appear as Israel's enemy, alongside the Philistines, especially in the Second Book of Chronicles (e.g. 2 Chr. 17:11; 21:16). An exact localization is difficult because *ʿarāb̲āh* also means "steppe/desert" in general in Hebrew. In one text there is the additional statement that it runs along both banks of the Jordan:

> "These are the words which Moses spoke to all Israel across the Jordan in the wilderness, in the Arabah opposite Suph, between Paran and Tophel and Laban and Hazeroth and Dizahab." (Deut. 1:1-2)

Furthermore, the designation "Sea of the Arabah" for the Dead Sea (Deut. 4:49; Joshua 3:16), is an indication that what is meant is probably not the biblical Arabia, which begins only towards the south of the Dead Sea. It is conceivable that the term designates the area from the Negev to Sinai, a territory inhabited by Nabateans. This corresponds to the information given in Paul's Letter to the Galatians: that "Mount Sinai" lies in "Arabia" (Gal. 4:25; Gal. 1:17 is vague, however, an area south-east of Damascus is suggested).

Ancient authors report different regions as Arabia.[5] In the case of Herodotus (died 430 BCE) it is Negev, Sinai and the territory situated to the east of Egypt, just as with Pliny the Elder (died 79 CE). The latter, however, also knows of an "Arabia of the Nomads" which can be found east of the Dead Sea. In Persian lists, especially since the time of Darius (died 486 BCE) an "Arabāya" has been mentioned which lies between Assyria and Egypt, an area probably ruled later from Ḥaṭra. According to Xenophon (died about 355 BCE), the Persian king Cyrus had troops march through Arabia, from Sardis to Babylon, east along the Euphrates.[6] Pliny also knew about this central Mesopotamian Arabia, east of the Euphrates and south of the Taurus Mountains.[7]

In the year 106 CE, the Romans also conquered the regions east of the Province of Judea and south of the Province of Syria, from about Damascus southwards until the northwesterly bank of the Red Sea. This region with both of its cities, Bosra *(Buṣrā)* in the north and Petra in the south (therefore also *Arabia Petraea*) was inhabited by Semitic Nabateans who used Nabatean, an Aramaic language with its own script as a written language, albeit with some kind of Arabic, – but not Classical Arabic –, as their spoken language, so the question whether they were genetically and linguistically Arabs is not so clear – at least if later definitions of "Arabs" and "Arabic" are used.

At the same time, there was an empire called "Arabiya" which was ruled by the king of Ḥaṭra, a city west of the upper reaches of the Tigris and near Assur (included in the Sassanid Empire in 241 CE), which stretched first of all from the Tigris in the west in the direction of or even up to the Euphrates.[8] The language of this "Arabia" was East Syriac, in the Sassanian period also Middle Persian. According to two homilies written by Isaac of Antioch in 459, "Arabs" conquered Bet Hur, a city situated in North Mesopotamia, around the middle of the 5th century.[9]

All of the Arabian regions mentioned up to now in which Arabs, also called *Ṭayyāyē,* lived,[10] have nothing to do with the *Arabian Peninsula* geographically, and the "Arabs" mentioned so far were ethnically more likely Arameans speaking variants of Aramaic or at least using Aramaic as their written language of choice.

In the Hellenistic period, the regions bordering on this region called "Arabia" in the south seem, occasionally, to be known as "Arabia deserta", a term probably designating the inner peninsula, and "Southern Arabia" or "Arabia felix", traditionally designating the Yemen. The equation "southern" and "felix" (Latin "fortunate; happy; lucky") goes back to the ambiguity in Latin (and also in Syriac and other Semitic languages) of the adjective *dextra,* which means "right = south (facing the sun at sunrise the *south* is to the *right*)", but also "happy; fortunate ("of the right [i.e., fortunate] hand")". The corresponding Semitic term is "yaman/yamīn", the root of which can be found in the names "Ben-jamin = 'son of the right/fortunate hand'" and "Yemen".[11]

Tribes from the Arabian Peninsula spread into the Middle East at a very early period:

> "Arabian dynasties established themselves everywhere on the land of the decaying Seleucid Empire. Arabian kinglets ruled not only in Emesa and Damascus, or the Itureans in parts of Syria, but also in Edessa and in Charax on the mouth of the Euphrates. In Egypt, where Arabs could be found in the desert to the east of the Nile as early as the early Achaemenid period, the district of Arabia, whose history can be followed through the centuries on the basis of papyrus discoveries, came about ... ."[12]

In the following centuries, these "migrations" continued. The ethnic and linguistic Arabs from the peninsula seem to have adopted the name "Arabs" from these new homes only in the course of these migrations to the north – into the Nabatean regions and into Mesopotamia. There, they continued to use their own language, although they also used the vernacular languages Syro-Aramaic or Greek for official correspondence and for their religious rites, depending on the environment.[13]

In the course of their settling down, these originally nomadic tribes – the Palmyrene empire is particularly known from the more recent pre-Islamic period –, then the Ghassanids in West Syria and the Lakhmids with their center Ḥīra at the end of the Euphrates, – but beyond that spread out over the whole of the Middle East, – largely took over the pre-Nicean Syrian Christianity common in the area.[14] The Ghassanids later converted to the Monophysitism of the Jacobites. There were Arab bishops and monks,[15] and Christianity "enriched that (*author's note: Arabic*) identity and raised it to a higher level".[16]

Later, when ʿAbd al-Malik and al-Walīd introduced Arabic as their official language, a process of re-discovery of their roots set in for the ethnic Arabs, so that the term *Arabia* was semantically narrowed to solely designate the Arabian Peninsula. At the beginning of the second half of the 8th century, Medina became the focus of attention, as a sanctuary was now erected there. Around the end of this century, the same happened in Mecca. This new vision was systematically solidified by the ostensibly historiographic literature of the 9th century written in Arabic, which shifted the alleged beginnings of their own – also religious – traditions on the Arabian Peninsula.

2.2 The Saracens

The Saracens are mentioned in many texts from the 2nd century CE on. Trying to clarify the etymology of this name, for which there is a series of hypotheses, Irfan Shahīd comes to the conclusion that this question cannot be clearly resolved. He quotes possible origins: Arabic *šarqī* = "western"; Arabic *sāriq* = "robber, looter"; Arabic *šrkt (šarikat)* = "company, confederation"; an Arabic tribe which Ptolemy called *sarakené* (Greek) and Stephanus of Byzantium mentions as *saraka* (6th century CE, Greek); Aramaic serak = barren land, emptiness, desert.[17]

Sven Dörper adds further derivations,[18] but agrees with Irfan Shahīd that none of the derivations is conclusive. Yet, Saint Jerome's explanation of the word added by S. Dörper is strange: the Saracens attribute their false name to their claim of descent from Sarah the mistress. Originally he understood Ismaelites, Agarenes and Saracens to be Midianites (*Maidanaei*).[19]

Then I. Shahīd examined the historical contexts in which the term originated and was developed.[20] As there were only two reliable early witnesses for the designation Saracens (Ptolemy[21] in the 2nd century and Ammianus Marcellinus[22] in the 4th century), assumptions can also be made here. Shahīd thinks that the most probable solution is the crucial date of the conquest of the Nabatean Empire by the Romans (106 CE) and its naming as "Provincia Arabia". The semi-nomadic and nomadic Arabs who did not belong to the

Roman province and its cities were then named "tent inhabitants", "robbers", "looters", perhaps after a tribe of a similar name or in a generally descriptive sense. This designation spread even more after the *Constitutio Antoniana* in the year 212, which awarded all male inhabitants of the cities of the Roman Empire Roman citizenship, but also spread after further Roman conquests (Osroene in 240 and Palmyra in 272). The Romans designated "eventually all Arabic nomads from the Euphrates to the Sinai Peninsula as *Saraceni*."[23] However, it is questionable as to whether these nomads could all be considered Arabs ethnically and linguistically.

Arabs in the North of the Ḥiǧāz and on the Sinai and, in addition to that, probably all Arabs outside of the cities to the east of the Euphrates are understood by Ptolemy to be Saracens.

From the 4th century on, Saracens appeared as nomadic groups, mostly with a negative connotation, who were perceived as robbers and looters. In his "Onomastikon" of biblical place names, Eusebius of Caesarea (died 339/340) equates the Saracens with the Ismaelites (and uses, somewhat unclearly, the terms *Pharan* and *Arabia*).[24]

Saint Jerome had written three biographies of monks before 393, which did him no credit because of their weird spirituality and obsession with miracles. In the fourth chapter of his *Vita Malchi*[25] he says that this Malchus was held up, plundered and brought into slavery along with a travelling group by the Saracens in the region between Nusaybin and Edessa.[26] In the same chapter, he also calls the Saracens "Ismaelites" without any further explanation – using the two terms synonymously.

In the 25th chapter of the "Vita Hilarionis – Life of the Saint Recluse Hilarion",[27] he speaks of Saracens again, this time in Southern Palestine, and narrates that they worship the morning star. There were also many "Saracens possessed by the devil", and Hilarion begs them imploringly "to worship God rather than stones".[28] This plea concerning astrolatry comes unexpectedly and is not explained further. In his comment to Amos in 406, Saint Jerome addresses the Saracens one more time.[29] In Amos 5:26, the cult of the "Sons of Horus" is criticized by the Israelites. Saint Jerome comments that this (male) God "has been worshipped by Saracens up to the present day".[30]

The worship of the "morning star", Venus, which is compared to the Greek goddess Aphrodite, is widespread in the whole of the Middle East and therefore also with the "Arabs". A. C. Klugkist thinks that this Venus cult was only current "in the North Arabian-Syrian desert (...) linked to al-'Uzza".[31] He explains in a footnote that al-'Uzza means "the strongest, most powerful". "Now we also find a god "Azīz, the strong, the powerful', the male equivalent of the same type of deity in the pre-Islamic Pantheon". In the northern border areas of the Syrian-Arabian desert both were worshipped. A. C. Klugkist assumes "that it was a matter of one original androgynous divinity" which "is distinguished as a male or female entity", depending on the area of circulation.[32] These observations could explain the change of the Saracens from the veneration of a female to a male deity, as Saint Jerome narrates.

2.3 The Biblical-genealogical Names of the Arabs: Ismaelites and Hagarenes/Hagarites

As Christianity was gaining more and more ground in the Middle East, the sacred scriptures of the Jews, the Old Testament of the Christians, began to have an ever greater impact on the way people thought in that area, not only in Jewish communities, but e.g. also among the Syro-Arameans, and later also with the Persians and "Arabs". Old Testament notions and patterns determined the "knowledge" of the world and its history. Accordingly, it was almost inevitable that (also) the terms "Arabs" and "Saracens" were paraphrased using the genealogical derivation of the Old Testament.

The tales of Abraham in the Book of Genesis are the point of reference, according to which his wife Sarah could bear him no children. Therefore, his wife asked him to go to her maidservant Hagar. She became pregnant and gave birth to a son, Ishmael (Gen. 16) and an angel announces to her that God will "greatly multiply your descendants so that they will be too many to count." (Gen. 16:10). Later, Sarah also gave birth to a son after all, the lawful heir Isaac (Gen. 21:9-21), through the influence of God. At Sarah's request, Abraham was – reluctantly – forced to cast out Hagar and Ishmael (Gen. 21:9-21). But once again God promised Hagar/Ishmael a large number of descendants (Gen. 21:13-18). Then it says:

> "20. God was with the lad [= Ishmael], and he grew; and he lived in the wilderness and became an archer. 21. He lived in the wilderness of Paran ..." (Gen. 21:20-21).

The most probable explanation is that the desert of P(h)aran is situated south-west of the Dead Sea.

The 25th chapter of Genesis is primarily about the descendants of Abraham, beginning with those of his son, Isaac. It is said of the "line" of Ishmael, "whom Hagar the Egyptian, Sarah's maid, bore to Abraham" (Gen. 25:12) that "the (twelve) sons of Ishmael" could be sub-divided "by their villages, and by their camps; twelve princes according to their tribes" (Gen. 25:16). Then it says "they settled from Havilah to Shur which is east of Egypt as one goes toward Assyria; he settled in defiance of all his relatives" (Gen. 25:18).[33] It is difficult to determine the area of settlement, it can probably be thought of as the territories south and south-east of Israel ("as one goes toward Assyria אַשּׁוּרָה – *ʾAšūrāh*").[34] Harald Suermann believes he knows more accurate details about *ʾAšūr*, – the ending "*-āh*" indicates direction –, however, has no evidence for this; "it more or less corresponds to the desert of Jathrib", later Medina.[35]

In any case, the tales about Hagar and Ishmael, the descriptions of their descendants as desert inhabitants, as well as the raids associated with them were enough to describe the "Arabs" and Saracens as Ismaelites for the purpose of the biblical derivation of peoples. Saint Jerome even considered *Ismaelites* (from Pharan) in connection with his translation of Eusebius' *Onomastikon* as the original designation for the Arabs who are "now (also) called Saracens."[36]

Apparently, Saint Jerome was also the first[37] to call the Ismaelites *Agareni*.[38] Likewise, in his Church History written between 443 and 450, Sozomen spoke of "Arabs who were called Ismaelites and later Saracens". He also specifically calls Hagar the mother of Ishmael.[39] Isidore of Seville also speaks about Ismaelites, Saracens ("*quasi a Sarra*") and Agarenes.[40] Thus all of these derivations were already common in pre-Islamic times.[41]

Other biblical genealogies are found more rarely. In the Syrian-Christian document "The Cave of Treasures"[42] from the 6th century, an "order of the derivation of the clans of Adam up until the Messiah" is allegedly provided.[43] Hagar and Ishmael are spoken of, but for the Arabs another derivation is suggested. In Genesis 25:1 it also says "Now Abraham took another wife, whose name was Keturah". She bore him six sons, one of whom was called Shuah (שׁוּחַ) (Gen. 25:2). Abraham sent his concubines' sons "away from his son Isaac eastward, to the land of the east" (Gen. 25:6). This is the passage the "Cave of Treasures" refers to, when it states that Keturah is the "daughter of Baktor, the king of the desert" and "the Arabs" descended from her son Shuah.[44]

How widespread this differing genealogy was, cannot be said. In any case, it did not affect the mainstream biblical classification of "Arabs" and "Saracens" as *Ismaelites* and *Hagarenes/Hagarites*, the only exception being the "History of Heraclius"[45], written by Pseudo-Sebeos, who once mentions "the children of Abraham, born of Hagar and Keturah". At least, both mothers were mentioned in the same place, however, without prompting any deeper reflection.

3 Christian Evidence under the Reign of the Arabs until about the End of the 8th Century

The documents normally used as sources for the historical and religious development of the Arabs are briefly introduced and checked for the *historical* information they actually contain. Beforehand, it should be taken into consideration that there are no critical editions to speak of and that there is often a very big time-gap between the oldest manuscripts and the presumed time of composition.

Likewise, the following interpretations can only be seen as provisional. It can be assumed that further material could still be found in libraries, museums and monasteries. So this short introduction is based on the texts that are already known and are being discussed at the moment. Precise distinctions of the character and theology of the publications conducted in this field cannot be introduced and analyzed here. Only what is said about the *ruling Arabs* in them will be examined.

Firstly, different pieces of evidence ("varia"), which are associated with an earlier and a later phase in literature, are introduced. Then the documents, representing the different genres and/or languages, are examined.

4 Different Texts up to the Middle of the 7th Century

4.1 Sophronius' Christmas Sermon

A Christmas sermon[46] is extant, written by Sophronius, Patriarch of Jerusalem from 634 to 638, of the year 634.[47] The Patriarch complained that the Christians of Jerusalem could not go to Bethlehem as usual at Christmas because of the Barbarians, especially the "godless Saracens" who blocked the way.[48] He interpreted this situation as a punishment for their own sins.

The Latin text extends the statements: He also calls the Saracens *Hagarenes* and *Ismaelites* and speaks of a siege and the occupation of Bethlehem.[49] The Greek text is only about the impossibility of going to Bethlehem, because Saracens are roaming about the whole area. The statements were added to the Latin text according to later Islamic historiography. Y. D. Nevo and J. Koren are to be agreed with, when they state that the bishop is not complaining about the *loss* of Bethlehem but the *impossibility of going on a pilgrimage* there at Christmas.[50] Obviously, no Arab occupation of the country had taken place yet, it was much more about the authorities' being unable to keep Saracen gangs under control. Saint Jerome had also reported about this in the 4th century, despite the Roman Empire, which was still functioning at the time. This was a "normal" or at least not unique situation of this period and was by no means evidence of a successful Islamic conquest. The fact that the Saracens are described as godless is not an indication of another religion, but a common insult for a gang of robbers, also for Christian gangs.

R. G. Hoyland presents another text by Sophronius from the year 636 or 637,[51] which addresses the aggression of Saracen troops who hurry from victory to victory, destroying villages and churches and looting cities and so forth, in the context of baptism. The manuscript is not publicly accessible, so its dating, the handwritten transmission and other questions must remain unclear (e.g. is it a matter of a later addition to a text about baptism?). This text, if it should exist, cannot come from the time of Sophronius, because it contradicts the archeological findings.[52] Also, a nice statement in the new "Encyclopedia of Ancient Christian Literature" should be registered:[53] "S.[ophronius] handed Jerusalem over to the Arab conquerors."[54] There is no historical source for this statement.

4.2 The Doctrina Jacobi Nuper Baptizati.

The document *Doctrina Jacobi nuper baptizati*[55] was allegedly written in the year 634, according to H. Suermann, however, only in 640.[56] It is a Christian and at the same time anti-Jewish piece of writing in which, however, only Jews are present. It is purportedly located in Carthage. Beforehand, it should be noted that in the opinion of Vincent Déroche, who critically edited the Greek text and compared it with all of the foreign translations, this text was handed down to us "in a hopelessly altered form" ("sous une forme irrémédiablement altérée")".[57] So, pieces of text can only be classified into the assumed historical contexts with the help of further criteria.

The anonymous author assumes that the forced baptism of Jews was ordered by Emperor Heraclius. H. Suermann summarizes the stories:

> "A Jewish merchant called Jacob who came to Africa refuses to be baptized at first, but is baptized, nevertheless, and thrown into prison. In prison he asks God to show him if it was good or bad for him to have been baptized. God reveals to him that it was good and that Christ is the Messiah".[58]

Consequently, he speaks to other Jews and wants to convince them of Jesus the Messiah. Another forcibly converted Jew reports of his brother from Caesarea (Palestine) and, according to the Doctrina Jacobi, he says:

> "Then my brother wrote to me that a false prophet had appeared. When (Sergius) Candidatus was killed by the Saracens, I was in Caesarea, said Abraham [my brother]. And the Jews rejoiced. They said that the prophet had accompanied the Saracens and he proclaimed the arrival of the Anointed One and Christ".[59]

The brother asked an "old man who was well-informed about scriptures" what he thought about the prophet of the Saracens.

> "He said, while sighing deeply: 'He is a fake because prophets do not come with swords and weapons'".

The man asked the brother to make some inquiries about the prophet. He did this and heard from those people who had met him

> "that there is nothing true about the prophet mentioned except where (people's) bloodshed is concerned. He (the prophet) claims namely to have the key to paradise which is unbelievable".

Although only "a prophet" is spoken about and the name Muḥammed is not mentioned, H. Suermann considers the Doctrina Jacobi to be the "oldest text which mentions Muḥammad".[60] It does indeed bother him that the dialogue does not mention the name of the prophet and moreover professes that he is still alive.[61] But he refuses suggestions to identify the prophet as someone else; it is about Muḥammad. No "particular role" was attributed to Muḥammad and the Muslims in the Jewish expectation of the Last Days. As revealed in the Doctrina Jacobi, they were only regarded as "part of the destruction precedent to the end of the world".[62]

What is to be made of this? First and foremost, it is a question of the text, which apparently, unlike the interpretation of H. Suermann, misconstrues almost all religious-historical contexts. The Jews could indeed associate hope with the takeover of the Arab autocracy and therefore the withdrawal of the anti-Jewish Byzantines, but not with the "prophet". Furthermore, the Muḥammad of the traditional account did not announce the coming of Christ or claim to possess the key to the kingdom of heaven and no longer moved around the Middle East with the conquering Saracens. Whether the information about the killing of the Byzantine representative, Sergios Candidatos, is historically true or a later addition must remain unclarified. Apart from that, it is first mentioned in the Chronographia[63] of Theophanes the Confessor in the 9th century and in a chronicle from the 13th century.[64]

It is out of the question that the prophet among the Saracens could have been Muḥammad, as the motto "*muḥammad*" was first brought to Palestine with 'Abd al-Malik's migration from the east where it originated. What is correct about the story is that the Arabian Peninsula is not spoken of, but the message is about a Saracen prophet who appeared in Palestine, in Caesarea where his brother Abraham lived.

It is possible to assume, as Y. D. Nevo and J. Koren do, that – due to the apocalyptic mood of that time – there could have been a real prophet on the Saracen voyages of conquest whom we know nothing about.[65] It is more probable, however, that the *Doctrina Jacobi* can be located at the time of the messianic expectations of "Abd al-Malik which are reflected in the construction of the Dome of the Rock at the end of the 7th century. At that time, the older expectations of the Last Days, linked to the tradition of Daniel, came to a head among Syrian and Arab Christians. Back then, Qur'ānic material, which indeed rarely talked about a man called "Muḥammad", but consistently spoke of a "prophet", was known in Jerusalem, Damascus and also in Caesarea. The prophet of the Saracens could have been understood by this. It is then obvious that the Jews shared the Syrian-Christians' expectations of the Last Days, which the apocalypses show and also the movement of ʿAbd al-Malik suggests.[66] But they also connected hope to the Saracen rule, although they thought it would instigate the catastrophe of the Last Days. The dialogue shows that they could not associate anything positive with the prophet; *this* prophet (of the Qurʾānic material and the Saracens) contradicted the Jewish idea of a prophet.

Likewise, it is conceivable for the time of ʿAbd al-Malik that non-Arab Christians wanted to use these contexts to do missionary work by means of fictitious dialogues by Jews. The backdating of the last years of Heraclius and his command for the forced baptism of Jews seems to have been consciously chosen as the "starter" of the dialogues. Historically speaking this is hardly "what really happened", as Heraclius separated the Middle East from the Byzantine Empire and had therefore revoked its immediate access. In the meantime Arab rulers had governed there.

It cannot be said for sure exactly what the historical truth is, as the problem of text transmission leaves many questions unanswered. On no account does the *Doctrina Jacobi* have anything to do with the prophet Muḥammad, nor does it reflect the circumstances in the later part of the first half of the 7th century. The localization in Carthage also seems to be fictitious and is appropriately relocated to Palestine through a narrative trick: the invention of a brother Abraham of Caesarea.

4.3 A Letter by Maximus the Confessor

Maximus the Confessor (about 580-622) was a fighter against the Christological doctrines of *monotheletism* and *monenergism* and probably lived in North Africa from 626. There, he enforced the dismissal of these Christological theses at synods and supported Pope Martin I in the same matter at a Lateran Council in Rome in 649. Therefore, as the Pope and Maximus the Confessor had gone against a *type* (edict) of the emperor, who had forbidden all discussions on this subject, both were arrested and brought to Byzantium in 653.[67] From there Maximus was first sent to Thrace in 655 but was then banished to the Black Sea by a synod in 622 because of his persistence after "his tongue had been cut off and his right hand had been chopped off".[68] He died in that same year.

This fate acts as a cynical comment on the alleged "culture of gentleness", in which he sees himself threatened by a "barbaric tribe of the desert", as he writes in a letter to Peter Illustrios (between 634 and 640):[69]

> "What is more wretched … to see a barbaric tribe in the desert who crosses a strange land as if it were their own? To see the culture of gentleness ravaged by

> horrible wild beasts? To see the Jewish people having for a long time enjoyed watching the blood of humans flow …?"[70]

What follows is an ugly anti-Jewish polemic. "The people of the desert" are not named more specifically. It could be about the Berbers but also, perhaps more likely, the Arabs. It is only mentioned in passing as the main direction of impact of the polemics is against the Jews. The accusations made against them are malicious stereotypes which cannot be historically verified. *They* are the real enemy for Maximus; the people of the desert at most only heightened the alleged misery.

If Maximus meant the Arabs, then he certainly did not consider them to be members of a new religion. His complete fervor was for the theological and especially the Christological conflicts of that time. He never mentions another religion.

The remarks about the people of the desert do not imply a conquest. Y. D. Nevo and J. Koren can be agreed with here, as they assume "a political vacuum" to be present in North Africa at that time, as "the previous owners (of the country) were effectively absent (and) could not keep control (…)."[71] So, barbaric people could roam the region.

In the year 632, Maximus interpreted the Book of Habakkuk 1:8[72] in which it is said of the Chaldeans that they are "keener than wolves of the steppe (NAS: "wolves in the evening"; Hebrew text: עֶרֶב *'äräḇ*, "evening"; with another vocalization *'araḇ* – "desert, Arabia"; Vulgata text: *velociores lupis vespertinis* = evening, west).

Maximus probably had a text version available in which "wolves of Arabia" were spoken of. He adds a commentary to this that the correct meaning is not "Arabia" but "the west". He explains that the wolves meant here are our sins of the flesh.[73] So this note has nothing to do with our matter.

4.4 The Dialogue between the Patriarch John and an Emir

The Syrian manuscript from the year 876 refers to a letter by the Patriarch John about a dialogue with an emir.[74] According to H. Suermann, it is about a dialogue between the Monophysite Patriarch John and the emir Sa'īd ibn Amīr, who is not mentioned by name in the text, which documents an early "debate between Christians and Muslims" in the year 644.[75]

Y. D. Nevo and J. Koren discuss different hypotheses on the people, location and date[76] and come to the conclusion that the dialogue must have taken place in 644, "in the years immediately following Mu'āwiya's acquisition of administrative control". According to them, the patriarch was John I and the emir or the chief administrator of Homs called 'Amr bn al-'Ās, but according to Michael the Syrian, it was Amru bn Sa'd.[77] The reason for this specification is that a conversation within this claimed context would have fitted to the year 644.[78]

In the letter, four topics are presented by the emir.[79] First, he asks if all Christians have the same gospel and why their faith differs so much. Secondly, it is about the Christological discussion and about the doctrine of the Trinity – was Jesus God or the son of God and which beliefs did Abraham and Moses have? Thirdly, it is explained that the Arabs accept Abraham and Moses as prophets, but not the rest of the Old Testament: hence the question whether the divine nature of Jesus and his birth of the Virgin Mary can be found in the laws (Pentateuch). Fourthly, he asks about the Christian laws (also the law of inheritance/succession) and calls on them to adhere to these laws or to comply with the rules of the Arabs.

Here an Arab, who holds the control, asks about the characteristics of the Christians. He asks the Monophysites, but also the Chalcedonians take part in the conversation. In the questions at no point does he show that he is a Muslim.

> "He is certainly not a Muslim. He shows no knowledge of or adherence to Islam and mentions neither Muḥammad or Islam nor the Qur'an."[80]

The emir simply wants to know what subject he is up against and what he should think of their teachings. He wants to know if they "possess enough adequately detailed laws" to govern their community themselves. "If not, they will have to comply with the Arab law which is now the new law[81] of the country".[82]

Y. D. Nevo and J. Koren think that the position of the emir, who only acknowledges the Pentateuch, was influenced by a non-rabbinical Jewish or Jewish-Christian or Samaritan sect.[83] After an unbiased reading of the conversation they are convinced that the emir did not take the Qur'ān into account because it did not exist; and the faith of the emir was not Islam but a form of "Basic Monotheism" with Jewish-Christian elements.[84]

So, if the document reproduces the conversation fairly reliably, then it will merely show the problems which the new Arab administration had with the many different groups of Christians and that they were looking to learn how to deal with them.

4.5 Letters by the East Syrian ("Nestorian") Patriarch Ishoyahb (Īšōʿyahb) III

Ishoyahb III (died in 659) answered the complaints of the clergy of Nineveh that the new Arab ruler preferred the Monophysites in one his 106 recorded letters. The patriarch answered that this was not true. God had given the control to the "Hagarene Arabs" (*tayyāye mhaggrāye*),[85] as they did not oppose "the Christian religion … but they praise our faith, they honor our priests and the saints of our Lord, they help the church and its monasteries."[86]

He also describes the status of the Christians, including the East Syrian ("Nestorian") ones, very positively: "The faith is at peace and flourishing".[87] Specifically, he states that the Monophysite thesis that "the almighty God suffered and died [on the cross – author], – for East Syrian Christians that Jesus, the Messiah, died",[88] is not supported by the Arabs.[89]

The context of this passage is translated in the following way by H. Suermann:

> "The heretics deceive you: what has happened was ordered by the zealots (Arabs). This is not true at all. In fact, the Arab Muslims do not come to the aid of those who say that the almighty God suffered and died. If it happens (...) that they help them, then you can tell the Muslims what is going on and convince them, as is right and proper".[90]

H. Suermann continues with laudable explanations on the relationship between Christians and Muslims.

Suspecting that the translation might not be appropriate – in any case it would be very difficult to explain why *Muslims* are mentioned this early – the Latin translation, which H. Suermann refers to, was checked by R. Duval. It turned out that in fact "Muslims" are never mentioned, the corresponding nouns to be found in the original being "*Arabes Mohammetani*" or simply "*Mohammetani*".[91] A comparison with the Syrian text, also edited by R. Duval, shows that in the quotation mentioned above "*Tayyāye m-Haggrāye*" (Hagarene Arabs) can be found twice and "*m-Haggrāye*" (Hagarene) once.[92]

This description of the Arabs as *Hagarenes* or *Hagarites*, which had been common since the time of Saint Jerome, has nothing to do with *Islam* and *Muslims*: It is a name for the Arabs according to biblical patterns. In the text, it is only said that at the time of Muʿāwiya, the Arabs gave the (other) Christians free rein and Christian life could flourish undisturbed. It remains a mystery, however, why translators do not simply translate what is clearly said in the text, instead of putting their own opinions, in this case that the Arabs of the time were, of course, Muslims, into the text.

In another text from his article, H. Suermann links his observations about "why Christianity was so weak and so many changed to Islam"[93] to a reference from a letter from Ishoyahb to Mar Simeon from the city of Rew Ardasir[94] which complains about deficits in spirituality and fervor in this region and calls for improvement. However, at no point in the letter can these claims be justified, not even in the Latin translation this time. The author of the letter refers to complaints and admonitions on behalf of the bishops responsible at given occasions, as was common at all times (and still is). Nothing can be read of a "conversion to Islam", but, however, of the danger of "losing faith". Here again, the "knowledge" of the seemingly true contexts, according to the Muslim historiography of the 9th century, is read into texts which themselves contain nothing of the kind. These texts are indeed valuable sources for their time, unless translators contaminate them with their own "knowledge".

We can conclude that Ishoyahb the Great was a witness for the life of the Christians under Arab rule at the time of Muʿāwiya, but he knows nothing of a new religion of the Arabs.

5 Various Texts Since the Second Half of the 7th century

5.1 Additions to the "Spiritual Meadow" (*Pratum Spirituale*) by John Moschus.

John Moschus (540/550–619/628) was the teacher and friend of Sophronius of Jerusalem (cf. text 1). He was a monk in a monastery near Jerusalem and went on journeys of many years in duration to visit monks in Egypt, on the Sinai Peninsula, and was at times accompanied by Sophronius. After the conquest of Jerusalem by the Persians in 614, he re-settled with Sophronius in the West and died in Rome.

Of course, he cannot contribute anything towards answering our questions himself, but he left his lifework behind, a spiritual book called *'hò leimón', Pratum spirituale* ("Spiritual Meadow")[95] which also provides reports and stories of his travels. This document was, however, edited for the first time much later, "possibly…by Sophronius".[96]

Thus we are concerned with this (at some time) finally-edited version of this text. It provides passages on our subject which can be traced back to John Moschus. He speaks, for example, of a "Saracenus gentilis",[97] of an abbot called John who stopped a destitute female Saracen from fornicating,[98] or about the rescue of a prisoner from the hands of three heathen Saracens.[99] These explanations, however, only give information about his lifetime, therefore "before Islam".

However, there is also an observation made which allegedly cannot be traced back to John Moschus, as he died too early. In the 19th story, it is explained that:

> "The godless Saracens conquered the Holy City of Christ, our Lord: Jerusalem… and they (wanted to) build this damn thing which they called a mosque (*midzgitha*) for their own worshippers."[100]

Only the Dome of the Rock can be meant by this "damn thing". These texts can only have been added as recently as 690, even if it is only the plans and not the finished construction which are being referred to. This was also way beyond the life of Sophronius (died 638). The anonymous person who added these passages to the Armenian translation could not have done this before 690/693.

Jerusalem was not "conquered", except in traditional reports. It was somewhat unknown Arabs princes, then Muʿāwiyah and later on ʿAbd al-Malik who "took over" the rule from the Byzantines. Accordingly, the 9th century is the most probable candidate for the interpolation.

The fact that the Dome of the Rock is also called "midzgitha" (Arabic: masǧid – lit.: "place of prosternation", Modern Arabic: "mosque"), which is a common term in Syrian Christianity for a church, indicates another religion just as inconclusively as the mention of their "own worshippers" – Protestants could also have spoken of Catholics in these terms and vice versa. The interpolator of these statements could only then have meant a *separate religion* of the Saracens if he belonged to it himself in the 9th century, when a conquest of Jerusalem is commented on.

5.2 The "History of Heraclius" by Pseudo-Sebeos[101]

Sebeos, to whom the anonymous and untitled parts, only extant in the Armenian version of the 'History of Heraclius', were wrongly attributed,[102] was bishop of Bagratunis in around 660. The document narrates the purported history between 590 and 661 CE, which is fit into a pattern of apocalyptic interpretation: The Last Days are initiated by the return of the Jews to the Promised Land and this return is achieved by the Jews' alliance with the Arabs, the "fourth beast" of the Book of Daniel[103] and a victory over Heraclius' troops. The author hopes that the Arabs will soon be defeated.[104]

In the 30th chapter[105] of the *History of Heraclius*[106], the author/editor provides information on the Arabs which he claims to have received from Arab prisoners of war.[107] The pieces of text that are interesting for our subject commence with talk of the descendants of the "slave" (Ishmael). It reads as follows (translated from the German translation by H. Suermann):

> "They (the Jews) took the path into the desert and reached the children of Ishmael in Arabia: they asked them for help and let them know that, according to the Bible, they were related. Although they readily believed in this kinship, the Jews could not convince the whole majority of the people because their cults were so different. [*beginning of interpolation; my gray shading*] At this time, there was a child of Ishmael, a trader named Muḥammad: He introduced himself to them, as God commanded, as a preacher and as the way of truth and taught them about Abraham's God, as he was very well-educated and versed in the stories of Moses. As the commandment came from above, everybody united under the authority of one for the unity of the Law and after they had left the cult of nothingness, they came back to the living God, who

> had revealed himself to Father Abraham. Muḥammad commanded them not to eat dead animals, not to drink wine, not to lie and not to go whoring. He added to this 'God promised this land to Abraham and his descendants under oath for evermore. He acted according to his promise, as he loved Israel. You are sons of Abraham and now God is carrying out his promise to Abraham and his descendants. Love Abraham's God, take possession of the region that God gave to your father Abraham and no-one can stand up to you in battle'[*end of the interpolation; my gray shading*].[108] Everyone from Weiwlay (in F. Macler: Ewiwlay; in R. W. Thomas: Ewila) to Sur came together against Egypt. They left the desert of Pharan split between 12 tribes, according to the race of their patriarch. They divided the 12000 children of Israel between the 12 tribes, 1000 per tribe in order to lead them into the region of Israel. They moved from encampment to encampment in accordance with the order of their patriarchs: Nabeuth, Keda (,) Abdiwl, Mosamb, Masmay, Idovmay, Mase, Koldat, Theman, Yetur, Naphes and Kedmay [Gen. 25:13-15, *author's addition*]. These were the tribes of Ishmael. They proceeded to Rabbath Moab in the territory of Ruben, because half of the Greek army was camping in Arabia. They attacked them unexpectedly, threw them to the wolves and routed Theodorus, the brother of Emperor Heraclius and went back to Arabia. Everyone who remained from the people of the children of Ishmael came to unite with them and they formed a big army. Then they sent a message to the Greek emperor which said: 'God promised this land to our father Abraham and his descendants: give it to us peacefully and we will not advance into your territory. If you refuse, we will take away with usury what you took for yourself'. The emperor refused and said, without giving them a satisfactory answer: 'The land belongs to me. Your inheritance is the desert. Go in peace to your land'."[109]

Pseudo-Sebeos refers to many details in his *History*. Regarding our issue, H. Suermann says:

> "He (the author) seems to be very informed about the history of the origins of Islam".[110]

Nevertheless, he regretfully notes that:

> "....the information on the location of places complies more with the biblical tradition than with the geography of that time. In Sebeos' book, Arabia is the area east of Sinai up to the other side of the Dead Sea. It is not the Arabian Peninsula, but the Arabia of Paul the Apostle. The ancestral homeland of the Arabs is, according to Sebeos, the desert of Pharan. This interpretation, however, leads to a wrong and incorrect geographical understanding of the happenings of that time."[111]

According to H. Suermann, the "right" geographical understanding would be the traditional report. If the standards of the 9th century are ignored, the anonymous author abides by biblical patterns, which are given in Gen. 25:12-18, so in this respect, he does not have any kind of "new" information on the "children of Ishmael" at his disposal. In principle, he also knows just as little about the historical contexts. The fact that the Jews moved to join the Arabs and united their own twelve tribes with the – according to Genesis 25:13-15 – twelve tribes of the Ismaelites, and formed "a big army" with them, contradicts all we know about history. In order to make this description historically plausible, reference is made to the "Constitution of Medina", according to which "Jews and Muslims made up a community",[112] which is historically audacious. Here, a fairytale – the "Constitution of Medina" is a much later idealization – is used to help provide historical reality for another fairytale.

All the same, this historical interpretation has a historical background. As (Christians like) the Jews were characterized by eschatological expectations in the 6th and 7th centuries, the Arab acquisition of autocracy initially triggered off eschatological hopes in the Jews. (A Jewish apocalypse confirms this [as already in text 2 above] with the Jewish hopes linked to Arab rule).[113] With the aid of the Arabs sent by God, the perspective of a triumph over the Greeks was possible, as Heraclius represented an anti-Jewish program.

However, the mention of a joint victory of the Arabs and Jews over Theodorus, Heraclius' brother, mixes up the historical contexts. Using clever propaganda, Theodorus succeeded in getting the Arabs, especially the Ghassanids, who had been disappointed by Byzantium up to this time, to support Heraclius with subsidiary troops in the battle against the Persians. The connection of Theodorus to the Arab troops is accurate, but policy of alliances is turned topsy-turvy.

The author's meager knowledge of historical contexts also becomes clear in the rest of the 30th chapter of the "History of Heraclius". All of the details about the activities of the Ismaelites, partly under King "Amr" ('Umar?), are inaccurate or wrong. It can only be said for certain that he (the author) knew that the Arabs had taken over the country of the Byzantines and he had heard several stories or rumors about battles, but not more.[114]

In Chapter 37, Pseudo-Sebeos mentions bloody conflicts amongst the Arabs themselves without locating or defining them more precisely, but these ended with Mu'āwiya:

> "When he had conquered them, he governed over all of the possessions of the children of Ishmael and made peace with everyone".[115]

At least Mu'āwiya's role in the establishment of peace among the Arabs is seen accurately; here the information is more exact on this point than in

Chapter 30, as it did not stem from an author so very dominated by biblical and theological thinking. However, the time before and after this remains unclear and without elaboration. On the other hand, it should be noted that no other religion of the Arabs is spoken of in these lines.

Having said this, Sebeos' entirely biblical-theological reflections in Chapter 30 contradict the remarks about Muḥammad and his preaching.[116] In doing so, information extending beyond the Old Testament, especially the name of the prophet, become important. Therefore, it must be assumed that subsequent interpolations were added to an older prototype. The older prototype uses several lines of Genesis as an aid when describing the speedy eventuation in terms of the apocalyptic expectation of the Last Days, according to the tradition of Daniel: the Jews gather themselves together to fight in order to seize possession of Palestine in the spirit of eschatological expectations. With this in mind, they join forces with the Arabs, the new eschatological threat, who, according to the model of the Book of Genesis, must be completely understood as the children of Ishmael from the Desert of Pharan – a concept which is conceivable in the context of Muʿāwiya.

If we understand the statements about Muḥammad to be later interpolations, then the strange disparity of the text in Chapter 30 can be explained. An older piece of biblical-apocalyptical historical interpretation that brings together Jews and Arabs as eschatological phenomena is then used by a scribe and/or a new editor as a starting point to add further information.

This can be attributed to a time in which the term "Muḥammad" was already historicized – without having been linked with the Arabian Peninsula yet – and Muḥammad was understood to be a preacher or a merchant. Chronologically, the use of the name Muḥammad is a hint that editorial work might have taken place in about the middle of the 8th century, or even two or three decades earlier or later. The assertions about the preaching of Muḥammad mention his demands "not to eat from a dead animal, not to drink wine, not to tell lies and not to go whoring". These individual instructions which can also be found in the Qur'ān – a general ban on wine only in later parts –, but the earlier statements of abrogated passages[117] are supplemented by explanations of the theological concept of Muḥammad, who was "very well-educated"; the proclamation of Abraham's living God[118] and the "unity of the Law", the abolition of a cult of nothingness, the right to Palestine "that God gave to your father Abraham" – a right – and here it is wrong again – that Muḥammad is said to have assured the Jews.

Side note

The notion that this prophet was also a merchant – which the Sīra and not the Qur'ān claims about Muḥammad – could go back to an old tradition about the establishment of Christianity in Southern Arabia, according to which a merchant in Ḥīra became a Christian and did missionary work after his return to Nağrān.[119] In the chronicle of Seert, also called Nestorian history, the following passage can be found; which refers to the 6th century:

> "In the era of Yezdegerd, there was a merchant called Hannan in the area of Najran in the Yemen who was well-known in the region. One day, he set off to do some trade in Constantinople and then returned to his country. Afterwards, he wanted to proceed to Persia, but when he got back to Hira he visited Christians frequently and got to know their teachings. He was baptized and stayed there for a while. Then he went back to his home country and invited the people to adopt his belief. He baptized the people of his house and many others of his country and the surrounding area. After that, he won over the inhabitants of Himar and the neighboring regions of Ethiopia with the support of several others who had joined him."[120]

The Nestorian history was written in the early 11th century. R. Tardy presumes, however, that the remarks about Nağrān were taken from another text, a much older book of the Himyarites, and are historically plausible.[121] In any case, the story of a preaching Arab merchant might be a kind of "wanderlegende", the prototype of a legend which spreads to many countries. This could explain the profession of the Prophet – merchant – both in Pseudo-Sebeos and in the Sīra. Likewise, the stories of the 9th century, that Muḥammad received revelations in the Cave of *Ḥirā'*, could go back to the above-mentioned religious re-orientation of the merchant/prophet of the story in similar sounding *Ḥīra*.

Pseudo-Sebeos' remarks about Muḥammad bear witness to a sympathy for this preacher and his teachings, but at the same time he is used for the confirmation of the Law and the Jewish right to the Promised Land. It is also striking that only motives from his preaching, that were positive in a Jewish sense, (except for the wine ban) were mentioned. Statements of this kind are rather strange in a Christian book of the time, which the *History of Heraclius* is everywhere else. The editor can neither have been a Christian nor a Muslim; the latter would hardly have assigned the Jews the Holy Land as a God-given property. The passages can most likely be explained if a Jewish editor[122] – in the first decades of the 8th century at the earliest – is presumed, who appreciated the Arab rule and the basic principles of their teachings – interpreted from a Jewish perspective –, believed it to be better than the Greek rule anyway and who then formulated Jewish demands using his "knowledge" of Muḥammad.

It is explained in another passage that the Jews lived in peace for a while so they decided to construct the Temple of Solomon again. But the Hagarites/ Ismaelites took away the Jews' place of prayer at this point and claimed it for themselves.[123] This passage implies knowledge of the construction (or the intended construction) of the Dome of the Rock.

A letter from Muʿāwiya to Emperor Constans mentioned by Pseudo-Sebeos calls on the readers to "Reject this Jesus and convert to the Great God whom I serve, the God of our father Abraham". According to the letter, Jesus could not even save himself from the Jews, how could he possibly save the Byzantines from Muʿāwiya?[124]

Since Y. D. Nevo and J. Koren do not only assume a "Basic Monotheism" for a part of the Arab population, but obviously also for Muʿāwiya, they do not deal with these passages critically.[125] The iconographical design of the coinage is, however, sufficient proof that Muʿāwiya was a *Christian* ruler, from whose mouth the demand for a rejection of Jesus is inconceivable. Whoever rejects Jesus and scorns him for his failure, will hardly have coins struck with crosses on them. This letter is a later invention and one of the not too rare interpolations. Due to the exclusive and positive emphasis on the belief of "our father Abraham", we must again assume the work of a Jewish interpolator.

5.2 Anastasius of Sinai

Anastasius Sinaïta (Anastasius of Sinai) (610-701?) was a "monk, priest (and abbot) in the Sinai Monastery".[126] He left behind an extensive work which, above all, was about the theological conflicts in Egypt and Syria, about Monophysitism and Monotheletism on the one hand and about the Syrian, occasionally new-Chalcedonian theology, which he represented, on the other. Moreover, he wrote edifying and exegetical publications.

As his works are attributed to the (later) half of the 7th century, it is amazing, given the traditional historiography, that he did not concern himself with the threat of an alleged *new religion* at all, let alone mention it by its name: *Islam!* Not even the Arabs were a problem for him, although they were the rulers of the country.

The latter are mentioned peripherally in his most important anti-Monophysite work, the "Hodegos" (Latin: "Viae dux"; before 690).[127] This document has an extremely complex transmission in manuscripts and has been edited many times. An originally independent treatise and scholia (glosses) seem to have been integrated into it.[128]

If the text is taken as it is now, short statements about the theology of the Arabs can be found. The reader is admonished to first reject some misconceptions that the opponents might have "about us" before conversing with them.

> "If we want to discuss with Arabs, we should anathematize the one who says '(there are) two Gods', or the one who claims that 'God carnally conceived a

> son' or the one who worships any other creature in heaven or on earth apart from God".[129]

What we are dealing with here are Monophysite convictions, whose theses both the Arabs and Anastasius himself reject.

There is nothing to be said against attributing these passages to Anastasius. Arab convictions at the time of ʿAbd al-Malik are correctly reproduced. As Anastasius is not in any way upset about this matter nor rectifies it, it can be assumed that he deemed the Arab wishes to be justified; they should not get the impression that he thinks like this. His Christology is so constituted that he does not believe in two Gods, nor in a conception of the flesh, nor in the worship of a creature – for him the human Jesus is "merely", a little inaccurately, united with the divine Logos in one hypostasis. Most notably, he does not describe the Arabs in any way as members of *another religion*, but as people *with a specific Christology*.

Another passage can also be understood in a similar way when he polemizes against the Severians. Severus was a more moderate Monophysite who rejected that Jesus Christ existed "in" two natures. He accuses the Severians of thinking about "ugly and unseemly things like the genitalia of men and women" when they hear the word "nature".

> "For this reason, they shun this word (nature) as if they were pupils of the Saracens, because when they hear about the birth and conception of God, they blaspheme immediately because they can only interpret this term as referring to marriage, fertilization and the union of the flesh."[130]

This drastic and untheological perception of nature may have helped the Saracens to defend their Christology – that Jesus was not God, but the Messiah and ambassador – in everyday discussions. Therefore, they could indeed be understood as Christians, like the (heretic) Severians.[131]

In his work *Quaestiones et Responsiones* (Questions and Responses),[132] Anastasius discusses 154 exegetical questions.[133] The short question 126 refers to the statement that the devil (Satan) was brought down because he did not want to kneel down in front of a man. Anastasius regards this as something coming from the myths of the Greeks and Arabs. Regarding the latter, this could, at least from hearsay, indicate knowledge of Qurʾānic material (cf. surah 38:71-78)

5.3 Jacob of Edessa (9)

Jacob (died in 708) was a significant Syrian theologian "one of the most productive authors and scholars of his time".[134] He was born near Antioch in around 633 and became bishop of Edessa in 684.[135] Evidently, he fell out with his surroundings again and again, and therefore, he resigned from his office of bishop after four years. For limited periods of time he lived in various Syrian monasteries and he was also active as bishop again for several months.

He wrote exegetical, canonical and philological books and chronicles, as well as translating Greek writings, including Aristotle, into Syriac.[136] However, "many of his works are passed on in fragments, mostly integrated into the works of later authors including Michael the Great".[137]

Islam is not mentioned in any of his writings! In one passage of a comment on the First Book of Kings 14:21-26, in which the sin of Judas under King Rehoboam and the following punishment of an attack on the part of the Egyptian king is spoken of, he comments

> "Christ hit us because of (our) many sins and wrongdoings and we are subjected to the hard burden of the Arabs".[138]

Jacob is not talking about battles at this point, but only about the Arab rule which he sees as a punishment for sins, just like John bar Penkaye (cf. text 12). Towards the end of the 7th century, the Arab rule was no longer felt to be positive, as in the time of Muʿāwiya, it was a now seen as a punishment. But conflicts with a *new religion* were probably not seen as problem, as he was not aware of any such thing.

Another chronicle is also attributed to Jacob of Edessa which is only extant in fragments in a manuscript from the 10th or 11th century.[139] Here, a person called Muḥammad is spoken of, who went around the regions of Palestine, Arabia (?), Phoenicia and Tyre as a merchant;[140] he is also called the first king of the Arabs who ruled for seven years and Abu Bakr for two years after him.[141] The information, however, that the Arab kingdom began in the 11th year of Heraclius and the 31st year of Ḳosrow, is more correct [142]

It is very difficult to explain that the same author, who writes of Muḥammad as a *merchant*, writes about him as a *king* a few lines later and also that the term inseparably linked to the name in Islam – "prophet" – with its religious meaning, is not even mentioned once. The fact that a person called Muḥammad is obviously seen as a historical figure would indicate that the text is from the 8th century, but then again he would have to appear as "prophet" and "messenger". Why is only a "merchant" and "king" spoken about here?[143] The text remains opaque, both in its meaning and in its chronological assignations. The isolated naming of Muḥammad, however, rules out an authorship of Jacob of Edessa.

5.4 Arabs as "heathens" in the late 7th century (10)

In 1902 J.-B. Chabot translated, commented on and published three volumes of Syrian synodal records. A synod from the year 676 prohibited a close coexistence with the (Arab) pagans; above all the intermarriage of Christian women with pagan men was disallowed. The custom of having two wives and being buried in magnificent clothes was likewise rejected.[144]

While the reference to two (instead of four) wives could be seen as Islamic to a certain extent, a burial in splendid clothes is strange in Islam. So it might indeed be "pagans" and their customs, which were obviously attractive for Christians, that this text warns about.

Likewise, in a letter to his priests, the Syriac-Orthodox patriarch Anastasius II advises against the participation in pagan festivals, their sacrifices and, above all, intermarriage of Christian women with pagans. He is, however, a little forgiving in the case that someone should return repentant.[145]

Arab rule and life with Arabs belonged to the religious milieu of these texts. Therefore, Y. D. Nevo and J. Koren come to the clear conclusion:

> "The local Arab population is pagan and they are holding pagan rites."[146]

However, the *Arabs* are not explicitly named. Y. D. Nevo and J. Koren think that the Syrian word "ḥanpē" used in the source is "a normal term for the invading Arabs".[147] Whether this is conclusive or not remains unclear. But as the existence of other pagan populations in traditionally Christian regions cannot be assumed, let alone that it exerted a kind of fascination, it seems very likely that what the text is dealing with, is Arab paganism.

However, it must be considered that the complaints of the bishops about paganism do not implicitly have to mean real pagans, but more likely people who were not baptized or non-Christians. This is how Isaac of Antioch, in two homilies of "about the year 459",[148] depicts the conquest of the city Bet Hur in Northern Mesopotamia by Arabs (about the middle of the 5th century).[149] He sees the capture as God's punishment for the fact that "the Christian inhabitants [of the city; *author's note*] still had memories of pagan cults. The devotion [of Christians; *author's note*] to pagan cults was the reason that the Arabs plague this city like a hostage of God".[150] In the following, Isaac goes into more details about these cults.

This look back into the past could convey that the much later synods could maybe also have referred to Christians who practiced pagan customs, ethics and cults with their accusations against "pagans". But it could also mean that larger groups of them, besides the Christian Arabs, were still "real pagans", as Nevo and Koren believe - perhaps with a "Basic Monotheism".[151] The connection with them and above all marriage with their women was considered a threat to Christianity on the part of the official church, probably because of the dominant position of the ruling Arabs.

5.5 Remarks in chronicles

Ancient chronicles should not be read with modern historical standards in mind. Apart from the continuous re-workings in the course of the handwritten transmission processes, they often offer a mixture of factual knowledge and fictional narratives, led by interests and religious interpretations, which serve to classify and master what was deemed history.

In any case, historical events are often reflected in those documents. Y. D. Nevo and J. Koren refer, for example, to a chronicle by Joshua the Stylite, which describes the years 395 to 506 CE, in which we can learn a lot about "battles, sieges, ambushes and attacks".[152]

The chronicles to be introduced now do not offer us much material, at least if we expect reports on Arab invasions, battles, their religion and so on, but the authors were at least contemporaries of the events. There can only be one reason that none, or hardly any of these things are reported: The things that are desired to be confirmed, did not happen in this way. The contemporaries simply did not know the narratives of the traditional report at that time.

5.6 A Syrian chronicle (11)[153]

In a Syrian chronicle[154] written by an East Syrian monk in South Iraq between 670 and 680,[155] the victory of the Arabs over Byzantium and the Sassanians is reflected upon:

> "Verily, the victory of the sons of Ismael, who conquered and defeated two of these strong kingdoms, was really God's (victory) who, up to this point, had not allowed them to seize Constantinople. Therefore, the victory is God's and should not be attributed to the Arabs. It is the Dome of Abraham which we have not found (nothing could be found out about what it is; *author's note*), but we know that the blessed Abraham, who was rich and wanted to remove himself from the desire of the Canaanites, preferred living in remote places and in the expansive open deserts, and as is common for those who live in tents, he built this place to worship God and to offer his sacrifices to him. Whichever (place) it happens to be that exists today, it got its name from him. The memory of the place survived along with that of the generation. For the Arabs are doing nothing other than maintaining this custom if they worship God at this place, as is proper for those who [offer] worship [to] the forefather of their race (lit.: the father who is the leader of their people; *author's note*). Hazor, who was called the head of the empire by the scriptures, belongs to the Arabs. It was called Medina, after the name Madian, Abraham's fourth son with Keturah, it. It was also called Yathrib."[156]

So the Ismaelites prevailed over two empires. This was seen as an act of God, who had not allowed them to "seize Constantinople" until then. In the year

674, Mu'āwiyah's attempt to conquer this city failed, and as Mu'āwiyah's loss of the East, which followed this event, is not yet spoken of, the chronicles seem to have been written in the year of preparation for the fight (?).

It is said of the Arabs that they worship God in the spirit of Abraham and at the place where Abraham built a cult site for God. Hence, even the Arabs are doing nothing new; it is even proper for them to continue maintaining the old customs and offer worship to their forefather Abraham. The author does not know anything else about the religion of the Arabs. By no means has he heard of a new Arab religion.

After this, thoughts follow on the cult site of Abraham, which the author admits "we" know nothing about. Then, biblical associations follow. According to Gen. 12, Abraham left his home country and built an altar in Canaan (Gen. 12:7), then he moved further away to the "mountain on the east of Bethel, (...) with Bethel on the west and Ai on the east; and there he built an altar to the Lord and called upon the name of the Lord," (Gen. 12:8) which he visited again some time later and called upon the name of the Lord there. (Gen. 13:4)

Then it says in the chronicle that "Hazor belongs to the Arabs". Hazor is situated, according to the Book of Joshua 11:10-15, in the northern half of Canaan and was "the head of all these kingdoms" which Joshua conquered (Josh. 11:10). This Hazor is put on a level with Medina – also an etymological, biblical derivation is found for this from Midian, one of Keturah's sons (Gen. 25:1-2, 1 Chr. 1:32) and then it is added that it refers to Yathrib.

All of this is very confusing, as one city in Palestine is equated with Medina/Yathrib. This can be explained in two ways: The author could have written this after the construction of the temple in Medina in the year 756, but then his remarks about the Arabs would have to be more precise and he could not have conducted his geography using only biblical references.

The second and more probable alternative is that a later scribe added Medina and Yathrib in the second half of the 8th century at the earliest. Unfortunately, this cannot be verified on the basis of the handwriting.

The author did not know where Abraham's cult site could be found and speculates with biblical references. But the scribe names Medina/Yathrib, so he knew more. He must have made the addition before the last third of the 8th century because Mecca was not made use of.

H. Suermann would disagree, he follows Islamic tradition:[157] "The author ...recognizes Mecca as the place where the tradition (of Abraham; *author's note*) has survived". Or: "Mecca is not mentioned by name, but the Dome of Abraham is identified as Mecca". H. Suermann thinks that the statements about Medina are comments "following" the remarks about Mecca.[158] As is so often the case, a source is re-interpreted according to the author's own beliefs, "knowledge" or taste. If sources are taken seriously so little, then why deal with them at all?

5.7 John (Jochanan) bar Penkayê

John bar Penkaye was an (East) Syrian Christian and probably a monk. At about the end of the 7th century (R. G. Hoyland: 687 CE)[159] he wrote a chronicle, a kind of world history of which only fragments remain. In these the Arab rule is depicted as God's punishment for the Christian heresies of Monophysitism and Chalcedonism. Then it said that they won two kingdoms "without a fight or a battle. (...) God gave them the victory".[160]

Obviously John knows nothing of the fights, but does indeed want to clarify that the Arab rule was wanted by God (and was therefore handed over peacefully). The Arabs seized their autocracy peacefully after the withdrawal of the Byzantines and the collapse of the Sassanian dynasty. He does report of conflicts between the Arabs which were ended by Muʿāwiyah: "Since Muʿāwiyah came to power, peace was established in the world henceforth."[161] We can agree with H. Suermann when he writes that John

> "sees the Arab Empire as the rule of an ethnic group and not the rule of a religious group."[162]

Other fragments attributed to the chronicle and documented especially by A. Mingana,[163] go into further detail about events after Muʿāwiyah's death which are evocative of details of the traditional report.[164] As their authenticity is questionable and cannot be judged at the moment, they should not be discussed further here.[165]

5.8 Thomas the Presbyter

A Syrian manuscript from the 8th century was attributed to a presbyter called Thomas.[166] It provides geographical references, ancestral charts and so forth. Statements about the *Arabs*, but not about a *new religion* can be found in it, although it is stated that they also killed many monks. Two remarks must be considered:

> "In the year 947 (635/636)....the Arabs invaded the whole of Syria, moved to Persia and conquered it."[167]
>
> "In the year 945 (634)....a battle took place between the Romans and the Arabs of Muḥammad in Palestine...12 miles east of Gaza....The Arabs devastated the whole region."[168]

The information given here causes difficulties: The rule of the Arabs in Persia did not begin until the end of the Sassanian dynasty, so much later, and cities, churches and monasteries were, according to archeological findings, not destroyed at that time. Whether a presence of Muḥammad at the battle should be pointed out by the term "Arabs of Muḥammad" or only the point of identification of the Arabs can remain unclear. The remarks can, by no means, go back to Thomas the Presbyter. The name was probably first given around the middle of the 8th century and a religious function of Muḥammad is not spoken of. Therefore, it must deal with statements which originated later, probably from the 9th century, in which the Arab rule is then traced back to an earlier invasion, without mentioning a new religion yet.

5.9 A list of caliphs (14)

A. Palmer records, in an English translation, a list of Muḥammad's caliphs (without ʿAlī) up to Al-Walīd[169] with details of their periods of government. A. Palmer assumes (with a question mark) that the fragments of a manuscript are from the 9th century and that the text was written in the years between 705 and 715.[170]

However, this enumeration requires knowledge of the traditional report. As it is said of Muḥammad "he came to earth (was born) (in the year) 932 (620/621)… and ruled for seven years"[171] and because ʿAlī is missing, there are uncertainties (A. Palmer thinks that the seven years were just – without thought? – taken over from Jacob of Edessa).[172] Apparently the order of the traditional report was not available in its complete form. Maybe the late 8th century can be presumed as the time of origin.

5.10 A further list (15)

A further list, translated from Arabic into Syriac – A. Palmer's[173] assumption – continued the list of caliphs up to Yazīd, a son of ʿAbd al-Malik.[174] Here, Muḥammad is also called the Messenger of God. On the one hand ʿAlī is also missing and, on the other hand, there are arithmetical problems with the times stated for Muḥammad. Also here, the time of origin is believed to be the end of the 8th century (at the earliest).

5.11 A Maronite chronicle (16)

This chronicle extends to the year 684 "and was probably written by someone who was alive then."[175] The fragmentary manuscripts from the 8th or 9th centuries[176] present ecclesiastical events at the time of Muʿāwiyah which cannot be checked. ʿAlī is also mentioned in one sentence:

> "Also ʿAlī again threatened to wage war against Muʿāwiyah, but they struck him down while he was praying in al-Ḥīra and they killed him. Then Muʿāwiyah wanted to go to Al-Ḥīra…."[177]

ʿAlī is neither mentioned in the Qur'ān, nor in inscriptions or coinage of the first two centuries. He first appears in the literature of the 9th century. Likewise, a Maronite church is first spoken about in the course of the late 8th century, even if it allegedly goes back to the early figure of Maron. This chronicle, and therefore also the fragment in question, can only have been written as recently as the 9th century.

5.12 A Spanish chronicle (17)

A small text from Spain which, however, "comes from the Orient" dates back to a chronicle which extends to the year 741. There it is said of Muḥammad that he belongs by birth to a "famous tribe of his people", he is "very wise" and the Arabs "respect and worship him because they consider him to be an apostle/messenger of God and a prophet".[178]

This text resembles the insertion in the "History of Heraclius" by Pseudo-Sebeos in its statement about Muḥammad (he is "wise"). The Arab estimation of Muḥammad is mentioned, but the author does not polemize against it. The Christian writer had no problem with this judgment. Due to the way the name of Muḥammad is mentioned and the way he is described, the text can be dated back to the last decades of the first half of the 8th century.

5.13 Syrian Apocalypses of the 7th and 8th Centuries

Apocalypses[179] are a very specific genre. They occur in times of severe affliction which are perceived as being hopeless. In such a situation, apocalypses preach hope for a speedy turnaround caused by God. The fact that this salvation is imminent is justified by looking back in history. Typically, an array of great empires are depicted, mostly following the Book of Daniel. After the annihilation of the last great empire and a dreadful plight under the rulership of the Anti-Christ, God will take action and cause a change.

In substance, apocalypses want to convey hope; they are a kind of "comfort and perseverance literature" at times of great distress. In order to support their reasoning, they work with biblical references and associations, into the patterns of which the course of history is adapted.

The Christian apocalypses have a model for their composition, the biblical Book of Daniel, which they are attached to. It is the "prototype of this genre (...) so that the interpretation of the Book of Daniel can be looked upon as a piece of world history."[180]

Aphrahat already commented on the vision in Daniel as a sequence of the four empires of the Babylonians, the Medes, the Greeks and the Romans without associating any hope with this story.[181] Ephrem, the Syrian, modified the empires: Babylon, Media, Persia and Macedonia, after which the reign of Christ comes to an end. Ephrem's second sermon[182] does not seem to be an apocalyptic adaptation of Daniel, but more a sermon with apocalyptic characteristics. An example of a complete apocalypse is the "pre-Islamic" "*Syriac Apocalypse of Daniel*"[183] from the 4th or 5th century.[184]

Apocalyptic moods and their corresponding literary manifestations could not only be found with Christians at that time, but also with Jews, who at first coupled their hopes with the Arab rulership, which had displaced the often anti-Jewish Byzantine regiment. But apocalyptic tendencies seem to be linked to the program of ʿAbd al-Malik as well; the construction of the Dome of the Rock and the expectation of a second coming of Christ in Jerusalem, some of which is also adopted into the Qurʾān. A kind of messianism linked to the apocalyptic literature can be proved for long periods of the 8th century and beyond:

> "During the first four centuries of Islamic rule, Messianic hopes ran high among the peoples of the Caliphate. Christians, Jews and Zoroastrians subjected (...) their traditions of a Messiah, (...) who (...) would come or return to the world (...) to the rule of a new and alien religion." (this does not apply to the first one and a half centuries; *author's note*)."

In the following, B. Lewis discusses comparable notions of a *mahdi* in Islam.[185]

The horrors which precede the anticipated end always follow the same pattern, as H. Suermann observes in Pseudo-Ephrem:

> "Sacrilege proliferates on the earth, the screams ascend to God who then intervenes…".[186]

The crimes of the wicked are atrocious; the scribes give free rein to their almost sadist imagination. As a rule, these stereotypical narratives bear no relation to historical reality; they are the inverted picture which gives the anticipated end an even more colorful intensity.

Just how little they are descriptions of real crimes on the part of the Arabs can be made clear by a reference to Ephrem, the Syrian, who writes in his second sermon (later re-workings, however, cannot be ruled out because the horrors are referred to after mentioning the people of Hagar):[187]

> "Behold! The adornment of men is destroyed, the jewelry of women is taken away. With lances (...) the old men are impaled, the son is separated from his father, the daughter from her mother, brother from brother, sister from sister. They will kill the bridegroom in bed and drive the bride out of the nuptial chamber (...), take the mother away from her child and imprison her. (...) The child is trampled by the hoofs of horses, camels and draft animals. (...) The ends of the earth will be ravaged, the cities will capitulate, there will be many people killed on the earth, all nations will be subjected… ."[188]

Remarks of this kind are present in all the apocalypses of the 7th and 8th centuries, now (also) with reference to the Arabs. These are not descriptions of historical events, but apocalyptic stereotypes with which the whole world history is proven to be wicked, corrupt, sinful and evil before the end.

5.14 The Sermon of Pseudo-Ephrem (18)

The sermon (Sermon 5)[189] that is incorrectly attributed to Ephrem, the Syrian, is problematic both concerning the time of its composition and the context of the text. As the Arabs are spoken of in Chapters 3 and 4, they are dated by some to be in the first half of the 7th century. G. J. Reinick suggests the last third of the 7th century (before 680 or 683);[190] but this dating applies at most to Chapters 3 and 4. W. Bousset had already realized that these Chapters could have been interpolated:

> "the alternative future prophesies in Chapter 5 do not take account of Chapters 3 and 4 anymore".[191]

Further parts of the apocalypse could also have been inserted later. According to the whole structure, however, – here H. Suermann can be assumed to be correct – "the content of the sermon [fits; *author's note*] into the 4th century"[192] and has been extended and edited many times. However, the displacement of the Romans by the "Assyrians", probably meaning the Persians,[193] and the Roman resistance, probably under Heraclius,[194] hint at the 6th and early 7th century – it is information that cannot be traced back to Ephrem. But even these few lines could have been inserted into an older manuscript. It may also be possible, however, that the conflicts between "Romans" and Persians meant here are events which had already taken place at the time of Ephrem.

It is Chapters 3 and 4 that are important to us, "about the Muslims", – or – as H. Suermann[195] correctly says: "about Hagar's offspring from the desert"[196] (neither Arabs nor Saracens nor Ismaelites appear by name, and definitely no Muslims!), – who were later inserted into the text that already existed. In Chapter 3, the descendants of Hagar, who come from the desert, are mentioned in an attachment, after general comments on the screams of the desperate which go up to heaven and cause God to intervene. These are described as the Sons of Hagar and Heralds of the Anti-Christ, drawing on the Book of Genesis.

> "And a people will emerge from the wilderness, the progeny of Hagar, the handmaid of Sarah, (the offspring) who hold fast to the covenant with Abraham (...) set in motion to come in the name of (...) Heralds of the Son of Destruction."

According to Matthew 24:30, there is talk of signs in heaven and the following wars of the disbelievers:[197]

> "And then the sign of the Son of Man will appear in the sky, and then all the tribes of the earth will mourn, and they will see the Son of Man coming on the clouds of the sky with power and great glory."

In Chapter 4, terrible proceedings are talked about. They could go back to a model or prototype. Only one reference to the "marauders" ("the marauding nation will prevail"[198]) could be understood as an indication of the offspring of Hagar – it cannot be decided if it was originally a part of the text or if it was added later. They loot, murder, take prisoners, raise tributes, enslave and tear families apart. The latter is based on Genesis 20 (Sarah's visit to Abimelech) and Genesis 37:12-41 (Joseph sold into slavery [by his brothers]). The hope is expressed that this captivity will end prosperously. However, this hope is not quite so clear for the present; at the end it is understood to be the work of the marauding nation;

> "And after the people have endured much on earth, and hope that now peace has arrived, they will start raising tribute and everyone will be fearful of them. Lawlessness will intensify on the earth (...)."[199]

Little information can be filtered out because of the biblical-apocalyptic patterns, actually only that the offspring of Hagar now rule and that this fact is evaluated negatively. The fact that they came out of the desert is not information, but biblical topos.

As in Chapter 4, hope for a positive outcome is expressed, following biblical references (Gen 20 and 37) and the editor does not contradict this. H. Suermann believes that he is of the same opinion regarding the current situation. Therefore, he is convinced "that the interpolation of Chapters 3 and 4 originated from the first instance of Arab attacks from the desert",[200] probably because it was hoped that a speedy end to the horrors was still possible.

Having said that, the coming of Hagar's descendants from the desert cannot be understood as a historical message. The interpolated text ends without a comforting perspective: they will raise tribute and injustice and godlessness will increase. Here, an establishment of Arab rule seems to be insinuated, which does not make the assumption compulsory that Chapters 3 and 4 were interpolated before the time of Muʿāwiyah, on the contrary.

Further reigns of terror follow (Chapter 5). The Huns cause terrible massacres (Chapter 6) and so forth. The 8th Chapter begins as follows:

> "Then the Lord will bring in his peace, which attests the glorification among the heavens, and once the empire of the Romans will spring and flourish in its place (...)."[201]

Nevertheless, the godlessness increases again and the "Son of Destruction", the Anti-Christ comes and enters Jerusalem.[202] He rules for a long time but finally God sends Enoch and Elijah, who are murdered (Chapter 11), then Gabriel and Michael and finally Christ (Chapter 12) "And Christ will reign forever and be king (...)."[203]

It is interesting that the anticipated and positively interpreted rule of the Romans is only mentioned in one sentence at the beginning of Chapter 8; this is overrun with new terror in the next sentence, and this is the way it stays until the coming of Christ. Statements of this kind do not seem to have arisen from a situation in which real hope was still possible for the Byzantines around the time of Heraclius; the Roman Empire appears to be an insignificant, although positive episode. It may be more easily assumed that the Romans no longer sparked any hope: that was in the past. The terror is much more established. However, it is not associated with the Arabs after Chapter 4.

Therefore, it is not surprising either that the Roman rule is not mentioned in Chapter 4. H. Suermann thinks:

> "The question arises whether the interpolator deliberately left this (the rebuilding of the Roman Empire; *author's note*) out for ideological-theological reasons or he simply forgot it".

H. Suermann believes that it is probable that it was forgotten.[204]

Now, it is very unlikely that an interpolator forgets something which is important to him. More likely it did not matter to him and this corresponds to the further description of the apocalyptic sermon. The text is strangely indifferent when it comes to historical places, and this also affects the detailed horror stories about the Huns. It is more likely to be assumed that a short-term dominance of the Romans, maybe under Heraclius, was already a matter of the past and had no bearing on the interpolator of Chapters 3 and 4. Nor is there any talk of "quick conquests that the Muslims made".[205]

Therefore, to summarize, we come to the conclusion that the editor must have believed that Chapters 3 and 4 about Hagar's progeny had to be inserted, because there was a negative assessment of the Arab rule. Nothing is said about *their religion* or even *Islam*. In the introduction of Hagar's offspring out of the desert at the beginning of the third Chapter, it merely says that they "hold fast to the covenant with Abraham". This might refer to Abraham's faith, which could not be judged negatively. It is, however, more probable that it was only said that this offspring continued to refer to Abraham and derive from him.

At this point, Ephrem's *Second Sermon*[206] should be considered. It also shows an apocalyptic pattern: there are conflicts among the peoples – the Assyrians (Persians) temporarily oust the Romans from their territories, many crimes take place,[207] Gog, Magog and the Huns wreak havoc and finally the Anti-Christ comes and seduces everyone. Enoch and Elijah are sent and killed by the Anti-Christ and then Gabriel and Michael follow and Christ, too.

At the beginning, after the Assyrians and the Romans are mentioned, the people from the desert are spoken of in a few lines; "and a people will come out of the desert, the son of Hagar, Sarah's handmaid, who received the covenant of Abraham, the husband of both Sarah and Hagar", a herald of the Anti-Christ.[208]

The terrors that followed are not verbally linked with this people so that it seems that an interpolation in a text existing already must be assumed. This original text itself could also be a later construction, but at least its composition in the time of Ephrem is not totally impossible, as the Syrian Apocalypse of Daniel was also written then (4th or 5th century). Sermons of this character were indeed possible at that time.

5.15 The Apocalypse of Pseudo-Methodius (19)

The apocalypse, which originated in Syria, probably near Edessa[209] and, according to F. J. Martinez, near the Sinjar Mountains in Northern Mesopotamia in the second half of the 7th century,[210] is available as a critical edition,[211] which is an exception for literature of this kind.

This text, which was apparently translated from several Syriac versions into Greek, of which there were also various adaptations before the end of the 7th century, and from the Greek, according to the opinion of G. J. Reinick, was translated into Latin[212] "before about 727". Therefore, it became "one of the most influential and widespread apocalyptic texts in Byzantium and the medieval West".[213]

All of the text versions available are, according to G. J. Reinick, from a Syrian original which cannot be reconstructed for sure, so that he makes do by taking one of the Syrian versions (from the Codex Vat. Syr. 58) as a basis and putting all the variants of the text from other Syrian manuscripts and also the Greek and Latin translations into the critical apparatus.[214]

The apocalypse of Pseudo-Methodius[215] is divided into 14 verses or chapters and deals with the stories from Adam to the end of the world. The first Chapters 1-10 provide a rather confusing "history of the world" which uses a series of other sources[216] beyond the Bible and awkwardly joins the respective motifs, names and associations together. In this order, Chapter 5, which is about Ishmael and his sons, that is the Arabs, seems to be interpolated. The fact that this is the case is shown in the following chapters, which return to the time before the Arabs and do not continue the narrative thread.

At the beginning of the 8th Chapter the apocalyptic pattern of the four kingdoms that followed one another is developed: the people of Cush[217] made way for the Macedonians, they, in turn, for the Greeks and the latter for the Romans. In the following, a lot of effort is made by the people of Cush to provide information on the background of Alexander the Great as well as the Kings of Byzantium and finally the Romans.

> "concerning this (kingdom [of the Greeks; *author's note*]), the blessed David spoke: 'Cush (Ethiopia) will quickly stretch out her hands to God.' [Psalm 68:31 – *author's note*]. For there is no people or kingdom on earth that can defeat the kingdom of the Christians".[218]

In Chapter 10, narratives about the Greeks and Romans follow who destroyed Israel under Vespasian and Titus after the death of the "Messiah". The last comment indicates an East Syrian author for whom the messiahship (not the divine sonship of Jesus) is important and the cross additionally a central date of salvation.[219]

The last two sentences of Chapter 10 lead on to Ishmael: "the sons of Ishmael, the sons of Hagar, whom Daniel called 'the Arm (forces) of the South' [Dan 11:15 – *author's note*] (...)."[220] (The sons of Ishmael are presented once again – without reference to the 6th Chapter). Hence, the last millennium begins in Chapter 11. This Chapter is entirely about the Ismaelites. In Chapter 12 general thoughts follow that not all Israelites are real Israelites, not all Christians are real Christians and that many Christians defect and many become weak in the final days.

> "And lots of those who were sons of the church will renounce the true Christian faith and the holy cross and the glorious sacraments. And without force and torture and blows they will deny Christ and will stand beside the disbelievers".[221]

There is always a (holy) "remainder" left.

In the 13th Chapter – the self-chastisement of the Christians, as addressed in the 12th Chapter, was connected with the sons of Ishmael who destroyed everything. Then the Greek king enters, defeats them and drives them back into the Desert of Yathrib where they also came from. A new Greek rulership is formed, the Byzantines, during which everything flourishes. It is "the last peace (before? – *author's note*) of the completion of the world".[222]

Then the gates "of the North"[223] will open and everything will be subjected to terrible atrocities again (Dan. 11). The king of the Greeks will go up to Jerusalem and "then the Son of Destruction will be revealed".[224]

Chapter 14 deals with the Anti-Christ who takes over the government in Capernaum and subdues everything. The Greek king erects the holy cross on mount Golgotha, which is then exalted to heaven. But everyone runs after the seducer who works miracles but otherwise only makes trouble. He enters Jerusalem.

> "And at the arrival of our Lord from heaven, he (the Anti-Christ) will be (...) at the mercy of (...) the Gehenna of fire (...) but our Lord Jesus Christ will find us worthy of his heavenly kingdom."[225]

G. J. Reinick believes that Pseudo-Methodius originated in the later period of ʿAbd al-Malik because of his religious propaganda documented "via the construction of the Dome of the Rock on Temple Square".[226] Reinick does not only see a separation from the Byzantine crown and the right to autocracy in ʿAbd al-Malik's activities, but also the proclamation of a new religion – Islam. According to him, this religion is then polemically antagonized in Pseudo-Methodius.[227] It is confronted with the ideal image of the (Byzantine) "last emperor", who governs "the final Christian empire";[228] he alone has claim to Jerusalem because of the cross. He is seen by Pseudo-Methodius as a second Alexander, a new Constantine or Jovian, who had followed the apostate Julian.[229] However, it must be noted that this "ideal Greek emperor" is only the *ruler before the end*. The term "last emperor" is a little inaccurate, as new terrors follow soon after.

Maybe Reinick's dating can be accepted and also the "Sitz-im-Leben" (position in life) that he designed for the formation of this apocalypse in ʿAbd al-Malik's conflict with Byzantium. But he assumes that the construction of the Dome of the Rock and particularly its inscriptions reveal an anti-Christian manifesto. However, this contradicts the contemporary sources. Therefore, the question has to be asked what can be read about the Ismaelites and their religion in Pseudo-Methodius, even if it is not the dominant opinion among the other interpreters.

If we begin with Chapter 11 (and the last sentences of Chapter 10), as well as further statements which probably belonged to the original text, the sons of Ismael would come, according to the exegesis of Daniel at that time, from the South (Dan. 11).[230] After the end of the Persian Empire, they would gather in the desert of Jathrib. According to Gen. 16:12 they are called "wild donkeys" (there the angel says to Hagar).

> "He [Ishmael] will be a wild donkey of a man,
> His hand will be against everyone,
> And everyone's hand will be against him;"

He is a fright for everyone. God let him and his sons "take possession of the Christian kingdom, not because he loves them to enter the Christian kingdom, but because of the injustice and sin committed by the Christians".[231]

The Ismaelites are dressed like harlots and commit sexual and unnatural digressions. Persia will be destroyed: Sicily (!), the country of the Romans, the islands of the sea, Egypt and Syria – so roughly the empire of ʿAbd al-Malik, with the exception of Sicily, which was first conquered in the 9th century. Tolls and poll tax are enforced upon everyone. They are led by tyrants who do not pity the poor and ridicule the Elders, on the whole a "chastisement"[232] for the Christians. Around the end of the Chapter, the crimes increase to apocalyptic standards; the "wild donkey" tortures everyone. "For these barbaric tyrants are not human, they are sons of the desert", they kill small children and priests and sleep with their wives and daughters; they are "a furnace of ordeal for all Christians".[233]

Noticeably, little historical information can be found about the Ismaelites, except regarding the wide area of their rulership and their crimes. What is historically certain is the aversion to them and the Christians' feeling of being menaced by them. The Ismaelites are confronted with and set against the (long-established?) Christians, but Chapter 11 does not provide evidence of *another religion.*

This seems, however, to be present in Chapter 12, which has a theologically-reflexive tone, in which "the ordeal/test" that the Christians were subjected to, is described. They renounce the Messiah freely and join the disbelievers. However, the apocalyptic statements are not linked verbally to the Ismaelites, but describe the lapse in faith expected at the end. If a link should be seen to the Ismaelites mentioned above, then the chronological attribution is difficult, as ʿAbd al-Malik documented a clear affirmation to the Servant of God, Jesus the Messiah; only the (Greek) teachings of the *divine sonship* are rejected. Chapter 11 can definitely be understood to be a complaint by the Christians about the hardship and certainly often inhumane foreign rule they experienced, as is imaginable at the time of ʿAbd al-Malik. In the opinion of almost all analysts, however, the narration in Chapter 12 goes beyond this, which would mean that a *new religion* of the Ismaelites could be referred to. This would first be conceivable at around the end of the 8th century at the earliest. But the text *itself* does not suggest this conclusion at all if the Bed of Procrustes of Islamic historiography of the 9th century is not taken into consideration. Chapter 12 probably simply provides an non-specific apocalyptic scenario according to the announcements from the New Testament; in the end many Messiahs are proclaimed and the big lapse in faith comes "at the end" (cf. the "Apocalypse of Mark" [Mark 13; cf. the parallels Matthew 24 and Luke 20]. If this should be the case, then these expectations have nothing to do with the history of the Arabs.

Initially this reflexive tone is continued in Chapter 13, and the Ismaelites are made responsible for the decline in Christian services and respect for the priests. The crimes described now are harmless in comparison to those mentioned previously in Chapter 12. Once again, the areas ruled by the Ismaelites are named[234] and in all of these regions it is said that "the Christians have no savior".[235]

According to Reinick, the term "savior" also has a "Christological connotation",[236] so it is not only the rescue/salvation from the oppressors. However, this is not clear unless, as Reinick does, a solid Islamic Empire ruling at that time is assumed. It should, however, be taken into consideration that the next sentence says: "the king of the Greeks will move against them (...) and he will throw the sword into the Desert of Yatreb and into the dwelling place of their fathers"[237] and take their wives and children prisoner. In Yathrib (Yaṯrib/Medina), the Ismaelites will endure great distress. If this, as it would seem, is meant by "salvation" of the Christians, then a *new religion* should not be spoken of. Instead it is a matter of "salvation" or rather "redemption" or "liberation" from foreign rule. The Christian-Ismaelite contrast can also be understood to reflect the polarity between the *long-established* Christians and the *new rulers*. If the term "salvation" is understood in a Christological sense, then this small sentence must have been interpolated later on, but the context does not suggest this point.

"Chapter 5", which is short, does not have to have come into existence later than the basic text by Pseudo-Methodius. It sounds very archaic but originally it was an individual item, as its motifs are not picked up on in the following Chapters. The train of thought is from the Old Testament, but adapted in a strange way. Thus the Ismaelites indeed rule Rome, Illyria, Egypt, Thessaloniki and Sardinia for 60 years,[238] which is quite a "western" vision. At the same time "the kings of the Hittites and the kings of the Hivites and the kings of the Amorites and the kings of the Jebusites and the kings of the Girgasites and the kings of the Canaanites and the kings of the Ammonites and the kings of the Philistines"[239] are all subordinate to them. These peoples were all long time gone at the time of the Arab rule. Then four Arab tyrants are mentioned by name. They are called "sons of the Arab woman Muya", and their names are taken from the Book of Judges 7:25, 8:3 and 8:5-11. It is added that "the sons of Ishmael were called Midianites", which alludes to Judges 7:23-25.[240]

It is said that King Samsasnakar (Shamaiaser; Šapur I, 309-379) makes captives of the sons of Ishmael who subsequently "(flee) the desert of Yatrib and (...) (enter) the civilized world".[241] They are described as barbarians on the basis of their terrible eating habits and their nakedness, who then conquer the whole earth and sail the seas with wooden boats.[242] But they are driven "out of the civilized world into the desert of Yathrib" again by Gideon.[243] The (first) exodus from the desert of Yathrib is announced again for the future, towards the end of the chapter as is the fact that they destroy the earth and take possession of the cultivated lands "from Egypt to Cush and from the Euphrates to India and from the Tigris to the sea", "because their yoke of oppression of all the peoples is twofold".[244] At this point the final editor, to whom Chapter 11 was already available, seems to have tried to explain the co-existence of two Ismaelite rules. We read that after ten weeks of rule "they will also be defeated by the kingdom of the Romans (...), because the (kingdom) will defeat all kingdoms (...) and cannot be vanquished by one of them".[245]

The assertions made in this chapter are not easy to understand. They seem to be retrojected in the past of the Book of Judges and, at the same time, the ancient Roman world, and yet outline the scope of the Arab rule from the end of the 7th century (and in the 9th century). At what time could the thesis of the invincibility of the Romans have been stated? It no longer seems to have been possible at the time of ʿAbd al-Malik or later on, despite the failure to conquer Constantinople. During antiquity, however, the Ismaelites (not even other Arabs) were not a power to be reckoned with. Alternatively, is it about re-projections from the future?

H. Suermann thinks "the author sees the eschatological invasion of the Ismaelites as prefigured in the eschatological descent of the Midianites on Israel".[246] If this is the case and Chapter 5 wants to provide an Old Testament prototype for the contemporary Arab rule in Chapter 11 – which would lead to the question of what sense that would make – then the apocalypse of two Ismaelite rulers, a biblical and a contemporary, would be recounted. But then it is difficult to attribute an Empire to the Midianites based on biblical traditions, which would cover roughly the same areas as that of the Arabs at the end of the 7th century.

Be that as it may, we only get to know allegorical-biblical matters about the Ismaelites in Chapter 5, and apart from the mention of the "desert of Yathrib", there is no talk of *new religion*. If Yathrib (Medina) first became the focus of attention towards the end of the first half of the 8th century, as is shown by the evidence of contemporary documents, then this passage could be dated as belonging to this period. An alternative would be an Arab orientation towards Yathrib, which did not leave traces known to us, which had already started some time before the construction of the temple there and which was the reason this place was chosen. A dating in the last decades of the 8th century can probably be ruled out as then Mecca would have occupied the position of Yathrib (Medina).[247] Due to the many uncertainties of the translation of the text, many questions cannot be resolved conclusively. Pseudo-Methodius wants to overcome the critical situation of the long-established Christians under Arab rule with apocalyptical methods and reveals a hopeful perspective. The real background may be the sectarian program represented by the rule of ʿAbd al-Malik, but at the same time, also the oppression and excesses of the soldatesca. The author(s) and editor(s) are of the opinion that legal control must belong to the Greek emperor.

However, the texts do not allow the conclusion that for Pseudo-Methodius "the crisis was brought about by the continuous presence of Muslim violence in the Christian world".[248] Indeed, Martinez also admits that Pseudo-Methodius ignores the Muslim faith.[249] However, due to the basic assumption that the dominating religion at the time the text was composed must have been Islam, the statements in the text are, as so often is the case, re-interpreted.

In all commentaries, *Islam* and *Muslims* are spoken of again and again. In doing so, Pseudo-Methodius is constantly misinterpreted in the light of the "knowledge" firmly established already. The apocalypse itself does not speak of it; the lapse in faith "at the end" is only spoken of in one single text. This is justified in Pseudo-Methodius using quotes from the New Testament, so it belongs to the eschatological scenario of the New Testament, independent of the Ismaelites, as no direct reference is made to them or their religion. The crimes, especially the corrupt sexual practices of the Ismaelites as well as the oppression and cruelty, are not information about Islam, but they belong to the repertoire of apocalyptic scenarios without immediate historical value. Similar things are also told about others, to some extent also about Christians. An example for this is the "pre-Islamic" Syriac Apocalypse of Daniel mentioned before. These stereotypes turn up again and again, sometimes they are described more colorfully, sometimes in a more reserved manner – this time they are described excessively and apply to the Ismaelites.

5.16 A fragment of Pseudo-Methodius (20)

In a fragment which can be attributed to the intellectual world of Pseudo-Methodius,[250] it is said that the sons of Hagar cause trouble; but that the Christian empire will soon come and the king of the Romans/Greeks will move against them. The sons of Hagar gather in Babylon and flee to Mecca where their empire comes to an end.

The empire of the Greeks will exist for 208 years and afterwards the sin will increase again. Gog and Magog arrive, a confinement (by Alexander) takes place, crimes are committed and so forth until the Son of Destruction seizes power. After some time Enoch and Elijah are sent and annihilate the corrupter. The Greek king, a person from Cush, comes up again and climbs mount Golgotha with a cross. After this, the end of the world will come together with the resurrection with heaven and hell.

This fragment is also very close to Pseudo-Methodius in its reasoning, although the order of events shows some changes. H. Suermann believes that this fragment is very old as "the Ismaelites suffered a resounding defeat by the Greek king in the year 694".[251] He advocates a time of origin before 694.[252] However, he fails to recognize that the victory – the defense of a siege of Constantinople – was not a *devastating* defeat for the Arabs, that the Greek king emerges triumphant many times in the course of the narrative and, likewise, that the final prospects – resurrection, heaven and hell are "more theologically" formulated than in the apocalypse of Pseudo-Methodius; Enoch and Elijah are not killed etcetera. Here a later contemplation of the material seems to be documented. The mention of Mecca instead of Yathrib (Medina) indicates the end of the 8th century.

Apart from the mention of Mecca "strong theological statements about Islam (,) or Muslims"[253] could not be found. There is no talk of a *new religion* of the sons of Hagar.

5.17 The Gospel of the Twelve Apostles[254] (21)

The Syrian manuscript which probably originated in Edessa and is dated by its publisher and translator, J. Rendel Harris, at the end of the 8th century, is titled "The Gospel of the Twelve Apostles together with the Apocalypses of each one of them".

The number twelve was important because, according to the text, the twelve apostles are associated with the twelve tribes of Israel from which they come, which causes a problem between brothers, and the matter of who will judge them. The apocalypses of Simon Kephas, James and John, the younger brother of James, who together were the sons of Zebedee, are all short texts.

"The apocalypse of Simon Peter probably deals with the Christological conflicts of the 5th century; the apocalypse of James is concerned with Jerusalem, the destruction of the temple and the re-building of the Church of the Resurrection by Constantine".[255] The apocalypse of John provides a complete apocalyptic pattern of world history and then devotes itself to the empire of Ishmael's offspring.

Whether there are also texts gathered in the "gospel" which are originally autonomous and can be dated differently, will not be taken into account here – H. J. W. Drijvers assumes an original entity,[256] – as our enquiry is only about the revelations of John. Regarding these, H. Suermann presumes that they "were written by a Jacobite in Edessa in around 700".[257]

According to J. R. Harris,[258] H. J. W. Drijvers[259] and H. Suermann,[260] the Apocalypse of John is about *Muslims, Islam* and *Muḥammad*, although H. Suermann has to admit that the name Muḥammad is not used and [261]

> "the religio-historical importance of Muḥammad and Islam are not addressed at all (...). The author does not say a thing about the teachings of Islam".[262]

At first, John was introduced in the apocalypse, who, moved by the Holy Spirit, knows all things, even those in the future. He sees the "kings of the north", and among them one, probably Constantine, who sees a sign. After him come the Roman kings (Byzantines) who are godless and wicked. Subsequently, God sends the Persians as a punishment. They are powerful but exploit people, so God sends the Medes as a punishment. This rule also ends because of their sins and God sends a wind from the south and a people who are ugly.[263] "And a warrior arises among them and they call him prophet and they are passed on to him."[264]

The historical interpretation entirely refers to the biblical book of Daniel (2:31-45; 7; 10:13-11:5). The "four kings" (Daniel 7:17) turn into the four consecutive empires of the apocalyptic tradition (Babylonians, Persians,

Greeks and Romans). Babylon and the Greeks have been omitted from the Apocalypse of John, the Persians and the Romans remain. The number four is reached by adding Medes and "Ishmael". In two cases the order of events is reversed; the Empire of the Medes lies chronologically before the Persians and also the "Romans" (Byzantines) were only pushed back by the Persians for a while, but not ousted. The rest is about the fourth empire.

"The south" subordinates Persia and destroys Rome, whereby the city of Constantinople cannot be meant, but the areas previously governed by the Romans in the Middle East. Everybody is afraid of them and "twelve renowned kings of them stand up, as it is written in the law".[265] Whether these are interpreted as twelve caliphs or are just quotes from the "law", i.e the Torah (Gen. 17:20 and 25:16 call the twelve sons of Ishmael "princes" or "kings"), remains undecided. The latter is more probable ("But it is more in accord with the tenor of the treatise to consider the meaning as symbolic"),[266] because the next sentence in the apocalypse refers to Abraham and Ishmael "He himself (Ishmael) is the people of the south of the earth".

Ishmael loots, takes prisoners "and all the end of the earth serve him and many principalities are conquered by him".[267] In the following, Ishmael's crimes are recounted in an apocalyptic fashion, which reproduces the stereotypes of this genre of literature, not historical events. In any case, Ishmael's rule is firmly established.

Several remarks must be considered because the purported facts cannot be found in the previous literature:

> "They (Ismael and his family) put all the more pressure on those who acknowledge the Messiah, our Lord, because they hate the name of the Lord until the end and they annul his covenant."

Subsequently, God is furious with them, as he was with the Romans, Medes and Persians before them. After this, there are "fights among them and many murders". "The North"[268] hears about this, extends an invitation to all people to prepare for battle and annihilates the evil ones.[269]

> "And the Lord turns the spirit of the south back to the place in which it became strong and destroys its name and its pride. And this happens when they enter the place which they had moved out of (...)."

On that day, the silver "that it is said they hid (...) in a place, the Tigris (J. R. Harris: Diglath)"[270] will be taken. "And they turn around and settle in the land that they came from" where they will fare badly.[271]

What do we learn about the historical background? The apocalypse was obviously written in the time of the Arab rule already long -established. The time of the "Romans", according to the Byzantines, is over in the Near

Eastern area, as are the victories of Heraclius: "Heraclius does not exist in this apocalypse".[272] The Ismaelite rule, which admittedly was God's punishment for the sins of the Persians, is perceived extremely negatively and the negative points are exaggerated in the apocalyptic images. The fact that the Ismaelites took over from the Persians and not the Romans indicates an East Syrian author.

The Arabs or Saracens are not named. They appear in biblical images as *wind, spirit* or people "of the south" or as Ishmael, who often appears in the plural, so that the personal pronoun changes from "he" to "they". Salvation is brought by the king of the "north".

It is not about the geographical terms north and south, for example the statement: the Arabs come from the south (from the Arabian Peninsula) and the salvation comes from the Byzantines in the north, it is about the allegories in the Book of Daniel (Dan. 11:5 "king of the south", v. 6 "king of the north", cf. ibid. verses 8, 9, 11, 14, 15 etcetera). If the apocalypse says: "He himself (Ishmael) is the people of the south of the earth", he interprets this people according to the Book of Daniel. The Apocalypse of John though seems to imply that the place which they (Ishmael) moved away from and must go back to is situated on the Tigris. The time of their rule, a big week and half a big week, seems to be taken from Pseudo-Methodius.[273]

Invasion and concrete battles cannot be inferred from the text,[274] only that Persia and "Rome" were conquered. The fact that before the "end", the children of Ishmael are fighting among themselves is not a reference to a particular event, e.g. an Arab civil war, but it is indeed a traditional topos for the imminent collapse of an empire (cf. e.g. Mark 8:24; Matthew 12:25 = Luke 11:17).

As already said, Muḥammad is not named and Islam is not mentioned. But the apocalypse knows of a soldier whom "they" call prophet. This means that it was known that the Arabs in Edessa at this time had a soldier and a prophet. This seems to correspond to a phase which only gradually began to change with the addition of the name Muḥammad in West Syria in the first half of the 8th century.[275] Perhaps it can be assumed that the naming of the prophet did not take place until later in Edessa and was therefore still unknown at the time the Apocalypse of John was written.

H. J. W. Drijvers states an exact time of composition (after Pseudo-Methodius in 692 and before the end of ʻAbd al-Malik's rule in 705).[276] However, the statements that "they" put pressure on those "who acknowledge the Messiah, our Lord", "hate" him and get rid of "his covenant" indicate the second half of the 8th century. On the one hand, these passages do not indicate a Jacobite, but an East Syrian ("Nestorian") author, like the whole of the Apocalypse of John; because he does not criticize the denial of the divine sonship of Jesus – the most important term for a Jacobite – but of *Jesus the Messiah*. On the other hand, "Ishmael's" separation and turning away from the Christian faith, which did not exist at the time of Muʿāwiyah or ʿAbd al-Malik and his sons, is documented here and neither was it present under the early Abbasids.[277] This being the case, a time of origin from about the middle of the second half of the 8th century might be suggested, at least for this passage. Only if it should be so that the text does not refer to a historical development, but simply reflects Mark 13, especially Mark 13:21-23 (and the parallels in Matthew and Luke), would an earlier composition come into question or even be probable.

5.18 Jewish historical interpretations of the apocalypse (20)

A Jewish apocalyptic scripture with the title "The Secrets of Rabbi Simon ben Yochai"[278] was not, as was thought by its publisher A. Jellinek, to be dated at the time of the first crusade, but according to H. Graetz, already at the end of the Umayyad era, around the year 750 (with the exception of one later addition).[279] Another later version of the "Secrets", which came from the "Midrash Ten Kings" and probably initiated the development of a further text "The Prayer of Rabbi Simon ben Yochai"[280] came into being in the Fatimid era of the 10th century or at the time of the crusades.[281]

"The Secrets" express apocalyptic hopes related to the Arab rule: "He (God) raises a prophet up over them, according to his will (...)."[282] It is explained that this prophet "should subject the Holy Land to them and they, the Arabs, will restore Israel". [283] Expectations of this kind are possible in the first part of the Arab rule as they almost match the remark in the 30th Chapter of Pseudo-Sebeos (cf. Text 7).

However, the remarks, which are confusing in parts, about the order of the empires and their kings, as well as the details of the reports, prompt questions. Thus B. Lewis, for example, basically agrees with the dating and interpretation of H. Graetz, but he thinks that correction and clarification could now be undertaken[284] "with the much greater knowledge of early Islamic history that we now possess" and he also does this. It is just a shame that this "more precise knowledge" is from the *traditional report* and not from *real history* (i.e.,, what really happened). So everything more or less leads to the confirmation of this traditional report, especially the history of the early "caliphs", which is possible by means of an almost allegorical interpretation of these dark texts, but is, unfortunately, not conclusive. An example is that B- Lewis interprets the "king of Hazarmaveth", who was murdered, as "ʿAlī in Iraq" who, according to the *Secrets*, was killed by Muʿāwiya, a fact inferred from the statement that he "profited from ʿAlī's death".[285] Now, the name ʿAlī does not appear in the Qur'ān, nor on the coinage of the first two centuries nor in the *Secrets*.

Anyway, the text provides no information on "Ishmael" to speak of, except on the names of several caliphs, and even less on the religion of these people. Perhaps there was an older version of the apocalyptic text before the end of the Umayyad era that sparked off Jewish hopes – perhaps the most plausible explanation. Nevertheless, it seems to have been revised many times and there is nothing in these passages which could provide information on our question. The same is also true of the "Prayer" of the Rabbi compiled much later.

5.19 Coptic sources

The following documents of Egyptian descent also belong to different genres, e.g. they are chronicles or apocalypses. However, here they will be dealt with together, not only because of their small number, but because they reveal a very specific character, courtesy of their Monophysite train of thought.

A sermon about the holy children of Babylon (21)

The motif of the "three young men in the fiery furnace" (Daniel 3:25-29) was often used in sermons of warning. An anonymously translated sermon[286] is extant in a Vatican manuscript of the 12th century. H. de Vis does not think that it is a translation from another language into Coptic: it was written in this language.[287] It features a Monophysite theology which is, however, not very "profound" and occasionally "very close to ridiculousness".[288] He assumes the first years after the establishment of Arab rule (in the language of Islamic historiography: "après la conquête" [after the conquest]"[289] to be the time of origin and R. G Hoyland dates them at around 640.[290]

The sermon calls on the people to pray and fast, but it should be different to the fasting of the "God-killing Jews" and the Saracens who are "oppressors who indulge in prostitution and carry out massacres… (also they said) We both (?) fast and pray at the same time". Likewise, the people should not fast like those "who deny the redemptive suffering of the son of God who died for us".

In the latter passage, it does not have to be the Saracens who are meant. A fasting in the manner of the apostles and the "ancient prophet Moses" of Elijah and John, the prophet Daniel "and (like) the three saints in the fiery furnace" is called for.[291]

This text is not clear. The accusation that the Jews had killed "God" and not just "Jesus" or the "Messiah", or that the suffering "of the son of God" is denied, reveals a Monophysite background. However, it remains unclear who the people are, who deny "the redemptive suffering of God's son", because the Saracens are no longer clearly named. Is it the Syrian Christians, who had reservations about the common statements made in the Monophysite churches that *God*, that is to say, *God's son* died for us (for them "Jesus the Messiah" died), or is it the Saracens who are meant here? As the latter did not know about 'Abd al-Malik's messianic scheme at this early stage, it could be about Syrian-Christian or "pagan" Saracens, perhaps with a "Basic Monotheism"? It must be admitted that the Saracens also claim to fast and, – according to R. G. Hoyland, to be "God-fearing".[292]

It is merely said of the Saracens that they oppress and kill as well as practice prostitution. These are accusations which almost always apply to a dominant band of soldiers (a "soldatesca"), who in this early period were not subject to close scrutiny, as was, however, soon to be the case under Mu'āwiyah's rule.

Benjamin of Alexandria (24)

Benjamin (born around 590) became patriarch of Alexandria beside a Melkite patriarch under Persian rule. In 631 he had to flee to Upper Egypt and first returned to Alexandria, which was "under Arab rule", in 643/644 and died there in 665. Of the "numerous scriptures" which he wrote in Coptic, many have been lost and others are only available in fragments and later translations and therefore a lot of things remain unclear.[293]

There are only a few pieces of information on our questions, e.g. that he was given the right to build churches by a certain 'Amr. According to the historiography of the 9th century, this was brought into the context of the Arab "conquest" of Egypt, which did not happen this way. Even R. G. Hoyland regards this source as historically uncertain.[294]

5.20 Further documents

H. Suermann examined further sources from the Coptic Church.[295] He states that a series of texts, like the "History of the Patriarchs of Egypt" and the "Chronicle of John (of) Nikiu", which are occasionally gathered together to obtain information on the "Muslim era", are unproductive and "many judgments might come from a later time".[296] This is certainly true for a part of the "History of Patriarchs",[297] a text in which "the rule of Islam" and the "year 96 of the Hijra (Islam)" are spoken of; this cannot have been added until the 9th century. At least the rule of Hišām (724-743?) is "described (as) fair towards everyone and a blessing for the Church."[298]

In a text from the "Chronicle of John of Nikiu", *Islam* and *Muslims* are also spoken about. Many Egyptian Christians abandoned their faith "and turned to the Muslim religion, the enemy of God, and accepted the despicable teachings of the monster Muḥammad". Two lines later there is talk of the "faith of Islam".[299]

The time and origin of the next text is completely unresolved. The chronicle was surely written in Greek and partially in Coptic, but it is now only available as an Ethiopian translation of an Arabic version (from the year

1602). Y. D. Nevo and J. Koren go to a lot of trouble to prove that the mention of Islam and Muslims cannot have been in the original[300] and then they come to the (wrong) conclusion that it could have been added in the era of ʿAbd al-Malik because they assume that there is talk of Muḥammad and Islam (as a religion) in the inscriptions in the Dome of the Rock. But this is not true, as an investigation by Chr. Luxenberg[301] has shown. Also no other text from the 8th century speaks of Islam and Muslims. The quoted insertion (in the Arab translation) must have taken place in the 9th century or later because of the new "knowledge" of the scribe.

The story "Eudocia and the Holy Sepulchre" and the "Cambyses Romance" are considered to be out the question because of their chronological attribution.[302] R. G. Hoyland points out later interpolations in a "Vision" (Pseudo-Shenute)[303] from the 5th century in which it is said of the sons of Ishmael and Esau that they rule and are constructing a temple in Jerusalem (again).[304] If the latter should refer to the Dome of the Rock, – Hoyland also believes that a simple biblical association is possible –, then the interpolator would not only have had to know about the Arab rule but also about the building of the Dome of the Rock. However, nothing more is explained.

H. Suermann thinks that the "Discussion of the Patriarch John III (with a Jew and a Melkite) before the governor ʿAbd al-ʿAzīz"[305] is a text which can be attributed to the late 7th century.[306] Apart from its very dubious handwritten translation (in Arabic and the Bohairic dialect of Coptic), it gives the impression that the discussion is literary fiction. Why should a Monophysite, a Melkite and a Jew of all people discuss questions about the understanding of the Eucharist before an Arab governor? "At the end of the discussion, the governor declares himself defeated (...)."[307] In other words, it is not about the reproduction of the actual conversation, but about a literary production – whenever this may have taken place.

A very legendary "Vita of the Patriarch Isaac" also deals with the relationships to the Arab governor. But even according to H. Suermann, "it is difficult to filter out the historical substance".[308]

A Coptic Apocalypse[309] (26)

A Coptic apocalypse – the fourteenth vision of Daniel – which is recorded in Bohairic and Arabic, provides hints on the reign of the Ismaelites. This is said to have ended before Gog and Magog and the Anti-Christ arrived.[310]

This apocalypse, which was written at the beginning of the second half of the 8th century at the earliest, "was edited again and provided with insertions[311] at the time of the Fatimid rule", so that the individual materials could not be historically located for sure. It is interesting that a text which originated in Egypt set its hopes on a Roman emperor.

At first, the fourth vision, the fourth animal, a lion, is interpreted by an angel:

> "The fourth animal (...) is the king of the sons of Ismael. He will rule over the earth for a long time (...) This kingdom is the progeny of Abraham and his maidservant Hagar (...) All Persian, Roman and Greek cities will be destroyed; nineteen kings of this people will rule over the earth."[312]

In the following, the author reports nineteen kings; "it is possible that he is talking about the Fatimids in Egypt."[313] For H. Suermann, several (the last?) of these could allude to the successors of ʿAbd al-Malik from Sulayman (from 715) up to Marwān. The only conclusion we can draw, unlike in the History of the Patriarchs, is that the Arab rule was perceived as a burden by the Copts and was depicted negatively in the apocalyptic interpretation of history in the first half of the 8th century (or the Fatimid period), although several of the kings are characterized positively. There is no information given on a *new religion* of the Ismaelites.

The Apocalypse of Pseudo-Athanasius (27)

The Coptic scripture that is most important for our questions is the "Apocalypse of Pseudo-Athanasius".[314] The Coptic manuscript, which was discovered at the beginning of the 20th century in a monastery near Faiyum (today in New York), is not dated and features many bigger gaps in the text which have been filled in from the Arabic version, which, however show considerable deviations. The text follows the pattern of a sermon (on the feast of St. Michael?) and has four parts: an introduction, an admonition to bishops and clergy, an "apocalypse", which complains about the moral decline of the Christians and announces the hard rule of the Persians as a punishment of God and gives explanations (particularly) about the Roman and Arab rule[315] and the last part, which continues with the apocalyptic descriptions of the previous part. The Roman kings were "godless" because of their religious policy and because of their propaganda of the doctrine that Jesus Christ existed "in" two natures. Again, a short Persian rule is announced, after which God will send another people, the Saracens.

Their rule is characterized in the usual negative apocalyptic stereotypes. They devastate everything, get rid of coinage with cross symbolism and raise taxes. God sends troubles (drought and famine), but the Christians do not convert and the clergy co-operates with the rulers.

A final perspective – the rule of a Roman emperor, the Anti-Christ and the second coming of Christ – is missing. In this respect, the text does not provide an "apocalypse", but is more a sermon with apocalyptic characteristics. The apocalyptic depictions should prompt the listener to persevere in times of hardship.

As Damascus is named (and Bagdad not yet),[316] H. Suermann advocates a time of compilation between 725 and 750.[317] This may be the case, but the possibility of later amendments and adaptations must always be considered.

The text reveals very little about the Saracens, except that they are Ismaelites and sons of Hagar. The replacement of the sign of the cross on the coinage (since ʿAbd al-Malik) with seemingly non-Christian symbols is criticized as ungodly or anti-Christian. However, nothing is said about the *religious ideas* connected with this act and just as little is said about the "invasions" or conquests of the Saracens, apart from the usual biblical reminiscences. Anyway, it is explained that:

> "Many Christians will join them in their faith (?), although they hope to be released from the oppressions which they (the Saracens) bring to the earth".[318]

If it should be the case that here it is *faith*, and not *loyalty*, trust or such like that is actually being spoken about (?), then this *faith* is obviously considered different to that of the Copts. This could mean that the teachings represented by the Saracens, no Trinity and no divine sonship", could be understood to be another heretical version of Christianity, as "ungodly" as, for example, the teachings of the Chalcedonians. A new non-Christian faith could also be meant. But nothing more is explained in addition to this, and an interpretation in the sense of a new religion is not necessary at all, especially as no important points of controversy appear in the rest of the text. If a *new religion* had really been noticed, should we not expect a *sermon* to be directed against a threat like this? But this is not the case.

5.21 Greek Texts from the First Half of the 8th Century

Germanus, Patriarch of Constantinople (28)

A note made by the patriarch Germanus of Constantinople (died between 730 and 733) is also interesting in this context. Because of the involvement of his father in a state scandal – previously a high-ranking official with Heraclius - Germanus was castrated and made a member of the clergy of the Hagia Sophia. In 705, he became Bishop of Cyzicus and Patriarch of Constantinople from 715 on. As he advocated the worship of images in the Iconoclastic Controversy, he was deposed in 729 or 730 and died soon after.[319]

Germanus spent most of his life in the capital city of the Byzantine Empire and certainly did not have any exact knowledge of the Arabs, unlike John of Damascus. Accordingly, the casual mention of the Saracens is inaccurate.

In the context of the discussion on image worship, in his dogmatic letters,[320] he briefly goes into the religious feasts and myths of the Greeks, the opinion of the Jews and the practices of the Saracens, and then the Christians.[321] He writes the following on the Saracens:

> "Considering that they themselves seem to have sworn to this [the previously mentioned observance of the laws by the Jews; *author's note*], it has brought shame and disgrace on the Saracens until the present day that they practice the cult offered to an inanimate stone in the desert (steppe, wasteland) – the worship of the so-called Chobar, and (likewise) the other ridiculous celebrations of the wicked customs practiced there and handed down by their fathers (like e.g.) at their notorious (renowned) festivals there."[322]

"Chobar" is the same term as the "Chabar" used by John of Damascus and is probably the Greek transcription of the root meaning "big (k-b-r)" in Arabic (cf. Text 29). Nothing is said about the meaning, unlike in John who associates "Chabar" with the old cult of Aphrodite (the "big"). With Germanus, it is merely a *baetylus*. The cult is, however, performed in the desert; he knows nothing about the function of the stone/rock on the Temple Mount that John addresses. He is probably referring to old stories about a Baetylus of the Saracens which, for example, Saint Jerome had witnessed. The reason for the assumption that this cult still exists could be the change from the clear and epiphanic Christian iconography to a stone symbolism which has been understood in this sense in Constantinople since the time of ʿAbd al-Malik; he would not have known anything about the Christological confession of faith documented in the Dome of the Rock.

Germanus complains that the Saracens still practice the cult with strange rites, although they are bound to the laws of the Torah like the Jews previously mentioned. The high estimation of the Torah could be attributed to the Saracens because they were connected with Abraham as Ismaelites/Hagarites; it is improbable that Germanus was aware of the Qur'ānic material in which Moses played a central role. "Empirical" information on the Saracens going beyond this cannot be recognized; it is probably more a matter of generally accepted stereotypes, e.g. about "*the* French" or "*the* English" etcetera, that are still common today.

John of Damascus (29)

John was born in Damascus in about 650. He came from a genteel Melkite family, maybe with Syrian roots, – his grandfather was allegedly the apostolic prefect of Damascus, his father head of the fiscal authority under Muʿāwiya – at first he was said to have been an official of ʿAbd al-Malik. Before 700 he secluded himself in the monastery of Mar Saba near Jerusalem. He later became a priest and was literarily active. He lived to a good old age, but the exact date of his death is not known (after 749, before 754).[323]

He left behind a series of scriptures written in Greek which show him to have been an important Byzantine theologian. As he summarized many areas of the discussion on late-antique Greek theology, he had also often been read since the period of High Scholasticism in the Latin Middle Ages. As late as 1890 he was pronounced a (Roman) Catholic Doctor of the Church.

In his time, there were intense discussions about Monophysitism and its effects on Monoenergetism and Monotheletism. Especially John devoted himself to this question and used a clear terminology for the diphysite Christology. In addition to that, he fought against dualistic trends, advocated image worship and composed ethical/ascetical writings.

Two documents, which are important for our questions, are associated with John: a book "Concerning Heresy" in which the faith of the Ismaelites is presented as the 100th heresy,[324] and a "Disputation" (verbal dispute) between a Saracen and a Christian.[325]

In the first four Chapters, the "Disputation" is structured as a direct verbal sparring match between a Christian and a Saracen. From Chapters 5 to 10, it is more about instruction as to how a Christian should answer Saracenic questions (e.g. Ch. 5, Line 1: If a Saracen asks you [...] answer him [...]).[326] The concluding Chapter 11 has the form of a dialogue again, apart from the resumptive concluding sentence: "The Saracen (...) did not know how to answer the Christian anymore and went away (...)."[327]

This dialogue cannot have come from the same author as the one who wrote Chapter 100 of the "Book concerning Heresy". Even if the word *Islam* or *Muslim* does not appear, (except in the French translation!), here the Saracens quite clearly belong to a new religion. The issues of dispute reveal a detailed knowledge of their religion. Therefore the dialogue must be traced back to a different author to the one of the "Liber de haeresibus", however not to "Theodore Abu Qurrah", – following a didactic talk by J(ohn)"[328] – either, as R. Volk considers possible. This work must be considerably more recent: it could only have been thought of and written in this way as recently as the 9th century or later, probably in about the middle of that century.

The "Liber de haeresibus" is generally considered to be authentic, although the manuscript translations did not exist until the 11th century.[329] It is not clear when this book was written, but probably not very much before 750. It discusses 100 Christian heresies. For the first 80 of them, John refers to the "Panarian Omnium Haeresium" ("medical case against all heresies") of Epiphanius of Salamis (died 403), while he deals with the remaining 20 "apparently independently"[330] and this is also true for the 100th heresy of the Ismaelites. John's fondness of the number 100 also speaks for the affiliation of this chapter.

One thing must be kept in mind from the start. John does not regard the concept of the Ismaelites as a *separate religion*, the term Islam cannot be found in his text, but considers their faith as a *Christian heresy*, like the other beliefs dealt with previously. This observation is important, because it was made by someone whose family was in the service of the Arab rulers in Damascus as was he himself for a while. But if he did not accept the religious orientation of the Ismaelites as a new religion, then it *was not one* at this time.[331] How could he of all people, an expert on doctrines in Damascus and at the same time a sophisticated theologian, misunderstand the intentions of the governing authorities in Damascus on such a central matter?

At the beginning, he goes into the cult of the Ismaelites of the obviously pre-Muḥammad period as described a few lines later. He says that the Ismaelites, also called Agarenes, are called this because Ismael was born to Abraham of Agar. They were also called Saracens (ἐκ τῆς Σάρρας κενούς) – here he attempts a play on words.[332]

It is said of the Ismaelites that in their language they used to worship idols and, in addition to that, the morning star and Aphrodite,[333] whom they called "Chabár", which means (the) "big one" (goddess).[334] They had been idolaters up to the time of Heraclius; since this time the Pseudo-prophet "Mamed (Machmed)",[335] who got to know the old and new covenant and was taught by an Arian monk,[336] "put together [his] own heresies."[337]

> "And he circulated again and again that a scripture (γραφή) had come down to him from heaven. But the order forced by him on this book (βίβλος) – it is laughable – he thus passed it on to them as an object of worship."[338]

So John knows about a (holy) book (kitāb?) that, however, probably was not known under the name Qur'ān at that time, but he traces this back to *Ma(ch)med.*

He then goes into the – in his opinion – most important heretical teachings. Admittedly, he (Ma[ch]med) teaches that there is only one God and creator.

> "He says that Christ is God's Logos and his spirit (pneuma), but that he was created and a servant, and that he was born of Mary, the sister of Moses and Aaron (cf. surah 19:27-28) without conception. He says that God's Logos and the spirit entered Mary and she bore Jesus, who was the prophet and servant of God. And (he says) that the Jews wanted to crucify him in outrageous ways. After they had seized him, they (only) crucified his shadow (simulacrum); but Christ himself was not crucified, as he says, and did not die. God took him up to heaven because he loved him".[339]

In the following, he summarizes part of Surah 5 (116-117). When Jesus had been taken up to heaven, God asked him:

> "Jesus did you say: 'I am the son of God and God?' Jesus answered as he (Ma[ch]med) said: 'Have mercy on me Lord; you know that I did not say this and did not want to seem (to be) more than your servant in any way.'"

People wrote that he had said such things but they lied and were mistaken.

> "And God answered him himself, as he said to (Ma[ch]med); 'You did not say this sentence'".[340]

He writes that lots of other superstitious things, which are worthy of laughter, can be found in something put together in writing in this way. In response to the question, e.g. how the scripture came down on the prophet, they (the Ismaelites) say that it happened while he was asleep, and in response to the question where the (holy) scripture bears witness to him (Ma[ch]med), they had to keep quiet.[341]

John responds to the accusation (of the Ismaelites), "that we associate God with a companion if we call Jesus the son of God and divine", which he denies with reference to prophets and scriptures.[342]

This is intensified further; "Again we say to them (the Ismaelites): 'You say (yourself) that Christ is God's *logos* and spirit (*pneuma*), why do you then reproach us as associaters?'"[343] This accusation is invalidated in the following:

> "They taunt us as idolaters because we worship the cross (...) But we say to them; 'Why do you rub (touch) a stone/rock of your (near you, under your) cave/cupola (Chabatá) and cherish affectionately the tip of the stone/rock?' Some of them say that Abraham lay on it with Hagar, but others say that he (Abraham) tethered his female camel to it when he wanted to kill Isaac".

John states that this contradicts the Holy Scripture (several details are mentioned below). "They worship it (the stone) but at the same time they say it is Abraham's stone/rock".

Once again the accusation concerning the worship of the cross is rejected. Then John attacks the Ismaelites: "But this thing, which they call stone/rock, is (in actual fact) the head of Aphrodite, whom they worship and also call Chabár (great) (...)."[344]

Explanation: The word 'Chabatá (Χαβαθά), masculine but declined like a feminine because of the 'a' ending [accusative: Chabathán Χαβαθάν) is difficult to interpret. John paraphrases the Arabic word "kabar" ([to be] big) with "Chabár" (Χαβάρ), thus transcribing the Arabic k-sound with the Greek "χ – chi" (Ancient Greek: aspirated [k^h]; Modern Greek: [x]). The term "Chabatá" might of course be interpreted as the equivalent of Arabic "kaʿba". There is, however, another possibility: For Arabic phonemes that do not exist in Greek the nearest possible equivalent must be used in the transcription. As the Arabic "q" (uvular plosive) might as well be transcribed with the letter *chi*, the term "Chabatá" might refer to the Arabic word "qubbat(a)". *Qubbat* means something like "cupola", "cave", "sepulchre (tomb)" (mausoleum). It suggests that the stone/rock worship (the touching or rubbing of a stone) which is associated with a cave or cupola can be understood as a reference to the Dome of the Rock, which has both a *cave* (tomb of Jesus) under the tips of

> the rock and a *cupola* above it and was well-known to John. Then the Greek katá (κατά) with the accusative (κατά τὸν Χαβαθάν) can be understood as a local preposition "under", "near" or "by". It has to be added that John, despite his other knowledge of Ismaelite statements, completely misunderstood the sense of the rock/stone, or wanted to misunderstand it for polemic reasons. Even so, he says that the stone was Abraham's stone for the Ismaelites but which he, with the reference to Aphrodite, does not want to accept.

The writer/editor of this text also knows Surah 4 "The Women (*al-nisā'*)" or, as he writes "the scripture (Surah) of the woman".[345] He says that it allowed "four wives (...) and in addition secondary wives, if possible thousands".[346] Divorce and marriage to someone else is also possible.[347] After this, he goes into the fact that Ma(ch)med coveted Zaid's "beautiful wife" and married her by order of God.[348] John judges this to be adultery and says that Ma(ch)med established a law after this: "Whoever wants to, should release his wife".[349] This cannot be found word for word in the Qur'ān, neither in this surah nor at any other place, but the following sentence is a quotation (cf. Surah 2:230): the rule that someone can only marry his divorced wife again after she has been married to another man.[350] Further aspects can be found as well.

The following remarks on a female camel (ἡ κάμηλος) are interesting. Considering the (short) length of Chapter 100, this is quite a broad and extensive explanation[351] of stories about the female camel, which was previously mentioned by John in the context of the sacrifice of Isaac by Abraham. John thinks it is a separate "scripture" (graphḗ), thus a surah or part of a surah written by a pseudo-prophet, like the previous evidence. This surah can no longer be found in the (later) canonized text of the Qur'ān.

But it has left its marks in the Qur'ān. This female camel appears in several places without stories closely connected to it.[352] Therefore it must have belonged to the narratives of a certain stage of development of the later Qur'ān. After the deletion of the surah referred to by John (or alternatively its insertion in one of the longer ones), the rest of the mentions in the Qur'ān remain unexplained. However, the stories of a female camel have not been completely lost, as they have lived on in the wealth of Arabic sagas. A. Sprenger has already meticulously gathered and reproduced them.[353]

Further references to Qur'ānic material are then mentioned in the following few lines.[354] The first sentence already points out that this can be traced back to Ma(ch)med:

> "On the other hand, Ma(ch)med says: The scripture [surah; *author's note*] of the table [Surah 5, The Table Spread (al-mā'ida); *author's note*] says that Christ requested a table from God and it was given to him (...)."[355]

Furthermore, John mentions "the scripture (graphḗ) of the cow" (Surah 2) in which he, Ma(ch)med, in addition, said "other ridiculous words which I believe have to be overlooked because of the sheer number of them". John briefly names several further motives and ends with the statement that "he has completely forbidden the drinking of wine" (surah 2:219).[356]

Chapter 100 ends abruptly, without a real ending and the Qur'ānic material addressed in the text is very selectively chosen. To sum up, it provides relatively short subjects of discrepancy of doctrine dealt with, however, in a rather "internal" Christian way, i.e., presented as if this faith was in fact a "Christian" heresy, thus e.g. on the question of God and Christology and several further peripheral aspects. The statements about marriage and the secondary wives seem to be based on the interpretation of Qur'ānic teachings in the schools of jurisprudence. The closing remarks of the fairly recent Surahs 5 and 2 were probably written later and do not match the rest very well. The passages which were added to Christological statements are probably amendments by scribes from the 9th century, who added everything that came into their heads at the time to the prototype and which was in circulation in the Christian polemics of that time against the *then new religion*. The strangely extensive stories of the female camel are more archaic, but these were indeed also in circulation in the 9th century.

Insofar as the text can be attributed to John, several important things can be discerned about his knowledge of that time: He knows the name of the "pseudo-prophet" *Ma(ch)med – "Maḥmad"*, not *"Muḥammad"* – and traces a book back to him. He probably does not know about the term *Qur'ān* or *surah*, but he describes some material as scriptures (*graphḗ*) of the Ismaelites and sees them compiled into a book. What he or later editors explain about it, finds its equivalent to a large extent in the Qur'ān as we know it today. Still there are some major discrepancies. The "Surah of the Cow" (al-Baqarah) is thought to be a separate book, and the stories of the female camel cannot be found in the Qur'ān today, so the Qur'ān as a collection cannot have been fixed when this text was written, not even when the last amendments were made.

The remarks on the stone/rock worship are important, which do not have anything to do with the future Ka'ba in Mecca, but with the Temple Mount in Jerusalem; the indication of stone/rock in the "Chabathá" can only be aimed at the Dome of the Rock. This corresponds to the practices since 'Abd al-Malik, but probably no longer in the second half of the 8th century. Likewise, John testifies to the probably vague, but roughly biblical Ismaelite interpretation of stone worship in the context of Abraham – instead of Jacob, as would be biblically correct. It seems as if this opinion really existed.

John of Damascus declines to go into further detail, he contrasts it polemically with the Christian worship of the cross and caricatures them as the continuation of the Aphrodite cult. Whether in the meantime this cult was ascribed to the Christian Arabs for polemic reasons or whether it actually still played a role under Christian cover, cannot be decided for certain. The claim that for John of Damascus the Arabs were "predecessors of the Anti-Christ"[357] is not supported at all in this text.

5.22 Non-usable Evidence

The following examples are exemplary for further texts[358] which deal in some way with Arabs and other related subjects and name them every now and again. Not all of them shall be discussed here, as they, as well as several of the passages discussed previously, are out of the question as contemporary historical sources, because of their apparent later time of origin, and because of their completely unresolved text attestation.

An Anonymous Commentary (30)

In a fragment of a Syrian gospel manuscript from the 6th century, which now only provides the Gospels according to Matthew and Mark, an addition can be found in the margin which speaks of conquests of (troops, followers?) of Muḥammad, the fall of Homs and Damascus and undefined battles.[359] Even R. G. Hoyland classified this text as unreliable.[360] Y. D. Nevo and J. Koren, however, consider the events he speaks about not to be consistent with traditional reports, but they think that a dating in the late 7th century is possible,[361] because in their opinion the name of Muḥammad has been known since the inscriptions in the Dome of the Rock, which is not true (the form was not a name yet).[362]

A dating of this commentary is difficult. As Muḥammad is obviously mentioned as a historical figure, it could only have been added around the middle of the 8th century at the earliest. The conquests and battles talked about in this text cannot be verified. There is also talk of an (otherwise unknown) battle of the people of Muḥammad against the Romans in "Gabitha". Many commentators equate this to the Battle of Yarmūk they are familiar with from the traditional report. So the (presumably legendary) mention of Gabitha makes the likewise legendary Battle of Yarmūk a historical event.

Gabriel of Quartmin (31)

Gabriel of Beth Kustan (593-667?) was the abbot of the Quartmin monastery for a long time and then bishop of Dara. In his biography, the "Life of Gabriel",[363] it is said that he met 'Umar (the caliph), the leader of the sons of Hagar. What is more, 'Umar granted all Christians, their churches and monasteries tax exemption.

As the problems mentioned first arose in the 8th century, according to R. G. Hoyland, he considers the narrative to be "a later fabrication" which was brought forward into the ʿUmar era in order to give it a higher authority ("authority by attributing it to Muslim figures").[364]

It can only be added to this that the fiscal questions mentioned only appeared around the end of the 8th century and the figure of ʿUmar only became "a famous figure" in the 9th century.

An Anonymous (West) Syriac Chronicle (32)

In an anonymous (West) Syriac chronicle from the year 819, of which fragments have survived (the manuscript was destroyed in 1915), about the year 945 (634) it is said:

> "Abu Bakr died and after him ʿUmar ruled (...) for 11 years. In the same year died (...) and Gabriel of Kustan became (...) bishop and abbot of Quartmin (...)."[365]

This chronicle could actually have already been written in 819. The names that he refers to from the traditional report could have been inserted into the Life of Gabriel, for which then a slightly later final edition must be assumed. However, it could also be possible that there were traditions in the last third of the 8th century which were first recorded in Islamic historiography in the 9th century. The chronicle does not provide relevant information on this.

Miracle Stories of the Saints Demetrius and George (33)

This also applies to the additions about Arabs occasionally mentioned in the "Miracles of the Saints Demetrius and George" which cannot be located historically and in addition to this, yield very little information. It may suffice to refer to R. G. Hoyland's remarks on their evaluation.[366]

5.23 Summary

Not all of the literature from the first two centuries concerning our questions could be introduced and examined, but this article discusses the most important texts in which there is talk of the Arab rulers that the Christian population were subordinate to.

As the Christian literature of this very complex region, both linguistically and culturally, has not been recorded nearly as completely and critically, as that of the Greek and Latin Church, it must be assumed that further unknown evidence exists. However, the sources up to now justify the reasonable assumption that the discovery of additional sources will not provide any completely new insights.

6 On the Arab Religion

6.1 Islam and Muslims Cannot be Found

The Christian literature of that time makes it clear that *Islam* is not named and is only indirectly dealt with as a subject of its own. The *Arabs/Saracens/Ismaelites/Hagarites* are not perceived as Muslims in the modern sense of the word. Instead, the substantial literary activities of theologians, clergymen and monks were still devoted almost exclusively to their "internal Christian" themes, conflicts and theological drafts.

If the Arabs should really have been *Muslims* and propagated a *new religion called Islam* in the Middle East, as the traditional report wants to make us believe, then these authors must have completely failed to notice it. Instead of dealing with this phenomenon literally, they went on about their usual business. This abstinence cannot be explained by a possible fear of repression because, apart from that, the new regime was often subjected to radical criticism. The Arab empire, for example, is caricatured and portrayed as the sum of all that is evil and is only surpassed by the Anti-Christ in the apocalyptic literature of this time. John of Damascus is not afraid of polemics which are also theological.

Indeed, these writers were never afraid. What should have prevented them from mentioning a new non-Christian religion or from fighting against it with theological arguments? This could have intensified the negative apocalyptic depictions. As numerous theologically highly sophisticated books about Monophysitism, Diphysitism, Monoenergetism, Monotheletism and so forth demonstrate, these authors possessed considerable literary and linguistic abilities. Why did they abstain from using them to face up to the new non-Christian religion of the new leaders if that really existed. But nothing can be read about this. This became different in the 8th century, although the Arab regime was now more stable and possibly more dangerous for the critics. However, real information about and conflicts with the new religion can now be found in the works of Christian authors writing in Arabic.[367]

Whenever the Arabs are insulted in the texts as sinful, wanton, murderous, oppressive and therefore also as "godless", it does not have anything to do with the *new religion* (yet). If they are confronted with "the" Christians, this can also refer to the "*old-established*" Christians. As nothing particular is explained about their religious idea at first, only indirect conclusions can be drawn.

6.2 Arabs as Christians, Heathens, Representatives of a Basic Monotheism

The key terms of the new religion – *Islam* and *Muslims* – cannot be found in the literature examined, as said before. According to all that is known, the majority of the ruling Arabs were Christianized and most of them would have advocated a Syrian-Aramaic Christianity in East Syria, but also a Monophysite-Jacobite Christianity in West Syria at first. This was especially true of the rulers in the Umayyad era, maybe even of those from later periods.

Occasionally the (Christian) Arabs are described as "pagan". Their characterization as "pagan", if the Arabs in the Syrian synods should be meant by this, should not be automatically understood as "a technical term". As already shown by "pre-Islamic" literature, *pagan* customs, rites and forms of worship were not rare among Christians, also Arab Christians. Modern institutions like carnival, Halloween and even Christmas are Christian re-interpretations of originally pagan cults. So if a Christian purist condemns Halloween as "pagan", that does not mean that young kids at a Halloween party are followers of a new religion. In addition, also John of Damascus, from whom we can learn a great deal about Qur'ānic ideas from the time before 750, admittedly sees the Ismaelites as *heretic Christians*, but likewise accuses them of maintaining their pagan traditions, especially the Aphrodite cult. Germanus of Constantinople criticizes their worship of stones, as Saint Jerome did before him.

The earliest evidence from the time of Muʿāwiya is difficult to evaluate. Y. D. Nevo and J. Koren assume a "Basic Monotheism" for some of the Arabs with an orientation toward the figure of Abraham.

In Biblical Studies there is a consensus that Abraham did not exist as a historical figure. But then the stories surrounding his name, from which the Arabs considered themselves to be Ismaelites/Hagarites and therefore descendants of Abraham, were all the more powerful, and even Syrian and Greek Christians classified the Arabs according to this biblical genealogy. Of course, "Abraham" as described in the Bible was not a monotheist, as monotheism in the modern sense first came into being in Judaism during or after the exile, i.e., from the 6th century BCE. But the Old Testament stories about Abraham had not been finally edited before this time so that they could be perceived to be monotheistic narratives.

It could indeed be that some of the Arabs advocated such a rudimentary monotheism relating to the "law", especially the Book of Genesis, because of their genealogical self-classification in biblical history. Should such a monotheism have been introduced in the Middle East, then it would not be surprising, but more to be expected that old Arab or common Near-Eastern practices, lifestyles and forms of worship would have survived in it, as mentioned by Saint Jerome or John of Damascus. These were not completely displaced by Christianity, as is shown by the sermons of Isaac of Antioch from the 5th century.[368] The reverse idea is also possible – or even probable: that some of the Arabs had not been Christianized (yet) and practiced their inherited cults. The environment shaped by earlier Syrian Christians, the narratives of the Bible, especially the Pentateuch from the Old Testament, developed their influence and let a *Basic Monotheism* emerge which then continued to be a basis for the pagan forms of worship still practiced. Through the religious and cultural dominance of Christianity, Judaism, Mandaeism and, in addition to this, the quasi-monotheistic Zoroastrianism and Zurvanism at that time, *Basic Monotheism* could be widely spread as a fundamental conviction in the whole of the Near East.

Muʿāwiya was a Christian ruler, as the distinctly Christian symbols on his coinage prove. It cannot be identified exactly which Christian orientation he leaned towards. He was first the ruler of West Syria and then later also of the East, moreover he was praised by contemporary Christian authors, so he must have been tolerant and have kept out of disputes. This was also true of his governors.

With the arrival of the "people from the east" in the west with ʿAbd al-Malik as the new ruler, a specific kind of Christianity came to this area which had developed in isolation and intensified its doctrines on a pre-Nicean Syrian basis. Now it was advocated in a firm, sectarian way, together with apocalyptic expectations which were focused on Jerusalem. This Christianity is documented in old Qur'ānic material, on coinage as well as in inscriptions in and on the Dome of the Rock and indeed on the Umayyad mosque in Damascus and on the temple in Medina (middle of the 8th century), albeit in altered form.[369]

The glorification (*muḥammad* – the praised one) of the servant of God (*ʿabd allāh*), prophet (*nabī*), messenger (*rasūl*), the Messiah (*masīḥ*) Jesus, son of Mary (*ʿĪsa bn Maryam*) – all these terms appear in the inscription in the Dome of the Rock – was connected to the radical rejection of the *divine sonship of Jesus*. Instead it was linked to a unitary monotheism (Monarchianism). The approach of the rulers is testified – positively – by Anastasius of Sinai and negatively by John of Damascus in 'Liber de haeresibus'.

6.3 The Beginnings of a New Arab Religion

The rejection of this program was only possible after the death of the sons of ʿAbd al-Malik. But obviously it took much longer before not only, as hitherto, the divine sonship of the messenger and prophet Jesus had been contested, but also his "final relevance" and his "uniqueness". However, then he still stayed integrated in the order of the prophets and was the most important figure apart from Moses, according to the evidence of the most recent Qur'ānic material. There was still a widespread, Christian-rooted messianism[370] until well into the 9th century, but now there was also a *Prophet of the Arabs* who was the *seal of the prophets* and whose proclamations offered a genuine revelation.

For the first time in this context - and exclusively in the apocalyptic literature - statements can be found which demand a dissociation of the rulers from the (sole) acknowledgement of Jesus as the (sole) Messiah. In these statements, which can be attributed to the last decades of the 8th century, the Arab religion appears as a *new, non-Christian religion*, without yet being described as *Islam*.

However, there is no certainty as to whether the apocalyptic remarks about a denial of the messiahship of Jesus actually reflect new religious-historical developments in the case of the ruling Arabs. Be that as it may, perspectives of this kind belong to the characteristics "of the end" given in the "Apocalypse of Mark" (Mk. 13 parr. [and passages in the other synoptic gospels]) in the New Testament. Christian apocalypses *had to* address these topoi: this eschatological scenario belongs to the apocalyptical repertoire, independent of the real activities of the Arabs.

If this should be the case, then the apocalypses, which have been the only documents that can be used for the historical evaluation of the Arabs up to now, provide no evidence of a new, non-Christian religion.

The occasional, but rather rare calls for the denial of the soteriological significance of Jesus or even the fact of Jesus' death on the cross might be a different matter. John of Damascus provides the earliest fairly certain evidence for this aspect. The denial of the death of Jesus and its soteriological relevance is not understood by him, however, as being *non-Christianity*, but as a heresy, and at the same time a peculiar form of Christianity. This aspect could not yet be understood as a complete turning away from Christianity until the texts from the last decades of the 8th century.

Now, the denial of the real death of Jesus on the cross had been widespread as an originally "*Docetic*"[371] motif in the whole of the Near Eastern and Greek Christianity for a long time. Also the function of the crucifixion is not the same in all culturally specific Christian theologies. The cross becomes the strongest, most crucial point of the salvation/justification in Latin Christianity ("staurocentrical Christology"), while in the Greek-Hellenistic theology ("incarnation Christology") the death of Jesus is ("only") a sign for the profound incarnation of the Logos and therefore the radical nature of God's love for us. In the Syrian tradition, which advocates a "probationary Christology (German: Bewährungschristologie)", Jesus' obedience to the Father is the focus, an obedience until (but not: through) death.

These ideas were advocated in the pre-Nicean Syrian Christology, but also in the post-Nicean Antiochene theology. However, the later opening of the Syrian church for "Western ideas" since the synod in Ctesiphon in 410, in which the Nicene Creed was adopted, also led to the acceptance of the soteriological significance of the crucifixion of Jesus in the Syrian church.

This was, however, not completely self-evident. The Syrian-Christian "Cave of Treasures", written in the 6th century, explains that the inscription that Pontius Pilate had attached to the cross ("the King of the Jews" Mark 15: 26 parr.) was "in Greek, Latin and Hebrew. And why did Pontius Pilate not write a word of Syrian on it? Because the Syrians did not have a share in the blood of the Messiah (...)."[372] Obviously the Christian Syrians had nothing to do with the death of Jesus. This is certainly not only to be understood historically, but it also shows that his death was not very important to them.[373] According to them we are redeemed through the probation of Jesus Christ in his life (up to his death) – "Jesus' passing the test" – and by trying to emulate him.

The undaunted probationary Christology in the pre-Nicean theology was taken on and maintained by Arab Christians with their (early) missionary work. It was especially the ʿArabī/Arab Christians who had been deported far away to the East of Mesopotamia, who developed and intensified these ideas further in their isolation. So a denial of the crucifixion can be found in the Qur'ān, despite the other places where the death of Jesus is mentioned.[374]

Thus the attested dissociation of the Arabs from the crucifixion of Jesus in (later) Christian literature cannot be interpreted as evidence for a new religion without further explanation. The crucifixion of Jesus, for example, was fundamentally important for the "Byzantine" theologian John of Damascus, despite his Syrian background. Nevertheless, he understands its denial in Qur'ānic material as "only" heretic outlandishness. It should not be ignored that a denial of the ability of Jesus Christ to die also existed in other Christian movements, even if for completely different reasons.[375]

The denial of the soteriological significance of the cross can only be recognized and understood as the sign of a *new religion* in passages of (interpolations in) apocalypses which must be attributed to the last decades of the 8th century. There is, however, still no talk of *Islam*:

> "It was perhaps only with Dionysios of Tellmahre (died 846) that we really get a full awareness of Islam as a new religion. Early observers had not been able to distinguish the religion of the Arabs from paganism (...)."[376]

This statement was only true for the Syrian-Christian authors, but it can be extended to Greek and Coptic writers and others. Islam can first be spoken of as a new religion in the 9th century. But the beginnings of such a development were already perceived and severely criticized in the last decades of the 8th century. Several of the bishops, monks and theologians who commented on the subject of the Arab rule were indeed quite capable of differentiating between paganism and Christianity, not like S. Brock thinks. As long as the accusation does not arise that the Arabs were not Christian, but only that they followed old pagan cults maintained from their time in desert, the basis for such an accusation was simply missing.

7 The Arab Prophet / Muḥammad

7.1 The Prophet of the Arabs

In the Christian literature of the first two centuries, a Prophet of the Arabs is occasionally mentioned, but rarely called by the name Muḥammad.

The chronological allocation of the corresponding passages, which can also be found in documents belonging to the 7th century, is difficult. But it must be assumed that they are more likely later amendments by editors/scribes who let their higher "knowledge" modify the text. Why?

Indeed the oldest testimonies talk about an Arab preacher and merchant or prophet who was a warrior. His name was still unknown and there is no conceivable reason why it would not have been mentioned if it had been known.

This evidence cannot come from the time before ʿAbd al-Malik because Qur'ānic material first became known in the course of its western migration." The "prophet" is always addressed in this material. Moreover, the more warlike statements, which were quite numerous, as well as the military activities of the Arabs could have brought about the designation "warrior".

These references to an Arab prophet, first possible since ʿAbd al-Malik, are easily recognized as later interpolations into the texts. In most cases the texts do not reveal any historical information about the Arabs/Ismaelites/Hagarites, apart from reports that – before Muʿāwiyah – there were gangs who took to looting, and that with Muʿāwiyah they seized control, which was mostly judged favorably. But from ʿAbd al-Malik onwards this rule was seen in a negative light. In addition to this, biblical patterns are almost exclusively used to describe the new masters. The insertions regarding a prophet seem to be contaminations in the context of the prototypical texts, because they exceed the biblical associations before and after the interpolations by using non-biblical notions.

In early texts the prophet is described as a warrior or a merchant. As already mentioned, the characterization as a warrior could be indirectly inferred from the unique character of the Qur'ānic statements. The Qur'ān itself – unlike the Sīra – knows nothing of the prophet as a *merchant* (cf. Texts 7 and 9).

"Warrior and merchant" were, however, descriptions of Jesus in the Marcionite literature, albeit in other contexts. They could have become popular in the Syrian-speaking area due to the anti-Marcionite works of

Ephrem the Syrian.[377] If they should have detached themselves from their origins and become mere motifs, then they might have influenced the description of the prophet. An old "wanderlegende" of a preacher and merchant who brought Christianity from al-Ḥīra to South Arabia might have influenced the emergence of such an idea.[378]

The mentions of a prophet "called Muḥammad" are even rarer and later. This name, which was originally a Christological title, was given to the prophet over time, in the last decades of the first half of the 9th century, as John of Damascus testifies.

For John of Damascus, Muḥammad is seen as the (pseudo-)prophet to whom the Qurʾānic material ("scriptures") can be traced back. However, in the first place, he is classed as a (Christian) heretic, not as the founder of a new religion. The latter can only have happened in the last decades of the 9th century, although he is not mentioned as the founder of a new religion by name in the Christian literature of this time.

7.2 Arabs, Saracens, Ismaelites and Hagarites

Due to the biblical character of the worldview of Christian authors, the *Arabs* only rarely appear under this designation. They appear occasionally as *Saracens*, but mostly as *Ismaelites* and *Hagarenes* in genealogical derivation from Abraham and his maidservant Hagar, as already mentioned in the "pre-Islamic" era. Even the term *Saracens* is occasionally traced back to the fact that they wanted to claim their descent from *Sarah*, the legitimate wife of Abraham.

Thus, the Arabs are paraphrased using biblical references, mostly from the Book of Genesis (and parallel passages in other Old Testament books) and also in the apocalypse ("kingdom of the south") from the Book of Daniel. These statements are the allegorical interpretation of biblical passages. They do not yield any historical information. If they are described as people who come out of the desert, this has nothing to do with the Arab invasion, but is rather relating to biblical statements that Ishmael lived in the desert (and so do his descendants). There is no geographical evidence given that a kingdom of the south is spoken of, but the Arab rule is classified within an apocalyptic scheme of history, described with patterns from the Book of Daniel.

Whenever we come across non-biblical indications of the home of the Arabs, it points to the "Arabs" from the Nabatean region as well as Mesopotamia, groups that were well-known in the pre-Islamic era, but *not* to the Arabian Peninsula. Yathrib/Medina is not mentioned until around the middle of the 8th century, and Mecca, the geographical location of which remains uncertain, even later.

In the literature examined there is no talk of an Arab invasion around the death of Muḥammad, as described in the traditional report. Occasionally battles are mentioned, sometimes with place names, which certainly happened during the acquisition of autocracy in West Syria and after the exclusion of these areas from the Byzantine Empire (622). These were finally lost for the Byzantines and firmly in the hands of the new Arab rulers after the death of Heraclius (640) and after the ultimate collapse of the Sassanian Empire in the East. At that time (in some cases up to the present day?), control could only be secured through violence. The conflicts which arise from it, as well as the place names given, do not correspond to the specifications of the traditional report and are therefore often re-interpreted by commentators (e.g. *Gabitha* into *Yarmūk* and the like).

In the time before Muʿāwiyah, uncertainty predominated in many areas of the Middle East because of the retreat of the Byzantines, but with his assumption of office, order is re-established, which is praised by Christian authors. The Arab rule is not perceived as a curse until the time of ʿAbd al-Malik and his sectarian movement and is described accordingly in the apocalypses, which also, at the same time, try to convey hope that this evil will – hopefully soon – end.

The overall fairly sporadic literary utterances by Christians under allegedly "Islamic rule" altogether show that both the political and the religious history took place differently to how the traditional report had constructed them until the end of the 8th century by projecting a later stage of the religion on a fictitious eon in Mecca and Medina. The examination of these historical processes, as well as their reflection in the Qurʾān, is a challenge to scholars of Islamic studies which they have not faced or have hardly faced up to now.

Bibliography

Primary Sources

Ammianus Marcellinus, Res Gestae, in: Ammiani Marcellini Rerum Gestarum capita selecta, ed. Joannes Baptista Pighi (Bibliotheca Neocomensis, 2), Neocomi Helvetiorum 1948.

Anastasius II, Patriarch, Brief an seine Priester, in: M.F. Nau, Littérature Canonique Syriaque inédite (Syriac text and French translation), in: Revue de l'Orient Chrétien, Tome IV (XIV), 1909, p. 113-130.

Anastasius vom Sinai, Quaestiones et responsiones, in: MPG 89, p. 311-824 (Greek and Latin).

Anastasius vom Sinai, Viae dux, in: Anastasii Sinaitae Viae dux, (critical edition of the Greek text) by Karl-Heinz Uthemann (Corpus Christianorum, series Graeca [CCG], Bd. 8), Turnhout, Brepols 1981 (Text: p. 7-320).

Anonyme (west)syrische Chronik von 819, in: ed. Palmer, p. 75-80.
Anonyme Glosse, German translation in: Theodor Nöldeke, Zur Geschichte der Araber im 1. Jahrhundert d.H. aus syrischen Quellen, in: Zeitschrift der Deutschen Morgenländischen Gesellschaft 1875, p. 76-82; English translation (with deviations if compared to Nöldeke) in: ed. A. Palmer, p. 2-4.
Aphrahat, Homilien, (about the vision Daniel 7) in: G. Bert, Aphrahates des persischen Weisen Homelien (TU III, 3/4), Leipzig 1888, p. 69-88
Chronicum ad annum Christi 1234 pertinens (CSCO 81; Scriptores Syri 36)
Chronik des Johannes von Nikiu, in: The Chronicle of John (c. 690 A.D.) Coptic Bishop of Nikiu, ed. and transl. by Robert H. Church, London 1916.
Chronik von Seert, in: Addai Scher (Arabic edition) und Pierre Dib (French translation), Histoire nestorienne (Chronique de Séert), première partie (II) (Patrologia Orientalis, éd. R. Graffin/F. Nau, tome V, fasc. 2), Paris 1950.
Dialog zwischen dem Patriarchen Johannes und einem Emir, in: M. F.(rançois) Nau, Un colloque du Patriarche Jean avec l'émir des Agaréens et faits divers des années 712 à 716 d'après le MS. du British Museum Add. 17193 ..., in: Journal Asiatique, 11e série, Tome 5, 1915, p. 225-279; Syriac text ibid, p. 248-256, French transl. ibid., p. 257-267.
Diskussion des Patriarchen Johannes vor dem Gouverneur 'Abd al-Aziz, in: Huge G. Evelyn White, The Monasteries of the Wadi 'n Natrun, vol. 2, New York 1932, p. 171-175.
Doctrina Jacobi nuper baptizati, Greek text and French translation by Vincent Déroche, in: Gilbert Dagron, Vincent Déroche (eds.), Juifs et chrétiens dans l'Orient du VIIe siècle (Travaux et Mémores 11, revised by Gilbert Dagron und Denis Feissel [Collège de France. Centre de Recherche d'histoire et civilisaton de Byzance]), Paris 1991, p. 47-229; following text: Gilbert Dagron, Commentaire, ibid., p. 230-273
Ephrem the Syrian, Hymnus De ecclesia and De crucifixo.
Ephrem the Syrian, Second Sermon (in: Sancti Ephraemi Syri. Hymni et Sermones ... edidit, latinitate donavit, variis lectionibus instruxit, notis et prolegomenis illustravit Thomas Josephus Lamy, Tomus III, Meclelinia MDCCCLXXXIV (ed. Lamy), p. 189-212.
Eusebius of Caesarea, Onomastikon (Greek text and St. Jerome's Latin translation in: Eusebius. Das Onomastikon der biblischen Ortsnamen, ed. by Erich Klostermann [Die griechischen christlichen Schriftsteller der ersten drei Jahrhunderte - GCS - 11,1]).
Evangelium der zwölf Apostel, in: The Gospel of the Twelve Apostles, Together with the Apocalypses of Each One of Them, ed. from the Syriac

Ms. with a Translation and Introduction by J. Rendel Harris (ed. J. R. Harris), Cambridge 1900.

Geheimnisse des R'Simon, firstly published in 1743 in Saloniki, then printed again by A. Jellinek, Bet ha-Midrasch, Leipzig 1855, vol. IV, VIII, IX and p. 117-126. English translation on the basis of A. Jellinek's edition in: B. Lewis, An Apocalyptic Vision, op. cit., p. 311-320.

Germanus, Patriarch von Konstantinopel, Dogmatische Briefe, in: Sancti Germani Patriarchae Constantinopolitani Epistolae Dogmaticae, in: MPG 98, 147A-222 B.

Hieronymus (St. Jerome), Commentariorum in Amos prophetam libri III (Corpus Christianorum, series Latina [CCL], LXXVI, Turnholti MCMLXIX, p. 213-348).

Hieronymus, In Hiezechielem.

Hieronymus, Liber de situ, Chapter on Genesis (GCS 11,1).

Hieronymus, Vita Hilarionis (MPL 23, p. 29-54); German: BKV 15, p. 33-72.

Hieronymus, Vita Malchi (MPL 23, 53-60); German: "Leben und Gefangenschaft des Mönchs Malchus", in: BKV 15, 1914, p. 73-83.

Homilie über die Heiligen Kinder von Babylon (Homily about the Holy Children of Babylon), as the first of three Coptic sermons edited on the subject and translated by Henri de Vis: Panégyrique des Trois Saints Enfants de Babylone, 1. Premier Panégyrique. Acéphale, in: Homélies coptes de la Vaticane II, texte copte publié et traduit par Henri de Vis (Cahiers de la Bibliothèque copte, Strasbourg), Louvain, Paris 1990, p. 60-120.

Isidore of Seville, Etymologia (in: Isidori Hispalensis episcopi Etymologiarum sive Originum libri XX, ed. by W.M. Lindsay, Tomus I: libri I-X [Scriptorum classicorum bibliotheca Oxonensis], Oxonii 1911 [without pagination]).

'Iso'yahw patriarchae III., Liber epistularum, edited and translated into Latin by R. Duval (CSCO, Vol. 12, Scriptores Syri II, Tomus 12).

Iso'yahw Patriarchae III liber epistularum (Syriac text), ed. by R. Duval (CSCO Vol. 11; Scriptores Syri, Tomus II).

Jacob of Edessa, Scholion on 1 Kings 14:21 ff., in: George Phillips, Scholia on Passages on the Old Testament by Mar Jacob, Bishop of Edessa, London 1864 (text and English translation).

Johannes bar Penkayê, Fragments, in: A. Mingana, Sources Syriaques, Leipzig 1907, p. 135-138.

Johannes bar Penkayê, Chronicle, chap. 14, in: German translation from the Syriac by Rudolf Abramowski, Dionysius von Tellmahre. Zur Geschichte der Kirche unter dem Islam (including translation of the books 14 and 15 of Johannes bar Penkayê), Leipzig 1940.

Johannes Damascenus, Disputatio Christiani et Saraceni, in: Die Schriften des Johannes von Damaskus, vol. IV Liber de haeresibus. Opera polemica, ed.

by Bonifatius Kotter (PTS 22), Berlin, New York 1981, p. 427-438. Greek and French translation in: Jean Damascène, Écrit sur l'islam, ed. by Raymond Le Coz (Sources chrétiennes, 383), p. 228-250.

Johannes Damascenus, Über die Häresien, Kapitel 100, in: Die Schriften des Johannes von Damaskus, vol. IV, op. cit., p. 60-67 (ed. B. Kotter).

Johannes Moschus, Pratum spirituale, Greek and Latin translation in: MPG 87/3, 2.847-3.116 (another Latin translation in: MPL 74, p. 119-240).

Koptische Apokalypse (zur 14. Vision des Daniel; Coptic Apocalypse on the 14th vision of Daniel), in: Henricus Tattam, Prophetae majores in dialecto Aegytiacae seu coptica, II, Oxford 1852, p. 386-405; French translation: Frédéric Macler, Les Apocalypses Apocryphes de Daniel, (Suite) III, in: Revue de l'histoire des religions 33, 1896, p. 163-176 (F. Macler, Les Apocalypses Apocryphes).

List of Caliphs, English translation in: ed. Palmer, p. 43-44.

List, from the Arabic into Syriac, English translation in: ed. Palmer, p. 49-50.

Maronite Chronicle, English translation in: ed. A. Palmer, p. 29-35.

Maximus Confessor, Epistula 14 (MPG 91, p. 533-544).

Maximus Confessor, Epistula 8 (MPG 91, p. 439-446).

Patriarchengeschichte der Kirche Ägyptens (History of Patriarchs of the Church of Egypt; Patrologia Orientalis 5).

Plinius Secundus, Naturalis Historia (ed. Pliny, Natural History [Latin and German], Volume II: Libri III- VII, ed. by H. Rackham, London und Cambridge (Massachusetts) 1947.

Plinius Secundus, Naturalis Historia V, XX 85, in: Die geographischen Bücher (II, 242-VI Schluss) der Naturalis Historia des Plinius Secundus, ed. by D. Detlefsen, Berlin 1904.

Pseudo-Athanasius, Apokalypse, in: Francisco Javier Martinez, Sahidic Apocalyse of Pseudo-Athanasius, in: id., Eastern Christian Apocalyptic in Early Muslim Period. Volume 1, Washington, D.C. 1985, p. 247-590 (Coptic/Arabic, p. 285-411).

Pseudo-Ephrem, Sermon 5, in: Des heiligen Ephraem des Syrers Sermones III, Syrischer Text, ed. by Edmund Beck (CSCO, vol. 320, Scriptores Syri, tomus 138), Löwen 1972, p. 60-71; Des heiligen Ephraem des Syrers Sermones III, translated by Edmund Beck (German transl.) in: (CSCO, vol. 321, Scriptores Syri, tomus 129), Löwen 1972, p. 79-94 (ed. E. Beck). Syriac text and German translation also in: H. Suermann, Die geschichtstheologische Reaktion, op. cit., p. 12-33.

Pseudo-Methodius, Die syrische Apokalypse des Pseudo-Methodius, ed. by G.J. Reinink (CSCO, Scriptores Syri, Tomus 220), Löwen 1993. German translation: Die syrische Apokalypse des Pseudo-Methodius, translated by G.J. Reinink (CSCO, vol. 541, Scriptores Syri, Tomus 221), Löwen 1993 (ed. G.J.Reinink). H. Suermann, text edition and German translation in: Id., Die geschichtstheologische Reaktion, op. cit., p. 34-85; French translation of the text of the Vaticanum: F.J. Martinez, Eastern Christian Apocalyptic in Early Muslim Period. Pseudo-Methodius and Pseudo-Athanasius, Volume 1, Washington D.C. 1985. Pseudo-Methodius: Part I, Chapter I: The Syriac Apocalypse of Pseudo-Methodius (MP), p. 2-205. About the Greek and Latin translations: Die Apokalypse des Pseudo-Methodius. Die ältesten griechischen und lateinischen Übersetzungen, ed. by W.J. Aerts und G.A.A. Kortekaas (CSCO, Vol. 570; Subsidia, tomus 98), Löwen 1998.

Pseudo-Methodius-Fragment, Syriac text and German translation in: H. Suermann, Die geschichtstheologische Reaktion, op. cit., p. 86-97.

Pseudo-Sebeos, Geschichte des Heraklius, in: Histoire d'Héraclius par l'Evêque Sebéos, traduite de l'Arménien et annotèe par F. Macler, Paris 1904 (ed. F. Macler); Armenian edition: Parmut'iwn Sebeosi, Ed. G.V. Abgarian, Yerevan 1979; The Armenian History Attributed to Sebeos, translated, with notes, by R.W. Thomson. Historical Commentary by James Howard-Johnston, Part I. Translation and Notes, Liverpool 1999 (ed. R.W. Thomson), Part II. Historical Commentary, Liverpool 1999.

Ptolemy, Geography, in: Claudii Ptolemaei Geographia. Edidit Fridericus Augustus Nobbe. Editio stereotypa, Tomus II, Lipsiae 1845 (ed. F.a. Nobbe).

Schatzhöhle, Die (The Cave of Treasure), Syriac and German ed. by Carl Bezold. First part: Translation; from the Syriac text of three unedited MSS translated into German and annotated by Carl Bezold, Leipzig 1883.

Sophronius, Weihnachtspredigt (Christmas Sermon) (in: two Greek manuscripts, München, 15th century and Paris, 10th century) edited by H. Usener, Weihnachtspredigt des Sophronius, in: (Rheinisches) Museum für Philologie, ed. by O. Ribbeke und F. Buecheler, NF 41. vol., Frankfurt a.M. 1886, p. 500-516. A Latin translation, Lyon 1677 (MPG 87/3, 3.201-3.212).

Synodicon Orientale, Canon 16, Canon 18, translat. and ed. by J.-B. Chabot, Paris 1902, vol. 2 (French translation), p. 488-489.

Syrische Chronik (Syriac Chronicle, before 680?), Latin version in: Chronica Minora, pars prior, ed. and transl. by Ignatius Guidi (SSCO, Scriptores Syri, series tertia, tomus IV), Paris 1903, p. 3-32.

Syrische Danielapokalypse (Syriac Apocalypse of Daniel). German translation and introduction: Matthias Henze, Apokalypsen und Testamente. Syrische Danielapokalypse (Jüdische Schriften aus hellenistisch-römischer Zeit. Neue Folge, vol. 1, Lieferung 4), Gütersloh 2006.

Tertullian, De carne Christi (CCL 2, 873-917).

Theophanes Confessor, Chronographia, ed. by C. De Boor, Hildesheim 1963 (reprint of Leipzig 1883-1885).

Thomas the Presbyter, English translation in: ed. Palmer, p. 15-21.

West-Syriac Chronicles, in: The Seventh Century in the West-Syrian Chronicles, introduced, translated and annotated by Andrew Palmer, including two seventh-century Syriac apocalyptic texts, introduced, translated and annotated by Sebastian Brock, with added annotations and historical introduction by Robert Hoyland, Liverpool 1993 (ed. A. Palmer).

Xenophon, Anabasis (ed. Books I-IV by M.W. Mather and J.W. Hewitt, Oklahoma [USA] 1962).

Secondary Literature

Abache, Samir, Les moines chez les Arabes chrétiens avant l'Islam, in: Patrimoine Syriac. Actes du colloque V: Le monarchianisme Syriaque. Aux premiers sciècles de l'Èglise IIe - Dèbut VIIe siècles, vol. 2, Antélias (Liban) 1998, p. 299-304.

Altheim, Franz und Stiehl, Ruth, Die Araber in der Alten Welt, first vol.: Bis zum Beginn der Kaiserzeit, Berlin 1964.

Bousset, W., Beiträge zur Geschichte der Eschatologie I, in: ZKG 20, 1899, p. 103-131.

Brock, Sebastian, VIII Syriac Views of Emergent Islam, in: Id., Syriac Perspectives on Late Antiquity, London 1984, 9-11; p. 199-203.

Bruns, P., Jakobus von Edessa, in: LACL 327-329

Bruns, P., Windau, B., Benjamin von Alexandrien, in: LACL, p. 107-108.

Cahen, Cl., Note sur l'accueil des chrétiens d'Orient à l'Islam, in: Revue de l'Histoire des Religions 2, 1964, p. 51-58.

Cahen, Claude, Note sur l'Accueil des Chrétiens d'Orient à l'islam, in: Revue de l'Histoire des Religions 2, 1964, p. 51-58.

Cowe, Peter, Philoxenus of Mabbug and the Synod of Manazkert, in: ARAM. A, Festschrift for Dr. Sebastian P. Brock, vol. 5, 1 and 2, Leuven 1993, p. 115-129.

Darling, R.A., The "Church from the Nations" in the Exegesis of Ephrem, in: IV Symposium Syriacum 1984. op. cit., p. 111-121.

Dörper, Sven, Zum Problem des Völkernamens Saraceni, in: Neue Romania. Veröffentlichungsreihe des Studienbereichs Neue Romania des Instituts für Romanische Philologie (Sonderheft [special edition], ed. by Chr. Foltys und Th. Kotschi), Nr. 14, Berlin 1993, p. 91-107.

Drijvers, H.J.W., Lavenant, R., Molenberg, C., Reinink, G.J. (ed.), IV Symposium Syriacum 1984. Literary Genres in Syriac Literature, Rom 1987 (quoted IV Symposium Syriacum 1984).

Drijvers, Han J.W., Christ as Warrier and Merchant. Aspects of Marcion's Christology, in: Id., History and Religion in Late Antique Syria, Aldershot (Great Britain), Brookfield (USA) 1994, XIII, p. 73-85.

Drijvers, Han J.W., The Gospel of the Twelve Apostles: A Syriac Apocalypse from the Early Islamic Period, in: Id., History and Religion in Late Antique Syria, Aldershot (Great Britain), Brookfield (USA) 1994, chap. VIII, p. 189-213.

Gahbauer, F.R., Anastasius Sinaita, in: LACL, p. 27.

Gahbauer, F.R., Germanus von Konstantinopel, in: LACL, p. 253-254.

Ginkel, Jan J. van, Jakob von Edessa in der Chronographie des Michael Syrus, in: Martin Tamcke (ed.), Syriaca. Zur Geschichte, Theologie, Liturgie und Gegenwartslage der syrischen Kirchen. 2. Deutsches Syrologen-Symposium (Juli 2000, Wittenberg; Studien zur Orientalischen Kirchengeschichte, vol. 17), Hamburg 2002, p. 115-124.

Graetz, Heinrich, Geschichte der Juden, vol. 5, (reprint of Leipzig 1909) Darmstadt 1998.

Hoyland, Robert G., Arabia and the Arabs, London 2001.

Hoyland, Robert G., Seeing Islam as Others Saw It. A Survey and Evaluation of Christian, Jewish and Zoroastrian Writings on Early Islam, Princeton, New Jersey 1997.

Klugkist, A.C., Die beiden Homilien des Isaak von Antiocheia über die Eroberung von Bet Hur durch die Araber, in: IV Symposium Syriacum 1984, op. cit., p. 237-256.

Lewis, Bernard, An Apocalyptic Vision of Islamic History, in: Bulletin of the School of Oriental and African Studies, vol. XIII: Part I, London 1949, p. 308-338.

Lexikon der Antiken Christlichen Literatur (LACL), ed. by Siegmar Döpp and Wilhelm Gerlings, Freiburg, Basel, Wien 1998.

Martinez, Francisco Javier, The Apocalyptic Genre in Syriac: The World of Pseudo-Methodius, in: IV Symposium Syriacum 1984, op. cit., p. 337-352.

Müller, D.H., Artikel "Agraioi 2", in: Paulys Realencyklopädie der Classischen Altertumswissenschaft, new edition by Georg Wissovar, vol. 1, Stuttgart 1893, p. 889.

Nevo, Yehuda D. and Koren, Judith, Crossroads to Islam. The Origins of the Arab Religion and the Arab State, Amherst, New York 2003.

Ohlig, Karl-Heinz, Das Syrische und Arabische Christentum und der Koran, in: Karl-Heinz Ohlig, Gerd-Rüdiger Puin (ed.), Die dunklen Anfänge. Neue Forschungen zur Entstehung und frühen Geschichte des Islam, Berlin [1]2005, [2]2006, p. 366-404.

Ohlig, Karl-Heinz, Fundamentalchristologie. Im Spannungsfeld von Christentum und Kultur, München 1986

Pauli, J. OSB, Johannes Moschus, in: LACL, p. 253-254.

Popp, Volker, From Ugarit to Samarrā' (first contribution in the present anthology).

Reinink, G. J., Der Edessenische "Pseudo-Methodius", in: Byzantinische Zeitschrift 83, 1990, p. 31-45.

Reinink, G.J., Pseudo-Ephräms "Rede über das Ende" und die Syrische Eschatologische Literatur des Siebten Jahrhunderts, in: Aram 5: 1 and 2, Oxford 1993.

Röwekamp, G., Sophronius von Jerusalem, in: LACL, p. 364-365.

Samir, Khalil, Qui est l'interlocuteur du Patriarche Syrien Jean III (631-648?), in: IV Symposium 1984), p. 387-400.

Samir, Samir K., The Prophet Muhammad as Seen by Timothy I. and Other Arab Christian Authors, in: David Thomas (ed.), Syrian Christians under Islam. The First Thousand Years, Leiden, Boston, Köln 2001, p. 75-106.

Shahîd, Irfan, Byzantium and the Arabs in the Fifth Century, Washington, DC, 1989.

Shahîd, Irfan, Nadjjran, in: The Encyclopaedia of Islam. New Edition, Volume VII, Leiden 1992, p. 871-872.

Shahîd, Irfan, Rome and the Arabs. A Prolegomenon to the Study of Byzantium and the Arabs, Washington, DC, 1984.

Shahîd, Irfan, The Book of the Himyarites: Authorship and Authenticity, in: Id., Byzantium and the Semitic Orient before the Rise of Islam, London 1988, p. 349-362.

Sprenger, A., Das Leben und die Lehre des Mohammed nach bisher grösstentheils unbenutzten Quellen, 1st vol., Berlin ^{2}1869.

Steinschneider, M., Apokalypsen mit polemischer Tendenz, in: Zeitschrift der Deutschen Morgenländischen Gesellschaft, 28. Band, Leipzig 1874, p. 627-659.

Suchla, B.R., Maximus Confessor, in: LACL, p. 433-435.

Suermann, Harald, Das Arabische Reich in der Weltgeschichte des Johannàn bar Penkàje, in: Nubia et Oriens Christianus. Festschrift (liber amicorum) für C. Detlef G. Müller zum 60. Geburtstag, ed. by Piotr O. Scholz und Reinhard Stempel, Köln 1988, p. 59-71.

Suermann, Harald, Die Apokalypse des Ps.-Athanasius. Ein Beispiel für die koptische Auseinandersetzung mit der islamischen Herrschaft im Ägypten der Ummayyadenzeit, in: Walter Beltz (ed.), Die koptische Kirche in den ersten drei islamischen Jahrhunderten (Beiträge zum gleichnamigen Leucorea-Kolloquium 2002, Hallesche Beiträge zur Orientwissenschaft), Halle 2003, p. 183-197.

Suermann, Harald, Die geschichtstheologische Reaktion auf die einfallenden Muslime in der edessenischen Apokalyptik des 7. Jahrhunderts

(Europäische Hochschulschriften, Reihe XXIII Theologie, vol. 256), Frankfurt a.M, Bern, New York 1985.

Suermann, Harald, Einige Bemerkungen zu syrischen Apokalypsen des 7. JHDS, in: IV Symposium Syriacum 1984, op. cit., p. 327-335.

Suermann, Harald, Juden und Muslime gemäß christlichen Texten zur Zeit Muhammads und in der Frühzeit des Islams, in: Holger Preißler, Heidi Stein (ed.), Annäherung an das Fremde. XXVI. Deutscher Orientalistentag vom 25. bis 29.9.1995 in Leipzig, Stuttgart 1998, p. 145-154.

Suermann, Harald, Koptische Texte zur arabischen Eroberung Ägyptens und der Umayyadenherrschaft, in: Journal of Coptic Studies 4, 2002, p. 167-186.

Suermann, Harald, Orientalische Christen und der Islam. Christliche Texte aus der Zeit von 632-750, in: Zeitschrift für Missionswissenschaft und Religionswissenschaft 52, 1993, p. 120-136.

Tardy, René, Najrân. Chrétiens d'Arabie avant l'islam, Beyrouth 1999.

Volk, R., Johannes v. Damaskus, in: LThK35, p. 896.

Willemsen, C.A., Sarazenen, in: LThK2 9, p. 326.

Volk, Robert, Johannes von Damaskus, in: LThK3 5, p. 895-899.

Volk, Robert, Johannes von Damaskus, in: LACL, p. 344-347.

Abbreviations

BKV O. Bardenhewer, Th. Schermann, (from vol. 35 on: J. Jellinger) and C. Weyman, Bibliothek der Kirchenväter, Kempten 1911 ff.

CCG Corpus Christianorum, series Graeca, Tournhout 1977 ff.

CCL Corpus Christianorum, series Latina, Tournhout, Paris 1953 ff.

GCS Die griechischen christlichen Schriftsteller der ersten drei Jahrhunderte, Leipzig 1897 ff.

GSCO Corpus Scriptorum Christianorum Orientalium, Paris 1903 ff.

LACL Lexikon der antiken christlichen Literatur, ed. by S. Döpp and W. Geerlings, Freiburg, Basel, Wien 1998.

LThK Lexikon für Theologie und Kirche, ed. by J. Höfer and K. Rahner, 2nd ed. Freiburg ²1957 ff.; 3rd ed. by W. Kasper, K. Baumgartner und H. Bürkle, Freiburg, Basel, Wien 1993-2001.

MPG Migne, Patrologia Graeca, Paris 1878-1890.

MPL Migne, Patrologia Latina, Paris 1878-1890.

PO Patrologie Orientalis, Paris 1903 ff.

From *muḥammad* Jesus to Prophet of the Arabs

The Personalization of a Christological Epithet

Karl-Heinz Ohlig

1. Preliminary Note

Whoever wants to investigate the term *muḥammad* by examining its genesis, history and meaning, cannot start by taking the Qur'ān as a basis, as this alleged name form appears here only in four places. According to both Muslim tradition, which originated from the 9th CE century on, and the majority of Western Islamologists, this sacred book had already been compiled and edited into its current form between the years 650 and 656 under the third Caliph ʿUṯmān: all other versions were forbidden. However, the oldest manuscripts stem from the second half of the 8th century, with the exception of one larger fragment found in Ṣanʿā', which might go back to the first half of the 8th century. These manuscripts show at least one thing, however: they do not draw on a finished codex, which, in fact, was only gradually emerging and would not be finished before the 9th century.[1]

It is true that in the case of New Testament manuscripts there is also a substantial time interval between the oldest extant manuscripts and possible autographs; but, in the meantime, they have been edited text-critically, i.e., displaying all variants that can be found in manuscripts, so that the presumed original, and if not that, then at least the oldest accessible form of the text, can be inferred. Furthermore, they can be arranged in a relatively exact chronological order as to their content and form, using methods of literary criticism, form criticism, history of tradition and other disciplines. Due to the fact that the traditional report concerning Muḥammad was generally assumed to be authentic without further questioning, this has hardly ever been attempted with texts from the Qur'ān, apart from a subdivision of the surahs into a Meccan period (with three phases) and a Medinan one. Moreover, it proves to be much more difficult than in the case of the New Testament because of the peculiarities of the revelations referred to in the Qur'ān, which hardly contain any regional, historical, "biographical" or other "contextual" details, if the texts are read plainly for what they are, i.e., without making use of the exegetical literature of the 9th century with all the stories built around dark and incomprehensible passages to give them some sense.

It is true that many Qur'ānic texts and materials are definitely older than their first attestation in later manuscripts, as is shown e.g. by the inscriptions in the Dome of the Rock; but these earlier versions are largely unknown to us and we have no information as to what they looked like; we neither know about their scope nor can we say in which language they had originally been composed.

Reports of Muslim authors from the 9th century, who tell us about a final edition of the Qur'ān under the third caliph 'Umar, must be considered a literary *topos*, the aim of which was to present the Qur'ān as very old and as close as possible to the time of the Prophet. This *topos* about the emergence of holy literature was current at that time; in a similar way, referring to even older traditions, it can be found in reports about the "Avesta", the collection of Zoroastrian sacred scriptures, and the "Zand", their corresponding laws and commentaries: By command of the Great King, the Avesta and Zand were to be compiled in the same way as Zoroaster himself had received his revelations from (God) Ohrmazd/Ahuramazda. According to tradition, his Majesty, the King of Kings Ardashir I, then followed the religious authority in his court, Tansar, and chose *one* version as canonic; the other versions were excluded from the Canon. Later on, scriptures on a large variety of themes important for Zoroastrianism, which were spread across India, the Byzantine Empire and other countries, were collected at the court of Great King Shapur I and then added to the Avesta.[2]

If the reports of the 'Uṯmānic final edition of the Qur'ān are understood as literary *topoi* of later times – analogous to the collection of Zoroastrian holy literature – then it must be assumed that the canonical text of the Qur'ān is composed of older and newer layers of texts; thus it is the product of a prolonged collection and compilation process, so that its individual texts have to be examined in detail for their possible temporal classification within the framework of history of tradition. Therefore, the path of the term *muḥammad* will be tracked first and foremost with the help of datable and locatable evidence of that time. Due to the absence of literary sources, only coins and inscriptions of the first two Muslim centuries[3] come into question for this purpose. Christian literature as a possible source of information about that time will be examined in another section.[4]

2. *muḥammad* as a Christological title

The term *muḥammad* appeared as an honorary title of Jesus on the coinage of Arab rulers and on inscriptions in the second half of the 7th century and in the first half of the 8th century. The Christological honorific epithet *muḥammad,* which, according to later Arabic understanding, means "the one to be praised" or "the praised one" has a history. The combination of letters *MḤMT* in Persian or Syrian writing was first found a little later than the term

"God's servant" (*'Abdallāh*) on coins in the area of East Iran around the year 40 H (661 CE).[5]

Since 241 (the conquest of the city of Ḥaṭra), Christians had been deported to this area under the Sassanids, first from the Eastern Mesopotamian Empire of 'Arabīya and later from other parts of the country, even from the city of Antioch.[6]

Apparently there were two regions of origin for these coins in which different concepts were represented. In the north-east, today's Turkmenistan and Afghanistan, the term MḤMT is linked to the concepts *'abdallāh* and *ḫalīfat Allāh*; this program would later be represented and enforced by 'Abd al-Malik, who came from Merv far north of Herat. In the south-east, i.e., the area around Kerman, east of Persis, the term MḤMT is equated with *walī allāh* and associated with the law of God, according to the Persian, i.e., mostly Imperial Aramaic, interpretation.

Coinage which documents a religious-political program requires two things: firstly a ruler who has the right or the power to mint such coins, and secondly a religious-political history of at least a few decades, during which the notions internalized by that ruler have had time to develop. As far as we know, 'Abd al-Malik was the first person to have minted MḤMT coins, while on his way from east to west.[7] In the east, however, possibly in his native region of Merv (Marw), this concept must have had a long tradition and affected the way of thinking; in any case, it seems to go back much further than the lifetime of a Prophet of the Arabs. As coins minted since the beginning of the 60s of the 7th century show, the notion of a *muḥammad* is older than the designation of a subsequent Prophet of the Arabs; moreover, this notion stems from a completely different region, which had nothing to do with the Arabian Peninsula.

If (among other languages) Syriac should have been spoken (and not only written) in this region, then MḤMT could be understood as a Syriac term *mḥmt* (MḤMT – *meḥmāt*). The ending "t" in MḤMT – instead of "d" (MḤMD) – could be due to phonetic spelling (hardening of end consonants like in German or Russian);[8] the whole form would then have to be correctly read as *meḥmād* ("the Desired/ Promised One"), which in Arabic led to the pronunciation *maḥmad*.

According to Volker Popp, the languages spoken in this region at this time were above all varieties of Middle Persian and to a lesser degree Parthian. If that were the case, then MḤMT could be understood as an Aramaic heterogram (i.e., a word written in Aramaic [e.g. *mlk*], but pronounced in Persian [*šāh* – "king"]). It could represent the Ugaritic "loan word" MḤMD in Aramaic, meaning "chosen" or "the chosen one" and pronounced in Middle Persian as *mehmet/mahmat*.[9] As power relations became increasingly dominated by Arabs and those entitled to coinage turned more and more to Arabic as their language of reference, the unvocalized term MḤMT had to be grammatically interpreted as an Arabic form, in our case the form "*muḥammad*" (passive participle of the second stem of "*ḥ-m-d*", meaning "the praised one" or "the one to be praised"). This is documented on bilingual coins from the year 60 AH (681 CE) on which *MḤMT* in Middle Persian and *muḥammad* in Arabic script are to be found side by side.[10] Since the 60s AH (680s CE) the Arabic term *muḥammad* in Arabic characters is nearly the only form to be found on coins in the whole of the Syrian region. When the Arabic transcription became common practice, the Syriac meaning "*the desired one*" was replaced by the Arabic understanding: "*the one to be praised*" or "*the praised one*".

The older phonetic interpretation of the Arabic consonantal skeleton "*mḥmd*", *Maḥmad,* seems to have been used for a long time alongside the form *Muḥammad*. In any case it is still used by the theologian John of Damascus (who died in about 750) for the "pseudo-prophet"[11] in texts written in Greek in West Syria. Furthermore, it is also conceivable that the Arabization of MḤMT could lead to the reading *aḥmad*. This version could certainly have emerged for theological reasons. The *Sīra* (biography of the Prophet) considers *Aḥmad* a synonym of *Muḥammad*. Therefore, Sprenger's observation is understandable that the terms/names *muḥammad* and (its approximate equivalent) *aḥmad* were exchanged freely:

> "Understandably traditions came into existence very early, according to which the prophet's mother or his grandfather were ordered to name the child Mohammed in a vision before his birth. In all traditions which refer to his name alone, a fluctuation between Ahmad and Mohammad can be found."[12]

Since ʿAbd al-Malik's reign and due to the increasing process of Arabization the form *muḥammad* became the dominant one. Something already indicated by the clearly Christian symbolism on coins, which rules out an "Islamic" understanding of the term *maḥmad/ muḥammad*, becomes certainty when the inscriptions on the interior walls of the Dome of the Rock from the year 72 (CE 693) and the relevant material from the Qurʾān are taken into consideration.[13] Here the Messiah is *Jesus son of Mary* (ʿĪsā bn Maryam); *muḥammad*, Servant of God *(ʿabdallāh)*, prophet, messenger, the word and the Spirit of God. At least up until this time, i.e., around 700 CE, probably even until 750 CE, the term "*muḥammad* Jesus" was current.

In areas close to the former Phoenician territories, the term *muḥammad* might go back to a loanword from Ugaritic, where the form means "desirable, precious", or another closely related Semitic language. The basic Semitic meaning of the verbal root might be "finding something desirable or precious on account of its form or splendor",[14] so the participle *mḥmd* might be translated as "(the) chosen (one)".[15] Such an understanding – Jesus is *the*

Chosen One, is close to biblical usage: the people of Israel considered themselves to be the "chosen people", a term still used in Paul's speech in the Acts of the Apostles (13, 17).[16] In his Epistle to the Romans (8:33) Paul calls everyone who believes in Jesus Christ a "chosen one (eklektós)". And in Deutero-Isaiah (i.e., chapters 40-55 of Isaiah), God calls the "Servant of God" (עַבְדִּי ʿab̲dī – lit.: my servant") "my chosen one" (בְּחִירִי – bᵊḥīrī), on whom he has put his Spirit. in the Second Book of Isaiah (42:1). The same verbal root appears in 49:7:

> "לְמַעַן יְהוָה אֲשֶׁר נֶאֱמָן קְדֹשׁ יִשְׂרָאֵל וַיִּבְחָרֶךָּ
> *ləmaʿan YHWH ʾašär näʾmān qəd̲oš yiśraʾēl wa-yyib̲əḥārāk̲*
> Because of the LORD who is faithful, the Holy One of Israel who has *chosen* You." (New American Standard, my emphasis)[17]

In the Gospel according to Luke, in the transfiguration scene, the voice out of the clouds calls Jesus the "chosen (*eklelegménos*) son", probably by analogy. The term is dissimilar to that in the Gospel of Mark (9:35), which served as a model for both Luke and Matthew, the term used there being "beloved one" (also in: Matthew 17:6). On the cross, Jesus is taunted by members of the High Council; having helped others he should now help himself, "if he be Christ, the chosen (*eklektós*) of God" (Luke 23:25 [King James]). The two Greek forms *eklelegménos* and *eklektós* are forms of the same verbal root: *ek-legō* – "to choose, elect". Thus, if *muḥammad* is understood as "the chosen one" then the term would reflect an important biblical and Christological tradition.

But also the other meaning, – "glorified, highly praised" or similar – which goes back to the Classical Arabic usage of the root, has a good biblical and Christological basis. In psalm 118:22, we read:

> – אֶבֶן מָאֲסוּ הַבּוֹנִים הָיְתָה לְרֹאשׁ פִּנָּה:"
> *ʾäb̲än maʾasū ha-bbōnīm hayᵊṯāh lə-roʾš pinnāh.*
> The stone which the builders rejected
> Has become the chief corner stone. (...)
> (verse 26): בָּרוּךְ הַבָּא בְּשֵׁם יְהוָה בֵּרַכְנוּכֶם מִבֵּית יְהוָה: –
> ***bārūk̲*** *ha-bbāʾ bə-šēm YHWH* ***bērak̲****nūk̲äm mibbēʾt̲ YHWH.*
> **Blessed** is the one who comes in the name of the LORD;
> We have **blessed** you from the house of the LORD. (NAS; my emphasis)"

The root "brk" meaning "to bless" used in these Hebrew verses is also common in Arabic, where the exact equivalent of the form "*bārūk̲*" (also used as a name, e.g. Baruch Spinoza) would be "*mu-bārak*" (the name of the former Egyptian dictator). Even modern speakers of Arabic will admit that *muḥammad* and *mubārak*, if understood as adjectives, are synonyms.

In the Gospels, this glorification of the psalmist is interpreted as a reference to Jesus: during the triumphal entrance of Jesus into Jerusalem, the following words are shouted to him:

> "blessed (*eulogēménos*) is he who comes in the name of the Lord." (Mark 11:9; as well as in the parallel verses of Matthew 21:9 and Luke 13:35).

According to Mark 14:61-62, the High Priest asks Jesus during his questioning before the High Council:

> "Are You the Christ, the Son of the Blessed One (*ho hyiós tou eulogētou*) ? And Jesus said, 'I am'."

So Jesus is the son of the Blessed One and himself the Blessed One who comes in the name of the Lord. In the so-called "Sanctus", a central hymn of the Latin mass liturgy, the wording is: *Benedictus qui venit in nomine domini – blessed is he who comes in the name of the Lord*, the corresponding form of *muḥammad*, – *benedictus* – is just as common a name in Christian countries as *Baruch* in Judaism and *Muḥammad* among Muslims. Moreover, this sentence is semantically not too far away from a second part of the *Šahādah*, the Islamic creed:

> "*muḥammadun rasūlu llāh* – commonly translated as: Muhammad is the messenger of God."

The Christian Arabic version of the biblical verse is:

"*mubārakun*	*al-ʾātī*	*bi-smi*	*- r-rabb*
a blessed one	the coming one	in the name of the Lord."	

We have already mentioned the fact that *muḥammad* and *mubārak* are synonymous. But even the first part of the Šahādah (*lā llāha illā ḷḷāhu* – there is no god but God) has a biblical basis: Deut 6:4:

> "שְׁמַע יִשְׂרָאֵל יְהוָה אֱלֹהֵינוּ יְהוָה ׀ אֶחָד –
> šmaʿ yiśra'ēl YHWH elohēnū YHWH eḥad
> Hear, O Israel! The LORD is our God, the LORD is one!

The same sentence is quoted in Mark 12:29:

> ἄκουε Ισραήλ κύριος ὁ θεὸς ἡμῶν κύριος εἷς ἐστί
> Hear, o Israel! The Lord our God is one God."

A third interpretation of *muḥammad*, which Alois Sprenger[18] takes into consideration and which fits the already mentioned meaning of the verbal root in Syriac and other old Semitic languages, can certainly be eliminated for the earlier contexts. He refers to the claim of the Qur'ān exegete Ibn 'Abbās "that Mohammad is mentioned in the Torah". Sprenger admits that the term in

Classical Arabic means "to glorify" or "to praise", but adds: "but in related dialects, also those contemporary with the Arabic that was spoken [...] in the Syrian desert ...", it can also mean "to wish for" or "to long for/desire". *Muḥammad* would then be "the one who is longed for".[19] Sprenger refers to Haggai 2:8 and Daniel 11:37:

> וְהִרְעַשְׁתִּי אֶת־כָּל־הַגּוֹיִם וּבָאוּ **חֶמְדַּת** כָּל־הַגּוֹיִם וּמִלֵּאתִי אֶת־הַבַּיִת הַזֶּה כָּבוֹד אָמַר יְהוָה צְבָאוֹת׃
> *"wə-hir^{ə}ʿaštī ʾäṯ-kāl [kɔl] ha-gōyim ū-ḇāʾū **ḥämdaṯ** kāl [kɔl] ha-gōyim ū-millēʾṯī ʾäṯ ha-bayiṯ ha-zzäh kāḇōḏ ʾāmar YHWH ṣəḇāʾōṯ*
> 'I will shake all the nations; and they will come with the **wealth** of all nations, and I will fill this house with glory,' says the LORD of hosts. (Haggai 2:8; my emphasis)
> וְעַל־אֱלֹהֵי אֲבֹתָיו לֹא יָבִין וְעַל־חֶמְדַּת נָשִׁים וְעַל־כָּל־אֱלוֹהַּ לֹא יָבִין כִּי עַל־כֹּל יִתְגַּדָּל׃
> *wə-ʿal ʾälohē ʾaḇoṯāw lōʾ yāḇīn wə-ʿal **ḥämdaṯ** nāśim wə-ʿal kāl [kɔl] ʾälō^{a}h lōʾ yāḇīn kī ʿal kāl yiṯgaddāl*
> He will show no regard for the gods of his fathers or for the **desire** of women, nor will he show regard for any other god; for he will magnify himself above them all. (Dan 11:37)"

The Hebrew form *ḥämdah* (in the NAS version translated as both "wealth" and "desire") here reflects the original Semitic meaning "something longed for/desired". For this reason A. Sprenger thinks that the "claim of Ibn ʿAbbas, that the prophet is foretold in the Old Testament under the name of Mohammad", is "at least partly" justified.[20] As this view is based on the opinion of a Qurʾān exegete of the 9th century, it can certainly be eliminated when it comes to the meaning of *muḥammad* in earlier texts.

The first two sources of the term *muḥammad* are linguistically, etymologically and theologically plausible. The Classical Arabic understanding of the form as "praised, blessed", which seems to have become increasingly dominant over time, fits most contexts in later attestations of the form. It also matches the use of the form in the inscription on the Dome of the Rock, where the praise of God (from the same verbal root: *ḥamd*) is followed by the praise (*muḥammad*) of God's servant.

In both cases the term *muḥammad* constitutes a *Christological predicate*, namely one which corresponds to both the Judeo-Christian and the common Semitic view. Within this Arab-Syriac mentality the historical figure of Jesus, who is intentionally called the "Son of Mary"[21], is valued highly in his role within salvation-history. This interpretation within the framework of salvation-history is even clearer with Aphrahat (died after 345), who did not yet know about the Council of Nicaea, when he speaks of the "Prophetess Mary [...] mother of the great Prophet", i.e., Jesus.[22] In the realm of

Hellenistic Christology, the predicates are different: the Majesty of Jesus is described in *natural categories*: Jesus is the (corporal) Son of God, the incarnate God.[23]

However, this view only became official doctrine in the Greek (and as a consequence also in the Latin) church since the Council of Nicaea in the year 325. In the Syriac church the outcome of the Council of Nicaea – a Christology assuming two natures of Christ and a Binitarian (later Trinitarian) concept of God – was only accepted at a synod in Seleukia-Ctesiphon in the year 410. Only after that these doctrines gradually adopted by Syriac theologians.[24] These doctrinal changes, however, did not reach the (formerly deported) Syro-Arabic Christians in the east of the Persian Empire. They stuck to their Syro-Arabic Christology, which they kept in the heartland of Iran and later in West Syria – after they had managed to gain power after the decline of the Sassanid Empire.

To sum up, we come to the conclusion that *muḥammad* expresses the "Majesty of Jesus" and reflects the Syrian and Arab-Syrian (pre-Nicean) Christology, which is also attested on coins, in the inscription on the interior walls of the Dome of the Rock and in Qur'ānic material: Jesus is the Chosen/ Praised One (*muḥammad*), the Messiah (*masīḥ*), God's servant (*'abdallāh*), the Prophet (*nabī*), the Messenger (*rasūl*), God's trustee/ procurator (*walī Allāh*), the Word and the Spirit of God.

But how did it come about that "*muḥammad* Jesus" gradually became the "Prophet of the Arabs"?

2 The Separation of Jesus from his Christological Predicate

2.1 Function and Possible Misunderstanding of Christological Predicates

Christological predicates serve as a way of putting into words the experience of the faithful that, through Jesus, their religious questions had been answered and the feeling of hope evoked – in spite of the ever present experience of deficiency in history. He is, for those who believe in him, the "mediator of salvation". Therefore, Christians adopt superlative topoi for Jesus, which is handed down from their religious and cultural traditions as perceptions of salvation.[25]

Jesus was either called the Messiah, the Messenger, the *muḥammad* and so forth, i.e., following the "Semitic" tradition within the framework of salvation history, or – ontologically – as the physical Son of God, God's Word incarnate, i.e., following the "Greek way". In either case, these predicates reflect concepts of religious ideals and hopes, which are definitely in contrast to Jesus as a "figure of poverty". Accordingly, it is understandable from the perspective of the psychology of religion, that these predicates were often more fascinating than Jesus himself.

In Hellenistic Christology there was the danger of the title taking on a life of its own. Jesus was perceived, above all, as God walking around on earth and the concrete person Jesus was neglected. Also in Jewish-Christian and Syrian-Arabic Christology, the majestic titles were so fascinating that the figure of Jesus receded. This process of a shift of interests to the majestic name and its gradual disengagement from its historical catalyzer Jesus, the original subject of all titles, is historically verifiable and attestable. In so doing, the focal point of our investigation will be the inscriptions that the respective rulers programmatically added to the sacred sites they erected, as these, more than anything else, reveal the official religious concept propagated by these rulers.

2.1 The time of ʿAbd al-Malik

In the programmatic Christological inscriptions on the interior walls of the Dome of the Rock in Jerusalem from the year 693, all of the titles named above are still explicitly linked to Jesus, the Son of Mary: it is for him that God's blessing is requested. A divine sonship is rejected. The inscription on the exterior walls of the building, done at approximately the same time, avows Allah as the sole deity without associated partners, and uses the same majestic titles *messenger, prophet, muḥammad, God's servant*: a divine sonship is equally dismissed. The blessing of God is craved for the messenger of Allah. However, the name *Īsā* (Jesus) or the term *masīḥ* (messiah), to which all these epithets refer according to the inscription on the interior walls, are not to be found in the text.[26] A possible explanation would be that the inscriptions on the exterior walls represent a second, somewhat later time layer. Here, the epithet is already detached from the name of Jesus. A text belonging to the same time layer might be the inscription on a milestone found close to Tiberias (AH 83/ CE 704), on which the only God – any partnership is rejected – and *muḥammad*, the prophet, is professed.[27]

Already at the time of Muʿāwiya the name "Jesus" is not to be found on coins, which, as a rule, reflect the central religious concepts of the current ruler in concise form. That, in fact, they *do* refer to Jesus is "only" recognizable due to the Christian symbols employed: one or more crosses, the depiction of a Christian ruler or of a reigning or alternatively apocalyptic Jesus, the head of John the Baptist in connection with a dove (symbol Christ's baptism) etc. Even during the early phase of Abd al-Malik's reign, when the Arabic motto *muḥammad* had already started to appear on coins, they nevertheless still displayed these undoubtedly Christian symbols (crosses or pictures of Christian rulers).[28] These symbols, although clearly Christian in origin, even though they are generally misinterpreted in Islamic numismatics as Islamic to make them fit the traditional report, soon receded in favor of a new symbol: stone pyramids, which were stacked up in tiers in the fashion of the Nabatean and Syrian steles. What does this stone symbol mean?

We do not know the theological developments of ʿAbd al-Malik and his advisors and therefore have to rely on indirect evidence. An important clue for interpretation purposes can be found in the erection of the building built over the rocks of Mount Zion and decorated with the inscriptions mentioned – the Dome of the Rock. According to its architecture as well as its Christological inscriptions this is a Christian building. Its location was motivated both by Jewish tradition (the Temple Mount as well as the myths linked to it: [Adam's grave and the place of the sacrifice of Isaac etc.]), and by specific Christian traditions (the Dome of the Rock as a Church of the Holy Sepulchre in contrast to the Byzantine Church of the Holy Sepulchre in the Old City of Jerusalem).[29]

The idea that Jerusalem already played a central role in Syrian-Christian projections is shown by the Syriac Apocalypse of Daniel, which was composed possibly as early as the 4th or 5th century CE, but is definitely "pre-Islamic".[30] According to Apocalyptic literature, in the Last Days everything will be concentrated on Jerusalem. After all, it is the Antichrist who is ruling there, before he is killed by an angel (syrDan. 21-24). The eschatological epiphany of God will happen on Mount Zion (syrDan. 26-29). Then Christ comes as a powerful warrior who brings peace to the world (syrDan. 30-32) and builds a new Jerusalem. Afterwards all nations go on a pilgrimage to Mount Zion (syrDan. 38-39). This tradition remained in force for centuries. The interest in Jerusalem – at that time the religious "center of the world" –

> "culminated at the end of the 7th century in the construction of the Dome of the Rock on the Temple Mount", which "stirred up the fiercest of emotions among the (*rather:* other [*my correction*]) Christians because this undertaking could be regarded as the reconstruction of the temple."[31]

One question which strangely enough has hardly been discussed up to now still remains: Why was the rock under the cupola of the cathedral not leveled out and the church building constructed in the conventional style, but rather the people entering were confronted with the bare rocks, lined and vaulted by the building? This only makes sense if it is the solid rock itself which is programmatically brought to the fore in this way. The central significance of the rock is equally apparent in the stone portrayals which were tiered and tapered up to the top on the coins of ʿAbd al-Malik as far as North Africa. Similarly, in his book against heresies, John of Damascus names as the one hundredth (Christian) heresy the "*Ismaelites*" (not "*Muslims*") and their prophet "*Machmed*" (not "*Muḥammad*"); he reports that they worship a stone[32] (which has nothing to do with the black stone in the Kaʿba).

The replacement of the cross depictions and comparable symbols by ʿAbd al-Malik should not be interpreted as apostasy from Christianity. It should rather be seen as the adoption of another Christian program, – as opposed to Syrian, Jacobite and particularly Byzantine Christianity, – and was supposed to demonstrate the foundation of the Arabic Church and its empire.

In order to recognize the patterns in effect here, it is necessary to go back to biblical, above all, Old Testamental traditions, the images and stories of which made up the background of all religious concepts and programmatic assertions of that time. So the question arises: Where in the Bible do we read about such a function of the "stone"?

Apart from archaic traditions (which had an effect on the Old Testament), the programmatic significance of stone and rip-rap revetment obviously goes back to Old Testamental concepts, in which important agreements and contracts were guaranteed using holy stones or stone symbolism. God promised Jacob prolific offspring in a "dream", which was understood to be a positive answer to the foundation of the people of Israel (Gen. 28:10-22). Consequently, Jacob "rose early in the morning, and took the stone that he had put under his head and set it up as a pillar and poured oil on its top (28:18)." The Hebrew word used for this memorial stone was מַצֵּבָה *maṣṣeḇāh*, which normally designates a stone pillar. He then called this location בֵּית־אֵל *bēṯ-'ēl (Bethel, i.e., "house of God").* The full form of the designation for God (*bēt 'älohīm – house of God*) appears in verse 22:

> "וְהָאֶבֶן הַזֹּאת אֲשֶׁר־שַׂמְתִּי מַצֵּבָה יִהְיֶה בֵּית אֱלֹהִים וְכֹל אֲשֶׁר תִּתֶּן־לִי עַשֵּׂר אֲעַשְּׂרֶנּוּ לָךְ:"
> wə ha-'äḇän ha-zo'ṯ 'ᵃšär śamᵊtī maṣṣēḇāʰ yihᵊhäh bēt 'älohīm wə-ḵāl [kɔl] 'ᵃšär titän-lī 'aśśer 'a'asᵊrännū lāḵ
> This stone, which I have set up as a pillar, will be God's house, and of all that You give me I will surely give a tenth to You."

In another place, Jacob erects a pile of stones as confirmation of his contract with his father-in-law, Laban (Gen. 34:45-48), which Laban (verse 47) named יְגַר שָׂהֲדוּתָא *Yəḡar Śāhᵃḏūṯā'* (NAS: Jegar-sahadutha). It is interesting to note that this is the only clearly Aramaic word in a text entirely written in Hebrew. It means "piles of evidence"; Jacob gave it a Hebrew name: גַּלְעֵד *Galᵊ'ēḏ* (NAS: Galeed), the Hebrew translation of the word: "a pile serving as a witness".[33]

The Christological adoption of this stone symbolism can be seen in the quotation of Psalm 118:22) in the gospels:

> "The stone which the builders rejected
> Has become the chief corner stone."

Instead of presenting speculative explanations, a sentence by the Syrian theologian Aphrahaṭ about the Christological significance of rock and stone from his book "Demonstrations" will be adduced:

> "Demonstration 1:3: And now hear concerning faith that is based upon the Stone, and concerning the structure that is reared up upon the Stone. [...][34]
> 1:6: But I must proceed to my former statement that Christ is called the Stone in the Prophets. For in ancient times David said concerning Him: –*The stone which the builders rejected has become the head of the building.* (*emphasis in the original English translation; the sentence is Ps. 118:22, see above*)[35]
> "[...]By these things they rejected the Stone which is Christ. And how did it become the head of the building? How else than that it was set up over the building of the Gentiles and upon it is reared up all their building (the German translator adds here: "as a foundation stone")."[36]

Aphrahat quotes further verses of the Old Testament with stone symbolism, which he understands from the perspective of Christology, e.g. Ezekiel 13:10 and 22:30 and above all Isaiah 28:16:

> "Therefore thus says the Lord God, 'Behold, I am laying in Zion a stone, a tested stone, A costly cornerstone for the foundation, firmly placed."

and adds Matthew 21:44:

> "And he who falls on this stone will be broken to pieces; but on whomever it falls, it will scatter him like dust."[37]

Then he explains (Demonstration 1:8):

> "And again Daniel also spoke concerning this stone which is Christ. For he said: 'The stone was cut out from the mountain, not by hands, and it smote the image, and the whole earth was filled with it (Daniel 2:34-35)".

Furthermore, he refers to Zechariah 4:7[38] and stresses the significance of the quote:

> "*Demonstration 1:9:* And definitely did He show concerning this stone:— Lo! On this stone will I open seven eyes (Zechariah 3:9)." *Demonstration 1:17:* And also Simon who was called Cephas because of his faith was called the firm rock (Matthew 16, 18)."[39]

Aphrahat's bible exegesis reads like an iconographic guide for the construction of the Dome of the Rock. Just to what extent ʿAbd al-Malik was familiar with the writings of Aphrahat evades our knowledge. But it can be assumed that a Syrian-Christian pictorial theology of this kind, based on Old Testament material, dominated his perception of the world. The significant role of Old Testament concepts for the doctrine of ʿAbd al-Malik is also visible in the depictions of utensils of Solomon's Temple on the coins he had struck.[40]

However, both areas of symbolism – stone and temple utensils – do not point to ʿAbd al-Malik's return to Judaism or adoption of a totally new religion, but are characteristics of his peculiar, Arabic Christianity.[41] Evidence that this is indeed so can be found in the very inscriptions added (by him) to the Dome of the Rock. For users of his coins, however, this symbolism was no longer self-evident as being Christian, as in the case of the former depictions of crosses. This lack of understanding can be read in a remark by John of Damascus about stone worship among the Ismaelites: He had not understood what it was all about. The result of this was that titles common on coins, and probably also as religious concepts, above all the predicate *muḥammad*, were no longer perceived as referring to Jesus.

2.3 The time of al-Walīd

ʿAbd al-Malik's successor, al-Walīd, had given up his father's apocalyptic ideas referring to Jerusalem and expanded the sanctuary of John the Baptist in Damascus, the *Ḥarām*, where the head of John the Baptist was preserved, a site which had already been treasured by Muʿāwiya.[42] Damascus is situated in the very north of the old ("Arabian") Nabatean Empire. The occupation of this tradition through John's sanctuary in the north had its counterpart in the south: the construction of a sanctuary in Medina, 49 years later. There are inscriptions on both buildings which document the religious and political program of the ruler and formally and conceptually follow the inscriptions on the Dome of the Rock. Space limitations prevent an interpretation of the entire texts of these inscriptions in the present study; but a formal analogy between these texts and the inscriptions on the Dome of the Rock and the majestic titles referred to is obvious.

The Umayyad Mosque constructed in the "Year of the Arabs" 86/87 AH (707/708 CE) in Damascus was certainly a Christian building/structure. The church previously located there was completely or partially torn down for the new construction. A programmatic inscription was affixed to the "mosque" by al-Walīd.[43]

At the beginning, al-Walīd renounced the religious bigotry of his father and explained that "there is no coercion in matters of the *dīn*" (according to conventional and current Arabic understanding erroneously translated as "religion"), and that from now on "the right path has been distinguished from the wrong one". The text is the same as surah 2:256:

> "*la ikrāha fī d-dīn. qad tabayyana r-rušdu mina l-ġayyi.*
> There is no compulsion in religion. The right direction is henceforth distinct from error. (Pickthall's translation)"

Christoph Luxenberg translates the term *dīn* trying to reconstruct the understanding of the time the text was written:

> "Whatever is true/ correct/ righteous (*dīn*) cannot be denied, the right way (*rušd*) is distinguished from the wrong way (*ġayy*; i.e., in the scriptures)."

This interpretation connects the two clauses logically.

Then the oneness of God without association of partners and the unity of the community is professed: in the following it is said that "our prophet is praised (*muḥammad*). May God incline to him and bless him". This blessing reflects the contents of the text on the interior and exterior walls of the Dome of the Rock. The following sentence states that al-Walīd, the servant of God, built the sacred site and (partially?) tore down the previous church.

Although the few majestic titles (*rasūl* and *muḥammad*), the rejection of partners associated with Allah and the "quoted" blessing refer to Jesus, he is not explicitly mentioned as "the Messiah Jesus, son of Mary" as in the Dome of the Rock. Here, the title has priority, comparable with the protocol of a religious sovereign. Like his father had done on a milestone not far from Tiberias and on coins, the new ruler al-Walīd calls himself "servant of God (*ʿabdallāh*)".

2.4 The Sacred Site in Medina

This tendency can also be found in an inscription on a sanctuary in Medina, which was erected in 135 (756), thus after the beginning of the Abbasid period.[44] However, the first centuries after the end of the Umayyad dynasty should be considered an interim period during which the traditional religious concepts and formulae were kept and complemented by legal regulations inspired by the Eastern Mesopotamian Arabs, who themselves had been strongly influenced by the Persians.[45]

In the inscription, the acknowledgement of a monotheism without association of partners is followed by the affirmation of the "correct" Christology through the repetition of the same Christological titles, which can already be found in the Dome of the Rock and, limited to only two titles, the Umayyad Mosque in Damascus. The remaining predicates are: *muḥammad, rasūl* and (as an addition not found in Damascus) *ʿabdallāh*, followed by a blessing of the messenger, as in Jerusalem and Damascus. Unlike the inscriptions on the interior walls of the Dome of the Rock, but like those on the exterior walls, there is no mention of the messiah, Son of Mary. The person who ordered the affixation of the inscriptions did not mention his own name but his title, to which *ʿabdallāh*, however, also belonged.

Here the question arises whether in these inscriptions Islam is already intended as a new religion of its own, or if Christian concepts still continue to be valid, albeit with more radical traits (emphasis on command and obedience, dominance of the new creed). Similarly it is not clear what exactly is to be understood by *kitāb allāh* (God's scripture) and the *sunna* of the prophet.[46]

There is good reason to assume that Jesus is still meant – and therefore the religion is still to be considered a kind of Christianity, as the predicate *'abdallāh* (servant of God) as a title, is not linked with the ruler, but also with the epithet *muḥammad*. Only in later Islam was it to become the designation of the prophet's father, so that now Muḥammad is the son of a "person called *'Abdallāh*". According to Volker Popp, the concept of *Muḥammad* as the name of the "Prophet of the Arabs" begins when, in inscriptions, the epithet "God's servant" is no longer used referring to him.[47]

There are also other reasons to assume this, above all, theological ones: the apparent formal coherence of the four inscriptions, which are constructed analogously, show that they document a comparable religious program, evolving on its way from Jerusalem to Medina, the themes being the nature of God and Christology. The four inscriptions on the interior and exterior walls of the Dome of the Rock, in Damascus and in Medina proclaim the religious and political program of the rulers who ordered them. What they have in common is the proclamation of the oneness of God in connection with a strong rejection of any association of God with partners or the concept of Jesus as his son. As the predicate "son of God" is thus impossible the alternatives *muḥammad, 'abdallah, rasūl* etc. had to be resorted to. In the inscriptions on the interior walls of the Dome of the Rock these are still explicitly linked to the messiah Jesus, son of Mary, on all other inscriptions only implicitly, as the words *'Īsā bn Maryam* or *masīḥ* are missing. A request for God's blessing on him always follows.

As the predicate *muḥammad* and other terms are confronted with the concept of an association of partners to God (i.e., trinity) or of Jesus as the Son of God, it becomes a key term of a theological and Christological program, of a "correct" view (i.e., *dīn*) of the nature of God and Christ. There might be some objection as we cannot be sure that these terms refer to Jesus. So let us assume that Jesus was not meant and that these terms refer to the founder of Islam, the Prophet of the Arabs: If that were the case, why then was it felt necessary to contrast the acknowledgement of "*Muḥammed, the Prophet of the Arabs*" with the (strongly rejected) association of partners to God or the view that Jesus was God's son? If in the central religious formula of the "new religion", which – according to the sunnah – was mainly preached to former polytheists, two views are explicitly mentioned (albeit rejected) that are in stark contrast to the intended propagation of an undifferentiated monotheism (i.e., "monarchianism"), this might have the adverse effect![48] The risk of a Binitarian and Trinitarian complication/ dilution of the strict monotheism, which is the core of Islam, was only present in forms of Christianity that were influenced by Hellenism. The Arabic Christians vehemently rejected this development, which had also been coming into the East

Syrian region since the synod of Seleucia-Ctesiphon. So in these texts, *muḥammad* is not the name of a person, but one of a number of predicates, which explicitly negate a Christological doctrine of the two natures of Christ or a Binitarian or Trinitarian view of the nature of God, i.e., they reflect exactly the "pre-Nicean" Syrian-Arab conception.

Maybe the inscriptions in Medina are the last to present *muḥammad* as a (Christological) title, as the concrete linkage to Jesus seems to have almost completely receded behind the predicates. Thus, the re-interpretation of the predicate *muḥammad* as the name of a Prophet of the Arabs called *Muḥammad* was made possible.

This gradual disappearance of Jesus behind his Christological predicates could also have something to do with the fact the Persian influence, which also played a role at the beginning of the Qur'ānic movement, had meanwhile become stronger. This is already shown by the inscriptions in Medina and all the more by the developments in and since the late 8th century.[49] It seems to be that Persian Christianity was more theocratic and methodical than its Syrian counterpart which led to a weakening of the position of Jesus. As the Syrian influence decreased, the figure of Jesus faded more and more into the background or out of sight.

2.5 *muḥammad* as a title in later Islamic tradition

It is interesting to note that the later Muslim tradition of the 9th century, contrary to the other current biographies of the prophet, seem to remember that *muḥammad* was originally a title, and only secondarily a name given to newly born children. In his "Book of The Major Classes (*Kitāb al-ṭabaqāt al-kabīr)*"[50] the famous Arab scholar Ibn Sa'd (died 845) reported about the different names of the prophet in a section of his biography entitled "Report on the Names and Patronymics of the Messenger of Allah".

Ibn Sa'd summarizes existing sources from different (fictional?) authors. According to one version, the prophet was at first named *Quṭam* at his birth by his grandfather 'Abd al-Muṭṭalib. It was later that his mother, Āmina, spoke about a dream with an angel and the grandfather renamed him Muḥammed.

In other sources cited by Ibn Sa'd in the same chapter, up to six other names are mentioned, of which *Muḥammad* was only one.[51] According to Ibn Sa'd six names were reported in two sources (in other sources it is three and five names). According to them, the prophet himself said that he had six names: *Muḥammad* (the Blessed/Praised One), *Aḥmad* (the Highly Praised One), *Ḥātim* (the Seal), *Ḥāšir* (the Awakener [of the dead?]), *'Āqib* (the last prophet; concluder) and *Māḥī* (the Redeemer [of sins]; also: the one who is awakened [to life]; the Eraser [of sins]). All of these are theologically significant names which would fundamentally fit Jesus more easily. In any case

Alois Sprenger should be agreed with when he concludes with reference to the reports in Ibn Saʿd:

> "In these traditions 'Mohammad' appears, in the same way as the rest of the other names, as an epithet of the prophet and not as a proper name."[52]

To sum up: Alois Sprenger already opined that *muḥammad* was a title and not a proper name. Of course, he relates everything to the Prophet of the Arabs. It is his opinion

> "It (Islam) is the only world religion about the formation of which we have reliable information, regardless of its age."[53]

If historical-critical methods are applied (a formal issue) and (only) contemporary sources are taken into consideration (a material issue), then this conviction begins to totter. However, the fact that Islamic sources as late as the 9th century know that Muḥammad (and other "names") are actually theological titles, remains noteworthy and is difficult to deny.

By the beginning of the Abbasid era, however, these had taken on a life of their own and, at least at first sight, had detached themselves from their original subject Jesus. Now a situation had arisen in which the former title *muḥammad* could and had to be connected to other material under new conditions and requirements which corresponded to the increasingly strong Arabic character that both the religion and the political leadership had meanwhile adopted.

3. The historicization of the title *muḥammad* as Prophet of the Arabs

There are numerous examples in the history of civilization of how basic initial processes are traced back and linked to people whose actions allegedly originated these processes; in some cases, narrative traditions evolve around these "founding fathers", because central aspects of what the new creed is all about can much more easily be made understandable and conceivable if these aspects are clad in a (albeit fictitious) biography with a message, or to use the Greek word, a *kerygma*.

The foundation of cities and empires can be based on initial figures (e.g. Romulus and Remus), as well as the derivation of a nation (e.g. Moses), a religion and so forth, but also central religious content can be turned into a legendary person of flesh and blood, for example "the three divine virtues", *faith, hope* and *love*, which are worshipped as concrete saints both in the Greek/Russian and in the Latin church.

Above all breaks and new beginnings in the evolution of a religion constituting a new phase of its history are often linked to narratives about their founder. In some cases, these characters are completely fictitious, like the Chinese "philosopher" Lao tsu (老子 Pinyin: Lǎozǐ, literally: "old one"), the biblical patriarchs, in other cases explanations of theological or philosophical views are connected to "historical" people, whose actual biography is hardly known at all, like Gautama Siddhartha or Zarathustra.[54] In the third case the sparse biographical material that does exist is recounted with a kerygmatic intention and extended for the purpose of propagation, the best example being the problem of the "historical Jesus" as opposed to the "kerygmatic Jesus".

Even sacred literature with central significance for a religion can be ascribed to fictitious founding figures and be established in their biography, like the *Gathas* of Zarathustra of the *"Five Books"* of Moses, a figure of central importance in Judaism, Christianity and Islam. In the latter case his authorship remained undisputed for more than two thousand years, although the "exodus" of the Jews (with the drowning of a whole army) is neither mentioned in any Egyptian text nor did their wandering in the desert and conquest of the Promised Land leave any archaeological traces.

So if we are to assess the understanding and probably only later "personalization" of the concept *muḥammad*, originally a central term to be found on all inscriptions and coins struck by non-Trinitarian Arabic Christians since ʻAbd al-Malik, we have to keep these facts in mind. At first, i.e., in the iconography of the coins and particularly in the Dome of the Rock, *muḥammad* only referred to the *Servant of God* and the *Messiah Jesus, Son of Mary*. Then the name of Jesus was mentioned less and less and was thus gradually overshadowed by the predicates, something that could easily happen, as most of the new members of the movement – unlike the old ruling class – did not know the original meanings and connotations of these terms. So it comes as no surprise that they got the impression that *muḥammad* was in fact a name and referred to a historically different person.

Above all opponents of the non-Trinitarian, explicitly "Arab" Christianity from other Christian denominations, i.e., mainly the Syrian and Byzantine Christians (e.g. John of Damascus), did not know the Christological title *muḥammad* from their own tradition. What could be more obvious for them than to understand the term as the name of the Prophet of the Arabs? Thus, they boosted a development within Arab Christianity which had presumably already started, although we unfortunately have no material proof of this.[55]

The titles "Messiah", "Servant of God", Bearer of "Word" and "Spirit", commonly used in "pre-Nicean" Christology and increasingly misunderstood, gradually receded. They were more and more replaced by the epithets *muḥammad* and the two titles "prophet *(nabī)*" and "messenger *(rasūl)*". Together they were interpreted as *muḥammad*, the *messenger* of God and the *prophet*, a person who stood for the beginning of a new Arabic religious movement: *Muḥammad, the Son of ʿAbdallāh* .

This development has a second origin: The Arab Christians from the East, who had determined the course of events since ʿAbd al-Malik, had brought with them at least the core constituents of the Qur'ānic material, let us call it tentatively the "Meccan" part. They edited, or in some cases maybe even had to translate it into the – at that time – only emerging Arabic language, the result being a kind of Arabic with a strong Syro-Aramaic imprint. In some passages it might even be fair to call it an *Aramaic-Arabic hybrid language*, as shown by the inscriptions on the Dome of the Rock in the 7th century. Further material was added to these core constituents in the course of the 8th century. These parts might be very roughly equated to the "Medinan" surahs and verses.

The authorship of a modern book is usually clear, but in the case of holy literatures their content is very often not connected to an "author", but rather to "creators", "guarantors" or "informants." Almost at the same time as the Qur'ān, the Zoroastrian traditions were gradually codified into a canon of scriptures. Their authorship was attributed to a man called Zarathustra, who, as the newest Iranological research shows, is a largely legendary figure. It might be that the oldest kernel of the Qur'ān, the "Meccan" surahs which the first generation of Arab Christians had brought along from the East, was assigned to a similar "informant/ transmitter" of the divine message, an idealized *Moses*. Even in the case of Jesus' *Sermon on the Mount* it is quite obvious that the model for this was the reception of the Ten Commandments by Moses on Mount Sinai, so that Jesus was portrayed as a "new Moses". Similarly, the *New Moses of the Arab Christians* from the East was expected to guarantee the long-awaited exodus from the isolated East Iranian enclaves into their new and old home country or even into the Holy Land. This conceptual "archaeology", in terms of history of ideas, was later forgotten due to two events: First, the "exodus" was successfully completed after the collapse of Sassanid rule and ʿAbd al-Malik's taking over of power, and secondly, Qur'ānic material was now available in Arabic language and script. Now *muḥammad* appears as the prophet and messenger addressed in the Qur'ān.

Furthermore, the Arabization of these Christians must be taken into consideration. Like in the case of the Nabateans, we might assume that the language of everyday intercourse of the Early East Arab Christians was a kind of Arabic, but that the written language they used was originally rather a kind of Aramaic (albeit with an Arabic substrate), which was then gradually replaced by a then only emerging written Arabic Koine (now with an Aramaic substrate). At the time of the "Arab" *Maʿāwiya* (Aramaic)/ *Muʿāwiya* (Arabic), – the Aramaic name form appears in the oldest "Islamic" inscription in Gadara in Greek letters (!) – this process was still "in statu nascendi", but it began powerfully with ʿAbd al-Malik and his successors. The new rulers perceived themselves as distinctly "Arabic", as heirs to, for example, the old ("Arabic") Nabatean Empire, during which programmatic sacred sites were built in the north (Damascus) and in the south (Medina), in addition to the "theological center" (Jerusalem). So it was more and more the *Arabic* character of this autonomous and, – at first still superficially (?) Christian – religion and the Arabic language of the Qur'ānic texts which increasingly became the dominant feature and served to establish a new identity: *muḥammad* now had to be understood as the normative *Prophet of the Arabs*, who stood *at the beginning* of the new movement, – "a messenger, (one) of yourselves (surah 9:128, Pickthall)" – at the same time the *Arab* transmitter of the meanwhile *Arabic* Qur'ānic revelation.

The emergence of the concept of a *Prophet of the Arabs* that the Qur'ānic sayings can be traced back to, can indeed have taken place as late as the first half of the 8th century, when Jesus was still (officially) the subject of the Christological titles in the inscriptions and on coins, as the report of John of Damascus shows, who talks about *Ma(ch)med* as a historical figure and who assigns several surahs, – in his Greek: *graphḗ* (scripture) – directly to him. However, the person he considers a "pseudo-prophet" for him is the founder of the *Christian heresy of the Ismaelites,* so when he discusses their doctrine, for him it is not a *new religion*, but *one of many heresies within Christianity.*

Accordingly, in an initial phase – until about 750, – Mohammed is indeed occasionally seen as a historical figure and initiator of the movement, but still in the context of Christianity. This is supported by the fact that this historicized *Muḥammad* is still probably seen as an "apostle" of Jesus Christ – the Christian Arabic term used for "apostle" is *rasūl*, the same word which in Islam means "messenger (of God)/ prophet", – whose task it is to confirm and enforce the Torah and the gospel, i.e., the scriptures (Arabic: *kitāb*), against the false interpretations of other "People of the Book (*ahl kitāb*; according to Muslim understanding: Christians and Jews)". Y. D. Nevo and J. Koren assume an earlier proclamation of *Muḥammed* as *Prophet of the Arabs*: 690-692.[56] For this assessment, their differing interpretation of the inscription in the Dome of the Rock is crucial. Whether the latter can really be interpreted as referring to a "prophet Muḥammad", is highly questionable.[57]

There does not seem to have been any personalization of the epithet *muḥammad* in the 7th century. The alleged evidence of Christian sources of this time cited by many authors for this purpose, in which *Muḥammad* is supposedly spoken of, are often uncritically analyzed and, in order to bring them into accordance with historiography, which is presumed authentic, wrongly dated. In the course of the first half of the 8th century, up to John of Damascus, there is evidence of an understanding of the term *muḥammad* as the designation of a Prophet of the Arabs named *Muḥammad,*[58] thus the earliest evidence of a historicization of *muḥammad.*

But it was not until relatively late in the 8th, or even as recently as the early 9th century, that the idea arose that the Arabic movement was a new and *no longer Christian* religion; however, it was not yet described as *Islām*). Due to this development, the Prophet of the Arabs named *muḥammad* becomes the autonomous preacher of a new religion who adjusts and surpasses the wrong teachings of Jews and Christians with a new revelation. The *Arab* preacher becomes the proclaimer of the *Qur'ān,* which is no longer a confirmation of the Torah and the gospels, but, – according to later surahs, – an autonomous text on a par with (and even above) these scriptures.

Since this time there have been attempts to biographically fill the life of the Prophet, which was supposedly spent on the Arabian Peninsula. Mecca and Medina, which are only seldom mentioned in the Qur'ān (Mecca once and Medina three times; in all cases it is not clear as to whether place names are meant!), become central locations in his life. In this process, the origin of this movement in the East Mesopotamian Empire *ʿArabīya,* a country which had meanwhile fallen into oblivion, was an advantage, as this location could now be equated with the *Arabian Peninsula.*

These early attempts from the second half of the 8th century are no longer available to us. The biographies of the Prophet cited today were all written down in the 9th and 10th centuries,[59] the collection of the *sunna* in the 9th century, but these later works may indeed have used sources from the second half of the 8th century; for their purpose of gaining credibility it was then only logical to backdate their sources and claim an uninterrupted chain of transmitters starting with the alleged "companions (of the Prophet)" (*ṣaḥāba*), his relatives and wives, in other words, to connect to the early days "of Islam." In this process, an amazing amount of historicizing material was collected from the stories in circulation, which were all linked to *Muḥammad,* apart from numerous newly created stories. The great pains taken to put together lists of informants and transmitters are clear indicators of the profound deficit felt due to these intentionally backdated traditions.

4. The Qur'ānic Material on the Figure of the Prophet[60]

4.1 The three phases of Qur'ānic development and the historicization of *muḥammad*

On inscriptions and coins, i.e., on contemporary material evidence, the term *MḤMT* (according to the extant evidence) appeared for the first time in the year 40 AH (661 CE), while the Arabic spelling *Muḥammad* can be found unvocalized no earlier than the year 60 AH (681 CE). Therefore, it would be astonishing if the term had already been used in the (few?) Qur'ānic materials which existed up to these temporal breaks. In fact, *muḥammad* appears in no more than four places in the Qur'ān, although the prophet is consistently addressed in the surahs as *rasūl* or *nabī*.

As we have shown, until at least 135 AH (756 CE = inscription in Medina), *muḥammad* was a Christological title, at least in official theology (according to Chr. Luxenberg's nomenclature "*Muḥammad I*"). However, even before this, in the first half of the 8th century, a historicization/ personalization of the concept might have been initiated ("Mohammed II").[61]

This historicization can only be detected in a few late ("Medinan") passages in the Qur'ān. It has to be mentioned that, according to later theologically inspired historiography, all places where God speaks to a *messenger* (rasūl) or *prophet* (nabī) or simply says "you", translators and commentators understand this as referring to the *Prophet of the Arabs* and add (mostly in brackets) the name *Muḥammad*. Therefore the topical index of most modern Qur'ān translations enumerates hundreds of occurrences under the entry *Muḥammad*. These comparatively frequent passages are, however, mostly short and as rule formulated in a very general and unspecified way, so that there is no clear indication as to whom they refer exactly. If the evidence on coins and inscriptions is taken into consideration, it turns out that whomever they might refer to, it can hardly have been the figure of the "prophet *Muḥammad*" as he appears in the biographies until the second half of the 8th century. However, the fact remains that it is always a "you" or a "prophet" who is addressed in the Qur'ān. As the oldest surahs, which originated in the far East of Mesopotamia, indeed assume a prophetic addressee, – unless these titles (*rasūl* and *nabī*) are not only literary *topoi* and the 2nd person relating to a "*typological 'you'*" (for the type "prophet in general") – then we can assume that there was a first (Aramaic) preacher in the land of origin whose name is not known. Therefore the claim is not "*the prophet Muḥammad did not exist*", – even the question "*did Muḥammad exist?*" is too simplistic, – but rather:

> ***There might have been a prophetic figure at the beginning of the religious movement that later became Islām, but his name was not Muḥammad, and his life was unlike the one described in the Sīra literature (biographies of the Prophet).***

When later the prophet's life was depicted with ever more concrete details, it might have been this prophetic leader that provided the personal kernel to which later generations added legends and stories, without, however, being aware of his possible historical beginning.

Biblical figures named in the Qur'ān are the following: Abraham (*Ibrahīm*): 79 times, Moses: (*Mūsā*): 136 times, Aaron (*Hārūn*): 20 times, Jesus

(*ʿĪsā*): 24 times, Mary (*Maryam*): 34 times, Adam (*Adam*): 25 times, Noah (*Nūḥ*): 33 times and Pharaoh (*Firʿawn*): 74 times; the term *nabī* (prophet) without a name: 43 times, "messenger/apostle of Allah" (*rasūl Allāh*) appears more than 300 times in different variations. The form *muḥammad* is named in only four places.[62]

As several Qur'ānic texts existed as early as the end of the 7th century in Arabic, the prophet addressed in them, whenever he speaks about Jesus or Moses/Jesus, can only be the already implied "unknown prophet" from the beginning of the Qur'ānic movement or a "typological prophet". In later texts from the first half of the 8th century, in contrast, the "prophet" might already designate the meanwhile personalized *Prophet of the Arabs*, i.e., to a purportedly historical figure. Nevertheless, even this latter person of reference still belongs to the context of Christianity, like an apostle, and must therefore be examined individually; this is certainly the case wherever his purpose is the confirmation of "the Scriptures", the Torah or the Gospel. So surah 62:2 assumes that God

> "hath sent among the unlettered ones a messenger of their own, to recite unto them His revelations and to make them grow, and to teach them the Scripture and Wisdom, ..." (cf. also e.g. surah 3:184; 7:10; 10:95; 28:52).

Most invectives against the "People of the Book *(ahl kitāb)*", who are reproached with having distorted the Torah and the Gospel, probably belong to this context. Statements of this kind do not mean that we are dealing with a new religion; it is, unfortunately, much more a matter of a common "debate culture" within Christianity to accuse people with different opinions, whether fellow Christians or Jews, of having a false understanding of the scriptures.

It is often claimed that the Qur'ān aims at replacing the Bible, one Ḥadīt even explicitly discourages Muslims from reading anything but the Qur'ān.[63] It is undoubtedly so that there are many references in the Qur'ān which assert that it was God himself who taught it (e.g. surah 55:2; surah 85:22; surah 59:21 and others) and (a little later?) the fact that the Qur'ān is written in clear Arabic is stressed (e.g. surah 41:44; surah 46:8-10 and others). Thus the new scripture claims to be a new norm and to possess literary authority. However, the Qur'ān never *contrasts* itself with the Torah or the Gospel, but always stresses that it *confirms* them. Moreover, the etymology of the word *Qur'ān* from Syriac *qəryāna*, i.e., "lectionary" (compendium of Biblical and liturgical texts), is generally accepted. So the Qur'ān should be understood as an *Arabic* (or Syro-Arabic) lectionary, the aim of which is to confirm the scriptures/ writing (*kitāb*) and interpret them in the right way,[64] so that even the djinns say:

> "1. Say (O Muhammad): It is revealed unto me that a company of the Jinn gave ear, and they said: Lo! it is a marvelous Qur'an,
> 2. Which guideth unto righteousness, so we believe in it and we ascribe unto our Lord no partner." (surah 72:1-2).

Or they say:

> "When before it there was the Scripture of Moses, an example and a mercy; and this is a confirming Scripture in the Arabic language, that it may warn those who do wrong and bring good tidings for the righteous." (surah 46:31; cf. 46:12).

The messenger/ transmitter of this Qur'ān says of himself:

> "I am no *new thing among the messengers (of Allah)*, nor know I what will be done with me or with you. I do but follow that which is inspired in me, and I am but a plain warner." (surah 46:9; my emphasis)

Elsewhere, he talks about himself as a "messenger making plain (*rasūlun mubīn*[un]" (surah 43:29), which probably alludes to the fact that the new scripture is written in Arabic, the normal language of intercourse of the target group, not Aramaic, the language of higher education. This *warner* (*mundir*), who saw himself as a true (i.e., non-Trinitarian) Christian, is not named; the obviously very important and often stressed fact that the Qur'ān was written in (clear, plain; Arabic: *mubīn*) Arabic, however, makes it clear that the "warner", prophet and messenger must have been an Arab. So the "Arabic Qur'ān (*Qur'ān ʿarabī*)" (surah 43:3) requires a "warner of their own (*mundirun minhum*)" (surah 50:2) – a clear indication of the concept of a Prophet of the Arabs; but he is still in the line of the preceding prophets. In some verses of surah 33, the prophet is portrayed as having a lifestyle which is definitely no longer "Christian", – e.g. in verse 28, he turns out to be a polygamist ("O Prophet! Say unto thy wives"). Concerning his religious orientation, however, even this surah sees him in line with the other prophets:

> "7. And when We exacted a covenant *(miṯāq)* from the Prophets, and from thee (O Muhammad) and from Noah and Abraham and Moses and Jesus son of Mary. We took from them a solemn covenant;
> 8. That He may ask the loyal of their loyalty. And He hath prepared a painful doom for the unfaithful."

It is interesting to note that Pickthall's rendering of the Arabic word *miṯāq* as "covenant" reflects the Biblical covenants between God and his prophets. The German translation by Max Henning,[65] does the same by translating the word as "Bund", whereas the prestigious translation by R. Paret[66] totally ignores this reference to the Bible and translates as "Verpflichtung (obligation)".

As soon as the movement that lived according to the Qur'ān was perceived as a new religion, the Qur'ān stepped up right beside the scriptures as possessing equal authority. It is even placed above the scriptures in so far as it is a "clear/ plain (*mubīn*)" book. For example in surah 9:111, the Torah, the Gospel and the Qur'ān are named side-by-side, but in surah 15:1 this fact is stressed:

> "9:111: It is a promise which is binding on Him in the Torah and the Gospel and the Qur'an."
> 15:1: These are verses of the Scripture and a plain Reading. (*tilka 'āyātu l-kitābi wa-qur'ānin mubīnin*)"

In verse surah 3:3 the significance of the Qur'ān that ("only"?) confirms the scriptures (Torah and Gospel), is strongly emphasized:

> "He hath revealed unto thee (Muhammad) the Scripture with truth, confirming that which was (revealed) before it, even as He revealed the Torah and the Gospel." (cf. also verse 4-9 and surah 4:136)

The nature of the Qur'ān as a revelation is repeatedly stressed, e.g. surah 16:102-103. Above all in the Medinan surahs, the Qur'ān appears as an important scripture of divine revelation, although even here the connection to the Torah, the Gospel, or to "scripture" is preserved.[67]

Now Jews and Christians can be contrasted with the followers of the Qur'ānic teachings (surah 9:30-31):

> "30. And the Jews say: Ezra (*'Uzayr*) is the son of Allah, and the Christians say: The Messiah is the son of Allah. That is their saying with their mouths. They imitate the saying of those who disbelieved of old. Allah (himself) fighteth against them. How perverse are they!
> 31. They have taken as lords beside Allah their rabbis and their monks and the Messiah son of Mary, when they were bidden to worship only One God. There is no god save Him. Be He glorified from all that they ascribe as partners (unto Him)!"

Just what made the author of these verses think that the Jews worship Ezra as the son of God is still not resolved. The polemics against Christians, however, sticks to the arguments and positions already brought forward in the inscriptions on the Dome of the Rock and on the temples in Damascus and Medina, as well as to the views advocated in other Qur'ānic texts. Up to this time, the controversy had, in the main, been a debate between Christian groups and individuals, – Syro-Arabian Christianity versus Hellenistic and Syro-Hellenistic Christianity. But now, in surah 9, the common Christian base seems to have been abandoned – both "the Jews" and "the Christians" are contrasted with the new creed as adherents of totally different religious orientations. A fundamental separation seems to have been announced. Similarly, in surah 2, verse 108 "your messenger" is contrasted with Moses as an autonomous figure and in verse 120 the following is said:

> "And the Jews will not be pleased with thee, nor will the Christians, till thou follow their creed."

According to Chr. Luxenberg's nomenclature this could be considered a case of "Muḥammad III"; but even here the messenger is still not mentioned by name.

It is worth noting that the Qur'ān stresses that the belief that only one god should be worshipped is identical to the (Biblical) command to Jews and Christians and that this belief is presented again and again within the context of identical successive revelation.[68] But the preaching of the Qur'ān appears to be the only one which completely corresponds to this original revelation.

This new step is now put into a theological-symbolical framework which begins with Abraham,[69] a figure recognized by both Jews *and* Christians and who preceded both these religions:

> "Abraham was not a Jew, nor yet a Christian; but he was an upright man who had surrendered (to Allah), and he was not of the idolaters." (surah 3:67)

A similar foundation myth had been used by Paul in his Letter to the Romans:

> "For the promise to Abraham or to his descendants that he would be heir to the world was not through the Law, but through the righteousness of faith." (Romans 4:13)

Choosing Abraham as a reference point allowed young Christianity to fall back on an authority which is older than Judaism (i.e., the law). The use of this fallback by the new movement is not only obvious from the parallels to Paul, but also from the perspective of Arabic tradition: long before the later Islam became established, the Arabs had been designated as *Ismaelites* – descendants of *Ishmael* (יִשְׁמָעֵאל yiśmāʿēl; Arabic: ʾIsmāʿīl), Abraham's son with his wife's Egyptian handmaid *Hagar* (הָגָר Hāgār, Arabic: Hāǧar), – or, after his mother, *Hagarenes* (Greek: *Agarēnói,* Syriac: *hagrāyē* or *mhaggrāyē*; the latter probably related to the *muhāǧirūn*, i.e., according to Muslim tradition those early Muslims who had fled from Mecca to Medina, as opposed to Medinan Muslims, the *anṣār*).[70]

Like in the case of Paul's epistles to the early Christian communities, relating to Abraham was an indicator that the religious movement had started to break away from the original religion. In Paul's case it was Christianity splitting from Judaism and in the later parts of the Qur'ān, the new religion Islam from Christianity. The fourteenth surah is entitled "Abraham" (the allegedly "Arabic" form *Ibrahīm* is probably a later misreading);[71]

the followers of the Qur'ānic movement represent the religious orientation of Abraham. (surah 2:130: "And who forsaketh the religion of Abraham save him who befooleth himself?"). They are not like the "Jews or Christians":

> "And they say: Be Jews or Christians, then ye will be rightly guided. Say (unto them, O Muhammad): Nay, but (we follow) the religion of Abraham, the upright, and he was not of the idolaters."(surah 2:135)

Abraham established "the house (*bayt*)" as "a resort for mankind and a sanctuary, (saying): Take as your place of worship the place where Abraham stood (to pray) (surah 2:125)". Muslim exegetes are convinced that by this "house", the *Ka'ba* in Mecca is meant, although the Arabic text of the Qur'ān offers no basis for this interpretation.

As the Arabic movement gradually became an independent entity, which reached out beyond Judaism and Christianity and based itself on the Qur'ān as the ultimate revelation, the transmitter of this scripture and thus (in retrospect) founder of the new religion acquired a new quality. The Prophet of the Arabs now appears as the final authority in the revelations from God. Like Mani, the "founder" of Manichaeism, who had claimed something similar, he is now called "Seal of the Prophets (*ḫatam al-nabiyyīna*) (surah 33:40)".

To sum up, we come to the following, slightly simplified conclusion: among the Qur'ānic texts we can distinguish between three consecutive phases which overlap at the edges: the oldest is the phase in which a Syro-Arabic Christianity is represented and where an unnamed preacher is addressed who points to either Jesus or Moses; in the next phase the material remains Christian, but is interpreted by the Qur'ān *in Arabic* (as far as it exists) so that a *Prophet of the Arabs* appears as its source – the first stage of a historicization of the epithet *muḥammad*; in the last phase the movement sticks to the biblical salvation-historical concepts, but sees the Qur'ān as the final and ultimate revelation. In this stage the movement considers itself to be a new "religion"[72] and the Prophet of the Arabs as the promoter of a new revelation and founder of this religion.

The detailed development and embellishment of the biography of *Muḥammad* first took place in the 9th and 10th century. By now the amount of alleged biographical material, anecdotes and sayings of the prophet on offer is so enormous that it already seems to exceed the possibilities of a single finite life.

4.2 The four places Where the Form *muḥammad* Appears in the Qur'ān

The four passages in which the term *muḥammad* is mentioned in the Qur'ān should be briefly discussed, beginning with the oldest passage – if the chronological assumptions based on the order and counting of the surahs should be correct. As there are no critical editions of the Qur'ān, the translations and transliterations are based on the Cairo edition of the Qur'ān, here in the English translation by Pickthall and Rudi Paret's German translation and commentary.

(1) Surah 48:29

> "Muhammad is the messenger of Allah. And those with him are hard against the disbelievers and merciful among themselves. [...]
> *muḥammadun rasūlu llāhi wa-llaḏīna maʿahū ʾašiddāʾu ʿalā l-kuffāri ruḥamāʾu baynahum*"

Surah 48 "al-Fatḥ (literally: "opening"; mostly translated as "victory; conquest"; Paret: "Erfolg [success]" can be subdivided into two parts. The first part, verses 1-28 is about combative conflicts, the displeasure of the Bedouin in having to fight, the divine determination of success and about reward and punishment. Verse 29, in the context of this surah unusually long, forms the second part. But length, – a purely formal feature, – is not the only difference between this verse and those of the preceding text, there is also its conciliatory content which has nothing to do with fighting. It seems to be a separate entity that was later inserted at this point. Perhaps the same is true for the likewise longer verse 25 which is about a holy site, sacrificial animals and the hindrance of sacrificial actions; this verse might have been inserted as in the previous sentence Mecca is allegedly mentioned:

> "And He it is Who hath withheld men's hands from you, and hath withheld your hands from them, *in the valley of Mecca*, after He had made you victors over them. Allah is Seer of what ye do.
> *wa-huwa llaḏī kaffa ʾaydiyahum ʿankum wa-ʾaydiyakum ʿanhum bi-baṭni makkata min baʿḍi ʾan ʾaẓfarakum ʿalayhim wa-kāna llāhu bi-mā taʿmalūna baṣīran.*"

The expression "*bi-baṭni makkata*" does not literally mean "valley" of Mecca, but rather "middle; orig.: belly" and the context of this verse does not give any hint as to whether Mecca is really a place name, let alone does it assign any features of the later sacred city to this place. If, furthermore, we consider that this is the only verse where the form "makka" appears, – in the often adduced second passage, the form is "bakka", not "makka", – then it becomes logical why it must have seemed necessary to insert verse 25.

Apart from the questionable mention of Mecca, the first part provides no concrete information that could serve to either historically or geographically localize the description, unless we adopt the views of the theological historiography of the 9th century. However, something special is found in this part: Mecca or "the valley in Mecca" is mentioned.

At this point we must take into consideration that, – contrary to common belief and to what can be found in most encyclopedias, press articles and school books, which only repeat the legends of the Traditional Account, – the Arabian Peninsula did not play a role up until the Abbasid period and Mecca was neither an important trade center before Islam, nor ever the capital of an Islamic State; Mecca is not even mentioned in any contemporary document about this new religious movement. The focus first switched to the south of the former Nabatean empire only after the construction of the sacred site in Medina. In the following decades, this area seems to have expanded even further. In any case, at the time of *Harūn (al-Rašīd)* (died 809) Mecca was a pilgrimage site and was enlarged as such.

If the mention of Mecca should belong to the original text and the word should really designate the later sacred city, then the whole first part of the surah might have to be dated far into the second half of the 8th century. For scholars from the historical and philological sciences, however, it is a very normal and frequent event that insertions into an old text are made in the process of the copying from one manuscript to another. In so doing, the new manuscript is brought "up to date" and now represents the "state of knowledge" of the writer. So does the mention of Mecca belong to these later additions or is it part of the original text? At present, this question cannot be answered because of the lack of a text-critical edition of the Qur'ān.

The second part, verse 29, opens with the sentence "Muḥammad is the messenger of God" (according to both Pickthall and Paret). If the sentence should have to be translated in this way, it would be an example for a consummated historicization, at least in relation to the name. Then this part of the surah would be connected to the subject of the first part.

But the sentence could also be translated as: "Blessed is the messenger of God"; in this case *muḥammad* would still be a predicate or title. But a title for whom? If we read the explanations following the first sentence, it is stated about those who are with the messenger that

> "Thou seest them bowing and falling prostrate (in worship), seeking bounty from Allah and (His) acceptance. The mark of them is on their foreheads from the traces of prostration. *Such is their likeness in the Torah and their likeness in the Gospel* like as sown corn that sendeth forth its shoot and strengtheneth it and riseth firm upon its stalk [...]. Allah hath promised, unto such of them as believe and do good works, forgiveness and immense reward. (my emphasis)"

These passages sound very Christian, apart from the second sentence: "And those with him are hard against the disbelievers and merciful among themselves." This indeed does not sound like a sentence Jesus would have said, but it is by no means unusual in the history of Christianity. In short: If we interpret verse 29 as an originally separate entity, which was secondarily added to the first part, then *muḥammad* can or must be understood as a *honorific title* for the messenger of God; the following context refers to the Torah and the Gospel and therefore to Jesus.

If the surah should originally have been an entity and the mention of Mecca belong to it, then *Muḥammad* would have to be understood as the name of the messenger and founder of a new "religion" for the first time; this would mean that this text belongs to a very late stage. If the first and second parts should form an entity and the mention of Mecca goes back to the interpolation of a later scribe, then surah 48 must be seen as the beginning of a "historicization" of the form *muḥammad* as a name, but it would not mean that the new movement had already split from Christianity.

Unfortunately, research about the Qur'ān is not at all based on the common text-critical method so well established in other disciplines, and even methods of comparative literature and form-criticism are rarely applied. Here new ground must be broken everywhere, even the beginnings of a truly scientific discussion are missing. If methodological reasoning is taken into consideration, as is usual in the study of literature and especially in biblical exegesis, then verse 29 has to be seen as an independent and theologically older entity and *muḥammad* as a title, not a name.

(2) Surah 47:2

Surah 47 is entitled *"Muḥammad"*. On the whole, it provides an only loosely connected collection of individual war-like sayings, ("Now when ye meet in battle those who disbelieve, then it is smiting of the necks", v.4), and of God's very unforgiving manner (God "surely will not pardon" the disbelievers, v. 34), of eschatological statements (heaven, hell) and ethical orders not to "hoard", and "spend in the way of Allah", verses 37 and 38). As regards their content, the verses do not intrinsically belong together and even their formal composition gives no indication of a concept. Therefore, it is hardly possible to assign a *Sitz im Leben* (roughly: "setting in life", i.e., context in everyday life) to them *as a whole*, and even for single verses such an undertaking would be rather hypothetical. The surah opens with the verse:

> "Those who disbelieve and turn (men) from the way of Allah, He rendereth their actions vain."

Then comes the verse containing the form *muḥammad* (47:2):

> "And those who believe and do good works and believe in that which is revealed unto Muhammad and it is the truth from their Lord. He riddeth them of their ill deeds and improveth their state.
> *wa-llaḏīna 'āmanū wa-'amilū ṣ-ṣāliḥāti wa-'āmanū bi-mā nuzzila 'alā*

> *muḥammadin wa-huwa l-ḥaqqu min rabbihim kaffara ʿanhum sayyiʾātihim wa-ʾaṣlaḥa bālahum*"

The third verse also belongs to this entity:

> "That is because those who disbelieve follow falsehood and because those who believe follow the truth from their Lord. Thus Allah coineth their similitudes for mankind."

But a completely new theme begins in verse 4:

> "Now when ye meet in battle those who disbelieve, then it is smiting of the necks until, when ye have routed them, then making fast of bonds;"

So the first two or three verses can or must be read separately. It is said of (the) *muḥammad*, that God sent a revelation down to him which is the truth of the Lord. Who is this *muḥammad*? If we use surah 19:30 as an aid, the infant Jesus says:

> "I am the slave (*ʿabd*, others translate as "servant") of Allah. He hath given me the Scripture and hath appointed me a Prophet, [...]"

Similar things are said in the Qur'ān again and again about Moses. Because of these Qur'ānic parallels, verse 47:2 should be translated as

> "those who believe in what has been sent down to the Blessed One (*muḥammad*) (as a revelation or scripture)."

In principle, the translation of *muḥammad* as a name would be conceivable if these verses could be attributed to the second phase and the beginnings of a historicization of the Prophet of the Arabs. But this possibility is ruled out by the last clause of verse 2: "And those who believe and do good works and believe in that which is revealed unto Muhammad/ the Blessed one, and it is the truth from their Lord. *He riddeth them of their ill deeds and improveth their state.*" The "redemption from sins" through faith is a "soteriological" concept, i.e., it refers to salvation as effected by Jesus Christ, not to a Prophet of the Arabs. The first three verses can obviously be considered Christian and *muḥammad* should be understood as a Christian title.

(3) Surah 33:40

The characterization of Surah 33, – "al-Aḥzāb", diversely translated as "the Clans, the Coalition, the Confederates or the Groups (Paret)" is the plural of "ḥizb", in modern Arabic meaning "(political) party" (cf. "*Hisb*ollah – the *Party* of God"),– as a whole is not intended at this point. It would appear sufficient to have a closer look at verses 37-40 as well as verses 50-59, as they are unambiguous and clearly belong together.

The Islamic tradition understands verses 37-40 as alluding to the story of Zainab: the prophet, who apparently must have coveted the (in the Qur'ān unnamed) wife of his adoptive son Zayd and at first wanted to relinquish any claims on her, because "*wa-taḫšā n-nāsa* – thou didst fear mankind" (verse 37). But God gave her to him as his wife after her divorce from Zayd was consummated. Verse 38 says that the fear of the prophet was unfounded:

> "There is no reproach for the Prophet in that which Allah maketh his due. That was Allah's way with those who passed away of old and the commandment of Allah is certain destiny."

Then, in verse 40, the form *muḥammad* is mentioned:

> "Muhammad is not the father of any man among you, but he is the messenger of Allah and the Seal of the Prophets; and Allah is aware of all things.
> *mā kāna muḥammadun 'abā 'aḥadin min riǧālikum wa-lākin rasūla llāhi wa-ḫātama n-nabiyyīna wa-kāna llāhu bi-kulli šay'in 'alīma*ⁿ"

In this context, *Muḥammad* seems to be the name of the Prophet of the Arabs if the traditional explanation is accepted. Here and in verses 50-59, the entirely historicized Prophet of the Arabs is portrayed in the context of new religious and ethical ideas which bear no relation to Jesus as a person, nor to his message, as he would have considered the described behavior of the Prophet as an especially abominable case of adultery.

In verses 50-59, without mention of further names, God's prophet is allowed to take wives from different groups of women, apart from the slaves ("whom thy right hand possesses [*wa-mā malakat 'aymānuhum*]"):

> "O Prophet! Lo! We have made lawful unto thee thy wives (*'aḥlalnā laka 'azwāǧaka*) unto whom thou hast paid their dowries, and those whom thy right hand possesseth of those whom Allah hath given thee as spoils of war, and the daughters of thine uncle on the father's side and the daughters of thine aunts on the father's side, and the daughters of thine uncles on the mother's side emigrated with thee, and a believing woman if she give herself unto the Prophet and the Prophet desire to ask her in marriage, a privilege for thee only, not for the (rest of) believers (*ḫāliṣatan laka min dūni l-mu'minīna*). [...]"

At the end it says:

> "It is not allowed thee to take (other) women henceforth nor that thou shouldst change them for other wives even though their beauty pleased thee, save those whom thy right hand possesseth (here a different wording: *'illā mā malakat yamīnuka*). [...]" (verse 52).

This is clearly no longer Christian, so both groups of verses must have come into existence very late. First, *Muḥammad* was already the "Seal of the Prophets"; secondly, rules that were diametrically opposed to the most basic ethics of Christianity had penetrated the new "religion", and thirdly, stories from the *Sīra* (the Prophet's biography) about his wives seem to be alluded to. However, surah 33 does not mention names of the women in question, nor does it reveal any biographical data about them. In the case of Zayd's wife, however, the information is quite specific. In verses 50-52, a kind of summary of marriage relationships is offered and in verses 53-59 instructions are given on contact with the wives of the Prophet and himself:

> "Linger not for conversation. Lo! that would cause annoyance to the Prophet, and he would be shy of (asking) you (to go);" (verse 53)

Some sentences might mean that the Prophet is presumed already dead:

> "Lo! Allah and His angels shower blessings on the Prophet. [...]."

Another hint at the prophet's passing away is the fact that in verse 6, the wives of *Muḥammad* are described as "mothers" of faithful believers ("The Prophet is closer to the believers than their selves, and his wives are (as) their mothers."), which is generally explained as a prohibition to marry them after the prophet's death. According to the *Sīra* it is hardly imaginable how especially older Muslims should otherwise have been expected to consider a (still at his death) teenager, like his favorite wife *ʿĀiša*, as their mother.

Whether these stories were attributed to a fictitious person *Muḥammad* or whether they are "true stories" about a historical Prophet of the Arabs (whose name was not Muḥammad!), which were preserved by Islamic tradition, cannot be determined. In the latter case, there must have been an "Arab preacher" either at the very beginning of the movement or over the course of time, who was later, secondarily, awarded the originally Christological honorific predicate *muḥammad* as a name, like Caesar's adopted son and later emperor Octavian was awarded the sovereign title "Augustus (the illustrious one; < augere – to increase)", which then became his name. This is one possibility. But it is also possible, or even probable, that stories of marriages, divorces and love affairs of e.g. a sheikh were in circulation, first independently handed down and secondarily added to the "Muḥammadan" tradition.

Until now there have never been any reasonable historical arguments to (answer) this question.

(4) Surah 3:144

The long surah 3, "āl ʿimrān – the Family of ʿImrān (Paret: die Sippe [clan] of ʿImrān)" provides an abundant range of statements, of which many relate to biblical texts or to Jesus, but which are only rarely indicative of a comprehensive context. Verses 144-148 can be treated as an entity, attached to verse 143, which speaks about death, probably applying the "Mnemonic Keyword principle". In the crucial verses (144 and the beginning of verse 145)[73] we read:

> "144. Muhammad is but a messenger (*wa-mā muḥammadun ʾillā rasūlun*), messengers (the like of whom) have passed away before him (*qad ḫalat min qablihi r-rusulu*). Will it be that, when he dieth or is slain, ye will turn back on your heels? He who turneth back doth no hurt to Allah, and Allah will reward the thankful.
> 145. No soul can ever die except by Allah's leave and at a term appointed. [...]"

Pickthall adds the words "the like of whom" to the "messengers that have passed away before him". Rudi Paret translates differently and refers the verse to Muḥammad:

> "Vor ihm hat es schon (verschiedene andere) Gesandte gegeben. –
> Before him there have been (several other) messengers"

In his commentary, he mentions an interesting parallel in surah 5:75, where exactly the same is said about Jesus:

> "The Messiah, son of Mary, was no other than a messenger, messengers (the like of whom) had passed away before him.
> *mā l-masīḥu bnu maryama ʾillā rasūlun qad ḫalat min qablihi r-rusulu*"

As we can see, the Arabic wording is exactly the same, a clear indication that the verse (at least originally) referred to Jesus. Moreover, it is interesting to note what remains of the sentence in surah 3, if the words in brackets of both Pickthall and Paret are merely left out: then a messenger is spoken of in verse 145 who is killed and dies; and this is according to God's will and according to the Scriptures. In Pickthall's translation "No soul can ever die except by Allah's leave and *at a term appointed*"; this does not become very clear, but Paret provides the literal translation in brackets:

> "Keiner kann sterben, außer mit Gottes Erlaubnis und nach einer befristeten Vorherbestimmung (w. Schrift).
> Nobody can die, except with God's permission and after a limited(-term) providence (lit.: scripture)
> *wa-mā kāna li-nafsin ʾan tamūta ʾillā bi-ʾiḏni llāhi kitāban*"

The Arabic expression "*ʾillā bi-ʾiḏni llāhi* – except with God's permission" is clear, the following word "*kitāban*" (accusative of *kitāb* – scripture) is a bit unusual. The only way to understand it is adverbially "scripture-wise", i.e., "according to scripture". This is clearly alluding to Jesus' statement that his death was inevitable, because the scripture had to be fulfilled (e.g. Mt. 26:24, during the last supper):

> "The Son of Man is to go, *just as it is written of Him*; but woe to that man by whom the Son of Man is betrayed!"

Especially the gospel of Matthew provides abundant examples of events that only happen so that "the prophet/ a prophecy is fulfilled":

> "2:17: Then what had been spoken through Jeremiah the prophet was fulfilled.
> 13:14: In their case the prophecy of Isaiah is being fulfilled, which says, [...].
> 26:54: How then will the Scriptures be fulfilled, which say that it must happen this way?
> 27:9: Then that which was spoken through Jeremiah the prophet was fulfilled: [...]"

So it seems quite clear that the Qur'ānic verse """Nobody can die, except with God's permission and *according to scripture*" applies to Jesus (and other prophets, cf. verse 146):[74]

That he can die and be killed, although he is the messenger, – though not more than only the servant of God (surah 3:51), – is justified in verse 59:

> "Lo! the likeness of Jesus with Allah is as the likeness of Adam. He created him of dust, then He said unto him: Be! and he is."

Therefore, there is no reason to "turn back on your heels" because of his death (verse 144) and to "turn back" and away from him. This is how "many a prophet" felt, so that "a number of devoted men/ *Paret:* many thousands of people, *ribbiyyūna kaṯīrun*" were therefore hit by misfortune and still did not "weaken, nor were they brought low" (verse 146); Then "their cry was only that they said: Our Lord! Forgive us for our sins (*ġfir lanā ḏunūbanā,* verse 147)"; the latter is an appeal requesting forgiveness almost identical to the one in the Lord's Prayer.

The verses are reasoning the violent death of Jesus, to whom God says in verse 55: "Then unto Me ye will (all) return,", so God "called him home" and (then) elevated him up to him; *elevation* follows death; the classic Jewish and Syrian-Christian "Elevation Christology (German: Erhöhungschristologie)".

It takes a fair bit of blindness to relate all of this to a Prophet of the Arabs named Muḥammad. The introductory sentence of verse 144 must therefore be translated: "*And the blessed One* (*Muḥammad*) is only a messenger (and can be killed)", the person meant being Jesus, like in the surah 5, 75 already mentioned: "*Christ, Son of Mary,* is only a messenger. There have been (other) messengers before him".

4.3 Conclusion

Three mentions of the form *muḥammad* (surah 3:144; surah 47:2; surah 48:29) can be related to Jesus, if not with certainty, – due to the opaqueness of the surrounding text, – then at least in all probability. They can only be understood as referring to a Prophet of the Arabs if they are read from the perspective of the traditional literature of the 9th century. A Prophet of the Arabs as a historical figure is only meant once (surah 33:40), although he is not described; nevertheless, in this verse *Muḥammad* seems to be meant as his name.

Of course, certain questions remain, which arise as a result of the literary characteristics of the Qur'ānic texts, the intended messages of which can only be deciphered imprecisely and for the interpretation of which so far no scientifically verifiable model is available. However, the Qur'ān seems to confirm the conclusions drawn from the evidence provided by contemporary coins and inscriptions: the historicization of the honorific predicate *muḥammad* and reinterpretation as a personal name was a very late event.

5. Further "biographical" Material about a Prophet of the Arabs in the Qur'ān

Not only traditional Islamic scholars, but also professors of Islamic studies in the West have looked for and found evidence of a biography of Muḥammad in the Qur'ān. As an example for this approach, an article entitled "Muḥammad" written by Adel Theodor Khoury shall be adduced:

> "The Qur'ān rates the marriage (*of Muḥammad; my addition*) to Khadidja as a divine act of grace for Muḥammad (93:7-8)."[75]

But is this really the information we may infer from the Qur'ān? The surah cited by Khoury contains only 11 verses and no names! The three verses cited plus the preceding one are the following:

> "6. Did He not find thee an orphan and protect (thee)?
> *'a-lam yağidka yatīman fa-'āwā*
> 7. Did He not find thee wandering and direct (thee)?
> *wa-wağadaka ḍāllan fa-hadā*
> 8. Did He not find thee destitute and enrich (thee)?
> *wa-wağadaka 'ā'ilan fa-'aġnā*"

According to surah 93, 6-8, the prophet addressed was an orphan, errant and poor: but God took him in,[76] led him and made him rich. As we "know" from the traditional Islamic literature (which was written a few centuries later based on chains of oral transmitters), Muḥammad became rich through his marriage with his elder rich cousin Ḫadīğa, whom he later married and who became the first human being the prophet converted to Islam. Nothing of all this can be found in the Qur'ān! But of course, the stories from the 9th century can easily be connected to Qur'ānic statements, which they match perfectly. The possibility that these later traditions were just invented in order to make sense of opaque Qur'ānic passages, is of course totally ignored, just as all of the other possibilities to make sense of particular verses are ignored, in our case: all the other possibilities *to become rich* or all of the other prophets who might be addressed in this surah without being named.

Rudi Paret, the famous German orientalist and translator of the Qur'ān shares the opinion of many Islamic scholars that the Qur'ān does not provide enough details to enable us to depict the life of Muḥammad.[77] However, despite all the reservations towards its late transmission, he still refers to the biography allegedly to be found in it. Likewise, W. Montgomery Watt believed that the attempt to reconstruct a description of Muḥammad's life solely from the Qur'ān was "beyond hope",[78] so that he drew on later narratives for his two volume biography.

The legendary character of the Ḥadīṯ collections of the 9th century has been recognized more and more since Ignaz Goldziher.[79] But as hardly anything can be said about Muḥammad without taking these texts at face value, this otherwise great and critical scholar still uses these narratives as if they were authentic, his excuse being "without this material, the Qur'ān is useless as a historical source."[80]

The preliminary decision makes an impartial examination of the Qur'ānic statements very difficult. Only if the mere "apparent" knowledge of the Sīra is dismissed in terms of its investigation, might the Qur'ān become valuable as a historical source again. But maybe then it becomes possible for other conclusions to be drawn.

In the following, several examples of "biographical" Qur'ānic notes will be discussed.

5.1 Surah 93:6-8

In the surah mentioned previously (93:6-8), God says about the prophet that he was an orphan, errant (in faith) and poor. These statements are written in the context of the short surah which can be considered to be the original entity. After an oath formula (verses 1 and 2: "By the morning hours – and by the night when it is stillest"), we read in verse 3:

> "3. Thy Lord hath not forsaken thee nor doth He hate thee.
> 4. And verily the latter portion will be better for thee than the former
> 5. And verily thy Lord will give unto thee so that thou wilt be content.
> 6. Did He not find thee an orphan and protect (thee)?

7. Did He not find thee wandering and direct (thee)?
8. Did He not find thee destitute and enrich (thee)?
9. Therefore the orphan oppress not,
10. Therefore the beggar drive not away,
11. Therefore of the bounty of thy Lord be thy discourse."

In the surah, God appears in the third person (except v. 9-11), instead of in the first person as is mostly the case. This makes it rather look like a (later) reflection of the life of a prophet. Obviously, the prophet must have had cause to feel abandoned and hated by God, a potential reproach which is countered by the promise of reward in the next world. The general situation of a prophet "in a crisis", who gets the impression that everything is in vain, is commonplace in biographies of prophets, so neither would it be astonishing for the *Prophet Muḥammad* – provided the author of these verses already knew of this concept.

The adduced good deeds that God had bestowed upon him up to this point contain the message that the prophet was *errant, poor* and an *orphan*, thus the number of prophets that could be meant here is limited. From biblical tradition, Moses is certainly a possible candidate. Before God showed himself to him at the burning thorn bush (e.g. surah 28:29-30), the Qur'ān says about him:

"He said: I did it then, when I was of those *who are astray.*
qāla faʿaltuhā ʾiḏan wa-ʾana mina *ḍ-ḍāllīn*[a]" (surah 26:20)

Apart from being "*errant*" as described in this verse, Moses was also poor (the son of a Hebrew slave) and a kind of orphan, as he had been put in a basket and set adrift on the Nile river. But like the prophet addressed in verses 6-8 he was saved and enriched: He went from being the poor son of a Hebrew to being the (rich) son of a pharaoh whose home was looked after by God (cf. e.g. surah 28:7-13). But it could also be Muḥammad who is meant, i.e., the figure described in the biographies of the 9th century, which certainly refer back to this surah and elaborated on it.

That this surah should refer to the Prophet of the Arabs, however, is rather improbable, as both the ethical consequences and above all the preaching of the mercy of God (instead of the threat of the Day of Judgment) are indicators that it belongs to an older layer of Qur'ānic texts. Considering the very frequent mentions of Moses in the Qur'ān, this surah would then be a sort of biblical meditation on the person and fate of Moses, whose life in "this world" was characterized by danger and distress, for which he was promised happiness in the afterlife (cf. e.g. surah 28:37).

Due to the starkness of the texts, which does not allow us to immediately recognize the associations originally connected with them, the question of which prophet was meant here cannot be determined for certain. If the internal logic of the Qur'ān is followed, the most likely candidate is Moses, because the Qur'ān provides stories which are appropriate to Surah 93. Considering the obvious age of the surah, which, among other things, is also reflected especially in its poetic style and its versification, Muḥammad (i.e., the later personification) is a rather unlikely candidate; at most an unknown Prophet of the Arabs (i.e., the prophet addressed in direct speech elsewhere in the Qur'ān, whose name was not yet Muḥammad) would be conceivable. But this is also difficult to imagine, as it is not supported by the text.

5.2 Surah 43:29-31

> "29. Nay, but I let these and their fathers enjoy life (only) till there should come unto them the Truth and a *messenger making plain (rasūlun mubin^{un}).*
> 30. And now that the Truth hath come unto them they say: This is mere magic, and lo! we are disbelievers therein."

The understanding of surah 43, 29-31 raises similar difficulties. Here the sending of a "messenger making plain" (v. 30), to whom the Qur'ān was sent down, is spoken of. The people standing around asked:

> "31. And they say: If only this Qur'an had been revealed to some great man of the two towns? (*rağulin mina l-qaryatayni ʿaẓīm^{in}*)"

According to this verse, the messenger was not a man who possessed power. If the "messenger making plain" is an Arab messenger and the Qur'ān a lectionary in Arabic (and not "the scriptures"), then the source behind the Qur'ān is seen as a historical figure, – even without being named, – and Moses is not meant. However, in surah 11:96 the same is said about Moses:

> "And verily We sent Moses with Our revelations and a clear warrant.
> (*wa-la-qad ʾarsalnā mūsā bi-ʾāyātinā wa-sulṭānin mubīn^{in}*)"

It is interesting to note that the Arabic word here corresponding to Pickthall's adjective "*clear*" is "*mubīn*", the same word that corresponds to the attribute of the prophet in surah 43:29 "*making plain*". Another question that arises concerns the "two towns" mentioned. Just which towns are meant cannot be determined here. The explanation given by Paret in his commentary that Mecca and Ṭā'if are meant is not proved by anything, – apart from much later traditions.

5.3 Surah 53:1-18 and 81:19-26

Three "visions" of the Prophet which are supposed to prove that his teachings are guaranteed from the outside are reported in the Qur'ān, although – apart from this case – the Qur'ānic texts are not normally justified with visions and do not report of anything visionary.

In Surah 53:1-12, the prophet "grew clear to view when he was on the uppermost horizon (v. 6-7)", i.e., on the border between the earth and the sky a person "which one of mighty powers hath taught him, one vigorous (v. 5-6)"; "10. And He revealed unto His slave that which He revealed. (*fa-'awḥā 'ilā ʿabdihī mā 'awḥā*)." Interestingly, the prophet is referred to as "*'ilā ʿabdihi – to his slave/ servant*".

In the same surah, verses 53:13-18, the prophet saw him come down "at the utmost boundary, (marked by) the lote-tree":

> "13. And verily he saw him, yet another time. 14. By the lote tree of the utmost boundary (*ʿinda sidrati l-muntahā*), [...]."

In surah 81:19-26, the prophet sees, on the other hand, an "honored messenger":

> "19. That this is in truth the word of an honored messenger (*rasūlin karīm*[in]),
> [...]
> 23. Surely he beheld him on the clear horizon. (*wa-la-qad ra'āhu bi-l-'ufuqi l-mubīn*[i])"

What is a little surprising is verse 22, which presupposes that at least some of his contemporaries considered the new prophet to be a lunatic:

> "22. And your comrade is not mad. (*wa-mā ṣāḥibukum bi-mağnūn*[in])"

The Arabic word used here, *mağnūn*, is derived from the same root as the noun "*ğinn* – ghost, spirit", thus meaning "*obsessed by a ghost*".

These visions are purely formal and do not provide any assertions regarding the content. In all of them, however, it is about providing legitimacy to what the preacher says by referring to someone *who has power (with God)*. Visions 1 and 2 do not make any further assertions, – here it could be God himself who is meant, – but Vision 3 explicitly calls this person an "honored messenger", probably an angel who has authority with God.

While Pickthall (correctly) does not mention the word "Qur'ān" in his translation of this surah, R. Paret adds this word in brackets (81:25: "Der Koran [w.: er *(lit.: it)*]). What is spoken about in all of these places in the Qur'ān is not "*the Qur'ān*", but more generally: "*revelation*". In verse surah 53:18 the wording is:

> "18. Verily he saw one of the greater revelations of his Lord.
> *la-qad ra'ā min 'āyāti rabbihi l-kubrā*"

The Arabic word corresponding to Pickthall's rendering "*revelations*" is "*'āyāt*", normally translated as "verses". But the "normal" word for "revelation (waḥy)", or at least the corresponding verbal root "'awḥā – reveal", also appears:

> "And He revealed unto His slave that which He revealed. (*fa-'awḥā 'ilā 'abdihī mā 'awḥā*)".

No further information is given about the preacher, but he is described twice as "your comrade (*ṣāḥibukum*)" (surah 53:2 and surah 81:22), a word translated as "euer Landsmann (your fellow-countryman)" by Paret. The translation is probably only based on the assumption that if it is about an Arab preacher, then he must certainly be a countryman of the Arab audience.

The place of appearance is mentioned twice as *on the horizon (bi-l-'ufuqi)*, in surah 53:7 "on the uppermost horizon (*bi-l-'ufuqi l-'a'lā*)" and in surah 81:23 "on the clear horizon (*bi-l-'ufuqi l-mubīn*ⁱ)". In one case, *a lote tree* is added to the description: 53:14. "By the lote tree of the utmost boundary (*'inda sidrati l-muntahā*)". The *lote-tree* (Arabic: *sidra*) belongs to the buckthorn plant, so it is a thorn-bush; this might allude to Moses and the burning thorn-bush (Ex. 3:2):

> "The angel of the LORD appeared to him in a blazing fire from the midst of a bush (סְנֶה – *sənäh*); and he looked, and behold, the bush was burning with fire, yet the bush was not consumed."

The story is alluded to elsewhere in the Qur'ān (e.g. surahs 28:29; 20:10; 27:7-8), but in all these verses a fire is mentioned, but no bush, e.g. 20:10:

> "When he saw a fire and said unto his folk: Wait! I see a fire afar off. Peradventure I may bring you a brand therefrom or may find guidance at the fire."

For linguistic reasons, Christoph Luxenberg believes that the translation "lote-tree" goes back to a misunderstanding, the correct translation should be "curtain/drape". In this case, the "curtain/drape" between heaven and earth could be what is meant, thus the same as "the uppermost of the horizon". Then the verse would have no direct connection to Moses.

The "comrade *(sāḥib)*" is called the slave/servant of God, a description claimed by Moses in surah 37:122. If Moses is meant, then the description "comrade/ (your countrymen)" in his speech would be directed at a Jewish audience.

If these texts are interpreted without all the legends of later biographies of Muḥammad and without all the fictitious explanations of the exegetes of later centuries, but rather only using Qur'ānic material, then Moses must have been the one who referred back to an authorization for his teaching from outside. Again and again the Qur'ān stresses that the revelations or *"the book/ the scripture (kitāb)"* came down to Moses from God.

Also the statement made in this context in surah 81:22 ("And your comrade is not mad") is to be found in the Qur'ān as an accusation made by the pharaoh about Moses:

> "(Pharaoh) said: Lo! your messenger who hath been sent unto you is indeed a madman! (*qāla 'inna rasūlakumu llaḏī 'ursila 'ilaykum la-mağnūn*[un])" (surah 26:27)

The Arabic term used for "mad" is "*mağnūn*" in all cases, which would indicate that surah 81 refers to Moses.

Briefly, if these three visions are read separately, they probably relate to Moses and not to the biography of Muḥammad, which was not yet known at the time these texts were written.

This also applies to the accusation of obsession which does not contain anything biographical, – for example epilepsy or such like, – but is common as a reproach against prophets, not only for Moses in the Qur'ān (surah 26:26), but also in the New Testament, e.g. for John the Baptist (Matthew 11:18; Luke 7:33) and Jesus (John 7:20; 8:48; 49:52) – thus "alleged madness/ obsession" is a topos of criticism of the prophets.

5.4 Surah 10:16

The only remaining piece of possibly biographical evidence can be found in surah 10:16. The topic of the preceding verses is the Qur'ān and its recitation. Then the prophet says:

> "16. Say: If Allah had so willed I should not have recited it to you nor would He have made it known to you. I dwelt among you a whole lifetime (*fa-qad labiṯtu fīkum 'umuran*) before it (*min qablihī*) (came to me). Have ye then no sense?" (the English words in brackets are Pickthall's explanations)

The "it" that "came to him" is explained by Paret in brackets: "i.e., the Qur'ān". Whether it is really the Qur'ān in its present form that is meant here is highly questionable, but Paret is certainly not too far from the truth if he presumes the existence of at least an early core version of the Qur'ān that this verse is alluding to. Should this be the case, then the transmitter of the Qur'ān is described as not very young, considering the "*lifetime ('umur)*" that he had spent with them "*before it*", i.e., the revelation. This would be an indication of a kind of historicization, albeit not one in line with the later biographies, as Muḥammad's alleged age of forty at the first revelation would make him too young to later utter such a verse. At the same time, the impression is conveyed that the Qur'ān, the scripture, was already finished during his lifetime. These verses should probably rather be considered as a posthumous assignment of the Qur'ān to the person who was its preacher. This was then adopted as the standard understanding of how the Qur'ān had come into being. Only in the 9th century was this beginning of the scripture located in the age of the third caliph, ʿUṯmān.

5.5 Conclusion about Biographical Material in the Qur'ān

As we have seen, the Qur'ānic texts offer no biographical information, or at least no unquestionable biographical information about the life of Muḥammad. Moreover, the insinuations of conflicts and the like are so vague that the events alluded to cannot be located; in most cases it is not even clear whether these verses are about "real" battles, the passages rather resemble descriptions of eschatological battles in the widespread Syriac apocalypses of the time. It was not until the biographies of the 9th century that the smallest insinuations and vaguest allusions in the Qur'ān were construed into veritable stories.

At least it can be extracted from younger layers of the Qur'ān that the source behind the Qur'ānic texts was presumed to be a *Prophet of the Arabs*. This is explained in several other places in the Qur'ān (e.g. surah 46:12; surah 26:195-199). But it is questionable as to what is meant by "Arabic".[81] Regardless of how the "Arabic" or the "clear (*mubīn*)" language is to be understood, a prophet must be presumed who is no longer identical to the biblical figures. But only once in the Qur'ān, in surah 39:40, can this "historicization/ personalization" be linked to the name *Muḥammad* with a reasonable degree of certainty.

6. Specific References to the Arabic Peninsula in the Qur'ān ?

The texts of the Qur'ān cannot easily be linked to the places named in later biographies. Muḥammad is believed to have been born in Mecca. He then is said to have lived first in Mecca, then in Medina and then in Mecca again, but the Qur'ān does not indicate this at any time. Muḥammad is said to have moved from Mecca to Medina (the so-called *hiǧra*) in the year 622, but the Qur'ān does not mention this at all, not even indirectly. Therefore the next chapter is dedicated to the question of just which geographical references the Qur'ān contains.

6.1 Mecca (Makka)

The "valley of Mecca ([*bi-*]*baṭni makkata*)" (surah 48:24) is mentioned only once in the Qur'ān. Theodor Nöldeke and Friedrich Schwally[82] consider this surah a very late one:

> "Surah 48 has to be considered as belonging to a time after the peace of Ḥudaibiya (in the month Ḏu'lqaʿda of the year 6), but only verses 1-17 stem from right after this period, i.e., probably after Muḥammad's return to Medīna, which is claimed by some for the whole surah." (1st part, p. 215 f.)

The traditional Islamic homepage "WikiIslam",[83] shares this view, classifying this surah (*al-fatḥ – victory, conquest*) as the fourth youngest one. Both the style and the contents of the surah make this late classification very probable. The context in which the alleged place name is mentioned is as follows:

> "22. And if those who disbelieve join battle with you (*wa-law qātalakumu llaḏīna kafarū*) they will take to flight, and afterward they will find no protecting friend nor helper. [...] 24. And He it is Who hath withheld men's hands from you, and hath withheld your hands from them, in the valley of Mecca (*wa-huwa llaḏī kaffa 'aydiyahum ʿankum wa-'aydiyakum ʿanhum bi-baṭni makkata*), after He had made you victors over them. Allah is Seer of what ye do. 25. These it was who disbelieved and debarred you from the Inviolable Place of Worship (*humu llaḏīna kafarū wa-ṣaddūkum ʿani l-masǧidi l-ḥarāmi*), and debarred the offering from reaching its goal."

First of all, nothing in this text indicates that *makka* is the name of a place. Even the word next to it, *baṭn*, does not originally mean "valley", but "belly" (like Hebrew *bäṭän*; with suffixes: *biṭn-*), from which the secondary meaning "middle" is derived. Compare Judges 3:21:

> "Ehud stretched out his left hand, took the sword from his right thigh and thrust it into his belly. – וַיִּתְקָעֶהָ בְּבִטְנוֹ – wa-yyiṯəqāʿähā bə-*biṭnō*"

So what the text says is: "in the middle (lit.: belly) of *makka*", provided the vocalization and doubling of the second consonant, which is not indicated in the original *kūfī* script, is correct. What might be taken as an indication that Mecca is meant, is the use of the term "the Inviolable Place of Worship (*l-masǧidi l-ḥarāmi*)". Literally, *masǧid* means the "place of prosternation" (today: mosque), and *ḥarām* means "forbidden". If we forget the modern designation of mosques in Mecca and other places, which is attested only much later, then again nothing indicates that *makka* or the *l-masǧid l-ḥarām* mean Mecca or even a specific mosque there. If the term *makka* (or rather its rasm: *m-k-h*) should already have been present in the earliest manuscripts of this Qur'ānic text, i.e., if it is not a later addition of a scribe, and if it should really have meant the city of Mecca, – not at all impossible considering the unchallenged late dating of the surah, – then this text might have been written as late as at the time of *Harūn al-Rašīd*.[84] However, no further information is given about this place, nor is the term mentioned in reference to the prophet.

But even if this verse does not (clearly) refer to a city called Mecca, later tradition undoubtedly does. But is it really clear that this city was on the Arabian Peninsula? This question has yet to be answered. In an addition to the *History of the Gothic, Vandals and Suebi Kings* of Isidore of Seville (died 636) from the second half of the 8th century (the "*Continuatio Byzantia Arabica*", which continues the account until 754), about the year 741 it is said that *Habdemale* wages a war against *Habdella*. The latter had also been fought by his father many times, the last time

> "*apud Maccam, Abrahae, ut ipsi putant, domum, quae inter Ur Chaldaeorum et Carras Mesopotamiae urbem in heremo adiacet* – at Mecca, Abraham's house, as they [the Arabs] believe, which lies between Ur in Chaldea and Carras, a city in Mesopotamia, in a wasteland (steppe, desert)".[85]

This addition ("addidamentum") to the Chronicle of Isidore is based on unknown sources outside Spain and provides possibly the oldest mention of a place called *Mecca,* linked to Abraham. However, it is not located on the Arabian Peninsula, but in "Mesopotamia". It is important to note here that the city Isidore, spelt *Carras,* is a Latin transcription of the Greek *Carrhae* which, on the other hand, is the Greek spelling of the biblical town Har(r)an (*Ḥārān),* which is mentioned in Genesis:

> "Terah took Abram his son, and Lot the son of Haran *(Hārān)*, his grandson, and Sarai his daughter-in-law, his son Abram's wife; and they went out together from Ur of the Chaldeans in order to enter the land of Canaan; and they went as far as <u>Haran</u>, and settled there. וַיָּבֹאוּ עַד־חָרָן וַיֵּשְׁבוּ שָׁם *wa-yyāḇō'ū ʿaḏ <u>ḥārān</u> wa-yyešəḇu šām.*" (Gen. 11:31; the name of the city is *Ḥārān,* not the same as the of Lot's father!)

The "house of Abraham" is therefore located between Ur and Harran, thus in Samarra.[86] This localization is quite plausible, both in view of the biblical stories of Abraham and the region of origin of the oldest Qur'ānic materials. If such an association is imaginable, then the mention of Mecca in the Qur'ān might even have taken place in an earlier phase of its genesis and therefore had nothing yet to do with the Mecca on the Arabian Peninsula.

6.2 Medina (*al-madīna*)

Medina (*al-Madīna),* the later meaning of the word is "city" [of the prophet], the name, however, contains the root "*dīn*" (law; religion) and might originally have meant simply "legal district; the place where a certain legal order is valid". This original meaning is still reflected in Hebrew, where the *State* of Israel is called "*mədīnaṯ Yiśra'ēl*". According to many interpreters the form *madīna* first appears first in surah 63:8:

> "They say: Surely, if we return to Al Madinah (*yaqūlūna la-ʾin raǧaʿnā ʾilā l-madīnati*) the mightier will soon drive out the weaker (*la-yuḫriǧanna l-ʾaʿazzu minhā l-ʾaḏalla*); when might belongeth to Allah and to His messenger and the believers; but the hypocrites know not."

R. Paret, however, does not consider the form to be a name yet, but translates it as meaning "city", but he still understands it as referring to the city Medina: "When we return to the city (in other words: Medina) …." At this point, it should be noted that other "cities/ towns" in the Qur'ān, especially those destroyed by God for their disbelief, are not called *madīna*, but *qarya* (plural: *qurā*; modern Arabic meaning: "village"), e.g. surah 6:123:

> "123. And thus have We made in every city (*wa-ka-ḏālika ǧaʿalnā fī kulli qaryatin*) great ones of its wicked ones, that they should plot therein."

Or in the plural:

> "And We set, between them and the towns which We had blessed, towns easy to be seen, [...] – *wa-ǧaʿalnā baynahum wa-bayna l-qurā llatī bāraknā fīhā quran ẓāhiratan*" (surah 34:18)

There are, however, exceptions, where *madāʾin*, the plural of *madīna*, is used:

> "They said: Put him off, (him) and his brother, and send them into the cities summoners – *qālū ʾarǧih wa-ʾaḫāhu wa-bʿaṯ fī l-madāʾini ḥāširīn*[a] [...]" (surah 26:36)

A variant of the sentence is found in surah 7, where the same story is told:

> "They said (unto Pharaoh): Put him off (a while) him and his brother and send into the cities summoners – *qālū ʾarǧih wa-ʾaḫāhu wa-ʾarsil fī l-madāʾini ḥāširīn*[a]" (surah 7:111)

In this story, *madīna*/ pl. *madāʾin* is used throughout:

> "Then Pharaoh sent into the cities summoners – *fa-ʾarsala firʿawnu fī l-madāʾini ḥāširīna*" (surah 26:53)

Even the singular *madīna* is found simply meaning "city":

> "Pharaoh said: [...] this is the plot that ye have plotted in the city that ye may drive its people hence. – *qāla firʿawnu [...]hāḏā la-makrun makartumūhu fī l-madīnati li-tuḫriǧū minhā ʾahlahā*" (surah 7:123)

Whether *qarya* and *madīna* were really synonyms is a question that cannot be answered with certainty. The two other cases of "*al-madīna*" are generally understood to refer to the city Medina, formally called *Yaṯrib,* and are to be found in surah 9:

> "And among those around you of the wandering Arabs there are hypocrites, and among the townspeople of Al-Madinah (there are some who) persist in hypocrisy whom thou (O Muhammad) knowest not. [...] – *wa-mimman ḥawlakum mina l-ʾaʿrābi munāfiqūna wa-min ʾahli l-madīnati maradū ʿalā n-nifāqi lā taʿlamuhum* [...]" (surah 9:101)
>
> "It is not for the townsfolk of Al-Madinah and for those there is none who can repel His bounty. – *mā kāna li-ʾahli l-madīnati wa-man ḥawlahum mina l-ʾaʿrābi ʾan yataḫallafū ʿan rasūli llāhi*" (surah 9:120)

R. Paret translates these passages using the name *Medina*, probably an appropriate translation in this case: after all, Medina had belonged to the territory characterized by Qur'ānic tradition since around the middle of the 8th century, much earlier than Mecca. There are other verses where the singular form *madīna* appears and which definitely do not refer to the city of Medina, e.g. in the story of the seven sleepers:

> "Now send one of you with this your silver coin unto the city [...] – *fa-bʿaṯū ʾaḥadakum bi-wariqikum hāḏihī ʾilā l-madīnati* [...]" (surah 18:19)

It is interesting to note that in the three cases where *madīna* probably refers to the town *Medina*, the connotations associated with the term are negative. There is nothing positive said about the Bedouin ("wandering Arabs"; in Arabic simply: *l-ʾaʿrāb*) in surah 9:101 and 120, which is a contrast to the ideal state claimed by the traditional literature. Apparently, the program of the sanctuary of Medina[87] did not find favor "among those around you of the wandering Arabs" (surah 9:101) or "the townsfolk of Al-Madinah" (surah 9:120).

6.3 Bakka

In many translations of the Qurʾān a second verse is cited as mentioning the name of the sacred city of Islam:

> "96. Lo! the first Sanctuary appointed for mankind was that at Mecca, a blessed place, a guidance to the peoples; – *ʾinna ʾawwala baytin wuḍiʿa li-n-nāsi la-llaḏī bi-bakkata mubārakan wa-hudan lil-ʿālamīn*[a]" (surah 3:96)

As the transliteration of the Arabic text shows, the term is not "*makka*", but "*bakka*", two words as distinct in Arabic as the wizard "Merlin" and the city "Berlin" in English. Even the "sanctuary" in Pickthall's translation is only a "house" (*bayt*) in the Arabic original. R. Paret interprets *Bakka* as *Mecca* as well, probably because Islamic tradition since Ṭabarī had done so, although a consonant shift from "m" to "b", or forms alternating between these phonemes are uncommon in Classical Arabic. The reason why Muslim scholars interpreted Bakka as Mecca is probably the reference to Abraham and a compulsory pilgrimage in the preceding and following verse:

> "95. Say: Allah speaketh truth. So follow the religion of Abraham, the upright. (*fa-ttabiʿū millata ʾibrāhīma ḥanīfan*) He was not of the idolaters. (*wa-mā kāna mina l-mušrikīna)* [...]
> 97. Wherein are plain memorials (of Allah's guidance) (*fīhi ʾāyātun bayyinātun*); the place where Abraham stood up to pray (*maqāmu ʾibrāhīma*); and whosoever entereth it is safe. And pilgrimage to the House is a duty unto Allah for mankind, for him who can find a way thither. (*wa-li-llāhi ʿalā n-nāsi ḥiǧǧu l-bayti mani staṭāʿa ʾilayhi sabīlan*)"

If these verses should really refer to *Mecca* and the *Kaʿba*, then several details are very surprising. First of all, the "memorials" are, in fact, "*ʾāyāt*", a word which means both "signs" and "verses" (e.g. of the Qurʾān), but does not designate a building. Moreover, these signs cannot relate to "Bakka" or "Makka", as both these words are clearly feminine, but the "*-hī*) in "*fīhī* – in it" is clearly masculine. Then the *maqāmu ʾibrāhīma* is the "place where Abraham stands/ stood/ dwells", a so-called *nomen loci* of the root "*q-w-m*" (to stand, dwell); a prayer is not mentioned. What made the translators add this prayer is clear: "to perform prayer" in Arabic is "*aqāma aṣ-ṣalāt*", the verb *aqāma* being the 4th stem of the same root "*q-w-m*" (lit.: to cause to stand prayer), but there are many expressions with derivations of this root, so there is no compelling reason for adding this noun. Furthermore, the word used here for "pilgrimage" is *ḥiǧǧ*, not *ḥaǧǧ*. Both forms are, of course, similar and have the same *rasm* (consonant skeleton), but it is unusual that one of the *Five Pillars of Islam* (*arkān-al-Islām*) should not appear in its proper form here. And finally, the destination of the pilgrimage is simply called "*bayt* – house", although no house has been mentioned before. Of course, every Muslim will equate the place where Abraham prayed (*maqāmu ʾibrāhīma*), this "house" and the *Kaʿba*, but again there is no text-inherent reason for doing so. As we will see in the next section, the word *kaʿba* only appears in surah 5.

So it must be assumed that *bakka* is not *Mecca*. But no other city of this name is known, unless we speculate, for example, that Bakka is a shortened form of *Baʿlabakk* (Baalbek) in the Lebanon constituting a pre-Islamic temple to Allah?).

So what does this mysterious word mean ? Christoph Luxenberg bases his new interpretation on an underlying Syro-Aramaic verbal root and translates surah 3:96:

> "The first sanctuary which was built for the people is the one which he *fenced in (defined)* as a holy (literally: blessed) (district) and (as) a guidance for the people".

Luxenberg continues:

> "This is confirmed by reading the following verse 97 which says that Abraham's residence (...) can be found in this (district)... and whoever enters it shall be secure."[88]

The context supports Luxenberg's translation. Thus it must be assumed that *Bakka* does not mean Mecca or any other city, but designates (some kind of) a fenced-in holy district.

6.4 Kaʿba

The form *kaʿba* appears twice in the Qur'ān, both cases in surah 5 (*al-mā'ida* – the table [spread]), in verses 95 and 97:

> "(the forfeit) to be brought as an offering to the Ka'bah (*hadyan bāliġa l-kaʿbati*)" (surah 5:95)
> "Allah hath appointed the Ka'bah, the Sacred House, a standard for mankind, and the Sacred Month and the offerings and the garlands. – *ǧaʿala llāhu l-kaʿbata l-bayta l-ḥarāma qiyāman li-n-nāsi wa-š-šahra l-ḥarāma wa-l-hadya wa-l-qalā'ida*" (surah 5:97)

This mention of *Kaʿba* twice in a coherent text could yield further specific information about localities. Apart from these verses, no comparable sanctuaries are named in the Qur'ān, they are only described:

> "And when We made the House (at Mecca) (*bayt*) a resort for mankind (*maṯābatan li-n-nāsi*) and a sanctuary (*'amnan*), (saying): Take as your place of worship the place where Abraham stood (to pray) (*wa-ttaḫiḏū min maqāmi 'ibrāhīma muṣallan*). And We imposed a duty upon Abraham and Ishmael, (saying): Purify My house for those who go around and those who meditate therein and those who bow down and prostrate themselves (in worship)." (surah 2:125)

Other epithets used for sanctuaries are "the ancient House (*[bi]-l-bayti l-ʿatīq*ⁱ)" (surah 22:29); "Thy holy House (*[ʿinda] baytika l-muḥarrami*)" (surah 14:37); "the Inviolable Place of Worship (acc.: *[a]l-masǧida l-ḥarāma*)" (surah 48:27). Mostly ritual duties and practices are reported in the context of these references. However, unfortunately, a localization of this house is missing; this is also true of the conceptual clarification of *kaʿba* in surah 5:95 and 97, as it is not said where it is located.

Hence, the questions arise as to whether it is always the *Kaʿba* in Mecca that is meant when the above-mentioned designations for cult sites are used and whether "the place where Abraham stood up to pray/ dwelt (*maqāmu 'ibrāhīma*)" is to be found in Mecca. After all, there were other *Kaʿbas* in the Middle East, which, according to the customs of that time, were circumambulated; in this respect the Qur'ān suggests no connection to Mecca at all. In a Syrian (Christian) chronicle written between 670 and 680 (?) in Southern Iraq, it says that no-one knows where the "house of Abraham" can be found.[89]

The thesis that "Abraham's dwelling place" can be found in Mecca on the Arabian Peninsula is indeed historically adventurous. But as the Arabs saw themselves as children of Ishmael, such a theological construction would be conceivable. But the Qur'ān itself provides no hints, the only source we have being the traditional literature of the 9th century. If the Spanish chronicle mentioned above is used as a basis and Mecca is presumed to be in Mesopotamia, then there would be no conflict with biblical geography and the "place where Abraham dwelt" would be located in Mesopotamia (more precisely in Samarra), roughly as in the Bible.

6.5 The direction of prayer (Qibla)

The Qur'ān contains sayings in which the direction of prayer is declared unimportant in view of correct behavior:

> "It is not righteousness that ye turn your faces to the East and the West (*laysa l-birra 'an tuwallū wuğūhakum qibala l-mašriqi wa-l-maġribi*); but righteous is he who believeth in Allah and the Last Day [...]"(surah 2:177)

Here the underlined preposition *qibala* is derived from the same root as the noun "*qibla*". surah 7:29 might point in a similar direction:

> "29. Say: My Lord enjoineth justice. And set your faces, upright (toward Him) at every place of worship (*wa-'aqīmū wuğūhakum 'inda kulli masğidin*) and call upon Him, making religion pure for Him (only)."

As already mentioned, "*masğid*", originally meaning only "*place of prosternation*", is the modern word for mosque; Pickthall correctly translated it as "place of worship". Whether "at every place of worship" really means that the direction is unimportant, is not entirely clear, but it is still surprising that it is not mentioned at all when, at the same time, the place of worship is declared generally unimportant.

The following verse seems to stress the omnipresence of God, irrespective of the direction of prayer:

> "(*about other gods*) And if they answer not your prayer (*fa-'illam yastağībū lakum*), then know that it is revealed only in the knowledge of Allah (*fa-'lamū 'annamā 'unzila bi-'ilmi llāhi*); and that there is no God save Him. Will ye then be (of) those who surrender? (*fa-hal 'antum muslimūn*[a])" (surah 11:14)

Surah 2:148 and 149 are somewhat ambiguous. In verse 148 the way of life is declared the most important feature of a good Muslim:

> "And each one hath a goal toward which he turneth; so vie with one another in good works. Wheresoever ye may be, Allah will bring you all together (*'ayna mā takūnū ya'ti bikumu llāhu*). Lo! Allah is able to do all things."

The phrase in Arabic, "*'ayna mā takūnū ya'ti bikumu llāhu*", literally means: "*Wherever you may be, God will come to you*", which sounds as if inspired by Matthew 18:20:

> "For where two or three have gathered together in My name, I am there in their midst."

But already in the next verse we read:

> "And whencesoever thou comest forth (for prayer, O Muhammad) turn thy face toward the Inviolable Place of Worship. (*wa-min ḥayṯu ḫarağta fa-walli wağhaka šaṭra l-masğidi l-ḥarāmi*)" (surah 2:149)

There are several preceding verses in the same surah which emphasize the importance of the (individual) direction of prayer:

> "142. The foolish of the people will say (*sa-yaqūlu s-sufahā'u mina n-nāsi*): What hath turned them from the qiblah which they formerly observed (*mā wallāhum ʿan qiblatihimu llatī kānū ʿalayhā*)? Say: Unto Allah belong the East and the West.(*qul li-llāhi l-mašriqu wa-l-mağribu* [...]" (surah 2:142)

R. Paret interprets the phrase "the qiblah which they formerly observed – *qiblatihimu llatī kānū ʿalayhā*" as referring to the *qibla* in the direction of Jerusalem, which is then changed to Mecca (see his commentary surah 2:142-150):

> "[...]And We appointed the qiblah which ye formerly observed (*wa-mā ğaʿalnā l-qiblata llatī kunta ʿalayhā*) only that We might know him (*'illā li-naʿlama*) who followeth the messenger, from him who turneth on his heels. (*man yattabiʿu r-rasūla mimman yanqalibu ʿalā ʿaqibayhi*) [...]" (surah 2:143)

It does not really become clear that the direction of prayer was actually changed from one city to another. Nor is it clear that qibla means "direction of prayer". Especially one of the following verses suggests a much more general meaning, maybe "customs, rituals" or such like:

> "And even if thou broughtest unto those who have received the Scripture all kinds of portents, they would not follow thy qiblah, nor canst thou be a follower of their qiblah; nor are some of them followers of the qiblah of others. – *wa-la- 'in 'atayta llaḏīna 'ūtū l-kitāba bi-kulli 'āyatin mā tabiʿū qiblataka wa-mā 'anta bi-tābiʿin qiblatahum wa-mā baʿḍuhum bi-tābiʿin qiblata baʿḍin wa-*

> *la-ʾini ttabaʿta ʾahwāʾahum min baʿdi mā ǧāʾaka mina l-ʿilmi ʾinnaka ʾiḏan la-mina ẓ-ẓālimīn*[a]" (surah 2:145)

Just what might be the reason why the word *qibla* was generally understood to mean "direction of prayer" is to be found in verses surahs 2:144, 149, 150):

> "[...] And now verily We shall make thee turn (in prayer) toward a qiblah which is dear to thee. (*fa-la-nuwalliyannaka qiblatan tarḍāhā*) So turn thy face toward the Inviolable Place of Worship (*fa-walli waǧhaka šaṭra l-masǧidi l-ḥarāmi*), and ye (O Muslims), wheresoever ye may be, turn your faces when ye pray toward it. [...]" (surah 2:144)

Verse 2:149 has already been mentioned above:

> "And whencesoever thou comest forth (for prayer, O Muhammad) turn thy face toward the Inviolable Place of Worship. (*wa-min ḥayṯu ḫaraǧta fa-walli waǧhaka šaṭra l-masǧidi l-ḥarāmi*)" (surah 2:149)

Exactly the same wording is found again in the following verse!

> "Whencesoever thou comest forth turn thy face toward the Inviolable Place of Worship [...] – *wa-min ḥayṯu ḫaraǧta fa-walli waǧhaka šaṭra l-masǧidi l-ḥarāmi* " (surah 2:150)

So here the expression "*fa-walli waǧhaka šaṭra l-masǧidi l-ḥarāmi* – turn thy face toward the Inviolable Place of Worship" appears three times in exactly the same form within a passage of six verses, without there being any textual reason for this: the phrase is definitely not a refrain! R. Paret always adds a set of brackets with the words "in Mecca" after his rendering of "*masǧid al-ḥarām* – die heilige Kultstätte (the sacred cult site)". But apart from Muslim tradition, there is no clear indication of either *qibla* meaning "direction of prayer", or of a change of the direction of prayer from Jerusalem to Mecca!

Apart from the unspecific verse surah 7:29, all relevant verses referring to the *qibla* are to be found in surah 2, which appears like an unconnected compilation of statements, mostly from much later. The interpretation of "*masǧid al-ḥarām* – the Inviolable Place of Worship / the sacred cult site" as referring to Mecca would make sense if these verses stemmed from the era of Hārūn al-Rašīd, the caliph who converted Mecca into a pilgrimage site. This interpretation is possible: but why is the simple phrase "in Mecca", which would make everything clear, never found in any of these verses referring to the *masǧid al-ḥarām*? The explanation might be that for the listeners/readers of the time it was perfectly clear that "the sacred cult site" was there.

Nevertheless, it is very difficult to bring the statements in line with one another; surah 2:142-143 speak of a "qiblah which they formerly observed (*[ʿan] qiblatihimu llatī kānū ʿalayhā*) and "which ye formerly observed (acc.: *l-qiblata llatī kunta ʿalayhā*)", which is now being changed. But also the previous direction of prayer – provided *qibla* means "direction of prayer here" – was arranged in this way "that We might know him who followeth the messenger, from him who turneth on his heels". This conveys the impression that this early direction of prayer was a specific feature of the Qur'ānic movement in contrast to the (other) Christians. It is by no means clear whether surah 2:144 refers to the changing of the *qibla* from Jerusalem to Mecca: "and now verily We shall make thee turn (in prayer) toward a qiblah which is dear to thee" is followed by "and ye (O Muslims), wheresoever ye may be, turn your faces (when ye pray) toward it". The two sentences do not necessarily refer to the same thing, nor does either of them clearly refer to prayer: the Arabic text of the first sentence says: "*fa-la-nuwalliyannaka qiblatan tarḍāhā*"– lit.: "and verily we will make you turn you (concerning) a *qibla* you will be content with it". Nothing is said about prayer, as Pickthall's translation suggests. The second sentence: "*fa-walli waǧhaka šaṭra l-masǧidi l-ḥarāmi*" literally means: "and turn your face in the direction of the forbidden/ inviolable place of worship".

If we did not know from the traditional literature and from modern Muslims that the direction of prayer is towards Mecca, in other words, if we just possessed this text, we would never translate and interpret it the way Paret and Pickthall did. The root the noun *qibla* is derived from is *q-b-l*, which means "to accept", the related preposition "*qabla*" meaning "in front of, before". The reason why qibla came to be interpreted as "direction" might be the preposition "*qibala* – towards" in the first verse mentioned in this section:

> "It is not righteousness that ye turn your faces to the East and the West (*laysa l-birra 'an tuwallū wuǧūhakum* <u>*qibala*</u> *l-mašriqi wa-l-maġribi*); but righteous is he who believeth in Allah and the Last Day [...]"(surah 2:177)

But even if all the above-mentioned verses should really refer to the direction of prayer, – this possibility cannot be ruled out categorically, – then the changing of the *qibla* from Jerusalem to Mecca would already have been the second establishment of a direction of prayer which, just like the earlier one, distinguished the new creed from the (Trinitarian) Christian one. So why change a feature to make it distinctive, if it is already distinctive?

Moreover, these statements only make sense if it is assumed that in the 7th and 8th centuries all Christian churches had altars which faced the East, which is documented, for example, in this region for the Church of the Nativity in Bethlehem, the Hagia Sofia in Constantinople and for churches in Northern Syria).[90] So at least in churches, Christians prayed in an eastbound direction. A first distinctive direction of prayer of the Qur'ānic movement could have been Jerusalem in the time of ʿAbd al-Malik, which was changed, later, towards the end of the 8th century, to the new sacred city of Mecca.

If all above-mentioned verses are understood in this "conservative" way, Mecca would appear as the spiritual center of the new creed in the latest parts of the Qur'ān. This is conceivable, but remains uncertain, because the Qur'ānic verses are so vague.

6.6 The Punishment Stories ("Straflegenden")

The Qur'ān offers a series of biblical and non-biblical stories ("from the ancient Arabian wealth of myths and legends"[91]) which are arranged according to a tight pattern: God sent a prophet into a city or to a clan or nation; the people dismiss him and do not believe, so God destroys them. Occasionally it is added that the prophet and a few who believed in him are saved. These stories are called to mind in the Qur'ān, that is to say they are told as if they are known to the audience already. They had probably been put into a collection before they were added to the Qur'ānic texts.

In the "punishment stories", – unlike everywhere else in the Qur'ān, – the names of the respective messengers as well as the clans and cities to which they were sent are mentioned. Those from the biblical tradition are known to us, but the ones from "ancient Arabic myths and legends" are not always familiar to us. A review of these legends has shown that real information indeed underlies several of these stories.[92] Frequently, catastrophes which had in fact already happened centuries before the composition of the Qur'ān were then interpreted using the theological pattern mentioned.

The verifiable non-biblical information refers to the area of the Midianites/ Nabateans in North-West Arabia. These stories seem to have been included in the Qur'ān at some time. This may have happened after Mu'āwiya had consolidated the early form of an "Arabic" empire, followed by 'Abd al-Malik, during whose reign the Qur'ānic movement established itself in the West-Syrian region as well.

These "pre-Islamic" stories, which were integrated into the Qur'ān, probably as a whole, display regional and local references, but reveal nothing about the geographical location of Qur'ānic preaching.

6.7 Conclusion

The little evidence that exists of cities, regions and landscapes in the Qur'ān does not provide a sufficient basis to link its preaching to the region of the Arabian Peninsula. The texts themselves are geographically vague in a strange way: they could have originated from anywhere in the Syrian-Arabic region which includes the Middle East.

Further information might be obtained through etymological research, e.g. determining the influence of the Syrian and Persian languages and notions on the Qur'ān, as well as by means of datable and locatable coinage which documents the beginning and further proliferation of Qur'ānic motifs.

A historicization of the title *muḥammad* can be recognized in later parts of the Qur'ān, following the notion of an Arab messenger or one "making plain (*mubīn*)", who represents the Arabic-Qur'ānic movement as their preacher – still without the separation from Christianity (but, however, from the *other* Christians). The historicization to a Prophet of the Arabs with the name *Muḥammad* can only be found with a certain degree of probability in one place (surah 33:40), as the views expressed there about marriage are definitely no longer Christian. But even in those passages from the later parts of the Qur'ān where the prophet is mentioned without a name, he gains a new individuality when compared to Jesus and Christians. At the same time the Qur'ān is placed next to or above the Torah and the Gospel.

However, this historicization does not indicate any geographical location in the region of the Arabian Peninsula.

After the manuscript was finished, I came across an article about Muḥammad by Patricia Crone on the internet.[93] She writes about the difficulties in locating the life of Muḥammad on the Arabian Peninsula ("the middle [of Arabia] was *terra incognita*) or in Mecca, which was unknown at the time: "In sum, we have no context for the prophet and his message", she concludes and suggests "the Dead Sea region" as the theater of all the events mentioned; an opinion, however, which is not backed by very much evidence.[94]

At least it must be conceded that she dares to utter critical thoughts, – an exception among scholars of Islamic Studies, although she still maintains the historicity of a prophet called Muḥammad,[95] which she bases on the (probably incorrect) testimony of Christian sources.[96]

Bibliography

Aphrahat, Unterweisungen. First and Second Part. From the Syriac translated by von Peter Bruns (Fontes Christiani, vol. 5/1 and 5/2) Freiburg, Basel, Wien et al. 1991.

Crone, Patricia, What Do We Actually Know about Mohammed?, www.openDemocracy.net. (31 Aug, 2006).

Die dunklen Anfänge. Neue Forschungen zur Entstehung und frühen Geschichte des Islam, ed. by Karl-Heinz Ohlig and Gerd-Rüdiger Puin, Berlin [1]2005, [2]2006.

Diodor von Tarsus, Fragmente bei Leontius, Contra Nestorium et Eutychen 3 (Greek: MPG 86, 1, 1865, 1388 A).

Diodor of Tarsus, Fragments 11, 13, 15, 18, 29 (Syriac and German: Rudolf Abramowski, Der Theologische Nachlass des Diodor von Tarsus, in: ZNW 42, 1949, 31, 33, 37, 47).

Ibn Saʿd, Kitāb al-Ṭabaqāt al-kabīr, Arabic Edition, Karachi (Pakistan) 1967; Arabic (with German commentary): Ibn Saad. Biographien Muhammeds, seiner Gefährten und der späteren Träger des Islams bis zum Jahre 230 der Flucht, Bd. 1, Theil I: Biographie Muhammeds bis zur Flucht, ed. by E. Mittwoch, Leiden 1905, und Theil II: Biographie Muhammeds. Ereignisse seiner medinischen Zeit, Personalbeschreibung und Lebensgewohnheiten, ed. by E. Mittwoch und E. Sachau, Leiden 1917.

Isidor, Geschichte der Goten, Wandalen und Sueben (History of the Goths, Vandals and Suevi, Add.(itamenta) IV.V: Continuatio Byzantina Arabica a. DCCXLI, on: Isidori iunioris episcopi Hispalensis historia Gothorum Wandalorum Sueborum ad a. DCXXIV, in: Monumenta Germaniae historica, tomus XI: Chronicorum minorum saec. IV, V, VI, VII, Vol. II: Chronica minora, edidit Theodorus Mommsen, Berlin 1844, p. 323-369.

Johannes Damascenus, Über die Häresien/About Heresies, Liber de haeresibus opera polemica, in: Die Schriften des Johannes von Damaskus, vol. IV, ed. by Bonifatius Kotter (PTS 22), Berlin, New York 1981, haer. 100, p. 60-67.

Kettenhofen, Erich, Deportations II. In the Parthian and Sasanian Periods, in: Encyclopaedia Iranica (ed. by Eshan Yarshater), Volume VII, Fascile 3, Costa Mesa (California, USA) 1994, p. 298-308.

Khoury, Axel Theodor, Muhammad, in: Ders., Ludwig Hagemann, Peter Heine, Islam-Lexikon. Geschichte - Ideen - Gestalten, vol. 3, Freiburg, Basel, Wien 1991, p. 543-566.

Koran, der, deutsche Übersetzung (German translation of the Koran): Der Koran. Übersetzung von Rudi Paret, Stuttgart [9]2004.

Koran, der, deutsche Übersetzung: Koran. Aus dem Arabischen übertragen von Max Henning, Stuttgart 1973.

Luxenberg, Chr., Die Syro-Aramäische Lesart des Koran. Ein Beitrag zur Entschlüsselung der Koransprache, Berlin [2]2004.

Luxenberg, Christoph, Neudeutung der arabischen Inschrift im Felsendom zu Jerusalem, in: Die dunklen Anfänge, op. cit., p. 124-147

Nevo, Yehuda D. and Judith Koren, Crossroads to Islam. The Origins of the Arab Religion and the Arab State, Amherst, New York 2003

Ohlig, Karl-Heinz, Fundamentalchristologie. Im Spannungsfeld von Christentum und Kultur, München 1986

Ohlig, Karl-Heinz, Evidence of a New Religion in Christian Literature "Under Islamic Rule"?, in the present anthology.

Ohlig, Karl-Heinz, Weltreligion Islam. Eine Einführung, Mainz, Luzern 2000

Paret, Rudi, Der Koran als Geschichtsquelle, in: Der Islam 37, 1961, p. 24-42.

Paret, Rudi, Mohammed und der Koran. Geschichte und Verkündigung des arabischen Propheten, Stuttgart, Berlin, Köln, Main 1957.

Paul von Samosata (died after 272), Fragmente aus dem Synodalbrief (nach 268), Nr.5 (Friedrich Loofs, Paulus von Samosata. Eine Untersuchung zur altkirchlichen Literatur- und Dogmengeschichte, Leipzig 1924)

Paul von Samosata, Akten der Disputation mit dem Presbyter Malchion, Nr. 8 (268; Greek and German: F. Loofs, ibid. 337)

Popp, Volker, Die frühe Islamgeschichte nach inschriftlichen und numismatischen Zeugnissen, in: Die dunklen Anfänge, op. cit., p.16-123.

Popp, Volker, From Ugarit to Samarrā' (in the present anthology).

Puin, Gerd-Rüdiger, Leuke Kome/Layka, die Arser/Ashab al-Rass und andere vorislamische Namen im Koran, in: Die dunklen Anfänge, op. cit., p. 317-340.

Puin, Gerd-Rüdiger, Über die Bedeutung der ältesten Koranfragmente aus Sanaa (Jemen) für die Orthographiegeschichte des Korans, in: Hans-Caspar Graf von Bothmer, Karl-Heinz Ohlig, Gerd-Rüdiger Puin, Neue Wege der Koranforschung, magazin forschung (Universität des Saarlandes)1, 1999, p. 37-40; p.46.

Reinink, G.J., Die syrische Apokalypse des Pseudo-Methodius, transl. by G.J. Reinink (Corpus Christianorum Orientalium, Vol. 541).

Sprenger, A., Das Leben und die Lehre des Mohammad nach bisher grösstentheils unbenutzten Quellen, Erster Band, Berlin ^{2}1869.

Syrische Danielapokalypse (Syriac Apocalypse of Daniel). German translation and introduction: Matthias Henze, Apokalypsen und Testamente. Syrische Danielapokalypse (Jüdische Schriften aus hellenistisch-römischer Zeit, Bd. 1, Lieferung 4), Gütersloh 2006.

Theodore of Mopsuestia, aus von Cyrill verurteilten Thesen (Mansi 4, 45 [219]).

Watt, Montgomery W. / Alford T. Welch, Der Islam. I Mohammed und die Frühzeit - Islamisches Recht - Religiöses Leben (transl. from English by Sylvia Höfer, Die Religionen der Menschheit, ed. by Christel Matthias Schröder, vol. 25,1), Stuttgart, Berlin, Köln, Mainz 1980.

Zaehner, R.C., Zurvan. A Zoroastrian Dilemma, Oxford 1955.

Zoepel, F., Ostung. II. Im Christentum, in: LThK2 1992, 1294, p. 1294-1295.

Relics of Syro-Aramaic Letters in Early Qur'ān Codices in *Ḥiǧāzī* and *Kūfi* Ductus

Christoph Luxenberg

1. Introduction

The following article is a continuation of a case study about a passage of the current edition of the Cairo Qur'ān, the first part of which was published in the anthology *"The Hidden Origins of Islam: New Research into Its Early History"*.[1] In this paper, entitled *"A New Interpretation of the Arabic Inscription in Jerusalem's Dome of the Rock"* (ibid., pp. 125-152 of the English edition), especially in the section *"Confusion concerning Syro-Aramaic Letters"* (ibid., pp. 134 f.), Arabic word forms were re-interpreted as an erroneous transcription of an earlier Syriac text, which later served as a model for the Qur'ān, into the more recent Arabic writing system. The core mistake was the mixing up of the similar Syriac letters ܠ (*lām*) and ܥ (*'ayn*), which led to the transliteration of the latter as an Arabic ل (*lām*). Thus, the first letter in the uncommon Arabic word لبدا (*l-b-d-'*; surah 72:19), reflects the Syro-Aramaic (*'ayn*). Thus the word was interpreted as "*libadan*" instead of the correct form عبدا (*'ibādan* – original pronunciation probably: *'ābidē;* originally < *'ābidayn* > *'ābidēn* > *'ābidīn*) = Syro-Aramaic ܥܒܕܐ (*'āḇḏē* < **'āḇḏayn* >*'āḇḏēn* >*'āḇḏīn*). The idea that the reading *libadan* does not yield a suitable meaning here, a fact that has been acknowledged by some of the most important western Qur'ān translators, can easily be seen in the context of surah 72: 18-20:

وان المسجد لله فلا تدعوا مع الله احدا /
وانه لما قام عبد الله يدعوه كادوا يكونون عليه لبدا /
قل انما ادعوا ربي ولا اشرك به احدا

Paret[2] *(486):* 18: "And the places of worship (*masāǧid*) are (solely) there for God. Thus, call upon no one (else) but God." 19: "And: as the servant of God [Note: i.e., Mohammed] rose to call upon him [note: Or: to pray to him], they nearly crushed him to death (out of intrusiveness?)(? *Kādū yakūnūna 'alaihi libadan*). [Note: The interpretation of the verse is very uncertain.] 20: "Say: My Lord (alone) I will call upon [Note: Or: I pray to my Lord alone] and I will not associate any partners with him."

Blachère (620): 18 "La Mosquée [*sacrée*][3] est à Allah. Ne priez donc personne à côté d'Allah! 19 Quand le Serviteur d'Allah[4] s'est levé, priant, [les Infidèles] ont failli être contre lui des masses (?) 20 Dis: «Je ne prie que mon Seigneur et ne Lui associe personne»."

Bell[5] *(II, 611 f.)* "18. And that, the places of worship belong to Allah; so along with Allah call not ye upon anyone; 19. And that, when a servant of Allah stood calling upon Him, they were upon him almost in swarms.[6] ; 20. Say: "I call simply upon my Lord, and I associate not with Him anyone."

A philological analysis of these three related verses would have revealed the following sense:

(The Ǧinn, invisible beings, spirits, report, that ...):
"18. and that worship (is solely for) God, you shall not call upon anyone but God; 19. and that, when the servant of God was resurrected and he (still) called on (= worshipped) him, they (the people) would almost have worshipped him (as God); 20. (to which the servant of God fendingly) said (*not: 'say!'*): I do call upon my Lord and do not associate him with another!"

The fact that here for the first time individual Syro-Aramaic letters could be discovered in the Qur'ān is not due to the study of any Qur'ānic manuscripts. It rather gradually revealed itself from the contextual philological analysis of the canonical Qur'ān text, using the method first outlined in my monograph "*Die syro-aramäische Lesart des Koran*[7] *("The Syro-Aramaic Reading of the Koran)*". The manuscripts meanwhile available, however, have helped to expose the sources of error in transcriptions from Syriac into the younger Arabic writing system. Moreover, they have led to the discovery of a particularly prominent Syriac letter, which will be discussed below. Methodologically, this means an extension of the previous method, which basically consisted of seven points. While the main problem of the Qur'ān has so far been seen in the absence of diacritical points in the early manuscripts (although the actual problem is more of a philological nature, with the diacritical points only playing a minor role), the range of research methods must be extended so that one does not only have to consider the confusion of Arabic letters, but also the erroneous interpretation of a number of Syro-Aramaic letters as Arabic ones. These letters, and the resulting re-interpretation of certain misspelled and misread words, will be addressed below.

So far our studies have shown that the following letters of the Syriac alphabet have given way to false transcriptions and readings, partly due to their similarity to Arabic letters:

1. A false transcription, which is not uncommon, concerns the confusion between the two Syriac letters (in the *serṭā* ductus) ܕ / *d* and ܪ / *r*. In the Syriac alphabet they are only distinguished by a diacritical dot above or

below them. It must have been inexperienced copyists who are responsible for a transcription using an incorrect corresponding Arabic letter. The letters in question, i.e., those reflecting the Syriac "rasm" are: ܕ / *d* and *ḏ* /ܕ݂ on the one hand, and ܪ / *r* and ܙ / *z* on the other. But even a transcription using an Arabic و / *w* is possible, due to the similarity of this letter with the Syriac counterparts: ܘ / ܙ.

2. Less frequently the confusion of the two similar Syrian letters ܠ / l and ܥ / ʿayn is encountered, where the latter was more commonly translated into an Arab ل / l, while the first, because of its articulated form, became an Arabic ع / ʿayn.
3. By far the most common confusion relates to the final forms of the letter ى Arabic / y / *ī* or *ā* and ن / n. Even though a confusion within the Arabic writing system based on the similarity of these handwritten stop signs had been suggested earlier, the graphic evidence that such a confusion goes back to the unmodified (i.e., accurate) transcription of the Syrian end ܢ / ܢ / *n* , was delivered by the early *ḥiǧāzī* and *kūfī*-Qur'ān fragments referred to below. This statement is the real discovery, which provides the concrete evidence of a drafted Qur'ān template originally written in Syriac (so-called *Garschuni* / *Karschuni*).
4. An incorrect interpretation of a Syrian ܣ / *s* as an Arabic ه / *h* (due to the similarity of the two letters) was found in two cases so far.

2. Concrete Examples

2.1 Faulty Transcription of the Syrian ܥ / *ʿayn* as an Arab ل / *l*

Following the first case study outlined above, further examples of such a transcription error in the canonical text of the Qur'ān will be shown (the incorrectly transcribed ل / *l* is underlined):

2.1.1 Example 2: Surah 104:1

ويل لكل همزه لمزه

Paret (517) translated according to the Arabic Qur'ān commentators: "Woe to all nitpickers and moaners ..."

Introductory Remark:

The Cairo edition of the Qur'ān reads: *waylun li-kulli humazatin lumazatin*. The following conjectures are necessary here:

a) The initial vowel *u* in the last two words is arbitrary and has no grammatical justification. In these two forms the Arabic Qur'ān readers did not realize that it had been a Syro-Aramaic *noun-agent* that entered Arabic as the pattern *faʿʿāl*. The Arabic grammarians must have been familiar with it. It must have been inexperienced readers, who read *hu* instead of *ha* and *lu* instead of *la*;

b) Following the pattern *fa"āl*, the middle consonant is doubled, and the following vowel A is spoken long;

c) The Arabic readers did not recognize that the final *-h* denotes the Aramaic article (originally the emphatic masculine ending) *-ā*, which is neither related to the Arabic feminine ending nor has it any emphatic effect, such as is explained by the *Lisān* (V, 407). The two diacritical points in the final *h* are just as wrong as the suffix *-īn*, since the Aramaic final *-h* (= *-ā*) cannot be inflected. In a first step, and in accordance with Surah 104, which has a rhyme in *-a*, verse 1 should be read without final vowels: *wayl <u>la</u>-kull* (not *<u>li</u>-kull*) *hammāza <u>la</u>mmāza*.

Philological Analysis:

The word ويل / *wayl* is composed of the interjection وي / *way* (< Syro-Aramaic ܘܝ / *way*) (woe, woe) and the preposition (expressing the dative) ل / la (< reduction from على / *'alā* losing the initial syllable *'a*). This preposition was merged as an enclitic with the exclamation particle وي / *way* (hurt / woe!) and thus formed a noun ويل / *wayl* (similar to the formation of مال / *māl* < ما / *mā* + ل / *l-* = *what (belongs)* + *to* [one] = possession, property). In front of the personal suffix the form وي / *way* with the following preposition ل / *la* is thus used as a proclitic forming an exclamation particle ويلكم / *way-lakum* (*woe to you!*) (surah 20:61) (= Syro-Aramaic ܘܝ ܠܟܘܢ / *wāy lə-ḵōn*), or as a noun (before or after the word of reference), like in ولكم الويل / *wa-lakum al-wayl* (woe to you!) (surah 21:18).

2.1.2 About the Incorrect Transcription of ل / l in لمزه (Previous Reading: lumazatin)

The Arabic ل / l is an incorrectly transcribed Syrian ܥ / 'ayn. The original spelling in Syriac script ܥܡܙܗ = Arabic عمزه / *'ammāza*. The ع / 'ayn, provided with a diacritical dot, results in the Arabic reading غمزه / *ġammāza*.

Lexically the verbal root لمز / *lamaza* in Arabic usage cannot be proven. Everything about it in the dictionaries dates back to the Qur'ānic transcription errors and should belong under the root غمز / *ġamaza*. The Lisān (V, 406b) does not know that لمز / *lamaza* was incorrectly transcribed as غمز / *ġamaza* (without diacritical point), when it explains the form لمز / *lamaza*: وأصله الإشارة بالعين (originally the twinkle = beckoning with the eye is meant). Thus the Lisān (V, 388b) repeats the definition of غمز / *ġamaza* والغمز: الإشارة بالعين والحاجب والجفن (*al-ġamz* = *to wink, meaning: to give a signal with the eye, the eyebrow and the eyelid*).

Because the verb لمز / *lamaza* does not exist in Arabic, the Arabic Qur'ān commentators and lexicographers resort to guesswork in their attempt to find a meaning in the Qur'ānic context. Thus, in *Ṭabarī* (XXX, 291 ff), as well as in the *Lisān* (V, 406b f.) a form *lumaza* (= *lammāza*) is *one who despises or vilifies others*.

The Qur'ān clarifies the actual semantics by self-reference. It is a common trait of the Qur'ān that many sentences appear again and again. If the expression in question with the suspected faulty reading should have been correctly transcribed in one passage, without the Qur'ān commentators noticing this, then this verse would prove the erroneous transcription. Such an example can be found in Surah 83:29-30:

> ان الذين اجرموا كانوا من الذين امنوا يضحكون
> واذا مروا بهم يتغامزون
> *traditional reading:* 'inna lladīna 'ağramū kānū mina lladīna 'āmanū yaḍḥakūna wa-'idā marrū bihim yataġāmazūna
> *Pickthall:* "29. Lo! the guilty used to laugh at those who believed, 30. And wink one to another when they passed them"

Paret (504) does not understand the latter nuance when he translates, "they (pinchedly) winked at each other (*yataġāmazūna*)". Although the twinkle can have different motivations, Qur'ānic context clarifies the intention, as the preceding verb in verse 29 means "to laugh". Thus, in the context, the noun agent غمزه / *ġammāza* must refer to the "taunter", who, in surah 104, mocks afterlife and sees his happiness in the prosperity of his earthly life, and who, however, is promised punishment in hell. The leitmotif of the unbeliever, who mocks afterlife in this world and who will meet laughing believers in the hereafter, is found several times in the Qur'ān with synonymous terms such as سخر / *saḥira* (mock), ضحك / *ḍaḥika* (laugh), استهزأ / *istahza'a* (mock), لعب / *la'iba* (make fun, have fun) and the like.

Concerning the previous form همزه / *hammāza* (which, due to the misreading, was chosen as the name of the surah: *humaza*): The Lisan (V, 425 b) considers the root همز / *hamaza* to be synonymous to غمز / *ġamaza* and adduces (426a) the present participle هامز / *hāmiz* and the *nomina agentis* همّاز / *hammāz* and همزة / *humaza* (= *hammāza*), for which the synonym الغيّاب / *al-ġayyāb* (*calumniator*) is given. This would mean that همزه / *hammāza* would have to be considered as an emphatic synonym of غمزه / *ġammāza*. However, it could also be that the root همز / *hamaza* is just a phonetic variant of همس /*hamasa*, which the *Lisān* (V, 426b) refers to the devil, who *whispers into* the heart of men. According to Mannā (176a), Syro-Aramaic ܗܡܣ / *hmas* and others means (4): شك. ارتاب / *šakka*, *irtāba* (to doubt, suspect). As the Qur'ān equates *doubt* with *disbelief* (as can be inferred, e.g. from Surah 34:21, where God has the devil test the men in order to find out who *believes* in the afterlife and who doubts), the form همزه /

hammāza = همسه / *hammāsa* = "doubter" would well match غمزه / *ġammāza* = "mocker", who *doubts* afterlife and therefore *mocks* it. That is why he is threatened with punishment in hell in surah 104.

The two examples from Meccan surahs so far discussed will now be followed by further examples with similar transcriptions from Medinan surahs.

2.1.3 Example 3: Surah 49:11

ولا تلمزوا انفسكم ولا تنابزوا بالالقب

> *Pickthall:* "Neither defame one another, nor insult one another by nicknames."
> *Paret (431):* "Und bekrittelt euch nicht (gegenseitig) und gebt euch keine Schimpfnamen!" (Do not criticize each other and do not give each other insulting nicknames!)

This part of a verse from the Medinan surah 49:11 is preceded by the admonition to the believers, not to *mock each other* (لا يسخر قوم من قوم / *lā yasḫar qawmun min qawm*). This clear statement makes the synonymous meaning of the following, incorrectly transcribed verb ولا تلمزوا / *wa-lā talmizū* evident. Like above, *Ṭabarī* (XXVI, 131) renders this incomprehensible phrase as "calumniate". In this case, the medial لـ/ *l* in تلمزوا is an incorrect transliteration of Syriac ܥ /*ʿayn* (without diacritical dot). If we replace the لـ / *l* by an Arabic medial *ʿayn* with a diacritical dot, we get the form ولا تغمزوا انفسكم / *wa-lā taġmizū anfusakum*: "and do not *wink* at each other (*tauntingly* with the eyes) = do not *mock each other*."

While the reconstructed verb غمز / *ġamaza* (*to wink*) is common in Arabic, the following verb ولا تنابزوا / *wa-lā ta(ta)-nābazū* is not. Therefore, *Ṭabarī* (op. cit., 132) thinks that it is a denominative form of a fictitious noun نبز / *nabz*, the plural of which allegedly is انباز / *anbāz*. He considers it as a synonym of the following, genuine Arabic word لقب / *laqab* (*sobriquet, nickname*), which has a plural according to the same pattern: ألقاب / *alqāb*. This unfounded explanation was adopted without further discussion by the *Lisān* (V, 413 a) and, as a consequence, H. Wehr (*Arabisches Wörterbuch*), who explains the suspicious word as follows: "to give a derisive or insulting name", and the purported noun *nabaz* pl. *anbāz*: "sobriquet, nickname". Therefore, Paret's paraphrasing translation "do not give each other insulting nicknames", which does not translate the unclear verb, is understandable.

Syro-Aramaic can provide the solution to the riddle. *Mannā* (427a) explains the root ܢܒܙ (*nḇaz*) as a dialect variant of ܢܘܙ (*nwaz*) (the opposite is the case). There (435b) he gives as the third meaning the Arabic rendering: خاصم. شاجر (*ḫāṣama, šāǧara* – to quarrel, bicker). If we take this Syro-Aramaic meaning as our point of departure, then the following phrase ولا

بالالقب تنابزوا / *wa-lā ta(ta)-nābazū bi-l-alqāb* would literally mean: "and *do not quarrel* with nicknames" (meaning: "do not insult each other with nicknames/ do not throw nicknames at each other"). The latter meaning certainly makes more sense here that "to quarrel". Moreover, the Syro-Aramaic root ܢܒܙ (*nḇaz*) turns out to be the etymologically corresponding form of Arabic نبذ /*nabaḏa* (*cast [out], throw away*), so the *lectio difficilior* suggests that ز / *z* is an erroneous transcription of Syriac ܕ / *d*, which is only distinguished by the similar letter ܪ / *r* by the diacritical dot below instead of above. If we transcribe it as an Arabic د / *d* (and add a diacritical dot: ذ / ḏ) then this simple conjecture yields the new reading: ولا تنابذوا بالالقب / *wa-lā ta(ta)-nābaḏū bi-l-alqāb* – "and do not throw *(insulting)* nicknames at each *other*". This reading is all the more plausible, as the root نبز / *nabaza* is not attested in Classical Arabic, unlike the common root نبذ /*nabaḏa*, which appears as often as twelve times in the Qur'ān, or rather thirteen times, if the new reading is included.

After this new interpretation, the passage of surah 49:11 should therefore be translated as follows:

> "and do not *wink* (*tauntingly* with the eyes) against each other (i.e.: *do not mock each other*) and do not *throw* (insulting) nicknames at each other."

2.1.4 Example 4: Surah 9:58

ومنهم من يلمزك في الصدقت

فان اعطوا منها رضوا وان لم يعطوا منها اذا هم يسخطون

> *Pickthall:* "And of them is he who defameth thee in the matter of the alms. If they are given thereof they are content, and if they are not given thereof, behold! they are enraged."
>
> *Paret (157):* „Und unter ihnen gibt es welche, die dich wegen der Almosenabgaben *(ṣadaqāt)* bekritteln. Wenn sie dann (?) etwas davon erhalten, sind sie zufrieden. Wenn sie aber nichts davon erhalten, sind sie gleich aufgebracht." ("bekritteln" – to criticize in a narrow-minded way)

The context of this passage excludes an understanding of the wrongly transcribed يلمزك (traditional reading: *yalmizuka*) = يغمزك /*yaġmizuka* with the same meaning as above: "to wink tauntingly". Paret's translation "to criticize" and Pickthall's rendering "to defame" do not make very much sense either, as petitioners can only hope to get alms if they behave accordingly. *Ṭabarī* (X, 156) thinks that this verb must have the meaning "to try" (to get something) or "to request" here. The "winking" would then consequently have to be interpreted as a gesture of humble request (maybe even with the wish whispered into one's hand), which aims at evoking sympathy in the person addressed. This interpretation can indeed be found in the *Lisān* (V, 388b) under the entry غمز / *ġamaza*. There we read that according to Ibn al-Aṯīr الغمز / *al-ġamz* (*winking*) was interpreted in several *aḥādīṯ* (pl. of *ḥadīṯ/hadith*) as الرمز / *ar-ramz* (*hint, sign*), so as "*a hint given with the eye, the eyebrow or the hand* (فسر الغمز في بعض الأحاديث بالإشارة كالرمز بالعين والحاجب واليد)". The above-mentioned verse should therefore be translated as follows:

> "Among them are some who *wink* at you (expressing a request with this friendly gesture) concerning the alms. If they are given thereof, they are satisfied; but if they are not given anything, they are upset."

2.1.5 Example 5: Surah 9:79

الذين يلمزون المطوعين من المومنين في الصدقت والذين لا يجدون
الا جهدهم فيسخرون منهم سخر اللـه منهم ولهم عذاب اليم

Pickthall: "Those who point at such of the believers as give the alms willingly and such as can find naught to give but their endeavours, and deride them Allah (Himself) derideth them. Theirs will be a painful doom."

Paret (159): " Die (Nörgler), die (einerseits) die zu *freiwilligen Leistungen* (und Spenden) bereiten Gläubigen wegen der (von ihnen zusätzlich dargebrachten) Almosengaben *(ṣadaqāt) bekritteln* [Anm. 86: Oder: Die (Nörgler), die (einerseits) die bei den Almosengaben zu freiwilligen Leistungen bereiten Gläubigen *bekritteln*], und die (andererseits) diejenigen (bekritteln), die (aus Mangel an Mitteln) nichts als ihren Eifer vorweisen können (?) [Anm. 87: Oder: die nur mit Mühe (überhaupt) etwas aufbringen können *(? allaḏīna lā yaǧidūna illā ǧuhdahum)*], und über sie spotten, – über die spottet (dereinst) Gott (wenn sie zum Gericht kommen), und eine schmerzhafte Strafe haben sie zu erwarten."

Note to Paret's translation: "freiwillige Leistungen – voluntary assistance; perks"; "bekritteln – criticize in a narrow-minded way"; Pickthall's rendering "naught to give but their endeavours" is given an alternative translation in Paret's annotation: "who only with much effort manage to raise something").

It would lead too far to analyze all aspects of Paret's rendering. But his complex translation with several alternative understandings and question marks demonstrates that the sentence is hardly comprehensible on the lexical, phraseological and syntactic level.

Philological Analysis:
First of all, the transcription of the word يلمزون / *yalmizūn*, as already explained in the previous paragraph, would have to be corrected as يغمزون / *yaġmizūn*. Semantically the taunting intention of this "winking " is made clear by the following synonymous verb سخر /*saḫira* (*to mock*), so that the meaning "to wink (tauntingly)" could be translated freely as "to deride, ridicule".

2.1.5 Example 6: *Wrong transcription of Syriac* ܠ / *l as Arabic* ܥ / *ʿayn*

It is quite a coincidence that the incorrectly transcribed word (يلمزون / *yalmizūn* = يغمزون /*yaġmizūn*) with a Syro-Aramaic ܥ /*ʿayn* erroneously transcribed as Arabic ل / *l* is immediately followed by an example of the reverse case, a Syro-Aramaic ܠ / *l* being transcribed as an Arabic ع / *ʿayn*. Thus, the form المطوعين (canonical reading: *al-muṭṭawwiʿīna*) must be corrected into المطولين / *al-muṭṭawwilīn*.

Philological and lexical explanation:
The Arabic verbal root طوع > طاع / *ṭawaʿa* > *ṭāʿa* has the basic meaning "to obey". In Modern Arabic, the fifth verbal stem تطوع / *taṭawwaʿa* is used to designate "to enlist in the army (as a volunteer)". This corresponds to the explanation in the *Lisān* (VIII, 243b) of المطوعة / *al-muṭṭawwiʿa*: الذين يتطوّعون بالجهاد /*allaḏīna yataṭawwaʿūna bi-l-ǧihād* ("those who volunteer for the *ǧihād* [holy war]"). The verbal noun تطوّع /*taṭawwuʿ* is explained in the *Lisān* as follows: ما تبرّع به من ذات نفسه مما لا يلزمه فرضه ("it is what somebody does on his own account (voluntarily) [or: by which somebody excels], which is not an obligation"). However, the basic meaning of تطوع / *taṭawwaʿa* is: "to behave obediently, to comply with one's duties."

Although the meaning "to enlist in the army (as a volunteer)" has become common in modern Arabic, a connection with the alleged Qurʾānic meaning "alms given willingly" is not felt by modern speakers, even if one should understand the term من تطوّع خيرا / *man taṭawwaʿa ḫayran* (surah 2:158, 184) like Pickthall does: "he who doeth good of his own accord" (Paret: "wenn jemand *freiwillig* ein gutes Werk *leistet*" [if somebody does a good deed of his own accord]. In the Qurʾānic context the fifth (reflexive) verbal stem تطوع / *taṭawwaʿa* seems to have adopted the meaning of the tenth stem استطاع / *istaṭāʿa* ("*to be able to*"), something indicated by the synonymous verb اطاق / *aṭāqa* in surah 2:184: وعلى الذين يطيقونه فدية طعام مسكين : "and for those *who can afford it* [Paret: who are able to] there is a ransom: the feeding of a man in need." The following phrase is: فمن تطوع خيرا فهو خير له "And whoever *is able to do better things* (i.e.: *even more*),[8] will *benefit* from it." (*Pickthall:* But whoso doeth good of his own accord, it is better for him; *Paret:* " Und wenn einer *freiwillig* ein *gutes Werk* leistet, ist das *besser* für ihn.")

If this explanation excludes the reading المطوعين / *al-muṭṭawwiʿīn* meaning “the *voluntary* (donors)”, then we have to check whether the reading المطولين / *al-muṭṭawwilīn* might have the latter meaning.

The Arabic verbal root طول > طال / *ṭawala* > *ṭāla* clearly has the meaning “to be long”. There are, however, three passages in the Qur’ān, which make another meaning more likely:

1) Surah 4:25: Referring to the dowry (morning-gift) *Ṭabarī* (V, 15 f.) understood the word طول (canonical reading *ṭawl* – in fact: *ṭūl*, Arabic = “length”) in the introductory sentence ومن لم يستطع منكم طولا correctly, although out of context: “Whoever of you cannot raise the (morning-)gift.”
2) Surah 9:86: The expression اولوا الطول (canonical reading: *ʾūlū ṭ-ṭawli*), equally out of context, has also been interpreted correctly by *Ṭabarī* (X, 207), who renders it as: “the *wealthy* ones”.
3) Surah 40:3: The same can be said about the right understanding of the divine attribute ذي الطول (*dī ṭ-ṭawli* / *dī ṭ-ṭūli*) in the following enumeration: غافر الذنب وقابل التوب شديد العقاب ذي الطول “the one who forgives guilt, accepts repentance, punishes severely (and) disposes of (many) favors” (Pickthall: “The Forgiver of sin, the Acceptor of repentance, the Stern in punishment, the Bountiful”). From the context, *Ṭabarī* (XXIV, 41) understands the expression similarly, while Paret (388) wavers in his translation: “und (auch) über genügend Mittel verfügt *(ḏī ṭauli;* [who disposes of enough means]*)* (um den Gläubigen zu helfen? [to help the believers?]).” Indeed, the current Arabic word (*ṭūl*) cannot mean “length” in the above-mentioned Qur’ānic verses. For this reason, the exegetes had to invent a fictitious reading (*ṭawl* instead of *ṭūl*), to justify the unusual understanding of the word in these contexts.

In reality and like in many other cases, the Qur’ān here applies a word which is a loan-translation from Syriac. In order to get the true semantics of the word we have to translate back into Syro-Aramaic. Two verbal roots seem possible:

1) ܐܪܟ / *eraḵ* (*lang sein*),
2) ܦܫܛ / *pšaṭ* (*strecken, ausstrecken, hinreichen*).

About the semantics of both verbs *Mannā* enumerates the following Arabic meanings:

1) (40a) طال سبغ / *ṭāla, sabaġa* (< Syro-Aramaic ܣܒܥ / *sḇaʿ*) (*to be long, be abundant*); under ܐܘܪܟ / *awre* : أطال / *aṭāla* (*to make long, extend*), in connection with ܛܝܒܘܬܐ / *ṭaybūṯā* (*mercy*): اسبغ نعمة / *asbaġa niʿma* (*bestow favor*).
2) (618b) : بسط . نشر / *basaṭa, našara* (*stretch out, extend, spread*), (3) . قدّم أعطى / *qaddama, aʿṭā* (*give, donate*).

The semantics of these two synonymous verbs suffices to explain the Qur'ānic expression طول /*ṭūl* (Arabic = *length*) meaning "*mercy, riches, fortune, gift, donation* " as a lexical loan-translation from the corresponding Syro-Aramaic term.[9]

Even if the meaning of طول /*ṭūl* did not survive in Modern Arabic, the information given in the *Lisān* demonstrates, that the Arabic term with the Syro-Aramaic semantics must have been in use as late as the 9th century, as can be inferred from several of the *ḥadīṯs* cited there. The *Lisān* (XI, 414) refers to two of the three above mentioned passages of the Qur'ān (surah 4:25, 40:3) and explains الطول /*aṭ-ṭūl* (erroneously vocalized as *aṭ-ṭawl*) with the synonyms: القدرة / *al-qudra (power, fortune)*, الغنى / *al-ġinā* (*riches*), الفضل / *al-faḍl* (*favor, mercy*). In a colloquial phrase the latter word is explained as a synonym of طول /*ṭūl*, which has the second meaning: المنّ / *al-mann* (*favor, boon, gift*). After that, the fifth verbal stem تطوّل /*ta-ṭawwala* in the sense of امتنّ / *imtanna* (< Syro-Aramaic ܡܢܐ / *mnā*) (*to bestow a favor, give [as a gift]*) is added. For the purpose of clarification several *ḥadīṯs* (with the verb تطوّل /*ta-ṭawwala*) are cited to demonstrate the phraseology of the word: تطاول عليهم الرب بفضله أي تطوّل (*the Lord bestowed his mercy on them*); قال لأزواجه أوّلكنّ لحوقا بي أطولكنّ يدا (*He said to his wives: The first of you, who are closest to me, are those, who have "the longest hand"*) – أراد أمدّكنّ يدا بالعطاء (*he meant: who stretch out their hands most in order to give offerings*); the following commentary is given: وكانت زينب تعمل بيدها وتتصدّق (*Zaynab used to donate from her own handiwork)*. Concerning the nominal form تطوّل / *ta-ṭawwul* (*donating, giving offerings*) the following saying is ascribed to Abū Manṣūr: والتطوّل عند العرب محمود يوضع موضع المحاسن (*at-taṭawwul* = "donating" is highly esteemed by the Arabs and is considered a praiseworthy deed). The following passages in the *Lisān* (op. cit.) attest the early use of تطوّل / *ta-ṭawwul* in the sense of "donating".

Even if this use of the root might seem strange to a speaker of Modern Arabic and its semantics will rather go back to a loan-translation from Syro-Aramaic than to the "language use of the Arabs", the well-attested fifth verbal stem تطوّل / *ta-ṭawwala* can be found in the form of its active participle متطوّل / *mu-ta-ṭawwil* (*donating one* = *donor*). The plural form of this word, in the reconstructed form المطولين is attested in the Qur'ān as a *Hapaxlegomenon*, which (in its Qur'ānic form) has to be read with *haplological syllable elision* (from المتطولين / *al-mu-ta-ṭawwilīn* > *al-mu-ṭṭawwilīn* (corresponding to Syro-Aramaic / *garschuni* ܐܠܡܛܘܠܝܢ = Arabic المطولين). A study of the Qur'ānic manuscript *Ḥiğāzī*- BNF 328a has shown, that there (Bl. 41b, Z.14) the ع / *'ayn* in the word المطوعين (*al-muṭṭawwi'īn*) already appears in its wrongly transcribed form, which is an indication that this manuscript is secondary. The discussion of this noteworthy Qur'ānic term leads to two conclusions:

1. A graphic analysis has shown for the first time that in the Qur'ān the Syro-Aramaic letter ܠ / *l* was wrongly transcribed as ع /*'ayn*.

2. The discovery of this wrong transcription was due to a philological analysis, not due to manuscript studies.

The method applied has shown once more that only the connection of two linguistic components leads to a conclusive result:

a) the Arabic use of the term in the Qur'ān coupled with a historico-linguistic investigation of the use of the term;
b) the semantics of the lexically corresponding Syro-Aramaic term.

A number of other cases of wrong transcription into Arabic from a Syro-Aramaic script (*Garschuni* / *Karschuni*), in which the respective Qur'ānic text must have been written in, will be analyzed with the same method.

In the above mentioned annotation 87, Paret refers to the hardly intelligible sentence, which is added in brackets *(? allaḏīna lā yağidūna illā ğuhdahum)*. He is right to do so, as the idiomatic expression وجد جهدا / *wağada ğuhdan* (lit.: *to find an effort*), which is not to be found in any Arabic dictionary, is a literal rendition of the two Syro-Aramaic idiomatic expressions: ܡܨܐ ܚܝܠܐ / *mṣā ḥaylā* and ܐܫܟܚ ܚܝܠܐ / *eškaḥ ḥaylā* (lit.: *to be able to + power/strength = to have the power = to be able to do something*). In the latter expression, the Syro-Aramaic verb ܐܫܟܚ / *eškaḥ* has two meanings:

1. *to be*
2. *to find*

The latter meaning is rendered in the Qur'ān as وجد / *wağada* (*to find*) instead of استطاع / *istaṭā'a* (*to be able to*). In another passage the Qur'ān translates the corresponding Syro-Aramaic expression with the Arabic equivalent: استطاع حيله / *istaṭā'a ḥaylā* (erroneously read as حيلة / *ḥīlatan*; surah 4:98: لا يستطيعون حيلة / *lā yastaṭī'ūna ḥīlatan;* lit. Arabic: "not to be able + a ruse"– Syro-Aramaic: "not to be able + strength, power (ḥaylā)" = *not to be able*). Thus, in many cases in the Qur'ān, the verb وجد / *wağada* (to *find*) is a misrepresentation (due semantic extension) of Syro-Aramaic ܐܫܟܚ / *eškaḥ* (*to find/ to be able to*) in the Arabic sense of استطاع / *istaṭā'a* (*to be able to*), e.g. in surah 58:4, where فمن لم يجد / *fa-man lam yağid* (lit.: and whoever does not *find*) replaces Arabic فمن لم يستطع / *fa-man lam yastaṭi'* (whoever *is not able to*). The verb وجد / *wağada* (*to find*) is thus a loan-translation of Syro-Aramaic ܐܫܟܚ / *eškaḥ* (*to be able to/can; to find*), which, according to context, corresponds to استطاع / *istaṭā'a* (cf. also surahs 2:196; 4:92; 4:121; 5:89; 18:53; 24:33; 58:4; 58:12). The expression وجد جهدا / *wağada ğuhdan* (lit.: *to find o's effort*), also a borrowing from Syro-Aramaic, corresponds to the Modern Arabic expression جهد جهدا / *ğahada ğuhdan* ("to do o's very best").

Syntactically speaking, Paret refers the second الذين / *allāḏīna* (*those who*) to the first demonstrative pronoun, which designates the subject. He does not see that the second one introduces a relative clause, which refers to the believers mentioned before.

After this philological discussion, and taking semantic, phraseological and syntactical aspects into consideration, the above cited verse from Surah 9:79 should be understood as follows:

> "Those who <u>*mock*</u> the <u>*donors*</u> among the believers concerning (their) alms, considering that they (raise these funds) according to <u>*what they are able to*</u>, so if those (still)[10] mock them, then God will mock them and (let them taste) a severe punishment."

2.1.6 Example 7: Surah 17:78

اقم الصلوة <u>لدلوك</u> الشمس الى غسق اليل

وقران الفجر ان قران الفجر كان مشهودا

Pickthall: "Establish worship at the <u>going down</u> of the sun until the dark of night, and (the recital of) the Qur'an at dawn. Lo! (the recital of) the Qur'an at dawn is ever <u>witnessed</u>. "

Paret (234): "Verrichte das Gebet *(ṣalāt)*, wenn die Sonne sich (gegen den Horizont) <u>neigt</u>, bis die Nacht dunkelt! Und die Rezitation des frühen Morgens *(wa-qur'āna l-faǧri)* ! Bei ihr soll man (allgemein) <u>zugegen sein</u> *(? inna qur'āna l-faǧri kāna mahšūdan)*." (*author's note:* "sich ... neigt – <u>inclines toward</u>"; "zugegen sein – <u>be present</u>").

The word to be discussed in this section is دلوك (canonical reading: *dulūk*). Referring to the sun, Pickthall understands it as expressing the idea of the sun "going down" or in Paret's case of the sun "inclining towards the horizon". Although some of the authorities cited by *Ṭabarī* (XV, 134 ff.), among others Ibn Mas'ūd and Ibn 'Abbās, understand this term as meaning the *sunset*, *Ṭabarī* sides with the majority who interprets the term as meaning "noon, midday". In his commentary, Paret (305) is right to assume that the term "generally refers to the time of evening prayer", but this assumption becomes certainty, when the wrongly transcribed Arabic ﻟ / *l* is replaced by the original Syro-Aramaic letter ܥ /*'ayn*. From Syro-Aramaic (*garschuni* / *karschuni*) ܕܥܘܟ = Arabic دعوك / *du'ūk* we get the Syro-Aramaic verbal root ܕܥܟ /*d'e*, which, according to *Mannā* (155b) means: (1) طفى /*ṭafi'a* (*to expire, vanish*), (4) غاب . غرب /*ġaba, ġaraba* (*to go down*). The meaning of this *Hapax-legomenon* دعوك / *du'ūk*, which has been shown to be a loan-translation from Syro-Aramaic, is thus "sunset".

The Arabic passive participle مشهودا / *mašhūdā* should not be understood in the Arabic sense of "*be witnessed, be present*", but in the Syro-Aramaic sense of "*admonished = prescribed*" (cf. *Mannā*, 480a, under ܐܣܗܕ / *ashed:* (3) نبّه . حذّر / *nabbaha, ḥaddara*). From this root the noun ܡܣܗܕܘܬܐ /

sāhdūṯā is derived, which means (3) شريعة. ناموس. وصية / *šarīʿa, nāmūs, waṣīya* (*law, commandment*).

The Arabic conjunction و / *wa-* in وقران / *wa-qurʾān* introduces a new, nominal clause, which is followed by a clause introduced with the particle ان / *inna*. The Arab readers did not understand this syntactic figure and therefore separated the verse. Thus, the above cited verse of the Qurʾān can be rendered as follows:

> "Perform the prayer at *sunset* until *dusk*. (As far as) the performance of Qurʾān recitation at dawn is concerned, it is *compulsory* (*prescribed*)!"

3 Graphic Analysis of Early Qurʾān Codices in the *ḥiǧāzī*- and *kūfī*-Ductus

(BNF 328a, British Library Or. 2165, Samarqand, Ṣanʿāʾ)

On the cover of my book *The Syro-Aramaic Reading of the Koran* (1st German ed., Berlin 2000) leaf 3b of the Qurʾān manuscript BNF 328a is depicted. In line 14 of this leaf the name *Johannes* (second word from the right, from surah 3:39) can be found, the writing looking very much like the Syriac word: ܝܚܝ (without prefixed preposition ܒ *bi-*). In the Cairene edition of the Qurʾān this word is written as يحيى – *Yaḥyā*. The last consonant, which was written in a *retroflex* manner in early versions of Arabic script, i.e., "turning around" toward the beginning of the word, was here replaced by the final *yāʾ* as we know it from Modern *nasḫī*: ى. The original graphemic structure was thus altered.

3.1 The hitherto Overlooked Graphemic Significance of Arabic *Retroflex* final ى (ے)

So far it has been common knowledge among researchers of the Qurʾān that both forms of the final ى are attested in Qurʾānic manuscripts as free variants (of final *ī* and *ā*). In fact both forms appear with the same word quite arbitrarily.[11] Therefore, researchers did not see any reason to assume two different graphemes for the two forms.

This idea, however, suggests itself, if we consider the Arabic reading يحيى *Yaḥyā*, which deviates considerably from the Syro-Aramaic ܝܘܚܢܢ *Yoḥannān*/ *Yuḥannān*, especially as this name is not attested in early Arabic literature (see A. Jeffery, *Foreign Vocabulary*, Baroda 1938, pp. 290 f.). In pre-Islamic times no trace of the name can be found (see Josef Horovitz, *Koranische Untersuchungen*, Berlin-Leipzig 1926, p. 151).

A. Mingana (*Syriac Influence*, p. 84) was the first who pointed out the misreading of Arabic *Qurrā'*, however, his point of departure was the current graphic representation: ىحىـ (يحيى), the final ى of which could also be interpreted as modern final ن. He writes:

> "I believe, with Margoliouth (*Moslem World*, 1925, p. 343), that the name (*Yaḥya*) is almost certainly the Syriac *Yoḥannan*. In the early and undotted Ḳur'āns the word stood as ىحىـ which could be read *Yoḥanna*, *Yoḥannan* or *Yaḥya*, and the Muslim *ḳurrā'* who knew no other language besides Arabic adopted the erroneous form *Yaḥya*. I am absolutely unable to agree with Lidzbarski (*Johannesbuch*, ii., 73: cf. also Nöldeke in *Z.A.*, xxx., 158 sq.) that this curious name is an old Arabic one."

From this we can conclude that in his assessment of the original *rasm*, Mingana referred to uniform final ى as we know it from the modern Cairene Qur'ān, which in its undotted version can well be misread as a secondary final -*ā* or final *n* (ن).

Although he was familiar with early Qur'ānic manuscripts, Mingana obviously did not notice the difference between the current modern yā' and the *retroflex* final ى (ܢ) in early codices. If, however, we take into consideration that the Arabic *retroflex* final (ى) (*ī*/*ā*) can hardly be distinguished from the Syro-Aramaic final ܢ (-*n*) (esp. in handwriting), and if we assume the latter as the basic form, then a handwritten form looking like ܝܚܢ excludes the readings *Yaḥyā* and *Yoḥannā* (with *ā* in final position). For if the Arabic *retroflex final* ܢ (= ى) of the passage in question is read as Syro-Aramaic final ܢ (-*n*) – (ܝܚܢ = يحنن), we automatically come to the Syro-Aramaic reading of the whole word: ܝܘܚܢܢ *Yoḥannān*. The fact that the Qur'ān does not transcribe the *mater lectionis* ܘ (*o*) of the Syriac form, can be explained by the (etymologically correct) perception of the speakers of this Early Arabic (who still understood Syriac), that the name is indeed a 3rd sg. of the imperfect. Therefore the vowel of the first open syllable, in analogy to the prefix of the third person of the Arabic imperfect form of the verbal stems II-IV, is short in Arabic, e.g. it is *yuḥibbu* ("he loves", short "u") and not *yūḥibbu*.[12] Thus the spelling of tran*scribed* (in this case *not* trans*literated*) Syro-Aramaic loanwords, the *mater lectionis* of which for short *u* is dropped by the Qur'ān, is not surprising. (see C. Luxenberg, *Die Syro-Aramäische Lesart des Koran*, 1st ed. 2000, p. 193, footnote. 228; 2nd ed. 2004, p. 226; 3rd ed. 2007, p. 227, footnote 267).

If this should be the case, similar cases of the Arabic *retroflex* final ى / (ܢ) as misreadings of original Syro-Aramaic final *nūn* should not only appear in a unique example like *Yoḥannān,* but other examples are to be expected in the Qur'ān. Such examples will be presented in the following:

3.2 Example of Misreading I: سـاى (سـا)

This word, which in the Qur'ānic manuscript in Paris BNF 328a is mostly written with a *retroflex* final ى (سـا) and is read as šaʾī or *šāy*, is normally considered to be a variant of the common modern Arabic word شـيء (*šay'*) (*thing, matter, something*) written in an *archaic orthography*. The long medial *Alif* (ـا) in the form سـاى was probably interpreted as a *mater lectionis* for the *hamza*, which should actually follow the ى. As, however, the final *hamza* in the modern spelling of شـيء is written without mater lectionis, the medial *alif* (ـا) of the Cairene Qur'ān was considered superfluous or even wrong and therefore dropped and replaced by the *hamza* without *mater lectionis*. Thus the modern spelling شـيء – as a purported correction of the supposedly *archaic* orthography of سـاى was fixed in the Qur'ān once and for all and accepted by scholars dealing with Qur'ānic research in East and West without further discussion.

In his *Untersuchungen zur frühen Geschichte der Arabischen Orthographie. II. Die Schreibung der Konsonanten* (in: Orientalia, vol. 49, 1980, pp. 67–106) W. Diem tries to historically explain this orthography, which is thought to be *archaic*:

> "§ 127 (line 7): Concerning شاى we have to note that this spelling must have been in current use, as the koranic attestation (18:23 لِشَاْىءٍ) suggests. According to a remark in ad-Dānī (footnote 92: *Muqniʿ* 45 above; cf. also *GdQ* III 49 footnote 4) the exclusive form to be found in the text of Ibn Masʿūd was شاي . The palimpsests of Lewis, apart from one exception, only display the spelling شاي (footnote 93: cf. *GdQ* III 56 above); this spelling also appears in the codex from Samarqand (footnote 94: cf. Jeffery-Mendelson: "Samarqand Qur'ān Codex" 187 and others); it is even attested in early Islamic records (see footnote 95). Concerning the question of phonetics, there can hardly be any doubt that شاي , as well as شى designates a form *šayy < šay'* (…).
> § 128 The explanations can be summarized: the written forms (…) شاي corresponded to the pronunciation (…) *šayy* (…) . This means that there is no reason to write the forms with *alif* due to hiǧāzī pronunciation habits. It is, however, conspicuous that the early form (...) *šay'*... did in fact contain a *hamza*, which, according to the early orthography, had to be written with an *alif*. The spelling, however, would then have to be…*شيا …, while the spellings attested in the Qur'ān appear as …شاي. Nevertheless, a historic connection between the two groups of spellings cannot be excluded. In the text of the Qur'ān there seems to be a rule that every time an *alif* that has *lost its phonetic function* was combined with the letters *alif-yā'* or *alif-wāw* when these express the actual pronunciation, then the order *alif-yā'* or *alif-wāw* was preserved, … i.e., the *alif* was retained and a letter *yā'* or *wāw* was inserted behind, never before. The spelling …*شيا … with their order of letters *yā'-alif*, contradicted

> the order *alif-yā'*, but for the scribes had to be assessed in a similar fashion, as they as well contained an *alif* without function and the letter *yā'* expressed the pronunciation. Thus, it might be imaginable, that the scribes, without knowledge of the etymology, which they could not have, changed the letters *yā'-alif* of the spelling …*شيا into the normal order *alif-yā'*, which led to the attested spelling…شاي … (see footnote 98: Rabin: *Ancient West-Arabian,* p. 140; he considers شاى as the result of an orthographic analogy…). In a case like this the deplorable fact that we do not possess any records of ḥiǧāzī Arabic during the long period of the latest Nabatean-ḥiǧāzī inscriptions and graffiti until the corpus of the Qur'ān becomes obvious once again."

To solve the riddle of this orthography, there is an easier explanation than these far-fetched speculations with questionable results: If the Arabic *retroflex* final ى is read as a Syro-Aramaic final *nūn* (ے), then the spelling ساے would not have to be read as *ša'ī* or *šāy,* nor as *šayy < šay',* but as شان (*šān /ša'n*). Thus God does not have power over every *thing*, every *object*, – على كل شيء قدير –, but على كل شأن about every *matter* (thus e.g. in BNF 328a, surah **2**: 282, 284: Bl.1b, Z. 7, 14; surah **3**: 5, 26, 28, 29, 92, 128, 154 (twice), 165, 189: Bl.2a, Z. 6; Bl.3a, Z. 6, 11, 15; Bl.4a, Z.16; Bl.6a, Z. 1; Bl.7a, Z. 12, 14; Bl. 7b, ultima; Bl.9a, Z. 10; surah **4**: 4, 32, 33, 59, 85, 86, 113, 126, 176: Bl.10a, Z. 5; Bl.12a, Z. 21; Bl.12b, Z. 2; Bl. 14a, Z. 4; Bl. 15b, Z. 5, 7; Bl. 17a, Z. 21; Bl.18a, Z. 4; Bl. 20b, Z. 12; surah **5**: 17, 19: Bl. 22a, Z. 9, 16, etc.).

A synopsis of the orthography of the oldest extant Qur'ānic manuscripts would certainly help to elucidate the original structure of the language of the Qur'āns. For the time being the attestations of alternating *plene* and *defective* spelling of ساے and سے (*š'an / šān*) in the accessible, fragmentary Qur'ānic manuscripts will be presented:

1) BNF 328a (in calligraphic *ḥiǧāzī*–ductus, covers about a fourth of the Cairene Qur'ān edition);
2) Samarqand (in *kūfī*-ductus, covers about half of the Cairene Qur'ān;
3) Ṣan'ā' (in ordinary *ḥiǧāzī*–ductus, except for later insertions, a bit more than a fourth of the Cairene Qur'ān edition).

1) BNF 328a:

a) Plene spelling with *retroflex final* ے (ساے) can be found in BNF 328a in the following 52 places in the Qur'ān (verse numbering according to the Cairene edition): Surah **2**: 282, 284; **3**: 5, 26, 28, 29, 92, 128, 154 (twice), 165, 189; **4**: 4, 32, 33, 59, 85, 86, 113, 126, 176; **5**: 19; **6**: 38, 44, 52 (twice), 69, 80, 91, 93, 99, 101 (twice), 102, 111, 148; **7**: 145 (twice), 156, 185; **9**: 115; **12**: 111; **13**: 8, 14, 16; **14**: 18, 38; **15**: 19, 21; **35**: 18.
b) Plene spelling with final Arabic ى (ساى) can be found in BNF 328a in 3 places: **5**: 17; **6**: 102 (2nd place); **14**: 21.

A comparison of the orthography of شان in Surah **5**:17, BNF 328a, leaf 22a, line 9 (with *ḥiǧāzī* final ى, i.e., bent down and turning left; سای) and **5**:19, BNF leaf 22a, line 16 (with *retroflex final* ي : سا) shows that the later copyist did not understand the graphemic difference between Syro-Aramaic final *nūn* (ـ), and *retroflex* Arabic final ى in all three above-mentioned cases. This becomes especially clear after an analysis of the alternating spellings in surah **6**: 102:

ذلكم الله ربكم لا اله الا هو خلق كل سا وهو على كل سای وكيل

Especially for the latter spelling (سای) the Ṣanʿāʾ codex (leaf 16a, penult.) has got سا, (*šān / šaʾn*) and for the first spelling defective: سـ (*šān*), while the Samarqand codex displays defective spelling for both (سـ). However, this does not mean that the copyist of manuscript BNF 328a is himself responsible for this change. It could as well be that he just took it over from an earlier model. In any case, we have to answer the question of the approximate dating of this Qurʾānic manuscript, which, for obvious reasons, does not belong to the first generation of written texts from the Qurʾān. So this change might be considered a litmus test for the age of a manuscript: Only manuscripts where the original form is used throughout can claim to be old.

c) Defective spelling of Arabic final ى (سى) can be found in BNF 328a in the following two places: **6**: 154; **7**: 89.

That in both places we are dealing with a misinterpretation of Syro-Aramaic final *nūn* (ـ), which was later rewritten as an Arabic final ى can be inferred in both cases from the Samarqand codex (leaf 327, 9 and leaf 377, 4), where the same word is written with a *retroflex final* ى, i.e., with Syro-Aramaic final *nūn* (ـ). Moreover, the context in **6**: 154, – وتفصيلا لكل شـ and in 7: 89: وسع ربنا كل شـ علما) makes the reading شـ (*šān*) (*matter, affair*) as opposed to شيء (*šay*ʾ) (*thing*) more likely, as Arabic شأن (*šaʾn*) covers a more comprehensive semantic field than شيء (*šay*ʾ).

Summary

In the last two cases we have assumed an originally defective spelling of شأن (*šān / šaʾn*). The adduced spellings from Samarqand prove that the plene spelling سای in the three above-mentioned cases in BNF 328a are a later misreading of the original form سا (*šān*). As a result, for the 55 cases of plene spelling in BNF 328a we can infer as the original form شان (*šaʾn / šān*), in two other cases the defective spelling شن (*šān*), so that in 57 cases the reading شان (*šaʾn / šān*) has to be assumed. In all 57 passages the form has been changed to شيء (*šay*ʾ) in the Cairene edition.

This leads to two conclusions: First, the Syro-Aramaic final *nūn* was not recognized as such by the Arabic copyist and re-interpreted as an Arabic *retroflex final yā'*. And second, such a confusion of two elementary Arabic terms with sufficiently different pronunciation contradicts the Islamic tradition of an uninterrupted chain of oral transmission of the Qur'ānic texts.

2) The Samarqand Codex (in kūfī ductus)

The spellings that can be found in this codex are the following:

a) Plene spelling (ساے) (*ša'n* / *šān*) with *retroflex final* ے (ى = ن) in the following 12 passages: **4**: 32; **6**: 38, 91, 93; **11**: 57, 101; **16**: 35, 75, 89; **18**: 23, 70; **20**: 50.

   The passage from the Cairene edition mentioned by W. Diem (18:23 لِشَاْىءٍ) has been explained with the help of the Samarqand codex as *retroflex final* ے, to be pronounced as a final *n* (ن) (لساے *li-ša'n* / *li-šān*).

b) In one place (surah **15**: 21) the Samarqand codex has got plene spelling (ساى) with an Arabic final ى. In the same place, BNF 328a, as mentioned above, has got plene spelling with *retroflex final* ے (ساے / *šān*). This seems to be a later change. The Samarqand codex does not belong to the first generation of Qur'ānic manuscripts.

c) Defective spelling (سے / *šān*) can be found in 56 places: **2**: 113 (twice), 148, 231, 259, 282, 284; **3**: 128, 165, 189; **4**: 33, 86, 113, 126; **5**: 97, 117, 120; **6**: 44, 52 (twice), 69, 80, 99, 101 (twice), 102 (twice), 111, 148, 154, 159, 164; **7**: 89; **11**: 72; **15**: 19; **16**: 35, 40, 48, 76, 77; **17**: 12, 44; **18**: 45, 54, 76, 84; **20**: 98; **27**: 16; **36**: 12, 15, 83; **38**: 5, 6; **40**: 7; **41**: 21; **42**: 36.

d) In one place (surah **5**: 94) Samarqand has got defective spelling (سى) with final Arabic ى. This passage is missing in the codices BNF 328a and Ṣan'ā'. In the context of ليبلونكم الله بشي من الصيد (Allah will surely try you somewhat (in the matter) it is certainly possible to read this ductus as بشيء (*bi-šay'*). The final Arabic ى is therefore correct here and makes the difference to the retroflex *nūn* even more conspicuous.

Summary

It can be stated that, – unlike in BNF 328a –, in the Samarqand Codex in the overwhelming majority of cases we find defective spelling (سے / *šān*) with 56 attestations (not including one case where *yā'* is correct: شيء / *šay'*), as opposed to twelve plene spellings (ساے / *ša'n* / *šān*; including the wrong spelling ساى).

3) Analysis of a manuscript from Ṣan'ā' (so far not indexed)

The analysis yielded the following results:

a) Plene spelling (ساے) (*ša'n* / *šān*) with *retroflex final* ے (ى = ن) can be found in 24 Qur'ānic passages: **2**: 155, 178; **5**: 68, 97, 117; **6**: 17, 19, 52 (2nd place), 91, 93, 102 (2nd place); **8**: 72; **16**: 75, 76, 77, 89; **51**: 42, 49; **57**: 29; **58**: 6; **66**: 8; **67**: 1, 9; **72**: 28.

b) In one passage (**8**: 60) the *retroflex* final ـے which we would expect was replaced by an Arabic final ى. The fact that this goes back to a change by a later, incompetent scribe is proved by a parallel passage (surah 34: 39) in the same Ṣanʿāʾ codex, where the word was written with final ـے, albeit spelt defectively (سـے / *šān*).

c) In the text from Ṣanʿāʾ, plene spelling (سا‍ے / *šaʾn* / *šān*), with 24 or 25 attestations, is less common than defective spelling (سـے / *šān*), which is found in 55 places: **2**: 20, 29, 106, 109, 113 (twice), 148; **5**: 120; **6**: 38, 44, 52, 69, 80, 99, 101 (twice), 102, 111, 148; **8**: 41 (twice), 75; **13**: 8, 14, 16; **14**: 18, 21, 38; **20**: 98; **21**: 30, 81; **22**: 17; **23**: 88; **33**: 54, 55; **34**: 16, 21, 39, 47; **35**: 1, 18, 44; **36**: 12, 15, 83; **38**: 5, 6; **48**: 21, 26; **50**: 2; **57**: 2, 3; **65**: 12; **67**: 19; **80**: 18.

d) The common final ى of Modern Arabic can be found in the second appearance of the word سى in surah **65**:12, where the form appears several times. That this is a later erroneous interpretation of the preceding final ـے (سـے / *šān*), is shown by the context:

لتعلموا ان اللـه على كل شـے قدير

وان اللـه قد احاط بكل شـي علما

"that ye may know that Allah is able to do all things, and that Allah surroundeth all things in knowledge." (what is meant is not *concrete things*, but rather *matters/ circumstances*)

The latter spelling shows that this codex (or at least the respective leaf) does not belong to the first generation of Qurʾānic manuscripts.

e) There are 8 spellings with the modern final ى (سى) on obviously more recent leaves, which were later added to the codex: **15**:19, 21; **16**:35 (twice), 40, 48; **20**:50; **49**:16.

In some of these places the reading شي (*šay*ʾ) in the sense of *thing, object* (**15**: 19, 21) or in the Syro-Aramaic sense of *somebody* (**16**:35, twice) seems justifies, as will be shown later. In all other cases the word meant by the spelling is شـن (= شـان / *šān* / *šaʾn*).

Conclusion

It can be stated that in the earliest Qurʾānic manuscripts written in both *ḥiǧāzī* and *kūfī* style the final Arabic ى appears in both variants with the same graphemic value. Up to this day it was not common knowledge that the Arabic *retroflex* final ى in early Qurʾānic manuscripts can also designate the Syro-Aramaic grapheme final *nūn*. Moreover, we come to the following results:

1) According to the analysis of the three manuscripts the plene spelling سا (with medial *alif* and *retroflex final* ى) is to be read as شان (*šān / ša'n*).
2) The defective spelling سى (with retroflex final ى) has two possible meanings:
   a) Parallel passages and in some cases the context suggest a reading as شان (*šān / ša'n*), like e.g. in Samarqand (Bl 454/55) in surah **16**:75, where لا يقدر على شي is written with plene spelling سا (= شان) once, but in the same sentence in the following verse 76 with defective spelling سى (= شن). The context and the meaning are the same.
   b) The reading شيء (*šay'*) can also be suggested by the context, as we will see below.
   c) The accusative ending makes it more difficult to distinguish between شيا (*šayy^{an} = šay'^{an} – something*) and شنا (*šān^{an} = ša'n^{an}*) (*matter, affair*). This graphic rendering (in defective spelling) is found 77 times in the Qur'ān.
   Wherever the context does not clearly indicate which noun is meant, parallel passages have to be considered. To confirm the reading شيا (*šayya^{n} / šay'a^{n}*) *something* in the sense of *somebody* (like in Syro-Aramaic ܡܕܡ *meddem*, which is rendered as both *aliquid / something* and as *quidam / somebody* (see Brockelmann, *Lexicon Syriacum*) the following phrase can be adduced: أشرك بالله شيا (to associate *something* = *somebody* with God; Pickthall: "Ascribe no thing as partner unto Him"; cf. surahs **4**:36; **6**:151; **22**:26; **24**:55; **40**:74: لم نكن ندعوا من قبل شيا / before we did not call anybody *(else)*; 60:12; Pickthall: "but we used not to pray to anything before").

The Syro-Aramaic meaning of شيء in the sense of أحد (*someone*) is confirmed in the Qur'ān with the phrase أشرك بالله أحدا (to associate someone, another one as partner to God) in the following parallel passages: surah 18: 38, 42, 110; 72:2; 72:18: فلا تدعوا مع الله أحدا / so pray not unto anyone along with Allah (as a parallel to the above-cited verse **40**:74); **72**:20.

A. Mingana, *Syriac Influence*, 92, already pointed out this meaning of شيء in surah **60**:11: وان فاتكم شيء من ازواجكم الى الكفار "*And if any of your wives escape from you to the unbelievers*".

Two spellings that appear twice in the Samarqand Codex (leaf 440 / 41) from surah **16**: 35 are interesting: the first one is سى , in the context ما عبدنا من دونه من شي (we had not worshipped anybody else beside Him [Pickthall: aught beside Him]), as explained above, as شيء (*thing* in the sense of *somebody*), the other one is سا = شان (in the sense of *matter*): ولا حرمنا من دونه من شا (nor would we have declared any *matter/circumstance* prohibited).

In the Cairene Qur'ān edition the reading شيء (*šay'*) appears 202 times, شيا 77 times, شان (*šān /ša'n*) only three times, and finally شأنهم only once. The latter one matches the orthography of surah **10**:61 with BNF 328a, leaf 48a, line 8 (with ḥiǧāzī final ن). This leads to the conclusion that the reading شيء

(*šay*ʾ) of the Cairene Qurʾān edition is mostly erroneous, even if this does not change the meaning. Even in places where the codex from Ṣanʿāʾ has شي (without medial *alif*) regularly with *retroflex final* ى (ـــ), as e.g. in surah **2**: 20, 29, 106, 109, 113 (twice) (Ṣanʿāʾ leaf 1b, line 2+25, leaf 4b, line 21, 27, leaf 5a, line 5+6), defective spelling of شا (= شان) (*šān / šaʾn*) must be assumed, as can be shown taking surah **2**:113 as an example. There we read (according to the Cairene edition):

وقالت اليهود ليست النصرى على شي

وقالت النصرى ليست اليهود على شي

Paret (18) and Pickthall paraphrase correctly:

> *Pickthall:* "And the Jews say the Christians' follow nothing (true), and the Christians say the Jews follow nothing (true);"
>
> *Paret:* "Die Juden sagen: 'Die Christen entbehren (in ihren Glaubensanschauungen) der Grundlage.' Und die Christen sagen: 'Die Juden entbehren (in ihren Glaubensanschauungen) der Grundlage.'" (lit.: they have no foundation in their view of faith)

This understanding, however, is only possible, if the corresponding term is not read as شيء – šayʾ (thing), but as شان (*šaʾn* or rather *šān [matter]*), in analogy to the lexically and semantically corresponding Syro-Aramaic term ܫܪܒܐ (*šarbā*), which *Mannā* (819a) renders in Arabic (under [3]) as أمر. شأن (*matter, affair*), and under (4) as علة . سبب (*reason*), while the *Thesaurus* gives us, among others, the following attestations (Thes. II, 4323):

> ܥܠ ܫܪܒܐ ܕܗܝܡܢܘܬܐ (ʿal šarbā ḏ-haymānūṯā) de re fidei; ܒܫܪܒ ܬܘܕܝܬܐ (ba-šreb tawdīṯā) causa fidei.

In this context the Qurʾān means the *cause/matter of (faith)*. To understand the Qurʾānic term شان the semantics of the lexically corresponding Syro-Aramaic term has to be checked, according to the context.

Another example which shows that شى can be considered as the defective spelling of شان can be found in the codex of Ṣanʿāʾ (leaf 11b, line 1) of surah **5**:120. The word شى in the stereotype sentence (according to the Cairene edition) على كل شي قدير is normally written plene as على كل شا (شان) قدير in BNF 328a (see e.g. the attestations mentioned above from BNF 328a from surahs **2**:284; **3**:26,29, 165,189; **5**:17,19 etc.). Even if this reading does not change the meaning, it will still add a nuance, as the term شان (*matter, affair, circumstance*) covers a wider semantic field than شيء (*thing, something*).

Even if the substitution of شيء (*šay*ʾ) by شأن (*šaʾn*) does not lead to a major change in meaning, it will still lead to three conclusions:

a) There was no authentic oral tradition when the text of the Qur'ān was fixed.
b) Scribes proficient in Syriac took part in the first redaction of the Qur'ān.
c) There was a considerable time distance to the earliest tradition of a Qur'ānic orthography, the investigation of which will help to understand the development of the language of the Qur'ān.

In order not to draw conclusions prematurely, more unusual readings in the Qur'ān have to be found and their orthography analyzed. This includes the search for other possible orthographic traditions of the Aramaic speaking world at the time of the emergence of the Qur'ān, which have to be considered in the assessment of Qur'ānic spellings.

A reason for this can be found in the conspicuous orthography of two spellings repeatedly appearing in BNF 328a (leaf 26a, line 16-17) from surah **10**:95: الحاى (*al-ḥāy,* with medial *alif*), while two other parallel passages from surah **3**:27 (leaf 3a, 8) and **10**:31 (leaf 46b, 16-17, the latter one with *retroflex final* ى) are written defectively and correctly as الحي (*al-ḥayy*). Although the first mentioned spellings are both written with *retroflex final* ى, their reading is certain due to unambiguous parallel passages, especially due to the contrast between الحي (*al-ḥayy – the living)* und الميت (*al-mayyit – the dead)*. Therefore, another interpretation of the *retroflex final* ى can be excluded in this case. But how can the medial *alif* be explained in these above mentioned spellings.

A possible explanation would be that the copyist (or earlier scribe) wrote a long *ā* by adding a medial *alif*, influenced by the pronunciation of the almost identical Syro-Aramaic word ܚܝ (> حي), which in West Syriac originally has a short vowel *a (ḥay)*, which in most monosyllabic[13] words, however, is lengthened to *ā* (*ḥāy*).

This *alif* designating a vowel in the Qur'ānic orthography has not been taken notice of so far. This feature, however, can be observed in the writing tradition of the Mandeans of Southern Mesopotamia. Thus, Nöldeke explains in his Mandaic grammar[14] how medial *alif* is used as *mater lectionis* for short or long *a* (§ 3, 1), ult.): "*a â* in medial or final position is א: (p. 4): מאלכא = מלכא (*m<u>a</u>lkā*); מאן = מן (*mān*)." (moreover § 9, line 5): similarly מהאיא for מהאייא ܡܚܝܐ (*m-ḥayyē*) (*to animate, cause to be alive*).

The latter example (active participle of ܚܝܐ / *ḥyā* = حيى) is orthographically analogous to our passage from the Qur'ān, as far as the use of medial *alif* designating a vowel is concerned. However, there is a phonotactic rule in West Syriac: a doubled *yy* is simplified to simple *y*, while the preceding *a* is lengthened to *ā* (= *m-ḥāy*). Thus the medial *alif* of the spelling الحاى might actually reflect this rule and designate the intended form *al-ḥāy*. The Mandaic spelling designates a secondary long *ā*, while the Syriac form, with identical pronunciation, is written defectively, as in most cases in the Qur'ān. The appearance of the plene spelling الحاى (*al-ḥāy*) in BNF 328a (from surah **6**: 95) is therefore rather exceptional, but reflect very well the Syro-Aramaic and Mandaic pronunciation, following Mandaic spelling tradition.

Such a medial *alif*, even to designate a short *a*, can sometimes be encountered in Syriac as well, as already Nöldeke remarked in his *Syrische Grammatik* (§ 35, line 4):

> "On the other hand ܐ is often used as a seemingly superfluous letter, where it should not be, as in ܡܣܣܐܒ for ܡܣܣܒ (*ma-ssab/ massāb*) 'to take…'" (see more examples).

What Nöldeke calls "seemingly superfluous" in the usage of *alif* in medial position, – from the perspective of the common Syriac orthography –, might go back to an earlier, so far overlooked Mesopotamian scribal tradition. It is noteworthy what Rudolf Meyer has to say about this in his *Hebräische Grammatik*[15] (p. 50, 3):

> "In the Hell(enistic) period, probably under the influence of Aram(aic) and also Greek influence, the linear vocalization in Hebr(ew) was strongly developed. The characters used are still those known from tradition: alef, he, waw and yod, but now their phonetic value is fixed, and they are not applied to designate long vowels, but also short ones. As the text of the sacred scriptures is not yet normatively fixed, this new form of vocalization, which, however, still is optional, enters the text of the Old Testament on a large scale. Even in places which deviate only little from the older, rather parsimonious use of vowel letters, the new principle can be observed. For the 2nd century CE the following picture can be described.
> Alef is above all used for a, more rarely for e, both in medial and in final position; he designates the long final vowels *ā* and *ē*, but no longer *ō*; waw represents *o* and *u*, yod *i* and *e* both in medial and in final position. As far as alef, waw and yod are used in the middle of words, they can designate both long and short vowels. "[16]

Thus we come to the following conclusions about Qur'ānic orthography:

a) Several scholars, among others A. Spitaler[17] expressed the opinion that *alif* as *mater lectionis* for medial long *ā* is a late, genuine Arabic development. This has to be dismissed.

The variation in the spelling of medial *alif* for *ā* in early Qur'ānic manuscripts as expounded by *GdK* I, 31 f. finds a parallel in the optional use of this letter in Hebrew as discussed by R. Meyer, who, however, is right in assuming an early Aramaic influence.

In fact S. Segert confirms this assumption in his *Altaramäische Grammatik* (4th edition, Leipzig 1990). In Chapter 2.4.4. *Vowel Letters in the Middle of the Word*: 2.4.4.3. *Use of Alef for long -ā-* he explains (p. 64):

> "The use of א to write long *-ā-* in the middle of a word, so common in later Aramaic texts was considered as due to a Persian model; earlier examples, however, can already be found in archaic inscriptions of Ja'udi in the 8th century BCE, e.g. גואם P 5." (see also p. 65, 2.4.7. *Use of Vowel Letters*: In medial position in Imperial Aramaic and Biblical Aramaic."

This is an important statement for future Qur'ānic research. The common assumption, which in an earlier publication was also shared by me,[18] that the use of *alif* to designate medial long *ā* is due to a later reform of Qur'ānic orthography, must be modified in the sense that this modification was only generally accepted at a later stage in the Arabic orthography. For Qur'ānic orthography we have to assume that this spelling was extant from the very beginning, albeit not regularly, which also explains the variation in the available Qur'ānic manuscripts. The problem, however, is that later, incompetent copyists inserted the alif in wrong places, which led to misreadings that can only be detected with the help of meticulous text-critical analysis of Qur'ānic texts.

b) The use of *alif* as *mater lectionis* for short *a*, as it is normal in Mandaic, could so far not be found in the Qur'ānic manuscripts available to us. The Cairene edition, however, contains a few examples. That the spelling الحاى with medial *alif* should be a piece of evidence in this case, is rather questionable, as this *alif*, as expounded above, can reflect the West Syriac (and Mandaic) pronunciation with a long *ā* (*al-ḥāy*).

If this form, – الحاى – were accepted as a piece of evidence which proves that medial *alif* was used for short *a*, then the explanation of the spelling شا for شان (*šān / ša'n*) would become obsolete and the common reading *šay* (or *šay'* resp.) could not be objected. The interpretation of the spelling يحى as يحنن (*Yōḥannān*) instead of يحيى (*Yaḥyā*) would then hardly convince as sole example for the misreading of *retroflex* Arabic final *y* as final Syriac *–n*. Other attestations of this misreading would be necessary to make this claim. This will be tried in the following:

3.4 Example of Misreading II (Surah 10: 53): اى وربي ('ēn wa-rabbī)

This particle, which in the modern Cairene edition is written with the modern final ى read as إي ('ī), can be found in BNF 328a (leaf 47 b, line 16), spelt with *retroflex final* ى (اى). It therefore corresponds to the *defective spelling* of Syro-Aramaic ܐܢ = ܐܝܢ (*'ēn* or *'īn – yes!*). In modern Arabic dialects, this term, which goes back to a common Aramaic substratum, is pronounced "*'ē*" or "*'ī*" resp., i.e., without the final *–n*, such a pronunciation, however, cannot be assumed for the Qur'ān.

This Aramaic particle can be found in defective and plene spelling (ܐܢ and ܐܝܢ = *'ēn*) in several places in the Qur'ān. I have repeatedly (op. cit. 288, 15.2, footnote 304; 2nd ed., p. 323, footnote 337; 3rd ed., p. 32,4 footnote

345) pointed to this spelling لين (*l-ēn*; consisting of the defective spelling of the Aramaic particle ܠܐ (*lā*) and the plene spelling of the conditional conjunction ܐܢ (*ʾēn*) in 61 cases, and to the spelling افاين (< ܐܦ ܐܢ / *ap-ēn = if then, so if*) in two cases of the Cairene Qurʾān edition. The assumption that the plene spelling لاين (*lā-ʾēn* > *l-ēn*) could be expected to be found in early Qurʾānic manuscripts is confirmed by the *ḥiǧāzī*-codex from Ṣanʿāʾ, where this plene spelling لاين (*lā-ʾēn* > *l-ēn*) is attested twice (surah **6**:109, leaf 16b, 10; surah **13**: 37, Leaf 31a, 10). Moreover, according to S. Segert (op. cit. 232, 5.5.6.1.4. f.), this nexus is attested in defective form (להן / *lā-hēn*) already in Early Aramaic:

> "In Early Aramaic the negation particle ל– is written together with the following word, e.g. S III 18; N II 4; Ass 8." (358, 6.5.3.3.2.a): 'The conjunction להן (*lā-hēn*) »if not« goes back to the combination of the negation *lā* with the hypothetical conjunction *hēn*." (the function of the latter was rather an interpretive particle; *author's note*)

The Qurʾānic spelling لين (*l-ēn*) therefore follows Old Aramaic writing traditions, but reflects a younger, Syro-Aramaic pronunciation (להן / *lā-hēn* > לין / *l-ēn*).

EXCURSUS: About the Origin of the Particle لـ (la-)

In this context the prefixed particle لـ / *la-*, which has hitherto been considered as a strange, emphatic particle of Classical Arabic,[19] turns out to be a borrowing from Old Aramaic. The particle must originally have had the function of an interjection, which led to the development of a range of semantic aspects, one of them being negation, another one the emphatic meaning in the Qurʾān (and in later, Classical Arabic, as well as in modern Arabic dialects[20]). Two conclusions can be drawn:

a) The particle لـ / *la-*, which, among other cases, is prefixed to the modus energicus, and has the function to introduce the main clause after a hypothetical conditional clause, is nothing but the *defective spelling* of لا. As can be seen in modern dialects, this word is closely linked to the following word, which led to the reduction of the originally long vowel *ā*.
b) In logical consequence the Qurʾān, as in the case of لاين, sometimes displays the *plene spelling* لا, especially when an oath is introduced: لا اقسم (8x)[21] in the following surahs: **56**: 75; **69**: 38; **70**: 40; **75**: 1, 2; **81**: 15; **84**: 16; **90**: 1. The translators of the Qurʾān had their problems with these passages. Paret translates: "Nein doch! Ich schwöre… (But no! I swear..."; Blachère: "Non! j'en jure…"; Bell considers it as a formal negation: "I swear not…". What we are dealing with, however, is only the original Aramaic particle לא (*lā*), in the Qurʾān alternatively spelt *plene* or

defectively, the latter spelling being adopted into Classical Arabic as a relic of Old Aramaic.

Other, similar relics, are the expressions ليس (*laysa*, actually the form *lays* would be preferable) and ليت (*layta*, better: *layt*), which are both variants of one and the same Aramaic expression in Arabic writing. In Arabic they were assigned to different meanings, like the English words "gentle", "genteel" and "gentile", which all go back to Latin "gentilis".

The form ليس (*laysa* – "not to be") is the connection of the defectively written prefixed Aramaic particle -ל (= לא) (*lā*), here having the meaning "*not*", with the Aramaic expression of existence יש (*ys / yš – to be extant, there is*). The Arabic sibilant س (*s*) goes back to the spirantized Aramaic ת (*ṯ*), so that Arabic ليس (*laysa*) is only a dialectal variant of Aramaic לא (*lā*) in connection with the expression of existence אית (*īṯ*). The spirantization of the latter goes back to the original separate pronunciation of these two elements in an earlier stage (MG S. 293 + 401).

The Arabic form ليت (*layta*) points to a more recent development, which formally and phonetically corresponds to Syro-Aramaic ܠܝܬ (*layt*), in so far as *Begadkephat*-consonants are not spirantized after a diphthong in Syro-Aramaic. Etymologically, both forms are identical, semantically they are not. In Syro-Aramaic ܠܝܬ (*layt*) the prefixed ܠ / *la*- expresses negation (*not to be*), Arabic ليت (*layta*) expresses a wish (*if only there would be*).

3.5 Example of Misreading III: هيى / يهيى

These spellings, which appear in surah 18:10 and 16 are read by the Cairene edition as *hayyiʾ* and *yu-hayyiʾ*. Here it has to be noted:

a) that ى in the Qur'ān originally does not function as *mater lectionis* for *hamza*.
b) that the Qurʾānic orthography excludes two consecutive و and ي (cf. about this question e.g. surah 2:28, where the Cairene edition – adapted to modern orthography – reads يحييكم , while the corresponding passage in the Ṣanʿāʾ-codex (so far without a designation), leaf 1b, line 23, displays an unambiguous يحيكم . This means that the adduced spellings هيى and يهيى have been misread.

Even a basic knowledge of Qurʾānic orthography should suffice to understand that the alleged final ى written as a *retroflex* ـ (-*n*) was only later interpreted as a final ي (-*y*). The original orthographic tradition inevitably leads to the assumption that here a final ن has to be read, thus instead of هيى (*hayyiʾ*): هيّن (*hayyin*), and instead of يهيى (*yu-hayyiʾ*): يهيّن (*yu-hayyin*) (*to alleviate*). In order to prove this new reading, attestations from earlier Qurʾānic manuscripts would be welcome, but they are not necessarily a requirement. Parallel passages and other criteria from the Qurʾān should suffice. First of all, we have to state that the verb هيّأ *(to prepare)* in this passage does not appear elsewhere in the Qurʾān. Instead the Qurʾān as a rule uses the root أعدّ (20x). Moreover, our assumed reading can be confirmed by parallels, if we consider the context of surah 18:10 and 16 (according to the Cairiner edition):

ربنا اتنا من لدنك رحمة وهيّء لنا من أمرنا رشدا

ينشر لكم ربكم من رحمته ويهيّء لكم من أمركم مرفقا

Paret (238) gibt diese beiden Versabschnitte wie folgt wieder:

> *Pickthall* (18:10): "Our Lord! Give us mercy from Thy presence and shape for us right conduct in our plight."
> (18:16): "Your Lord will spread for you of His mercy and will prepare for you a pillow in your plight."
> *Paret* (18:10): "Herr schenke uns Barmherzigkeit von dir und bereite uns in unserer Angelegenheit einen rechten Weg (*rašadan*)." (bereiten = prepare)
> (18:16): " Dann wird euer Herr euch (etwas) von seiner Barmherzigkeit zukommen lassen und euch in eurer Angelegenheit für Abhilfe sorgen (*yuhaiyi' lakum min amrikum mirfaqan*)." (für Abhilfe sorgen = to find a remedy)

That this questionable verb should not be read as هيىء (*hayyi'*), but as هيّن (*hayyin*) can be seen in a parallel passage from surah 20:25-26, where the synonym يسّر (*yassara* = هيّن *alleviate*) appears in connection with أمر (*amr* = *matter*). There we read:

رب اشرح لي صدري / ويسّر لي أمري

> *Pickthall:* "My Lord! Relieve my mind. And ease my task for me."
> *Paret* (255): "Herr! Weite mir die Brust (26) und mache es mir leicht." (Eigentlich: mache mir meine Angelegenheit = was mich betrifft – leicht [actually: make this matter easy for me]).

Another criteria to confirm this reading is the fact that the verbal root هيّن (*hayyana*) appears twice in the surah Maryam as an adjective (surah 19:9,21: هو علي هيّن *huwa 'alayya hayyin / It is easy for Me*). Together with the new readings there would be four attestations. The verses from surah 18:10 and 16 would have to be read as follows:

ربنا اتنا من لدنك رحمة وهيّن لنا من أمرنا رشدا

ينشر لكم ربكم من رحمته ويهيّن لكم من أمركم مرفقا

The new translation would have to be:

> (18:10): "Our Lord, let us receive your mercy and make the right path easy regarding the matters that concern us (lit.: *concerning our matter*)."

> (18:16): "Thus your Lord will give[22] you from his mercy and make the bearing of your suffering[23] easy. concerning your matter (of what *concerns you*)." (i.e., *God will help you with his mercy to bear the suffering of the ordeal to come*).

In the Qur'ānic fragments we are referring to these passages are missing. It can, however, be expected that other manuscript attestations of the *retroflex* spelling of final ى in the forms هيى (= هين) and يهيى (= يهين) will be found.

The meanwhile published of Qur'ān codex Or. 2165 (f. 1–61) of the British Library has a final *alif* in both passages: surah 18:10: وهيا (leaf 43a, line 21); surah 18:16: ويهيا (leaf 43b, line 9). According to East Aramaic/ Babylonian orthography the final *alif* can represent a final *nūn* (which has nothing to do with the Arabic *nunation*), as is the case in the Qur'ān in the spelling of the *Energicus* وليكونا / *wa-la-yakūnan* (surah 12:32) as well as لنسفعا / *la-nasfaʿan* (surah 96:15). More examples from the Qur'ān will be found and reasons for this strange spelling of final *n* with a *nūn* will be explained.

Summary

This preliminary analysis of Qur'ānic orthography provides the first piece of evidence which clearly indicates that the Qur'ān, or at least parts of it, was originally written in Syro-Aramaic script. These findings might be met with surprise at first glance. But whoever investigates the cultural, linguistic and religious-historical milieu from which the Qur'ān and early Islam emerged, will more likely find confirmation of an old conjecture.

For although the Qur'ān might be the first book composed in Arabic, – albeit an Arabic with a strong Syro-Aramaic imprint –, this does not mean that it was also originally written in Arabic *script* as we know it today. Moreover, if we assume that the initiators of the written Arabic language were educated people, then it is certainly not too far-fetched to also assume that they had received this education before the emergence of the Qur'ān and within the boundaries of the Syro-Aramaic civilization. The fact that the Syro-Aramaic script is a core element of this civilization is self-evident. For scholars of comparative cultural studies or comparative linguistics it is furthermore a very common phenomenon that a culture is more likely to adopt and adapt an existing writing system than to create one from scratch. In other cases the writing system is later replaced by another one, which results in typical orthographic mistakes, not unlike those we have come across in the present study: Within a hundred years, most Turkic languages of the former Soviet Union switched from the Arabic script to first the Latin, then the Cyrillic alphabet and after the end of the Soviet Union back to the Latin script (e.g. Uzbek). Romanian was written in both the Cyrillic script (in Romania until the end of the 19th century and in the Soviet republic of Moldavia until recently, the language there called "Moldavian") and (in Romania proper) in an adapted Latin script. Some older Romanian texts are extant in which both scripts are mixed. Something similar can be assumed for Qur'ānic texts. It is very likely that the scribes and copyists of Qur'ānic texts were Syro-Arameans or at least Arabs who had received an education in Syro-Aramaic, and if they wrote in Arabic, they certainly were also able to write in Syriac.

There is a well-known tradition in Christian circles up to this day to write Arabic using the Syro-Aramaic script, above all in liturgical books. This script is called *Garshuni* or *Karshuni*, and a copious Christian-Arabic literature is extant in it, a part of which can be accessed in European libraries.

The idea that the "Ur-Qur'ān" (or at least parts of it) was written in this script has been proved with the present analysis. A further, more detailed study will confirm and expand the preliminary results.

It should be noted that there is a rumor that in a library in Egypt, some claim at the Azhar University, there is such a Qur'ān written in *Garshuni*. It would not be surprising, considering the fact that Islamic tradition claims that the caliph 'Umar had had Ḥafṣa's Qur'ān manuscript destroyed, which had served as the master copy for scribes. The story of 'Umar and Ḥafṣa might just be a legend, but is it not conceivable that in the process of the end redaction of the Qur'ān there was once a *master copy in Garshuni*? This would also explain the cautious respect Muslims traditionally show toward the Syro-Aramaic language (in Arabic: السريانية / *as-suryānīya*).

In this rather short contribution not all potentially misread and incorrectly transcribed Syro-Aramaic letters to be found in the Qur'ān could be discussed. A more comprehensive treatment of the subject will follow.

Bibliography

Bell, Richard, The Qur'ān, translated, with a critical re-arrangement of the surahs, vol. I, Edinburgh 1937, vol. II, Edinburgh 1939.

Blachère, Régis, Le Coran, traduit de l'arabe, Paris 1957.

Brockelmann, Carl, Lexicon Syriacum, 2nd ed., Halle 1928.

Brockelmann, Carl, Syrische Grammatik, Leipzig 81960.

Déroche, François et Sergio Noja Noseda (eds.), Sources de la Transmission du Texte Coranique, I. Les manuscrits de style ḥiǧāzī, Volume 1: Le manuscrit arabe 328(a) de la Bibliothèque Nationale de France, Paris (Bibliothèque Nationale de France) 1998; Volume 2, tome I, British Library, London 2001.

Grohmann, Adolf, Arabische Paläographie, vol. I, Wien 1967, vol. II, Wien 1971.

Horovitz, Josef, Qur'ānische Untersuchungen, Berlin, Leipzig 1926.

Horovitz, Josef, Jewish Proper Names and Derivates in the Qur'ān, Ohio 1925 (reprint Hildesheim 1964).

Jeffery, Arthur, The Foreign Vocabulary of the Qur'ān, Baroda 1938.

Manna, Jacques Eugène, Vocabulaire Chaldéen-Arabe, Mossoul 1900 (reprinted with a new appendix by Raphael J. Bidawid, Beirut 1975).

b. Manẓūr, Abū l-Faḍl Ǧamāl ad-Dīn Muḥammad b. Mukarram al-Ifrīqī al-Miṣrī, Lisān al-ʿarab ("Zunge" der Araber), 15 vols., Beirut 1955–1956.

Meyer, Rudolf, Hebräische Grammatik, 3 vols., 3rd ed., Berlin 1966.

Mingana, Alphonse, Syriac Influence on the Style of the Kur'ān, in: Bulletin of John Ry-lands Library, 11 (1927), pp. 77– 98 (see also Ibn Warraq, What the Qur'ān Really Says, Amherst 2002, pp. 171–192).

Nöldeke, Theodor, Geschichte des Qorâns, Göttingen 1860.

Nöldeke, Theodor und Friedrich Schwally, Geschichte des Qorâns, I., Über den Ursprung des Qorâns, 2nd ed., Leipzig 1919; III. Bergsträßer-Pretzl, Die Geschichte des Qur'āntextes, 2nd ed., Leipzig 1938 (reprint Hildesheim 1961).

Nöldeke, Theodor, Kurzgefasste syrische Grammatik (reprint of the 2nd ed., Leipzig 1898, in the appendix: Die handschriftlichen Ergänzungen in dem Handexemplar Theodor Nöldekes und Register der Belegstellen, bearbeitet von Anton Schall), Darmstadt 1977.

Nöldeke, Theodor, Mandäische Grammatik (photocopy of the edition Halle an der Saale [1]1875, in the appendix: Die handschriftlichen Ergänzungen in dem Handexemplar Theodor Nöldekes, bearbeitet von Anton Schall), Darmstadt 1964.

Ohlig, K.-H./Puin, Gerd-R. (eds.), Die dunklen Anfänge. Neue Forschungen zur Entstehung und frühen Geschichte des Islam, Berlin, 2005.

Paret, Rudi, Der Qur'ān. Übersetzung, 2nd ed., Stuttgart, Berlin, Köln, Mainz 1982.

Paret, Rudi, Der Qur'ān. Kommentar und Konkordanz, Stuttgart, Berlin, Köln, Mainz 1971.

Qur'ān karīm, Kairo 1972.

Segert, Stanislav, Altaramäische Grammatik, Leipzig [4]1990.

Swithh, Payne (Hrsg.), Thesaurus Syriacus, Tomus I, Oxonii 1879, Tomus II, Oxonii 1901.

Spitaler, Anton, Die Schreibung des Typus صلوة im Qur'ān. Ein Beitrag zur Erklärung der koranischen Orthographie, in: Wiener Zeitschrift für die Kunde des Morgenlandes, 56th vol. (Festschrift [liber amicorum] Herbert W. Duda), Wien 1960.

Syriac Bible (63DC), United Bible Societies, (London) 1979.

al-Ṭabarī, Abū Ǧaʿfar Muḥammad b. Ǧarīr, Ǧāmiʿ al-bayān ʿan ta'wīl al-Qur'ān (Qur'ān commentary; 30 parts in 12 vols.), 3rd ed., Kairo 1968.

Wehr, Hans, Arabisches Wörterbuch für die Schriftsprache der Gegenwart, 5th ed., Wiesbaden [5]1985.

Read Anew: Islam and Parsism

(Islamisme et Parsisme)[1]

Ignaz Goldziher

Speech held September 6, 1900 at the General Assembly of the first International Congress for the History of Religion at the Sorbonne in Paris.

For the German version of the present anthology, the text of the speech had been translated from French into German by Werner Müller, who, together with the editor Karl-Heinz Ohlig, had amended some of the bibliographical data in the footnotes.

The present English translation was done by me, the main body of the text having been translated from the French original, the footnotes from both the German and the original version[2].

For qur'ānic quotations Pickthall's English version was mainly used, except in cases where Goldziher's own translation differed substantially. The transcription of Arabic proper names was slightly adapted to normal usage in the present anthology. My own explanatory additions are in brackets and have been marked by the added word "transl."

The French version of this article was published in: Ignaz Goldziher, Gesammelte Schriften (collected writings), edited by Joseph Desomogyi IV, Hildesheim 1970, p. 232-260, the text originally having appeared in: Actes du premier Congrès international d'histoire de religions. 1900, p. 119-147).

Markus Gross, editor of the English edition

Ladies and Gentlemen!

For a long time we have been content with the simple assertion: "All of a sudden Islam came into existence and immediately appeared in its perfected form." – Literally: "in broad daylight" (in French: *"au plein jour"*).

The more we advance in the critical examination of ancient documents of Islam, as it has been undertaken during the past few years, the more we have to come to the conclusion that Muslim tradition (Ḥadīṯ), which is our oldest source of information after the Koran, can lead us back to the early childhood days of this religion only in a very limited way:[3] It rather offers us a picture of often conflicting tendencies, which have not yet taken the inflexible form adopted by Islamic Orthodoxy in the current rigidity of the system and the crystallization of rites.

This conviction is spreading more and more. By using the rich materials of this tradition, which Muslims see as documents corroborating their sacred book, we go far beyond the critical-rational method employed by Muslim scholastics since the second century of hijra.

Regarding this literature we have become much stricter and more circumspect. Nobody amongst those who are seriously engaged in Islamic Studies would dare to naively browse the sayings attributed to Mohammed and his companions in order to use the information drawn from this source to reconstruct the old state of affairs and the primitive doctrines of early Islam. Modern historical criticism protects us from such an antediluvian method of approach. The struggles of political and religious factions are the clue to a better understanding of these documents and reveal to us the assertions and intentions behind them, to be confirmed or proven wrong in such and such a saying of Mohammed or such and such a piece of information of one of the "companions" of the prophet.

The critical investigation of Muslim Tradition helps us to comprehend the fundamental problems of religious history in the realm of Islam and to find solutions. But they represent no more than one single group of observations the knowledge of which is of paramount scientific importance for our research.

Another group of elements must complement our historical investigation. While the first group primarily refers to evolution due to *internal* forces, we must at the same time direct our attention to *foreign* influences decisive in the emergence and development of Islam. In this context I haven't only got *popular Islam* in mind, as constituted in the different provinces of the Islamic faith, at times incorporating pre-Islamic elements, I am also thinking of its *universal*, canonical formation since the earliest times of its existence.

Every elementary textbook of mediaeval history teaches us that Islam, from its very beginnings, was subject to Jewish and Christian influences, and that Mohammed himself based his work on Jewish and Christian foundations. These influences continued to be perceptible as either positive or negative, even during the first generations that followed the death of the prophet. The presence of Jewish and Christian elements[4] has always been somehow admitted without ever having been properly acknowledged; on the other hand, in spite of loudly proclaiming this view, the doctrines and practices of Judaism and Christianity were rejected; they were removed and not responded to any more. "*Ḫalīfū-hum* – be different from them" became the usual formula.[5] But even this reaction must be seen in its own right as a symptom of a spiritual relationship and as the result of intimate influence.

Up to the present time, one of the most important ingredients of the religious development of Islam – the Persian element – has been widely neglected. It was a determinant factor in the characteristic formation of Islam, both in the form of *borrowing* and of *reaction*. The influence of Parsism on Islam is one of the first issues to be dealt with by scholars of our discipline. In order to be done properly, its study requires an equally profound knowledge of the Islamic and the Persian religions. In this field, M. Blochet is as yet the only one to have touched upon this question in some of the articles in the "Revue de l'Histoire des Religions,"[6] and who has provided us with important materials for the solution to the problem; both from the point of view of philology and of the study of religions, I take the liberty to point to the excellent study of his, in which he demonstrated the Persian origin of the Muslim notion of *al-Burāq*, the winged horse on which the prophet is said to have accomplished his ascension.[7]

Although I am not a professional expert on Iranian studies myself, I would like to give you an impression of the scope of the problem as well as to present some of the main data to this conference.

One of the most thrilling chapters of cultural history is the investigation of the varied influences exercised by the Sassanian civilization on the different parts of the human race, even those separated geographically. Even in the language and the works of art of the nation to which I belong, very noticeable traces of these influences can be observed. To adduce an example from religious terminology: Since the time of the migrations of the ancient Hungarians, before they had entered the Carpathian Basin and up to this day, we have been calling *God* using a Persian loan-word: *isten* (Pers.: *izd-ân*); the *devil*, the *principle of evil*: *ördög* (Pers.: *druga*); even in the mundane world, a remnant of *daêva* (*dévaj* – rascal) has been preserved. Our archaeologists and our art historians are finding more and more traces and remnants of Persian elements in the ancient monuments of our art.

A similar influence on the civilization of the Arabs is virtually palpable. It was the immediate and permanent contact with the civilization of the Sassanians which gave the Arabs, who had little more than their poetry, the first stimulus which would trigger the development of a more profound intellectual life. I stick to the thesis I once formulated and which M. Brockelmann adopted in his "History of Arabic Literature", namely that the historiography of the Arabs has its origins in the literature of the Royal Annals of the Persians and that there would be no Arabic historiography without the impetus Arabic literature had received from Persia, which led it to research and preserve the memories of their nation.[8] Pre-Islamic Arabs had no sense of history. Their oldest records hardly go back to an era predating the 6th century AD, apart from traditions related to migrations of Southern Arabian tribes to the North. Even events of recent history were shrouded in mystery and blurred by a mythological cloud for them.

It was contact with the culture of the Persians – a contact which goes back to the earliest times of Islam[9] – which was to determine the direction the development of intellectual life the Arabs would follow and its destination.

As soon as Islam had established its rule – by the sword – over the geographical domain of ancient Parsism and had brought the faith of the Prophet of Mecca and Medina to the Zoroastrians, the impact of the Persian element on the formation of the religion began to be very deep. The occupation of Iraq by the Muslims is one of the most decisive factors of the religious formation of Islam.

Persian theologians introduced their traditional notions into their newly adopted religion. The conquerors enriched the poverty of their own religious background with elements provided by the experience of a profound religious life, like that of the conquered Persians. Therefore the importance of the intellectual movement which had emerged in Iraq and which was connected to the schools of Basra and Kufa cannot be overestimated for the formation of Islam. It is not surprising that this local development involved a considerable number of Persian elements.[10]

These influences had fully evolved by the time of the great revolution that the Islamic state was to undergo in the year 128 of its era, namely the transition from the Umayyad to the Abbasid dynasty.

This was not only the politically motivated overthrow of a dynasty; it was a far-reaching religious revolution. The mundane government of the Umayyads, who had preserved Arabic traditions in their capital Damascus, adjacent to the desert, was replaced by the theocratic regime of the Abbasids, who founded their state on both political as well as ecclesiastical principles. They established their residence in Anbar and Baghdad, the center of the Sassanian Empire, which had been overthrown by Islam. From the latter they adopted the traditions. Their title is no more that of an Arabic sheikh, but that of a Persian king; as "children of the prophet" they base their authority upon *legitimacy*, exactly as the Sassanians of the Persian Empire had based their power on legitimacy. Like them, the Abbasids now wanted to restore the true religion, which had decayed under their predecessors. Their kingdom is an ecclesiastical state; they are no longer secular, but religious leaders. They considered themselves, in a manner of speaking, as *bâghî*, "divine ones", like the Sassanians;[11] this is how the latter had chosen to be depicted on coins. Their entourage was fully aware of this connection between the new institution of the caliphs and the concept of Persian royalty. Whereas the Umayyad caliph ʿAbdalmalik reproaches his court poet with employing the attributes of a Persian king to glorify him[12] – the issue was merely about a diadem (*tāǧ*)[13] –, the Abbasid prince and poet celebrates the caliph in a didactic historical poem as follows:

> "He resembles the Persian Ardeshir, when he restored an annihilated kingdom."

From the very beginning this restoration was linked to the notion of dignity of the caliphs. Not only their court, their administrative organization, the system of dignitaries of the state and the etiquette were modeled after the Persian royalty; the *internal* signification of the caliphate, however, is formulated according to the Persian concept: they are guardians of the *divine economy*. The State itself becomes a religious institution, a universal church, headed by the legitimate follower of the prophet, the caliph of God ("*ḫalīfat Allāh*"). The government regards religion with the highest consideration. A government worthy of its name acts in accordance with religion. Due to their perfect union, government and religion are like close relatives; that is why it can be said that government and religion are the same, that religion is the government of the people.[14] These are entirely Islamic maxims, which, however, were not extracted from the book of a Muslim legislator, but from a book written in Pehlevi (*Middle Persian, transl.*), the *Dēnkard*, dated in the final stage of productive Parsism.

So you can see how deep the influence of the Sassanian concept of the State was on the Abbasid royalty and just how far it emphasized the theocratic idea. You see how the latter emerged in a Persian atmosphere. Similarly, in its application as well as in its practical consequences, it betrays the inspiration of Persian tradition. In lieu of the confessional indifference current among the Umayyads, it is now *confessionalism* which becomes the reigning principle of government and which takes its place on the scene of the Empire.

The historian must therefore consider the confessionalism, which was officially established in Islam in the 2nd century, as a fruit of Persian influence. Thus, the caliphate did nothing but follow the tradition of the Persian *bâghi* kingdom. Whereas the Umayyads looked down on theologians who opposed them with aplomb,[15] from the very beginning it is dogma which is the primary concern of the first Abbasids. They inaugurate their Empire endeavoring to preserve the *Sunna* in the government, formulating dogmas about transcendental questions, while fanatics like Ma'mūn try hard to enforce them, and finally, prosecuting heretics and dissidents. Among their political acts it will suffice to mention the prosecution of the Anti-Muʿtazilites and the *Zindīqs,*[16] a Persian designation for a group of heretics who fell victim to a sort of Islamic inquisition briefly after the establishment of the Abbasid caliphate.[17]

> "God girded the Abbasids with two swords: one destined to defend and to enlarge the borders of the State; the other to strengthen the law in its dogmatic form and to punish infidelity and heresy."[18]

Thus the Abbasids inherited religious prosecution from their Sassanian predecessors as well as the system of confessionalism and intolerance. Like them, they base their power on the religious views of their subjects.[19] As a consequence, the Persian distinction between *bih-dīn* and *bed-dīn*, i.e.,good and bad believer, becomes a vital principle of Islam: It does not belong to the original Arabic movement, which had become constituted in the confessional indifference of the Umayyads.

II

Persian influence is not limited to the transformation of the public spirit of Islam; it also left traces in some legal peculiarities.

Without going as far as the Grandmaster of Persian philology, *Frédéric Spiegel*,[20] who asserted that the roots of Islamic tradition, the basic form of religious precepts, are already permeated by Parsism, we still cannot fail to recognize, when studying the *Ḥadīt*, the influence of the Persian element on details of its contents.

This does not only apply to the importance of Iraq, the classical country of the Old Persian culture, with its successful theological efforts in the development of Islamic faith and law; we must also think of the role played by the populations of this country in the development of Islamic spirit, keeping in mind that their fathers had still been loyal adherents of the religion of Zoroaster and that they introduced all their Parsee piety into their new confession.

I cannot imagine that you would be very much interested in an enumeration of all the analogies between religious and ritual details as described by traditional Islamic literature and the precepts of the Persian religion. The chapter on ritual purity and impurity, – provided that these are not remnants of ancient pagan taboos, – came into being due to the influence of Persian religious concepts; Islamic tradition has safeguarded these traces, although, at the time when this ritual legislation developed, the natural need was felt to not slavishly copy Persian views about purity and impurity.

You know about the Persian notion, also to be found in Judaism, of the defilement incurred by a dead body. To demonstrate the Islamic reaction, I will simply quote the following passage from the *Ḥadīṯ*;

> "A client of the Anṣārī Abū Waḥwaḥ narrates: We washed a dead body. Then we wanted to clean ourselves by washing. The Abū Waḥwaḥ came forward and said: By God, we defiled ourselves neither like the living nor like the dead."[21]

This simple report allows us to observe the trace of a kind of influence which had not yet taken a definite shape. It is a sign of opposition against the infiltration of Persian habits.

Today is not the day to give you a proper presentation of all these elements; however, I hope you will allow me to cast an entirely aphoristic look at some formal data and some aspects of religious thinking in Islam, which point to the profound Parsee influence that took place in the era after Muḥammad.

1) – From the very beginning of Islam, the very recitation of sacred texts, especially of the Koran, was considered as a meritorious religious act. It is not prayers or religious formulae we are dealing with, but the very recitation, either personally or by others, of the revealed book or considerable portions of it. Those familiar with Islamic literature will often have read remarks, at the end of commentaries about a special surah, about the merit incurred and rewards to be expected from the recitation of a single chapter or of the whole Koran.[22] In my view this notion of merit accrued by recitation of a revealed text echoes the Persian notion of merit accumulated through the recitation of the Vendidad.

> "A short Yasna as well as the longest Vendidad-sade can be recited for the benefit of individuals, either for the dead so that their sins be remitted, or by proxy for the living, with the same aim; for as a man cannot live on the earth without committing sins, it is necessary, from time to time, to recite the Vendidad in order to get rid of one's sins."[23]

For a Muslim, the recitation of his sacred book must lead to the same result for the salvation of his soul. As in the case of the Persians, Muslims practice the recitation of their holy book during several days after the death of a family member; even nowadays this custom can be observed (ḳirāje, vulg. grâje) in Muslim families, on the occasion of a visit of condolence. To demonstrate the Persian link to this custom, it shall suffice to point to the study by M. *Söderblom* about the *Fravashis*, as far as the Persian custom of Vendidad recitation of the Feast of the Dead is concerned.[24]

As we are dealing with a mourning custom, you will allow me another observation along the way. I once explained in detail just how far Muslim ethics severely condemn certain expressions of mourning for a deceased and I will not reproduce the verdicts of the prophet in which this idea is expressed.

At the time I tried to find the reason for this in the submission Islam demands of the believers;[25] however, I cannot help pointing out the striking similarity with Parsism in this respect:

> "The distress of the soul should not be increased by mourning; in the ceremonies and benedictions dedicated to them the Fravashis of the believers

ask for neither lamentations nor wailing. Those who lament for the dead will suffer the punishment in hell of crying with their heads cut off."[26]

2) – The eschatological doctrine of the scales (*mizān*), on which every good and every bad deed of a human is weighed after his or her death, is a borrowing from Parsism and implies an *arithmetic* evaluation of ethical and religious acts. (William Jackson[27] gave evidence for the Aryan origin of this notion). As in the sacred books of the Parsees[28], the value of good and bad deeds is calculated in weight units in Islam[29].

"A ḳintār of good deeds will be credited for the one who reads a thousand Qur'ān verses in one night."[30]

The prophet says: 'whoever says a prayer (ṣalāt al-ğināza) at the bier of a deceased, accrues the merit of one qirāṭ; but the one who attends the ceremony until the deceased has been buried, is rewarded with two qirāṭ, of which one is as heavy as the mountain Uḥud'.[31] 'The small ablution, (wuḍū', like the one performed before prayer) has the value of a mudd (modius), a complete ablution (ġusl) is worth a ṣa'.'[32]

'Prayer in a community is worth twenty-five times as much as individual prayer.' That is why al-Muzanī, an excellent disciple of Imām al-Šāfi'ī, one of the chief authorities of the 2nd century, had the habit of saying twenty-five individual prayers as compensation, if by coincidence he missed a community prayer.[33] 'Abdallāh b. 'Abbās taught his children the following: 'Perform the pilgrimage on foot; for whoever walks to the sanctuaries on foot, gains 700 meritorious virtues of that sanctuary with each step he takes, of which each single one has the value of 100,000 others.'[34]

There is no lack of practical considerations linked to such measures. If a pious man emigrates from Mecca to Jerusalem, he is aware that his prayers will lose three quarters of their value. In Mecca they are worth a hundred thousand ordinary ones; in Jerusalem not more that twenty-five thousand ordinary ones.[35]

You can add other arithmetic considerations to this. For example, certain quantities of the previously accrued merits can be lost.

"Whoever has a dog in his house, unless it should be a shepherd's dog, diminished his bona opera (*good deeds, transl.*) by two qirāṭ."[36]

Here one can easily recognize the calculation of good and bad deeds, calculated according to predetermined weights. The same can be found in every line in the religious books of the Parsees.

"Every step taken in order to accompany the dead body of a deceased is a good deed to the value of 300 stīr; every stir has the value of four dirham; so that the equivalent of 300 stīr is 1,200 dirham."[37]

Someone who, under ritually inadmissible conditions, defiles the ritual fire by his look has committed a sin worth twelve dirham; the weight of the sin of each more intimate contact is expressed in a precise figure; the progression can go up to fifteen tanāwar.[38]

"To take a step without wearing a belt is a sin worth one farmān, to take four steps a sin of one tanāwar." One tanāwar equals 1,200 dirham[39].

3) – The Islamic Ḥadīṯ has borrowed the formal characteristics of numerical relations from the Persian system in yet another respect. Even a mere superficial look at the holy scriptures of the Parsees reveals the importance of numerical analogies, where the same numbers appear on each numerical level (units, tens, hundreds, thousands). And sometimes these figures are very high. The book entitled Mainôgi-Khirad (XLIX, 15) counts 99,999 protecting spirits of the just and just as many demons and fiends, who fight the good heavenly world, while the Sad-der (XIII, 4) is contented with 9,999. The same numerical relations can be found regarding ritual actions. As a sacrifice for the dead, "33 beans and 33 eggs" are prescribed; at this point I refer to what James Darmesteter brought forward regarding the signification of the number 33 to the Iranians.[40] Now compare the corresponding Muslim form of the equivalent data. I intentionally quote the oldest information provided by the Ḥadīt: 33 angels carry the praise of humans to heaven. Concerning the merit accrued by pious litanies, the value mentioned is 33 tasbiḥ, 33 taḥmīd and 33 takbīr etc.,[41] a figure still current in the litanies of many mystic communities.[42] Faith has 333 ways.[43] When a believer bends his knees for prayer, 333 bones and 333 nerves praise God.[44] As you can see, hundreds of statements regarding the formation of such numbers are attributed to the prophet.

As far as these formal elements are concerned, it would lead us too far to give you a detailed presentation of material borrowings of Persian elements into Islamic law and customs. On the other hand, I would not like to end this chapter without facts, so I hope you will allow me to at least choose two examples from extreme poles, to demonstrate the scope of the problem that historical studies of Islam are still facing in this field: the greatest and the least important from a religious point of view. As the greatest I consider the Islamic institution of prayer, the homage that the servant of God pays by prostrating himself in the dust before the rabb al-ʿālamīn, the master of all the worlds. The fixation of the *number* of daily repetitions of this ritual, which must have emerged under the influence of Jewish-Christian traditions, is certain to go back to Persian origins. The prayer, as instituted by Muḥammad himself, was originally fixed at two times of the day: later, but still in the Qur'ān, a third time was added, which Muḥammad called the middle one (al-wusṭā): the morning prayer, the evening prayer and the middle one, correspond very well to the *shacharīth, minchāh* and *ʿarbīth* in Judaism.

But this no longer sufficed when Parsee religious institutions started to penetrate the circle of founders of Islamic ritual more and more. Regarding the quantity of religious expression, one did not want to lag behind when compared to the adherents of Zoroastrianism. Thus, as James Darmesteter saw it,[45] the five gāhs (prayer times) of the Persians were adopted, which raised the original three fixed prayer times to five.[46] So you can see how an old and fundamental institution of Islam, in its essential injunctions, came under Persian influence and was finally shaped in its definite form, which is still valid today.

Only a small step has to be taken from the most to the least important religious act. I ask your indulgence at this point, as we will no longer deal with a pious community prostrating themselves in the dust before God five times a day, but with a small and insignificant everyday object, the toothpick; it is hard to believe how much religious benediction has been attributed by Muslim tradition to this ordinary object. Muslims attribute such a high religious value to it, that they charge pious pilgrims with bringing them one as a sanctified souvenir from sacred places of Islam.[47] We are on the verge of drowning in an embarras de richesses when considering the myriad of adages demonstrating how far the miswāk (its Arabic name) was valued in ancient Islam; so I will have to limit myself to just a few.

The use of the miswāk counts as a preparation for prayer on a par with the canonical Aḏān (*call to prayer, transl.*). It belongs to the "Sunan al-mursalīn", i.e.,to practices of prophets who had lived before Muḥammad.[48] Their privileges are proclaimed by the Prophet in some characteristic sayings:

> "A prayer before which a toothpick has been used is worth more than 75 ordinary prayers."
>
> "If it were not too much of a burden for my believers, I would prescribe them to perform a siwāk *(use of the toothpick, transl.)* before each prayer."[49] The ancient tradition assesses this usage as so valuable that it makes the prophet say: "God insisted so strongly on me performing the siwāk that I almost feared that he was prescribing it to me as a revealed law."[50]

In jest, the prophet is made to say that Gabriel had charged him with the use of the toothpick so often that he was afraid of losing his teeth because of all the rubbing. One of the effects of the siwāk is to infuriate the devil; this pleases Allāh and is hated by Satan (marḍāt lil-rabb, mušīṭah lil-šayṭān).[51]

The use of a toothpick has the additional advantage of making it easier for a dying person, in his last moments, to profess his faith and shorten his agony.[52] In fact, the prophet, in his last hour, asks for a miswāk, and one of his assistants narrates that never in his whole life had he made an equally serious use of it as in his last moments.[53] The poetic literature of the Muslims soon took possession of this sacred object; there is even a kind of genre poetry of the miswāk. According to the testimonial of the Shiite scholar Abū l-Qāsim Murtaḍà ʿAlam al-hudà, we owe the most beautiful poem about this matter to the plume of the poet Abu Ḥayyā al-Numayrī (era of transition from the Umayyads to the Abbasids).[54]

Ladies and Gentlemen, a short indication should suffice. The miswāk and the high value attributed to it, which can hardly be explained from the religious conditions of Islam, lead us onto Persian territory. It stems from a ritual disposition attached to this object in the religious everyday life of Parsees,[55] which then evolved freely in Muslim dicta, of which some have come down to us as sayings of the Prophet.[56]

But we also have to consider the other side of the coin in reports of Muslim tradition under Persian influence.

From time to time there are signs of opposition as a reaction of Islam against Persian ideas. As evidence, a typical example can be adduced, the change of Muslim feelings towards the dog, our most loyal domestic animal. As you know, from time immemorial, Islam considers the dog to be a despicable animal.

> "The angels never enter a house where there is a dog or an image."

The Prophet is said to have ordered the killing of all the dogs of Medina, especially those of a certain dark color.[57] Muslim theologians find it hard to give a reason for this action. It is reported that the caliph Abu Ǧaʿfar al-Manṣūr (this information goes back to Ibn Qutayba) had received information concerning this point from an important scholar of his time, ʿAmr b. ʿUbayd. The latter could not give him any other explanation except for this one:

> "This is what tradition tells us; I do not know the reason."

The caliph is said to have expressed the following idea:

> "Because the dog barks at guests and scares beggars."[58]

There is certainly room for doubt as to whether the Prophet really took this action or not. At the time of the Prophet, the dog was not yet a despised animal; the believers had far more tender feelings towards it than could be inferred from the contempt shown for it during later generations. For example, we know that at the time of the Prophet, dogs would run around in mosques and that this fact was not considered to be a profanation of the sacred place.[59] Even later sayings, which have been preserved, reveal a friendly disposition of Muslims toward this animal, the contact with which, according to the law, constitutes one of the worst defilements. The dog – according to one Ḥadīṯ – sees things invisible to us, i.e., demons. If you hear your dog bark at night, ask God for his assistance against Satan.[60] This way of thinking is entirely Persian:

> "As often as a dog barks, the demons and evil enemies flee."

The dog shares this feature with the rooster,[61] about whom Muslim tradition makes Muḥammad state that he is Satan's enemy and that his crowing indicates that he has seen an angel.[62]

In a saying attributed to Ḥasan Baṣrī (died 110/728)[63], which has been adopted in Persian poetry[64] in several variants, the practicing Ṣūfī (faqīr) is compared to a dog in a way which strongly reminds us of a well-known description in the Avesta:[65]

> "The dog has ten laudable features, which all have to be present in a faqīr:
> 1 – It is always hungry – this is the custom of the believers.
> 2 – It has no permanent residence – this is the custom of those who confide in God (mutawakkilīn[66]).
> 3 – It sleeps very little at night – this is the custom of those immersed in God's love.
> 4 – When it dies, it leaves no heritage – this is the custom of the ascetics.
> 5 – It never leaves its master, even if he chases it away – this is the custom of the adepts (murīdīn).
> 6 – It is content with the smallest earthly goods – this is the custom of the most abstemious people.
> 7 – When it is chased away from one place, it will withdraw and look for another one – this is the custom of the humble.
> 8 – When it is beaten and chased away, but later recalled, it obeys – this is the custom of the modest.
> 9 – When it sees nourishment, it stands upright at a distance – this is the custom of those dedicated to poverty.
> 10 – When it leaves, it does not take any provisions for the road with it – this is the custom of those who have withdrawn from the world."

How is it possible that, at the time of Muḥammad, this animal was even tolerated in mosques and that even later it was found worthy of being compared to holy men due to its qualities, but that suddenly it started to inspire a feeling of horror which can hardly be reconciled with the tenderness for domestic animals prescribed by Islam? The answer is quickly found if we think of the high esteem it enjoys with the Parsees, among whom the Muslims settled. For them, it is the animal that chases away demons;[67] the dead body of a Parsee on his last voyage to the daḫmah (funerary tower) shall even be exposed to its views (segdīdeh); in the old days pious foundations established for the livelihood of this animal, in order to be sure of its help when the moment for the deceased would come, to cross the bridge of Sinvat, where the decision between eternal bliss or damnation would be taken.

Muslim tradition, in opposition to the religious esteem for this animal, ascribed the measure of extermination of the dogs to the Prophet and thus, for religious motives, turned a formerly much esteemed domestic animal into a despised one.[68]

III

The influence exerted by either the borrowing or rejection of foreign elements goes back to the earliest stages of the theological movement of Islam and is just as old as the efforts of lawmakers to formulate the norms of religious life.

We are not referring to the era when the conquests of victorious Islam lead to an encounter and subsequently to permanent contact with the Persian population.

We might (and maybe this little word "might" ought to be underlined here) be able to go back even further in the history of Islam and the effect of Parsee elements on the formation of Muḥammad's thinking. This leads me to a hypothesis to which I would like to direct your attention and the attention of all those interested in historical research of principles that exerted an influence, not only on the development, but also on the very origin of Muḥammad's work.

Up to this moment it has been above all Judaism and Christianity which have been considered sources of Qur'ānic teaching; the much celebrated essay of Abraham Geiger (1833) opened a new path to investigations which ever since have had a bearing on all kinds of details. Moreover, there has been research about the role played by apocryphal Jewish and Christian literature in the emergence of the Qur'ānic religion. In his work on Apocrypha, our colleague René Basset provided numerous useful indications concerning this matter that can stimulate scholars of the history of early Islam to attain a deeper insight into this domain.[69] One will find out that the concept of a "well-guarded tablet (*al-lawḥ al-maḥfūz*)", on which both the original version of the divine revelation and the destiny of mankind are engraved, has as its source a current notion in the *Book of Jubilees*; that the depiction of the Last Judgment, as it can be found in the Qur'ān, has its prototype in the Book of Enoch.[70] The connections with Ethiopian Christianity, in which these Apocrypha played an important role, have brought these concepts within the horizon of the Prophet of the Arabs.

It is equally not impossible that he had a Persian element at his disposal, which he then only had to take and reshape. This is not the first time that this idea is put forward. It is generally recognized that eschatological elements of the Qur'ān, even apart from Persian elements that had spread through Judaism and Christianity as intermediaries, betray direct borrowings from the Persians. The places and occasions where Persian concepts could penetrate Arabia at the time of Muḥammad were very numerous.

Persian culture was within the range of the inhabitants of Central Arabia, at a time before the appearance of Muḥammad. The commerce of Meccan traders, which had extended to Persian territory,[71] as well as the travels of poets-errant led them to the very boundaries of the Persian civilization. Al-Aʿšā is not the only Arabic poet whose excursions made him enter the Sassanian Empire; he is just one of many. And finally Ḥīra, the residence frequented by poets and inhabitants of Arabia, in spite of its Arabic court, offers a veritable large-scale painting of Persian life. From there, elements of Persian culture could easily enter the cities of the North and the center of Arabia; moreover, they can undoubtedly be recognized in Persian words and expressions which can be found in great number in the language of Ancient Arabia.

Allusions to Persian life, Persian clothes, and Persian customs abound with Pre-Islamic poets, who – of course – reject them with a typically Arabic arrogance, which, however, attests the knowledge these Arabs had of what appeared foreign to them.[72] In order to insult his enemy, a pre-Islamic poet, ʿAws b. Ḥağar, precisely uses the expression *fārisiyya*, i.e., Persian fashion, to designate a blemish on his family life.[73]

The Arabs did not have to transgress the boundaries of their geographical area in order to enter the sphere of the Persian element. In several locations of the peninsula, there were Persian traders living close to them. Already at the beginning of our era, Persians exploited gold mines in a number of places of the country.[74] Concerning the extent of the influence exerted by Persians on the Arabic population, this can be assessed by the fact that a part of the Arabic tribe established in Baḥrain, the Banū ʿIğil, totally adopted Persian nationality,[75] which proves the strength of the Persian element as an ethnographic factor in the middle of Arabic territory.

From a religious point of view, Southern Arabia (Yemen) also has to be taken into consideration. At the time of Muḥammad, it was a province under the influence of the Sassanian Empire. We know the names of the Persian dignitaries who ruled in the name of the Sassanians in Southern Arabia at the time of the Prophet. Commerce between the North and the Southern Persian-Arabic provinces could easily bring not only goods from Southern Arabia to the North, but also a school of thought. There is certainly justification for the assumption that trade was not limited to fine cloth that merchants would transport to the North from the South where it had been woven.[76] Neither was it limited to wine from Yemen and rainy Ḥaḍramawt,[77] rich in grapes, the vineyards of which were so frequently mentioned by poets whenever they sang about this wine that refreshed the burning throats of desert dwellers after the long hardships they had had to bear. People from the South will probably have exchanged a few words on religion and will have had some sort of contact, even if only superficial, with the ideas of the country they entered. Moreover, the opinion has already been uttered by Jes. Halévy that many a typically Christian expression later adopted in Islam, was imported from Southern Arabian Christianity.

Be that as it may, there was ample occasion for the Persian religion to have an impact on the thinking of the founder of Islam. In fact, the Prophet knows the *mağūs* and places them on the same level as the "Jews, the Sabeans and the Christians", as opposed to those who "practice idolatry". (surah 22:17).

This rapprochement is, at the least, evidence that the *mağūs* were part of the world within the religious horizon of Muḥammad, as he, from a religious point of view, did not see in them a heterogeneous element like in the idolatrous pagans of Arabia and faraway countries. Certainly, around him they were not numerous enough to give him a chance to observe their religious system profoundly like that of the Jews and the Christians, whose masters, Ḥabr and Ruhbān, furnished him with direct information. For this man, who was dominated by the idea of absolute monotheism, the notion of God as blurred by the dualism of the magi could not be a source of religious teaching like the religious systems around him, which he considered degenerated forms of the *dīn-Ibrahīm* (the religion of Abraham).[78]

Nevertheless some of the smatterings that Muḥammad adopted from Persian culture, without being conscious of it, did not fail to have their impact on Muḥammad's temperament, open to any religious impulse. – He had not gotten to know Parsism in a form that was practiced by a living community; it was rather a matter of latent influences that had their effect in a completely unconscious way, which combined with his own religious concept without ever organically uniting with it, and which only slightly modified some points of his system, the basis of which is Judeo-Christian.

The prosecution raging much later under the Abbasids against incredulity and heresy, at a time when theocracy developed under Persian influence, can already be found as indications in Qur'ānic sayings. The kāfir of the Qur'ān, however, is not the copy of the unbeliever and the heretic as we find him in Judaism or Christianity. Muḥammad introduced the Persian notion of material impurity. Here we have a truly Parsee thought:

> "An evil biped, for example an impious Ashemaogha, defiles the creations of the Good Spirit by direct contact, defiles them by indirect contact."[79]

Such a concept must have inspired this sentence in the Qur'ān:

> "*Innamā-l-mušrikīna nağisūn* – truly, the polytheists are *impure*."

At the beginning, this maxim is taken literally only in theory, and the older generation of exegetes (Ibn 'Abbās hereby being the authority) in fact comment this Qur'ānic sentence word by word:

> "The substance of the unbelievers is impure," and, "one has to perform ritual purification after having been in contact with them."[80]

It is true that the law of the Sunnites removed this inhumane interpretation from the text of the Qur'ān and explained the "impurity of the infidels (nağāsa)" in a moral sense.[81] But in Shiite circles, in which the Persian tradition had never ceased to exert a more pronounced influence, the literal understanding has been preserved with all its strictness, and in every Shiite code (I refer to Querry's Compendium[82]), you will find the "kāfir" mentioned as one of the ten causes of ritual impurity (deh neğāsāt). The consequences of this manner of interpreting in a strictly legal way become stricter the more the respective Shiite community, which as a whole is split up into numerous branches, has deviated from orthodox Islamic dogma. The more one of these sects is permeated by non-Arabic traditions, the more violently it is exclusive and intolerant regarding those that it considered as unbelievers.[83]

Similarly, those attributes of the phraseology and terminology of the Qur'ān that refer to infidelity and unbelievers, betray considerable similarities with the religious languages of the Parsees, and could easily lead to the hypothesis that a former infiltration from this source had taken place. But let us refrain from going too far and let us not expose ourselves to the danger of missing the target in our efforts to find analogies at any cost.

In his reprimanding sermons, Muḥammad often uses an epithet for unbelievers and sinners which, if understood in its original meaning, does not pertain to the domain of religious life proper, but is rather a borrowing from the terminology of civil law, which deals with disputes among private individuals. The unbeliever is called *ẓālim*, i.e., "oppressor, violent, tyrant". This term was later adapted to the religious domain according to the following procedure: the one who transgresses the commandments of Allāh, *ẓalama nafsahu*, "commits injustice and violence with regard to his own soul."

We will not give in to the temptation to see the prototype of *ẓālim* in the Parsee *sāstarān* (oppressor), while keeping in mind that the biblical term *râšâʿ* attests the same process of transition from a juridical to a religious notion, and that the term "*sinner who does violence to his soul*", in the original biblical text can be found as "וְחֹטְאִי חֹמֵס נַפְשׁוֹ *wə-ḥōṭəʾî ḥōmēs nafšō* (Prov. 8:36) – whoever sins against me, does violence to his soul (*Hebrew* ḥāmās = *Arabic* ẓulm)".

Ladies and Gentlemen, you might now ask the well justified question as to whether traces of specifically Parsee concepts can be found in the doctrines of the Prophet of Islam. If I adduced the eschatology of the Qur'ān, which, as I already mentioned above, shows traces of Parsee influence, and then repeated facts that have been well-known for a long time, I would exceed the time allowed for my talk. I would rather summarize a hypothesis that I recently formulated in an anthology dedicated to the memory of a dear friend [D.

Kaufmann] who prematurely passed away.[84] Unless I was mistaken, it underlines the latent influences Persian ideas had on the doctrine of Muḥammad. In the specific case I had in mind, they merely modify an institution borrowed from Judaism and Christianity by giving it a nuance that had not originally been present, but which was to be of lasting importance.

As you all know, the Islamic Friday is a copy of the biblical Sabbath. Nevertheless, it is distinct in one essential point from the biblical institution. The latter is destined to continuously remind the believers of the divine work of creation as its completion of a six day period: it is a day of rest for mankind and no work may be done, as the creation of the world was finally accomplished on this very day.

Certainly, Muḥammad also wants to maintain the belief among his believers in "the work of creation in six days", but his Friday is not a commemoration day. Neither is it a day of Sabbatical rest, nor a day of preparation for this rest. It is a "day of reunion" for the weekly celebration of the cult; since the very beginning, it had never been conceived as a day of rest:

> "O ye who believe!" says Muḥammad in the Qur'ān (surah 62:9-10), "When the call is heard for the prayer of the day of congregation, haste unto remembrance of Allah and leave your trading ... And when the prayer is ended, then disperse in the land and seek of Allah's bounty. (*transl.: Pickthall*)".

Muḥammad strictly rejects the idea that God had a rest after completing his work of creation. This idea is so deeply rooted in the Muslim consciousness that the following words of the Qur'ān (surah 50:37) have always been seen as direct polemics against Judaism:

> "And verily We created the heavens and the earth, and all that is between them, in six days, and naught of weariness touched Us (*wa-mā massana min luġūbin; in Pickthall's verse numbering verse 38; transl.)*"

I have given you an example of what I would call latent Persian influence. According to the doctrine of the Parsees, the universe was created in six periods.[85] Festivals were instituted to commemorate each of these periods of creation, but none with its accomplishment in view; similarly, no festival resembled the Jewish Sabbath in any way. Their theologians antagonized the Jewish concept of Sabbath and especially the idea that God had a rest after completing creation. It is true that the document called *Pāzend*, which J. Darmesteter[86] made known and in which the Parsee polemic against the institution of the Sabbath had found the expression of a dogma (*chikand gûmânik viyar*), dates from the 9th century; but probably it only reflects older theological discussions.

This opposition to the biblical creation account seems to have been noticed by Muḥammad. The Prophet of the Arabs' mind was permeated with the idea of the almightiness of God. It was the *root idea* determining his thoughts. So when adopting the institution of the Sabbath, he did not hesitate to seize the opportunity to modify it by vigorously rejecting the idea of a god who *has a rest*.

Ladies and Gentlemen! By allowing myself to draw your attention to this brief sketch for an hour, I absolutely did not intend to completely exhaust a topic that is so important for the historical study of Islam. Even less did I pretend to have found the final scientific answer by exposing my ideas on this matter to you. At this point it is rather my heartfelt wish to repeat the word that you might remember I began the last chapter of my talk with: *we might*. Whatever I have tried to present to you in this final chapter, I do not consider it an accomplished doctrine; I rather see it as a *hypothesis*. – *Valeat quantum valere potest*.

This learned assembly seemed to offer a good opportunity to draw your attention to a series of phenomena, the exact investigation of which will enable us to gain a deeper understanding of different elements concurring during the formation of early Islam. Allow me, Ladies and Gentlemen, to conclude by expressing my sincere appreciation for the friendliness and patience with which you have lent me your attentive ears.

The Influence of Persian Religious Patterns on Notions in the Qur'ān

Volker Popp

The notion of a connection of Iranian religious patterns with notions in the Qur'ān must cause disconcertment among those who know the traditional reports of the eventful life of a prophet of the Arabs, who came from the Arabian Peninsula, was born in Mecca and acted as the herald of a divine revelation in Medina. In the process it is often forgotten that the Arabian Peninsula had been strongly influenced by the Iranian civilization over long periods of time.

The annunciation of the prophet of the Arabs is believed to have been reduced to writing and thus turned into the Qur'ān long after his death. Here we must distinguish between Iranian religious patterns, which can already be found in previous revelations and which are kept in the Qur'ān, though partially re-interpreted, and those Iranian religious patterns, which can only be found *hidden* in the text of the Qur'ān.

An example of the former is the notion of the existence of paradise and the work of angels.

1 The Notion of Paradise to Syrian Christians of the First Centuries – From Syrian Paradise to Iranian Garden

According to the account in Genesis, paradise is a synonym for the Garden of Eden, from which God banned the first humans after their fall from grace. The early Jewish designation *Paradise* for the Garden of Eden comes from Avestan – in transliteration *pairidaêza* ("surrounded by a wall") – the Old Iranian language in which the teachings attributed to Zarathustra have survived. The contact of the Babylonian Jews with Iranian culture is probably the cause of the penetration of the notion of paradise, along with its corresponding name, into the Biblical text.

According to the New Testament the term also designates the eschatological state of happiness (Luke 23:43; 2 Corinthians 12:4; Revelation 2:7).

The Qur'ān follows this interpretation. However, the "walled" Paradise with its small, designed gardens, in the midst of a non-paradise-like environment, is expanded to a vast garden compound, the "Ğannat". It is a merger of two concepts, the Biblical with a Gnostic concept of the "Invisible" behind a gnostic veil. From the Avestan word for paradise – *pairidaêza* – via the Middle Persian form *fairidaêz,* we come to the Arabic *firdaws*. This is considered an Arabic plural form of the word, so consequently an Arabic singular is formed: *farādis*. Within the context of semantic expansion from the notion of *paradise* to a *Ǧannat,* the old site of the *firdaws* gradually becomes a part of the new Qur'ānic compound.

The expansion of the notion of paradise of the New Testament, in the Syrian Christian version, enlarged by Iranian elements, is symptomatic for the method of approach of the authors of Qur'ānic materials. In terms of a collection of all expressions of the "*Dēn* (Iranian)/*Dīn* (Arabic)[1]" (i.e. the divine and human wisdom), the Iranian conception of the eschatological state of happiness must be added to the ones known from the scriptures. From the perspective of the early Syrian Christians living in an Iranian environment the writings require a *Sunna*. Only then is it possible to do the working of *Dēn / Dīn* justice as a process of progressive realization of divine and human wisdom. The work of the *Dēn / Dīn* forces a continuation of the scriptures in the form of new collections of the experience of divine and human *sophia*. Hence, the Qur'ānic materials contain references to this extension from the idea of paradise of the early Syrian Christians to that of the Iranianized Syrians of the sixth century.

2 How can the Syrian view of Paradise be identified in the Text of the Qur'ān?

Since the Syriac understanding of the early Qur'ānic materials had been lost and a new approach from an Iranian point of view was only sought after the formation of a new Iranian state religion following the religious turmoil of the time known as the Caliphate of al-Ma'mūn period (after 840 CE), an Islamic tradition emerged in the interpretative literature, which led to an indistinguishable merger of Syrian and Iranian traditions.

The way to a solution was not found until Christoph Luxenberg's approach[2] first made it possible to distinguish between the interpretation of the Syro-Aramaic originals and the superimposed Iranian coining. Thus it is of fundamental importance that we permanently dismiss the fiction that the language of the Qur'ān is Classical Arabic (*ʿArabīya*). The language of the Qur'ān is a mystery only in mainstream Islamic studies.

Since the Qur'ān is a product of the expansion and dynamics of *Dēn / Dīn*, its linguistic form is as fluid as its contents, its scope and the tendencies of the collection of wisdom displayed by it. This collection has no end point, in so far as it does not have a final linguistic form. Its language reflects the historical development of collecting material, but is not the product of an announcement within an assessable time period in a specific region of the Arabian Peninsula. Therefore, there can be no linguistic form which could be presented as canonical. It is well imaginable that many centuries of language development lie between the creation of Qur'ānic materials and the release of the earliest grammar of Arabic by the Persian Sībawayh of Baṣra (757 [?] –796 [?] CE). Since the Iranians were confronted with the historical dimension of language throughout their sacred writings, it is not surprising that they were aware of the historical contingency of the linguistic form of a tradition. Being great experts on the history of language, their aim was not standardized uniformity, but on the contrary, they used even the most remote expressions and forms of the rich Indo-Iranian linguistic heritage to vividly portray the historicity of the experience.

The mysteries regarding the language of the Qur'ān are similar to the philological puzzles the readers of the Avesta are confronted with. The following example of a statement referring to a problem of Gatha-tradition should make this clear:

> "The influences the texts were exposed to first of all result in a lot of Young Avestan peculiarities entering into an originally Old Avestan text. A large number of phenomena must be added to this, which, in their present form, can neither be directly assigned to Old Avestan, nor to Young Avestan. These phenomena may have been adopted into the text at various times."[3]

These findings regarding the linguistic circumstances of the Gatha-tradition can, by analogy, be applied to the linguistic problems in the tradition of the Qur'ānic materials. Old Avestan here only has to be replaced by Old Aramaic, Young Avestan accordingly by the Aramaic dialect underlying the language of the Qur'ān, which is commonly mistaken for Arabic. Here too we see phenomena which cannot directly be assigned to Old Aramaic nor to an Aramaic element of the Qur'ānic language. These phenomena may have entered the text at very different times. The only possible conclusion to be drawn is that the Qur'ān reflects a historical stage of language development in the Western Iranian area, an analogous development of which can be found in religious texts from the Iranian East. Western Iran is the area of *'Arabīya* (The West); the generic term for the languages spoken there is *'Arabī* (the Western). It consists of elements from Aramaic and another language which was common from the West of the Tigris to the Mediterranean.

3 Luxenberg's depiction of the paradise of the Syrians in the Qur'ān

The starting point for the development of the notion of wide-eyed houris serving the male inmates of the paradise garden compound is the Qur'ān (44:54, 52:20). The translation by R. Paret reads:

> "So (this is). And we give them wide-eyed houris as wives (44:54). They lie (comfortably) on lounges arranged in rows. And we give them wide-eyed houris as wives (52:20)."

This interpretive reading of the text marked with diacritics, which leads up to the desired reading "wide-eyed" is, of course, in the spirit of Indo-European studies. Where, if not in the sacred cow of the Indo-Aryans, can we find the wide-eyed? The animal sacrificed to Hera, wife of Zeus, was the cow. The idea of the cow-eyed/wide-eyed Hera is historic. The cattle grazing Iranians, the Zoroastrians feasting on sacrificial cattle, of course must find the wide-eyed in their Qur'ānic paradise garden.

The urban Syrians, however, did not require this dewy-eyed gaze. Their idea of paradise was frugal. This can be demonstrated by Luxenberg's reading of the same parts of the Qur'ān text. Luxenberg's Syro-Aramaic reading uncovers the early understanding of the text. There is no mention of wives in the form of wide-eyed houris, but

> "We will make them comfortable under white, crystal clear grapes."[4]

This naturally leads to the early Syrian Christian belief in paradise. They were content if their souls were safe in the bosom of the patriarchs Abraham, Isaac and Jacob, and if they refreshed them with cool, white grapes from the vines of Paradise. In life one was prepared for this paradise, because in the mosaic decoration of the churches in Syria, the vine and grape motifs were widely used. The mosaic decoration of churches depicted the birds of heaven, which cavorted above the vegetal decoration. So it is not surprising that these are on the menu card of the blessed. R. Paret translates this as "and meat from poultry, what(ever) pleases them" (Qur'ān 56:21). This reading is an Iranian import as well. Scenes of hunting boars and birds are common motives of Sassanian art. Luxenberg reads here just "Fresh food". This produces an interesting turn. Accordingly the inhabitants of the invisible world feast on freshly prepared food. So it becomes evident, that they are with us in this world until the day of the Last Judgement, when the world will be cleaned by the fire that goes before Him. The invisible world is described in the books from the Nāǧʿ Ḥammādī library. The concept of the Gnostic veil is present in the Qu'rānic materials.

However, ideas are changing: not only are the houris represented in the text of the Qur'ān today, thanks to the diacritical marks, but following the Iranian reading of the Qur'ān, also their male counterparts, the Persian temple slaves (*hierodules*), are there as part of the feast. R. Paret translates:

> "Forever young boys make the rounds among them. When you see them, you think they are sown (or unmounted?) pearls (they are so perfect in form)." (Qur'ān 76:19).

Again Luxenberg's Syro-Aramaic reading is quite different:

> "There circle among them fruits, that are (such) as if they were pearls (still) entrapped (in the shell)."[5]

In his final assessment of what he regarded as a philological reading of the current misinterpretation of the Qur'ān text using diacritics, Luxenberg has highlighted the extent of the alienation of the Qur'ān exegesis from the original Christian symbolism of the text.

Fig. 40: The patriarchs of the Syrian Paradise feed the souls of the deceased with grapes. Monastery of the Syrians in Egypt (Wādī Natrūn). Fresco of the 6th century CE (Photograph by: Andrea B. Schmidt).

What is a sign of alienation to Luxenberg is a testimony of approach and appropriation to the Iranians. By means of diacritics a new text is created which reflects the Iranian understanding. A way had to be found to introduce the "Divine Virgin" of Zoroastrian mythology into the text, just like the temple slaves, without whom the conversion of a Syrian-Christian paradise into an Iranian paradise of a different character would have been impossible; for without song, the Iranians could not imagine a feast in paradise.

4 The Iranian concepts of paradise as a supplement to the Syrian tradition

The eternal Iranian life in paradise is present in many places of the Qur'ān. The importance of the family and the sanctity of marriage, an important institution among Iranians ("Go with your wives into Paradise ..."), are also reflected in the new concept of life in paradise. (Qur'ān 13:23; 36:56, 40:8, 43:70).

The Iranian paradise of the newly interpreted Qur'ān has no poor people. All residents enjoy the privileges and luxuries of the Iranian gentry (Qur'ān 76:12-20). The clothing of *diqans* is a general standard. This means that there are large robes, gold chains and fragrances (Qur'ān 22:23, 35:33) for all.

Around the time when the Qur'ānic materials were compiled, the representatives of the former state religion of the Sassanid Empire were reworking their materials. A member of one of the most important families of the Zoroastrian clergy and the highest office holder of the clergy in Fars and Kerman was Manûjir. He was active around 880 CE. The following message about the Iranian Paradise is in an excerpt of his writings:

> "... it says that the inhabitants of Paradise are linked together in love and friendship and are thinking only of themselves. Manûjir provides inter alia the following definitions: '[Paradise] exalted, elevated, brightest, most fragrant, purest, most beautiful, most desirable, at best, and [it is] the abode of the gods'. In it there is only peace and joy, happiness and blessing and kindness [and indeed] more and greater than the largest and highest quality and the largest and highest-peace in the visible material world (gêtig pad). In it there is no desire and no pain, no suffering, no discomfort (Dd 25.2-4) ... [Hell is] at the bottom, facing downward, and the darkest, stinkiest and most horrible, evil and superfluous, the dwelling place of demons and devils (dewân du druzân). In it there is no peace, no kindness, and no joy. In it there is only stench and filth, pain and punishment, suffering and sorrow and evil and inconvenience." (Dd 26.2 to 4; this description was taken from Manûjir's work 'Dâdestân î Denig' [The religious judgments]).[6]

5 The description of Paradise as an example of the development of the Qur'ān text

1) An early layer includes the description by the early Christian-Syriac tradition.
2) The frugal idea of paradise of Syrian Christians is enriched with Iranian ideas. The notion of paradise of a Syrian Christian community inculturated in Iran emerges. Here the founders of the community are promised paradise as well, despite the fact that they were deported (Qur'ān 3:195, 9:100).
3) The description of the early layer is no longer understood, neither from a linguistic standpoint nor for contextual reasons. Iranian notions dominate over early Syrian Christian symbolism. The result is that by means of diacritics, the early material is re-read and adapted to concepts of the Iranian tradition. White grapes are intentionally misread and turned into

"celestial virgins", hence an approach towards the Iranian vision of the "Divine Virgin", who guides the souls to paradise. Fruit being served to the inhabitants of paradise must therefore be turned into (equally juicy and seductive) girls and boys, so that paradise is enhanced with singing and other favors granted by the hierodules.

In the end, the text took on a form, which is reminiscent of the form of the Avesta. An earlier and a later form of language can be found in the same codex, not including the reading on a third level, which is achieved by the addition of diacritical marks.

6 Angels in the Qur'ān

In the New Testament, angels are messengers of God. Angels play an important role in the texts of the Qumran community. Even in the New Testament, the report about the capture and liberation of Saint Peter (Acts 12:1-19) betrays the influence of Iranian angelology:

> "They said to her, 'You are out of your mind!' But she kept insisting that it was so. They kept saying, 'It is his angel.' (Acts 12:15)"[7]

One cannot help feeling that even in the New Testament angels were perceived as having the nature of the Iranian *fravahr*. The *fravahr* is the

> "(M.P.) heavenly, immortal counterpart of earthly beings, tutelary genius; immortal soul of Magians, guardian angel during one's lifetime."[8]

Another description is:

> "Voting decision; anthropological and cosmogonal / cosmological principle, at the same time (probably more helpful) spirit of the dead; Middle Persian Frawahr."[9]

Today, a month of the calendar of the Islamic Republic of Iran is still dedicated to this idea of the *fravahr* as a ghost from the dead; it is the month *Farwardîn*. It is reminiscent of the Christian notion of *All Saints' Day* and *All Souls' Day*.[10]

In the Qur'ānic text, God makes his angel speak to the prophets. Moses is the exception. There is no consensus as to who the "speaker" is in the Qur'ānic text. One might be tempted to think that in this case we see the *fravahr* of God.

There are good reasons for making such considerations. If Iranian notions are dissected and presented in conjunction with the Qur'ānic materials, then this does not mean that such beliefs were only common in the area that we now call Iran. Iranian religious notions were also at home in the area of the Upper Euphrates. For example, the central concept *Dīn / Dēn* in the Qur'ān is found on a Greek inscription from the 2nd Century BCE, from Cappadocia. Therefore it is not necessary to go so far as to posit an inculturation of Syrian Christians as deportees in eastern Iran and Chorasan in order to locate the home of the basic patterns of the Qur'ān. This may have been situated anywhere between Jerusalem and al-Marwa.

The upper Euphrates was the location of the Commagene kingdom with its capital Samosata (now flooded). The remains of the cult site on the Nimrud Dagh are well known. They stem from the first century BCE. The King of Commagene, Antiochus I, states in an inscription that he had made the statues and friezes on the Nimrud Dagh "in many ways according to the old tale of Persians and Greeks". Thus, if we see the area of the upper Euphrates as the first hub of such concepts of the first century BCE, then we can also assume that "Persian" ideas were received in this area. That is probably also true of the Iranian terminus *Dēn/Dīn,* known from a Greek inscription of the 2nd century BCE from Cappadocia, and preserved to date as a central concept in the text of the Qur'ān.

If Antiochus I felt committed to the Persian way of representing the gods in his inscription, then this means that Antiochus did not depict the gods, but their *fravašis*. Moulton has already suggested this possibility. Moreover, Moulton has pointed out the proximity of the term *fravaši* to the terms *Di Manes* and *genius*, while connecting the term *genius* to the concept of *iuno* (...), which he translated as "young woman". He writes:

> "It is remarkable how great the general similarity is between the genius and the Fravashi. The genius, with his female counterpart, the Juno, is the special patron of birth, a function belonging to the Fravashis. Both seem to combine the ideas of an inborn part of the individual and a power which watches over him."

On the other hand, Söderblom wrote:

> "Les Fravashis font en effet concurrence aux divinités reconnues par la littérature la plus classique du mazdéisme. Les Gáthâs. (The Fravashis in fact compete with deities recognized by the most classical literature of Mazdaism: The Gathas.)"

Compare Nyberg's view:

> "The Fravashis are the omnipotent powers, the sustainers of heaven and earth, the guarantors of the order of nature and of social life, the victors in dispute, the prop of man from the moment when he is formed in the womb, the masters of historical process. The Fravashis of the gods are also invoked, the gods themselves being Fravashis by their inner nature."
> "(...) Just as the term fravashi can help us understand the cult of ancestor worship in Commagene, as far as it goes back to Persian ideas, similarly it can

> make their concept of a God-King intelligible. The Commagenic kings neither equate their own higher spiritual self with one of the purportedly pre-existing, unnamed Fravashis, nor with the Fravashis of any of the main gods, but with the royal god par excellence, Mithras."[11]

The idea of the Fravashis is not only reflected in today's commemoration of the dead in Iran. The concept of the "speaker/spokesman" in the Qur'ān might be connected with the idea of the Fravashis. The existence of the *speaker* is indeed still a mystery. The attempt to see the text as a proclamation of a prophet of the Arabs can only succeed if it does violence to the text of the Qur'ān. The *Prophet* can only be read into the Qur'ān if we assume that a third reading based on a new positioning of diacritical marks was imposed on the original text.

The Qur'ān has to be seen in the context of the Messianic and later on Chiliastic movements of ʿAbd al-Malik and the Abdallāh from Merv (Marw) in Chorasan. The *fravashi* of the royal god (malik) is of course no longer Mithras, but the eschatological Jesus. This pre-existent Jesus (to be equated with the Greek *logos,* the Aramaic *memrā* and the Arabic *'amr* in the Qur'ān) with his predicates *saffāh, manṣūr* and *mahdī*, was the higher spiritual self of the rulers of Merv, who refer to themselves as *bn amīr al-mu'minīn.*

7 The central concept of the Qur'ān: *Dēn / Dīn*

The Qur'ān makes statements about faith and how faith should be. It does not make any statements about "religion". The view that the term *Dēn / Dīn* in its connection with *islām* designates the religion of Islam is historically wrong.

Only the modern academic discipline of Islamic Studies interprets the term *Dēn / Dīn* to mean "religion".[12]

According to the view expressed in the Qur'ān, *islām* is what emanated from *Dēn / Dīn.* The Iranian concept of *Dēn*, a manifestation of the divine and human wisdom, cannot tolerate any dispute over the interpretation of the Scripture. It is an injunction of *sophia* (*Dēn*) to make the concord of the understanding of scripture a duty. Therefore, in the Qur'ān we read: one must stand up against the dispute (*mā* ⁽ⁱ⁾*ḫtalafa*) among the "people of the book (*ahl kitāb*)" and make concord (*al-islām*) one's obligation, "for as far as believing in God, he calls for unity" (*'in[na] d-dīn[a] ʿind[a] llāh[i] l-islām*, surah 3:19).[13]

The text of the Qur'ān does not reveal any more material about the new religion of Islam. These materials emerged in the area of Merv (al-Marwa), and Jerusalem. The *Prophet of the Arabs in Mecca* belongs to a later Iranian interpretation, when the text of the Qur'ān was aligned with the expectations of the new recipients. The Qur'ānic materials had an Iranian fate: From the hands of the editors they got into the hands of the Pharisees (Arabic: *šarīfs*). And the *sunnah* of a Christian community became the collection of traditions of an Iranian orthodoxy.

> "Ahura Mazda created man with his vision (*daênâ*; Y. 46.6). The bond of religion (*paywand î dên*), which denotes 'adopting a righteous authority in time and not deviating from this authority', (...)."[14]

8 About the Kufic inscription inside the Dome of the Rock.

The text is as follows:

> "*bi-sm(i)-llā(i) r-rahmān(i) r-rahīm / lā ilāh(a) illā llāh(a) wahda(ū) lā šarīk(a) la-h(ū)* according to the re-reading of Christoph. Luxenberg: 'In the name of the merciful and compassionate God (...) / There is no god but God alone, he has no partner/associate'."[15]

The question of who the "partner/associate" may be, has already led to many discussions. According to popular belief, there is an "anti-Trinitarian" reflex here. But if we consider the objective of the Mazdayasnic concept of *Dēn*, which aims at purifying / dividing what has been (unlawfully) mixed, then we can understand it as an indication that no *confusion* in the sense of understanding the *Dēn* is what is meant here.[16]

9 The *Dīn Ibrahīm* of the Qur'ān

Varied attempts have been made to clarify this term. Mostly, it is considered to refer to the historical Abraham, who is said to have founded a religion. This religion of Abraham, which could also be called "*hanīf*dom", is still being sought. Moreover, there are constant attempts to connect this term with a concept of "Abrahamic religion". This is all wrong.

Taken to be understood in terms of the Iranian *Dēn,* the *Dīn Ibrahīm* is the "faith of Abraham". It is the *faith* of Abraham, about which Paul speaks in his Epistle to the Romans (4; 3:11-16). This "faith of Abraham" is evoked in the Qur'ān.

The Abraham of the Qur'ān avoids the company of the *mušrikūn*, here not meaning "those who associate partners with God", i.e. either Trinitarians or polytheists, but rather "those who mix and jumble". A true believer prefers to be entitled *ḥanīf* (heathen) than to go to church with those who cannot keep things apart in a lawful way.

In this sense the Qur'ānic concept of "*dīn al-ḥaqq* – the right faith" is also to be understood as opposing the "*dīn kulli*" (the common-made, contaminated faith).

10 About Qur'ān 2:256

Pickthall translates as follows:

> "There is no compulsion in religion. The right direction is henceforth distinct from error. And he who rejecteth false deities and believeth in Allah hath grasped a firm hand hold which will never break. Allah is Hearer, Knower."

Rudi Paret as usual adds words in brackets:

> "There is no coercion in religion (i.e., no one can force you to [right] faith). The right way (of faith) has become clear (through the proclamation of Islam) (so that it is distinct) from aberration (of pagan unbelief) (...)."

Here we are dealing with a statement that has to be attributed to the general Iranian view of the world. It is interesting to note that this verse appears in the inscription in Damascus. This fact is understandable from a historical point of view if we consider it as referring to a time before the expected *Parousia* (the second coming of Christ) fails to materialize in the year 77 according to the Arabs (i.e. 698 CE). After this failure it became opportune to confine oneself to very general doctrines.

Whereas Rudi Paret, and with him the whole community of Islamologists, consider this verse a commandment of tolerance, an ancient Iranian man, who did not go to the church of Islamology, would have seen it as an ancient Iranian concept of how faith ought to be.

Using Qur'ānic rhetoric and by explaining a phenomenon through pairs of opposites (unity [*islām*] vs. dispute [*iḫtilāf*]) here it is stated: "fi d-dīni / lā ikrāha": *if your faith is present, it is not difficult to see*. In other words: Once the right faith is there, it takes no effort to see the truth (*lā ikrāha fi d-dīni*). The *right way of faith*, which R. Paret sees here, is nothing more than an Avestan concept according to the *Dēn yašt*. In this text the goddess of the straight path, "sophia", is praised as the embodiment of true wisdom. The name of this goddess (*Razišta*) has led to the Qur'ānic designation of such behavior: "rušd". The Qur'ānic notion *rušd* corresponds to what the goddess called Razišta meant to the Mazdayasnian Iranians. It embodied the straight path, the right way in the sense of *Dēn / Dīn*.

11 In the End, the Reward for the Effort is Given

The believer receives the reward of God – *Rizq Allāh*. A Syrian living far away from home had to rely on his *daily wages*. Since he was not a country gentleman (*diqān*), he had to settle for one day's pay or wages.

In Middle Persian, the Persian language contemporary to Qur'ānic exegesis, "daily wage" is translated as *rôzik*. Etymologically, it designates what belongs to a *rôz* (day).

These few examples should suffice at this point. A more detailed study could demonstrate the Iranian background of many Qur'ānic ideas even more clearly.

12 Bibliography

12.1 Standard Works of Reference

EIr.= the Encyclopaedia Iranica, Costa Mesa, Ca. 1994.

EI = the Encyclopaedia of Islam. New Edition, Leiden 1960-.

F. Steingass, A Comprehensive Persian- English Dictionary, London 1892.

12.2 Further Literature

Christoph Luxenberg, Die Syro-aramäische Lesart des Koran, Berlin 2004.

Id., Neudeutung der Arabischen Inschrift im Felsendom zu Jerusalem, in: Die Dunklen Anfänge, Berlin 2005, p. 124-139.

Michael G. Morony, Iraq after the Muslim Conquest, Princeton 1984.

Johanna Narten, Zum Vokalismus in der Gatha-Überlieferung, in: Studia Grammatica Iranica, München 1986, p. 257-279.

Rudi Paret, Der Koran, Stuttgart 1979.

Mansour Shaki, Artikel "Dēn", in: EIr, II, p.279-281.

Michael Stausberg, Die Religion Zarathushtras, Stuttgart 2002.

Hellmut Waldmann, Der kommagenische Mazdaismus, Tübingen 1991.

Id., Heilsgeschichtlich Verfasste Theologie und Männerbünde, Tübingen 1994.

New Ways of Qur'ānic Research

From the Perspective of Comparative Linguistics and Cultural Studies

Markus Groß

1. Introduction: Aims, Procedure and Scope

How can we, who have painstakingly tried to immerse ourselves in the language of such an ancient people, whose way of thinking is so far removed from our own, contradict men who have imbibed their feeling for the Arabic tongue with their mother's milk and scholars of whatever origin living among the Arabs who completely devoted themselves to the study of the Arabic language and its monuments? We have, however, one particular advantage over them: freedom from religious prejudice or bias. And furthermore, we have grown up in the school of scientific criticism.[1]

Theodor Nöldeke

The aim of the present study is the examination and evaluation of some of the central results of recent Qur'ānic research, above all of the findings brought forward by Christoph Luxenberg[2] concerning what he called the mixed Aramaic-Arabic language. One of the main points of interest here is the issue of the putative *primarily oral transmission* of the text of the Qur'ān, the text of which was only *secondarily* fixed in writing at the time of caliph 'Uṯmān. But it is especially this last question which can hardly be answered from the commonly accepted narrow perspective of the Qur'ān and its linguistic and cultural environment in isolation.

In fact it would be much more appropriate here – and the same applies to the study of virtually all languages and cultures – to examine the Qur'ān and its language from a "universal" standpoint, i.e., in comparison to the situation in other civilizations, language families and religions.

Unfortunately, this is hardly ever the case, partially due to a lack of open-mindedness, but in many cases it is also attributable to insufficient knowledge of the objects of comparison.

In the discussion about the controversial publication of Christoph Luxenberg, which continues in unabated intensity also on the internet, arguments against the phenomena described by him have been adduced which totally ignore the fact that these very phenomena are normal, in some cases even very frequent in other languages.

From a universal perspective it is by no means too far-fetched to assume the existence of a mixed language like the 'Arabic bearing a strong Aramaic imprint' in Luxenberg's theory, the borrowing of word forms from different dialects of the same language (in Luxenberg's case: Eastern and Western Syriac), the taking over of elements from another (or predecessor) religion (in Luxenberg's case an example being the Eucharist) or the use of misunderstood "winged words" (in Luxenberg's case: "qāba qawsayn" – allegedly: "two bow lengths"). These are ubiquitous phenomena which can easily and frequently be found.

What, however, cannot be counter-argued is a reproach like the following against one of Luxenberg's predecessors, to be found on an apologetic Islamic homepage[3]:

> "One such example of an orientalist belonging to this class was that of Reverend Alphonse Mingana. Mingana attempted to teach Muslims about the transmission of their sacred Book down to even the Arabic alphabet!" (my emphasis)

In other words: It is not acceptable for non-Muslims to criticize the Holy Scriptures of Islam.

However, in the article just cited from the Internet Luxenberg's theory is also the object of ostensibly scientific counter-arguments. Above all the enormous influence of Aramaic and especially of Syriac is flatly denied.

To support their view the authors adduce some old Arabic-Nabataean inscriptions where diacritical dots can allegedly be found, which is supposed to prove that Arabic letters can in fact have developed without Syriac influence. Moreover, they cast doubt on the assumed geographical distribution of Syriac/Aramaic, the influence of which, according to the authors, must have been much smaller.

A look beyond one's own nose and a bit of logic might have quickly provided the apt answer: Whether there were diacritical dots in some inscriptions or not – nothing unusual in quite a number of defective writing systems – is irrelevant in so far as the oldest Qur'ānic manuscripts *do not have any* diacritical dots!

And the "international" impact of Aramaic can easily be seen in the widespread use of writing systems based on Aramaic. In fact all Middle Iranian writing systems, above all those for Manichaean Middle Persian and Parthian, derive from an Aramaic model. And even for Central Asian languages like late Tocharian an Aramaic writing system replaced the older Brahmi script for while. And last but not least the Mongolian script is based on Aramaic turned by 90°, i.e., written vertically. Moreover, the administrative language of the Achaemenid (Persian) Empire was Aramaic – not Persian, which was only used for representative inscriptions. And although in the later Sassanian Empire this task was performed by Middle Persian, this latter language is not only written in Aramaic script, but this writing system contains hundreds of so-called Aramaic *heterograms* – words written as if they were Aramaic, but read as Persian, a bit comparable to the Latin heterogram in English "e.g. (exempli gratia)", which is pronounced/ read as "for example".

Inscriptions in the Aramaic language can be found from Afghanistan to Egypt and even in Old High German there is a well-known Gospel harmony attributed to the Syrian monk Tatian, which goes back to the Latin translation of the Syriac original called by the Greek name "diatesseron".

Taking all these facts into consideration it is next to ridiculous to doubt the enormous impact of Aramaic as a global *lingua franca* at that time. What, however, is a bit surprising is the fact that hardly any of the critical replies to Luxenberg's assumptions ever deal with his Aramaic parallels, or – in clearer terms – why most critics show such little knowledge of Syriac. The answer is simple as well as astounding: Syriac-Aramaic is largely unknown, because all grammars and dictionaries use the Syriac script.

Whoever is interested in Sanskrit (Old Indian), Gothic or Tocharian is not forced to learn a new and complicated script beforehand. For Sanskrit there are voluminous textbooks, grammars, dictionaries and even editions of its classical literature in or with transliteration.

But should you desire to learn Syriac, you will be faced with textbooks and grammars with an introductory chapter *on* the writing system and the rest is then *in* that writing system. In case you failed to master it perfectly, you will not be able to use the grammar. To make the situation even more complicated, there are at least two totally different vocalization systems in general use and two quite different ductūs of the script in use in the standard grammars. Healey[4] for instance and most of the older grammars use the Western Syriac Serṭā ductus (with Western vocalization based on Greek vowels) and Muraoka[5] the older Estrangela with Eastern vocalization (dots).

This deplorable situation is similar for Old Ethiopian (Geʿez) and (the Indo-European language) Classical Armenian[6]. The academic disciplines dealing with these languages have thereby become hermetic orders, unintentionally barring access to their treasures to most scholars of neighboring disciplines.

For this reason all examples in the present study will be transliterated and vocalized. Moreover, for almost all text samples an analysis of each grammatical form in the text is given in a right hand column, often accompanied by etymological explanations.

In order to widen the angle of the perspective parallel examples of a wide range of languages, religions and regions concerning the respective phenomena in question will be discussed.

The general structure of the study can be summarized as follows: The first part will deal with the problem of primarily oral or written transmission of religious texts. In addition to Qur'ānic passages a number of ancient texts from other civilizations will be examined with regard to their *transmission* history and possible evidence for either primarily oral or written transmission.

As the key notion "oral poetry" has often been mentioned when discussing the history of the Qur'ān, examples of this phenomenon from cultures which until recently did not possess a written literature will be given, e.g. poetry of the Tswana and Kazakh.

A more general part will then deal with poetic devices and their use in different languages, in order to obtain a yardstick for judging their use in the Qur'ān, the examination of which will follow at the end of the chapter.

In order to widen the perspective within Classical Arabic, a text sample from the famous "Burda (the mantle)", an Arabic religious poem from the Middle Ages, will be analyzed for comparison.

A further chapter is dedicated to the often asserted, but nowadays hardly ever questioned "beauty of the Qur'ān".

In order to make it possible to assess claims made for Early Arabic and its script several defective writing systems from the Middle East will be briefly sketched.

The paramount importance of the concept of a "mixed Arabic-Aramaic language" as postulated by Luxenberg – for simplicity's sake we will keep using this misnomer – will be taken into consideration in so far as a number of attested language forms will be presented and discussed which would fall into the same category, as e.g. BHS (Buddhist Hybrid Sanskrit) as a parallel case of a language form emerging from the literal transposition of words from one language into another.

Another chapter will deal with the position of Qur'ānic Arabic within the Semitic language family. Above all the assessment of grammatical forms which – according to Luxenberg – were misread will be of special interest.

Several pages will be dedicated to the linguistic form of *the* central word/concept of Islam, the name of God: *Allāh.* This name or word will be analyzed etymologically, which inevitably involves comparison with corresponding forms in neighboring, especially adjacent Semitic languages.

In Islamic countries religions other than Islam are hardly studied in any profound way, let alone valued – in Saudi-Arabia the practice of any religion but Islam is downright forbidden – so it is not surprising that their very study is also hampered[7] in most Islamic countries. One might adduce Judaism and Christianity as exceptions, but even here it is not unbiased *research about* these religions as such which is usually intended, but it is rather a search for evidence of the Islamic prophet in early Jewish or Christian texts. All the achievements of modern theology and philology like text and form criticism, the investigation of the historical and linguistic context of those texts and last, but not least, the science of comparative religion is mostly ignored in departments of Islamic Studies. Therefore, the last chapter but one is dedicated to the processes that take place during the emergence of a new religion, especially the frequent use and reinterpretation of elements of predecessor religions. Here, as in other chapters, a widened perspective is considered indispensable for a true assessment of the Qur'ān and the formation of Early Islam.

It is precisely this aiming at a broadened horizon which is the theme that runs through all the highly heterogeneous chapters of the present study. The presentation of phenomena which are being observed from a universal perspective allow the Arabic tongue and the religion of Islam to be located on a "phenomenological world map".

2. Oral or written tradition, which one is primary?

In the summary of his much debated book "The Syro-Aramaic Reading of the Koran" Christoph Luxenberg casts strong doubts on the primarily oral tradition of the Qur'ānic texts as postulated by Islamic tradition. In his opinion the text of the Qur'ān was not passed on orally, but in the form of undotted and unvocalized written manuscripts. Islamic tradition is not very consistent on this question, considering the special position of the so-called *rasm* (track, outline), i.e., the Arabic text without diacritical dots and vowels. Although the *rasm* does not possess the rank of a canonical text of reference, its importance for Islamic theologians is still considerable, as text variants are considered rather negligible as long as they do not affect the *rasm*.

Until today Muslims hold the axiomatic and unquestioned view that the Qur'ān was not *created* or even *authored*, but *revealed* to the prophet as the *literal* word of God. According to this view the original text is pre-existent to the created world and was preserved in a tablet in heaven. From there the angel Gabriel (Ar. Ğibrā'īl) transmitted it orally and in small portions to the prophet Muḥammad in the course of many years. The latter, who, according to tradition, was unable to read and write (Ar. *ummī*[8]), likewise passed it on orally. However, there are reports of early written manuscripts of surahs, mostly on improper writing materials such as bones, but their selection and the final redaction of the Qur'ān allegedly took place only at the time of the third caliph, 'Uṯmān[9], who reigned from 644 to 656 CE. Yet again, the primary text of reference during this alleged recension process is said to have been the phenomenal memory of the Arabs, not the extant written texts, a procedure already mentioned in reports about some incidents of text correction during the prophet's lifetime. To sum up, the traditional view holds it that oral tradition has always been *primary* and written tradition *secondary* in rank and importance.

This traditional Islamic view, however, contradicts a passage in the *Sīra* (biography) of the prophet about how 'Umar Ibn Al-Ḫaṭṭāb (581-644 CE, caliph after 634 CE) became a Muslim. The story presupposes very early written manuscripts of surahs:

> "('Umar is still a polytheist, his sister already having converted to Islam without him knowing about it; on the way to the prophet in order to kill him he meets an acquaintance whom he tells about his plans, only to get the following answer:) 'You deceive yourself, 'Umar', he answered, '[...] Had not you better go back to your own family and set their affairs in order? [...] Your brother-in-law, your nephew Sa'īd, and your sister Fāṭima, have both become Muslims [...], so you better go and deal with them.' Thereupon 'Umar returned to his sister and brother-in-law at the time when Khabbāb was with them with the manuscript of Ṭā Hā, which he was reading to them. [...] ... and he seized his brother-in-law Sa'īd, and his sister Fāṭima rose in defence of her husband, and he hit her and wounded her. [...] When 'Umar saw the blood on his sister he was sorry for what he had done and turned back and said to his sister, 'Give me this sheet which I heard you reading just now so that I may see just what it is which Muhammad has brought', for 'Umar could write. [...] (She is reluctant at first, but eventually gives him the sheet.) So 'Umar rose and washed himself and she gave him the page in which was Ṭā Hā, and when he had read the beginning he said, 'How fine and noble is this speech.' (On the same day he converts to Islam.)"[10] (the explanations in italics are my additions)

According to the text 'Umar was surprised and overwhelmed by an unknown text, moreover it is explicitly stressed that 'Umar could write, so there can be no doubt that what is described of him is definitely his "reading", not his "reciting" the surah. And finally it becomes clear that the manuscript mentioned in the text (the "sheet") was used for missionary purposes.

So even traditional Islamic scholarship is undecided about the core topic of the present contribution – the question about what is primary, the oral or the written transmission of the Qur'ān. My own study will investigate this matter in two steps:

In the first part the *rasm* (undotted Arabic text) of an exemplary Qur'ānic passage with attested variants will be analyzed and interpreted, in the second part the same question will be discussed departing from the analysis of texts from other traditions which are generally considered to have been transmitted only orally for a longer period of time.

These are Homer's Odyssey as the oldest literary monument of Ancient Greek, the Avesta as an Old Iranian (Zoroastrian) text and finally the Rigveda as the oldest document of Old Indian literature. In addition, an example from the Pāli canon, the oldest layer of Buddhist writings, will be discussed briefly.

In all these examples we may not take the information garnered from tradition about their composition at face value. Most of it was formulated centuries after and the authors of traditional reports about the transmission of early texts might have had an agenda of their own. Therefore, "text-inherent" evidence, i.e., evidence found exclusively within the text itself, *not* in accompanying traditions, is to be considered much more reliable if in conflict with such traditions. Such *text-inherent* evidence is, of course, not easy to find.

One example are *archaisms* that were *not recognized as such* at the time when the text was first written down. "Normal" archaisms are nothing special and rather numerous in most languages. An English sentence like "thou shalt not kill" is an archaism that might be heard in a Sunday sermon, but every native speaker knows it is the language of a few centuries ago, many will even know it is the wording of the King James Bible. An "undetected" archaism is much harder to find, first because it must be interpreted by the average modern speaker as something else, e.g. a foreign form, and second, because in order to detect it, the researcher must know a lot about older stages of the language. Whoever has watched the film "Forrest Gump" will remember the proverb "*stupid is as stupid does*". The fact that many modern native speakers do not really understand the grammar of this sentence can be seen in discussions on the internet[11]. Especially the meaning of "*as*" in this sentence seems to be a problem. The use of this little particle in expressions like "*as big as*" might mislead one to think that the meaning is something like "you are stupid *to the extent of* your stupid deeds". It is obvious that this meaning makes sense and is not too far away from the truth, yet the *grammatical interpretation* is flatly wrong. "*As*" here is an old *relative pronoun*, the sentence would have to be paraphrased as: "Stupid is *the one who* does stupid (things)".

In Chaucer's Middle English, this use was quite normal: "... we may do nothing but oonly swich thyng as we may doon rightfully", and Shakespeare wrote sentences like "... Maids as we are (As you like it)", "In every county as we go along (The Third Part of Henry the Sixth)". This use of "*as*" as a relative particle can still be found today in sentences like "even such *as* have ..." for "those who have ...", but nobody would say a sentence like "a topic *as* we talk about" today.

So how do such cases relate to our analysis of old texts? The answer is that we have to find peculiarities in the way the texts are written, which at the time of the first codification were considered to be oddities of the scribes, divine language or even mistakes, but which turn out to be *hidden archaisms* if analyzed with our modern knowledge of historical linguistics. This would be a litmus test for a considerable time gap between the *composition* of such texts and their first written attestation and thus prove a period of only oral transmission.

As the discussed languages will probably only be known to part of the readers, all texts will be presented in transliteration and two interlinear translations, one very literal, the second more readable, but still close enough to the text to enable the reader to comprehend the original syntax. In most cases at least a part of the text will also be given in the original script. In a separate right-hand column each grammatical form from the text will be analyzed and in some cases etymologized. Whenever a standard or at least well-known English translation exists, it will be added at the end of the text, together with interpretations from literature.

2.1 An example against the oral transmission of the Qur'ān

Before the example itself is discussed a general question must be answered: How can we *in general* decide whether the primary path of transmission was oral or through the written medium?

One way is to look at mistakes and variants in the manuscripts. What that means can be demonstrated with the help of a "constructed" English parallel as follows:

Let us assume that we have got a text written in English in an alphabet like the one used for Qur'ānic Arabic, i.e., with only about a dozen different letters and without vowel signs. Moreover, let us imagine that the following sentence is found in the oldest extant manuscript:

TH BK 'BT LR

And finally we assume that only later generations added diacritics and vowels to this sentence, but not consistently, so that in two different editions we have the following interpretations (in the case of Qur'ānic manuscripts they would be called *variants*):

1. The book about *lore.*
2. The book about *Larry.*

The two words sound very different, but the consonants are the same: "l" + "r". Therefore a logical conclusion would be that the variants "lore" and "Larry" represent different interpretations of the same defectively written form "LR".

One more thing could be said in this case, namely, that double consonants like in "Larry" must have been written as single consonants; otherwise the word could not have been confused with "lore". In any case, it is clear that the transmission must have been through the *written medium*, not the spoken word.

The situation, however, would be totally different, if the two variants were as follows:

1. The book about *lore.*
2. The book about *law.*

The two words "lore" and "law" go back to different "consonant skeletons", but they sound *almost* alike, some speakers of British English even pronounce them *exactly* alike[12]. Therefore the only logical explanation in this case would be that the primary path of transmission was through the *spoken medium.* One might even suspect that one of the transmitters had been an Englishman (or an old-fashioned New Yorker or Bostonian), whose pronunciation of the word "lore" was interpreted as "law" by the next member in the chain of transmitters.

The matters become even more complicated if we consider the ambiguity of Arabic consonants. If we apply this to our example, the letter "L" could e.g. represent both "r" and "l". Variant interpretations of the combination "LL" could therefore include words as different as *Larry, lorry, roar, rear, Lear, real, role, Laura* etc.

As we will see, examples like the one cited above with 'Larry' and 'lore', which make the assumption of a transmission through the written medium very probable and totally exclude oral transmission, abound in early manuscripts of the Qur'ān. One would expect Western scholars who deal with the history of the Qur'ān to unanimously dismiss the idea of its primarily oral transmission, but on the contrary, they nearly all accept the traditional view. And even when they dare to cast doubts on at least some of the details of 'Uṯmān's alleged redaction of the Qur'ān,[13] they do it very cautiously:

> "Their account, according to which the corpus of the first Koranic collection by the prophet's scribe Zaid ibn Ṯābit under Abū Bakr (reigned from 11-13/ 632-634 CE) or alternatively 'Umar (reigned 13-23/ 634-644 CE), from scattered fragments such as palm stalks, ostraca, shoulder bones and similar things, and only additionally amended from witnesses' memories, cannot withstand the results of literary analysis of the Koran and must be considered as strongly exaggerated."

The primarily oral transmission, however, is not questioned as a matter of principle:[14]

> "There are many traditional reports which state that parts of the Koran were memorized by numerous private people for liturgical purposes, in Medina even larger groups of surahs by official Koranic reciters. Their written codification thereby plays the role of a mnemonic device for the oral tradition (my emphasis; in German: 'Stütze für die mündliche Tradition'), functioning as aide memoire for teaching and learning purposes. As such it was a necessary prerequisite for the preservation of the long verses of Medinan surahs."

Only recently, especially following the publication of Christoph Luxenberg, some well-established orientalists have started to question the axiom of the primarily oral transmission of the Qur'ān, e.g. Manfred Kropp.[15] In the overwhelming majority of textbooks, encyclopedias, introductions and documentaries, however, the alleged oral transmission of the Qur'ān is still treated as a fact.

As one example of evidence to the contrary a Qur'ānic verse with an interesting variant, which had considerable impact on translations, will be discussed in the following (surah 13:31)[16]. The verse, to which Gerd-R. Puin directed my attention several months ago in a private conversation,[17] is only one of dozens of similar cases, a discussion of which he has meanwhile published.[18]

The text of the Cairene edition is as follows:

وَلَوْ أَنَّ قُرْءَانًا سُيِّرَتْ بِهِ ٱلْجِبَالُ أَوْ قُطِّعَتْ بِهِ ٱلْأَرْضُ أَوْ كُلِّمَ بِهِ ٱلْمَوْتَىٰ ۗ بَل لِّلَّهِ ٱلْأَمْرُ جَمِيعًا ۗ

أَفَلَمْ يَاْيْـَٔسِ ٱلَّذِينَ ءَامَنُوٓاْ أَن لَّوْ يَشَآءُ ٱللَّهُ لَهَدَى ٱلنَّاسَ جَمِيعًا

> wa-law 'anna qur'ānan suyyirat bihi l-ğibālu 'aw quṭṭiʿat bihi l-'arḍu 'aw kullima bihi l-mawtā bal li-llāhi l-'amru ğamīʿan 'a-fa-lam yay'asi llaḏīna 'āmanū[19] 'an law yašā'u llāhu la-hadā n-nāsa ğamīʿan

The gray form *yay'asi* is traditionally interpreted as 3rd sg. masc. jussive of a verb 'ya'isa (a,i) – to despair'. Pickthall and Paret[20] translate this verse differently:

> *Pickthall:* Had it been possible for a Lecture to cause the mountains to move, or the earth to be torn asunder, or the dead to speak, (this Qur'an would have done so). Nay, but Allah's is the whole command. Do not those who believe know that, had Allah willed, He could have guided all mankind?
>
> *Paret:* (...) For is it not so that those who believe have despaired (that everybody should immediately accept the right faith, and put up with it), that God, had he so desired, could have guided all mankind?
> (in the German original: Haben denn diejenigen, die glauben, nicht die Hoffnung aufgegeben (daß jedermann sogleich den rechten Glauben annehmen wird, und sich damit abgefunden), daß Gott, wenn er gewollt hätte, die Menschen allesamt rechtgeleitet hätte).

The reasons for these competing interpretations are found in Paret's commentary:

> "It is no wonder that the commentators have tried to reinterpret the verb ya'isa or ayisa respectively as its contrary, or to read the consonantal text (y'ys, variant yys) as a different verb (yatabaiyana, from tabaiyana (V) 'to become evident/ find out' or even to assume a downright lapse of the scribe."

As we can see, the latter reinterpretation presupposes a variant reading, which, according to Jeffery, can be found in Ibn Masʿūds edition:[21] *yatabayyan*.

In order to be able to understand why two phonetically and – in the modern writing system – graphically diverse forms (*yay'as* - يَا۟يْـَٔسِ vs. *yatabayyan* - يَتَبَيَّن) – can be confused, we have to have a closer look at their unvocalized form, their *rasm*:

	yatabayyan	yay'as
fully vocalized	يَتَبَيَّنْ	يَيْأَسْ
without vowels and diacritical dots	ٮٮٮٮں	ٮاْٮس
after elimination of the Sukūn	ٮٮٮٮں	ٮٮس

In the second line the *alif* in *yay'as* carries a "neutralising" *sukūn*, which is eliminated in the third line, thus giving us the resulting rasm of the form. If this *rasm* is compared to the one of the alternative form *yatabayyan*, it turns out to be identical, as the distances between the little hooks are only distinctive in certain fonts.

Therefore it is understandable that the alternative *reading* is in fact only a *reinterpretation* of the same *rasm*. Of course this does not exclude the existence of even more alternative interpretations, especially as the "classical" interpretation *yay'as* shows highly unusual orthographic traits, as Paret mentioned. The decisive conclusions we may draw from this example are the following:

- If the primary tradition had been oral, that would logically mean that while memorizing the Qur'ān, the two forms were mis-*heard*, i.e., *phonetically* mixed up.
- This, however, can absolutely be ruled out: Except for the first consonant, which is only a conjugational prefix, all other (root) consonants are different.
- The two forms consist of 2 vs. 5 syllables, so even their length is drastically different.

The only thing these two forms have in common is their *rasm*, which means that at the time of Ibn Masʿūd (allegedly died 32/ 653 CE) it must have been the *written text* and not *oral tradition* which had the highest authority among the Muslim scholars!

2.2 Parallel Case: The Homeric Epics

The Homeric epics – the Iliad and the Odyssey[22] – were composed in their final version around the year 800 BCE, which makes them the oldest literary monuments not only of Greek, but also of European literature. They display a number of extremely archaic traits, which were recognized as such already in the classical period and which are irrelevant as to the question of primarily oral or written transmission of the epics.

There is, however, one phenomenon hidden in the text, which must have been a problem for Greek reciters of the Classical period, the linguistic explanation of which was not found until the 19th century: In both epics there are a considerable number of verses, where short syllables appear in places where long syllables would be necessary for the meter, e.g.: Iliad 3, verse 172, where Helena says the following words:

αἰδοιός	τέ	μοί	ἐσσι	φίλε	ἑκυρέ	δεινός	τε
aidoiós	**te**	**moí**	**essi**	**phile**	**hekuré**	**deinós**	**te**
– – | –	˘	˘	| – ˘	˘ | ˘	˘ ˘ | ˘	– | –	˘
revered	*and*	*to me*	*you are*	*dear*	*father in law*	*terrible*	*and*

"Revered art thou in mine eyes, dear father of my husband, and dread."[23]

In the case of the two marked syllables the meter would require a long syllable. But if we look at the etymology of the word *hekurós* (father-in-law), we find out that it goes back to an older form **svekurós*, Sanskrit (the sacred language of Old India) *śvaśuras*, connected to German *Schwieger-* (*-in law*).

If we assume this older form to be the original one, we get our long syllable for the meter: phile + svekuré (short vowel + double consonant). The same applies to the second problematic word – *deinós*[24] –, which is preceded by a short syllable that, according to the meter, should be long. The word, however, goes back to *dveinós*, which explains this putative irregularity: The etymologically reconstructible consonant cluster "dv" at the beginning automatically makes the preceding syllable long, as required by the meter.

The v-sound, which in the oldest Greek written texts (the so-called Linear B) is still written as a Ϝ (the Greek letter is called *digamma*), was a normal phoneme in some Greek areas until the classical period and can be found in a number of dialect texts. So the word for king (classical Greek: ánax) is written as Ϝάναξ - wánax.

Cases like the one mentioned above, i.e., of a reconstructible *digamma* with metrical effects have been counted in Homer. It was found out that in 3354 cases such a digamma had a metric effect vs. 617 cases in which it did not[25]. A text-critical analysis might even shift the ratio further to the "archaic" side as many of the supposed cases of *digamma without metrical effect* can be explained away if we assume that the disturbingly short syllables were "repaired" by later scribes with the insertion of a short "filler" like δ or ῥ.

The side-by-side existence of digamma with and without metrical effect points at a minimum of two layers of composition. The verses containing a *digamma with metrical effect* must belong to the oldest layer, except in those cases where only a poetic formula[26] with such a digamma was used in a later verse. The style of the epics thus makes it quite difficult to cut the new verses from the old, but the fact remains that there must be a layer of older and one of younger verses.

But for our study we are less interested in the question of when these verses were *composed*, but rather in answering the question whether they were primarily *transmitted* through the *written* medium or *orally*. And the case of the digamma clearly leads to the conclusion that when the overwhelming majority of verses were first *sung*, the sound was still pronounced, but when they were first *written* down, it was no longer spoken. As such a sound change (total loss of a phoneme) usually takes centuries, during that period of time transmission must have been *oral*.

When mentioning Homeric epics, another phenomenon should be mentioned: Many later authors, the first one being Hesiod, imitated the mixed Homeric language – the basis being the Ionian dialect with strong Aeolian admixture wherever it suits the meter. Especially poetic formulae and proverbial quotations become current in later literature and can even be found in Platonic dialogues. As we will see, this is also relevant for the interpretation of Qur'ānic elements in later Arabic texts, as many *winged words* from the Qur'ān are used as fixed lexical items irrespective of their original meaning. A winged word like *qāba qawsayn* (two bows' length) might be chosen as a name of a newly founded company, but that does not necessarily mean that this putative meaning is what is meant in the Qur'ān.

A parallel example of a syntactic connection can be found at the beginning of the Iliad:

διαστήτην	ἐρισάντε
diastḗtēn	erisánte
they separated	*quarreling*
3rd sg. dual aor. ind.	dual pres. participle

The two dual forms were no longer in current use in the classical period. The finite form of the verb *diistēmi* was not recognized as a form of the aorist, as it did not have the otherwise obligatory augment *e-* as the first syllable (like *epáideusa* from *paidéuō*), apart from the fact that the dual as a number had become archaic in the classical period.

The following dual participle *erisánte* was equally or even more unintelligible, so it comes as no surprise that later generations erroneously interpreted it as an obscure finite form meaning "they quarreled", which would fit the context. What remained was the now superfluous first part **diastḗtēn.** Here again the context could help because the quarrel between Achilles and Agamemnon as described in the verse was about Briseis, the favorite slave girl of

Achilles. So the opaque form had to be reinterpreted so that it made sense: dià **stḗtēn** – because of a **Stete**. This imaginary "ghost word" *stētē* was later used in two poems of the 2nd century with the meaning "girl".

2.3 Parallel case: The Ancient Indian Rigveda

The Rigveda (< ṛc – praise song) is the oldest literary monument of Old Indian (Indo-Aryan[27]). It was composed from around 1500 BCE in a very archaic form of Sanskrit, which diverges from the later classical language about as much as Homeric Greek differs from the language of the New Testament. Therefore it is normally referred to as *Vedic Sanskrit* or simply *Vedic*.

The Rigveda consists of altogether 1028 hymns in ten books (Maṇḍalas), which are mostly hymns for different gods. Its emergence can be located in the Punjab (panj-āb – five rivers; etymologically connected to Greek *pente* [five] and Latin *āqua* [water]). The youngest books are the first and the tenth, so their order is not chronological.

The preservation of single hymns was originally the task of certain families, the term *preservation* here not only referring to the exact *wording*, but even to the exact *phonetic reproduction*, without which, according to pious Hindus, the magical effect of the texts is lost. The understanding of texts, however, was much less resistant to the ravages of time. So the commentary of Sāyaṇa (14th century CE) contains many explanations which, from a modern linguistic point of view, are untenable.

The Rigveda still is the holiest text of Hinduism and its hymns are still memorized by modern Brahmins, especially in the South of India. The first written records, however, are just a few hundred years old, and even if there should have been an earlier fixation of the text in writing, the information contained cannot have been the same as in the latest edition, as we will see. The oldest extant written monuments of Ancient India are the inscriptions of King Aśoka from the 2nd century BCE, so they are on average a millennium later than the Rigveda. Moreover, they are not in Sanskrit, but in Early Middle Indian (Prakrit) languages, which differ from Sanskrit like Old French from Latin. The Devanagarī alphabet, which is today used for Sanskrit, is again more than a millennium later and stems from the 9th century CE.

Classical Sanskrit, the already-mentioned later form of Vedic, is still a language of erudition and one of the official languages of India. Most, but not all its phonemic inventory and morphology is identical with Vedic, but its syntax shows very strong influence from Middle Indian languages, especially the nominal style and a predilection for passive constructions without finite verbal forms is typical.

Moreover, Vedic is based on a rather Western dialect, while Classical Sanskrit has features which point in the direction of the Ganges valley.

The most important meter of the Vedic hymns is the Gāyatrī, in which about 25% of the total text was composed. It consists of 3 verses containing 8 syllables each and is based on the following pattern:

⏑ – ⏑ ⏓ |

Some arguments for the primarily oral transmission of Vedic texts have already been mentioned, above all the fact that the oldest attested written documents of Ancient Indian are so much later than the Rigveda, but also the fact that they were not even written in the sacred language. Another important argument in favor of a late written fixation, however, is something much more difficult to detect: the *allophonic orthography* of Sanskrit.

Whenever a language is reduced to writing the normal problem is that the information fixed in its written form is less than what would be necessary to reconstruct the spoken word perfectly, in other words the writing system is *defective*. Russian has got a free accent (i.e., every syllable in a word might theoretically be stressed), but these accents are normally not written. So when learners of Russian are supposed to read a Russian text, even if they know the rules of pronunciation and orthography perfectly, they will make mistakes whenever they come across a word the stress position of which they do not know. Very few languages are exceptions to this tendency (Finnish is an example) and even a language like Latin is written in a defective writing system, e.g. *malus* – 'bad' (with a short a) and *mālus* – 'apple tree', (with a long ā) were written the same. Greek was better in this respect as far as short and long o/ō (ο - ω) and e/ē (ε - η) are concerned, but it did not distinguish the short and long versions of the vowels α, ι and υ. Moreover, the Greek accents were normally not written until a long time after the classical period.

Written Sanskrit, by contrast, does not only display all phonemically relevant differences, but also all assimilation processes, which therefore – even in Western linguistics – bear the Sanskrit name *Sandhi* (Sanskrit: *saṃdhi* (**संधि**) – "putting together"). In most languages, some of these processes may be reflected in the writing system, Greek *syn-* (with) becoming *sym-* before bilabials like in '*sym*-pathy' being an example, but most of them are neglected in orthographic systems, e.g. the devoicing of voiced consonants ("Auslautsverhärtung") in Russian or German. An English example is the so-called *intrusive R* in combinations like "I saw it", where many British speakers will insert an r-sound after "saw". In written Sanskrit, even the most minute assimilations are written, so that its orthography is more similar to a narrow phonetic transcription than to any "normal" spelling system.

So the two words *tat* (this) + *śrutva* (having heard), when appearing together, are written as *'tacchrutva'*, which does not make pronunciation easier, as the assimilation comes rather naturally: [tat + ɕrʊtʋɐ > tatɕʰrʊtʋɐ]. But it makes reading much more complicated, as all single elements are "glued together" in one *phonetic word* (in French there is the term 'mot phonétique'[28] for this phenomenon), which sometimes stretches over a whole line and has to be decoded and broken down into its original elements by the reader. Even "inevitable" assimilations like the palatal pronunciation of *n* [ɲ] before "c [tɕ]" and velar n/*ṅ* [ŋ] before velar consonants (*k, g, kh, gh*) are indicated by the separate letters transliterated as *ñ* and *ṅ*. Unlike in the Greek example mentioned above, where *sym-* replaces *syn-*, there are no *phonemes* that correspond to the letters *ñ* and *ṅ* (as opposed to the Greek phonemes /n/ and /m/), both sounds only being *allophones* of the same phoneme /n/. This would be tantamount to distinguishing *dark* and *light L*[29] or the difference in aspiration of the /t/ in "*take* [tʰeɪk]" and "*mistake* [mɪsˈteɪk]" in English.[30]

This 'much too exact' way of writing is a clear indication that the first fixation of the written text was felt to be a kind of *phonetic transcription* of the text for speakers/ readers who as a mother tongue spoke a different language already,[31] in order to preserve the exact *allophonic structure* of the language, without which the *magical* effect of the text recitation would be lost. The writing system that emerged was subsequently used for all texts written in Sanskrit.

The most meaningful argument for a primarily oral tradition of Rigveda texts, however, is to be found in the accent marks in the later editions – small horizontal strokes above and underneath the syllable, which interestingly did not denote stressed, but unstressed syllables. Classical Sanskrit as well as Middle Indian Languages like Pali did not possess phonemic stress or pitch accents, the stress position usually being on the penultimate if long, otherwise on the antepenultimate – much like in Latin or Classical Arabic. So the Sanskrit word corresponding to English *over*, Latin *super*, Greek *hyper* is *úpari*, with the stress on the first syllable. In the Rigveda, however, the form is *upári*, with the stress on the second syllable. This stress position is exactly the same we find in Greek: *hypér*. In Vedic Sanskrit, the accent is phonemic, i.e., words can be distinguished by it, like in Russian or Greek. The Vedic form *śatá-* (hundred) corresponds to the Greek *hekatón* and the Russian *sto*, which all have an accentuated last syllable.

These are, of course, only two examples of thousands of which prove that in Vedic Sanskrit, unlike in the later classical language, stress (or probably rather pitch) was phonemic and its position was mostly the same as in other Ancient Indo-European languages.

But could it not be – one might object – that there had been a long tradition of accent marks in Old Indian languages? That this cannot have been the case is demonstrated by the oldest written documents we have of Indo-Aryan languages, the already mentioned Aśoka rock edicts (2nd century BCE). They were written in a number of Early Middle Indian languages (very similar to, but not identical to Pali), the alphabet not indicating the accent position. Neither did other older alphabets, e.g. the Central Asian Brahmi script or the Karoṣṭhi alphabet dispose of any accent marks. The first accent marks are attested at a time roughly *two millenia* after the composition of the first hymns of the Rigveda. During the interim period the transmission *must necessarily have been oral.*

Even more convincing are cases where the exact nature of the accent is revealed not by the horizontal accent marks, but by the meter, as in the following example (first hymn of the Rigveda[32], verse 8):

8. rā́jantam **ad^{h}varā́ṇāṃ**
to the ruling *of sacrifices*
(to thee), ruling over sacrifices,

gopā́m **ṛtásya** **dī́divim /**
the guardian of world order the shining
the shining guardian of order,

várd^{h}amānaṃ **své** **dáme //**
to the growing *own* *in house*
growing in thine own house.

rā́jantam - acc. sg. part. pres. act. 'rāj - rule'
ad^{h}varā́ṇāṃ - metrically: ad^{h}varā́ṇāaṃ - gen. pl. 'ad^{h}vará- masc. sacrifice'
gopā́m - acc. sg. 'go-pā́ - guardian' < 'go fem. - cow'+'pā - protect'
ṛtásya - gen. sg. '**ṛtá** neutr. - settled order'
dī́divim - acc. sg. 'dī́divi - shining' < 'dī - shine'; cf. Latin *di*es - day
várd^{h}amānaṃ - gen. pl. part. med. 'vṛd^h - grow'
své - metrically bisyllabic: **suvé** - loc. sg. 'svá - poss. pronoun. - own' (cf. Latin 'suus')
dáme - loc. sg. 'dámas n. - house'; cf. Latin 'domus'

For metric reasons the last syllable of the genitive plural form *ad^{h}varā́ṇāṃ* counts as bisyllabic. This becomes logical, when we consider that the ending -*āṃ* corresponds to Greek -*ῶν* with a circumflex, a prolonged intonation responsible for the bisyllabic nature of the syllable. MacDonell therefore writes it "metrically restored" as: *ad^{h}varā́ṇā̃ṃ*.

The bisyllabic metrical value of this syllable parallel to the Greek form furthermore shows that the Vedic accent was a *pitch* rather than a *stress* accent (like in Ancient Greek or Lithuanian). The old intonational pattern on this accent (the term used in German publications: *Schleifton*) does not appear in the writing system at all, but the comparison with Greek proves that it is an old feature preserved *only by the meter* – not a tradition conscious of its nature – thus a *hidden archaism*.

A last argument for the oral transmission is the very rhythmical recitation of the Rigveda which is characterized by a strong differentiation of short and long syllables and an extremely elaborate memorization technique, which among other things inspired the Bulgarian linguist Georgi Losanov to his method of *suggestopaedia*[33].

2.4 Parallel case: The Old Iranian Avesta

The Avesta is the collection of religious texts of Zoroastrianism. It is written in the Old Iranian Avestan language, closely related to Old Persian, even though written in a totally different script, but also to a certain extent mutually intelligible with Old Indo-Aryan (Sanskrit): Whole passages of the Avesta can be transposed word by word into Vedic Sanskrit.

Two linguistic variants can be distinguished in the Avestan texts, so-called Older and Younger Avestan, their difference probably not only being that of different time layers, but also of different dialects, not unlike in the case of Vedic and Classical Sanskrit. The Avestan script is written from right to left and designates all consonant and vowel phonemes. It ultimately goes back to the Middle Iranian "Book Pahlavi" script, which itself is an offshoot of the Aramaic script. However, two major changes took place in the adaptation process. First, the so-called *heterograms* were no longer used. *Heterograms* are words written in Aramaic, but read/ pronounced in Persian, roughly comparable to cases like "e.g." from Latin *"exempli gratia"*, which is read as *"for example"*. The second problem to be solved in the adaptation of the foreign script was the fact that Book Pahlavi is very defective and in order to render the sacred text unambiguously several Book Pahlavi letters had to be differentiated. The Pahlavi letter  for example could designate the following phonemes: *a, ā,* x^v, *h* and x^i.

The newly created Avestan letters based on the Pahlavi letter with added diacritics[34] were the following:

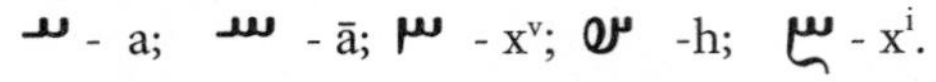

And finally the many ligatures of Book Pahlavi were abolished, which enormously facilitates reading the script. The following very short text sample of Old Avestan is the beginning of the most esoteric and difficult to understand Gatha, which, however, is interesting for both linguists and historians of religion and culture: Yasna 29. The text begins with a lamentation of the cow, who reproaches man of abusing her.

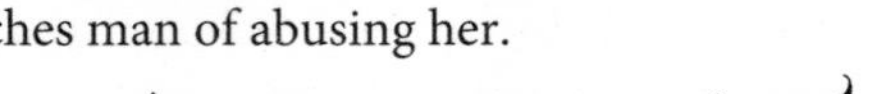

āuuru šuǝ g a ii b i a m ṣ̌ x

xṣ̌maibiia gǝuš uruuā

Paragraph 1
xš̹maibiiā gə̄uš uruuā gərəždā
with you of the cow the soul complains
The soul of the cow complains about you

xš̹maibiiā - pers. pron. 2nd pl. loc. 'with you' (alternative form: yūš̹maibiiā)
gə̄uš - gen. 'gāuš - cow' = vedic: goḥ
uruuā - 'soul'; etym. unclear
gərəždā – 3rd sg. injunctive medium 'complains = ved. gṛh - to complain'

The same argument for the primarily oral transmission that we found in the case of Vedic, namely the extremely exact, allophonic designation of sounds, is also applicable in the case of Avestan, the only difference lying in the fact that at the time of the first written fixation of Avestan texts the language was no longer spoken, not even as a language of learning, whereas Sanskrit as a late form of Vedic is still used as a medium of instruction in some Indian universities today! So the pronunciation of Avestan at the time when it was reduced to writing was certainly much more influenced by later Iranian languages than was the case with Vedic Sanskrit.

A good example is the written combination *"ərə"* or *"rə"* like in the word *gərəž-* = vedic *gṛh-* 'to complain' or *ərəzuuō* - 'right' = vedic *ṛjú-*. As the underlying phoneme, syllabic /ṛ/ [r̩], was not extant in Middle Iranian languages, it had to be replaced by the nearest equivalent.

In some cases, the intended pronunciation can hardly be reconstructed. Two allophones of /t/ can be found in Avestan: 't̰' und 'ϑ', but it is not clear what sounds they represent. The same applies the allophones 'š̹' and 'š́'.

Moreover, some originally short syllables are written as long ones, probably because during the recitation they were lengthened for euphonic reasons.

To sum up, what we have in written Avestan today is an attempt at transcribing Avestan pronunciation with a Middle Iranian accent. Although the writing system stems from the *Book Pahlavi*[35] script, the latter is much harder to read due to the heterograms[36] and its highly defective character.

All aspects of Avestan so far mentioned relate to the script and the question of the nature of transmission of sacred texts. But Islam and Zoroastrianism share more common ground, as even Zoroastrian concepts have found their way into the new religion. To adduce an example, the central concept, which today is usually translated as "religion", in Arabic is *dīn*. This word is thought to be of Avestan origin with Aramaic as intermediator.[37] The original Avestan form of the word is:

"*daēnā-*" fem. – (lit. "insight, conscience") religion; also deified; "self, personality"; cf. also *daēman* n. – eye (the seeing one)

< *dāy* – (ved. dī́dhye, dī́dhyaya) – pres. "*diδā, diδay* – to see, look at"

The word is connected to Modern Persian "*dīdan* - to see".

The original meaning here might be described as "the right view/ way of seeing things". Only later, under the Middle Persian form *dēn*, it adopted a meaning which comes close to the modern concept of *religion*, yet is not identical with it. However, there also seems to have been a truly Semitic root *d-y-n*. In Biblical Aramaic it bears the meaning "right, justice" as well as "tribunal, court", e.g.:

Dan. 4:37: וְאֹרְחָתֵהּ דִּין - wə-ʾōrḥāṯēh dīn - and His ways (are) *just*,

Dan. 7:22: וְדִינָא יְהִב - wə- ḏīnā yəhīḇ – and *judgment* was passed (Greek (LXX): καὶ τὴν κρίσιν ἔδωκε)

In Syriac, *judgment day* is *yawmā ḏə-ḏīnā*, which is the exact equivalent of Arabic *yawmu d-dīn*. The meaning "religion" does not make sense here at all. So the only logical conclusion is that two different roots, Semitic *d-y-n* (right, just[ice], judgment) and Iranian *dēn* (orig. "the right view", later "religion") merged into a new term, which bears both original meanings. The word was no longer perceived as an import, so that when the root served as a basis for new words, these reflected mostly the Iranian, not the Semitic meaning, e.g. "*dāna* - to profess a religion", "*dayyān* – pious".

2.5 Parallel Case: The Buddhist Pali Canon

The Pali Canon, the collection of scriptures of Theravada Buddhism,[38] was committed to writing on the island of Ceylon during the reign of Vaṭṭagāmaṇī (ca. 89-79 BCE) or even later. Before that the transmission is said to have been oral. The territory of emergence of the bulk of the texts might be located in the modern Indian states of Madhya Pradesh, the language of the written texts being the Middle Indian language *Pālī* with some admixture of *Māghadī*, the alleged mother tongue of the Buddha. The two 'languages' were in fact very close dialects probably not more divergent from each other than American and British English. They differ from Sanskrit like Italian from Latin.

The collection is also called *Tipiṭaka* (= Sanskrit *Tripiṭaka* = Three Baskets) and has the size of a large encyclopedia, thus being much more voluminous than both the Bible and the Qur'ān. Written transmission of Buddhist texts is a tradition in many monasteries, one of the reasons probably being the fact that in order to become a monk, one must be over 19 years old, an age too late to memorize a large text corpus (Hindu Brahmins start to memorize the Vedas as boys). Nevertheless I have had the opportunity to meet Buddhist monks in Thailand who dispose of a considerable repertoire of memorized Pali liturgical texts for recitation. For the following text sample the recitation was available on tape,[39] the most interesting aspect being the style of the recitation.

itipi[40]	*so*	bhagavā	**arahaṃ**
and so	this one (is an)	exalted one	worthy one
vacca		*so*	*bhagavā*
and this (should be said)		this (is an)	exalted one

itipi so bhagavā **sammā-sambuddho**
(the fully self-enlightened one)
vacca so bhagavā
itipi so bhagavā **vijjā-caraṇa-sampanno**
(perfect in knowledge and conduct)
vacca so bhagavā
itipi so bhagavā **sugato**
(having walked a good path)
vacca so bhagavā
itipi so bhagavā **lokavidū**
(who has known the world)
vacca so bhagavā

The pronunciation on the tape is strongly influenced by the Thai mother tongue of the reciters, as – due to a sound shift in Ancient Thai – some of the Indian letters are pronounced with their modern Thai values. The following shifts are the most conspicuous:

B and *bh* are pronounced as [p^{h}], analogously *d, dh* become [t^{h}] and *g, gh* change to [k^{h}]. The final syllable (long) -o is usually diphthongized to [o:^{a}], e.g. in *dhammo* - [t^{h}am:o:^{a}] (= dharma; religion, eternal law).

The tapes display an extremely rhythmical recitation style, the long vowels being very clearly enunciated and the underlying intonation being a monotonous singsong with alternately rising and falling rhythm. While actively participating in such a recitation in Thailand I could witness the desired "hypnotic" effect of the rhythm.

It should be noted that only a small part of the Tipitaka can be recited in such a way, the bulk of the text material being in narrative prose, which does not make it very apt for memorization. Nevertheless there must have been a certain period of time, presumably a few centuries, during which the texts were transmitted orally. The sheer size of the corpus and the fact that many stories, e.g. the biography of the Buddha, appear in several parts of the corpus and in very different versions, make it very likely that the number of people involved in the transmission must have been considerable, much like in the case of the Rigveda, the hymns of which were transmitted by several families. Unlike in the case of the latter, which is a text collection well preserved from modifications by its meter, the main body of the Tipitaka is much more likely to have been changed, adapted or amended.

2.6 Parallel Case: Classical Chinese literature before the Qin (秦) dynasty (221 - 206 BCE)

After the unification of China under the emperor Qín Shǐ Huáng 秦始皇, who has become famous in the West for his terracotta army in Xian, a number of important and useful reforms are said to have taken place in China, among others a land reform. Confucianism and the ideas connected to its philosophy, however, were seen as a potential danger – much like under Mao two millenia afterwards. So following the advice of his chancellor, the emperor allegedly ordered the burning of books and burying of scholars in the year 213 BCE, which led to the loss of a considerable part of the ancient literature. One of the few exceptions is said to have been the annals of the Qin state and several scientific books. According to the "Records of the Grand Historian" (Shǐjì 史記; written appr. 100 BCE), about 460 scholars were buried alive due to this order.

During the following Han (汉) dynasty part of the lost scriptures must have been reconstructed, even if with some distortions, allegedly as a lot of literature was transmitted orally.

Against this traditional view of an early oral transmission of Chinese literature, however, several arguments can be adduced:

- The numbers and the depiction of the events are considered to be exaggerated by modern scholars. The emperor might have seen scholars as his enemies and literary and scientific production declined under his reign, yet one should not forget that the reports about his cruelties and the burning of books were written long after his death and the end of his dynasty.
- Paper had not yet been invented, the main writing material being bamboo and wooden strips; the number of written books certainly was very small, furthermore the order might have been executed only locally.
- The private libraries of over 70 scholars are said to have survived.

For these reasons it seems very unlikely that it was primarily oral transmission which saved Chinese literature from oblivion.

Moreover, there is another strong argument against the exaggerated importance of oral tradition, an argument which lies hidden in the nature of the Chinese writing system itself: The Chinese script is originally a pictographic system, where every character represented a picture. Later, the combination of pictograms, often one designating the sounds, the other the meaning, completed the system, as can be seen from the following examples:

Character	*Pinyin*[41] *- IPA*[42] */ Basic Meaning*	*Analysis* *M = Middle Chinese*[43]
不	bù [`b̥u]- 'not'	Basic character without phonetic component; according to some authors the horizontal line designated an obstacle that prevents a tree from growing; one reading: M: 'pi̯e̯u'; 2nd reading: puət
人	rén [ˊɹə̃n] - 'man, human'	Basic character, also a radical (i.e., used as part of other characters, in this case slightly different: 亻 – picture of a stickman M: ˛ńźi̯ĕn
星	xīng [¯ɕiŋ]- 'star'	Sound-meaning compound: 日 - rì - 'sun' + phonetic element: 生 - shēng - 'be born' M: ˛sieng
安	ān [¯an] - 'peace(ful)'	2 meaning elements: 宀 - miān - 'roof' + 女 - nǚ - 'woman' ("peace is where a woman is under a roof" or "quiet like a woman in the house"; cf. the old word designating a wife: 内人- nèirén (inside + human) or the current Japanese word 家内 - kanai - 'wife (of the speaker, not the one spoken to)': the Chinese reading would be: jiānèi (not used in Chinese); i.e., 'family' + interior'); M: ˛˙ân
問	wèn [`wə̃n]- 'ask'	Modern simplified: 问 phonetic element 門 - mén - (simplified: 门) + meaning element: 口- kǒu - 'mouth'; M: mi̯uən'

These few examples should suffice to demonstrate that the script does not merely reflect the sounds of words, but conveys a whole gamut of extra information, in some cases even philosophical views and "Weltanschauung". So for a poet the choice of words has always been the choice of *characters*!

As the Chinese writing system is not phonetic – the phonetic elements in the compounds reflect the pronunciation at the time the characters were invented and they do not adapt – sound shifts in the course of the centuries are ignored. This means that many of the poems, which in Chinese make ample use of rhyme, will lose this literary device if sound shifts make rhyming words dissimilar. This is a bit like the English ending *-ough*, which in the modern stage of the language does not rhyme any more in words like *through*, *cough* and *although*. But whoever memorizes songs or poems knows that rhymes "stick" in your memory much better than prose. So sound changes would have destroyed this memorization aid.

Another negative effect of sound changes is the fact that many words will become phonetically indistinguishable. "Boy" and "buoy" would be an example in English, "saw" and "sore" only in British English. The tactics employed in such a case are the use of word combinations as a good means to disambiguate: "let's eat rice" instead of "let's eat", "look-see" instead of simple and ambiguous "look".

How far this phonetic neutralization of phonemic oppositions could go can be demonstrated by a quotation from Karlgren:[44]

> "Ancient Chinese **k^{y}i** 'bench', kyei 'already', kyie 'singing-girl', kiei 'hen', **ki̯ĕt** 'lucky', **ki̯ət** 'finish', **ki̯əp** 'to reach', ki̯ək 'urgent', **kiek** 'to beat', tsiei 'to cross a stream', **dz'i̯əp** 'to collect', **dz'i̯ĕt** 'sickness', **tsi̯äk** 'spine', **tsiek** 'to spin', **tsi̯ək** 'immediately' have all coincided in Pekinese **chi.**" *(my emphasis)*

Karlgren reconstructed the common ancestor of modern dialects with the help of dialect comparison, comparison with other languages from the same linguistic phylum, e.g. Tibetan, and by using old rhyming dictionaries. The reconstructed language – "Ancient Chinese (today usually called Middle Chinese)" – was spoken around 600 CE.

An even older stage of the language, in Karlgren's terminology "Archaic Chinese (today: Old Chinese)" was used in the oldest extant literary monuments like the Shījīng (诗经, appr. 600-800 BCE). Karlgren even tried to reconstruct this stage with the help of rhymes. An example of the sound shift from Old to Middle to Modern Chinese can also be found in Karlgren:[45] *(Karlgren's transcription)*

出 - Old Chin.: *t'i̯wət - Middle Ch.: tś'i̯uĕt - Mandarin: chū [¯tʂ^{h}u]

For all these reasons it is more than doubtful that Chinese literature was primarily transmitted orally and could therefore be saved in spite of the burning of books. The latter event is either a legend or an exaggeration.

2.7 Examples of recent oral literature

The well-known theory of oral composition is connected with the names Milman Parry und Albert B. Lord, which was first applied to reconstruct the history of the Homeric epics, later to assess other forms of oral literature, has been summarized by Renate Jacobi as follows:[46]

> "The epic singer of tales does not recite a fixed text, but creates his poem as a kind of 'improvisation bound by tradition' anew every time he recites it. Emergence, recitation and tradition of the epic constitute one process, the phases of which cannot be separated. Therefore, the search for the urtext or the original in oral literatures is doomed to failure, for every epic text can possess several authentic versions, which during the transition from the oral to

> the written literary period come into being through the fixation of different recitations."

The Parry-Lord theory is, among others, based on the comparison of homeric with contemporary Serbo-Croatian epics, which the two researchers had recorded and transcribed.[47] In this context Parry explicitly mentions the preservative character of rhyme, which makes it next to impossible to create a new version during the recitation.[48]

However, oral literature is not confined to poetry; prose can also be transmitted orally. An excellent example are the stories of Jefet Schwili, a Yemenite Jew, of whom about 200 short and medium-sized prose narratives were recorded a few years after his emigration to Israel. Studying the collection can tell us a lot about how the human brain works and how it does not. When he told the stories, his memory oriented itself sequentially around the respective plot, *not* the wording, which becomes evident from the fact that the stories he had learnt during his youth in Arabic could be transposed into Hebrew without any problem. The contents of the stories, however, did not remain totally unchanged. So in his stories the narrator uses words for modern pieces of furniture that were not used in the Yemen he grew up in. In some cases, two versions of the same story are told, which, however, he considers two different stories because of some minor details. So it is obvious that hardly any of the stories had remained unchanged. Without the preserving effect of rhyme and meter a prose story can muster very little resistance to modifications and adaptations[49].

In this context the notes of Alois Musil about war poems of the Rwala tribe[50] (Northern Arabian Peninsula) are certainly interesting. According to Musil the poems originate first as a number of verses, which are recited within the family. Then the comments of the listeners lead to additions and modifications, e.g. about events not mentioned. Around different campfires different versions of the same poem are then told, depending on the reactions of the listeners and the mood of the reciter. In the case of criticism verses are left out or exchanged for others.

As most poems do not really contain many individual traits – hunting, raiding, being brave and fathering sons are not very distinctive activities – it is very common that whole passages can be taken over from already existing poems by just replacing the names.

The recitation takes place with the so-called "Rbâba" as a background instrument, the verses being sung. The meter is based on vowel length and end rhyme[51].

The following two examples represent literature which is without the trace of a doubt oral, as they were only recorded in the 19th century by linguists, one in Kasakh, a Turkic language of the former Soviet Union, the other one in the Bantu language Tswana (Southern Africa).

More examples to exemplify the use of respective memory aids, – rhyme, meter, alliteration etc. – are from Old Germanic languages, Thai, Somali and Finnish.

2.7.1 Praise Poems of Tswana Chiefs

The following short text samples from Tswana[52] are praise poems on former and current chiefs at the time of the recording. According to Schapera the texts have neither meter nor rhyme, yet "metric rhythm/dynamic stress" plays an important role as a stylistic means during the recitation and distinguishes the texts from prose. This involves clear emphasis on the penultimate with periodic additional accentuation of the penultimate of certain words, followed by a pause. Thus, the poem can be subdivided into smaller units, which can be uttered in one breath, which creates an additional rhythmic element.

Another feature of these texts are intentionally chosen archaic words or archaic meanings of words, which are felt to appeal to the listeners. The "verses" are marked by pauses; accentuation is indicated by vowel-lengthening. The transcription does not reflect the phonemically relevant tones of Tswana.

Of many praise poems several versions exist, e.g. three versions of the poem on chief Pheto of the Kgatla have been recorded, all by the same poet (Klaas Segogwane), but of different length.

In another case a poem was composed from parts of other poems of another author. In one case some verses of another poet were used, but 11 lines (of originally 156) were left out. Moreover, the order of verses was changed, which was not much of a problem, as no coherent story is told.

In the analysis in the right hand column the single forms are given in the form they have in Brown's[53] dictionary. The modern orthography differs in some cases, e.g. compound word forms are often written separately, which is not the case in the poem, probably in order to preserve rhythmical units. The translation at the end of each verse is the one from the anthology:

dile kwasakêng jagabômogolo
they were in Kraal of maternal kin
they were in the Kraal of his maternal kin

dile kwasakêng jaga Tshukudu
they were in Kraal of Tshukudu
they were in the Kraal of Tshukudu

kwasakêng - 'kwa ... eng' + (le)saka - a cattle kraal
jaga-bô-mogolo - 'of (*ga* before kinship terms) + 'bô - prefix of collective kinship terms' + '(mo)goloo - elder brother/ sister (or brother/sister-in-law'
Tshukudu - personal name

The interesting feature here is the parallelism of the first three words of the two verses; cf. also chapter 3.6 and its use in Finnish.

In the next example another stylistic device can be found: chiastic structure, i.e., the end of the first line is resumed in the following line:

Batho	**bakilê**	**batsênwa**	**kelegorwe**
people	*once*	*were entered*	*green tree-snake*

People were once attacked by a tree snake,

kenôga	**etala,**	**tlhômaganya-batho**	
by snake	*green*	*dogger*	*man*

by a green snake, dogger of people

ba-tho - pl. '(mo)tho - man, human'; corresponds to 'Bantu'); ba - class prefix plural
ba-kilê - class pref. + 'kile - then'
ba-tsênwa - class pref. + pass. 'to be possessed, entered'
ke-legorwe - 'by' + 'green tree-snake'
ke-nôga - 'by' + 'snake'
e-tala - adj.-conjunctive prefix + 'green'
tlhômaganya-batho - 'add to; go to one place or thing after another' + 'man' = 'man dogger'

In some cases, the last word is virtually resumed for want of a matching synonym:

oême	**fôo,**	**ketlê**	**kegolaêlê,**
stand	*there*	*that I*	*send you with message*

halt there, that I may command you,

kegolaêlê,	**kegonêyê**		**dikgang**
send you with message	*that I you*	*give*	*news*

may command you and give you a message

o-ême < 'èma - stand'
ke-tlê - pref 1st sg. + aux. verb fut. subjunctive
ke-go-laêlê - 1st sg. + 2. obj. affix + 'laèla - send with a message, give a charge'
ke-go-nêyê - 1st sg. + 2nd pers. + 'naea - give'
di-kgang - class pref. pl. pl. + 'kgañ - news'

Note: The prefix of the 2nd person "go" is spelled "gu" in modern orthography, in order to distinguish it from the infinitive prefix "go", their pronunciation being the same.

One last feature of this short example of oral literature should not remain unmentioned: The older the poems (especially after the chiefs have died), the shorter they become!

2.7.2 Kyz Zhibek – A Kazakh Love Poem

The next example is from Kazakhstan[54]. Contrary to popular belief, nomad life is rather boring. The only distraction for Kazakh nomads before the introduction of modern mass media were the shows of vagrant minstrels (in Kazakh: ақын/aqın, Kyrgyz: акын/akyn, Russian: акын). During the recitation the minstrels ad-libbed a sung version of the epic, always accompanied by the *dombra*, a mandolin-like string instrument. The plots of most epics center around a hero (in Kazakh: batyr).[55] Probably the most famous Kazakh epic, Kyz (= girl; cf. Turkish: kız) Zhibek, however, is a love story.

It tells the story of a girl named Zhibek and her fiancé Tölegen, who is mortally wounded by Bekejan, a former rejected admirer of Zhibek and member of the rival Kipchak tribe. Before he dies he asks to tell the event to his brother Sansyzbai. Meanwhile Zhibek finds out about the murder and six of her brothers kill Bekejan. After that two followers of Bekejan tell the Kalmyk Koren about Zhibek's beauty and one of her brothers, fearing Koren's power, promises her in marriage to him. When Koren arrives to demand his right, he pressures her and has her arrested. She is saved by Sansyzbai at the last minute and escapes together with him. When Koren follows them, Sansyzbai kills him in a duel and finally marries Zhibek.

This basic plot is narrated in several totally different versions, a Russian translation always accompanying the Kazakh original in the edition used. Although the plot is the same, the wording must have emerged independently, as can be seen in the two beginnings of two of the versions:

1st Text sample: Version recorded in 1887:

Emendations of the redactor are in pointy brackets, words to be deleted in square brackets, the lines correspond to the verses in the text.

Бұрынғы өткен заманда
Burɨnɣɨ ötken zamanda
formerly having passed time-in
Once, a long time ago,

<Қалың> қазақ ішінде,
<Qalɨŋ> qazaq išinde,
stout Kazakh middle-in
amongst numerous Kazakhs

Базарбай деген [бай] бар еді,
Bazarbay degen [bay] bar edi,
Bazabay named master there was
there lived a master (Bey) named Bazabay.

burɨnɣɨ- formerly
öt-ken - 'pass + part.'
zaman-da - 'time + loc.'
qalɨŋ - stout, deep, thick
qazaq - Kazakh
iš-i-n-de - 'interior + 3rd sg. + connecting cons. + loc.'
Bazarbay - pers. name
de-gen - 'say, name + partic. suff.'
bay - rich; master
bar - there is/are
e-di - 'to be' + 3rd sg. pret.
tört - four
tuwlik - cattle

Төрт түлік малға сай еді,
Tört tuwlik malɣa say edi,
four kinds of cattle abundant was
Of all four kinds of cattle he had abundantly,

[Төлеген деген] Бір баласы бар еді.
[Tölegen degen] Bir balasɨ bar edi.
Tölegen named one child-his there was
and he had a child named Tölegen.

Translation of the Russian Version:
A long time ago
amongst [numerous] Kazakhs,
[lived] a Bey (chieftain) named Bazarbai.
cattle he had in great abundance,
someone called Tölegen was his only son.

mal-ɣa - 'cattle + dat.'; tört tuwlik mal - four kinds of cattle (horses, camels, sheep and horned cattle)
say - abundant
edi - see above
Tölegen - personal name (possibly < töle - pay, make up a loss)
degen - see above 'named'
bir - 'one'
bala-s-ɨ - 'child + connecting cons. + 3rd sg.'
bar - 'there is/are'
edi - 'was'

The last sentence, in which Tölegen appears as his only son, is in slight contradiction to a later episode, in which Tölegen calls Sansyzbai his "only brother".

The second version, recorded in Kazan in 1900, can also be found in an illustrated edition with big letters, probably made for children[56], which comes close to a certain "canonization". The beginning gives us an impression of how a recitation must have taken place amongst nomads and underlines that "vagrant minstrel" was in the first place a *profession* aiming at *making money*:

Мен сөйлейін, жарандар
Men söyleyin, jarandar
I will say people
Folks, I want to tell you something!

Тындап құлақ салыңыз
Tɨndap kulaq salɨŋɨz
listening ear prick
So prick up your ears and listen!

Аз әңгіме қозғайын
Az əŋgime qozɣayɨn
a bit talk I will stir
I will make a bit of a fuss,

men - 'I'
söyle-yin - 'to speak + jussive 1st sg.'
jaran-dar - 'people (-dar - pl. - suffix)'
tɨŋda-p - 'to listen + converb'
kulaq - 'ear'
salɨŋɨz - 'sal- to build; put; listen + 2nd pl. imper.'; 'kulaq sal- - to listen'
az - 'a bit'
əŋgime - 'conversation'
qozɣa-yɨn - to stir, excite + jussive 1st sg.'
kel-gen-in-še - 'kel - to come + pres. part. + 3rd

Келгенінше	**халіміз.**
Kelgeninše	**xalimiz.**
as far as reaches	*our strength*

as far as I can.

Зекетсіз	**болса**	**пайда**	**жоқ**
Zeketsiz	**bolsa**	**payda**	**joq**
without donation	*if were*	*profit*	*there is no*

Whatever riches you might have gathered

Қасықтап	**жиған**	**малыңыз.**
Qasɨqtan	**jiɣan**	**malɨŋɨz**
from spoon	*gathered*	*your cattle/ belongings*

what is it worth without donation(to me)!

Қыз	**Жібекті**	**тыңдаңыз,**
Qɨz	**Jibekti**	**tɨŋdaŋɨz**
girl	*Zhibek*	*listen*

Listen (to the story of) the girl Zhibek!

Замандас	**еркек,**	**ұрғашы,**
Zamandas	**erkek,**	**urɣašɨ**
of same age	*man*	*woman*

(You old) man and woman of the same age (as myself)!

Ақ	**сақалды**	**шалыңыз ...**
Aq	**saqaldɨ**	**šalɨŋɨz...**
white	*bearded*	*you old men*

You white-bearded old men

Қыз	**Жібектің**	**сөзіне**
Qɨz	**Jibektiŋ**	**sözine**
girl	*Zhibek-of*	*speech-her-to*

Now totally satisfy your curiosity

Енді	**әбден**	**қаныңыз ...**
Endi	**əbden**	**qanɨŋɨz...**
totally	*now*	*quench your thirst*

about the story of the girl Zhibek!

sg. +še'; a bit unclear: - gen+še - 'as long as'

xal-imiz - 'power, ability + 1st pl.'; possibly from Ar. ḥāl - state

zeket-siz - '= Ar. zakāt (?) - almsgiving + 'without', i.e., 'without donation (to the minstrel)'

bol-sa - 'to be + conditional (3rd sg.)'

payda - 'benefit, profit < Ar. fā'ida'

joq - 'there is/are no

qasɨq-tan - 'spoon' + abl.

ji-ɣan - 'to collect + part.'

mal-ɨŋɨz - 'cattle+2nd pl.'; probably < Ar. māl - belongings

qɨz - 'girl'

Jibek-ti - personal name (jibek - silk) + acc.

tɨŋda-ŋɨz - 'to listen + imp. 2nd pl.'

zamandas - 'person of the same age < Ar. zamān - time'

erkek - 'man'

urɣašɨ - 'woman'

aq - 'white'

saqaldɨ - 'bearded' < 'saqal - beard'

šal-ɨŋɨz - 'old man + 2nd pl.'

Jibektiŋ - Jibek + gen.

söz-i-n-e - 'speech+3rd sg. poss. + connecting cons. + dat.'

endi - 'now'

əbden - 'totally'

qan-ɨŋɨz - 'to quench thirst + imper. 2nd pl.'

Translation of the Russian version:

Folks, I will tell you (something),
so listen well!
I will tell you bit by bit,
as far as I can!
Unless you give *zeketa* (i.e., a donation; my emphasis)
what is the use of riches (literally: the things gathered on a spoon)
Listen about the girl Zhibek,
you of the same age (as me), men and women,
white-bearded old men!
For the story of the girl Zhibek
now quench your thirst!

The Russian version also contains sheet music with parts of the epic, which give a good impression of how it was recited for the recording.

2.8 Indo-European Poetic Language

Already in the 19th century comparative linguistic and literature studies in the field of Indo-European linguistics yielded parallels between the old Indo-European epics which could hardly be explained as independent developments, i.e., a Greek form like μέγα κλέος (méga kléos) "great glory" has an exact equivalent in Sanskrit *máhi śrávas*, which both go back to Indo-European *méĝəh$_2$ ḱléu̯os; another example is Sanskrit *sū́rasya cakraḥ* - wheel of the sun - Greek: ἡλίου κύκλος *(hēlíu kýklos)* - Old Norse *sunnu hvél*, Old English *sunnan hweogul*[57].

These and many other examples justify the assumption that already at the time of the Indo-European *ursprache* (protolanguage), i.e., several millenia before any of the later daughter languages were first reduced to writing, a poetic tradition must have existed, which logically must have been exclusively oral.

Moreover, even some characteristics of this poetic language can be inferred by comparing the later daughter languages. So in Vedic, as well as in Greek poetry, which both are characterized by quantitative meters, there are sequences of verses with – ˘ ˘| and – ˘ |.

Avestan seems to be an exception, as its meters are not based on quantity, but on the number of syllables per verse. This, however, can easily be explained by the fact that in final position the vowels of polysyllabic words lose their fixed quantity[58].

Another parallel can be found in the names of gods, e.g.: Greek Ζεῦ πάτερ (Zeû páter) – Latin: Jupiter – Vedic: dyauṣ pitā (Zeus father)[59].

Even in the topics there are parallels. In the Indian *Vanaparvan*, which is a part of the national epic *Mahābhārata*, the god of death Yama hands over a supernatural weapon to Arjuna, so that "the earth should be disburdened".

What is meant becomes clear later: to alleviate the earth, which is suffering from overpopulation.

The same concept of an overburdened earth can be found in a scholia of the Cod. Venetus A about the fifth verse of the Iliad:

> "It is said that the earth, burdened by the number of men, asked Zeus to be alleviated; therefore Zeus first caused the war of Thebes, which caused many to ... ."[60]

And finally there is a common Indo-European designation for the poet himself, describing him as "builder of verses":

Greek: ἐπέων τέκτονες (epéōn téktones) – "builders of words"

Rigveda: (6, 32, 1 d) vácāṃsy āsā́ sthávirāya takṣam –
"I will put together words with my mouth (in the following song) for the portly one (the god Indra)".

Avestan: vacastašti – "putting together of words (Fügung von Worten)" < * ék^{u}os - word + *tek's - to carpenter.[61]

2.9 Concluding Remarks about the Evidence

The question asked at the beginning of the present study – "Oral or written tradition, which one is primary?"– can be answered as follows for the single texts investigated:

Generally speaking, a clear indication of primarily oral transmission of a text are *hidden archaisms*, which only centuries later are detected as such. Moreover, it must be taken into consideration that not every text is equally well suitable for memorization. Decisive memory aids are features like rhyme, a plot and above all meter, in other words the possibility of following a rhythm during the recitation.

The latter point is especially conspicuous for all texts investigated except for the Qur'ān, in a way that for normal Western listeners their performance resembles singing more than text recitation.

Of course it might be adduced that the Qur'ān is also "sung" by sometimes famous reciters (in Arabic: qāri', pl. qurrā < qara'a - to read, recite), who follow the complicated rules of *taǧwīd*, but as will be shown later, this never happens in a clearly fixed rhythm, at least not for the vast majority of verses. Instead certain syllables (according to the reciter) are held for seconds and sung to a mostly improvised melody, which inevitably destroys even the slightest remnant of text-inherent rhythm and replaces it by new, recitation-based rhythmic patterns.[62]

To put it in a nutshell: The recitation of the Pali-Canon, the Rigveda, the Odyssey or the epic Kyz Zhibek could easily be accompanied by a drum (which was definitely done in the case of the homeric epics and Kyz Zhibek), in the case of the Qur'ān this would not be possible.

The second litmus test, the hidden archaisms, could only be detected in three of the investigated texts.

In the Rigveda it is the inherited Indo-European accent positions and its allophonic spelling which reflects very archaic speech habits. All things considered the memory of the Old Indians or rather their mnemotechnics, especially as far as phonetic exactitude is concerned, must have been phenomenal and far exceed anything else in human history.

Qur'ānic recitation, on the other hand, seems to be of much more recent origin and did not even retain the old pronunciation of the letter *ǧīm*, which used to be pronounced as a [g] like in modern Egyptian Arabic.

In the case of the Homeric epics it is especially the metric effect of the old Digamma, which is the main piece of evidence pointing at a long oral transmission of at least a major part of their verses.

The main argument for originally oral transmission in the case of Avestan is its exact allophonic writing, which, however, betrays traces of the later, Middle Iranian mother tongue of the reciters at the time the texts were reduced to writing.

If again the language of the Qur'ān is compared to Classical Arabic, then the deviations in vocabulary, grammar and spelling do not support the view that old features were retained, but rather – especially if Christoph Luxenberg's findings are taken into consideration – that Syriac served as donor language for both words and grammatical constructions.

The main argument for the primarily written transmission of the Qur'ān, however, is the authority of the *rasm*-text (undotted consonant skeleton text) on the one hand, and the alternative readings on the other. These readings cannot possibly be explained by mis-*hearings*, i.e., erroneous *oral* transmission, but only by mis-*readings*, i.e., erroneous interpretation of the undotted consonant text.

At this point, orthodox Muslims would certainly adduce the argument that memorizing the Qur'ān is still a flourishing art in the modern Islamic world, and especially the fact that many famous reciters are blind clearly proves the mainly oral text transmission. It is undoubtedly true that today probably more than ever the Qur'ān is being memorized. Qur'ānic recitation in the media is downright ubiquitous, as a bit of channel hopping on satellite TV quickly shows. The question, however, is not whether it is possible – with incredible effort – to memorize the Qur'ān, but rather whether the *Qur'ān in its modern form* of the Cairene edition can be traced back to the 7th century with the help of an uninterrupted chain of transmitters who primarily relied on the spoken, not the written word. The answer to this latter question is a clear NO. The modern tradition of memorization emerged only *after the final written fixation* of the Qur'ānic texts and is consequently secondary.

This does of course not exclude the possibility of some kind of oral tradition *before* this written fixation, but then again it was probably rather the transmission of texts written in a language strongly influenced by Syriac, and not in what was later to be standardized as Classical Arabic. If the Qur'ānic verses are reconstructed in this Syriac-imprinted Qur'ānic language (probably without many of the classical endings), it might well be that at least some verses will get a meter![63] Lüling actually did reconstruct Arabic without endings and with a meter. He presumed that pre-Islamic Christian hymns, which originally had a meter, were *intentionally* turned into prose in order not to betray their origin. The way in which Günter Lüling's career was destroyed after publication of his findings has been described among others by Ibn Rawandi.[64]

After the first, still defective reduction to writing of Qur'ānic verses the general understanding of this Syriac-imprinted Arabic must have started to quickly fade away, which would explain the numerous misreadings.

The two text samples from Tswana and Kazakh have been chosen to clarify a common misunderstanding about oral literature. If somewhere in the world a linguist or anthropologist records hitherto unknown stories, poems or myths, then that is not *the* oral literature of a people, but at best *one version* of this literature, in most cases only an *ad hoc* version created during the recording. Powell[65] arrives at similar conclusions for the Homeric epics:

> "... since the Iliad and the Odyssey, though products of oral composition, could not have been preserved in the form we have them without the aid of writing. This conclusion is a necessary consequence of the fact that for an oral poet there is not such a thing as a fixed text. Even if, contrary to his training, an oral poet wanted to memorize a song 'word for word', he could not have done so, because verbatim memorization is the result of endless repetition and before writing there was no fixed text to be repeated. Hence the Iliad and the Odyssey that we possess today represent a single version, the one that was written down. The moment of recording of the Iliad and the Odyssey is also the moment of their creation."

The Kazakh and African examples furthermore demonstrate that Homer's "profession", which must have existed already in Proto-Indo-European times, has not yet died out.

3. Some Preservatives of Oral Literature

The following section will be dedicated to important poetic devices, which – as a side-effect – facilitate memorization. Moreover, it will be demonstrated that not all of these devices are possible or make sense in every language.

3.1 Metre, Syllable Counting, Refrain and Repetition

Some sort of meter is possible in every language of the world, its simplest form being based on syllable counting. Quantity-based meters like the Greek hexameter or the Old Indian Gayatrī, however, are only possible in languages which distinguish long and short syllables, which again normally means that there must be an opposition between long and short vowels.

In some tone languages like Thai there are further restrictions concerning the position of tones or the repetition of tones in a verse.

Another very common stylistic device is refrain, e.g. in the text sample from the Pali canon. In many fairy tales a whole passage is told several times with minor variations, e.g. the wishing-table, the gold-ass, and the cudgel in the sack (in German: "Tischchen deck dich, Goldesel und Knüppel aus dem Sack") in Grimm's famous fairy tale.

Symbolic numbers are also favored by many cultures, just think of the *twelve* ("dozen" does not fit in the metric system, but also: 12 disciples, 12 tribes of Israel), *forty* (the Hebrews spent 40 years in the Sinai, Moses spent "forty days and forty nights" on Mount Sinai, Jesus fasted in the desert for 40 days etc.), *seven* (7 heavens, 7 mortal sins, 7 Samurai), *five* (5 wounds of Christ on the cross, 5 precepts and 5 skandhas in Buddhism), *three* (*Trinity* in Christianity, *Tipitaka* [Three Baskets; the name of the canon] in Buddhism, *Trimūrti* [the Hindu triad of Brahmā, Viṣṇu and Śiva]).

A whole chapter of an article by I. Lawrence Conrad is dedicated to the symbolic use of the number "forty",[66] which (like 400 or 4000) often only means "many".

3.2 Rhymes

Rhymes can be found in a vast number of languages, their importance[67] or appeal, however, differs greatly.

What follows now are examples from English and German to demonstrate a few rhyme schemes. The first example is from Jonathan Swift's poem Stella's birthday (1719):

Stella this day is thirty-four,	A
(We shan't dispute a year or more:)	A
However, Stella, be not tr*oubled*,	B
Although thy size and years are d*oubled*,	B
Since first I saw thee at sixteen,	C
The brightest virgin on the green;	C
So little is thy form decl**in'd**;	D
Made up so largely in thy m**ind**.	D

Rhyme schemes do not have to be so simple, however, just take Edgar Allan Poe's famous poem *The Raven*:

Once upon a midnight dreary, while I pondered, weak and weary,	AA
Over many a quaint and curious volume of forgotten lore	B
While I nodded, nearly napping, suddenly there came a tapping,	CC
As of some one gently rapping, r*apping* at my chamber door	CB
'Tis some visitor," I muttered, "tapping at my chamber door	B
Only this and nothing more."	B

Common schemes in both German and English are ABAB - ACAC, ABBA or AABB. Rhymes usually affect between one and in rarer cases three syllables. The sound correspondences do not have to be perfect, especially in German many "impure" rhymes, e.g. l*ei*de - Fr*eu*de, sch*ö*n - g*eh*n, are very common. In English poetry this corresponds a bit to so-called *forced* or *oblique* rhymes, e.g. mine – bind. If only the vowels are the same, we talk about *assonances*, e.g. grea*t* - brea*k*, a German example would be "Schwindsucht und Bindung". It is typical for Spanish poetry, but is also found in Old High German literature, German Romantic poetry and the Qur'ān, where it is called *loose rhyme* (in Arabic: *sagʿ*).

Another very special kind of rhyme are *spoonerisms* (German: Schüttelreim), where consonants are switched intentionally or unintentionally, a phenomenon very common in linguistic change, e.g. Russian kto vs. Croatian tko; Latin miraculum – span. milagro; French Roland vs. Italian: **Or**lando.

The term goes back to Reverend William Archibald Spooner (1844–1930), who was notorious for speech errors like "the Lord is a shoving leopard" instead of "loving shepherd". It is common as a stylistic device in many languages, e.g. in Thai, where it is the basis of many puns and a bread-and-butter device for stand-up comedians. In German it can also be found in verses like the following:

Ist das dort nicht der Suppen***h***ahn,
den gestern wir noch ***h***uppen sah'n?
or:
Wenn liebenswert ihr hübschen Zofen ***s***eid,
dann finden selbst die Philo***s***ophen Zeit.

As we could see in cases like Roland - Orlando, it also appears with vowels. The famous German philosopher Schopenhauer remarked after the death of his landlady: "Obit ***a***nus – ***a***bit onus." (The old woman is dead, the burden is gone.)[68]

Spoonerisms are less a kind of rhyme than a special form of the next phenomenon: alliterations.

3.3 Alliteration

In many languages, virtually everywhere in the world, alliteration as in the English "*P*eter *P*iper *p*icked a *p*eck of *p*ickled *p*eppers" plays an important role, e.g. in old Germanic poetry (im German called *Stabreim*), but also in non-Indo-European languages. As we will see, it is a regular poetic device in Somali, Thai and Finnish.

In English, the word "rhyme" is used both as a noun and as a verb. Something similar can be found in other Germanic languages. In German the verb "staben" is the verb corresponding to "Stabreim" (alliterative verse). Alliterative verse as the binding agent in old German poetry emerged around the middle of the first millennium BCE, mainly because the accent position shifted to the first syllable, which thus gained a prominent position and made a recitation with a lot of emphasis possible, especially on the initial consonant. This shall be demonstrated with a few examples:

Example: Old Germanic

Alliterative verse was recited or sung based on a melody, possibly accompanied by instruments. In England it survived longer than on the continent and started to disappear only around 1500 CE, in Iceland it still flourishes today.

A verse consists of two halves bound together by alliteration. Every single half verse must necessarily contain at least one alliterative sound. The German term *Stabreim* comes from *Stab* (pl. Stäbe; English: staff). A "Stab" is a stressed syllable with the initial consonant or consonant cluster (e.g. sp, st, sk, sw, br) to be found in other stressed syllables[69], examples would be:

Old High German:[70] *Otfried of Weissenberg's Evangelienbuch (Gospel Book, around 870, II. 14,1)*

Sīd	**thō**	**thésen**	**thingon**	||	**fuar**	**Krist**	**zēn héimingon**
since	there	those	things		went	Christ	to (his) home

= after these events

Old Englisch:[71] *The Battle of Brunanburh, 937*

ofer	**bráde**	**brímu**	||	**Brýtene**	**sōhtan**
over	the broad	sea		the Britons	(they) sought

Bēowulf[72] (my translation)

Bēowulf	**wæs**	**brēme,**	||	**blǣd**	**wīde**	**spranȝ**
Beowulf	was	famous		(his) fame	widely	spread
Scyldes	**eafera,**		||	**Scedelandum in.**		
of Scyld's	son			to the Scede-lands (Danish lands)		

Old Saxon (= Old Low German)

suuīdo	**fród**	**gumo**	||	**frấon sīnum**	... thíonon thórfti)
the very old	[=wise]	man		to Lord his	(=the Saviour) should serve

Old Norse:[73] *from the Codex Regius of the Older Edda*

Þic	**hefir**	**Brynhildr**	||	**bǫl**	**at**	**gerva**
thee	has	Brynhild		havoc	to	wreak
heiptar	**hvattan,**		||	**harm**	**at**	**vinna**
to hatred	provoked			harm	to	win

Alliterations are ubiquitous, even in everyday language (e.g. "busy as a bee", "rack and ruin", German: "Feuer und Flamme", "Land und Leute" etc.). It is especially often used in proverbs and slogans:

English:	Dunkin' Donuts, Coca-Cola
	You'll never put a better bit of butter on your knife."
	(advertising slogan for butter)
German:	Milch macht müde Männer munter
Latin:	veni vidi vici
	Ceterum censeo Carthaginem esse delendam.
Greek:	Πόλεμος παντῶν μεν πατὴρ ἐστι
	Pólemos pantõn men patḗr esti (Heraclitus)
	(War is the father of all things.)
Lithuanian[74]:	Dẽwas dãwė dantìs, dẽwas dű́s ir dű́nos.
	God gave teeth God will give also bread

The alliteration would survive in the Latin translation:

Deus dedit dentes, deus dabit et panem.

Arabic:	Lā 'ilāha illā llāhu

Example: Thai

Thai is an isolating (i.e., non-inflecting) language belonging to the Tai-Kadai-language family. Contrary to common belief Thailand does not belong to the Chinese, but to the Indian civilization, which a brief look into a dictionary will show: The number of Sanskrit (and to a lesser degree Pali) words is comparable to the number of French and Latin words in English. In the sample text[75] the respective alliterative sounds are shaded gray or underlined. The tonemes, for which complicated limitations have to be applied, are indicated, the corresponding rules, however, will not be analyzed.

รูปแร้งดูร่างร้าย	รุงรัง
rûûp **r**έέŋ duu **r**ââŋ **r**áάj	**r**uŋ **r**aŋ
ภาคนอกเพียงพึงชัง	ชั่วช้า
phââk nɔ̂ɔ̂k phiaŋ phɯŋ chaŋ	chûa cháá
เสพย์สัตว์ที่มรณัง	นฤโทษ
sèèp sàt thîî moranaŋ	narɯ thôôt

Analysis:

รูป	แร้ง	ดู	ร่าง	ร้าย
[rûûp	**rέέŋ**	**duu**	**rââŋ**	**ráάj]**
image	*vulture*	*looks*	*form*	*bad*

By outer looks vultures are ugly and disheveled.

rûûp - figure, picture < Sanskr. rūpa
rέέŋ - vulture
duu - to look (like)
rââŋ - form
ráάj - cruel, wild
ruŋ raŋ - unorderly

\- รุง รัง
[ruŋ raŋ]
unorderly

ภาค นอก เพียง พึง ชัง
[phââk nɔ̂ɔk phiaŋ phuŋ chaŋ]
appearance outer even one must abominate
The appearance is even disgusting

\- ชั่ว ช้า
[chûa cháá]
evil shameless
evil and shameless

เสพย์ สัตว์ ที่ มรณัง
[sèèp sàt thîî moranaŋ]
eat animals which dead
(But) it eats only animals, which are already dead,
นฤ โทษ
naruı thôôt]
without guilt
(therefore) it is without guilt (= bad karma)

phââk nɔ̂ɔk - outside appearance < Sanskr. bhāga + **nɔ̂ɔk** - outside
phiaŋ - until, even
phuŋ - one has to
chaŋ - to abominate
chûa - evil
cháá - shameless
sèèp - devour
sàt - animal < Sanskr. satva
thîî - place; relative indicator
moranaŋ - dead < Sanskr. maranaṃ
naruı - free of, without
thôôt - guilt < Sanskr. doṣa

The poem is recited with a marked melody, which is also determined by the tonemes, and an equally marked rhythm.

In the poem the (ugly) vulture is contrasted against the (beautiful) ibis. But while the ugly bird lives on dead animals, his beautiful counterpart has to kill his prey. The contents reflect the Buddhist view that killing of animals creates bad karma. So the author draws the conclusion that it is preferable to be reborn a vulture, even if the price is ugliness, than to accrue bad karma as a beautiful bird.

Example: Somali

In the following text sample from Somali oral literature[76] alliteration (Somali: higgaad) is the by far most important stylistic device.

The same alliterative sound is kept throughout the whole poem, so that up to 100 lines of text are dominated by a "g":

Dhaachaan ka gabanggaabsaday e **waygu geliseen e**
Gooddiga Ban Cawl buu fakhrigu **geed ku leeyahay e**
Gaajada huggeedii miyaa **galabta i saaray?**

Translation in the anthology
I lately sought this plight for myself and you put me into it,

On the edge of the 'Awl Plain, poverty has a tree (to sit under)
Have the garments of hunger been put on me this evening?

Analysis:

Dhaachaan ka gabanggaabsaday e
lately of decided for myself and
Recently I decided for myself and

waygu geliseen e
I in you entered (= you entered in me) and
you urged me to it.

Gooddiga Ban Cawl buu fakhrigu
side the plain gazelle it poverty the
On the edge of the Gazelle Plain, poverty

geed ku leeyahay e
tree in has and
has a tree, and

Gaajada huggeedii miyaa
hunger the clothes his is it so that he/it
have the clothes of hunger been donned on me

galabta i saaray?
evening the me has put on
tonight?

dhaachaan = dhawaan (?) - recently
ka - prep. of, from
gabanggaabsaday - 1st sg. pret. gabagabsasho (?) (< 'gabagabeyn - decide') 'decide for yourself'
e - 'and then'
wa-y-gu - 'waa - focus particle + i (obj. pron. 1st sg. + ku - prep. in'
geliseen - 2nd pl. pret. 'gelin - enter'
gooddi-ga - 'side + defin. article'
ban - m. 'plain'
cawl - f. 'gazelle'
buu - focus particle 'baa + suff. 3rd sg. uu
fakhri-gu = 'faqri m. - poverty + def. art.' < Ar. faqr
geed - m. 'tree'
ku - prep. 'in'
leeyahay - 'has' < 'leh - having' + 'yahay - 3rd sg. 'to be'
gaaja-da - f. 'hunger'
hug-geed-ii - 'xuga m. - clothes' + poss. 3rd sg. + determinative suffix
miyaa - question particle ma + 3rd sg.
galab-ta - f. 'afternoon + def. article'
i - 1st sg. obj. pron.
saaray - 3rd sg. pret. saarid - put (on)

Notes:

The text was recorded before the introduction of modern Somali spelling (for the creation of which the author of the collection, B. W. Andrzejewski, was asked for advice). Moreover, the text might have some dialect admixture, which makes some forms a bit unclear. The grammatical term *preposition* in the analysis is a bit misleading in Somali, as their position is not in front of the noun they refer to, but in front of the verb! On page 45 Andrzejewski makes the following remarks about oral tradition:

> It is only natural that in this process of transmission some distortion occurs, but comparison of different versions of the same poem usually shows a surprisingly high degree of fidelity to the original. This is due to a large extent to the formal rigidity of Somali poetry: if one word is substituted for another, for instance, it must still keep to the rules of alliteration, thus limiting very considerably the number of possible changes.

This clearly shows the importance of the "preservative" alliteration in Somali poetry.

3.4 Parallelism in the Finnish Kalevala

The Kalevala, the national epic of Finland, is also a good example for the use of alliteration (in Finnish: alku-sointu), there is, however, yet another important stylistic and at the same time mnemotechnical device: *parallelism*, for which it is even more typical. The Kalevala consists of 50 songs (in Finnish: runo) with a total of 22795 verses. The basic text consists of old Finnish heroic songs, which were composed during the early era of Scandinavian Christianity, the oldest ones even before the 12th century in the south-west of Finland. The collection was gathered and recorded by Elias Lönnrot and his assistants on eleven field trips through the country from the oral tradition of singers and published in the years 1835 and 1836. The most characteristic meter (runo-mitta) is the trochaic tetrameter:

– ˘ | – ˘ | – ˘ | – ˘ |

According to the rule, the first syllable of the word must be long, i.e., must contain a long vowel or a diphthong and end in a consonant. The poetry was performed in a kind of singing feud, accompanied by music.

The first text sample is from the internet (Wikipedia – search word "Kalevala") and is the beginning of the Kalevala, the second was quoted from Robert Englund's[77] textbook of Finnish. The analysis and translation were made by myself.

1:1-9)[1]

Mieleni minun tekevi,
temper my me makes
My desire urges me

mieleni - 'mieli - mind, temper + 1st sg. poss.
minun - pers. pron. 1st sg. gen.
tekevi = tekee < 3rd sg. pres. 'tehdä - do,

aivoni **ajattelevi**
brain my *thinks*
(and) my brain thinks (of it)

lähteäni **laulamahan,**
beginning my *to sing*
to start singing

saa'ani **sanelemahan,**
ability my *to recite*
to be able to chant

sukuvirttä **suoltamahan,**
clan-songs *to let glide*
to let (you) hear the songs of our clans

lajivirttä **laulamahan.**
kinds-of-songs *to sing*
to sing the kind of songs of old.

John Martin Crawford translated this verse as follows (1888):
Mastered by desire impulsive,
By a mighty inward urging,
I am ready now for singing,
Ready to begin the chanting
Of our nation's ancient folk-song
Handed down from by-gone ages.

A few lines from the Aino myth:

Tuopa Aino, **neito** **nuori**
Tuopa Aino, *girl* *young*
Tuopa Aino, a young girl,

Sisar **nuoren** **Joukahaisen**
sister *of young* *of Joukahainen*
sister of young Joukahainen,

Läksi **luutoa** **lehosta,**
went out *of brooms* *from grove*
went out to fetch brooms from the grove

make'
aivoni - 'aivo - brain' + poss. 1st sg.
ajattelevi - 3rd sg. pres. 'ajatella - think'
lähteä-ni - 'lähtea - begin; go away' + poss. 1st sg.
laulamahan - inf. III illative of 'laulaa - to sing, to verse (runoillen)'
saa'ani = 'saada - get; can; move' + poss. 1st sg.
sanelemahan - inf. III illativ 'sanella - recite' < sana - word
sukuvirttä - 'suku - clan, family' + part. sg. virsi - song
suoltamahan - inf. III illative 'suoltaa - to let glide'
lajivirttä - 'laji - kind (of)' + part. sg. virsi - song
laulamahan - see above

Tuopa Aino - pers. name
neito - girl, virgin
nuori - young
sisar - sister
nuoren - gen.
Joukahaisen - gen. sg. pers. name 'Joukahainen'
läksi - 3rd sg. pret. 'lähteä - go out'; to be added: hakemaan - inf. III Ill. 'hakea - fetch'
luutoa = luutaa - part. sg. 'luuta - broom'
lehosta = lehdosta - elative sg. 'lehto -

Vastaksia varvikosta. *of birch-twigs from brush-wood* *birch-twigs from the brush-wood.*	grove' **vastaksia** - partitive pl. 'vastas, -ksen birch-twig **varvikosta** - elative sg. 'varvikko - brushwood'

Notes:

The Kalevala was written in the dialect of Karelia, therefore *saa'a* = *saada*, *luutoa* = *luutaa* (partitive), *laulamahan* = *laulamaan*, *tekevi* = *teki* (impf.).

The alliterations are shaded in gray, parallelisms can be found in the paraphrase at the beginning of a verse of an idea propounded at the end of the preceding verse, e.g. "... brooms from the grove" – "... birch-twigs from the brush-wood".

3.5 The use of poetic devices in different languages

Not all theoretically – i.e., phonetically or grammatically – possible poetic devices are used in a specific language. In order to have an appealing effect, it may not be too easy to use them and they may not occur too often by chance. In Bantu-languages like Tswana or Kiswahili for example, alliterations occur automatically, as the class prefixes of the subject have to be attached to adjectives, verbs and even particles, e.g.:

Kiswahili: The simple question and answer "How old is the big child now? - 3 years, and the small child 2 years." would be rendered in Kiswahili as follows:[78]

m-toto m -kubwa mi-aka mi-ngapi sasa? -
child big years how many now
mi-aka mi-tatu, na m-toto m-dogo mi-aka mi-wili.
years three and child small years two

So here alliteration is downright inevitable, thus it would not be considered much of an "art" to use it.

In Qur'ānic Arabic it actually does appear, its appearance is, however, rather sporadic and never regular as in Finnish or Thai. The most famous example is the beginning of the *šahāda* (creed): لا إله إلا الله – lā ilāha illā ḷḷāhu – *there is no God except Allah.*

Rhymes occur in a great number of languages, but again their appealing effect is vastly different: as a rule of thumb the importance of rhymes grows with the number of syllables which are possible in a language.

For this reason rhymes were probably too uninteresting in Classical Latin (unlike in Medieval Latin), because too many words ended in -us, -um, -a etc., so it was very easy to find a fitting rhyme. Instead the verse was based on syllable quantity. In the Middle Ages this had to change, as vowel quantity (*mālus - apple tree* vs. *malus - bad*) had disappeared, because it was not reflected in the written language. Therefore Latin poets of that era started to use the poetic device they knew from their mother tongues: rhyme.

Rhyme is of utmost importance in German with its many syllables, which is mainly due to the fact that consonant clusters are allowed at the end of a syllable, e.g. in the 2nd sg. pres. of "schrumpfen": du schrumpfst – "you shrink". For a poet it would be very difficult to find a word which would rhyme with such a form. In French, on the other hand, consonant clusters do not occur in this position and most syllables end in a vowel, of which French has fewer than German. So the phonotactic[79] peculiarities of a language determine the usefulness and ultimately the use of this poetic device.

In Arabic, most syllables end in a vowel (except if *in pausa*, when case endings are dropped). The relatively small number of vowels (six) and diphthongs (two) diminishes the appeal of rhymes. So it is not surprising that in Arabic poetry rhyme is more based on the last *consonant* than on the last syllable ending as in European languages. In the Qur'ān, what is called *loose rhyme* (sağʿ) should rather be called assonance, as will be shown in the next section.

3.6 Poetic devices in the Qur'ān

The following text samples from several surahs of the Qur'ān will demonstrate which poetic devices are used in the Qur'ān and which are not. The transcription is a bit unusual as it will reflect some of the phonemically relevant assimilations. It is not a real transliteration of the graphemic structure of the Arabic script. So the defective writing of the long "ā" will not be marked. Assimilations will be explained in the right-hand corner. The translation in the third line is Pickthall's.

Example 1: Surat al-Fatiḥa 1: 1-7

بِسْمِ اللّهِ الرَّحْمَنِ الرَّحِيمِ

الْحَمْدُ للّهِ رَبِّ الْعَالَمِينَ

الرَّحْمنِ الرَّحِيمِ

مَالِكِ يَوْمِ الدِّينِ

إِيَّاكَ نَعْبُدُ وإِيَّاكَ نَسْتَعِينُ

اهدِنَا الصِّرَاطَ المُستَقِيمَ

صِرَاطَ الَّذِينَ أَنعَمتَ عَلَيهِمْ غَيرِ المَغضُوبِ عَلَيهِمْ وَلاَ الضَّالِّينَ

1. bi-smi-llāhi -r-raḥmāni -r-raḥīm^{i}
In the name of God the benevolent the merciful
In the name of Allah, the Beneficent, the Merciful.

2. al-ḥamdu li-llāhi rabbi -l-ᶜālamīn^{a}
*the praise to God Lord of the worlds**
Praise be to Allah, Lord of the Worlds,

3. ar-raḥmāni -r-raḥīm^{i}
the benevolent the merciful
The Beneficent, the Merciful:

4. māliki yawmi -d-dīn^{i}
king/ruler of day of judgment
*Owner of the Day of Judgment, **.*

5. iyyāka naᶜbudu wa
(it is) you we worship and
Thee (alone) we worship;

iyyāka nastaᶜīn^{u}
(it is) you we ask for help
Thee alone we ask for help.

6. ihdinā -ṣ-ṣirāṭa -l- mustaqīm^{a}
guide us the path the straight
*Show us the straight path****,*

b-ismi - 'in/ through' + gen. sg. 'ism - name'
-llāhi - gen. 'god'
-r-raḥmāni - def. art. + gen. raḥmān- benevolent'
-r-raḥīm^{i} - def. art. + gen. 'raḥīm - merciful'
al-ḥamdu - def. art. + 'praise'
li-llāhi - 'zu' + gen. 'god'
rabbi - gen. 'rabb - lord'
-l-ᶜālamīn^{a} - gen. pl. 'ᶜālam - world'*
ar-raḥmāni - def. art. + gen. merciful'
māliki - gen. 'mālik - ruler'; variant: 'malik - king'
yawmi - gen. 'yawm - day'
d-dīn^{i} - def. art. + gen. 'dīn - religion; judgment'
ʾiyyā-ka - particle introducing an acc. + suff. 2nd sg.
naᶜbudu - 1st pl. impf. 'ᶜabada - serve, adore'
wa - 'and'
nastaᶜīn^{u} - 1st pl. impf. X. St. 'istaᶜāna - ask for help' < 'ᶜawn - help'
ʾihdi-nā - imp. 2nd sg. 'hadā - lead (the right path)' + suff. 1st pl.

ṣ-ṣirāṭa - def. art. + 'ṣirāt - way'
l-mustaqīm^{a} - def. art. + 'mustaqīm - upright, straight' = part. 'istaqāma - stand upright'

7. ṣirāṭa **-llaḏīna** **anʿamta** **ʿalayhim**
the path *of those* *you bestow favor* *on them*
The path of those whom Thou hast favored;

ġayri **-l-maġḍūbi**
another one (than the one) *the angried*
*Not (the path***) of those who earn Thine anger*

ʿalayhim **wa-lā** **-ḍ-ḍāllīn**^{a}
upon them *and not* *(the one) of those astray*
nor of those who go astray

ṣirāṭa - acc. sg. 'way'
-llaḏīna - gen. pl. rel. pron.
anʿamta - 2nd sg. perf. IV. St. ',anʿama ʿalay - bestow favor on' < 'naʿima - live without sorrows'
ʿalay-him - 'prep. 'against' + suff. 3rd pl.
ġayri - gen. sg. 'ġayr - other, different from'
l-maġḍūbi - def. art. + gen. part. pass. 'ġaḍiba ʿalay - be angry about'
wa-lā - 'and not'
ḍ-ḍāllīn^{a} - def. art. + gen. pl. 'ḍāll - going astray' < 'ḍalla'

It should be noted that many Qur'ān commentaries interpret "those who earn thine anger" as referring to Jews and "those who go astray" as referring to Christians. Paret mentions in his commentary that *ʿālamūn* is an Aramaic loanword and means "Bewohner der Welt" (inhabitants of the world).

Notes about the translation:

Final vowel written as superscript letters are dropped in pausal position.

* According to Luxenberg[80] "**ʿālamīn**^{a} (the worlds)" should be read as a dual, i.e., "**ʿālamayn**^{a} (two worlds)", of which both have the same *rasm* (undotted consonant skeleton). What is meant is *this world* and the *afterworld.*

** The translation "*Day of Judgment*" for *yawmu d-dīn*, which sounds very Christian, is indeed so, because it perfectly corresponds to the Aramaic "yawmā ḏ-ḏīnā (ܝܘܡܐ ܕܕܝܢܐ)", which occurs several times in the New Testament (e.g. Mt. 11, 22).

***Luxenberg[81] does not consider *ṣirāṭa* as a Latin loanword from "strata", but as one from Syro-Aramaic, which is still used in modern Arabic: *saṭr* - line (with metathesis); if this should be the case, the word *mustaqīm* would have to be translated as "straight".

Poetic devices:

- This surah is the best known and most recited one of the whole Qur'ān. It must be known by heart before a conversion and is recited during the five compulsory prayers a total of 17 times per day. What is very conspicuous throughout the whole Qur'ān is the already mentioned *loose rhyme.* In the above example the rhyming syllables are shaded in grey. Some of them are impure rhymes (-īm vs. -īn) or their occurrence might be interpreted as following a pattern: (-īm - īn - īm - īn)[82].
- There is also a case of parallelism to be found in this surah: *allaḏīna anʿamta ʿalayhim* vs. *ġayri l-maġḍūbi ʿalayhim.*
- The formula *ar-raḥmāni -r-raḥīm^{i}*, which occurs twice in the surah must have been interpreted by some German orientalists as an alliteration, otherwise the German rendering "Allah der Allerbarmer" cannot be explained.

Example 2: Surat al-Baqara 2: 2-3

ذَلِكَ الْكِتَابُ لاَ رَيْبَ فِيهِ هُدًى لِّلْمُتَّقِينَ

الَّذِينَ يُؤْمِنُونَ بِالْغَيْبِ وَيُقِيمُونَ الصَّلاةَ وَمِمَّا رَزَقْنَاهُمْ يُنفِقُونَ

2.2	**ḏālika**	**-l-kitābu**	**lā**	**rayba**
	that	*the book*	*no*	*doubt*

This is the Scripture whereof there is no doubt,

fīhi	**hudàl-**	**li**	**-l-muttaqīn^{a}**
in it	*guidance*	*to*	*the righteous*

a guidance unto those who ward off (evil).

ḏālika - nom. sg. 'that' - kitābu - def. art. + 'kitāb - book'

lā rayba - 'no' + acc. 'rayb - doubt, suspicion, uncertainty'

fī-hi - 'in' + suff. 3rd sg. m. hudàl = hudan (assim.) - acc. sg. 'hudan - (right) guidance'

li -l-muttaqīn^{a} - 'for' + def. art. + gen. pl. 'muttaq - righteous' = part. VIII. St. 'ittaqā - fear God; to beware of' < 'waqà - protect'

2.3 allaḏīna	**yu'minūna**	**bi-**
who	*believe*	*in*

Who believe in the unseen,

-l-ġaybi	**wa- yuqīmūna**	**-ṣ-ṣalāta**
the unseen and	*constantly* keep up*	*the prayer*

and establish worship,

wa-mim-mā	**razaqnāhum**	**yunfiqūn**^{a}
and of what	*we bestowed*	*spend / donate*

and spend of that We have bestowed upon them;

allaḏīna - gen. pl. rel. pron.
yu'minūna - 3rd pl. m. impf. IV. St.''āmana - believe'
bi- l-ġaybi - 'in, by, at' + def. art. + gen. 'ġayb - the unseen'
wa- yuqīmūna - 'and' + 3rd pl. impf. IV. St. 'aqāma - put up, fix, perform'*
ṣ-ṣalāta - def. art. + acc. 'ṣalāt - prayer'
wa-mim-mā = 'and' + 'min - of (assim.) + mā - what'
razaqnā-hum - 1st pl. perf. 'razaqa - bestow' + suff. 1st pl.
yunfiqūn^{a} - 3rd pl. impf. IV. St. 'anfaqa - spend (money), donate'

* the addition of the adverb "constantly" reflects the meaning of the Syriac equivalent of the word *'aqīm* - to keep constantly.

Poetic devices:

The most striking point in the above surah is the use of the gray shaded verbal forms, because they represent both rhymes as well as alliteration (a nasal radical). Arabic poets usually consider the endings *-īna* and *-ūna* as rhyming, which might cast some doubt on the nature of Arabic case endings in general. All languages which possess rhymes usually make allowances for consonantal variation (the rhymes thus become assonances), but are much stricter with vowels. That two vowels as different as [u:] (back and rounded) and [i:] (front and unrounded) should be able to form a rhyme is phonetically unthinkable.

Example 3: Surat az-Zalzala 99: 1-5

إِذَا زُلْزِلَتِ الْأَرْضُ زِلْزَالَهَا

وَأَخْرَجَتِ الْأَرْضُ أَثْقَالَهَا

وَقَالَ الْإِنسَانُ مَا لَهَا

يَوْمَئِذٍ تُحَدِّثُ أَخْبَارَهَا

بِأَنَّ رَبَّكَ أَوْحَى لَهَا

99.1. iḏā zulzilati -l-ʾarḍu zilzāla-hā
when is shaken the earth her quake
When Earth is shaken with her (final) earthquake

2. wa- aḫrağati -l-arḍu aṯqāla-hā
and unloads the earth her burdens
And Earth yieldeth up her burdens,

3. wa-qāla -l-insānu mā la-hā
and speaks the man what to her
And man saith: What aileth her?

4. yawmaʾiḏin tuḥaddaṯu* aḫbāra-hā
on that day will tell messages her
That day she will relate her chronicles,

5. bi-anna rabbaka awḥā la-hā
because your lord revealed to her
Because thy Lord inspireth her.

iḏā - 'if, when'
zulzilati - 3rd sg. perf. pass. f. 'zalzala - cause to tremble'
l-ʾarḍu - def. art. + nom. 'arḍ - earth'
zilzāla-hā - acc. sg. 'zilzāl - earthquake' + suff. 3rd sg. f.
wa-ʾaḫrağati - 3rd sg. Pf. IV. st. 'aḫrağa - to take out, unload'
l-ʾarḍu - see above
ʾaṯqāla-hā - acc. pl. 'ṯaql - burden' < 'ṯaqula - be heavy
wa-qāla - 'and' + 3rd sg. perf. 'qāla - speak'
l-ʾinsānu - def. art. + nom. sg. 'ʾinsān - human, man'
mā la-hā - 'what' + 'to' + suff. 3rd sg. f.
yawmaʾiḏin - 'on that day' < 'yawm - day'
tuḥaddaṯu - 3rd sg. impf. f. 'ḥaddaṯa - tell, narrate, speak'
ʾaḫbāra-hā - acc. pl. 'ḫabar - message, news' + suff. 3rd sg. f.
bi-ʾanna - 'because, that' < 'by, in, at' + particle (with acc.)
rabba-ka - acc. sg. 'rabb - lord' + suff. 2nd sg. m.
ʾawḥā - 3rd sg. perf. m. 'ʾawḥā - reveal'
la-hā - 'to'+ suff. 3rd sg. f.

* according to the rules of Arabic grammar the form to be expected would be the II. stem. "tuḥaddaṭu" with "a".

It should be noted that Luxenberg considers all forms with *yā'* as a carrier for *hamza* as highly suspicious. This would mean that the form يَوْمَئِذٍ "*yawma'iḏin*" might be an Aramaic loanword.

Poetic devices

The most striking feature is the gray shaded rhyme at the end of the verses. As the ending *-ā* is extremely common in Arabic and nearly all rhyming words are identical (i.e., the personal pronoun *-hā*), the charm of this rhyme cannot be rated very highly. Still, the surah has a certain rhythm, as the number of syllables in each verse are nearly the same (12 - 11 - 9 - 12 - 10). So it would not be too far-fetched to assume that this text was originally a poem, the form of which, however, would still have to be reconstructed.

Example 3: Surat al-Kāfirūn 109:1-6

قُلْ يَا أَيُّهَا الْكَافِرُونَ

لاَ أَعْبُدُ مَا تَعْبُدُونَ

وَلاَ أَنتُمْ عَابِدُونَ مَا أَعْبُدُ

وَلاَ أَنَا عَابِدٌ مَّا عَبَدتُّمْ

وَلاَ أَنتُمْ عَابِدُونَ مَا أَعْبُدُ

لَكُمْ دِينُكُمْ وَلِيَ دِينِ

109:1. qul yā ayyuhā -l-kāfirūna
say oh oh the disbelievers
Say: O disbelievers!

2. lā aᶜbudu mā taᶜbudūna
not I worship what you worship
I worship not that which ye worship;

3. wa-lā antum ᶜābidūna mā aᶜbudu
and not you worshipping what I worship
Nor worship ye that which I worship.

qul - imp. 2nd sg. m. 'qāla - say'
yā 'ayyuhā - double vocative particle 'oh'
l-kāfirūnª - def. art. + pl. nom. 'kāfir – disbeliever'
lā 'aᶜbudu - not' + 1st sg. impf. "ᶜabada - serve, adore, worship; all following verbal forms of this verb'
mā taᶜbudūn - 'what' + 2nd pl. impf. m.

4. wa-lā anā ʿābidum -mā ʿabadtum
and not I worhipping what you worship
And I shall not worship that which ye worship.

5. wa-lā antum ʿābidūna mā aʿbudu
and not you worshipping what I worship
Nor will ye worship that which I worship.

6. la-kum dīnu-kum wa-liya dīn(ī)
to you religion your and to me religion my
Unto you your religion, and unto me my religion.

wa-lā - 'and + not'
antum - 'you (pl.)'
ʿābidūna - nom. pl. part. act.
mā - 'was'
aʿbudu - 1st sg. impf.
wa-lā - 'and not'
anā - 'I'
ʿābidum -mā = ʿābidun (assim.) - indet. part. act.' + 'what'
ʿabadtum - 2nd pl. pf. m.
ʿābidūna - nom. pl. part. act.
mā ʾaʿbudu - 'what' + 1. sg. impf.
la-kum - 'to' + suff. 2. pl. m.
dīnu-kum - nom. sg. dīn - Religion' + poss. 2.pl. m.
wa-li-ya - 'and' + 'to' + suff. 1st sg.
dīn-ī - 'religion' + poss. 1st sg.

Notes

In a later Inârah anthology (Inârah 4: *Vom Koran zum Islam*) this surah will be treated again under a different aspect. As the main focus here is on style, the new findings will not be taken into consideration. Moreover, it must be remembered that the translation of *dīn* as "religion" was chosen for simplicity's sake for the time being. 'Religion' is a European concept of the era of enlightenment. One should not be misled by the Latin word 'religio', which is also old. But its meaning was quite distinct from the etymologically derived word 'religion' in modern European languages. The Latin word designated a *set of duties*, not a *conviction* or a *faith*. Moreover, as we have already seen, in *yawmu d-dīn*, *dīn* means "judgment" (an old Semitic root) and definitely not 'religion'. The later meaning "religion" (or rather "faith', a way to "see the world") goes back to the Iranian *dēn* (Middle Persian from Avestan *daēna*, orig. "the right view").[83]

The word "say" at the beginning of many surahs, which translates the short Arabic imperative "qul", is probably a later emendation as otherwise the following verses could not be considered the literal word of God. With this little trick a big problem could be solved: in the Qur'ān God sometimes speaks in the 1st person, sometimes he is talked to and finally he is also talked about!

Paret in his commentary dedicated a paragraph to what he considers to be a case of "*Parallelismus membrorum*" of verses 2-5, which, however, he finds unsymmetrical, otherwise verse 5 should read: *wa-lā antum ʿābidūna mā ʿabadtu* (perfect). He explains why this verse was not appropriate:

> "This breach of symmetry is due to objective facts. Mohammed could not reproach the infidels with not worshipping what he (formerly) had worshipped. Because just like they (still) avow themselves polytheists he himself had also done so formerly."

According to Luxenberg this is an erroneous interpretation due to a wrong interpretation of tenses, an idea not sufficiently elaborated and discussed. The question whether the term "mušrikūn" really means "polytheists" was discussed by G. R. Hawting,[84] who came to the conclusion that the term rather refers to monotheists who were regarded as Trinitarian heretics and not true monotheists by the first Muslims. This view is corroborated by the enormous number of verses that refer to the Old and New Testament, the frequent mentioning of Christians and Jews in the Qur'ān and the negligible archaeological traces in the Ḥiǧāz that point at a flourishing polytheist cult in the area. All these facts make it very difficult to assume a strong pagan religion (i.e., the prophet's alleged enemies) on the Arabic peninsula in late antiquity, as the Islamic orthodoxy does.

Poetic devices

The most conspicuous device here is the use of the same verbal root in opposing clauses, which would be appealing in Arabic, if the root appeared in different stems (verbal or nominal), which is, however, not the case. All forms are finite forms or participles of the root in the first stem, which makes the surah rather monotonous and difficult to recite.[85]

Example 4: Surat an-Nās 114: 1-6

قُلْ أَعُوذُ بِرَبِّ النَّاسِ

مَلِكِ النَّاسِ

إِلَٰهِ النَّاسِ

مِن شَرِّ الْوَسْوَاسِ الْخَنَّاسِ

الَّذِي يُوَسْوِسُ فِي صُدُورِ النَّاسِ

مِنَ الْجِنَّةِ وَ النَّاسِ

1. qul aᶜūḏu bi rabbi -n-nās[i]
say I seek refuge in lord people
Say: I seek refuge in the Lord of mankind,

2. maliki -n-nās[i]
king (of) people
The King of mankind,

3. ilāhi n-nās[i]
god of people
The God of mankind,

4. min šarri -l-waswāsi -l-ḫannās[i]
from evil (of) the whispering of the [devil]
From the evil of the sneaking whisperer,

5. allaḏī yuwaswisu fī ṣudūri n-nās[i]
who whispers in breasts (of) the people
Who whispereth in the hearts of mankind,

6. mina -l-ğinnati wa -n-nās[i]
of the (single) ghost and the people
Of the jinn and of mankind.

qul - imp. 2nd sg. 'qāla - say'
aᶜūḏu - 1st sg. impf. 'ᶜāḏa bi min) - seek refuge (in/ with - from)
bi rabbi - 'in/with' + gen. 'rabb - Herr'
n-nās[i] - def. art. + gen. 'nās - people'
maliki - gen. 'malik - king'
ilāhi - gen. 'ʾilāh - god'
min - 'of, from'
šarri - gen. 'šarr - evil'
l-waswāsi - def. art. + gen. 'waswās - whispering'
l-ḫannās[i*] - def. art. + gen. 'ḫannās - unclear (epithet of the devil)'
allaḏī - sg. m. rel. pron.
yuwaswisu - 3rd sg. impf. m. 'waswasa - whisper'
fī - 'in'
ṣudūri - gen. pl. 'ṣadr - breast, heart (fig.)'
n-nās[i] - see above
mina** = min + connect. vowel + def. art. 'of', meaning here maybe: be it that ...
al-ğinnati*** - def. art. + gen. 'ğinna - (single) ghost; derived from collective noun 'ğinn - ghosts, jinees' < 'ğanna - hide'
wa -n-nās[i] - 'and' + def. art. + 'nās – people'

* *ḫannās* is a word of unknown meaning, the root of which is not used outside the Qurʾān; a good candidate for a misreading.

** *min* in the last verse is unclear and the commentators interpret it in different ways; according to the context it has been translated here as "be it ... or".

*** *ǧinnati* according to Luxenberg a misreading; he thinks the correct form should be the Aramaic plural *ǧinnē;* what is meant is that the evil can wreak havoc as a ghost or in human form.

Poetic devices

In early Islam it was a matter of debate whether this surah, the preceding one (together called "*al muʿawwidatayn* - the verses of refuge") and the first surah (actually a prayer) belonged to the Qur'ān or not. Ibn Masʿūd did not have them in his codex. One reason is that the beginning of the second surah (al-Baqara) looks very much like the intended beginning of a book, the last surah before the two debated ones – Sūrat al-iḫlāṣ – sums up the main tenets of Islam in one line. So it would make a perfect ending. One explanation why these three surahs might have been added would be that they were something like additional pages at the beginning and at the end of the Qur'ān to protect the core text from dirt and scratches, a bit like the so-called *bastard title* in modern bookbinding (the first page of the book carrying nothing but the title; in German called "Schmutztitel" = dirt title).[86]

In this last surah the rhyming syllables end in *-ās,* six of them in verse-final position, five of them in the same word. The loose rhyme in this surah certainly does not betray poetic mastery. Moreover, the parallelism in lines 2 and 3 is conspicuous. The introductory "say" is certainly a later emendation. Obviously, and in this case even in accordance with Muslim tradition, the surah was originally a prayer. The "whisperer" might indeed be the devil, who (according to the gospels) also tried to seduce Jesus during his 40 day fasting.

3.7 An example from Arabic Poetry: The Burda

According to the definition of Arabic poetics it is meter and rhyme which distinguishes poetry (šiʿr) from prose (naṯr). The Arabic system of metrics, which goes back to al-Ḫalīl (died 175/791) contains 15 meters, of which fifteen are attested in the older poetry. The rhythm of the verses is based on syllable quantity; furthermore, several researchers assume a verse accent. Every meter is composed of partially equal, partially different metrical feet which contain an unchangeable, mostly iambic core (˘ ‒), around which changeable syllables gravitate. All verses of a poem have the same meter and the same rhyme, which appears for the first time after the first half verse. As the morphological structure of Arabic facilitates the formation of rhymes, poems of up to a hundred verses pose no difficulty to the poets.[87]

The Qur'ān has to be assessed against the background of this short characterization of Arabic poetry by Renate Jacobi, as it can be assumed that the listeners or readers of Qur'ānic texts were familiar with text similar to the ones described above. There has been some debate about the question whether the alleged old Arabic poetry is really pre-Islamic or not. Doubts have been cast on its authenticity mainly because of its very late written attestation on the one hand and its obvious linguistic influence from the Qur'ān on the other. An alternative view would be that their composition, which certainly must have taken some decades or even centuries, overlapped the compilation of the Qur'ān, if we assume more than one author and different layers for the latter.[88]

But even if these texts should turn out to be later than the emergence of Islam, then the use of poetic devices are sufficient reason to infer the existence of a prolonged poetic tradition even before the first Qur'ānic texts were composed.

The oldest form of poem in ancient Arabic is the so-called Qaṣīdah ("intention"), which had a form that can be summarized as follows:[89]

A Qaṣīdah consists of 70 - 100 lines with the same meter and the same rhyme (only final consonants rhyme, vowels are ignored!). The following parts can be discerned:

1. Introduction (*nasīb*): Complaint of the poet about the departure of his loved one (with flashbacks)
2. Connecting motive A
3. Transition to the description of a riding camel / the landscape during a ride through the desert
4. Connecting motive B
5. Final part: 3 possibilities
   - *maḍīḥ*: praise of a mighty person
   - *faḫr*: praise of the author's own tribe
   - *hiğa'*: vilification of an opponent

In later phases of Arabic poetry there are more complicated rhyme schemes, e.g. in the form "Muḫammas", strophes of five half verses with the rhyme scheme *aaaaR, bbbbR* are the rule.

Rhyme and meter can be found all through the history of Arabic language and literature and seem to be deeply rooted in the Arabs' feeling for style[90].
In order to give the reader an impression of what an Arabic Qaṣīdah was like, a short sample from one of the most famous Arabic poems, the so-called Burda ("mantle") will be discussed. On the internet several sound files can be downloaded.[91] The content of this poem is religious and there is a tradition of reading it in mosques, therefore it is not inappropriate to compare it to the Qur'ān.

The text of the Burda (qaṣīdatu l-burda) was composed by the Egyptian Sufi Imam al-Būṣīrī (died after 694/ 1296).[92] It is recited all over the world for magical purposes, e.g. a man who wants a male offspring should recite it 116 times. The written text is sometimes worn as an amulet and it has been translated into many languages of the Islamic civilization.

The Burda consists of 160 verses, which all rhyme in the letter "*mīm*". They are subdivided into 10 chapters, each verse consisting of two half verses of 14 syllables each.

It should be mentioned that a Burda recitation can be "enjoyed" even without knowledge of Arabic, as the text is sung to melody and is accompanied by drums. The text sample is verses 26 and 27 (according to an alternative numbering verses 27 to 30 from chapter two). The translation and analysis were made by myself.

26. *a.* **astaġfiru** **-llāha** **min**
I ask for forgiveness *God* *because of*
I ask for Allah's forgiveness because of

qauwlin **bi-lā** **ʿamalil**
speech *without* *action*
talking without acting,

b. **la-qad** **nasabtu** **bi-hi**
for verily *I ascribed* *by it*
for verily I have thereby ascribed

naslal **-llaḏī** **ʿuqumi**
offsprings *which* *of the barren*
offsprings to the barren.

astaġfiru - 1st sg. impf. X. st. 'ask for forgiveness' < ġafara - forgive
-llāha - acc. 'god'
min - 'of, because of'
qauwlin - gen. sg. indet. 'qawl - speech'
bi-lā - 'without'
ʿamalil = ʿamalin (assim.) - gen. sg. indet. 'ʿamal - action'
la-qad - 'verily'
nasabtu - 1st sg. perf. 'nasaba - ascribe to'
bi-hi - 'by + pron. 3rd sg. '
naslal = naslan (assim.) - acc. sg. indet. 'nasl - offsprings < 'nasal - beget'
-llaḏī - sg. rel. pron.
ʿuqumi - gen. pl. 'ʿaqīm - barren, useless' < ʿaqama (u, i) - or pass. 'ʿuqima' - be barren'; one would rather expect: ʿuqima

27. *a.* **amartuka** **-l-ḫayra** **lākim**
I ordered you *the good* *but*
... and I have given you orders to do good,

-mā **-ʾtamartu**** **bi-hi**
not *I executed* *by it*
but have not carried them out myself.

amartu-ka - 1st sg. perf. 'ʾamara - order, remind' + pron. 2nd sg. m.
l-ḫayra - def. art. + acc. sg. 'ḫayr - the good'
lākim = lākin (assim.) -

b. **wa**	**-mā**	**-staqamtu**	**fa-mā**
and	*not*	*I stood upright*	*and not*

and I have not stood upright, so what use

qawlī	**laka**	**-staqimi**
my talking	*to you*	*stand upright*

are my words to you: stand upright!

German translation of Ralfs:[93]

26. Möge Gott es mir vergeben, dass ich Worte ohne That gepredigt; fürwahr. In diesem Beginnen legte ich jenen Unfruchtbaren eine Nachkommenschaft bei.
27. Ich befahl dir das Gute, kam jedoch selber diesem Befehl nicht nach, und stand nicht gerade - was soll es da heißen, dass ich zu dir sagte: "Stehe gerade!"

but'
mā - 'not'
-ʾtamartu - 1st sg. perf. VIII. st. of ʾamara: 'iʾtamara - to carry out (orders)'*
bi-hi - see above
wa - 'and'
mā -staqamtu - 'not' + 1st sg. perf. X.st. 'istaqāma - stand upright, do the right thing'
fa-mā - 'and' + 'what'
qawl-ī - 'speech' + poss. 1st sg.
la-ka - 'to' + suff. 2nd sg. m.
-staqimi - impf. 2nd sg. 'istaqāma - stand upright, do the right thing'

* Luxenberg pointed out that the *t*-stem in Aramaic is used for the passive voice, which would also fit the context here, so an alternative translation would be: *I reminded you of the good, but did not want to be reminded of it myself.*

3.8 Summary and Conclusion about Poetic Devices

A comparison of the above text samples has yielded the following results: Poetic devices, which do not only serve to appeal to the readers or listeners, but also facilitate memorization, are very rare in the Qurʾān. There is neither a meter, nor a consistent rhyme or alliterative scheme, let alone a plot.

The loose rhyme that is used is hardly useful as a mnemonic device, as most rhymes are in fact either assonances or the rhyming words are particles or grammatical endings. Pure rhymes that extend over more than one syllable can hardly be found. Alliterations do exist, e.g. in the *basmallah* (bi-smi-llāhi r-raḥmāni -r-raḥīm) or in the formula "lā ilāha illā ḷḷāhu", but even their occurrence is rather sporadic and never regular as in Finnish or Thai. Like in the case of rhymes, alliteration is rather frequent in the form of assonances, i.e., imperfect alliterations, where the sounds repeated are not identical, but only similar (e.g. in sura 2:3: allaḏīna *yuʾminūna* bi-l-ġaybi wa-*yuqīmūna* -ṣ-ṣalāta wa-mim-mā razaqnāhum *yunfiqūna* – Who believe in the unseen, and establish worship, and spend of that We have bestowed upon them).

The probably best preservative for oral literature – rhythm – which requires a meter and a similar verse length, is only found sporadically, – especially in the short Meccan surahs at the end of the Qur'an *(ğuz' 'ammā)* –, although modern reciters bend over backwards to squeeze it into a text which hardly allows a rhythmical recitation, as we will see in the next section but one. Especially the long juridical Medinan surahs were certainly not meant to be rhythmically recited, its verses being of very different length and in most cases too long.

There is no pattern in the sequences of long and short syllables or vowels as in Greek or Sanskrit, and even a meter based on the number of syllables per verse (as in Avestan) can only be assumed in a few short surahs, as Lüling tried to demonstrate.

The fact that the Qur'ān seems to consist of stylistically very divergent layers is another argument for its late compilation.

Recitation of the Qur'ān must follow the rules of *tağwīd* ("elocution", from the verbal root *ğ-w-d* - make beautiful/ good), which often greatly differ from normal Classical Arabic phonetics. These rules affect almost exclusively the segmental phonetics and phonotactics of the text to be recited (e.g. assimilations, pharyngealizations etc.), but give hardly any hint as to the melody and rhythm of a recitation. Therefore it comes as no surprise that different reciters differ much more on this field than for example Buddhist monks who recite their chantings. The very existence of several recitation traditions or schools[94] is therefore yet another argument against a primarily oral transmission. It is tell-tale that the main criteria to make a recitation style canonical is the fact that it coincides with the *rasm* of the written Qur'ān. For an oral chain of transmitters – i.e., for only phonetic transmission – the *rasm* is absolutely irrelevant: an undotted "yā'" in the middle of the word can represent sounds as phonetically different as the *vowel* [i], the *semivowel* [j], the *nasal consonant* [n], the *voiced plosive* [b], the *unvoiced plosive* [t] or the *fricative* [θ]!

What the recitation schools primarily differ in are all those features not reflected in the *rasm*, e.g. the positions of hamza (the glottal stop), vocalizations etc. Thus the name of the archangel Gabriel appears in the forms *Ğabrīl, Ğibra'īl* or *Ğibra'il.* Even a word of such paramount importance as "Qur'ān" is pronounced by some without the glottal stop as "Qurān". And, at the same time, all these schools cite as authorities uninterrupted chains of transmitters which all go back to the prophet himself. To sum up, if they (or at least the canonical schools) should *all* be right, this would mean the following:

The prophet, who could not read or write, taught different pronunciations to different people, who then passed on these individual teachings to later generations. When later these oral traditions were reduced to writing, it miraculously turned out that they *all* yielded the same undotted consonant skeleton in writing![95]

Certainly, orthodox Muslims will not see this as a problem and, on the contrary, take it as yet more proof of the divine origin of the Qur'ān (God is almighty). If a religious person having grown up in the Islamic tradition should choose to believe this, it is understandable, but that such a ridiculous axiom should be the basis of Qur'ānic research in practically all major universities in the West, that every encyclopedia, every book about religion(s) and every documentary uncritically spreads this obviously late concept of oral tradition shows that the normal rules of scholarly methods as known and accepted by historians and philologists of all disciplines are widely ignored by Islamologists.

3.9 The alleged Beauty of the Qur'ān

A last paragraph is dedicated to the often claimed "beauty of the Qur'ān", which is directly opposed to the view expressed by the German orientalist Schwally, who wrote about the "schauerliche Öde (eerie wasteland/ boredom)" of the Qur'ān. When the first German edition of the present book was written (in 2006), "beauty of the Quran" was typed in as a Google search and yielded 657,000 hits. The same search was repeated in July 2012 and yielded 21,400,000 results! There does not even seem to be a discussion about this allegation, non-Muslims readily admitting that the Qur'ān must be a beautiful piece of literature, the "best Arabic ever written" etc.

The topic cannot be separated from the view that the Qur'ān is the miracle attesting to the prophethood for the Prophet of Islam, a view primarily based on the concept of *iʿǧāz*, i.e., the *inimitability* of the Qur'ān.[96]

"Inimitability", though at first glance it might seem to be a very noble feature, if boiled down to its very basic meaning, is actually a characteristic of *any peculiar* style (good as well as bad style!). Whoever sees the often pathetic attempts to imitate pop icons like Marilyn Monroe or Elvis Presley during "look-alike contests" knows what is meant by *inimitability*. But in a religious context such an everyday feature is quickly equated with "unsurpassability".

A short summary of the aesthetic virtues of the Qur'ān from an Islamic point of view can be found on the internet.[97]

> "(...) At the time the Qur'an was revealed, the Arabs recognized that the language of the Qur'an was unique and that it was distinctly different from the language normally used by the Prophet Muhammad, peace be upon him. The Arabs of that time, by the way, were known for their beautiful poetry and Muhammad was known to be an illiterate man! (...) It is also interesting to note that even though the Qur'an is not poetry, the Arabs more or less gave up writing poetry after it was revealed. It could be said that the Qur'an is the piece

> of Arabic literature par excellence – and Muhammad's contemporaries realized that they couldn't outdo it."

In other words: The literary qualities of the Qur'ān surpassed that of all previous poetry to the extent that poets of Arabic tongue gave up poetry altogether for a long time!

In the traditional Islamic literature, many cases of conversion after listening to the recitation of a Qur'ānic surah are attested. In contrast to this there are a number of reports about the Qurayš (the prophet's tribe), according to which these were not so impressed by the Qur'ān. Moreover, the prophet even had poets (who had dared to oppose him) killed (thus ridding himself of a yardstick).[98] The inconsequence of the traditional report can easily be demonstrated with a simple unanswered question: If the impression of the Qur'ān (as an aesthetic miracle) on the listeners of its dawn should really have been so overwhelming, why then did Muḥammad have to escape from Mecca?

The German Islamologist and author of fiction, Navid Kermani, himself of Iranian descent, wrote his doctoral thesis[99] about the "Aesthetic experience of the Qur'ān", the main title being "God is beautiful". In about 500 pages, written in good German style, he presents a very useful history of the reception of the Qur'ān and of the views of later writers about it. Interestingly, he only dedicates about 77 pages in the second chapter to the *text* of the Qur'ān itself. Although he does not rank the Qur'ān among the works of Arabic poetry[100] (*šiʿr*), – a view well in accordance with Muslim orthodoxy – he still mentions stylistic devices from poetry in the Qur'ān, e.g. "oaths, puns, parallelism of members, frequent use of the dual, onomatopoeia, word accents, rhythmic homogeneity". Kermani also mentions the sometimes scathing critique of European scholars, e.g. Thomas Carlyle's verdict, who called the Qur'ān a "wearisome confused jumble" and continued:

> "I must say, it is as toilsome reading as I ever undertook. [...] Nothing but a sense of duty could carry any European through the Qur'ān."

It seems a bit illogical, however, that, on the one hand, Kermani portrays the "openness" of the Qur'ān,[101] – what is meant is probably its unclearness and unintelligibility – as an exceptionally fascinating characteristic of the Qur'ān, but, on the other hand, he often mentions that Islamic scholars insist on the fact that the Qur'ān was written in "a clear Arabic tongue *(bi-lisānin ʿarabīyin mubīn)*". This is obviously a contradiction – a text is either *clear and precise*, or *enigmatic and open*, but never both. Kermani seems to sense this conflict, but prefers not to treat the matter in more detail.

In German there is a proverb: "Unverständlichkeit erweckt Ehrfurcht - unintelligibility inspires awe". It could have been the motto of all those scholars of all eras who keep on emphasizing the "openness" and "inimitability" of the Qur'ān, which in many cases is only due to erroneous dotting and vocalizing of the *rasm*.

As an example of a very poetic passage in the Qur'ān Kermani quotes surah 100 with a slightly modified translation of Rückert,[102] the famous German polyglot poet and translator of the Romantic Period, who tried to imitate the style of the surah in his German. Kermani also quotes his doctoral adviser Angelika Neuwirth, who underlines the "emotional choice of sounds" in this passage.[103] The passage in Arabic with Rückert's German translation and Pickthall's English one underneath is as follows (gray shading is my emphasis):

1. wa-l-ʿādiyati ḍabḥā	Bei den schnaubend Jagenden
2. fa-l-mūriyāti qadḥā	Mit Hufschlag Funken schlagenden
3. fa-l-miġīrāti ṣubḥā	Den Morgenangriff Wagenden, ...

1. By the snorting coursers,
2. Striking sparks of fire
3. And scouring to the raid at dawn,

Another example is from surah 111 (al-Lahab):

1. tabbat yadā Abī Lahabin wa-tabb
2. mā aġnā ʿanhū māluhū wa-mā kasab
3. sa-yaṣlā nāran ḏāta lahab
4. wa-mraʾatuhū ḥammālatal-ḥaṭab
5. fī ǧīdihā ḥablun min masad

Rückert tries to imitate the loose rhyme:

1. Ab sind die Händ' Abulahab's, und er ist ab;
2. Es half ihm nicht sein Gut und Hab.
3. Heizen wird er des Feuers Br<u>ast</u>,
4. Zuträgt sein Weib des Holzes L<u>ast</u>,
5. Um ihren Hals ein Strick von B<u>ast</u>

Pickthall makes no attempt to imitate the original style:

1. The power of Abu Lahab will perish, and he will perish.
2. His wealth and gains will not exempt him.
3. He will be plunged in flaming fire,
4. And his wife, the wood carrier,
5. Will have upon her neck a halter of palm fibre.

It must be admitted that these examples were well chosen, especially Rückert's imitation of the style in German is admirable. But apart from the fact that these surahs are not very clear – especially surah 100 is full of *hapax legomena* (words only attested here) – they are not very humane either: surah 113 is about the punishment of Abu Lahab (if this should really be a name, which is highly questionable!) and his wife in hell, about chopping off hands and burning people alive!

Nobody should be forbidden to enjoy these lines, and we might even admit that these surahs are *highlights* of Qur'ānic style, but only if *compared to the rest of the text*; a bit like the princesses in the paintings of Goya and Velazquez are only *relatively* pretty, because these painters always surrounded them with ugly dwarfs. In the more legalistic Medinan surahs such examples are hardly to be found.

Angelika Neuwirth, Kermani's teacher, in her study about Meccan[104] surahs, analyzed several of them according to form and contents and subdivided them into their structural elements, which she called in German "Gesätze". This extremely unusual and badly chosen German word – it sounds exactly like "Gesetze – laws" and is hardly known even to well-educated German speakers – in this context it means something like "strophe, verse, paragraph". What she found was marked groups of three and four. As an alternative to subdividing surahs into verses of very uneven length she suggests the subdivision into syntactically joined "cola".

A very similar idea could be found in Lüling's already mentioned book "Über den Urkoran"[105] a few years before (without being mentioned by A. Neuwirth).

Another one of her findings is very interesting and worth mentioning: While early Meccan surahs display a variety of up to 80 different types of rhyme, in what she considers to be the third phase only 8 types remain!

If we add the fact that in 29 (!) surahs a word as central as *Allāh* is not found (instead: *rabb* – Lord), that many verses in Medinan surahs if compared to their Meccan counterparts are super-long, and that the contents of different surahs drastically contradict each other[106] (e.g. concerning the consumption of wine), then it is well astounding that scholars like Angelika Neuwirth, who were educated in the European Academic tradition, do not jump to the most natural logical conclusion that every scholar of Ancient Greek or Latin would jump to: namely *that the Qur'ān is composed of different texts, written by different people with different views, probably over a prolonged period of time!*

Instead she (and almost all of her Western colleagues) stage an incredible performance of mental gymnastics to explain away these facts ("dialogue between the prophet and the community", "abrogation" etc.).

If the Qur'ān had been found in the ruins of an old library in the plains of Central Asia, or if it were the diwan of a poet and not the sacred book of an often bellicose world religion, then nobody would ever assume that it was *one* book written by *one* author within a period of *only 20* years, let alone a *beautiful* or even *divine* text!

Concerning the alleged *beauty of the Qur'ān* Angelika Neuwirth emphasizes the even proportions in the sequence of "Gesätze" (strophes). All the things that normally disturb a Western reader of the Qur'ān, the breaks in the arguments, the unfinished sentences and thoughts, the mind-numbing repetition of typical phrases – for *her* these are *intentional caesurae*, and more than that, *well-chosen* breaks.

But not all Western scholars find the Qur'ān so beautiful. A good summary of the often diametrically opposed assessments by Western scholars was put together by Stefan Wild.[107] He mentions the poetic devices that Angelika Neuwirth had emphasized, "parallelism of members, clause endings with different functions, as well as meditative insertions, which evoke a meditative atmosphere".

When the quality of literature is chosen as a matter of debate then the normal criteria for quality should be applied and the usual reasons for the choice of poetic devices considered. In his famous book "Principles of Literary Criticism", written in 1924,[108] I.A. Richards adduces psychological reasons why rhythm and meter are able to evoke predictable feelings in readers and listeners:

> "Rhythm and its specialized form, meter, depend upon repetition and expectancy. Equally, where what is expected recurs and where it fails, all rhythmical and metrical effects spring from anticipation. (...) Evidently there can be no surprise and no disappointments unless there is expectation, and most rhythms perhaps are made up as much of disappointments and postponements and surprises and betrayals as of simple, straightforward satisfactions. (...)"

He adds that meter is the most suitable way of connecting words in a way that they influence each other. Moreover, according to him, rhythmical recitation unconsciously creates a "horizon of expectations" which is much more focused and offers by far fewer possibilities than prose, an effect even much stronger when rhymes come into play.

The argument that Qur'ān reciters well prove the "musicality" of the Qur'ānic text, belongs to an otiose discussion. What is called "musicality" of Qur'ānic recitation is created by the lengthening of consonants and the "drawing" of vowels over periods of several seconds, adding an ad-hoc melody to them. On closer inspection this has nothing to do with the musicality of the *Qur'ānic text,* as this method could be applied to almost *any* text. Moreover, there are good reasons to assume that this way of reciting is rather new: The famous medieval Islamic scholar Ibn Taymīyah (1263–1328 CE) strongly discouraged the recitation of the Qur'ān in a "melodious way" (in Arabic: التغنّي *al-taġannī*) so that it resembles a song, calling it an *innovation.*[109]

So the beauty of the recitation is created by the reciter, whose motivation to make the text sound solemn and awe-inspiring is mainly religious, not primarily aesthetic[110].

As an example of the (missing) rhythm in most of the Qur'ān and the extreme lengthening of single sounds we will adduce the waveforms (oscillograms) of the recited verses of the Burda and the last surah of the Qur'ān. The x-axis shows the time in seconds (1000 = 1 second).

Notes:

The Burda: The amplitudes before the vertical line (at about 3000 on the x-axis) go back to the beat of the drum. The Burda has follows a fixed basic melody, which is sung by a choir encompassing several bars (if it were written as sheet music). The more prominent amplitudes are mostly vowels. The waveform shows a rather regular pattern which goes back to the strict rhythm of the recitation.

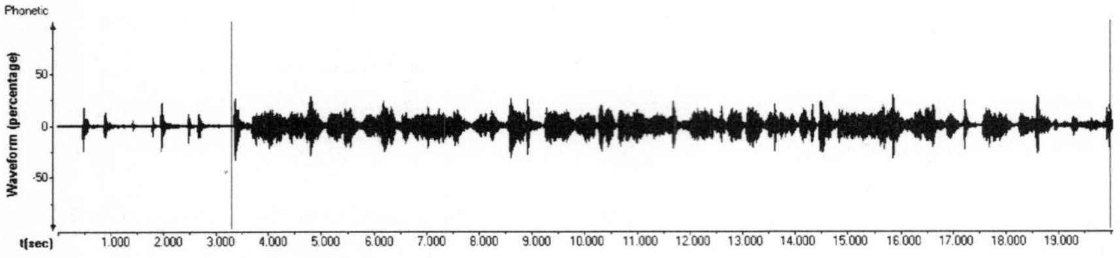

The Qur'ān: The sample text is the last verse of the last surah (see section 3.6.5): *qul aʿūḏu bi rabbi n-nās.*

The graph underneath the waveform shows the pitch of the single sounds of the graph above. If the verse is transcribed so that each letter corresponds to the sound in the waveform, we get the following picture:

qul aʿūūūūūḏu bi rabbbbinnnnnnnnnnnnnnaaaaaaaaaaaas

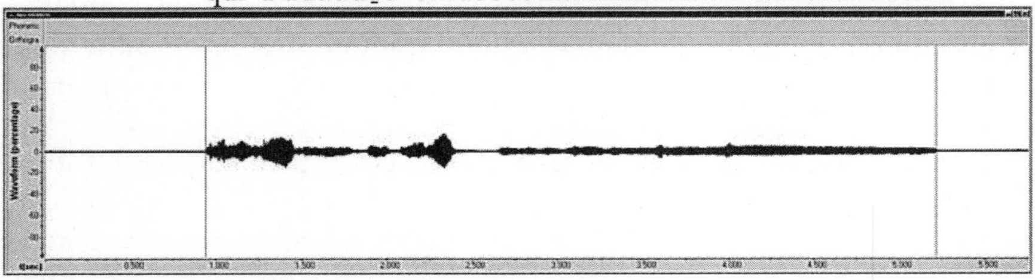

The total recitation of the verse takes about 4.3 seconds. Of these about 1.8 are taken up by the words "*qul aʿūḏu bi rabbi*". The last word, "*nās*", is much longer: around 2.5 seconds (= 58 %!), of which more than half is dedicated to the utterance of the nasal consonant "n" (= 29 % !).

In other words: about a third of the total verse, which consists of 18 phonemes, including 7 vowels, is taken up by a single sound, which itself is *not a vowel* and which in normal speech would not last longer than the lateral consonant "l" in the first word "qul"!

Now the question arises whether listening to such an unnatural and unrhythmical way of reciting can actually lead to enjoyment, which would justify the adjective "beautiful" (as referring to aesthetics) or whether it is rather the conviction on the part of the listeners that they gain *religious merit*, which leads to *elation* or *edification*.

Or to adduce an example to make the point clearer: It is well possible to read the Odyssey – whether in the Greek original or one of the many excellent translations – and enjoy it, even if one does not at all believe in the Greek gods. But it remains very questionable whether anybody who does not believe in the tenets of Islam can enjoy the Qur'ān – whether in the Arabic original or one of the many translations which Muslims claim are all not half as good as the original.

Of course against this view one could object that the beauty of a text does not necessarily have to be one of poetic devices, that it could well be that the aesthetic value of a text lies in its clear or surprising train of thought, the wits it displays, the unusual metaphors and puns or its ability to evoke images and feelings. It is in fact true that the Qur'ān, in innumerable places, threatens disbelievers with hell and torment, thus *evoking the feeling* of fright and fear, but these feelings are only evoked in *believers*, not in *listeners/ readers* in general.

We shall leave the summary about the aesthetic values of the Qur'ān to the famous German orientalist Nöldeke,[111] whose observations contain almost everything to be said about Qur'ānic style:

> "If he (i.e.: Muḥammed) was already struggling in the description of his religious thoughts and even legends, it was even harder for him to express himself as a lawmaker and ruler."

About the Qur'ānic use of rhyme, he had to say the following:[112]

> "Muḥammad took from the soothsayers (kāhin), along with a number of other things, the use of short rhyming sentences. Already with the little care he takes with regard to rhyme and assonance, he shows his lack of understanding of form (...). On account of the rhyme, however imperfect it may be, the speech was subject to much constraint, while the individual verses of the same passage often varied greatly in length."

Moreover, he criticizes:[113]

> "The fact that the Qur'ān repeats its fundamental principles, readily using the same words, often makes it very boring for us."

And what he has to say about the train of thought in the Qur'ān is not very flattering either:[114]

> "The fact that the Koran has a tendency to switch rapidly from one subject to another will not have disconcerted the Arabs; they were accustomed to this with their poets. Certainly Muḥammad sometimes goes rather too far in this respect: he breaks off from one subject, takes up another, drops this one and goes back to the first, and so on."

He sums up the assessment of Qur'ānic style by Arabic poets as follows[115]:

> "Although they (i.e.: the Arabic poets) saw in it (i.e.: the Koran) the most magnificent merits or attributes of the unmatchable word of God, it did not occur to them to incorporate them into human speech. (explanations in brackets by myself)."

And last, but not least, here is his opinion about the value of Qur'ānic loose rhyme:[116]

> "Thus rhyme in prose was always formed in a pure fashion and never in the incomplete manner of the prophet."

So why is it so that the "beauty of the Qur'ān" is so obtrusively repeated by so many Muslims who adduce this very feature as utmost proof of the divine origin of the Qur'ān. And – what is even more astounding – why is this argument accepted by so many Western scholars of Islamic studies (apart from all the journalists, fiction writers etc.) without even a trace of doubt and without even the slightest attempt to question this allegation. The attitude of Nöldeke – who, in spite of his critique, was certainly no enemy of the Muslims – is unthinkable in the era of "political correctness", in which any tenet, belief or allegation is automatically labeled *sacrosanct*, as soon as it belongs to a major religion or ethnic group. In order not to jeopardize "peace among civilizations" or to keep alive what is called "dialogue" (or its unetymological even more politically correct counterpart "trialogue")[117] – whatever that may mean – the alleged characteristic "beauty" is readily taken over and reiterated to the point of making it a generally accepted notion. If asked to produce some examples to exemplify this assessment, the normal answer is a long list of Muslim scholars from many centuries who wrote about the beauty of the Qur'ān ("we as non-native speakers cannot really appreciate this beauty like they can") and the last resort is the argument that beauty is always in the eye of the beholder – or here in the ear of the listener, so if Muslims find it beautiful, then it must be beautiful.

To understand how ridiculous this attitude is, one should only imagine the cream of the crop of Western chefs from the major five-star hotels of Paris, Berlin, London and New York unanimously stating that if devout Hindus drink cow urine (a common thing in India) and claim that it tastes good, then it must actually be delicious and we have no right to doubt it!

In this example, as in the case of the beauty of the Qur'ān, *aesthetic appreciation* and *taste* are confused with the *feeling of religious merit*. We do have a right to doubt! Moreover, it should be mentioned that this constant talking about the beauty of the Qur'ān does not really do justice to the text itself either: The Qur'ān does not intend to be beautiful! It is rather a collection of theological, liturgical, explanatory and juridical texts written with quite divergent intentions in mind, none of them aesthetic. If compared to other old texts with some sort of religious content, e.g. the Rigveda with its strict meter, the Biblical tales of Joseph or Samson and Delilah with plots that have inspired Hollywood studios to make motion pictures about them, or – strict meter and a thrilling plot combined – in the Odyssey, nobody can seriously claim that reading the Qur'ān leads to aesthetic enjoyment.

If one considers the questions of the path of transmission of the Qur'ān (*communis opinio* among both Western and Islamic scholars: "primarily oral") and of its aesthetic value ("beautiful"!) then one is inevitably reminded of the fairy tale "The Emperor's New Clothes", with one difference: Even if a child (or even an unbiased scholar) should cry out "But he isn't wearing anything at all!", the pretense would not cease to be maintained!

Be that as it may, the following conclusion of the preceding section seems to be justified to me (even if that should mean that I – like somebody not able to see the emperor's new clothes in the fairy tale – should appear "unfit for my position"):

Whoever reads the Qur'ān from beginning to end without *a priori* considering it to be the literal word of God, but employing all the well-established methods, techniques and standards of philology, linguistics and the historical disciplines, can only arrive at two conclusions:

1. The transmission of the Qur'ān was primarily through the written medium. Oral transmission developed only after the written text had been established.
2. The Qur'ān is not a poetic text meant to be beautiful. It is a collection of divergent texts from different authors written over a prolonged period of time.

3.10 Defective Writing Systems: A Comparative overview

In the following section a number of historical writing systems of the Middle East will be briefly presented with a short sample text. The aim is to provide the readers with a background for comparison with the highly defective Qur'ānic orthography, which does not possess more than just about a dozen different graphemes.

When writings systems "are invented" – in fact such events were much rarer than generally believed, as most writing systems develop from already existing systems – the first phase is usually pictographic, never phonetic. The second phase is typically one of syllabaries (like in Japanese) or of consonants[118] (like in Ancient Near Eastern systems). The third step, in which phonemes including vowels are represented, is only taken by very few systems. Usually the representation of all or at least most phonemically relevant differences is best at the beginning of this phase, in order to prevent misunderstandings, but this aim is hardly ever achieved perfectly, so that most writing systems are to some extent defective. As writing systems are as a rule more conservative than phoneme systems, i.e., the actual pronunciation of the language, the orthography of most languages must necessarily become less and less phonemic as time goes by.

This also applies to the use of the Latin script in modern European languages. The only language which makes perfect use of it – in the sense that the relation between grapheme and phoneme is 1:1, so that the spoken word can perfectly be rendered in writing and vice versa – is Finnish. Modern Hausa (and many other African languages) makes very defective use of the Latin script, as both vowel length and tonemes are ignored when writing the language.[119]

As already mentioned, many languages have strongly historicizing orthographies, just think of the Irish or English spelling ("scent", "sent", "cent"), which often transmits more information about the history of the word than about its pronunciation. Another good example is Thai with many silent consonants that go back to Sanskrit. So the morpheme จันทร์, pronounced [can] and meaning "moon", [120] is written "candr", the letter originally meaning "d" now being pronounced as an aspirated "t" (when at the beginning of a word) and the "r" having a neutralizing superscript sign (in Thai: "garan") on top of it. The Sanskrit word it comes from is "candra", which makes the orthography logical. The phenomenon of allophonic systems like in Sanskrit and Avestan has already been mentioned, but even in modern European languages many allophonic features can be found in some systems.

Arabic, however, is quite a special case: fully vocalized and with all distinctive dots it perfectly reflects all phonemes and – at least when applying all extra symbols of the Cairene Qur'ān edition – it even indicates some sandhi phenomena like assimilations. In its unvocalized form (like in modern books and newspapers) it is highly defective. This defective character is even more conspicuous when considering the spelling of the first generation of Qur'ānic manuscripts. No more than about a dozen graphemes (written symbols distinguishing words) can be discerned. In the middle position the undotted letter *yā'* in its medial form can represent consonants as different as as the vowel [i], the diphthong [ai], the semivowel [j], the nasal consonant [n], the voiced plosive [b], the unvoiced plosive [t] or the fricative [θ]. Luxenberg calculates altogether 23 cases of possible misreadings on the letter level, on the word level this number would, of course, be much higher (see section 2.2).

On the following pages several writing systems from the Middle East will be discussed, thus providing the reader with a framework for a better assessment of the defective nature of the Arabic script. The first example will be the Ugaritic script, the first pure consonant script of the Ancient Near East.

3.10.1 Ugaritic Cuneiform

Ugaritic is an old Semitic language once spoken in the town of Ugarit in modern Syria and written in the easiest of all cuneiform systems, which only designated consonants, not syllables or even morphemes like in Sumerian. Ugaritic texts are attested from the 14th to the 12th century BCE. The town was destroyed in the year 1180/70 BCE.

Ugaritic Script: Table of Consonants[121]

Translit.	Ugaritic	Translit.	Ugaritic	Translit.	Ugaritic
a	𐎀	ḥ	𐎈	š	𐎝
i	𐎛	ḫ	𐎃	ʿ	𐎓
u	𐎜	t	𐎉	ġ	𐎙
b	𐎁	ẓ	𐎑	p	𐎔
g	𐎂	y	𐎊	ṣ	𐎕
d	𐎄	k	𐎋	q	𐎖
ḏ	𐎏	l	𐎍	r	𐎗
h	𐎅	m	𐎎	š	𐎌
w	𐎆	n	𐎐	t	𐎚
z	𐎇	s	𐎒	ṯ	𐎘

Word divider: 𐎟

Text sample: From the Baal Cycle (1.4:IV:20-39; cf. Gordon 51:IV; IIAB,IV)[122]

20. 𐎛𐎄𐎋 𐎟 𐎍𐎚𐎚𐎐 𐎟 𐎔𐎐𐎎
i d k . l t t n . p n m

21. 𐎓𐎎 𐎟 𐎛𐎍 𐎟 𐎎𐎁𐎋 𐎟 𐎐𐎅𐎗𐎎
ʿm . i l . m b k . n h r m

22. 𐎖𐎗𐎁 𐎟 𐎀𐎔𐎖 𐎟 𐎚𐎅𐎎𐎚𐎎
q r b . a p q . t h m t m

23. 𐎚𐎂𐎍𐎊 𐎟 𐎏𐎄 𐎟 𐎛𐎍 𐎟 𐎆𐎚𐎁𐎜
t g l y . ḏ d . i l . w t b u

24. 𐎖𐎗𐎌 𐎟 𐎎𐎍𐎋 𐎟 𐎀𐎁 𐎟 𐎌𐎐𐎎
q r š . m l k . a b . š n m

25. 𐎍𐎔𐎓𐎐 𐎟 𐎛𐎍 𐎟 𐎚𐎅𐎁𐎗 𐎟 𐎆𐎚𐎖𐎍
l p ʿn . i l . t h b r . w t q l

26. 𐎚𐎌𐎚𐎈𐎆𐎊 𐎟 𐎆𐎚𐎋𐎁𐎄𐎅
t š t ḥ w y . w t k b d h

27. 𐎅𐎍𐎎 𐎟 𐎛𐎍 𐎟 𐎋𐎊𐎔𐎅𐎐𐎅
h l m . i l . k y p h n h

28. 𐎊𐎔𐎗𐎖 𐎟 𐎍𐎕𐎁 𐎟 𐎆𐎊𐎕𐎈𐎖
y p r q . l ṣ b . w y ṣ ḥ q

The grammatical analysis including the vocalization of the text follows Segert's explanation, the translation being mine.

Context: The goddess Athirat is on a journey on the back of a donkey to the highest god Il. She is being accompanied by two servants. Her aim is to intercede in favor of the young god Baal, who needs a palace.

20. **idk.** **lttn.** **pnm** /ʾiddāka la-tatinu panīma/ *then* *in fact she gave* *face* *Then she (really) turned her face*	**idk /ʾiddāka/** - 'then; really' **lttn /la-tatinu/** - 'la - pref. 'in fact' or 'lā - not'[123] - 3rd sg. impf. 'y-t-n - give' **pnm /panīma/** - acc. pl. 'face'; cf. Hebr. panīm - id.
21. **ʿm.** **il.** **mbk.** **nhrm** /ʿamma ʾili mabbaka naharēmi/ *to* *Il* *source* *of two rivers* *to Il (at) the source of the two rivers*	**ʿm /ʿamma/** - 'with, to' **il /ʾili/** - gen. 'god; name of the god Il', cf. Hebr. 'ēl(ohīm); Ar. ʾaḷḷāh **mbk /mabbaka/** - acc. < '*manbak- source' **nhrm /naharēmi/** - Du. gen./ acc. 'river'; cf. Hebr. mibbəkē nəhārōt (Job 28,11)
22. **qrb.** **apq.** **thmtm** /qarba ʾapiqi tahāmatēmi/ *in the middle of* *headwaters* *of ocean* *In the middle of the headwaters of the ocean*	**qrb /qarba/** - 'in the middle of' **apq /ʾapiqi/** - gen. 'channel, headwaters'; cf. Ar. Afqā - East of Byblos, myth. home of Il **thmtm /tahāmatēmi/** - du. gen. '("Ur-") ocean'
23. **tgly.** **ḏd.** **il.** **wtbu** /tagliyu ḏāda ʾili wa-tubāʾu | / *enters* *realm* *of Il* *and goes into* *she entered his realm and went into*	**tgly /tagliyu/** - 3. f. sg. impf. 'g-l-y- go into/ (out of?)' **ḏd /ḏāda/** - 'territory (or pavilion)' **il /ʾili/** - gen. 'Il/ god; Il' **wtbu / wa-tubāʾu/** - 'and' +3. f. sg. impf. 'b-w-y- come; enter' **qrš /qarša/** - 'area, domain' **mlk / malki/** - gen. 'king' **ab /ʾabī/** - gen. sg. 'father'

24. **qrš.**	**mlk.**	**ab.**	**šnm**
/qarša	malki	ʾabī	š-n-m-/
domain	*of king*	*of father*	*years*

the domain of the king, the exalted father,

šnm /š-n-m-/ - pl. 'šnt - year'; cf. Hebr. šanīm; pl. in Ug. mostly 'šnt'; alternative: ab. šnm - the elevated one

25. **lpʿn.**	**il.**	**thbr.**
/lē-paʿnē	ʾili	tahburu
to feet	*of Il*	*bows down*

she bowed down to Il's feet

wtql
wa-taqūlu/
and drops to the ground
and dropped to the ground,

lpʿn /lē-paʿnē/ - 'to' + du. gen./ acc. 'foot'
il /ʾili/ - gen. 'Il'
thbr /tahburu/ - 3rd sg. impf. 'h-b-r- bow down'
wtql /wa-taqūlu/ - 3. f. sg. impf. 'q-w-l- drop to the ground (?)'

26. **tštḥwy.**	**wtkbdh**
/taštaḥwiyu	wa-takabbidu-hu/
kneels down	*and honors*

she kneeled down and honored him.

tštḥwy /taštaḥwiyu/ - 3rd sg. f. impf. probably. Št. of 'ḥ-w-y- live'; here: 'ask for o's life; kneel down in front of'; cf. the corresp. Hebr. form 'tištaḥwe'[124]
wtkbdh /wa-takabbidu-hu/ - 3. f. sg. impf. 'k-b-d - be heavy, honored' (D-st. - 'honor') + suff. 3rd sg. m.

27. **hlm.**	**il.**	**kyphnh**
/halum(ma)	ʾilu	kī-yiph-ha/
behold	*Il*	*he sees her*

And lo and behold, Il sees her,

hlm /halum(ma)/ - interj. 'behold'
il /ʾilu/ - nom. 'Il'
kyphnh /kī-yiph-ha/ - 'kī - emphatic part. 'probably' + 3. m. sg. impf. 'p-h-y - see, perceive' + suff. 3rd sg. f. '-(n)h'; cf. 'phy - he saw'

28. **yprq.**	**lṣb.**	**wyṣḥq**
/yaparriqu	liṣba	wa yiṣḥaqu/
opens	*mouth*	*and laughs*

opens his mouth and starts laughing.

yprq /yaparriqu/ - or: **/yapruqu/:** 3rd sg. m.impf. 'p-r-q- cut off, open wide'
lṣb /liṣba/ - acc. sg. 'tightness (?) (mouth or throat)'
wyṣḥq /wa yiṣḥaqu/ - 3rd sg. m. impf. 'ṣ-ḥ-q - laugh'; cf. name 'Isaak = Yiṣḥāq - he laughs'

Notes:
In both the interlinear and the "readable" translation in the line underneath the imperfect forms have been translated tense-neutral with the English present tense. In early Ugaritic the imperfect was not a tense, but rather an aspect, thus being able to designate actions in the past, present and future. Only later, parallel to other Semitic languages, did it become the tense of the present.

3.10.2 Old Persian Cuneiform

Old Persian:
At the time the following inscription was written, the administrative language of the Persian Achaemenid Empire was so-called *Imperial Aramaic.*

Like Ugaritic cuneiform (a pure consonant script) the Old Persian cuneiform alphabet can hardly be more than loosely connected to the Sumerian and Akkadian writing systems, with which it does not share more than one single character, which is only used in borrowings. It consists of little over 60 characters including numbers, each character representing a consonant to which a vowel can be added. If no vowel is added, a short optional "a" is inherent by default. This rule is almost identical to the one valid in most Indian writing systems, including the Devanagari-script normally used for Sanskrit. So 𐎴 can designate either *n* or *na*, 𐎭 *d* or *da etc.* A long *ā* is written as 𐎠, which is added to these characters on their right: 𐎴 𐎠 meaning *nā* and 𐎭𐎠 *dā*.

The question inevitably arises why one would invent a new system if so many well established writing systems (Aramaic, Elamite, Akkadian) had been in use, of which one could easily have been adapted, something that actually did take place a few centuries later, when Middle Persian was written in two different adaptations of the Aramaic script.

The answer lies in the prestige of Old Persian itself, which was never used for practical purposes. Old Persian inscriptions are normally monumental stone inscriptions meant to be representative and demonstrate power. Aramaic, which could easily be written on papyrus with a calamus, could, of course, be used for stone inscriptions as well, but would never have had the same awe-inspiring effect as cuneiform letters!

To give an impression of the nature of the Old Persian cuneiform, a short text sample from the Behistun Rock inscription will be analyzed.

Source:
Titus Homepage (see bibliography); the sample text in Brandenstein's and Mayrhofer's "Handbuch des Altpersischen"[125] was also used. In the readable translation the Greek forms of the names have been chosen.

𐏐 𐎠 𐎭 𐎶 𐏐 𐎭 𐎠 𐎼 𐎹 𐎺 𐎢 𐏁 𐏐 𐎧 𐏁 𐎠 𐎹 𐎰 𐎡 𐎹

| a – da- ma | da - a - ra -ya -va - u - ša | xa - ša - a -ya -ϑa-i -ya
| a – d - m | d - a - r - y -v - u - š | x - š - a - y - ϑ- i - y
| adam | dārayavāuš | xšāyaϑiya

𐏐 𐎺 𐏀 𐎼 𐎣 𐏐 𐎧 𐏁 𐎠 𐎹 𐎰 𐎡 [𐎹 𐏐 𐎧 𐏁 𐎠 𐎹]

| va -za-ra- ka | xa- ša-a - ya- ϑa-i- ya | xa -ša -a- ya-
| v - z - r - k | x - š -a - y - ϑ- i- y | x - š - a - y-
| vazərka | xšāyaϑi ya | xšāya

𐎰 𐎡 𐎹 / 𐎠 𐎴 𐎠 𐎶

ϑa -i - ya / -a - na-a -ma
ϑ -i - y / -a -n - a - m
ϑiy/ānām

(mp. = Middle Persian; mod.p. = modern Persian; PN = personal name)

adam | dārayavāuš | xšāyaϑiya | vazərka |
I Dārayavauš king great
I, Dareios, the great king,

xšāyaϑiya | xšāyaϑiy/ānām |
king of kings
king of kings, ...

adam - nom. 1st sg. pers. pron. 'I'
dārayavāuš - PN Greek 'Dareĩos' < *dāraya-vahu - 'holding firm the good'
xšāyaϑiya - m. 'king' < 'xšāy- rule' > mp./mod. p. 'šāh'
vazərka - 'great' > mod. p. 'buzurg' > mod. p. 'bozorg'
xšāyaϑiya xšāyaϑiy/ānām - 'king of the kings' > mp. 'šāh ān šāh' > mod. p. 'šāhanšāh'

It should be mentioned that the ending of the genitive plural - **ānām** led to the Modern Persian plural ending (mostly used for humans) -**ān**, like in '**ṭālib-ān** - students', the correct Arabic plural of this borrowing being '**ṭullāb**'.

3.10.3 Zoroastrian Middle Persian (Pahlavi/ Pehlevi)

Middle Persian is a descendant from Old Persian and was spoken between the 3rd century BCE and the 8th/9th century CE. As a sacred language of the Manichaeans, however, it survived until the 13th century in the Turfan oasis in Chinese Turkestan. The alternative designation *Pahlavi* or *Pehlevi* should be avoided for two reasons: Strictly speaking it refers more to the writing system and in the form *pahlavīk* it can also designate the related, yet distinct Parthian language. Apart from some inscriptions, Middle Persian was written in three different alphabets:

1. In later, Manichaean texts a rather easy to read consonant script derived from Aramaic was used, which reflects the pronunciation at the time when the texts were written down, albeit without vowels. Manichaean Parthian, a North-Western Iranian language – Middle-Persian belongs to the South-Western subgroup – was also written in this script.
2. In later texts, when spoken Middle Persian had begun to drift away from the old written standard and started to become an early form of Modern Persian, an adapted form of the already mentioned allophonic Avestan script called *Pāzand* was used. The Avestan script itself, however, is only an enhanced offshoot of the so-called Book Pahlavi script explained in the next paragraph[126].
3. The (Zoroastrian) Book Pahlavi script is also derived from an Aramaic script and thus runs from right to left. The largest Middle Persian text corpus is written in this script, although of the three alphabets mentioned it is by far the most difficult to read, for several reasons:
   - It is almost as defective as the Arabic script of the earliest manuscripts, only possessing around a dozen graphemes.
   - As a pure consonant script it does not reflect vowels, and even the orthography of the consonants is archaizing, as it often seems to represent the phonemic structure of an older stage of the language, e.g. **npšt** – to be pronounced: **nibišt** < Old Persian: **nipišta.**
   - There is a considerable number of often confusing ligatures.
   - About a thousand so-called heterograms are used, i.e., words written in Aramaic, but to be read as Middle Persian, roughly comparable to cases like English "e.g." from Latin "exempli gratia", but read as "for example", or "i.e." (Latin: *id est*), read as "that is". A few hundred of these heterograms are obscure to this day.

Such heterograms can also be found in other languages of the area like Old Persian, Hittite or – more contemporary to Middle Persian – Parthian, where the Aramaic words often follow Middle Iranian syntax, e.g. MLKYN MLKA for Parthian "šahān šāh". The correct Aramaic form would be "meleḵ malkē". The -YN of MLKYN reflects the normal Aramaic plural ending *-īn*, which in this case, however, would be incorrect.

So the form MLK is not a real borrowing from Aramaic. Such "putative" borrowings are quite common in many languages, if one considers cases like German "Handy" (for "mobile phone"), "Beamer" (for "LCD-projector") or "Oldtimer" (for "vintage car"). It is not exactly the same case as with heterograms, but the fact remains that foreign morphemes are recombined to make a new word, which is uncommon in the language the morphemes come from. In other cases a fixed expression is syntactically adapted, e.g. "Standing ovation" (in German only in the singular!).

Still, the emergence of a system with as much as 1000 heterograms needs a clarification. One possible way it might have developed is bad reading habits. Originally purely Aramaic texts were read out loud mainly in Aramaic with a growing number of words being pronounced in Persian. Due to this mixed character of the recitation, scribes, whose mother tongue was Persian, started to use more and more syntactic constructions from Persian when writing Aramaic, which in turn made it easier to replace even more words by their Persian equivalent when reading the texts aloud. In a further step, a growing percentage of the text was spelled in Persian in the first place, so that in the end only the heterograms remained as the Aramaic element. The "missing link" might be found in many documents from the Arsacid[127] era (e.g. from Nisā and Awrōmān). These texts were thought to be basically Aramaic with an Iranian admixture. Because of the very un-Aramaic syntax, however, it is quite possible that they were basically Iranian texts written heterographically.[128]

Sample text: Middle Persian (Book-Pahlavi)
Kārnāmag-ī Ardaxšīr-ī Pābagān (deeds of Ardaxšīr, son of Pābagān), chapter 1; source: Titus-Homepage (including translation)[129]:

The original text in the first line is part of a scan from the Titus homepage,[130] the transliteration in the second line displays all heterograms as capital letters. In the right-hand column the Old and Modern Persian equivalents of single words are given.

tyNWMYWḴY t špn nwty ͗ n ͗k p̄ ͗p y ryšxtr ͗ kMŠ r ͗k NWP
(*OP. = Old Persian; Mod. P. = Modern Persian; Av. = Avestan)*

PWN k͗r ŠMk ͗rtxšyr y p͗p̄k͗n
pad kārnāmag ī ardaxšīr ī pābagān
In the Book of Deeds of Ardašīrs, the son of Pāpak,

PWN - pad - 'to(ward)' < OP. 'pada - Stelle, Stätte'; Mod. P. pa-
k͗r + ŠMk - kārnāmag + Book of Deeds < 'kār - deed' = Mod. P., Av. kāra° (doer of an action; pref.) + 'nāmag - book ("something to make a name for yourself with") - Mod. P. 'nām - name'
ī - ezafe (connecting particle) < OP. haya

ʾytwn	npšt	YK̲WYMWNyt
ēdōn	nibišt[131]	ēstād
so	*written*	*stands*

(dem./rel. pron.)
ʾrtxšyr - ardaxšīr - personal name = OP. ṛta-xšaϑra - 'truth and reign', see above
y - ī - ezafe (connecting particle, see above), 'of'
pʾpkʾn - pābagān = patronym 'son of Papak'
ʾytwn - ēdōn - 'so' < OP. 'ai̯ta - dem. pron.'; cf. 'čigōn - wie'
npšt - nibišt - written (nibištan/ nībēs)'; OP. 'ni-pišta down + written'; > Mod. Pers. 'newestan/ newīs'
YK̲WYMWNyt - ēstād - Aram. yqym √ qwm /qām/ - stand; Middle P. ē̆stādan - stehen; Mod. P. 'īstādan/ īst' < OP. 'abiy - to(ward)' + stā -stand, put'

Notes:

In this Middle Persian narrative, written during the Sassanian period (224 - 642 CE) in Iran, the adventures of Ardaxšīr, the founder of the Sassanian Empire, are told.

The question arises, why such a highly complicated and defective writing system could survive for such a long time, considering that at the same time other writing systems – e.g. the phonetically very exact and easy to learn Avestan script – were in use.

It is true that after some time the introduction of a number of diacritics made reading book Pahlavi somewhat easier, and – as already mentioned – a few Middle Persian Zoroastrian texts *were* actually written in the Avestan script (the so-called Pāzand), as the knowledge of Middle Persian declined. But this proves that the shortcomings of the system *and* the possible solution were clearly seen, but the latter only very half-heartedly adopted. The writing system used for the vast majority of texts remained the complicated and defective book Pahlavi with its cumbersome heterograms, which burden the reader and slow down understanding.[132]

The solution, however, to this enigma might be found in the Far East: Japanese and Korean are both written in a mixture of phonetic and logographic elements: The phonetic characters in Japanese are the syllabaries *Katagana* and *Hiragana*, hardly interconnected and both derived from Chinese characters, whereas in Korean the so-called *Hangul*-script is a unique invention. The logographic elements are the thousands of Chinese characters (in Chinese: *Hànzì*; Japanese: *Kanji*; Korean: *Hanja*), e.g.

日本	**え**	**来た**
Ni┌hon ┐	**e**	**ki├ta┤**
Japan	*to*	*came (he/she/ I came to Japan*[133]*)*

Only the gray shaded characters are phonetic (Hiragana), the others are Chinese logograms (Kanji). As all speech sounds can be perfectly represented in the syllabaries, it would be well possible to write Japanese without using any Kanji. That this is not done, however, is often explained by the fact that too many Kanji are pronounced identically, so by abolishing the Kanji these homophones would become indistinguishable. But the fact that in *spoken* Japanese these homophones do not pose a big problem shows that the possible misunderstandings to be expected would be limited to a fairly small number of cases. Chinese characters in Japanese, however, are also ambiguous as for every Kanji there are at least two different readings, one going back to the Chinese pronunciation of the borrowing, one being the Japanese semantic equivalent. So Chinese 人 (rén) has got the Sino-Japanese reading "jin" or "nin" in compounds like 人口 – jin-ko (Chinese: rénkǒu, = population). Standing alone it is pronounced as "hito". If English were written with the same system, the character would be pronounced "man" in a sentence like "this man is big", but "human-" in a word like "human-ity". So by dropping the Kanji, the difficulty of homophones might be increased, the difficulty of multiple pronunciations for the same Kanji, however, would be eliminated!

Moreover, the fact that Japanese in Kanji *can* actually be read, can be proven with an example: the autobiography of the former Geisha Masuda Sayo,[134] who had never attended a school and taught herself to write in Hiragana, was written without the use of Kanji. When it was sent to a publisher they did not have problems to understand it, the question was rather in which form it should appear in book-form. The sample sentence at the beginning (*Nihon e kita* - came to Japan), by the way, would be absolutely clear even in a phonetic script, although there are dozens of Kanji other than **日** which are pronounced "ni", simply because there is only one compound "Nihon = Japan".

In North Korea Chinese characters (Hanja) have virtually been abolished, and even in South Korea they are used less and less, their last sanctuary being the above-mentioned cases of homophones.

The often adduced argument that older literature would be much harder to understand, as the elliptic style greatly increases the homophone problem, is to be taken a bit more seriously. But even here there is a solution which can make everyone happy. A short look at a modern Japanese bible will show that next to every (!) Kanji, the pronunciation is indicated with a small superscript Hiragana letter, which makes it excellent teaching material for everybody not yet perfect in the system and willing to improve his or her reading skills.

But what is the *real* reason for this obstinate adherence to a difficult writing system? The case of the publisher of the geisha's autobiography reveals the truth: Whoever has invested years of arduous learning in order to master a difficult writing system, the perfect mastery of which – like in ancient China – might be a synonym to climbing up the social ladder or at least universal respect, somebody who feels superior to every peasant or manual laborer merely because of his knowledge of writing, such a person has absolutely no interest in exchanging this difficult, yet cumbersome system for a handier one, which can easily be learnt by these very peasants or manual laborers.[135]

3.10.4 A parallel case: Runic alphabets

It might be a bit surprising to mention Runic alphabets in a study about the writing systems of the Ancient Near East. But the evolution of this script displays a striking parallel to the evolution of the Arabic writing system, if considered within its Syriac context. Syriac had a moderately defective writing system of 22 consonants, where only two consonant letters merged, which later were distinguished by dots (namely: "d" and "r"). Its apparent offshoot, the Arabic script, consisted of originally only about a dozen letters and was enormously defective. Only later was it *disambiguated* with the help of *diacritic dots.*

The oldest Runic[136] alphabet, the so-called *Elder Futhark*, consists of originally 24 runes, which well represented most phonemic distinctions of Old Norse, e.g. "k - ᚲ", "g - ᚷ" and "ng- ᛜ".

A few centuries later, a much reduced alphabet (the so-called *Younger Futhark*) consisting of only 16 characters, was the dominant alphabet in use. All three above mentioned letters had merged in one: ᚴ.

After the 12th century, this latter system was disambiguated with the help of *diacritical dots*, so that "k" and "g" could now be distinguished again:

"k - ᚴ" vs. "g - ᚵ".

3.10.5 A defective cipher from fictional literature

From a universal perspective an orthography like the one in use in the earliest Qur'ānic manuscripts with a mere dozen graphemes is hardly to be found in any language, apart from cases like modern Polynesian languages, which are written with about a dozen graphemes, simply because they do not possess more than a dozen phonemes!

Stenotype machines might be adduced as yet another counter-example, as they have by far fewer keys than a normal keyboard. But here it is the combination of simultaneously pressed keys (called "chording/ stroking") which leads to the output of not only letters, but even syllables and words.

The fact that a writing system as defective as the early Arabic script must have been in use even in more modern times, and at the same time an explanation why such a system would be used, can be inferred from a passage in fictional literature.

Rudyard Kipling, the author of famous novels like the *Jungle Book* or *Kim*, which betray his intimate knowledge of the Indian society of the Victorian era, described an interesting cipher consisting of no more than a dozen graphemes in his novella *The man who would be king.*[137]

> "'The letter? - Oh! - The letter! Keep looking at me between the eyes, please. It was a *string-talk letter*, that we'd learned the way of it from a blind beggar in the Punjab.'
> I remember that there had once come to the office a blind man with a *knotted twig* and a *piece of string* which he *wound round the twig according to some cipher of his own*. He could, after the lapse of days or hours, repeat the sentence which he had reeled up. He had *reduced the alphabet to eleven primitive sounds*; and tried to teach me his method, but I could not understand. (...) *(my emphasis)*"

It is worth noting that the cipher described here intentionally renounces on distinctions to make the message unintelligible to outsiders!

3.10.6 Defective Scripts: Summary and Conclusion

When assessing the orthography of the oldest Qur'ānic manuscripts, above all when comparing it with the ones used for Hebrew, Syriac, Middle Persian or even much older scripts like the ones in use for Ugaritic or Old Persian, it does not take much reasoning to consider it – speaking in terms of progressiveness of a system – a *huge step backwards*.

No other system in the area has or had a comparably small number of graphemes, and even in other eras and areas of the world it will be difficult to find anything even remotely as defective. Even in Kipling's cipher only similar sounds would be grouped together under one letter, unlike in Arabic with the five totally unrelated sounds being represented by undotted *yā'*.

So the question arises why somebody who has learnt one of the moderately defective writing systems of the Ancient Near East (as must be assumed for the "inventors" of the Arabic script), like one of the scripts used for Aramaic or Epigraphic South Arabic, would transform it in such a way that texts written in it – unless they are very simple or standardized – can only be read by somebody who roughly knows the contents anyway?

One explanation would be the already mentioned aim to make the religious texts, which later would be edited as the Qur'ān, only accessible to the inner circle of readers familiar with them. Thus the Qur'ānic orthography would be a kind of cipher. But on the other hand, why should a religious group use a highly ambiguous writing system, while much clearer systems were available, considering that one of their aims must have been the preservation of supposedly divine texts. Regarding the typology of religions, the case of the Avesta, the Rigveda and the Masoretic punctuation point in a different direction: generally speaking, transmitters of religious texts rather have a tendency to disambiguation and clear transmission, for fear of falsification. Furthermore, the idea that such a tendency is not alien to Islam is well proven by the extremely detailed punctuation and vocalization of later Qur'ān editions, not to mention all the additional symbols which even indicate assimilations, obligatory and non-obligatory pauses etc. But the mistakes in these punctuations and vocalizations clearly show that this natural tendency belongs to a much later phase.

A final and conclusive solution of the enigma will certainly require a much more detailed and unbiased research of the early manuscripts with the ultimate aim of a text-critical Qur'ān edition, including all deviating readings, preferably with facsimiles of all corresponding passages in old manuscripts.

4. Mixed Languages as a Linguistic Phenomenon

In his book "The Syro-Aramaic Reading of the Koran", Christoph Luxenberg concludes that the Qur'ān was originally written in what he called an Arabic-Aramaic *mixed language.* On the homepage of the prestigious Summer Institute of Linguistics (SIL), entitled "The Ethnologue", there is a page about "mixed languages"[138] with a list of 21 such languages. According to their implicit definition, a mixed language is a language, in the case of which it is difficult to say which of the normally two parent languages is the prevailing one. If this narrow criterion is used, then the language of the Qur'ān is not a mixed language *strictu sensu,* as it is predominantly Arabic with an Aramaic admixture, even if modern, as well as classical Arabic authors kept on insisting on its purity.

But in a *wider* sense, the term *mixed language* for the reconstructible original idiom used in the Qur'ān – which is not identical with the language of modern Qur'ān editions – is certainly not unjustified.

So in this section we want to have a short look at different types of mixed languages, if a less strict definition is applied.

First of all, in a way every human language is to a certain extent mixed, as every language contains elements borrowed from other languages, however, in very varying degrees. Modern Chinese has hardly got any borrowings –

even modern devices like a "telephone" get a name the elements of which are purely Chinese (in this case: 电话 dìan-hùa – lightning + speech). But on closer inspection even Chinese will reveal influences from other languages, e.g. the increasing use of a syntactical construction which distinguishes real and irreal conditional clauses, an influence mainly due to translation from European languages. Moreover, even if the elements in a compound are purely Chinese, the choice of these elements often shows the phonetic influence of the donor languages, e.g. discotheque 迪斯科舞厅 "*dísīkē* wūtǐng", the second element meaning "ball room", the first one only imitating the English sounds.

English is at the other end of the spectrum and absorbs anything to the extant that it does not even have a real designation for these borrowings, unlike German, which distinguishes (clearly discernible) foreign words ("Fremdwörter"), e.g. Tabu (taboo), Tomahawk, Pyjama etc. from "adapted foreign words" ("Lehnwörter"), e.g. Münze (coin) < Latin "moneta". For many Germans it is quite surprising to hear that very "German-sounding" words like "Keller" (cellar; < Latin "cella"), "Mauer" ("wall" < Latin "murus"), "kaufen" (to buy < Latin "caupo – landlord") are indeed borrowings. English has such cases, too, e.g. "church" (German "Kirche", Scots English "kirk" < Greek "kyriaké"). In other cases the speakers might know that the word is of foreign origin, but it is no longer "felt" to be so, e.g. "chocolate" from Nahuatl (the language of the Aztecs), "pyjama" from Hindi/ Urdu.

Another special case are so-called *calques* (in German: "Lehnübersetzung = loan translation"), i.e., compounds made up from "indigenous" elements, where every element is a translation of an equivalent in the donor language, e.g. "loanword" from German "Lehnwort".

Sometimes, even whole sentences are "loan-translated" like this, e.g. "long time no see" is an exact literal rending of a Chinese phrase, which entered the English language through Chinese Pidgin English.

In German, calques, especially from Latin, are extremely numerous, e.g. "Ein-fluss" (influence) < Latin "in-fluentia".

Something less known is the fact that many modern standard languages possess words and phrases from different dialects. The French word for "love", "amour", is not a nominal form of the corresponding verb "aimer". If it were, it should be spelled "aim-eur", *-eur* being the abstract suffix like in "chal-eur", "haut-eur" etc. The form "aimeur" does actually exist in at least one moribund French dialect, but it means "rut", not "love", although there is of course a semantic overlap.

The word is taken from the closely related Occitan (by some called Provençal), a language or rather group of dialects once spoken in the southern half of France. Although the modern forms are rather moribund, it was once the major European language of love poetry, its "troubadours" inspiring both the Northern French "trouvères" (actually the Northern

French equivalent of the word), the Galician-Portuguese "trobadores", the German "Minnesänger", the poets of the "Scuola Siciliana" of Emperor Frederick II as well as Dante and other authors of the "Dolce Stil Nuovo". So it is not surprising that the Occitan word "amor", pronounced [a'mur] and phonetically spelled in French as "amour" was borrowed into French.

In the Old English period large parts of England were occupied by Danes, who spoke a variety of Old Norse, which to a certain extent was mutually intelligible with Old English. In the course of the following centuries many words from Old Norse replaced the Old English words, e.g. Old English "niman" (German: "nehmen") was replaced by Old Norse "tacan", which later developed into Modern English "to take".

When dialect words are borrowed it is quite common that the dialect word does not totally replace the genuinely inherited word (as in the case of "aimeur" in standard French), but that both forms live side by side as a doublet with slightly different meanings or in different environments. In Modern English we have the forms "ship" (the inherited form Old English) and the Norse form "skipper". A less clubbable German example would be the word "Titten" (tits), which is of Northern German origin. The form to be expected according to the sound change rules of the "High German Consonant Shift" (t > z [ts]) would be "Zitze". The word does exist in standard German, but it means "dugs, teats".[139]

At this point another interesting phenomenon deserves to be mentioned: lexical re-import. "Tennis" is an English foreign word in French, the English word itself being derived from the French "tenez!". French "casino" (with the same meaning as the identical English word, but with the stress on the last syllable as normal in French) goes back to the Italian word "casino" (with the stress on the penultimate). In Italian it is still in use, but means "brothel". If, however, it has the stress on the last syllable (spelled "casinò"), then it means the same as in English and French. Another example involving German is the originally French word "chic", which is meanwhile also used in other European languages including German as a loanword of putative French origin. Originally it goes back to the German "schick", which until now is an acceptable orthographic variant in German, although most Germans think that "schick" is a non-cosmopolitan, hillbilly version of a more correct spelling "chic". The word, however, belongs to the originally German root "-schick-" that we find in words like in "schicklich (seemly)", "sich schicken (to be seemly)" and "geschickt (adroit)".

Semantic adaptation, i.e., the act of enlarging the meaning of a word following the use in another language, – Christoph Luxenberg claims numerous cases of especially this phenomenon between Arabic and Aramaic – is also very common. The English word "to realize" has two major meanings: in "to realise a project" it means to "make come true/ to give physical form to", while in "I realized it was over" it means "to become aware of". The German equivalent "realisieren" could be used in the first sense, but not in the second until maybe thirty years ago. At that time more and more journalists living in English speaking countries did not bother to look for a good German word with that meaning (e.g. "einer Sache gewahr werden; bemerken; sich einer Sache bewusst werden", all rather long equivalents), but simply used the German (etymological) equivalent of the English word with the adopted meaning.

A similar, maybe even more common case is the borrowing of words from older stages of the language, e.g. Latin words like "a priori" in French (and most European languages). In some cases, the modern form of such a loan-word, i.e., the form inherited from Latin which underwent all the different sound-shifts, is also used, e.g. French "légal" (legal) from Medieval Latin "legalis" and "loyal" from the Gallo-Romance variety of Latin.

A rarer case of how a word can come into being is erroneous etymology or interpretation by scribes, something parallel to the interpretation of the consonants of Aramaic derived stems as Arabic radicals. In French we find a similar case in the Old French spelling "scavoir" for modern "savoir". A velar plosive was never pronounced in this word, the spelling with "sc-" going back to the idea that the word is derived from the Latin word with the same meaning: "scire", while in fact in comes from Latin "sapere" ("to be wise" like in "homo sapiens").

After a while even such wrong spellings can be corroborated by linguistic reality. The English word "debt" is normally pronounced [dɛt], only less educated speakers using the variant [dɛbt]. Originally, there had never been such a pronunciation, as the word goes back to French "dette" [dɛt]. The spelling with "b" goes back to the erroneous idea that the word came from Latin "debitum". The fact that it is especially less educated speakers that pronounce the "b" again demonstrates the awe-inspiring effect of writing.

In the case of English another phenomenon can be observed: lexical material from different sources is automatically associated with a certain social class or different levels of sophistication, the Germanic element being lowest in the ranking, just consider the following examples:[140]

"Pure Germanic English":

The man in the wilderness asked of me
How many strawberries grow in the sea?
I answered him as I thought good.
As many red herrings as grow in the wood.

"French English":

People prefer travelling in groups particularly during certain seasons despite very considerable reasons favoring possible contrary arrangements.

"Latin English":

Devastating conflagrations, incinerating vast rural areas, inflicted incalculable, irremediable destruction, exceeding prevalent popular expectation.

In all these cases the differentiation of different levels is not phonetic, but mostly lexical and grammatical only to a very limited extent, although it must be admitted that pronunciation can also greatly serve as a distinctive indicator of social origin, in England, however, much more than in the United States.

If two languages are in close contact, the mutual influence often goes much further. Substrate and superstrate languages in most cases mix on all levels, although not always in the same way. One of the reasons for this interference is the fact that if people speak two languages, either from early childhood on or because one of them was learnt in later stages of their lives, they hardly ever master them both equally well. In most cases one of them is dominant, but even if both are on an equal footing, they will inevitably be influenced by the respective competitor language. Many Hispanics in America will use phrases like "*Tengo que ir al bus stop para pick up mi hija*[141]" or they will use the verb "remover" as equivalent for "to remove", not the correct "sacar". An extreme case of grammatical simplification is the emergence of Pidgin and Creole languages, a topic we will refrain from discussing in the present paper, as it has little relevance for the language of the Qur'ān. Moreover, the case of *Mixed Languages* according to the definition of the *Summer Institute of Linguistics*[142] must be excluded for the same reason. In these cases the two or more parent languages are not at all or only remotely akin, unlike in the case of Luxenberg's postulated language composed of Syro-Aramaic and Arabic, which differ as much (or as little) as maybe Dutch and English. The situation here would be much more comparable to the case of the mixed Russian and Belorussian language spoken by many less educated people in Belarus called трасянка (trasjánka - forage).[143] The difference, however, is that of both parent languages well defined and excellently described standard varieties exist, which could be said of Syriac at the time of the writing of the earliest Qur'ānic texts, but certainly not of Arabic.

Another example of a similar situation is the present state of the "broad" forms of German dialects. In many areas they are gradually yielding to "regional forms" of standard German, i.e., variant forms of standard German with phonetic traits, grammatical constructions and lexical elements from the corresponding dialect or better a number of regional dialects. A similar development has taken place in France, where most dialects are moribund and have been replaced by regional varieties of Standard French. e.g. "Francitan" in the South (a word composed of elements from "français – French" and "Occitan – the Romance language of the Southern half of France"). As a rule of thumb in Germany, the dialectal element becomes stronger the more you go to the south, depending on social origin, education and emotional relation to one's home area, the only area where more or less pure forms of the dialects are the normal medium of communication between all generations being Switzerland and Luxemburg, where, however, the "dialect" has meanwhile become an official and standardized "language".

In some areas there is or was a kind of intermediate form between standard language and dialect which itself had a specific name and a social status. In Bavaria it was so-called "Honoratioren-Bairisch" ("dignitaries' Bavarian"), in Northern Germany so-called "Missingsch", a German variety strongly influenced by Low German ("Plattdütsch"), which some forty years ago became quite popular all over Germany because of televised theatre productions from the "Ohnsorg Theater" in Hamburg. Although this theatre usually stages a large variety of performances in pure Low German, for the nationwide TV productions the intermediate language form was chosen, as it was both clearly regional and understandable for the average German speaker. The younger generation of Germans, who did not grow up with such TV programs, might find Missingsch much harder to understand than the generation of their parents.

At this point it should not be forgotten that the German standard language ("Hochdeutsch" = High German) itself does not go back to one German dialect, but is mainly based on East Middle German dialectal forms with phonetic habits and lexical elements added from other areas. Yiddish, which branched off from German only in the Middle Ages, shows an equal variety of roots as standard German and does not go back to one dialect.

The notion "Sprachbund" is another phenomenon which is certainly relevant when researching linguistic interference, its best known example being the *Balkan Sprachbund.*[144] "Sprachbund" means a number of languages which are unrelated or at best remotely related, but share common features, which are typical for the whole area in which they are spoken. Often there is a kind of epicenter, where all features can be found and more marginal areas with less common ground. In the Balkans the most typical languages are Albanian, Bulgarian (with the closely related Macedonian) and Romanian (including the smaller variants like Aromanian). Serbian and Croatian on the one hand and Greek on the other belong to the outskirts of the Sprachbund. While there is a very limited "Balkan" vocabulary, in most cases shepherd terminology, the bulk of the shared features, however, is to be found in parallel constructions, e.g. the postponed article, e.g. "*the* river" - Albanian "lum-*i*", "the man" – Romanian "om-*ul*". Semantic parallels can also be found, e.g. the semantic enlargement of the verb meaning "to pull" which also means "to suffer" (Bulgarian teglja, Dako-Romanian "a trage", Modern Greek "travó", Albanian "heq"). The most conspicuous characteristic of Balkan languages, however, is the loss of the infinitive, which is replaced by a subordinate clause with a finite verb form e.g.: *"How long do you want to stay?"*

Greek :	πόσο	καιρό	θέλετε	νὰ	μείνετε
	'pɔsɔ	kjɛ'rɔ	'θɛlɛtɛ	na	'minɛtɛ
Bulgarian:	до кога		искате	да	останете
	do ko'ga		'iskate	dɐ	o'stanete
Romanian:	Cît	timp	vreţi	să	rămineţi
	how long		*you want*	*that*	*you stay* [145]

The isogloss boundary of the Balkan Sprachbund concerning the use of the infinitive vs. subordinate clause construction can be drawn right between two variants of the same language:[146] "I want to go": Serbian: *želim da idem* ("Balkan type": *I want that I go*) vs. Croatian: *želim ići* ("Middle European type": *I want to go*). The same boundary goes through the Albanian dialects: While standard Albanian, which is mainly based on the Southern (Tosk) dialects follows the Balkan type, the Northern (Gheg) dialects, e.g. those spoken in the Kosovo, use "me" together with the preterit participle passive as an infinitive. The sentence "he begins to look" would be "ay fillon *të shikojë* (he begins that he looks) in standard Albanian and "Aj fillon *me shikjue*" in Gheg.[147]

A last phenomenon must be mentioned here, which refers especially to the situation in areas with related languages spoken by nomads and their classification. Menges[148], in his standard overview of Turkic languages, classifies Qyrgyz both as member of his subgroup A.I.6 and of A.VI.14. The reason for this at first glance contradictory procedure is the fact that related languages with a high degree of mutual intelligibility which are in contact over a large area, as is the case among nomads, often tend to absorb features of different subgroups of the language family, which often makes it quite hard to decide which affiliation is the primary one. The family-tree of such a language group is much harder to draw than of a group the members of which are clearly divided by large rivers, deserts or mountain ridges.

As most Semitic dialects were once spoken by city dwellers as well as by nomads, the existence of such intermediate dialects must be taken into consideration.

In the following, two examples of mixed languages in the widest sense of the word will be presented to make a fair assessment of the postulated Arabic-Aramaic mixed language easier. The first example is the so-called *Buddhist Hybrid Sanskrit* (BHS), a language form which emerged after the transposition of Middle Indian (Prakrit) texts into the corresponding Old Indian (Sanskrit) forms. The second example is Modern Norwegian, which once had two clearly distinguished variants, Nynorsk and Bokmål, which in the past hundred years have moved closer and closer together.

4.1 Example: Buddhist Hybrid Sanskrit (BHS)

Buddhist Hybrid Sanskrit (BHS) emerged as a language form of its own when Buddhist texts originally written in Middle Indian languages were not translated, but rather transposed word by word, replacing the Middle Indian forms by the corresponding, but not always correct Sanskrit forms. Three levels of adaptation can be distinguished:

1. Texts written in correct Sanskrit prose with verses in BHS.
2. Texts in Sanskrit interspersed with hybrid forms.
3. Texts entirely written in BHS.

According to the alleged word of the Buddha (from the Vinayapiṭaka), the teachings could be spread in the corresponding local languages. For this reason canonical texts in various Middle Indian languages (or rather dialects, as they were mutually intelligible) were composed. Of these collections only the Dharmapada in Gandhāri (rather a small texts of less than a hundred pages) and the Pāli Canon (in the Bangkok edition of 1996 consisting of 45 thick vols.) have been preserved. The oldest written texts in an Indo-Aryan language are the edicts of King Aśoka (304 BCE to 232 CE) of the Mauryan dynasty, mostly carved on pillars and boulders. The language, however, is not Sanskrit, but are the respective local Middle Indian (early Prakrit) languages, apart from one inscription in Greek and one in Aramaic, which might also be heterographically written Iranian, as its syntax is very un-Semitic. In these edicts the king, who, after a battle, had allegedly become a Buddhist, proclaims his new faith.

The older stage of the language from which these Middle Indian languages derived – Sanskrit – experienced a kind of renaissance from around the first century BCE, which had a major impact also on Buddhist literature. Buddhist texts now had to be translated into the old sacred language of Hinduism, which had meanwhile become the lingua franca of scholars. When prose texts had to be translated, it did not pose a problem, provided the translator's competence in Sanskrit was sufficient. But versified texts would have required poetic skills. So texts with a meter were transposed as described above, but only to the extent that the meter was not affected, which often resulted in hybrid forms, e.g. a Middle Indian (Prakrit) form "hoti - he/she is" could not easily be replaced by the Sanskrit form "bhavati", as the extra syllable would have destroyed the meter, so the original form was kept in the (hybrid) Sanskrit text. In prose, of course, such a compromise was not necessary.

But the replacement of Prakrit forms by the corresponding Sanskrit forms in general was not unproblematic either. It was rather as if someone "re-Latinized" a French sentence like "*je l'ai vu*" ("I have seen him") by replacing each form by its Latin counterpart, which would yield "*ego illum habeo visum*" (instead of the correct "*eum vidi*").

From a certain moment on the canonical texts of certain sects, e.g. the Sarvastivādins, were recited and read entirely in more or less correct Sanskrit. The mixed language that had thus evolved was then no longer a medium for translation, but was used for the composition of new, original texts, which did not have a Middle Indian model. As most Prakrits share their main syntactical traits it is very difficult to derive BHS from a specific Middle Indian dialect, as the deviations from "normal" Sanskrit – which itself is a very peculiar case, as will be shown later – have parallels in several Prakrit varieties.

Moreover, it should be noted that the Mahayana Canon was not translated into Tibetan and Chinese from a model text in Pāli, but from a Sanskrit original. Only parts of this Sanskrit Canon – if compared to the enormous Pāli Canon, it is hardly more than fragments – have been preserved, so that modern Mahayanists have to resort to the Chinese and Tibetan collections, with very few exceptions like the famous Heart Sūtra (Sanskrit: Prajñāpāramitā Hṛdaya), which is recited both in Sanskrit and the later Tibetan and Chinese translations.

Given the enormous discrepancy in size and number, it is quite surprising that the first Buddhist texts translated into European languages were not from the (older) Pāli-Canon, but from Sanskrit originals, so that the most central Buddhist terms in common use in European languages are Sanskrit and not Pāli, e.g. *Nirvana* (Pāli: *nibbāna*), *Dharma* (Pāli: *dhammo*), *Karma* (Pāli: *kammo*), *Gautama* (Pāli: *Gotama*), *Siddartha* (Pāli: *Siddhattha*). The only ambiguous term is "Buddha", which is the same in both languages.

In the case of Pāli there is still some debate going on whether it was a true local dialect or rather a koineized lingua franca based on Western Early Middle Indian. The alleged home of the Buddha would make the closely related dialect Māghadhī his mother tongue, of which a later form was used in the classical drama, as we will see later. But even in the Pāli-Canon some "maghadisms" did survice, e.g. the Buddha usually adresses his disciples as "*bhikkave*" (voc. pl. of "bhikku" [Sanskrit: bhikṣu]). The correct Pāli form would be "*bhikkavo*", the "-e" being a typical Māghadī feature. This, however, might as well be considered a "trick" to localize the origin of the new religion in an area where Māgadhi was spoken, a bit like a fictional character in an English or American novel would automatically be labeled Australian, if his direct speech is "peppered" with words like "mate" or "godday".

Tradition is said to have been oral for a long time, with specialists for each kind of text called "bhāṇaka". The fact that the same story often appears several times with divergent details shows that this oral tradition cannot have been too reliable.

When the text collections were finally canonized, the material was arranged with regard to content and divided into three so-called "baskets" (piṭaka), the entire canon then being called "Tipiṭaka (three baskets)" in Pāli.

The homeland of the Pāli Canon is said to be the area which roughly corresponds to the modern Indian state Madhya Pradesh, but up until the second century CE texts were added in Ceylon (modern Sri Lanka).

Sample text: Dhammapāda 393,[149] *from chapter 23 - Brāhmanavaggo*

1. Text in Pāli (corresponding Sanskrit forms are to be found in the right-hand column; skt. = Sanskrit)

Na jaṭāhi na gottena *not by matted hair not by clan* *Not by wearing matted hair, nor by lineage,*	**na** - 'not'; skt. id. **jaṭāhi** - instr. pl. 'jaṭā - matted hair'; skt. jaṭābhiḥ **gottena** - Instr. sg. 'gotta n. - clan, ancestry
na jaccā hoti brāhmaṇo, *not by caste (one) becomes brahmin* *nor by caste, does one become a brahmana;*	**jaccā** = jātiyā - instr. sg. 'jāti - birth, caste'; skt. jātyā **hoti** - 3rd sg. pres. 'bhū - to be'; skr. bhavati **brāhmaṇo** - nom. sg. 'brāhmaṇo - brahmin, man of the Brahman caste'; skt. brāhmanaḥ
yamhi saccañ ca dhammo *at which/in whom truth and morality* *only he who realizes the Truth and the Dhamma*	**yamhi** - lok. sg. m. 'yo - rel. pron.'; skt. yasmiṃ **saccañ** - nom. sg. 'sacca n. - truth'; skt. satyaṃ **ca ... ca** - 'as well as; skt. id. **dhammo** - nom. sg. 'dhammo - religion, norm, doctrine, morality'; skt. dharmaḥ
ca so sucī so ca brāhmaṇo. *and this pure this and brahmin* *is pure; he is a brahmana.*	**so** - nom. sg. 'this'; skt. 'saḥ' **sucī** - nom. sg. 'pure, holy'; skt. śucī

The corresponding BHS variant[150] of this text is nearly identical, the only difference being that instead of "gotteṇa" the correct Sanskrit form "gotreṇa" is used. The BHS version has 414 verses as opposed to the 423 of the Pali original. Moreover, there are some differences in the order of verses.

In Central Asia the so-called "Gandhārī Prakrit" had a similar position as a lingua franca as Pali in the South. It was written in the comparatively hard-to-read *Karoṣṭhī* (donkey's lip) script. The above text was also transposed into this language,[151] the fourth line of the following interlinear comparison being correct (but not attested) Sanskrit.

Gandhāri:	na	jaḍa'i	na	gotreṇa
Pali:	na	jaṭāhi	na	gottena
BHS:	na	jaṭāhi	na	gotreṇa
Sanskrit (reconstructed):	na	jaṭābhiḥ	na	gotreṇa

Gandhāri:	na	yaca	bʰodi	bramaṇo
Pali:	na	jaccā	hoti	brāhmaṇo.
BHS:	(not attested)			
Sanskrit:	na	jātyā	bhavati	brāhmaṇaḥ

Another good example of BHS for a comparison with Pali is the following text from Mahāvagga I, 6, 19-22 (Pali) and Mahāvastu III 332, 1,5,7,9 (BHS)[152] respectively.

P = Pali, S= Buddhist Hybrid Sanskrit

P: Idaṁ kho pana bhikkave
S: tatra bhikṣavaḥ katamaṁ
this well but monks
there which
"This, monks, is

P: dukkhaṁ ariyasaccaṁ:
S: duḥkam āryasatyaṁ tad yathā:
suffering noble truth
this how
the noble truth of suffering

P: jāti pi dukkhā, jarā pi dukkhā,
S: Jātiḥ duḥkaṁ, jarā duḥkaṁ,
birth but suffering old age but suffering
birth is suffering, getting old is suffering,

P: vyādhi pi dukkhā, maraṇaṁ pi
S: vyādhi duḥkaṁ, maraṇaṃ
illness but suffering death but
illness is suffering, death is

P: dukkhaṁ
S: duḥkaṁ
suffering
suffering.

words only in the Sanskrit version:
tatra -'there' (Pali: tathā)
katamaṁ - 'which' (= Pali)
tad - nom. n. 'this' (= Pali)
yathā - how (= Pali)

idaṁ - nom. sg. 'this'; skt. id.
kho - 'well, then'; skt. khalu
pana - 'but, however'; not attested in skt.
bhikkave - voc. pl. 'bhikku - monk'; skt. bhikṣavaḥ
dukkhaṁ - nom. sg. n. 'suffering'; here: Bahuvrīhi: "having suffering = woe-begone"; skt. duḥkam
ariyasaccaṁ - 'ariya - noble' + 'sacca - truth'; skt. āryasatyaṁ
jāti - 'birht'; skt. id.
pi - 'but; also; emphatic particle'; skt. (a)pi
dukkhā - 'suffering' (pausal form)
jarā - 'old age'; skt. id.
vyādhi - 'illness'; skt. id.
maraṇaṁ - 'death'; skt. id.

The transposition of a text from a later stage of a language into an earlier one might seem a rather singular case to the average linguist. But within the realm of Indo-Aryan language this phenomenon is by no means limited to Buddhist Hybrid Sanskrit, as the linguistic history of Classical Sanskrit clearly shows. If Classical Sanskrit and Vedic – the oldest stage of the language – are compared, it is obvious that the latter is much closer to Homeric Greek in syntax than the former. Classical Sanskrit has a conspicuous tendency to nominal constructions, which is typical of later forms of the language, often called Prakrits. In his standard survey about Indo-Aryan languages, Colin Masica[153] writes the following about the stages of the language:

> "VEDIC: based apparently on a far-western dialect, perhaps influenced by Iranian; further substages may be distinguished, the language of Books II-VII of the Rig Veda being the most archaic, that of the Brāhmaṇas and Sūtras the least.
>
> VEDIC CLASSICAL SANSKRIT: based on a dialect of the midland (western Ganges valley, eastern Punjab, Haryana), although influenced by Vedic. Later literature was much influenced by MIA (with which it is contemporary), remaining OIA only in phonetics and morphology."

MIA here means Middle Indo-Aryan, OIA Old Indo-Aryan. On page 55 Masica writes:

> "The oldest Sanskrit inscription, that of Rudradāman, a Śaka king – a foreigner – in what is now Gujarat, dates only from AD 150. The habit of making inscriptions in Sanskrit thus gradually ousts that of making them in Prakrit and not the other way around. It is as if Latin had replaced (Old) French."

What this means is the following: what happened in the case of Buddhist texts is the same phenomenon we can observe here: a later form of the language (Prakrit dialects) were trans*posed* into the corresponding forms of an older language, the syntax and phraseology remaining more or less the same. How far this went can be seen in Sanskrit drama, characterized by Masica as follows (p. 56):

> "The so-called Dramatic or Literary Prakrits (the main representatives of the Second MIA stage: Sauraseni, Magadhi, and Maharashtri) are highly stylized dialects prescribed for certain types of stage characters or literary genres, written according to formula."

What is interesting in the dramas is the fact that different people speak different languages and dialects depending on their social status: men of higher status speak *Sanskrit*; women speak *Śaurasenī*, but sing their songs in *Māhārāṣṭrī* – the Prakrit *par excellence*. Men of lower status speak *Māgadhī*.

These three Prakrits must have been mutually intelligible – otherwise it is unimaginable that they were displayed in the same drama, but the sentences were not necessarily authentic. The author probably only spoke one of them well and just transposed his words into the other Prakrits according to sound rules, a bit like modern British comedians imitating Americans by pronouncing all the R's and changing a few vowels, thus leaving aside all the other differences that exist between these two variants of English. In some modern editions of Classical Sanskrit dramas, the original Prakrit text is then accompanied by a translation into Sanskrit, as modern Indian students who want to perform the drama might know Sanskrit and modern Indian languages, but not the Prakrits of Kālidāsa's time. These Sanskrit translations of the Prakrit passages are often only transposed much like in the case of Buddhist Hybrid Sanskrit, but with by far fewer mistakes. The Sanskrit that comes out is pure Classical Sanskrit, a clear indication that that is exactly how Classical Sanskrit originally came into being: *by morphologically and phonetically transposing Middle Indian into Old Indian.*

What this means can best be exemplified with the help of India's most famous drama: Abhijñāna-Śākuntalam of Kālidāsa[154] ("The recognition of Śākuntala"). Although Kālidāsa is probably the most famous classical Indian poet, not even the century when he wrote his masterpieces is known, the estimations varying between the first century BCE and the fourth century CE. The following sentence is from Act 5 and is first given in its original Prakrit form (as in Woolner, p. 101) and an interlinear version underneath is the Sanskrit translation as in Devadhar and Suru's edition (transliterated from Devanagarī by myself):

(Situation: Śakuntalā before the king, who has forgotten her due to a curse):

Imaṃ	avatthantaraṃ	gade	tādise
idaṃ	avasthāntaraṃ	gate	tādṛśe
this	*changed condition*	*gone*	*thus*

aṇūrāe	kiṃ	vā	sumarāvideṇa.
'ṇūrāge	kiṃ	vā	smāritena.
affection	*what*	*then*	*having reminded.*

"When such love has so changed, what use is there in bringing it to mind?"

The form *sumarāvideṇa* is the past participle causative of '*sumaredi, sumaradi* – remember' = skt. 'smarati'; it should be mentioned that a noun derived from the same root, *smṛti*, means "(everything) *remembered*" and designates the Hinduist *tradition* as opposed to "*śruti* - (everything) *heard*", which designates *revealed texts*, the two concepts thus being exactly equivalent to *Qur'ān* and *Sunna* in Islam.

If Christoph Luxenberg should be right, then something similar as in Buddhist Hybrid Sanskrit would have happened in the case of at least some Qur'ānic texts: they were originally conceived in Syriac and imperfectly rendered in Arabic by transposing word by word into the corresponding (or putatively corresponding) Arabic form. As these forms, however, were written in a defective writing system and later generations could not make head or tail of this hybrid Arab-Syriac, many were misunderstood and erroneously re-interpreted[155].

4.2 Example: Norwegian

Between the years 1380 and 1814 Norway was united with Denmark, the closely related Danish being the official language, Norwegian being confined to private use. The pronunciation of Danish in Norway, however, was strongly influenced by Norwegian, so that after independence two alternatives to create a modern written Norwegian language were discussed: on the one hand, the standardization of "pure" Norwegian dialects, on the other the "Norwegization" of Danish.

In the end both alternatives were adopted simultaneously. The following table shows how these two language variants, which at the beginning were quite distinct, have meanwhile moved closer and closer to each other. This development will be shown with the help of an example: the sentence "the children went out through the door"[156]. In 19th century Danish the sentence would have been rendered as:

Børnene gik ud gennem døren.

The corresponding sentences in the two variants are as follows:

	*former "Riksmål" = today "**Bokmål**" = norwegized Danish*	*former "Landsmål" = today "**Nynorsk**" (lit.: New Norwegian), based on 'pure' dialects*
1907	Børnene gik ut gjennem døren.	Borni gjekk ut gjennom dyri.
1917	Barnene gikk ut gjennem døren.	Borni gjekk ut gjennom døri.
1938	Barna gikk ut gjennom døra.	Borni gjekk ut gjennom døra.
1959	Barna gikk ut gjennom døra.	Barna gjekk ut gjennom døra.

Notes:

In Danish there are only two genders ("utrum", [Latin: both of the two], i.e., masc. + fem. on the one hand and "neuter" on the other), in Norwegian dialects, however, the three original Germanic genders (masc., fem., neuter) have been preserved. Bokmål adopted the distinction only in the year 1938.

As can be seen in the table, the two variants of Norwegian are gradually coalescing, with "discrete leaps" in the years 1907, 1919, 1938, when language reforms took place.

5. The Language of the Qur'ān, Protosemitic and Modern Arabic Dialects

When investigating the language of the Qur'ān it is imperative to consider it not only from the perspective of Classical Arabic, but also within the framework of Semitic languages on the one hand, and Middle Arabic and modern dialects on the other.

The Semitic languages are themselves only one of a number of branches of a much larger phylum, the so-called "Afro-Asiatic" languages. This latter designation became popular only after the publication of Greenberg's famous book "The Languages of Africa",[157] in which he radically reduced the number of mutually unrelated linguistic groups in Africa to only four. Before this, the designation commonly in use was "Semito-Hamitic Languages",[158] a term which seems to imply that there is a subgroup "Hamitic" which is opposed to the Semitic branch, which is not the case. Comparative studies have shown that the branches of the macrophylum are all branches of equal status, i.e., there was no *Hamitic* protolanguage.

Deplorably, however, no new discipline "Comparative Afro-Asiatic Studies", – comparable to the well-established "Comparative Indo-European Studies" – has emerged. There are several reasons for this:

First of all, the attestation of older stages of Afro-Asiatic languages is much weaker than that of Indo-European languages. Although the oldest preserved texts in Afro-Asiatic languages – Akkadian (Semitic) and Old Egyptian – are much older than the oldest Indo-European texts (Hittite), it is hardly possible to reconstruct more than a handful of Afro-Asiatic protoforms. This is mainly due to the defective nature of most writing systems employed, in the case of Semitic languages even to this day. Another reason is the fact that the different branches of Afro-Asiatic are much more distant to each other than those of the Indo-European languages.

While in many cases it is not too difficult to reconstruct an Indo-European protoform if the Greek and Sanskrit corresponding forms are known, the situation is drastically different even between such well attested languages as Akkadian and Old Egyptian: the undisputed inherited Afro-Asiatic forms easily fit on one page. Moreover, in most cases it is quite clear that there must have been a protoform, but it is nearly impossible to reconstruct it with any degree of certainty.

An aggravating factor is the numerous borrowings between branches, languages and dialects within the macrophylum as well as the branches and subgroups. The latest wave of borrowings came after the Islamization of large parts of the Middle East and Africa, which filled the vocabularies of many languages of those areas, – of course not only Afro-Asiatic ones – with Arabic words.

Apart from Semitic and Old Egyptian no other subgroup of the macrophylum possesses significant texts in older stages of the language, and the subgroups themselves are so heterogeneous (and little investigated so far) that it is very difficult to even reconstruct Proto-Cushitic, Proto-Omotic or Proto-Chadic.

A third problem connected with research of Afro-Asiatic languages is the fact that many of them were first researched by Semitists, which can be seen from the misleading designation "Semito-Hamitic" and a general attitude which considered Semitic as the most archaic type and everything differing from it as deviations from this prototype. If e.g. Egyptian or Cushitic had roots which shared only two radicals with the normally three-radical Semitic roots, the conclusion was that *these families* certainly must have *lost* a radical, not that *Semitic* could have *added* one.

Regarding Afro-Asiatic languages an interesting and very common linguistic mistake should be mentioned: Let us imagine someone claimed that Russian and Australian English are related languages. How would the average linguist judge such a statement? Certainly, almost everyone would smile and reply that Russian doubtlessly is a Slavic language and English clearly a Germanic language, so either *all* Slavic languages are related to *all* Germanic languages or they are not related; but to pick out one language from a well-established group and link it to a language from a totally different group is a methodological blunder.

Such a linguist might add a little reservation pointed at the possibility that by "related" a different kind of link between the two languages is meant, the already mentioned relation within a *Sprachbund*. This, however, would be a different case, as it does not mean that the two languages go back to the same protolanguage. Although this seems to be quite self-evident, it is especially subgroups of the Afro-Asiatic phylum, which are often linked to single languages outside the phylum, e.g. Berber to Basque, Egyptian to Wolof etc.

The case would be a bit different within a group of languages that are at least to a certain extent mutually intelligible. In such a case a dialect might be transplanted into a different area by emigration and subsequently adopt features of the new neighboring dialects, something that can be observed in Sicily, where there are linguistic enclaves where North Italian dialects are spoken. Although North Italian dialects belong to a well-established subgroup of Romance languages, the dialects of such an enclave might be characterized as having *links* to South Italian dialects, maybe even *intermediate forms*, but they are not *related* in a "genealogical" sense.

If two language groups are related in a genealogical sense, then it must be possible to link any language of the first group lexically and morphologically with any language of the second one.

A good example of a view which was often to be found in popular publications about the languages of Asia, and which violates this rule, was adduced by the already mentioned linguist Greenberg:[159] Until the 1940s – and sometimes even today – Thai (Siamese) is described as genetically related to Chinese, which seems very logical to most readers, as both languages are tonal, isolating and even share some common words like the one for "horse" (Chinese: mă - 馬; Thai máá - ม้า) and other domestic animals, some of the basic numbers etc. Such common words, however, can only be found in Thai and Chinese, but not between other languages of the language families to which Thai and Chinese belong. Chinese belongs to the Sino-Tibetan phylum, so if Thai and Chinese were genetically related, i.e., went back to the same proto-language, then there should be a similar number of common words between Tibetan and Thai, which is not the case. Moreover, Tibetan shows that the isolating character of Chinese is probably a secondary development. And finally, "cultural words" like those for instruments, domestic animals and religious notions and rituals are next to worthless to establish a genetical relationship between two languages, as these are normally the first words to be borrowed in case of cultural contact. Therefore, the suspicion that the common vocabulary of Chinese and Thai goes back to cultural borrowing is certainly justified. A closer look at the shared numbers corroborates this view: in Chinese the number "21" is pronounced (in the pinyin transcription of Mandarin) *èr-shí-èr*, which sounds quite unlike Thai [*jî: sìp èt*]. If, however, we compare the latter to Cantonese "*yi*^{2} *sap*^{6} *yat*^{1}" (in the Yale transcription), it quickly becomes clear that their source is a late Southern Chinese dialect[160].

The evidence of lexical similarities has much higher value if words from the basic vocabulary, – e.g. words to be found on the "Swadesh-list"[161] – can be found in the two (or more) languages investigated. But even that is not enough to prove a relationship. To do that the common lexicon must display clear sound correspondences and it should be accompanied by morphological and structural similarities.

To sum up, a sentence like "Thai and Chinese" are related, "Basque and Berber" have a common origin, or "Indo-European and Semitic belong to the same family" have to be banned from linguistic literature. Either *all* Tai-Kadai languages, to which Thai belongs, are related to *all* Sino-Tibetan languages, or the isolated Basque is related to *all* Afro-Asiatic languages, or there is *no* genetic relationship whatsoever.

To come back to Afro-Asiatic languages, here is a simplified diagram to show which language families belong to it:

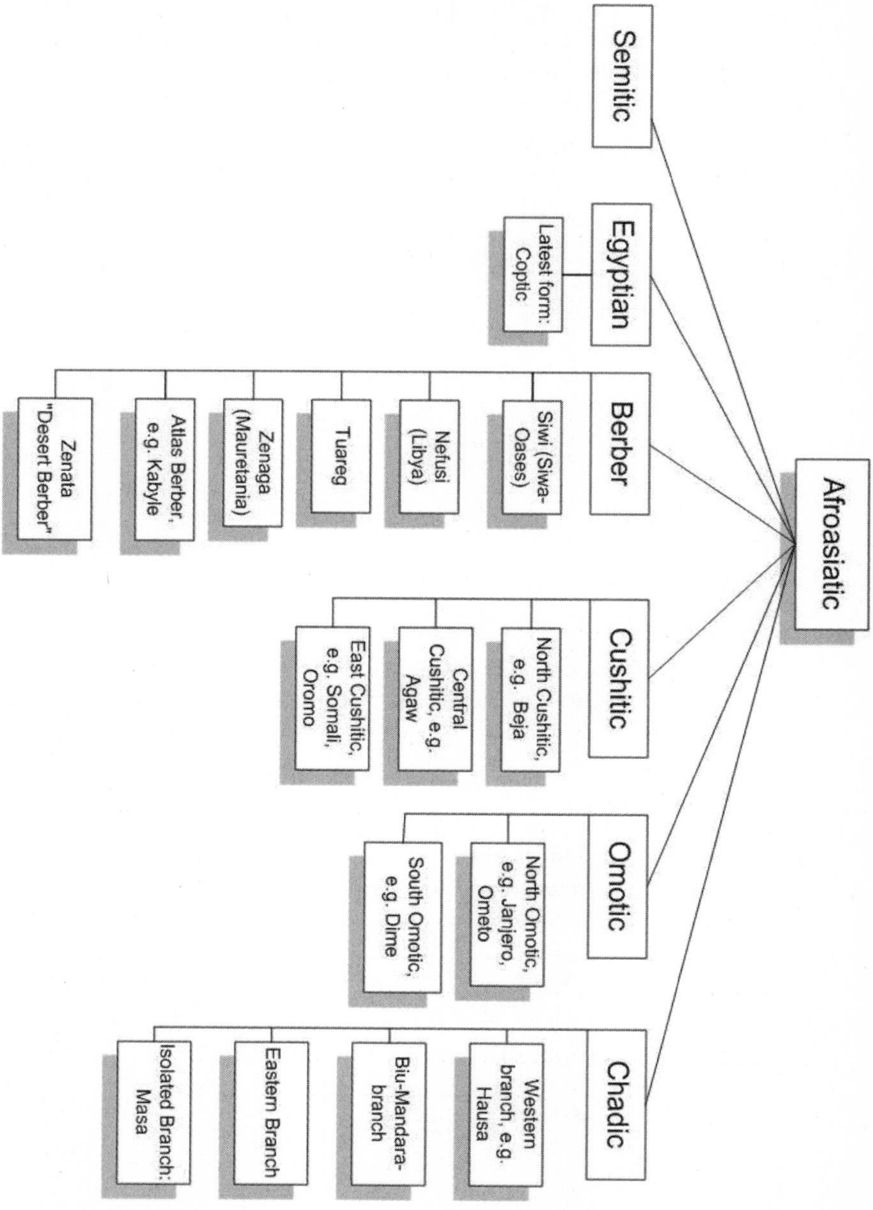
Afroasiatic
Semitic
Egyptian
Latest form: Coptic
Berber
Siwi (Siwa-Oases)
Nefusi (Libya)
Tuareg
Zenaga (Mauretania)
Atlas Berber, e.g. Kabylie
Zenata "Desert Berber"
Cushitic
North Cushitic, e.g. Beja
Central Cushitic, e.g. Agaw
East Cushitic, e.g. Somali, Oromo
Omotic
North Omotic, e.g. Janjero, Ometo
South Omotic, e.g. Dime
Chadic
Western branch, e.g. Hausa
Biu-Mandara-branch
Eastern Branch
Isolated Branch: Masa

The following chart of the Semitic languages is mainly based on that of Stempel.[162] He declines to clearly assign Eblaite to any subgroup and considers Hebrew and Aramaic not to be more closely related to each other than e.g. to Arabic, their common traits, – e.g. the dropping of case endings and the sound rule initial w>y – going back to borrowing, retention of older features and parallel development (like in the case of the so-called *begadkefat*-letters). This view is not universally accepted, but as there is a tendency amongst linguists to establish or adopt subgroups all too often without sufficient evidence I have preferred to be as conservative as possible here.

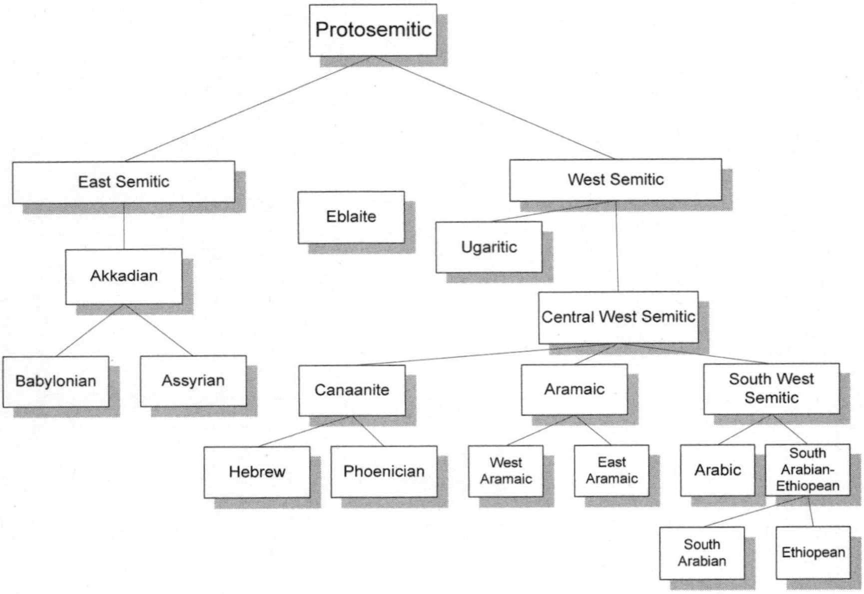

The genetic relationship between the different groups of Afro-Asiatic languages can be seen in verbal prefixes, e.g.:[163]

	Semitic		Berber	Cushitic	
	Akkadian	**Arabic**	**Tamazight**	**Beja**	**Somali**
sg. 1.	a-prus	'a-ktub-u	dawa-ₒ	'a-dbíl	i̧-qiin
2.m.	ta-prus	ta-ktub-u	t-dawa-d	ti-dbil-à	ti̧-qiin
2.f.	ta-prus-ī	ta-ktub-īna		ti-dbil-ì	
3.m.	i-prus	ya-ktub-u	i-dawa	'i-dbíl	yi̧-qiin
3.f.	ta -prus	ta-ktub-u	t-dawa	ti-dbíl	ti̧-qiin

In Old Egyptian these prefixes were lost and replaced by forms based on participles with added personal suffixes. Interestingly, the fate of these prefixes in Modern Eastern Aramaic and in Somali was almost the same, of course an unrelated parallel development[164], which goes back to internal forces of linguistic change. The similarities between Semitic languages can be seen in the lexicon as well as in the morphology, e.g. in the already mentioned verbal prefixes, which are separated by a hyphen. The Aramaic forms from the root *k-t-b* are Biblical Aramaic (and common Syriac), those from *š-q-l* (cited in cases where the corresponding Biblical Aramaic form was not attested) are Syriac. The West Aramaic forms would be: ʾeḵtūḇ, tiḵtūḇ, yiḵtūḇ, tiḵtūḇ, niḵtūḇ, tiḵtəḇūn, (tešqəlān), yiḵtəḇūn, yiḵtəḇān.

	Akkadian *pres.*	*pret.*	*Ugaritic*	*Aramaic*	*Hebrew*
sg. 1.	a-prus	a-parras	a-qbr	ʾe-ḵtoḇ	ʾe-ḵtoḇ
2.m.	ta-prus	ta-parras	t-qbr	te-ḵtoḇ	ti-ḵtoḇ
2.f.	ta-prus-ī	ta-parras-ī	t-qbr-n	(te-šqəl-īn)	ti-ḵtᵊḇ-i
3.m.	i-prus	i-parras	y-qbr	ye-ḵtoḇ	yi-ḵtoḇ
3.f.	ta-prus	ta-parras	t-qbr	te-ḵtoḇ	ti-ḵtoḇ
pl. 1.	ni-prus	ni-parras	n-qbr	ne-ḵtoḇ	ni-ḵtoḇ
2.m	ta-prus-ā	ta-parras-ā	t-qbr-n	te-ḵtᵊḇ-ūn	ti-ḵtᵊḇ-ū
2.f.			t-qbr-n	(te-šqᵊl-ān)	ti-ḵtóḇ-nā
3.m.	i-prus-ū	i-parras-ū	y/t-qbr-n	ye-ḵtᵊḇ-ūn	yi-ḵtᵊḇ-ū
3.f.	i-prus-ā	i-parras-ā	t-qbr(n)	ye-ḵtᵊḇ-ān	ti-ḵtóḇ-nā

	Arabic	Geʿez indicative	subjunctive
sg. 1.	ʾa-ktub-u	ʾəqabbər	ʾəqbər
2.m.	ta-ktub-u	təqabbər	təqbər
2.f.	ta-ktub-īna	təqabrī	təqbərī
3.m.	ya-ktub-u	yəqabbər	yəqbər
3.f.	ta-ktub-u	təqabbər	təqbər
pl. 1.	na-ktub-u	nəqabbər	nəqbər
2.m	ta-ktub-ūna	təqabrū	təqberū
2.f.	ta-ktub-na	təqabrā	təqbərā
3.m.	ya-ktub-ūna	yəqabrū	yəqbərū
3.f.	ya-ktub-na	yəqabrā	yəqbərā

Common Semitic word forms

	Protosemitic	Akkadian	Ugaritic	Aramaic	Hebrew	Arabic	Geʿez
to open	*ptḥ	petū	ptḥ	ptaḥ	pātaḥ	fataḥa	fatḥa
Lord	*baʿlu	bēlu	bʿl	baʿl(ā)	baʿal	baʿlu	baʿāl
dog	*kalbu	kalbu	klb	kalb-(ā)	keleb	kalbu	kalb
camel	*gamalu	gammalu		gaml(ā)	gāmāl	ğamalu (eg. g-)	gamal
to bury	*qbr	qabāru	qbr	qbar	qābar	qabara	qabara
five	*ḫamišu	ḫamšu		ḥammeš	ḥāmēš	ḫamsu	ḫaməs
to set (sun)	*ġrb	ʿerēbu		ʿəreb	ʿārab	ġaraba	ʿaraba
land	*ʾarśu	erṣetu	ʾarṣ	ʾarʿ(ā)	ʾereṣ	ʾarḍu	
name	*šimu	šumu	šm	šm(ā)	šēm	ismu	səm
ear	*uďnu	uznu	udn	ʾedn(ā)	ʾōten	ʾuḏnu	ʿəzn(?)
bull	*ťawru	šūru	ṯr	tawr(ā)	šōr	ṯawru	sōr
brother	*ʾaḫ	aḫu	aḫ	ʾaḥ(ā)	ʾāḥ	ʾaḫ	ʾəḫ^{w}

The question now is how to investigate the language of the Qurʾān – supposedly the best Arabic ever written – in a linguistically sound and unbiased way. The first step to answer this question would be a definition of the term "Arabic". Should Christoph Luxenberg be right, then the language the original version of many Qurʾānic texts was written in was basically a kind of Arabic, however strongly influenced by Syriac. The term "a kind of Arabic" has been used here intentionally to indicate that this language was not identical – even in the non-Syriac forms – with what later was to become Classical Arabic, which contains many words and grammatical forms that ultimately go back to misreadings. This Arab-Syriac mixed language – in the sense discussed in previous sections – is not a fixed idiom, but can rather be defined within a spectrum with the extreme points "pure Syriac" or rather "pure Syriac varieties" at the one end. But what exactly was at the other end, how would the "pure" Arabic element of the Qurʾānic language have sounded?

At this point we must be aware of the fact that "pure" forms or varieties of a language are abstract entities rather than subsystems of a language that exist in the reality of spontaneous speech. Good examples of the above-mentioned spectrum on which individual speakers move are the linguistic situation in Jamaica and that in many German-speaking areas.

The first language most people in Jamaica[165] grow up with in their early childhood is "Patois", an English-based Creole language not mutually intelligible with English. This is the one end of the spectrum. At school Standard (British) English is taught, the other end. An example of sentences in pure Patois would be:

a ɹon mi dida ɹon; a ɹon mi ben(w)en a ɹon - *I was running*

dem a fait fi wi - *they are fighting for us*

But hardly any spoken statement in Jamaica is pure Standard English or pure Patois, most utterances can be placed somewhere between these extreme points, even with the same speaker. Intermediate stages between English and Creole would be:

English:	I didn't eat any
Intermediate:	ai didn it non
Patois:	mi na bin nyam non

A good example of the practical toggling between these varieties is Bob Marley's famous song "No woman, no cry". Contrary to common belief the title does not mean "if you stay away from women, you will have no reason to cry", but: "No, woman, don't cry!" This sentence is quite close to the Patois end of the spectrum. A few lines below in the lyrics we find "obaserving the 'ypocrites". This is Standard English with two phonemic features of Patois: the insertion of a vowel to prevent a consonant cluster and the dropping of the "h". One of the following sentences, "In this great future, you can't forget your past", is an almost pure Standard English sentence, which, however, is pronounced with a strong Jamaican accent, especially with regard to the pure (non-diphthongized) vowels, a deviation from Standard English, however, which does not affect is phonemic structure, i.e., all minimal pairs can still be distinguished. So what language then was this song written in? The answer would be as difficult as for the Qur'ān!

In order to investigate this spectrum it is necessary to first know what the extreme ends are, and that can be quite problematic, if these positions are taken by hitherto unwritten languages. As most utterances in the language have to be located *on* the spectrum and not *at the ends* it is of course very difficult to find out what the "pure" system would be like. A good method to overcome this problem was found by the German linguist Lothar Steitz[166] who investigated the dialect situation in the South West German town of Saarbrücken. In recent decades, the pure form of German dialects, which are not all mutually intelligible, have given way more and more to "regional colloquials", i.e., intermediate forms between dialect and standard German, especially in bigger towns, much like in the case of Jamaican Patois and English. The mixture between dialect forms, hybrid forms and standard forms is due to context, education, mood and age. Whether a new "standard" will ever emerge remains to be seen. In order to write a grammar of the "pure" dialect of Saarbrücken, Steitz used a method from classical philology, which is normally applied to manuscripts: the search for the "lectio difficilior" (most difficult reading). This means that if several alternative forms are in common use, the one that looks least like the standard German one has the highest probability of being the original dialect form, at least of coming closest to it.

If this method is applied to Qur'ānic studies it would mean that whatever deviates most from Syriac (without being a clear borrowing) has the best chances of being original Arabic. The problem here is the defective writing system and the impending danger of falling into the trap of a misreading. As a corrective factor, however, comparison with modern dialects might be useful. It should also be mentioned that the use of a hybrid language is not confined to the Qur'ān, but can also be found in Christian and Jewish Arabic (and Aramaic).

In the following, this method – in combination with other approaches – will be used to investigate remarkable forms in the language of the Qur'ān, especially alleged archaisms and features that set Arabic apart from other Semitic languages. The aim is to find out in the first case, whether these are real archaisms, i.e., characteristics inherited from Protosemitic, and in the second case whether these typically Arabic features go back to a real development in the spoken language or rather to misreadings and the resulting analogous formations.

The term "remarkable forms" in this context designates words and forms which do not occur in modern dialects (e.g. the passive) or in other Semitic languages (e.g. the numerous broken plurals). If they neither occur in the one, nor in the other group, the probability is very high that they never existed in a spoken language and rather go back to misreadings.

During the investigation the following points have to be taken into consideration:

1. The language of the Qurʾān as a sacred text has influenced and keeps influencing Modern Standard Arabic and even the dialects, i.e., misreadings might have been adopted and possibly even re-interpreted at a very early stage.
2. Modern dialects – with the exception of some urban varieties – have little prestige as opposed to Classical Arabic and are often considered a debased form of the latter.
3. Already in so-called Middle Arabic,[167] which was partially written in Samaritan, Syriac and Hebrew script, many of the "typical" features of Classical Arabic are dropped: the *iʿrāb* (the case and modal endings) are not pronounced like in Modern dialects, the genitive and status constructus-construction are replaced by a construction with *bitāʿ* (or alternatively *mtāʿ*) etc.

A last word shall be said about the alleged pre-Islamic poetry, often adduced to prove the old age of a form or word. It was written down only centuries after the rise of Islam and even much longer after the time when these poems were composed, so their authenticity is very doubtful, to say the least. Even if they – or part of them – should have been written before the composition of the first Qurʾānic texts, we must assume major changes in the process of reducing them to writing.

5.1 Case study: Indicative, Jussive and Subjunctive moods

The first phenomenon to be briefly discussed is the existence of altogether four moods in the language of the Qurʾān, which are in use to this day in Standard Arabic, e.g. *indicative:* yaqburu – *subjunctive:* yaqbura – *Jussive:* yaqbur – *Energeticus:* yaqburan(na)

In his article about the position of Arabic within the Semitic language family in the prestigious German "Grundriss der Arabischen Philologie" ('Handbook of Arabic Philology') Karl Hecker[168] does not make a commitment as to whether these go back to secondary developments or to Protosemitic:

> "In Arabic the suffixed 'tense' is contrasted with a form of prefixed formation (yaktubu), to which modal forms of declaration have access (subjunctive, jussive, energicus yaktuba, yaktub, yaktubanna). This Arabic verbal scheme with its strict distinction of prefix and suffix conjugation might give the impression of being a self-contained system, nevertheless it seems to be the result of a secondary systematization."

The context here does not reveal whether "secondary systematization" refers to the two conjugational types or the modal endings. The full set of the latter is as follows (the energicus ending in *-an(na)* is well attested in Hebrew and will therefore not have to be discussed):

	indicative	**subjunctive**	**jussive (apocopatus)**
sg. 1.	a-ktub-u	a-ktub-a	a-ktub
2.m.	ta-ktub-u	ta-ktub-a	ta-ktub-u
2.f.	ta-ktub-īna	ta-ktub-ī	ta-ktub-ī
3.m.	ya-ktub-u	ya-ktub-a	ya-ktub
3.f.	ta-ktub-u	ta-ktub-a	ta-ktub
pl. 1.	na-ktub-u	na-ktub-a	na-ktub
2.m	ta-ktub-ūna	ta-ktub-ū	ta-ktub-ū
2.f.	ta-ktub-na	ta-ktub-na	ta-ktub-na
3.m.	ya-ktub-ūna	ya-ktub-ū	ya-ktub-ū
3.f.	ya-ktub-na	ya-ktub-na	ya-ktub-na

The plural ending *-ū* for the indicative instead of *-ūna* can be found as early as the 9th century CE (885-6), e.g. yasmaʿ*ū*, yatakallam*ū*.

In modern dialects modal endings are non-existent, unless one takes into consideration the opposition of forms with and without "b-", the latter prefix indicating the indicative (e.g. in Egyptian and Syrian Arabic):

	Standard Arabic	**Maltese**	**Algerian**	**Tunisian**	**Egyptian**	**Syrian**
sg. 1.	aqra'u	naqra	nekteb	nekteb	b-aktib	b-iktub
2.	taqra'u	taqra	tekteb	tekteb	b-etiktib	b-tiktub
3.m.	yaqra'u	jaqra	yekteb	yekteb	be-yiktib	b-yiktub

As the comparative tables of old Semitic verbal forms on page 123 ff. shows, the other old Semitic languages (Akkadian, Hebrew, Aramaic and Geᶜez) do not possess forms with corresponding modal endings. Therefore, it would be well admissible to doubt the authenticity of these forms as being derived from Protosemitic. On closer inspection, however, there is one old Semitic language which proves that these endings are genuine and do not go back to misreadings or false analogies: Ugaritic.

Although Ugaritic, as we have seen, is normally not written with vowels and thus these modal endings (*-u, -a, -/*) would not appear in writing, there is, however, an exception: the glottal stop, which corresponds to the Hebrew aleph (' in transliteration), has three distinct forms in Ugaritic, according to whether it was accompanied by a following *a, i* or *u*. Therefore in many transliterations of Ugaritic these variants are written as "*a, i, u*". As a consequence, traces of the modal endings can only appear in verbs with aleph as third radical, which is in fact the case:[169]

1. Indicative: 1st pl. nmlu /namalliʾu/ < √"mlʾ/ D (ful)fill"; Hebr. Pi. id.
2. Jussive: 3rd pl. tǵr(k) /taǵǵurū(-ki)/ < √ "nǵr - to guard" (if it were an indicative another *-n* would have to be there)
3. Subjunctive: a few problematic cases, e.g. yqra - yiqraʾa – call
4. Energeticus: e.g. 1st sg. iqran /ʾiqraʾan(na)/

To sum up we can conclude that the modal system of Arabic is a real archaism inherited from Protosemitic.

5.2 Case study: Nominal Inflection of Arabic

The Classical Arabic system of case endings, which are non-existent in almost all modern dialects – apart from a few remnants like adverbial accusatives, proverbial expressions adopted from the written language is as follows: (Ugar. = Ugaritic, Arab. = Arabic, Akkad. = Akkadian)

	masc.			*fem.*		
	Ugar.	Arab.	Akkad.	Ugar.	Arab.	Akkad.
sg. abs./constr. nom.	-u	-u	-u(m)	-(a)tu	-atu	-(a)tu(m)
gen.	-i	-i	-i(m)	-(a)ti	-ati	-(a)ti(m)
acc.	-a	-a	-a(m)	-(a)ta	-ata	-(a)ta(m)
du. abs. nom.	-āmi	-āni	-ān	-(a)tāmi	-atāni	-(a)tān
gen./ acc.	-ēmi	-ayni	-ēn/-īn	-(a)tēmi	-atayni	-(a)tēn
du. constr. nom.	-ā	-ā	-ā	-(a)tā	-atā	-
gen./ acc.	-ē	-ay	-ī	-(a)tē	-atay	-
pl. abs. nom.	-ūma	-ūna	-ū	-ātu	-ātu	-ātu(m)
gen./ acc.	-īma	-īna	-ī	-āti	-āti	-āti(m)
constr. nom.	-ū	-ū	-ū	-ātu	-ātu	-āt
gen.-acc.	-ī	-ī	-ī	-āti	-āti	-āt

The forms of Ugaritic are those to be found in Segert's grammar, many of which, however, are "postulated" forms, especially in the feminine. The fact that masculine nouns ending in "ʾ" do distinguish the case endings (there are three letters according to the following vowel), makes these forms quite probable.

So as we can see, the endings for nominative (*-u*), genitive (*-i*) and accusative (*-a*) are attested in at least two other Semitic languages, Ugaritic and Akkadian. In Hebrew some relics of case endings were preserved, e.g. the suffix *-ā*, which indicates direction and was derived from the accusative ending. Moreover, the opposition of absolute and construct endings in the Dual *–ay(i)m* vs. constr. *–ē*; f. abs. *–tay(i)m*, constr. *–tā* might be indications of a former case system.

In Ethiopian genitive and accusative coalesced and are formed with the suffix *-a*, somehow comparable to so-called diptotic nouns in Arabic (see below).

In Aramaic, like in Hebrew, the case system had collapsed before the vocalization of the first text corpora had been started, there are, however, some remnants in less well known varieties of the language. In Ya'udi-Aramaic a pl. masc. nom. in *–w (ū)* and a gen.-acc. in *–y (ī)* are attested.

It is interesting to note that the masculine plural ending *-īn* (just think of borrowings in English like *mujahid-een*), which is identical with the Aramaic ending and similar to the Hebrew equivalent *-īm* goes back to the oblique case, not the nominative, a parallel development to the old Latin accusative plural in *-ōs* (masc.) and *-ās* (fem.) which became the general plural ending in Spanish and Portuguese (cf. amig*os* / amig*as* - friends).

Summing up we come to the conclusion that the Arabic case system as such goes back to a Protosemitic system of endings and is a true archaism. This, however, does not preclude the possibility that, when the oldest Qur'ānic texts were composed, they did not possess case endings and these were only later added to make the text look more archaic. This, of course, would imply that the donor language must have been an archaic dialect of Arabic. It cannot have been Syriac, which had long lost those endings. The oldest manuscripts were of course not vocalized and show no traces of most of these endings.

5.3 Case study: Diptotic Nouns

A difficulty of the Arabic nominal inflection are the so-called "diptotic" nouns, i.e., nouns which do not possess three endings for the nominative (*-u*), genitive (*-i*) and accusative (*-a*) like the so-called "triptotic nouns", but only two, an indeterminate (!) ending *-u* and an ending *-a* for genitive and accusative. The following groups of nouns are diptotic:

1. Proper names like e.g. bayrūt-*u* (Beirut) - gen. *-a*, Aḥmad-*u*/- *a* (but not: Muḥammad-*un,* an indicator that it is not originally a proper name)
2. Comparative forms of adjectives like: akbar*u* - gen. akbar*a* and the related terms for colors: aḥmar*u* - gen. aḥmar*a*
3. Several broken plural patterns: indeterminate: madrasa - madāris*u* instead of *-un*, gen. madāris*a* instead of *-in*; as a determinate noun the endings are as with triptotic nouns: al-madāris*u* - gen. al-madāris*i*

Some scholars have tried to interpret this as a reflex of an old Semitic adverbial case in -u (relics can be found e.g. in Arabic prepositions like "munḏ*u* – since"). But apart from Arabic, only Ugaritic might have something comparable, the evidence being more than weak. In his grammar, Segert briefly mentions diptotic endings for proper names and geographical terms, but adds that their use is not consistent and gives the following example (p. 50):

rap-a-nu (rap'ānu) – gen.-acc. *rap-a-na /rap'āna*, possibly also *u-ga-ri-ta*, which he then compares to Arabic Makkat*u* – Makkat*a*.

It is certainly not too far-fetched to cherish some doubts, as Ugaritic "invites" the researcher to interpret it as if it were Arabic. So we can conclude that there is no undebatable parallel in other Semitic languages of this class of nouns.

Moreover, what surprises in Arabic are the complicated rules, which do not seem to be reflected in the semantics of these forms. A possible explanation is that different Arabic dialects lost their case endings at different speeds. Some might have first coalesced the genitive and accusative – like Ethiopian – while others retained the full fledged system for a while. In case of the adoption of a proper name or of dialect mixing, this special noun class might have emerged in a secondary development.

5.4 Case study: Masculine nouns in *-a(tun)*

Another peculiar class of words in Arabic are masculine nouns ending in *-a(tun)*, a suffix normally considered to be feminine, e.g. *ḫalīfatun* - caliph.

Masculine nouns with the feminine ending are hardly attested in other Semitic languages, e.g. in the Hebrew form קֹהֶלֶת "qōhélet", mostly translated as "preacher" and the Hebrew name of the Biblical book "Ecclesiastes". It is believed to be an epithet of Solomon, derived from the noun *qāhāl* - assembly, so it could be understood as a personified assembly of elders. This, however, would make it an abstract term rather than the designation of a person. So the original meaning of this rare word is debatable.[170]

So this opaque parallel can hardly prove the authentic Semitic character of the noun class in question.

The explanation of traditional grammarians is that Arabic masculine nouns with a feminine ending are intensified forms, e.g. ʿullām*atun*, rāwiyy*atun* - traditionarian (alternative form: rāwin). This is semantically not very likely. Apart from making a masculine noun feminine (*sāriq* - thief vs. sāriq*a[tun]* – female thief), the addition of the feminine ending normally makes collective nouns (ism ǧamʿ) individual, e.g. *šağar* – tree(s) vs. šağar*a(tun)* – (one single) tree. As collective nouns and masculine agents belong to different categories, these two meanings of the suffix will hardly ever lead to misunderstandings. That the same suffix should be used as an intensifier added to masculine nouns is very unlikely, as this would inevitably lead to misunderstandings. How would an Arab have expressed the concept of "female traditionarian (transmitter of traditions)"? It is especially very suspicious that there are nouns attested with *and* without this ending.

A similar problem is posed by nouns ending in اء -*ā'u*, e.g. "ṣaḥr*ā'u* – desert", "kibriy*ā'u* - glory (of God), pride (of a man)", "ʿaḏr*ā'u* – virgin" and nouns ending in *alif maqṣūra* like "ذِكرى ḏikrā – memory". It is remarkable that the spelling of elatives alternates between different endings, which in modern dialects all coalesce and become -ā: 'afʿalu - fem. faʿl*ā* or faʿl*ā'u* (spelled: فعلى or

فعلاء). One interpretation could be that the spelling *-ā'u* must be interpreted as designating a phoneme /o:/, which only later coalesced with /a:/. That such a phoneme must have existed in very early Arabic is indicated by the use of the letter *wāw* with superscript hamza, e.g. ṣalāh *(modern:)* صلاة / *(Qur'ānic:)* صلوة .
A similar point can be made for the phoneme /e:/, which Arabic grammarians called "a with *imāla* (inclination)". This pronunciation was well described for certain words, but it is also found in some roots used in the Ḥiğāz, e.g. "ẖēfa - to fear", "ṭēba - to be good", "mēta - to die", where it perfectly corresponds to the vowel found in Hebrew: *mēṯ*. So the two vowels /e:/ and /o:/ can well be assumed as phonemes of both Protosemitic and Early Arabic[171].

Christoph Luxenberg's assumption is that all above mentioned endings (-*a(tun)*, *-ā'u* and *-ā*) are all reflexes of the Syriac emphatic ending (used like a definite article) *-ā*, which was later misunderstood as belonging to the word form itself. Thus, the form "خليفة ẖalīfatun – caliph" should actually be written with an undotted ـه as خليفه or even better as خليفا and pronounced as *ẖalīfā*. That this is not too far-fetched is proven by the corresponding Syriac form with emphatic suffix: *ܚܠܝܦܐ (ḥlīpā), which itself is a substantivized participle passive masculine: *the one put in a place, substitute, deputy, surrogate, successor*.

This originally emphatic ending, which in Biblical Aramaic functioned as a definite article, would later become more and more an inseparable part of the noun without any deictic or determining function, a stage fully reached in the Babylonian Talmud.[172] In all modern Aramaic languages this ending is part of the word and in some a new equivalent of the definite article emerged: in Turoyo[173], a daughter language of West Syriac, *u-* is used as a definite article: "*u-*ṭuro - *the* mountain" (Classical Syriac: *ṭūr* – mountain vs. *ṭūr-ā* [pronounced ṭūr-ō] – *the* mountain).

So it is not at all surprising that Aramaic words in the Qur'ān mostly appear in this originally determined form, the suffix of which was felt to be part of the word, so that the Arabic definite article could be added.

Linguistic plausibility, the fact that the Arabic words ending in *-a(tun)* usually have a Syriac equivalent and finally the fact that clearly parallel forms in other Semitic languages are missing, make Luxenberg's assumption much more likely than the explanation of the old grammarians.

5.5 Case study: The Demonstrative Pronouns *hā'ulā'i* and *'ulā'ika*

These two forms, *hā'ulā'i* and *'ulā'ika* were not discussed in Luxenberg's book, but with his theory in mind they look especially suspicious due to the hamzas on original *yā'*, which might be an indicator for an old /e:/.

In his article about early attestations of modern forms of Arabic, Wolfdietrich Fischer[174] stresses as a common trait of the otherwise quite heterogeneous Arabic dialects that they dropped the glottal stop (written as a *hamza*) in most cases and replaced this phoneme by *y* or *w* or by lengthening of the adjacent vowel.

He opines that this phonetic change could be old and the classical grammarians described this process as a peculiarity of the dialect of the Ḥiǧāz.

Because of the complicated rules of hamza orthography – the hamza (ء) can be written alone, i.e., without a carrier, or can be placed on the so-called weak consonant letters for " ʾ - w – y", the explanation of most traditional Islamic scholars is that the Prophet's tribe, the Qurayš, – unlike other tribes – had dropped the glottal stop and replaced it by *w, y* or vowel lengthening. So when the Qur'ān was written down, this was done with Qurayš consonants. When later vowels were added, the "original" consonantal skeleton was reconstructed by the addition of *hamzas*. This sounds very unlikely. If the Islamic tenets are taken seriously – the Qurʾān having been considered the original word of God, word by word – how then could later generations dare to tamper with it, why was it not vouchsafed exactly as it had been revealed: in the dialect of the Qurayš!

But even the tradition about the alleged "*hamza*-less" pronunciation of the Qurayš is by no means clear:[175] the general assumption is that this dialect did not possess a glottal stop, and that the latter had been re-introduced following the usage in the prestigious more central Arabic dialect of the Tamīm. This later insertion would make sense from a grammatical point of view, because it makes the radicals easier to recognize (e.g. √ *q-r-ʾ* in forms like *Tamīm:* qarātu vs. *Qurayš:* qaraʾtu).

The information concerning this alleged feature of the dialect of the Tamīm, however, is highly contradictory. To adduce an example, as the Tamīm equivalent of the form **yarʾä* ("he sees", Hebr. *yirʾeh*) a grammarian mentions the form *"yarä"* without a hamza, while in the allegedly "hamza-less" dialect of the Ḥiǧāz, the word 'ṣalāya – forehead' is said to have been pronounced as *ṣalāʾa*[176]. The form pl. *ʾūlä* mentioned as a Tamim form is contrasted with Ḥiǧāzī *ʾūlāʾi* with hamza. Of course, one explanation would be that the latter form was influenced by Qurʾānic usage and might have been *ʾūlay* or *ūlā* originally.

Be that as it may, the weakest point of those believing the old grammarians is the fact that there are no attested old dialect texts apart from the contradictory quotations of those same grammarians.

In modern dialects the glottal stop either has vanished as a phoneme altogether or has been limited to very few positions, e.g. in Syrian Arabic the 2nd sg. of the verb *ʾamar* is *təʾmur*, the same form of the verb *ʾakal*, however, is *tākul* and not – as would be analogous – *taʾkul*.

However, the glottal stop is attested as a middle radical, e.g. 3rd sg. perfect *sʾal* - to ask.[177] In normal nouns, however, the glottal stop has been dropped in this dialect.

In the following, we will investigate the plural forms of the demonstrative pronoun – *hāʾulāʾi* and *ʾulāʾika* – and compare them with their old Semitic counterparts on the one hand, and their modern Arabic dialect equivalents on the other:

Modern Dialects

Proximal Deixis – "this/ these"

(Order: Classical Arabic, Middle Arabic, Moroccan, Algerian, Tunisian, Egyptian, Syrian, Iraq, Maltese)

	Cl. Ar.	*Middle Arabic*[178]	*Morocco*[179]	*Alg.*[180]	*Tunis.*[181]
sg. m.	hāḏā	hā, dā, dē, hādā, hēdē	hâd; subst. hâda	hâda	ha:ða
f.	hāḏihi	hādī, dī	hâd; subst. hâdi	hâdi	ha:'ði
pl.	hā'ulā'i	dōl, dōle, hadōli/ hādōle, ūlā	hâdum	hâdu	ha:'ðu:la

	Egyptian[182]	*Syrian Arabic*[183]	*Iraqi Arabic*[184]	*Maltese*[185]
sg. m.	da	haad(a); haida; ha + def. art.; subst. heek	haaδa	dak
f.	di	hayy(e), haadi; haidi	haaδi, haay	dik
pl.	dôl (mostly postponed)	hadôl, haudi	δool, δoola, haδool, haδoola	dawk

Notes:

- The forms cited by Bauer[186] about the dialects of Lebanon and Palestine resemble those of the Syrian dialect:
  Proximal (this)
  Palestine: m. *hāđa*, f. *hāđi* – pl. *hađōl, hađōla*
  Lebanon: m. *haida*, f. *haidi* – pl. *haudi*
  Distal (that)
  Palestine: *hađāk*, f. *hadīk* – pl. *hađōlāk*; f. *hađōlīk*
- In Syrian there is a short form: *ha* + article, the full form can optionally follow: *hal-bint' haidi* – this girl
- In Classical Arabic the rare forms "*ḏāka, tīka, 'ulāka*" are also attested; the "l" can thus be interpreted as an insertion: *ḏālika, tilka, 'ulā'ika* < *'ulālika*
- In Cl. Ar. there is also an alternative form *ḏālikum* in sentences with "*antum* - you (plural)".

Distal Deixis – "that"

Not all languages and dialects have separate forms (order: Classical Arabic, Middle Arabic, Moroccan, Algerian, Tunisian, Egyptian, Syrian, Iraq, Maltese).

	Class. Ar.	*Middle Ar.*	*Morocco*	*Algerian*	*Tunisian*
sg. m.	ḏālika	dāk, dālik, dēlik	dâk, hâdāk hâdīk	(hâ)dak	ha:ða:'ka
f.	tilka	dīk, tilk	dîk,	(hâ)dik	ha:ði:'ka
pl.	'ulā'ika	dīk	dûk, hâdūk	hâ(duk)	ha:ðu:'ka

	Egyptian	*Syrian*	*Iraqi*	*Maltese*
sg. m.	dik-hâ, duk-hâ, duk-hau'wa	hadâk, haidâk	δaak	dan
f.	dik-hâ, dik-hai'ya	hadîk, haidîk	diič	din
pl.	duk-ham'ma	hadolîk, haudîk	δook, δoolaak	dawn

A comparison of the forms appearing in the dialects yields a very heterogenous overall picture. On closer inspection, however, it turns out that all forms appearing in the tables are composed of a limited number of elements (morphemes), by re-combining, doubling and slightly transforming them. These elements are the following:

1. '*hā*' as prefix, suffix, or in combination with the article
2. the connective morpheme "*ḏā, ḏī, ḏū*", which corresponds to the Aramaic relative particle "*ḏ-*". In Classical Arabic it appears alone and is mostly translated as "owner of; having ...", e.g. "*ḏū faḍlin* - owner of excellence = excellent". The corresponding plural is "*ulū*".
3. A deictic element "*ula*" or short *-l-*, which might have the same origin as the definite article in Arabic.
4. For the distal deixis the element "*ka*" or short "*k*", which in Maltese indicates proximity versus "*n*" for distance.

Old Semitic forms

These findings have to be compared to the oldest layer of Semitic languages[187]. The Ugaritic forms are rare and not totally unambiguous. Real demonstrative pronouns can only be found in late prose texts in the form: 'this – *hnd, f. hndt*'. There is, however, a terminative/ relative particle sg. m. *du-ú /dū/* f. *dt /dāt/* (?) - Pl. m. *dt /dūt/* (?) f. *dt /dāt/ (?)*

Proximal Deixis – "this"

(Order: Akkadian, Hebrew, Phoenician, Biblical Aramaic, Syriac, Arabic, Old South Arabic, Ethiopian [= Geʿez])

	Akkadian	*Hebrew*	*Phoen.*	*Bibl. Aram.*	*Syriac*
sg. m.	annū	zē	z(')	dənā dēḵ, dikkēn	hān(ā), haw,
f.	annītu	zōt		dā, dāḵ, dikkēn	hād(ē), hāy
pl.m.	annūtu	'ẹllē	'l	'ẹl(ē), 'illēn	hāllēn, hānūn, f. hānēn
f.	annātu				

	Arabic	*Old S. Ar.*	*Ethiopian*
sg. m.	(hā)ḏā	ḏn	zə(ntū)
f.	(hā)ḏihi, ḏī, tī	ḏt	zā(ttī)
pl. m.	(hā) 'ulā('i)	'ln/t	'əllū(ntū),'əllōntū
f.			'əllā(ntū)
Du. m.	(hā)ḏāni		
f.	(hā)tāni		

The Syriac forms with double "ll" have been taken over from Moscati, their vocalization looking West Syriac. Common Syriac would rather be: hālēn, enōn, hānōn.

Distal Deixis– "that"

Like in Arabic dialects not all Old Semitic languages have separate forms.

	Akkadian	*Bibl. Aram.*	*Syriac*	*Arabic*	*Ethiopian*
sg. m.	ullū	dẹ̄k, dikkẹ̄n	hāw	ḏā(li)ka	zəkū
f.	ullītu	dāk, dikkẹ̄n	hāy	tī/āka, tilka	'əntəkū, 'əntāktī
pl. m.	ullūtu	'illẹ̄k	hānōn	'ulā'ika	'əllekū
f.	ullātu		hānēn		

The "*-n*" at the end of the Biblical Aramaic form is emphatic, the spirantization of final *-k* has not been indicated.

In general, it should be mentioned that in Semitic languages in general personal pronouns can often be used instead of demonstratives.

After a comparison of these forms the following conclusion can be drawn: protosemitic demonstrative pronouns cannot be inferred from these forms, but like in the case of Arabic dialects, the existing forms have been composed of a limited number of deictic elements:

1. *(h)ā* as indicating proximity
2. *ḏ/z /d* as a connective and relative particle
3. *-l-* , also with vowels: *il, el, əl, li*
4. *k* or *ka*, especially for the distal deixis
5. *n* with unclear meaning

Burkhart Kienast comes to similar results in his copious book on historical Semitic linguistics.[188]

If this conclusion is compared with the situation in modern Arabic dialects, it is conspicuous that in both cases no protoforms can be reconstructed, but that at the same time, the deictic elements are next to identical.

This seems to indicate that the Arabic language that spread over the large area it covers today was no uniform language, but rather a continuum of dialects, in which a large variety of combinations of these deictic elements were in use, possibly even several alternatives simultaneously in the same dialect.

In later stages of the language only some of these alternatives survived, in other cases new formations might have emerged.

The forms *"hā'ulā'i"* and *"ulā'ika"* (spelled أُوْلاٰئِكَ and أُوْلَٰٓئِكَ) with two glottal stops each, however, have no real equivalent, neither in modern dialects, nor in any of the old Semitic languages. It is highly probable that they go back to misreadings. It is a telltale fact that they possess the alternative forms *"hūlā'i* and *ulāka"*, so it seems justified to assume original forms that might have sounded *"hawlā, hawlay"*or *"hawlē"* and *"ulēk(a)"* for the distal deixis.

6. Some General Remarks about how Religions Emerge

If the interested reader seeks information about a specific religion or about religions in general, the notion conveyed by most introductory books is that they are "founded": Moses founded Judaism, Jesus Christianity, Buddha Buddhism, Lao Tse Taoism, Zarathustra Zoroastrianism, Muḥammad Islam. But is this really so?

Of course, it might be argued that in recent times religions actually *were* founded: Joseph Smith Jr. founded Mormonism, Yong (Sun) Myung Moon the *Unification Church*, L. Ron Hubbard the *Church of Scientology*, Bahá'u'lláh the *Bahá'í Faith*, Maharishi Mahesh Yogi founded *Transcendental Meditation* and Anton Szandor LaVey the *Church of Satan*.

So this notion seems to be based on empirical data. On closer inspection, however, a totally different picture emerges. So we first should have a short look at "modern" religions: *Mormonism* is an offshoot of Christianity and the style of its sacred book is nearly identical to that of the Old Testament of the King James Bible. *Transcendental Meditation* is clearly derived from Hinduism with an admixture of other old Indian religions, while the *Bahá'í Faith* is derived from Islam as much as Christianity from Judaism, however with a much more friendly attitude towards other religions. Whether the *Church of Satan* is a religion *strictu sensu* is debatable, as Satan here is rather a symbol than a being that actually exists, but a short look at the rituals quickly reveals how much they are patterned on Christian rituals, albeit turned upside down. So all these newly found religions might have an *initiator*, but they do not come out of thin air, they are heavily dependent on already existing religions.

But what about the founders of the ancient world religions? Even here the picture looks quite different from popular belief, as hardly any of these founders is attested in *contemporary* sources. The exodus of Israelites has neither left any archaeological traces nor was it mentioned in any Egyptian text. Lao Tse (= 老子 Lǎo-zǐ "old master") was almost certainly a mythological figure, Zarathustra very probably so. The oldest text mentioning Buddha are the Aśoka inscriptions written more than 200 years after he was born. Jesus was almost certainly a historical figure – around the year 75 CE the Jewish author Flavius Josephus mentions "the brother of Jesus, who was called Christ, whose name was James" – but it is very questionable whether he had in mind to *found a new religion* opposed to Judaism. So the only founder remaining seems to be Muḥammad, who was allegedly raised as a polytheist – not a Christian or Jew, – and received the revelation these two religions had received before, but (according to the Muslim view) had later altered and falsified. For Muslims, the original Torah and the original gospels are divine texts, but they are not identical with the modern editions. So common Muslim belief assumes that the similarities between Islam on the one hand and the predecessor religions on the other do not go back to the "religious environment" (or "milieu", in Wansbrough's terms), but directly to God's direct speech itself, which had been uttered before twice in vain.

Therefore, it is unimaginable for a Muslim to even discuss Christian or Jewish texts as possible "sources" of Islamic precepts, tenets or rituals. Islam for the Muslims came – not out of thin air, but directly out of heaven.

So if certain elements are similar in Islam, Christianity and Judaism, this is not surprising for Muslims, as they will claim that these elements belong to the non-falsified parts of the divine message still present in Judaism and Christianity. If Western scholars link the word "*qur'ān*" to Syriac "*qəryānā* – lectionary", this will not arouse too much commotion, as it can be explained as a pure linguistic borrowing. But if Christoph Luxenberg links core Christian institutions like Christmas,[189] the Eucharist[190] or Eastern to Islamic texts, then this is unacceptable to Muslims.

The fact that Muslims believe this is nothing one can reproach them with – as a key tenet of the religion they are expected to do so, but that *Western scholars* of Islam base their whole research on these foundations is a scandal. So on the following pages we will – from a universal perspective – have a look at a few examples which demonstrate how religions in general transform predecessor material and reinterpret it.

The typological conclusions to be drawn from these examples are, of course, no proof in favor of or against any theory concerning the Qur'ān – a singular development cannot easily be excluded – but at least they provide a background in front of which the "typological likelihood" of a claimed phenomenon can be better judged.

The phenomenon that elements from former religions are actively adopted and reinterpreted into a new religion in order to make proselytism easier, is well known. Christmas, which – unlike Easter – was unknown in early Christianity, goes back to the festival of the Roman *sun god* ("Sol invictus"), which took place on 25th December. The prominent position of the sun god can be seen in the fact that even the "Christian" emperor Constantine (christened on his deathbed) had coins struck with the sun god on the one side and the *Chi Rho* (*X+P*; for Greek *XP*ΙΣΤΟΣ = Christ) on the other. By reinterpreting this festival as the birthday of Christ it made the new religion much more familiar for former adherents of the sun god. Amongst Islamic festivals one would immediately think of the Hadj as a parallel case for the adoption of a ritual of a predecessor religion, although Muslims would vehemently deny this.

There are other, less obvious similarities between the legends woven around the founders of religions: in many cases the legends mention women as their first adherents: Muḥammad's first wife, Ḫadīğa, is said to have been the first human being to convert to Islam. In the New Testament both Jesus and St. Paul receive major support from women – three women stood near the cross of Jesus, while all his disciples except for John were in hiding. And even Buddha is said to have received support from an elderly lady named Visakha (Viśākhā, one of his lay disciples) and from the hetaera Āmrapāli, who donated a garden to the sangha (monastic order).

In the following, a few examples will be discussed of how elements from one religion were adopted, transformed and sometimes reinterpreted in a newly emerging religion.

6.1 Example: The "Oneness of God"

The first example concerns the core tenet of monotheism, the "oneness of God", for which Islam possess a central term: *tawḥīd*. This term – at least in its etymological form –, however, is not confined to Islam, it is also found in the official name of the Ethiopian church: "Ethiopian Orthodox *Tewahedo* Church". Here *tewahedo* – although etymologically the same as the Arabic term – goes back to Geᶜez "ተዋሕዶ *tawāhidō* "being made one" and designates the *unifying nature of Christ*, which combines his human and divine side.

The Arabic term finds its clearest expression in the concise formula لا إله إلا الله – lā ilāha illā ḷḷāhu - literally: "there is no deity except God".

The idea that there is only one God, that the gods of neighboring tribes are not *weaker* than our God, but simply *do not exist*, is not to be found in older parts of the Old Testament. It finds its expression, however, in the famous formula (Deut. 6:4):[191]

שְׁמַע יִשְׂרָאֵל יְהוָה אֱלֹהֵינוּ יְהוָה ׀ אֶחָד -
šmaᶜ yiśra'ēl YHWH elohēnū YHWH eḥad
hear Israel Yahweh (is) God our Yahweh (is) one
Hear, O Israel: The LORD our God is one LORD (King James Bible)

The last word of this formula, "eḥad – one" belongs to the same root as "tawḥīd". The sentence is also quoted in the New Testament (Mark 12,29):

ἄκουε Ισραὴλ κύριος ὁ θεὸς ἡμῶν κύριος εἷς ἐστί
hear Israel (the) lord the God our lord one is
Hear, O Israel; The Lord our God is one Lord (King James Bible)

The fact that the Hebrew original had a linguistic effect on the language of the Qur'ān is visible in an inscription in the Dome of the Rock: "Aḷḷāhu aḥad – God is one", which has a counterpart in surah 112 (al-Iḫlāṣ) in the formula: *qul huwa llāhu aḥad*. According to the rules of Classical Arabic the correct form of the numeral here would be "wāḥid"[192].

But apart from Judaism, Christianity and Islam there is also a fourth religion in which this notion or tenet is of exceptional importance: Sikkhism. This Indian religion is based on ideas and tenets of both Hinduism (e.g. reincarnation) and Islam (monotheism). The central formula, which is also to be seen as a kind of logo is the following:

ੴ

Ik Onkar
one God (lit.: the "Om-maker")

It is interesting to note that although the idea of only one God stems from Islam, the word chosen to designate that deity is made up of words taken from Sanskrit (the sacred language of Hinduism), one of them designating the holy syllable of Hinduism: *Om*, which also can be seen in many places as a logo:

ॐ

So the borrowing of word formative elements is accompanied by the taking over of visual elements. Here it should be mentioned that for a phonetician the syllable Om itself has nothing sacred about it. Although in many old Indian texts lengthy explanations are given as to the meaning of every little aspect of this syllable – the Māndukya Upanishad is entirely devoted to this syllable – the explanation of its connection to religious activities is very obvious: When meditators relax their whole body including their speech organs, the tongue will be in a neutral, central position, the velum relaxed. If they then breathe out slowly and let their vocal chords vibrate, the sound produced will inevitably be a [ə̃] or [ɐ̃]. When closing the mouth with an open velum, the sound automatically produced is [m]. If the closing happens very slowly and the lips are a bit rounded, a short [ũ] might be audible beforehand. The syllable thus uttered – taking into consideration some leeway in its actual realization – is identical to how this syllable is described by the ancient Indians. The syllable does *not* go back to *revelation*, but to *observation*!

At this point one might object that in the case of the Sikh word for God Hinduism cannot have been the source of the designation of a monotheistic deity, as it is the most clear case of a polytheistic religion. As we will see later, this is only partially true. It is true that the hymns of the Rigveda are dedicated to a large number of gods and goddesses. But already in the Upaniṣads the original polytheism gave way to a special kind of monism, in later literature a whole range of different notions can be observed, including henotheism and even monotheism. So it is not surprising that in his famous speech at the Parliament of the World's Religions in Chicago in 1893,[193] Swami Vivekananda (ca. 1863-1902) quoted Rigveda 1.164.46: "*ekaṃ sad viprā bahudhā vadanti* - That which exists is One: sages call it by various names" and adds:

> "In all these cases where hymns were written about all these gods, the Being perceived was one and the same; it was the perceiver who made the difference."

It is highly questionable whether the authors of the Rigveda really had this meaning in mind, but any interpretation *ex post* of a religious term tells us more about the notions of the interpreter and his time than about the term.

6.2 The Jewish "Qaddish (קדיש)" and the Lord's Prayer

The second example is the central prayer of Christianity, which shows striking resemblances[194] with one of the most important Jewish prayers, the "Qaddish", sometimes called "the Mourners' Kaddish". Interestingly, the Qaddish is not recited in Hebrew, but in a Western variety of Aramaic.

What follows is a comparison of the relevant passages of the Qaddish[195] and the Lord's Prayer of the *Pšiṭṭā*.

יִתְגַּדַּל וְיִתְקַדַּשׁ שְׁמֵהּ

yiṯgaddal	**wə- yiṯqaddaš**	**šmēh**
shall be exalted	*and sanctified*	*name his*

His name shall be exalted and sanctified

בְּעָלְמָא

(congregation: ʾāmēn)	**b-**	**ʿālmā,**
verily	*in*	*eternity*

truly eternity.

וְיַמְלִיךְ מַלְכוּתֵהּ

(...) wə-	**yamlīḵ**	**malḵūṯēh (...)**
and	*may reign*	*kingdom his*

and his kingdom may reign

יְהֵא שְׁמֵהּ רַבָּא מְבָרַךְ

yəhē	**šmēh**	**rabbā**	**məḇārāḵ,**
shall be	*name his*	*Lord*	*blessed*

the name of the Lord shall be blessed,

yiṯgaddál - 3rd sg. impf. Etp. 'gdl - be exalted, praised'; influenced by Hebrew

wə- 'and'

yiṯqaddáš - 3rd sg. impf. Etp. 'qdš - be sanctified

šmē-h - 'name' + poss. 3rd sg. m.

ʾāmēn - amen; cf. ʾamīn - constant'

b- - 'in'

ʿālmā - emphat. 'eternity, world'

yamlīḵ - 3rd sg. impf. Aph. 'mlk - to reign'; cf. 'malkā - king'

malḵūṯē-h - kingdom + poss. 3rd sg. m.

לְעָלַם וּלְעָלְמֵי עָלְמַיָּא

l-ʿālam	**ū-**	**l-ʿālmē**	**ʿālmayā**
in eternity	*and in eternities*		*of eternities*

forever and in all eternity.

The translation in Wikipedia is as follows[196]:
May His great name be exalted and sanctified, (amen) in the world, (...). May He establish His kingdom (...) May His great name be blessed for ever, and to all eternity!

yəhē - 3rd sg. impf. 'hwā - to be'; cf. syr. nehwē; Hebr. yəhī
šmēh - his 'name'
rabbā - 'Lord'
məḇārák̠ - part. pass. 'brk - bless'
l- - 'to'
ʿālam - 'eternity'
ū-l- - 'and + to'
ʿālmē - 'eternities (stat. constr.)'
ʿālmayā - pl. 'eternities'

Notes:

From a Syriac perspective some of the grammatical forms are a bit surprising:
"*yiṯgaddál*" is strongly influenced by Hebrew; the genuine root designating "great" in Aramaic is "*rabbā* - be/become great" vs. "gadōl – great" in Hebrew, so the correct Etpael form would be *yiṯrabbay*. A root *"gdal"* does exist in Syriac, but it means "to plait, to weave", the Etp. form is "*eṯgdel* - to plait one's hair". It is conspicuous that the verbal form *"yiṯgaddál"*, unlike the following one, does not appear in the Lord's Prayer.
The Syriac equivalent of Aph. *yamlīk̠* would be *yamlék*. As the second vowel was stressed, in Western Syriac it was likewise lengthened to [e:], which is not a phonemic change.
The "k" in *"malk̠ūṯē-h"* is not spirantized in Syriac.
Instead of the form "məḇārák̠" one would rather expect a form with gemination: "məḇarrák". The lengthening of the preceding vowel instead of a following gemination might be a Hebrew peculiarity or go back to Arabic *"mubārak"*.
The *"ū"* instead of *"wa"* might also go back to Hebrew influence.
Instead of *"ʿālmē"* the form *"ʿālmay"* (with identical "rasm") would be correct in Syriac.

The Lord's Prayer in (West) Syriac[197]

abūn	**ḏ-ḇa-šmayā**	**neṯqadaš**	
father our	*who in heaven*	*be sanctified*	
Our father	*in heaven*	*hallowed be*	
šmāk̠	**tīṯe**	**malkūṯāk̠**	**(...)**
name you	*shall come*	*kingdom your*	
thy name	*thy kingdom come ...*		
lᵊʿālam	**ʿālᵊmīn**	**amīn**	
to eternity	*of eternities*	*amen*	
forever and ever amen			

abū-n - 'father' + poss. 1st pl.
ḏ-ḇa-šmayā - 'who (rel.)' + 'in' + 'heaven'
neṯqadáš - 3rd sg. impf. Etp. 'qdš - be sanctified'; East Syr. neṯqaddaš
šmā-k̠ - 'name' + poss. 2nd sg. m.
tīṯe - 3rd sg. f. impf. 'eṯā - come'; East Syriac: 'tēṯe'
malkūṯāk̠ - 'kingdom' + poss.

2nd sg. m.
l'ᶜālam - 'to' + 'eternity' (status constructus); cf. emph. ʿālmā
ᶜālᵊmīn - pl. 'eternities'
ʾāmīn - 'amen; truly'

Notes:

In West Syriac there are several cases of allophonic lengthening of a phonemic short /a/ (the etymologically long /a:/, which remained in East Syriac, has here become an /o:/. In most cases this is equivalent to a preserved geminated consonant in East Syriac: West Syr. "ḏḇašmáyā" [āyo] vs. East Syr. "ḏḇašmayyā", West Syr. *neṯqadáš* [a:], vs. East Syr. *neṯqaddaš.*

In the form "*amīn*" the /a/ is also pronounced as [a:], although there was never a geminated vowel. The reason is probably the sacred character of the word.

The equivalent form *yiṯqaddaš* – *neṯqaddáš* in Jewish Aramaic and Syriac display the typical difference of the two dialects of Aramaic in the 3rd masc. sg. of the Semitic prefix conjugation. While Western Jewish Aramaic (like Biblical Aramaic) retains the old Semitic prefix *y*- (cf. Arabic "*y*-aktubu") Syriac changed it to "*n*-", while the Eastern Aramaic of the Babylonian Talmud changed it to "*l*". (cf. section 7.6. about the name *Yahwe*).

6.3 Example: Mani and Jesus in Central Asia

Manichaeism is an extinct former world religion, which for a long time was only known due to secondary sources and which goes back to a founder named Mani, whose father had become a member of the Aramaic-speaking Christian sect of the Elchasaites. Just how far the report of his life is to be taken as historical remains to be discussed.

Having received two vocational visions, Mani is said to have left his community in order to "found" his own religion. So from 240-241 he traveled to Afghanistan and India for missionary work, where he got to know Hinduism and Buddhism. The propagation of the new religion was made much easier due to his good relations with the Sassanian ruler Shapur I. Several books written in Aramaic, of which no fragments remain, have been ascribed to Mani. As a parallel to the life of Jesus, he was captured and executed in a prison in the year 276.

Although Manichaeism considered itself a revealed religion, it appears as the syncretistic religion par excellence, as elements from Christianity, Buddhism, Hinduism and Zoroastrianism were adopted alike.

This turned out to be an enormous advantage in its missionary work, as it could always portray itself as a more elaborate and developed form of the respective predecessor religion, the core elements of which it had amongst its own tenets. Therefore, it is not surprising that Manichaeism in Mediterranean countries resembles Christianity, while in Central Asia it portrayed its founder as a reincarnation of Buddha or Lao Tse.

This adaptation to regional traditions of other religions had a major impact on the vocabulary of the texts, e.g. in Manichaean Parthian[198] the following Christian terms are attested:

Gospel: 'wnglywnyg /ewangelyōnīg/ (= Latin: evangelium– gospel)
Jesus: yyšw' /Yišō'/

The name of Jesus goes back to an Aramaic form (Syriac: yešū').

In the description of Mani's death (p. 47), however, the following combination of words can be found:

... qdyxwd'y prnybr'd ... /...kadexwadāy parniβrād ...) – "master of the house gone to paradise"

"parniβrād" here is a denominative verb and goes back to the Buddhist term "parinirvāna - Supreme Nirvana; lit.: be totally blown out (candle), be extinguished; cease to exist".

Moreover, in the Indo-European languages Tocharian, spoken in two varieties (A = Eastern and B = Western) in the oases on the northern part of the Tarim Basin (currently Xinjiang Uyghur Autonomous Region of China) until the early Middle Ages, we have the interesting case of a hymn for Mani, which has been preserved in a fragmentary bilingual version Tocharian B (Western T.) / Old Uyghur (also called Old Turkish). Therefore, it is not surprising that this hymn is nothing more than a "re-directed" hymn written for Jesus, in which the addressee was exchanged. But even this is not the original version, because Tocharian had already become extinct as a spoken language at the time when this hymn for Jesus was composed, as can be seen from several mistakes in the text (line breaks not between words, which would have been possible, but in the middle of a morpheme). It was only chosen as the medium of a sacred text because of its high prestige as the sacred language of Buddhist texts of the area. The Manichaen and Christian texts make up only a minute (and very late) fraction of the whole corpus, while the whole of the rest is almost exclusively Buddhist literature (apart from some mundane texts). The Tocharians, or at least a part of them, seem to have converted from Buddhism to Christianity and a bit later to Manichaeism, when their language was already moribund. So it is highly probable that the hymn for Jesus itself goes back to an even older hymn for Buddha.[199]

The allusions in the text of the Mani hymn include Hinduist, Buddhist as well as Zoroastrian terminology, the latter e.g. in line 12 in the form "xormuz-da – gen. god", which goes back to the Zoroastrian designation "Ahuramazda". Similarly in the combination:

mn aryaman fristum - *me, Aryaman Frestum*

On p. 12 the Toacharian text is illegible, but the Old Uyghur version displays an interesting text passage:

qangïm mani burxan

my father Mani Buddha (line 21)

qaŋ-ïm – father + suff. 1st sg.

Burxan, Burɣan – from Chinese "fo - 佛" = bvyr - Buddha + xan - leader; Khan"

It is remarkable that the Old Uyghur form *Burxan* for *Buddha*, which is well attested also in other texts, is still used as a common first name in modern Turkey, although most Muslim bearers of this name might be quite shocked at its etymology.[200]

In the same bilingual text we find the following phrase in Tocharian B, written in defective Manichaean consonant script.[201]

... bramñikteṃse pässak ram.

... *of Brahma wreath like – like the garland of Brahma (or Brahmin)*

bram-ñäkte - god Brahman; cf. pa-ñäkte – Buddha god

pässak = pässakw - garland

ram(t) - like

So here the divine name Brahma connects Manichaeism to Hinduism. Similarly in line 24, a central Buddhist term is used:

nerwāṃše taṃ šañiññe

nirvāṇa-like your nature

But an inherited Proto-Turkic word for "god" (originally probably designating one specific god) is also used in Tocharian:.

kʔsy b'ḍḍy tngryy

käsi bäddi tngri

teacher Buddha god

käṣṣi - teacher

t(ä)ŋri – heaven, god, cf. Modern Turkish: Tanrı - god

Mani himself is mentioned on p. 31:

lkā[s]i śukye pidär- m[āni]

to see shining father Mani

Refrain: **tu sa tu sa pällāmar**

therefore therefore I praise you

lkātsi – inf. läk – to see

śuke – taste < śu – to eat

tu sa – therefore

√ päl – to praise

The parallel hymn for Jesus can be found in the so-called Fragments of Henning (Henningsche Fragmente), written about 1000 CE. The reconstructed text is as follows:

yiṣwe	**lkāsi**	**śukye**	yiṣwe
Jesus	to see	shining	Jesus

Refrain: **tu sa tu sa pällāmar**
therefore therefore I praise you

It should be noticed that the spelling of the name of Jesus is entirely Aramaic: *yšw'yy*. This piece of evidence for the influence of Aramaic in an area as far away from the Near East as Modern Chinese Turkestan can also be seen in the traditional Mongolian writing system, which is based on Aramaic turned by 90°. So here we have got an example of an originally Buddhist text, which was first made Christian and then Manichaean by simply exchanging the names of the respective prophet/ founder of the new religion.

6.4 "Gods" and "Demons" in the Avesta and the Rigveda

At this point a comparison between Zoroastrianism in its oldest form and Hinduism might be interesting as it will demonstrate the evolution of designations for positive and negative transcendental beings. In the Rigveda (appr. 1400-1000 BCE), which is several centuries older than the Avesta (appr. 1000-900 BCE) two groups of such beings are mentioned, both with a rather positive connotation, the *Devas* and the *Asuras*, the latter term being used to designate a number of gods, among others Agni, Indra, Soma and Savitṛ.

Of special interest is Rigveda (RV) 8,25,4, where the two *adityas* Mitra and Varuṇa are called "*devav asurā* – the two spiritual Devas", as well as 7,65,2, where they are called "*dev nām ásurā* – the two spiritual ones among the Devas".[202]

In later parts the word *ásura-* adopted a more and more negative meaning, e.g. RV 8, 96, 3 "*ásurā ádevāḥ* - the ungodly Asuras".

This can be seen in connection with the etymological origin of the word: "*ásu* (Avestan. *aŋhu*) life" is semantically narrowed more and more to the rather negative meaning "life of the deceased", e.g. RV10,15,1 "*ásum yá īyuḥ ... pitáraḥ* - the (fore)fathers who have gone to the (other) life".

The next step in the development can be seen in RV 10,53,4:

"*tád ... yén surāṃ abhí dev ásāma* – that by which we Devas might be superior to the Asuras".

Thus the polarization of these two groups of celestial beings, which at the beginning had been on nearly equal footing, gradually leads to a clear favoring of the "Devas".

In Avestan the process took place in the other direction. The Avestan "Daevas" (*daēuua*, f. *–ī* [skr. *devá-*, f. *deví-* Gott] – name of false gods, demons, devils and evil spirits) are nothing else but "evil spirits", the (main) god to be venerated now being "*Ahura Mazdā*", alternatively "*Mazdā Ahura*" – "the wise

Ahura/ Asura". In the later Sanskrit translation of the Avesta the name was translated "*mahājñānin svāmin* – the wise Lord" by avoiding the equivalent Vedic term *ásura*.

The *Daeuas*, on the other hand, are insulted, e.g. the following imperative is attested in the Avesta: "*nista daēuuō* – so abuse the Daēvas!".

So here the reverse process that we have seen in the Rigveda took place: the "evil spirits, demons" here are the *Daeuuas*.

6.5 Mutual influence between Hinduism and Buddhism

Buddhism, which emerged in an area where Hinduism in its oldest (Vedic) stage was the major religion – if the modern term *religion* is justifiable in this case at all – shares many important notions with the latter, e.g. reincarnation. As we have seen in section 5.1, however, some Hinduist concepts were reinterpreted, e.g. the term "Brahmin", which in Hinduism means the *member of a caste*, and which now describes a person displaying a *certain behavior*.

In the course of time, however, especially after Buddhism had become a major competitor in South Asia, Hinduism (in a later form) started to adopt typical Buddhist notions and concepts, which it transformed and reinterpreted, as the following example from the *Bhagavadgītā* will show. This text is officially a part of the *Mahābhārata*, the national epic of India, although the plot is only loosely connected to it. It is no exaggeration to say that it is maybe the most famous text of Indian literature.[203] The *Bhagavadgītā* narrates the conversation between the military leader Arjuna and his charioteer Kṛṣna, a reincarnation of Viṣṇu, before the decisive battle, after Arjuna refuses to fulfill his duties as member of the warrior (Kṣatriya) caste and fight against the enemy (from the same family) on the ground that it is better to die than to kill one's relatives. The dating of the poem is highly unclear, which is due to the Indian lack of a historical tradition, but it is generally considered to have been composed after the emergence of Buddhism. Mylius,[204] in his edition, mentions datings ranging between the 4th and 2nd century BCE, which does not exclude the possibility that different layers are possible. The text shows the transition from a former Vedic-Brahmanic ritualism ("do ut des") to a Viṣṇuist theism with Viṣṇu as main god.

chapter 2,verse 72[205]
एषा ब्राह्मी स्थितिः पार्थ नैनां प्राप्य विमुह्यति ।
स्थित्वास्यामन्तकालेऽपि ब्रह्मनिर्वाणमृच्छति ॥२- ७२॥[206]

eṣā **brahmī** **sthitiḥ** **pārtha**
this *Brahma-* *abode* *o Pṛtha-son*
This, o Pṛtha-son, is the state og Brahma!

eṣā - nom. f. this
brahmī - 'sg. loc. m.
brahman- Brahman
sthitiḥ - f. location,
abode; order, rule <

naināṃ	**prāpya**	**vimuhyati** ||
not this	*having obtained*	*goes astray*

Whoever has obtained it does not go astray.

sthitvā	**'syāmantakāle**	**'pi**
having stayed	*in this end time*	*even*

Whoever stands fast in it in his hour of death,

brahmanirvāṇamṛcchati ||
Brahma-nirvana-enters
enters the dissolution into one with Brahma.

sthā - stand; here: Bahuvrīhi: having the abode of
pārtha - voc. sg. 'oh Pārtha (= son of Pṛtha)'
naināṃ - < na - not + enāṃ. - acc. sg. f. this'
prāpya - absolutivum pra + āp– to get'
vi-muhyati - 3rd sg. 'vi+muh- go astray'
sthitvā - abs. sthā – having stayed
'syām-anta-kāle - asyām sg. loc. f. "this" – in this + anta- last; end; death + kāle – loc. kāla – time (of death)
'pi < **api** – emph. part.
brahman- m/n. Brahman (orig.: growing); universal soul
nirvāṇam- being blown out
ṛcchati - 3rd sg. pres. ṛ - enter

Translation of Swami Swarupananda:
This is to have one's being in Brahman, O son of Pṛthā. None, attaining to this, becomes deluded. Being established therein, even at the end of life, a main attains to oneness with Brahman.

German translation of Mylius:
Das ist der Brahma-Zustand, oh Pṛthā-Sohn!
Wer ihn erreicht hat, wird nicht (mehr) betört.
Wer auch in der Todesstunde dabei ausharrt, erlangt Seligkeit im Brahman.

Here Kṛṣna connects the originally Buddhist term "nirvāṇa" (blowing out [of craving]) with the Hinduist concept "bráhman (n.)", which covers a whole range of meanings: the word appears as a neuter noun ("brahman"), as well as in a masculine form (in English often written as "Brahma"). In the first case it reflects a non-personal, in the second case a more personal concept of god. It is translated with such different equivalents as "the god Brahmā", "Universal

Soul", "the Vedes", "Brahmin caste"; "(ultimate) heavenly happiness"; "creator of the world (above all in the Upaniṣads)". In compound words it appears in the form "brahma-".

The term "brahma-nirvāṇa - extinction in Brahmā; absorption into the one self-existing Spirit; lit.: being blown out in Brahma" turns the original Buddhist term upside down.

In Buddhism, which denies the existence of an immortal soul (see the doctrine of *an-ātman – not-soul*), Nirvana means "extinction, being blown out", i.e., entering the realm of non-existence by freeing oneself of all attachments, defilements and cravings for earthly things ("nirvāṇa - be blown or put out, extinguished, calmed" < nir + vā - blow [wind], cease to blow, be blown out, be refreshed). The Bhagavadgīta, in contrast, interprets it as "attaining one-ness" of the individual soul (*Ātman*) with the universal soul (*Brahman*).

Another Buddhist term, the "setting in motion of the wheel", which in Buddhism means the "beginning of the teaching of Buddhist dharma (doctrine)", appears with a totally different meaning in *chapter 3, verse 15:*

एवं प्रवर्तितं चक्रं नानुवर्तयतीह यः ।
अघायुरिन्द्रियारामो मोघं पार्थ स जीवति ॥३- १६॥

evaṃ **pravartitaṃ** **cakraṃ** *thus* *set in motion* *wheel* *Whoever does not turn around the wheel*	**evaṃ** - thus **pravartitaṃ** - pra + vṛt – set in motion **cakra** -n. - wheel
nānuvartayatīha **yaḥ** || *not here turns around* *who* *set in motion here (one the earth)*	**nānuvartayatīha** - 'na – not' + 3rd sg. pres. caus. 'anu-vṛt + iha - here'- follow; vṛt – to turn (cf. Lat. vertere) **yaḥ ... sa** – who ... this one
aghāyurindriyārāmo *sinful senses lover* *relishing in sinful sensual pleasures*	**aghāyur-indriyā-rāmo** - 'sinful + pl. senses + rāmah - lover < √ ram – to relish
mogham **pārtha** **sa** **jīvati** *in vain* *o Pṛtha-son* *this one* *lives* *such a person, o Pṛtha-son, lives in vain.*	**moghaṃ** - in vain **pārtha** – o Pṛtha-son **sa** - this **jīvati** - 3rd sg. pres. 'jīv - live'

Translation of Swami Swarupananda:
He who here follows not the wheel thus set revolving, living in sin, and satisfied in the senses, O son of Pṛtha – he lives in vain.

German translation of Mylius:
Wer dieses in Bewegung gesetzte Rad
nicht rollen läßt hier auf Erden,
sündig, sich an den Sinnen freut,
der, o Pṛthā-Sohn, lebt vergeblich.

From these four examples it should have become clear that religions do not come out of thin air, they are usually based on material taken from predecessor religions, which is transformed and reinterpreted.

6.6 "Muḥammad" and the Semitic Root "ḥ-m-d"

In this section the attempt will be made to consider the purported name or alternatively the epithet *Muḥammad/ Mḥmt*, as discussed in several contributions in the present anthology and its predecessor volume, within the framework of other Semitic languages.[207] The form *Muḥammad* is normally derived from the root "*ḥ-m-d* – to praise". This interpretation, however, is based on the prior acceptance of the *Traditional Account,*[208] as the concept of praise in Semitic is usually not expressed by *ḥ-m-d*, but by *s/š-b-ḥ*, and seems to have developed late, being of Aramaic origin.[209] Nevo and Koren describe the corresponding Arabic root *s-b-ḥ* as follows (p. 261):

> "It denotes the verbal expression of devotion: declaring the divinity's greatness, perfection, justice, etc. Thus Q.15:98: fa-sabbiḥ...rabbika wa-kun min-al-sājidīna means: ‚but do praise your Lord's ... and prostrate yourself in prayer'."

They suggest the translation "to pray; invocation of God, supplication". The Hebrew root *š-b-ḥ*, according to Nevo and Koren, provides words with the various meanings "praise, bless, thank". The Semitic root *ḥ-m-d*, on the other hand, originally means "to desire, covet, wish or have to acquire for oneself". For Hebrew they mention 16 attestations for the root in the basic stem, e.g. in the ten commandments: "*lo taḥmōd* – thou shalt not desire ...". In Arabic, the semantic boundary between "desired" and "praised" was crossed only much later, as part of the *Tafsīr*, but not so in other Semitic languages like Ugaritic. They quote a sentence from Gordon's Ugaritic Manual:[210] "*bʿl ḥmdm yḥmdm* - Baʿal verily covets (them)". Furthermore, Nevo and Koren point out the frequency of names and designations for prophets in the Qur'ān, which is totally unbalanced:

Muḥammad: 4 times, *rasūl Allāh*: (including suffixed forms like *rasūluhu* etc.) 300 times; *nabī*: 43 times; *Ibrāhīm* 79 times; *Mūsà* 136 times; *Hārūn* (Aaron) 20 times; *ʿĪsà* 24 times; *Maryam* 34 times, *Ādam* – 25 times; *Nūḥ* - 33 times; *Firʿawn* 74 times.

Above all the fact that the alleged prophet of the new religion, according to these statistics, should have been called *rasūl Allāh* as many as 300 times, but only four times *Muḥammad* sounds very suspicious; especially as next to no clear personal information is given about him in the Qur'ān itself. So the conclusion does not seem too far-fetched that *muḥammad* is not originally a name, but an epithet, originally meaning "the desired one (desideratus)" and only later "the praised one (*benedictus*)".

A similar conclusion is drawn by Christoph Luxenberg in his new interpretation[211] of the inscription in the Dome of the Rock. For him, *muḥammad* is an epithet of Jesus and was only later personalized.

The root in "*ḥ-m-d – to covet*" is also discussed in great detail in Botterweck and Ringgren's Theological Dictionary of the Old Testament.[212] At the beginning of their article they come up with an interesting etymological explanation (p. 452):

> "The root ḥmd has not been the subject of etymological study. Possibly, if the middle radical is ignored as a liquid (l, m, n, r), it is connected with an originally bilateral root ḥd, a rare root from which Biblical Hebrew derives the verb ḥdh I, 'rejoice (qal)', 'make happy' (piel), and the noun chedhvāh, 'joy'."

In the following paragraph, they give several examples of roots which appear with and without a "liquid (l, m, n, r)" as middle radical:

> "...pls, 'make level', pas, 'flat'; šmd, 'destroy', šōdh 'violence', (...) 'ānaph, 'be angry', 'aph II, 'nose', 'anger'..."

They have the following to say about the frequency of the root:

> "The root ḥmd appears in Biblical Hebrew in the qal (16 times), the niphal participle (4 times), and the piel and hiphil (once each). It is also attested generally in the other West Semitic dialects: Egyptian Aramaic, Jewish Aramaic, Samaritan, Old South Arabic, Mandean, Ugaritic, Phoenician, and the Amarna letters. This root does not appear in East Semitic, which makes use instead of other roots with various nuances; erēšu, 'wish'; ..."

They also mention that outside Biblical Hebrew, the root also appears "in the book of Sirach as well as in the Dead Sea Scrolls". But the root does not always have exactly the same meaning:

> "As we shall see, all these roots coincide only partially with the semantic content of Heb. ḥmd. In contrast to simple 'rejoicing' (chādhāh), ḥmd expresses the notion of 'finding something desirable or precious on account of its form or splendor'."

On page 454 he specifies the meaning:

> "The word chāmadh refers not to the 'desire' that is inherently human (concupiscence), but to the specific act of desire that is generated by emotion.

> This act begins with the visual impression made by the desired object or person: 'the eye desires grace and beauty' (Sir 40:22). (...) Consequently the qal passive participle of chāmadh is applied to things that seem especially valuable, i.e., desirable. (...) In similar fashion, all the derivatives of ḥmd refer to outward appearance, the beautiful exterior that suggests high value: chemedh: pleasant fields (Isa. 32:12), pleasant land (...) machmādh: describing the sanctuary (Ezk. 24:21) or its cultic furnishings (...), considered as Yahweh's treasures, then applied to human property (Hos. 9:6; Lam. 1:7,11: machmōdh) and finally to the high value and beauty of human life (...). The same meaning finally, attaches to the personal name chemdān, attested in various Semitic dialects (Gen. 36:26; cf. 1 Ch. 1:41; also 'Muhammed')."

A last interesting point mentioned in this publication is the appearance of the form "*ḥwby ḥmdy* – sin of desire" in the "*Fragmententhargum*", i.e., in Aramaic, which obviously means less the desire itself, but rather the "*act as carried out*".

Gesenius in his famous dictionary[213] gives the following translations for the etymologically connected words:

> maḥmād - 1. object of desire; 2. grace, charm; 3. preciosity, treasure, e.g. 1 Kings 20:6: כָּל־מַחְמַד עֵינֶיךָ - *kāl [kɔl] maḥmad ʿēnejḵā* - whatsoever is pleasant in thine eyes – Greek/ LXX (= Septuagint): τὰ ἐπιθυμήματα ὀφθαλμῶν

Apart from this, there is a form only attested in the plural: "*maḥ^{a}mod* – preciosities" as well as the noun "*ḥemed* – grace, beauty". The root these nouns are based on is "*ḥāmad* - I demand, desire, praise; start to like". Especially the passive participle "desired, desirable (lat.: desideratus)" has to be taken into consideration, e.g. Job 20:20:

> בַּחֲמוּדוֹ - *ba-ḥ^{a}mûḏo* - Greek/ LXX: ἐν ἐπιθυμίᾳ αὐτοῦ – "of that which he desired".

Attestations of the root in other old Semitic languages have already been mentioned in the quotations, e.g. Old South Arabic "*ḥmd* – to praise", the language of the Amarna-letters "*ḫamudu*, probably Canaanite", (Egyptian and Jewish) Aramaic "*ḥmād/t* – to desire (passionately)", its passive participle in the 2nd/ 3rd stem being "*meḥmād*"; the form is identical with the infinitive of the 1st stem. The fact that it is not attested in Classical Syriac might be due to the fact that a verb meaning something like "to be horny" was considered too vulgar for religious texts.

The oldest attestation, however, seems to be Ugaritic. The following short text sample is from Segert's grammar[214] and is part of a text, in which the narrator tells the story of how god "Il[215]" allows god "Baal" to build a house. The translation was made with the help of Segert's grammar and glossary, including the vocalizations found there:

15. **tblk.** **ǵrm.** **mid.** **ksp.**
bring you *mountains* *much* *silver*
The mountains will bring you much silver

16. **gbʿm.** **mḥmd.** **ẖrṣ**
hills *desirable* *gold*
and the hills desirable gold.

tb - 3rd sg. f. - bring' (?)
l-k – to you
ǵr-m - pl. mountain
mid - ma'd - much
ksp - kasp - silver
gbʿm - pl. gabʿ - hill
mḥmd - 'desirable, precious (thing)'; pass. part.
ẖrṣ - 'ẖurāṣu - gold' (acc. id.); cf. Greek chrysós

According to Segert's grammar the form "*mḥmd*" is the regular passive participle of the factitive/causative stem. Whether the form *mḥmd* in Hebrew (not the root itself) is a loanword (or calque) from Ugaritic (or another Semitic language) or an inherited form from *Proto*semitic is hard to decide.

The fact that the Hebrew participle of the root is *ḥamûḏ* (like "kəṯūḇ"), not *mḥmd*, which, however, does appear at the same time as the noun "*maḥmād* - object of desire; grace, charm; preciosity", the meaning of which is next to identical to the Ugaritic meaning "desirable, precious (thing)", rather suggest a calque from Ugaritic or another Semitic language with similar morphology as the latter.

If this should prove correct, this would mean that two processes of borrowing took place simultaneously: on the one hand, a Ugaritic participle *mḥmd* would have been loan-translated as *raḥūm* and, at the same time, borrowed as a noun: *maḥmad*. The formation of the Syriac form is identical with the Ugaritic one. Why and how the original meaning of the root, – "to desire" – was changed to "to praise" in Arabic – and only here – remains to be investigated. It is not impossible that the answer lies in the theological concepts developed in the Tafsīr literature, as Koren and Nevo surmised.

6.7 "Aḷḷāh" and other names for God

The last section shall be dedicated to the central concept of Islam – the designations for God. As we will see, this will make it necessary to insert a relatively lengthy excursus about Arabic phonology, without which one important aspect of the divine name cannot be etymologized.

6.7.1 The Arabic term *Aḷḷāh(u)*

In Arabic the divine name – Aḷḷāh(u) – appears as a phonetic, or rather phonological singularity: The geminated consonant "ḷḷ" is pronounced as "emphatic (pharyngealized)", which is normally possible only in cases of another emphatic phonemes appearing in the same word, because there is neither a phoneme "emphatic *l*" not a letter for it. This would mean that that the divine name would be in phonological opposition to "non-emphatic *l*" in the form "*'allā* < *'an lā* – (so) that not". This again would make "ḷḷ" a "lexicalized phoneme", which would appear in only one word, which would contradict everything we know about language universals. It should be added that other Semitic languages do not possess such a phoneme either.

This emphatic pronunciation, however, is only audible after the "dark" vowels "*a, ā,* and *u*", i.e., not before a syllable containing /i/, thus "aḷḷāhu – God" – [ɒ'lˤ:ɒ:hu], but "*bi-smi-llāhi* – in the name of God" [bismi'l:æ:hi], where the double "ll" is pronounced without pharyngealization. This will have to be dealt with in more detail.

The explanation Muslim scholars give for the origin of the divine name is that it is a contraction of "*al-ilāh* – the deity", due to the frequency of its use (Arabic: *bi-kaṯrati isti'mālihā*). This is obviously wrong: Contracted forms like "*don't*", "*won't*", "*didn't*" in English, are rarely compulsory, so the full form "*do not*", "*will not*", "*did not*" will also appear in slow and accentuated speech (remember Bill Clinton's famous sentence: "*I* ***did not*** *have sexual relations with that woman.*") The French form "*j'ai*" might be adduced as an example to prove the contrary, but this example is badly chosen, as it is not a *contracted* form, but a form going back to the elision of a final [ə] *due to a general phonetic rule* in French, which also has an effect on the definite article (*le* + *ami* > *l'ami*). A *contracted* form would rather be the colloquial pronunciation [ʃɥi] (written "*chuis*") for "*je suis*". So if it were true that *Aḷḷāh* was derived from *al-ilāh*, then the original form should at least sometimes appear, especially as the divine name would certainly be pronounced with special care. This is *never the case*, the only form we have is *Aḷḷāh*. Moreover, it would be a very singular case of a contracted form, had the equally important word *al-islām* be treated the same way, it would have become *a(ṣ)ṣlām.*

Moreover, the name is never explained in the Qur'ān, which is an indication that it was in current use among the audience of the first Qur'ānic texts.

The genuine Arabic noun designating the category "god(s)" is "*ilāh* - pl. *aliha* – god, deity" with a female form "*ilāha* – goddess" and many derived forms, e.g. "*ta'līh* – apotheosis", "*ālih* – (pagan) god", "*āliha* – (pagan) goddess", "*ulūhīya* – divinity, divine power"; a common vocative for God is "allāhumma". The written form has not always been the same either. In older manuscripts the spelling " *'lyh*" appears, the "yā'" being *mater lectionis* for long "*ā*".[216]

6.7.2 Excursus: The Phonology of Qur'ānic Arabic

The phoneme system of modern written Arabic – i.e., a form of Arabic which does not betray the origin of the speaker, has corresponding phonemes for all letters of the written language and would be classified as both "neutral" and "pronounced by a native speaker" in the vast majority of Arabic speaking countries - can be sketched as follows (the transliteration symbol is followed by the respective phoneme in IPA):

Plosives:	ʾ-/ʔ/ ʿ-/ʕ/ b-/b/ t-/t/ d-/d/ k-/k/ q-/q/
Fricatives:	f-/f/ ṯ-/θ/ ḏ-/ð/ s-/s/ z-/z/
	š-/ʃ/ ḫ-/x/ ġ-/ɣ/ ḥ-/ħ/
Affricates:	ǧ-/ʤ/ Nasals: m-/m/ n-/n/
Lateral:	l-/l/ Trill: r-/r/
Semivowels:	w-/w/ y-/j/
Vowels:	a-/a/ i-/i/ u-/u/

Remarks:

1. In older grammars of Arabic the pharyngal /ʕ/ is described as a fricative, which is also the usual meaning of the employed IPA symbol. Both Kästner[217] and Thelwall[218] agree, however, that the sound is a plosive, Thelwall describing it as a "retracted tongue root glottal stop".
2. There are two seeming lacunae in the plosive system, /p/ and /g/. In modern borrowings, e.g. "urub(b)a/ urupa" however, /p/ can be found, at least as an alternative pronunciation. Moreover, comparison with other Semitic languages shows that the Arabic /f/ regularly corresponds to /p/ in most of the other languages. In some areas, e.g. in Egypt, the affricate /ǧ/ is pronounced as a [g], a pronunciation which can be proven to be old by comparison with other Semitic languages.
3. Long vowels can be interpreted as sequences of two vowels, e.g. [aː]-/aa/ or vowel plus semivowel, e.g. [iː]-/ij/, [uː]-/uw/. The same applies to the diphthong [aj]-/aj/.
4. The following phonemes are usually called "emphatic sounds" and will be the main topic of the present excursus: ṭ, ḍ, ṣ ẓ (transliteration symbols). Thelwall describes their main characteristic as "Retracted Tongue Root, involving simultaneous pharyngalization and greater or lesser degrees of velarization", the IPA symbols to be used being [tˠ, dˠ, sˠ, ðˠ] (velarized) or [tˤ, dˤ, sˤ, ðˤ] (pharyngealized). Velarization in general means that during the pronunciation of a sound the back part of the tongue is raised against the soft palate or the velum. In English this can be observed in the case of the "dark l" at the end of a syllable like in the word "dull" (as opposed to the "light l" in initial position like in "lead"). In the case of pharyngealization the back part of the tongue moves even further back and forms a narrowing in the pharynx. Velarization and pharyngealization are rather similar and are quite difficult to distinguish, as the latter usually inevitably involves a bit of the former.

Realization of Emphatic Phonemes in Modern Arabic

The opinions of different phoneticians about these sounds, however, differ considerably. Mitchell[219] sees their main distinctive feature in what Arabic phoneticians described as "lidding", i.e., the widening of the tongue root, which automatically leads to pharyngealization, whereas the shape of the tongue is rather longitudinal when non-emphatic consonants are being pronounced. Most Arabists assume the same pronunciation for Classical Arabic as well.[220]

The medieval phonetician, mathematician and philosopher Avicenna (Ibn Sīnā (980/ 1037 CE)[221] describes this category of sounds as pharyngealized. It is interesting to note that Ibn Sīnā, like Kästner in his description of Modern Arabic, considers /q/ as part of this group of sounds, although a *uvular* sound like /q/ cannot normally be velar*ized*, as the two positions (*velar* and *uvular*) are too close for a secondary articulation to be performed.

One of the main characteristics of emphatic sounds is their enormous impact on both neighboring consonants and vowels. This impact differs to some extent in different dialects, in the most extreme cases each word becomes either emphatic or non-emphatic, i.e., all other consonants are pharyngealized, the vowels /a i u/ becoming /ɒ ɨ ʊ/. It should be noted that after /q/, /a/ is pronounced [a], in most other positions as [æ].

The surprising fact here is that this assimilation has no effect on the writing system. A word like "ṣadara" is pronounced [sˤɒdˤɒrˤɒ] with all consonants being "emphatic", and although there is a letter for emphatic "ḍ", the phoneme is interpreted as a non-emphatic "d", which is only assimilated.

Two of the mentioned consonants, ẓ and ḍ, are not distinguished any more today, neither in any modern Arabic dialect, nor by the vast majority of Arabic native speakers in the written language, their common realization being mostly [ðˤ], [dˤ] or [zˤ].

This is also surprising, as all three realizations, [ðˤ], [dˤ] and [zˤ], can be found in the respective dialects, namely as (assimilated) allophones of the non-emphatic phonemes "/ð d z/", e.g. in the aforementioned example "ṣadara".

One of these two sounds, "ḍ"" (Arabic: ḍād) was considered the most typical sound of the Arabic language, the Arabs even being called "people of the ḍād". The fact that originally it cannot have been a simple [dˤ] is clear to see in its description by Avicenna, who mentions an "l-like" pronunciation, in Gairdner's[222] words they are "*... pronounced laterally, against the (left) side teeth, with strong affriction.*" This pronunciation must have survived for quite a few centuries, as can be seen in the word "judge - *al-qāḍī*", which was borrowed into Spanish as "alca*ld*e – mayor" and into Somali as "qa*ll*i (Somali spelling)".

In nearly all modern dialects the phonemes /ḍ/ and /ẓ/ coalesce, the pronunciation of the merged new phoneme displaying a range of realizations[223]. The only reported example of a dialect which keeps both phonemes apart (in Daṯīnah) has been doubted by Otto Jastrow.[224]

The already mentioned sound "ḷḷ" in the divine name would belong to the class of "emphatic" sounds, although not as a fully-fledged phoneme, as it only occurs in one word. As we will see the term "emphatic" is not very well chosen, as it means something quite different both in phonetics, where it can also mean "bearing stress", and in the study of other Semitic languages, where it can mean "ejective".

The reason given by some Arabic scholars for the irregular emphasis in the divine name is the assumed effort to underline God's glory by pronouncing his name with emphasis. This latter explanation can only be understood by the polysemy of the Arabic word for "emphatic sounds - *al-mufaḫḫama*", which is a participle of the verb "*faḫḫama* - to honor; to pronounce emphatically."[225]

For the above reasons it seems very unlikely that the modern realization of this group of consonants, which is furthermore responsible for almost all allophones of Arabic, is the original one, i.e., the one current at the time of the first use of the alphabet.

The first question to be answered now is how this group of consonants was pronounced in Protosemitic. In modern Semitic languages the realization is either *pharyngealized*, e.g. in Arabic and most Aramaic languages, or *ejective* as in the Semitic languages of Ethiopia.

For Protosemitic[226] and probably also for Early Arabic an ejective pronunciation like in Ethiopian languages seems more likely. Ejective – another term used is "glottalized" – consonants are voiceless plosives, which are articulated with a closure and opening of the glottis simultaneous or nearly simultaneous to the main articulation, e.g. the closure and opening of the lips [p'], the tongue against the dental ridge [t'] etc. Phonetically speaking, the first explosion takes place totally independent of lung air, the effect exclusively going back to the difference in air pressure between the main point of articulation and the glottis. Only after this explosion has taken place, or nearly simultaneous to it, the second chamber of air, – the one behind the glottis, – is opened and lung air is ejected. For a phonetically untrained person they sound a bit like plosives with an immediately following glottal stop. Apart from (Semitic) Ethiopian languages they are typical of quite a number of languages including Georgian and Quechua (dialect of Cuzco).

In different languages different degrees can be distinguished, in some languages the sounds are called "tense" (e.g. Korean[227]), as the explosion at the main closure takes place exactly at the same time as that of the glottis, which makes them sound "stronger". Moreover, the closure at the glottis can be imperfect. Vowels with this kind of glottalization are often called "creaky voiced". In the Northern pronunciation of Vietnamese two of the six tones are *creaky voiced*: orthographic "ạ" (low, glottalized) and "ã" (rising, glottalized; here with the vowel "a").

A slightly ejective pronunciation of plosives has also been described as an individual variant of French ("occlusives prononcées à glotte fermée").

For the oldest attested Semitic language of Ethiopia, Geʿez (ግዕዝ), the following emphatic phonemes are assumed (in original script, transliteration and reconstructed pronunciation): ጰ p̣ [p'], ጠ ṭ [t'], ቀ ḳ [q, k'], ቈ ḳʷ [qʷ, kʷ'], ፀ ṣ́ [ɬˤ], ጸ ṣ [ʦ']. In modern Ethiopian languages further symbols for "emphatic" phonemes (realized as *ejective* consonants) can be found, e.g. the Amharic ጨ [ʧ']. The arguments that would explain why the Protosemitic and possibly early Arabic realization of the emphatic consonants was rather ejective/ glottalized than pharyngealized can be summarized as follows.[228]

1. Pharyngealization has got enormous impact on both neighboring consonants and vowels. This impact differs to some extent in different dialects, in the most extreme cases each word becomes either emphatic or non-emphatic, i.e., all other consonants are pharyngealized, the vowels /a i u/ becoming /ɒ ɨ ʊ/. In some it only covers the following syllable, in others it can also be regressive, e.g. "nurse – mumarriḍa [mu'mˤɑrˤːɨdˤɑ]". In some dialects the whole word is either emphatic or non-emphatic.[229] It should be noted that after /q/, /a/ is pronounced [a], in most other positions as [æ]. Hebrew, by contrast, does not indicate any vowel differences between emphatic and non-emphatic sounds, although it does so, e.g. for the subtle differences of realizations of *šwa*. The surprising fact here is that this assimilation has no effect on the writing system. A word like "ṣadara" is pronounced [sˤɒdˤɒrˤɒ] with all consonants being "emphatic", and although there is a letter for emphatic "ḍ", the phoneme is interpreted as an assimilated *non-emphatic* "d". As already mentioned, two of the mentioned consonants, ẓ and ḍ, are not distinguished any more, neither in any modern Arabic dialect, nor by the vast majority of Arabic native speakers, their common realization being mostly [ðˤ], [dˤ] or [zˤ]. This is also surprising, as all three realizations, [ðˤ], [dˤ] and [zˤ], can be found in the respective dialects, namely as *assimilated allophones* of the *non-emphatic phonemes* "/ð d z/", e.g. in the aforementioned example "ṣadara". So why should the phonemes /ẓ/and /ḍ/ merge, if their main allophones – [dˤ] or [zˤ] – survive, albeit as allophones of non-emphatic consonants? To adduce an example: In the word صد *ṣadda* probably every native speaker of Arabic pronounces the second consonant as an emphatic [dˤ] (although written as non-emphatic), the whole word being pronounced as [sˤɒdˤæ] or [sˤɒdˤɒ]. Two questions now arise, firstly, why the consonant is interpreted by original speakers/ scribes as a *non*-emphatic /d/ (Arabic: د) and not as an emphatic ḍ (Arabic: ض), and secondly, if words like this exist, why did the phoneme "ḍ" become indistinguishable from the phoneme "ẓ", or in other words: How can it be that a *phonemic distinction* is lost, if the corresponding *realizations (i.e., the allophones)* survive?

To make the point clearer: In some dialects, the phoneme /d/ (Arabic: د) is pronounced as a pharyngealized [dˤ] (the realization of the phoneme /ḍ/), if in contact with emphatic phonemes, but the phoneme which should have this pronunciation – /ḍ/ (Arabic: ض), is pronounced as a [ðˤ], i.e., exactly like the consonant /ẓ/ (Arabic: ظ)! The only fitting explanation is that the modern pharyngealized pronunciation is secondary and due to later phonetic change.

2. The strong impact of pharyngealized consonants on neighboring sounds would have had another consequence for early Arabic. One would expect variant spellings of words, e.g. of a short form like "ḍidda – against", in which both consonants are pronounced more or less alike. In the oldest manuscripts, however, only the "standard" orthography (concerning emphatic consonants) can be found. Ejective consonants, on the other hand, have hardly any assimilatory effect, their secondary articulation being much easier to limit to only one sound. It must be remembered that in manuscripts from the 8th century on, confusion of these phonemes did take place, so at that time the "emphatic" sound were actually pharyngealized.
3. It is easier to explain the evolution of pharyngealized consonants from ejective consonants than the other way round. If the release at the main organ of articulation and at the glottis become more and more simultaneous instead of sequential, then, due to the inevitable tension in the pharynx area, ejective sounds gradually become pharyngealized.
4. Universally speaking, pharyngealized consonants as phonemes seem to be rarer that ejective ones, which can be found in a variety of well described languages, e.g. Georgian, Quechua and Armenian.
5. The Hebrew "ṣ" (צ) is pronounced [ts] by European (Ashkenazi) Jews, a sound much closer to the Geʿez pronunciation of the corresponding phoneme, [ts'], than to the Arabic counterpart [sˤ].
6. In Syriac (Aramaic) texts emphatic sounds do not undergo the usual spirantization of the so-called "Begadkepat" sounds (/p t k b d g/), e.g. in intervocalic position. Pharyngealized consonants can easily be spirantized, i.e., pronounced as the corresponding fricative, ejective and at the same time fricative sounds are hardly to be found at all, except for "s".
7. For the Proto-Afro-Asiatic[230] language, the parent language of Semitic, it seems more probable to assume ejective than pharyngealized consonant phonemes. Both in Chadic languages like Hausa and in many Cushitic languages there are ejective correlations, the case for Egyptian being somewhat unclear. Hannig[231] seems to prefer the interpretation of a certain set of phonemes as ejectives, an interpretation which is, however, not very clear due to missing cognate words with other Afro-Asiatic languages.

In Somali, a Cushitic language (a subgroup also belonging to the macro-phylum "Afro-Asiatic"), a number of inherited words (i.e., not borrowings from Ethiopian Semitic languages) have a sound which has a peculiar articulation affecting the involved air-stream. The Somali phoneme written orthographically as "dh" has been characterized as a retroflex post-dental voiced plosive with an ingressive initial phase.[232] Hausa, (a so-called Chadic language) also possesses ingressive sounds. From these examples one might surmise that the Afro-Asiatic protolanguage must have had classes of phonemes the distinctive feature of which was the nature, direction and timing of air-stream (ingressive, ejective), but not the raising of the rear part of the tongue (as in pharyngealized sounds).

8. The ancient interpretation of /q/ as belonging to this same group of consonants (i.e., as the ejective counterpart of "k") would make more sense if they were interpreted as ejective. The counterparts of /q/ in modern dialects have been described by Mitchell as follows[233]: [q], [ʔ], [k], [g], [ʤ], [dᶻ], [ɟ]. It is interesting to note that all voiceless variants stem from sedentary, all voiced varieties from nomadic dialects. Especially realizations in the front part of the mouth can more easily be explained from an original [k'] than from [q] and also the realization as a glottal stop resembles an ejective much more than a uvular stop. Furthermore, it is interesting to note that the name of the drug "qat - celastrus edulis" appears in an Ethiopian chronicle of the 14th century in the form ጫት ç̣ āt [tʃ'āt].[234]
   Another argument is that in the ancient Central Arabian dialect of the Tamīm, which medieval Arabic grammarians regarded as exceptionally archaic, the "q – Qāf" is said to have resembled a "k", a pronunciation often reflected in writing. However, the voiced pronunciation is also attested as rather old. The poet Baššār bn Burd (died 167/ 783 CE) wrote the Aramaic word "gamlā – camel" as "qaml."[235]
9. In Latin transcription of place names, Syriac "ṣ" is rendered sometimes as "ts", and at least in one case as "ps", e.g. Buṣra (south of Damascus) - Greek/ Latin: Bo*st*ra; Maṣṣiṣtā - Latin: Mo*ps*uestia[236]. It is especially the vacillation between "p" and "t" which clearly indicates that the Romans and Greeks heard a strange sound, the place of articulation of which they could hardly localize, namely the ejective [ts'] and not the pharyngealized [sˤ].
10. A last argument concerns less phonetics, but rather phonology: Rabin[237] interprets the correlations of the ancient Arabic phoneme system as follows: t - d - ṭ; s - z - ṣ; ṯ - ḏ - ẓ (= ḏ̣); (probably) š - l - ḍ [probably meant: ɬ - l - tɬ'], the distinctive features being "voiceless - voiced – emphatic". Because "emphasis" here appears as independent from voice, it points to ejective rather than pharyngealized consonants. This would also explain how /q/ could become a voiced or unvoiced consonant in different

dialects. Rabin also mentions the fact that the lateral character of the "ḍ" was also a feature of the phoneme " š - /ʃ/", which can be seen in parallel forms like "ʿillaud - ʿillauš - jackal; nāḍa - nāša – carry". The "š" was originally a [ɬ] (like in Welsh "ll", then became a [ç] (like in German "i*ch*") and finally a [ʃ].

According to Stempel, the realization of the phoneme "ḍ" was probably the ejective affricate [tɬʾ], a sound which can still be heard in South Semitic languages like e.g. Mehri.[238]

It should be noted that in modern Aramaic languages the emphatic consonants are mostly realized as pharyngealized plosives.[239] An exception seems to be the Jewish Neo-Aramaic dialect of Persian Azerbaijan, which has given up the opposition "emphatic – non-emphatic" in the pronunciation, but not in the spelling. However, examples like "slola – prayer" (< Syriac "ṣloṯā") clearly show, that the initial consonant rather goes back to pharyngealized [sˤ] than to ejectives [tsʾ]. We can therefore assume that the replacement of glottalization by pharyngealization in Aramaic is a very old phenomenon, probably even older than the branching off of dialect groups, but definitely later than the upcoming of spirantization of non-emphatic plosives (the so-called Begadkephat letters) and also later than the transcription of Syriac names like Bostra and Mopsuestia.

The sound shift in Arabic seems to be of a later date, considering the fact that in the earliest manuscripts (unlike in later ones) non-emphatic phonemes in syllables with emphatic phonemes are always written as non-emphatic (e.g. ḍidda is never written as ḍiḍḍa). Therefore the conclusion seems justified to ascribe this sound shift in Arabic to Aramaic influence. An independent parallel development would not be unimaginable, but taking into consideration the universal rareness of this sound shift the assumption of Aramaic influence seems much more likely.

Now the question might be asked why this realization of so-called "emphatic"[240] phonemes is relevant for the investigation of the divine name. Phonetics will provide the answer: ejective sounds are normally *plosives*, in some rarer cases *sibilants*. Laterals like the "ll" in Allāh cannot really be made ejective. So if the original pronunciation of the earliest layer of Qurʾānic texts still had ejectives and not pharyngealized consonants, then how was the divine name pronounced and why was the "ll" interpreted as emphatic? The answer to this question will be given later.

On the other hand, in a language with pharyngealized (not ejective) sounds, the "introduction" of a pharyngealized (lexicalized) *phoneme* "ḷ" [lˤ] into the language would not have been a big problem for the speakers, as this sound already existed (and still exists) as an *allophone* of /l/ in words with *emphatic phonemes*, e.g. ẓill (shadow) – [ðˤɪlˤː]. An ejective sound [lʾ], in contrast, whether as a phoneme or an allophone, never existed. So the existence of an "emphatic ḷ" only makes sense in a phoneme system with pharyngealized consonants, i.e., at a *later stage* of the language.[241]

This, in turn, would mean that the "ll" in the divine name had only become a "ḷḷ" *after* the originally *ejective* consonants had already become *pharyngealized*, i.e., sometime after the oldest Qur'ānic manuscripts had been written!

6.7.3 The root "Il" in older Semitic Languages (Akkadian, Ugaritic, Phoenician)

In order to investigate the divine name within the framework of Semitic languages, we will have a brief look at its attestation within the oldest layer of languages of this family. As the discussion of the Hebrew etymon will show, the root underlying the Arabic version – "ʾ-l-h" – is a lengthened form of an older, only bi-radical root "ʾ-l", which appears in the following languages:

Akkadian: ilu (DINGIR) - god - pl. *ilū* or *ilānū* (rare in Old Babylonian, normal in late Babylonian); see also: *lā ilu* – hostile god; *ilūtu* – deity; *iltu* –f. goddess; cf. *bābilu* - Babylonian < *bābu* – gate + *ilu* – god's gate; moreover: "*ilai, ilaḫi, iluḫa*" in Aramaic and Hebrew names written in cuneiform.

Ugaritic: 𐎛𐎍 *il* – pl. ilm – god, deity, name of god Il'; *ilt* - goddess

Phoenician/ Old Aramaic: ʾl

Old South Arabian: ʾlh

6.7.4 The root "Il" and its formations in Hebrew

In Old Testament Aramaic and Hebrew a number of different name forms appear, which ultimately go back to the Semitic root "ʾ-l": *ʾēl, ʾēloh* and above all its plural *ʾēlohīm*. These forms will be discussed in the following, the primary semantic explanations being the one given by Gesenius.[242]

1. אֵל ʾēl

The root has a number of meanings, which is an indicator of the merging of originally separate roots:

1. mighty one (< ʾayil)
2. tree (<ʾayil)
3. pillar of the wall (<ʾayil)
4. power, strength
5. God/ god, pl. ʾēlīm

Etymologically, there could be a connection with "ʾwl – up front" or "ʾlh – to curse". The form is often used with a qualifying epithet,[243] of which some are linked to locations like Shechem or Jerusalem, e.g.:

- *El, the god of Israel:* [244]אֵל אֱלֹהֵי יִשְׂרָאֵל – ʾēl ʾ^{e}lohē yiśraʾēl – griech./ LXX: θεὸν ισραηλ (Gen. 33: 18-20) "El-elohe-Israel (King James Bible)"
- *El, the seeing one:* אֵל רֳאִי – ʾēl r^{o}ʾi – Greek/ LXX: ὁ θεὸς ὁ ἐπιδών – '*Thou, God, seest me*' (Gen. 16: 13)

- *El, the Highest:* אֵל עֶלְיוֹן – ʾēl ʿelyon – Greek/ LXX: τῷ θεῷ τῷ ὑψίστῳ – "the most high god" (Gen. 14:18-20)
- *El, the Eternal* אֵל עוֹלָם – ʾēl ʿolām – Greek/ LXX: θεὸς αἰώνιος – "the everlasting God" (Gen. 21:33)
- *El, the Almighty:* אֵל שַׁדַּי – ʾēl šaddaj – Greek/ LXX: (...σου) εὐαρέστει – "the Almighty God" (Gen. 17:1; 35:11); often used in the book of Job.
- *El Berith:* אֵל בְּרִית – ʾēl bərit̲ – Greek/ LXX: βαιθηλβεριθ – "the god Berith" (Jdc. 9:46) (Shechem)
- *El Bethel:* אֵל בֵּית־אֵל – ʾēl bēt̲ ʾēl – Greek/ LXX: τοῦ τόπου βαιθηλ –"El-beth-el" (Gen. 31: 14; 35,7)

Forms with "El" are much rarer than those with "ʾelohim", but this syllable is widespread as part of names, of which some are very common to this day, e.g.:

Daniel: Hebr./ Aram. דָּנִיֵּאל – dāniʾēl – Greek/ LXX: δανιήλ (Dan 1,6); the name also appears in Ugaritic as "dnil /dānī-ʾil/", as well as in the Amorite form "Da-ni-AN" and in Babylonian "Dânilu"; for comparison the form in the Arabic bible: دَانِيَالُ - dāniʾālu

Gabriel: גַּבְרִיאֵל – gab̲riʾēl ("man of god"; one of the three archangels) Greek/ LXX: Γαβριὴλ (Dan. 8:16 (i.e., in the Hebrew part), Lk. 1:19); Arabic: جِبْرَائِيلُ - Ǧibraʾīlu

2. אֱלֹהַּ - ʾᵉlōᵃh

< ʾlh (?): the Hebrew phonemes indicate that it is the exact equivalent of Arabic "ʾilāh" and Aramaic "ʾelāh(ā) / ʾalāh(ā)".

1. god (as a generic term)
2. *God* as proper name of the true God (around 40 times in the Book of Job); pl. ʾᵉlohīm as normal plural of the generic term, i.e., "gods", idols; with a meaning in the singular: god as a generic term; might have been an archaic vocative of *ʾēl*. The singular *ʾēl* is relatively common in the Book of Job (over 40 times) as opposed to the plural *ʾᵉlohīm* (over 2500 times) elsewhere.

   The form can be negated and then means "un-god", similar to the already mentioned Akkadian "lā ilu – hostile god":

   לֹא אֱלֹהַּ - lo ʾᵉloᵃh – Greek/ LXX: οὐ θεῷ - "...(unto devils), not to God" (context: ...they sacrificed to an un-god/ non-god) (Deut. 32:17)
3. אֱלֹהִים – ʾᵉlohim - pl. of ʾᵉloᵃh (see above)

   This form can have a range of meanings:

– *idols:* אֱלֹהֵי כֶסֶף וֵאלֹהֵי זָהָב - ʾᵉlohim k̲ese p̄ wēlohē zāhāb̲ – Greek/ LXX: θεοὺς ἀργυροῦς καὶ θεοὺς χρυσοῦς – "gods of silver/ gods of gold" (Ex. 20: 23)

– *the one and only God:* with the definite article: הָאֱלֹהִים - hā-ʾᵉlohim – Greek/ LXX: ὁ θεός - '(the LORD he is) God ' (Deut. 4:35)

- *gods* (the formerly venerated ones): וַיֹּאמֶר אֱלֹהִים נַעֲשֶׂה אָדָם בְּצַלְמֵנוּ - wayo'mer (sg!) ᵓᵉlohim naᶜᵃśe(h) (pl!) ᵓādām bᵊṣalmē*nu* – Greek/ LXX: καὶ εἶπεν ὁ θεός ποιήσωμεν ἄνθρωπον κατ' εἰκόνα ἡμετέραν
  And God said, Let us make man in our image, after *our* likeness (Gen. 1:26);[245] elsewhere in the Bible, when speaking about himself, God always uses the singular!
- *demons, gods* (of other peoples):
  יִזְבְּחוּ לַשֵּׁדִים לֹא אֱלֹהַ אֱלֹהִים
  yizbᵊḥū la-ššeḏīm lō 'elōḥ ᵓᵉlohīm
  they sacrificed to demons (which are) non-god to gods, (whom...)
  Greek/ LXX: ἔθυσαν δαιμονίοις καὶ οὐ θεῷ θεοῖς - 'They sacrificed unto devils, not to God; to gods whom ...' (Deut 32, 17)
- In at least one case this designation for god is used in a kind of pun:
  כָּל־אֱלֹהֵי הָעַמִּים אֱלִילִים וַיהוָה שָׁמַיִם עָשָׂה כִּי
  wə YHWH šamajim ᶜaśā: kī
  and Yahweh heaven created because

  kɔl ᵓᵉlohē ha-ᶜammim ᵓᵉlilim
  all gods (of) the peoples (are) weaklings
  Greek/ LXX: ὅτι πάντες οἱ θεοὶ τῶν ἐθνῶν δαιμόνια – 'For all the gods of the nations are idols; (but the LORD made the heavens.)'. (Ps. 96:5)
  "ᵓᵉlilim" originally might have actually meant "gods", later it adopted the meaning "nothingness".

The use of *Elohim* together with the Tetragrammaton *YHWH/ Yahwe,* which will be discussed below, can be found e.g. in:
אֲנִי יְהוָה אֱלֹהֵיכֶם - 'ani YHWH ᵓᵉlohēḵem – Greek/ LXX: ἐγώ εἰμι κύριος ὁ θεὸς ὑμῶν "I am the LORD your God." (Lev. 18:2)

6.7.5 The Tetragrammaton "YHWH – Yahweh"

Gesenius explains the Tetragrammaton YHWH, the Samaritan pronunciation of which has been described by Theodoret of Cyrus as Ἰαβε (Iabe), as a verbal form 3rd sg. m. of a root "hyh" (to be), which is an older Hebrew form identical to the common Aramaic form. Proper names in the form of the 3rd sg. m. are very common in the Bible, e.g. Isaac = יִצְחָק - yiṣḥāq – "he laughs". Gesenius assumes two alternative interpretations, either from the verb in the basic stem (*qal*) or in the causative stem (*hiphᶜīl*), the meaning thus being "*the one who is*" in the first case, and "*the one who creates* (makes to exist)" in the latter. As the causative stem of this verb is not attested elsewhere in the Bible, Gesenius prefers the first interpretation. This divine name appears as part of proper names in the following form: "-jāhū (f. jahw)" or shorter "–jā" at the end of the name or "Yəho-", later "Yō-" in initial position, e.g.:

Jonathan: וִיהוֹנָתָן - יוֹנָתָן- *jon*āṯān / *jəho*nāṯān (God gave) (1 Sam 13:16; Chr. 17:8) - griech./ LXX: ιωναθαν/ ιωναθαν; Arabic: يُونَاثَان وَيَهُونَاثَان - yūnāṯānu / yahūnāṯānu

Elijah /Elias: אֵלִיָּהוּ - ʾēliyāhu (my God is Yahwe) – Aram.[246]: ܐܠܝܐ ʾeliyā - ʾēliyyā (Mt. 11,14); Greek/ LXX: ηλιου (Elijah); Mt.: ʾΗλίας; Arabic: إِلِيَّا - ʾīliyyā

The formula *(H)alleluja* (praise the Lord), current in many languages, also contains a shortened form of this divine name:

הַלְלוּ־יָהּ - hallǝlu-*jā* (hallǝlū – 2nd pl. imperative "praise" + Yahwe) – Greek: ʽΑλληλουϊά - Syriac: ܗܠܠܘܝܐ - halǝluya' (West Syr.) - hallelūyāh (East Syr.), e.g.: Ps. 104:35; Acts 19:1); Arabic: هَلِّلُويَا - hallilūyā

The reading "Jehova" goes back to a misreading. After the Babylonian exile the pronunciation of the divine name in full was forbidden for Jews, so when reciting a text the name was replaced by אֲדֹנָי "ʾadonaj – my Lord".[247] The vowels of this form were then added to the Hebrew consonant text to remind the reader to replace the original word by the surrogate term.

In the Septuagint the theonym was translated as "kýrios – Lord", a form Martin Luther wrote with two capital letters at the beginning: "HErr". The reading of the hybrid Hebrew form (consonants YHWE of "Yahwe" and vowels "*a-o-a*" of "*ʾadonaj*"[248]) led to the pronunciation "Jehovah". Already in the 14th century this vocalization was known as an erroneous reading. Gesenius explains the word as follows:

> "formerly the proper name of the tribal god of Israel, esp. the god who helps Israel against other peoples, only later the absolute God; in later times this name was more and more avoided."

In the interpretation of this name as a form of the verb "to be", a passage in Ex. 3:14 was certainly instrumental:

וַיֹּאמֶר אֱלֹהִים אֶל־מֹשֶׁה אֶהְיֶה אֲשֶׁר אֶהְיֶה
wa-y-yoʾmer ʾelohim ʾel mošeh ʾehyeh ʾašer ʾehyeh
and spoke God to Moses I am who I am
וַיֹּאמֶר כֹּה תֹאמַר
wa-y- yoʾmer koh toʾmar
and spoke so you (shall) say:
אֶהְיֶה שְׁלָחַנִי אֲלֵיכֶם לִבְנֵי יִשְׂרָאֵל
liḇnē jiśraʾēl ʾehyeh šǝlāḥani ʾalēḵen
to the sons (of) Israel "I am" sent me to you
Greek/ LXX:
καὶ εἶπεν ὁ θεὸς πρὸς μωυσῆν ἐγώ εἰμι ὁ ὢν καὶ εἶπεν οὕτως ἐρεῖς τοῖς υἱοῖς ισραηλ ὁ ὢν ἀπέσταλκέν με πρὸς ὑμᾶς

King James: And God said unto Moses, I AM THAT I AM: and he said, Thus shalt thou say unto the children of Israel, I AM hath sent me unto you.

It is noteworthy that the edition of the Syriac Pshiṭṭā used for this article, which in the Old Testament section is normally not vocalized, renders this sentence as follows:

ܘܐܡܪ ܐܠܗܐ ܠܡܘܫܐ ܐܗܝܗ ܐܫܪܐܗܝܗ

transliterated: w-'m(a)r 'lh' l-mš' 'ahiyah 'ašra'hiya'
and spoke God to Moses "'ahiyah 'ašra'hiya'"

The Hebrew formula "*I am who I am*" is not translated, but transliterated in vocalized form in Aramaic script. This is even more surprising, as a literal translation into Aramaic would have been easy. It seems to indicate that the Hebrew original was felt to be strange.

In his philologically exact and commented German translation, the famous Hebraist Kautzsch,[249] translates this sentence as follows: '

> "Da erwiderte Gott Mose: ‚Ich bin der ich bin, und sagte: So sollst du den Israeliten sagen: der 'Ich bin' hat mich zu euch gesandt.' "
> (Then God replied to Moses: 'I am who I am, and said: You shall say to the Israelites: the 'I am' sent me to you.'"

In the commentary he discusses the difficulty of the sentence:

> "...the usual assumption that God had wanted to point at his real name *(jahwè)* by using a verb in the 1st person of the imperfect *('ehjè)* is not sufficient; in contrast, the form jahwè must have been present in the text, but was later replaced by an encoded term, as the normal surrogate *'adônaj*, Lord, was not applicable in this context. As god of the Sinai, the name Jahwe (about this form of the name cf. 2a, note 1) in its pre-Israelite veneration probably does not belong to the Assyrians, nor to the Egyptians, but to the Midianite, more precisely to the Kenites native in that area. There is still a debate going on about the original meaning of the name. What is certain is the fact that the explanation underlying our passage insinuates an imperfect Ḳal of the verb *hāwā* (older form for *hājā*) meaning "he is". This will hardly be an attempt to portray him as the "truly being one" in the philosophical sense, but rather as the eternally being and unchanging one. Of alternative explanations the derivation from a Hiphil of *hājā* (= the one causing to be, the creator) or of hājā as an alleged variant of *ḥājā* to live (= the one causing to live) can be excluded for both linguistic and objective reasons. What would rather be possible is the derivation of a further meaning of *hājā*: "to fall". According to this latter interpretation Jahwe was interpreted sometimes as the falling one (in the form of a meteor from the sky/heaven), sometimes assuming an active verb as the one causing to fall (with lightning, as god of tempest). But this is all just as uncertain as the derivation of a verb *hāwā* (to blow [wind]) which is not attested in Hebrew (= the one traveling the air). – Knowledge of the theonym has a practical impact: without it veneration in a cult is impossible; at the same time the

use of the divine name has a protective effect. – This passage makes Moses the founder of Israelite Jahwism."

The following points should be noted concerning this opinion: First of all the imperfect of the Hebrew verb *hāyā* as copula meaning "I am" is not usual. Luther's translation "I will be" follows the temporal use of Hebrew tenses more closely, but it should not be forgotten that the semantics of tenses underwent radical changes in the course of the centuries, so that the original aspectual character was gradually replaced by a more temporal one. In modern Ivrit the imperfect (one should rather call it *prefix conjugation*) it is only used as a future tense (as Luther also understands it). Moreover, other examples from the Old Testament show that in order to express the phrase "I am", a competent Hebrew speaker would rather have chosen a construction with a personal pronoun, e.g.:

Gen. 27:24: "... And he said, Art thou my very son Esau? And he said, *I am.*" – griech./ LXX: the Hebrew equivalent of "ὁ δὲ εἶπεν *ἐγώ*" is: וַיֹּאמֶר אָנִי – way-yo'mer *'ani* (lit.: and he said: *I*)

An alternative solution would be to interpret the form "'ehje" as a jussive, which in Hebrew is hardly distinguished from the imperfect. The meaning would then be: "be I whoever I might be", i.e., "it is none of your business what my name is". This statement would have to be seen as a parallel to Ex. 20:4:

"Thou shalt not make unto thee any graven image, or any likeness of any thing that is in heaven above, or that is in the earth beneath, or that is in the water under the earth."

Examples of the verb "*h-y-h*" without preceding *waw* (the so-called *imperfectum consecutivum*) in the whole Hebrew Bible almost exclusively have to be interpreted as having a jussive meaning, e.g.:

Jdc 6:39: וְעַל־כָּל־הָאָרֶץ יִהְיֶה־טָּל - wə-'al kāl [kɔl] hā-'āreṣ yihye ṭṭāl

Greek/ LXX: καὶ ἐπὶ πᾶσαν τὴν γῆν γενηθήτω δρόσος - '(let it now be dry only upon the fleece), and upon all the ground let there be dew.'

"Yahwe" as a proper noun can also be found outside the Hebrew Bible, in Egyptian sources from the era of Amenhotep III (1408-1372 BCE), the so-called texts of Soleb, which contain a list of lands and peoples, one of them being the "land of Shasu-yhw". The same name is also attested from the era of Ramses III (1198-1166 BCE). In his Egyptian dictionary, Hannig[250] translates the corresponding attestations as follows (in the German original, translation of relevant passages in brackets):

" – *T3- š3sw Yhw* (*Yhw3*) (fremdsprachlich), [syllabische Schreibung] Jahu, Land der Schasu *(e. Örtlichkeit in Syrien-Palästina)* [cf. Jhwjw] *(English transl.: of foreign origin; syllabic writing; Jahu, land of Shasu (location in Syria/Palestine)*

 – Jhwjw [mittelägyptisch] e. Gebiet *(wo leuchtendes Metall gewonnen wird) (English transl.: Middle Egyptian: area (where brilliant metal is dug out)*

 – *š3sw* - [neuägyptisch] Schasu-Beduinen (im Nordosten Ägyptens; *vielleicht die Beni Qedem, *(unsicher) inkl. Midianiter, Amalekiter, Moabiter, Edomiter, Ammoniter und Kederiter)" *(English transl.: Shasu-bedouins, in the North-East of Egypt)*

Moreover, the name is attested on the "Mesha-Stele" (9th century BCE), where the following sentence appears: "And from there I took Yahweh's vessels, and I presented them before Kemosh's face."[251] In Phoenician and Ugaritic a similar name has appeared.[252]

Like many gods in the Greek and Egyptian pantheon the original Yahweh had a consort, named "Asherah". She is mentioned in the Bible, however, not explicitly as Yahwe's companion, but as the wife of his "competitor" Baal, e.g. 2 Kings 23:4:

> לַבַּעַל וְלָאֲשֵׁרָה - la-baʿal wə lā ʾašērā – (all the vessels that were made) for Baal, for Asherah, (and for all the host of heaven).

She is also called Elat (Ugaritic : il-t – goddess [feminine of Il = Allah]). The notion that in fact she was originally considered Yahwe's consort can be inferred from an inscription on a storage jar, which shows three human figures and displays an inscription to "Yahweh … and his Asherah".[253]

A clear indication concerning the pronunciation of the divine name can be found in the Aramaic part of the Book of Daniel, where a form לֶהֱוֵה - ***lehewēh*** appears for the 3rd sg. m. of the verb "hwh – to be" (throughout the whole book, e.g. Dan. 4:25).

The Book of Daniel is written in West Aramaic (not in Syriac Aramaic). This form, however, belongs to the East Aramaic dialect of Babylonia, the language of large parts of the Babylonian Talmud.[254] The corresponding Syriac form is "***neh**ewēh*", the West Aramaic form *to be expected* would be "***yeh**ewēh*" (prefix: *y*- like in other Semitic languages as opposed to *l*- and *n*-). Everywhere else in the Book of Daniel the prefix for the 3rd sg. m. imperfect is *y*-. The only explanation for this irregularity is that the correct dialect form sounded too much like the divine name and had to be replaced by the corresponding form of another dialect.[255]

6.7.6 The Divine Name in Aramaic

It is interesting to note that in spite of the borrowed dialect form mentioned in the previous section to avoid a homonymous form with the Tetragrammaton YHWH, this latter form of the divine name never appears in the Book of Daniel itself. The form used in the Hebrew part is הָאֱלֹהִים "ha-ʾelohim" with the definite article, whereas in the Aramaic part the forms used throughout are אֱלָהּ – "ʾelāh (without emphatic ending)" or אֱלָהָא – "ʾelāhā (with emphatic ending, e.g. Dan. 2:18)". In some cases, the name appears with an epithet: אֱלָהָא חַיָּא – "ʾ^{e}lāhā ḥayyā – the living God", e.g. Dan. 6:26. A plural form "ʾelohīn", which is the exact equivalent of Hebrew "ʾ^{e}lohīm" also appears, but means "gods".

In Palestinian Aramaic a form "*ʾəlāhū* – deity" is attested. In the Syriac Bible (Pšiṭṭā) the only form appearing has the emphatic ending, a clear indication of how much it had lost its original function, e.g. Gen. 1:1:

ܒܪܫܝܬ ܒܪܐ ܐܠܗܐ ܝܬ ܫܡܝܐ ܘܝܬ ܐܪܥܐ

b-rēšiṯ brā ʾalāhā yāṯ šmayyā w-yāṯ ʾarʿā.

in the beginning created God as well the heaven and as well the earth

Syriac text and transliteration from Muraoka[256].

The corresponding text passage in other old Semitic languages is as follows:

Hebrew:

בְּרֵאשִׁית בָּרָא אֱלֹהִים אֵת הַשָּׁמַיִם וְאֵת הָאָרֶץ :

bə-rēʾšiṯ bārā ʾ^{e}lohim ʾēṯ ha-ššāmayim wə ʾēṯ hā-ʾāreṣ

in the beginning created God (dir.obj.) the heaven (pl.) and the earth

according to the Samaritan pronunciation:[257]

Bằrắšit bắrằ ǣlůwĕm it eššắmem wit ắreṣ

Arabic:

فِي الْبَدْءِ خَلَقَ اللهُ السَّمَاوَاتِ وَالأَرْضَ

fī-l badʾi ḫalaqa ʾallāhu s-samawāti wa- l- ʾarḍa

in the beginning created God the heavens and the earth

The only language of the family which does not use an etymologically related name for "God" is Old Ethiopian (Geʿez):

በቀዳሚ ፡ ገብረ ፡ እግዚአብሔር ፡ ሰማየ ፡ ወምድረ ።

ba-ḳadāmi gabra ʾegzīʾabḥēr samāya wa-medra

in the beginning created God (Lord of the world) the heaven and the earth

The Greek version is as follows:

ἐν ἀρχῇ ἐποίησεν ὁ θεὸς τὸν οὐρανὸν καὶ τὴν γῆν

en archễ epoíêsen ho theòs tòn uranòn kaì tền gễn

In the beginning created the God the heaven and the earth.

In the beginning God created the heavens and the earth. (King James)

In the New Testament the designation of God is usually the Greek word *theós*, either with or without the article. There is, however, one phrase in which the divine name in a Semitic form appears : Jesus' last words on the cross (Mt. 27:46 and Mk. 15:34). According to most theologians[258] the phrase is a quotation from psalm 22:1-2, in the Hebrew Bible as follows:

אֵלִי אֵלִי לָמָה עֲזַבְתָּנִי - ʾēli ʾēli lāmā ʿazaḇtāni - My God, my God, why hast thou forsaken me? Greek/ LXX: ὁ θεὸς ὁ θεός μου πρόσχες μοι ἵνα τί ἐγκατέλιπές με

The Aramaic version of the Pšiṭṭā renders it as follows:

ܐܠܗܝ ܐܠܗܝ ܠܡܢܐ ܫܒܩܬܢܝ

In our edition of the Pšiṭṭā the Old Testament is not vocalized; as the consonant text, however, is identical with Jesus' words on the cross in the (vocalized) New Testament quotation, there cannot be any doubt about the vocalization:

ʾalāh^{y} ʾalāh^{y} ləmānā šḇaqtān^{y}

The King James Bible translates the two passages in the gospels as follows: Mt. 27:46:

> "Eli, Eli, lama sabachthani? that is to say, My God, my God, why hast thou forsaken me?"

Mark 15:34:

> "Eloi, Eloi, lama sabachthani? which is, being interpreted, My God, my God, why hast thou forsaken me?"

The Greek text of the two Evangelists differs in modern editions. On closer inspection, however, it turns out that in manuscripts of both of them, the diverging version of the respective other Evangelist appears as well, so the conclusion seems justified that the original text must have been the same. The two versions are the following:

Matthew:

Ηλι ηλι, λεμα σαβαχθανι; τοῦτ' ἔστιν, Θεέ μου θεέ μου, ἱνατί με ἐγκατέλιπες (Novum Testamentum graece);

The Aramaic text in transliteration would be:

ēli ēli, lema sabachthani

The following variants can be found in manuscripts: λαμα - lama, ελωι - elōi, ηλει – ēlī (ει was pronounced as "ī" in New Testament Greek). The form "ēli" reflects Hebrew "אֵלִי - ʾēl-i (God-my)" and is not Aramaic. According to Metzger[259] the form ελωι – "elōi" is the equivalent of Aramaic אֱלָהִי ʾ^{e}lāhī, the long "ω" /ō/ betraying the influence of the corresponding Hebrew form אֱלֹהַי ʾ^{e}lohaj.

The versions in the Pšiṭṭā are:

ܐܝܠ ܐܝܠ ܠܡܢܐ ܫܒܩܬܢܝ

West Syriac:	ʾīl ʾīl	l^{ə}mānā šḇaqtān^{y}
East Syriac:	ʾēl ʾēl	l^{ə}mānāh šḇaqtān^{y}

So this passage perfectly corresponds to the verse in psalm 22. The version of the Arabic gospel is:

« إِيلِي، إِيلِي، لَمَا شَبَقْتَنِي؟» أَيْ: «إِلٰهِي، إِلٰهِي، لِمَاذَا تَرَكْتَنِي؟

" ʾīlī ʾīlī, lamā šabaqtanī?" ʾay "ʾil(ā)hī, il(ā)hī, li-māḏā taraktanī?"

Mark:

The passage in Greek editions is as follows:

Ελωι ελωι λεμα σαβαχθανι; ὅ ἐστιν μεθερμηνευόμενον Ὁ θεός μου, ὁ θεός μου, εἰς τί ἐγκατέλιπές με;

The Aramaic phrase in transliteration: *elōi, elōi, lema sabachthani.*

The variants in manuscripts are roughly the ones already mentioned above. The form λεμα goes back to Aramaic "l^{ə}mā", while λαμμα reflects the corresponding Hebrew "l^{a}mmā".

A variant from Codex Bezae should be noted: instead of "sabachthani" it has "ζαφτανει", which is the exact Greek rendering of Hebrew "עֲזַבְתָּנִי – ʿazaḇtāni".

The wording of the respective passages and especially the last variant are clear indications that the phrase is definitely a quotation from psalm 22 and not an outcry of desperation. The sentence in the Pšiṭṭā is:

ܐܝܠ ܐܝܠ ܠܡܢܐ ܫܒܩܬܢܝ ܕܐܝܬܘܗܝ ܐܠܗܝ، ܐܠܗܝ، ܠܡܢܐ ܫܒܩܬܢܝ

West Syriac: ʾīl ʾīl l^{ə}mānā šḇaqtān^{y} dʾiṯeh ʾalāh^{y} ʾalāh^{y} ləmānā šḇaqtān^{y}

East Syriac: ʾēl ʾēl l^{ə}mānā šḇaqtān^{y} dʾiṯēh ʾalāh^{y} ʾalāh^{y} l^{ə}mānā šḇaqtān^{y}

The translation in this passage only applies to the form *El*, which is rendered as *ʾalāh^{y}*.

The translation in an Arabic Bible is:

أَلُوِي أَلُوِي، لَمَا شَبَقْتَنِي؟» أَيْ: «إِلهِي إِلهِي، لِمَاذَا تَرَكْتَنِي؟

ʾalūy ʾalūy, lamā šabaqtanī? ʾay "ʾil(ā)h(i)y, ʾil(ā)h(i)y, l(i)-māḏā taraktanī?

If we try to reconstruct the original Aramaic wording of Jesus' last word – provided they were ever pronounced as such – we might come to the following version:

əlāhí əlāhí ləmā šḇaqtānī

At this point it might be objected that Jesus spoke the dialect of Galilee. But all phonetic differences between the dialects of Judea and Galilee, as mentioned e.g. in Beyer,[260] e.g. the weakening of pharyngeal consonants (ʿ and ḥ) in Galilee, are irrelevant for this short sentence, as these sounds do not appear. Another difference to Syriac, the retention of final '-í - my', which in Syriac is written as a *silent* letter, is a characteristic of both dialects.

6.7.7 Other Names for Gods and Deities

In Arabic a number of other names for gods are attested, e.g. "hubal", which Wahrmund[261] in his dictionary translates as "Name eines mekkanischen Götzen (name of a Meccan idol)". So it looks like designation for a local deity. In his biography of the prophet, Ibn Isḥāq mentions that Hubal was located in the middle of the Kaaba.[262]

In the article "Did the Meccans Worship Yahweh God?"[263] the name is linked to the common Semitic god "Baal/ Akkadian: bēlu". The first syllable "hu" could reflect the definite Hebrew article as in "hā-baʿal – the lord, (the) Baal".[264]

Moreover, the frequent Qurʾānic form "raḥmān – merciful[265]" should be mentioned. It also appears in a number of old Semitic languages:

Akkadian: rēmēnû < rêmu – to take pity on so.; the dropping of ḥ in Akkadian is a regular sound shift.

Hebrew: raḥūm (Greek/LXX: ἐλεήμονος) merciful (usually together with ḥanūn), e.g. Ex 34:6: יְהוָה אֵל רַחוּם וְחַנּוּן YHWH ʾēl *raḥūm wə ḥanūn* – The LORD God, *merciful and gracious*

This word has also been linked to an epithet of the old Semitic weather god (H)adad.

6.7.8 Syriac *Alāhā* and Arabic *Aḷḷāh*

In order to etymologize the Arabic form "ʾAḷḷāh" it is important to take into consideration the fact that in West Syriac the long "ā" of the form "ʾAlāhā" was written with the Greek letter omicron. Even today in the recitation of liturgical texts the pronunciation of this vowel is a long, open "o" [ɔ:]:

ܐܠܗܐ - ʾalāhā [a'lɔ:hɔ:]

The phonetic problem with the Arabic theonym *Aḷḷāh* – the emphatic pronunciation of the "ll" – was discussed in connection with the vocalism of West Syriac by Arne Ambros.[266] As far as the Syriac pronunciation of etymological /ā/ as [ɔ:] is concerned, he assumes as the point in time *post quem* the 5th century, but notes that up to the 7th century this phoneme was occasionally written with an Alpha, which indicates a vowel shift in progress. He concludes that the emphasis, i.e., the pharyngealization of "ll" in Arabic *Aḷḷāh* should be interpreted as a hybrid development going back to the West Syriac form with [ɔ:] and a contracted form "allāh" from "al-ilāh", which he considers unproblematic.

In his article, he also dwells upon the medieval Syrian philologist Bar Hebraeus, who mentions the velarization/pharyngealization (Arabic: tafḫīm) of "l" in the divine name as being due "lᵉ-rūrāḇeh – to his glorification", but limits this phenomenon to West Syriac. Ambros considers this pronunciation as an "acoustic prop" for a new concept of God. In this context he mentions the interesting fact that in as many as 20 surahs, nearly all from the oldest layer, the word *Aḷḷāh* does not appear, but instead *rabbī* is used.

Ambros' article contains many interesting points, but some of his linguistic views cannot be accepted without reservation:

The vocalism of phonemic long /ā/ in Syriac has to be seen within the framework of language universals. In general it can be said that languages which distinguish *quantities* without major differences in vowel *quality* tend to either drop this distinction or alternatively to strengthen the opposition by adding a different vowel quality as a further distinctive feature. So, for a while, the originally *long-short* opposition might, for example, become a *long, lowered – short, raised* difference. Good examples of languages at this stage are English and German. Both have phonemically long /i:/ and short /i/ [ɪ]; but the phonetic realization of both, e.g. in the English words "beat" and "bit" (or the German "biete" and "bitte") reveals that the short vowels are lower (referring to tongue position) than their longer counterpart, the pronunciation thus is: /i:/ [i:] vs. /i/

[ɪ].[267] Most French speakers will pronounce the English "bit" with a much more closed vowel, the word then resembling the French (not clubbable) word pronounced [bit].

Then, in the next step, the length difference between the two sets of vowels is reduced – to distinguish these phonemes it is no longer necessary – and what remains as a distinctive feature is vowel *quality*, in our example *lowered* and *raised*. Probably the clearest example for this development is Modern Persian. The inherited vowel system, which is also reflected in the spelling, is /iː/ [iː] vs. /i/ [i]; /uː/ [uː] vs. /u/ [u]; /aː/ [aː] vs. /a/ [a]. Vowel quantity was added as a distinctive feature, so the new pronunciation (at the same stage as English or German) was: /iː/ [iː] vs. /i/ [e]; /uː/ [uː] vs. /u/ [o]; /aː/ [ɒː] or [ɔː] vs. /a/ [æ]. Meanwhile, vowel length is hardly important anymore, so the modern vowel system could phonemically be re-interpreted as purely qualitative: /i/ – /e/ – /u/ – /o/ – /ɔ/ – /æ/.

Another example is Vulgar Latin of the late Empire. Whereas Classical Latin had vowel length as an important distinctive feature, – e.g. populus - people vs. pōpulus - poplar tree – during the Roman Iron Age these minimal pairs, which had formerly been distinguished only by length, were more and more distinguished by vowel quality, to be more precise, longer vowels were more closed, shorter vowels more open: /oː/ [o] vs. /o/ [ɔ]; /eː/ [e] vs. /e/ [ɛ]; /iː/ [i] vs. /i/ [ɪ]; /uː/ [u] vs. /u/ [ʊ]. The phonetic closeness of [e] and [ɪ] on the one hand, and [o] and [ʊ] on the other then allowed these vowels to merge. So the phenomenon that in most Romance languages "short *i*" and "long *e*" on the one hand, and "short *u*" and "long *o*" merged, can be explained very easily through the basic laws of natural phonology.

The only exception to this rule was the vowel pair "ā – a", the vowel quality of which was too small to serve as a distinctive feature. As a sequel to the general collapse of vowel quantities the two phonemes merged.

Such processes usually take many generations with many intermediate stages. Moreover, the process is very often not equally fast everywhere, so one should not be surprised at spelling fluctuations like in the case of the West Syriac long /ā/, as mentioned by Ambros: the fact that the vowel was written with an alpha instead of omicron in late Syriac text does not necessarily mean that it was still pronounced as a clear long (phonetically speaking *cardial*) [aː]. It only means that the scribe responsible for this text had the impression that the vowel he heard in the Syriac words he was writing, resembled a Greek /aː/ (alpha) more than a Greek /o/ (omicron). That both interpretations are possible in case of an *intermediate* vowel [ɒː] or [ɑː] is not surprising, but *to be expected*.

Another problem is rather geographical, as the area where the East Syriac variety was spoken, i.e., those regions, in which the original vowel quality of /ā/ was retained as [aː], are much closer to the relevant Arabic-speaking areas at the borders of Mesopotamia than those areas where West Syriac was spoken. This would make an impact of the latter on Arabic less likely.

The variety of Aramaic that Christoph Luxenberg favors as a source for most borrowings is also East Syriac,[268] probably together with East Aramaic (e.g. Mandaic), but even he found a few Arabic words that he considers borrowings from the West Syriac variety, e.g. kūṯārā (as opposed to East Syriac ku*tt*ārā), which led to Arabic "kawṯar" with a spirantized "ṯ" (IPA [θ]), a word only appearing in the surah of the same name.[269] In general, borrowing from two (or more) varieties of a language is quite common. In Thai, most English words come from American English: there is a Thai word derived from "apartment" (meaning "apartment block"), but none from "flat". "A period of six months at a university", however, is not called "semester" in Thai, but "term", certainly because the British word is easier to pronounce for Thai speakers than the American equivalent with its consonant clusters.

To come back to the problem to be discussed in this article, in order to explain the pharyngealized "l" in *Aḷḷāh* and its connection to the pronunciation of the long /aː/ as [ɔː] in Syriac 'alāhā [a'lɔːhɔː], we must again return to the already mentioned impact of emphatic consonants on neighboring sounds.

Close to an emphatic consonant, the Arabic phoneme /aː/ is pronounced lower and further back in the mouth, i.e., as an [ɒː], which is next to inevitable due to the different initial tongue position caused by pharyngealization. After /q/, in Modern Arabic, the pronunciation is more or less the one of the cardinal vowel [aː], in all other cases [æː], i.e., like "a" in "bad".

So in order to comprehend the phonetic interference processes between (West) Syriac and early Arabic we have to put ourselves in the position of an Arabic native speaker of the Early Middle Ages. At the time of the first manuscripts with Qur'ānic texts his mother tongue still possessed the phonemes /oː/ and /eː/, in Arabic the latter is called "ā with *imāla* (slanting)". Several words have been described by Arabic grammarians as requiring a pronunciation with *imāla*, e.g. kāfir ['kɛːfir] and ṣiyām [sˤijɛːm]. As the phoneme /aː/ is possible in the same position, /ɛː/ or /eː/ must here be considered a phoneme (and not merely an allophone or free variant). In other cases, the spelling with *wāw* for *ā* – /aː/ indicates that the pronunciation was [ɔː] or [oː], so here the existence of a phoneme /oː/ must be assumed. It can clearly be seen in spellings like "*ṣlwt* - modern spelling: *ṣalāt* – prayer", which indicates a pronunciation [ts'a'lɔːt] (with initial ejective) or [sˤa'lɔːt] (with initial pharyngealized consonant). The corresponding Syriac form is "ṣlotā", which indicates that the word is originally Syriac. For the early Arabs it was therefore no problem to pronounce the divine name correctly, i.e., as ['a'lɔːhɔː].

As time went by, however, the ejective consonants became pharyngealized and, – independently –, the two phonemes /oː/ and /eː/ were dropped, so that it became more difficult for an Arabic native speaker to imitate the West Syriac pronunciation of the divine name. The only way for him to produce a vowel resembling the intended [ɔː] was to turn the preceding consonant, in this case "l", into a pharyngealized one, which automatically "darkens" adjacent vowels. This would not have been too difficult for him, as a pharyngealized "l" did exist in his language, albeit only in words with other pharyngealized (emphatic) consonants. To make the pharyngealization as strong and "emphatic" as possible (in the true phonetic sense of the word), he would geminate the "l", not a very difficult task in slow and solemn speech, the result being the form *Aḷḷāh.*

The velarized/ pharyngealized pronunciation in West Syriac which Arne Ambros mentioned as being that of Bar Hebraeus, might go back to phonetic interference with Arabic – Bar Hebraeus lived in an already predominantly Muslim and Arabic-speaking world, something which might have to be investigated in more detail.

Should this interpretation be correct, then it would have major implications for the "relative chronology" of the history of Arabic: it would mean that in the earliest phase of Arabic (the time of the first manuscripts) the "technique" of turning the "l" of the divine name into an emphatic in order to produce a vowel similar to [ɔː] or [ɒː] was not yet *possible*, because the emphatic phonemes were realized as ejectives, a class of sounds which does not darken adjacent vowels. Moreover, the trick was not yet *necessary*, as the Arabic language at that time still possessed the phoneme /ɔː/. When this phoneme merged with /aː/ and at the same time the ejective sound class became pharyngealized, the trick became both *possible* and *necessary*.

What remains to be explained is the fact that in the modern pronunciation the "ll" is *not* emphatic after the front vowel "i": one explanation would be the raised tongue position of the [i], which makes the pharyngealization of the following consonant more difficult. A counter-argument would be the existence of pharyngealized syllables with short [i] in modern Arabic, the [i] itself here being strongly pharyngealized: *ẓill* - shadow.

At this point it should not be forgotten that the main Syriac influence was from its Eastern variety, which did have a pronunciation of the name with cardinal vowels: [a'laːhaː]. The situation might have been a bit like the one in contemporary Germany, where English has impact on everyday German in both its British and its American variety. In a common pseudo-English word like "Oldie Dance Night" the average German will pronounce the vowel of "dance" like in American English, i.e., as an [æː]. In contrast, when talking about university degrees, the word "master" is always pronounced with an [ɑː], i.e., like in British English. For the computer game "Master of the Universe", however, the situation is not so clear. Sometimes it is pronounced with the British, sometimes with the American vowel. That the pronunciation of the two varieties can also be mixed can be demonstrated with the word "Derby". The normal German pronunciation is ['dəːbɪ] (without an *r*-sound/ retroflexion of the vowel!), which is a hybrid form between the correct British form ['dɑːbɪ] and the American form ['dɚːbɪ]. The reasons are clear: most Germans cannot pronounce a retroflex [ɚ].

The situation might have been similar for speakers of early Arabic: in different areas where it was spread there was influence from both varieties of Syriac. Whenever a word was adopted and there was a choice to make, the variant easiest to pronounce would be chosen, the default source being East Syriac. In the case of the divine name, the pronunciation of West Syriac sounded more solemn for the Arabic taste, so it was adopted for the name in isolated position, where it could easily be imitated with the trick of turning the "l" into an emphatic consonant. In a phrase like بسم الله الرحمن الرحيم – "bi-smi -llāhi r-raḥmāni r-raḥīm"[270] this effort was not made and the Eastern variety was chosen instead.

6.7.9 Final Remarks about the Divine Name

Summing up we come to the conclusion that the Arabic form *Aḷḷāh* is a borrowing from Syriac *Alāhā*, the inherited Arabic word being *ilāh*. The pharyngealized pronunciation of the "ll" shows that the donor language was West Syriac, except in phrases where the name follows a genitive.

The classical interpretation of "aḷḷāh < al-ilāh" is totally untenable. Firstly, the uncontracted form never appears in the Qur'ān, secondly, a contraction of the name of God is rather improbable, as it can be expected to be pronounced with ultimate care, and finally there are no other cases of such a contraction. The word itself is well attested in old Semitic languages (as Il, El, Eloh etc.) and originally designated one of a number of gods, similar to the word YHWH. The common Semitic character of the latter form makes it difficult to state which language the name originally came from, but an Aramaic origin is at least possible. The two gods were identified and their names used as near-synonyms only after the emergence of monotheism, which is a rather late development.

7. Final Conclusion

In our conclusion we must go back to the initial question concerning the primarily oral or written tradition: was there ever a time when the Qur'ān existed only in the memories of men, but not in a written form (at least not in one that was used as a basis for memorization)?

The judgment of scholars concerning the value of oral tradition differs considerably. While the Swedish theologian Gerhardson[271] was convinced that the gospels go back to Jesus himself, considering the painstaking transmission of texts within Rabbinical Judaism, the Africanist Jan Vansina casts doubts on the reliability of oral traditions as messages:

> "When sources are intangible, such as oral tradition, ethnography or linguistic sources, they must be reproduced from the time of their first appearance until

> they are recorded. Oral history and oral tradition are the only ones among them which are also messages. That means that they accumulate interpretations as they are being transmitted. There is no longer an original encoding interpretation and a decoding one, but there are many encoding and decoding interpretations."[272]

With these reservations in mind a new heuristic method was applied in the present study to find out whether texts were transmitted primarily through the spoken or the written medium. The method consisted of checking the texts in question for *hidden archaisms* and other *text-inherent* pieces of evidence for primarily oral tradition.

In the case of the Homeric epics the above question would have to be answered affirmatively, transmission was primarily oral, at least for a large part of the epic. The same applies to the Rigveda and the Avesta. In the case of the Qur'ān the answer is equally clear: the very existence of the *rasm*, its impact on variant readings, and the nature of the variants clearly show that the primary medium of reference was never the memory of the Arabs, but written manuscripts!

It is much more likely that originally Syriac or at best mixed Syriac-Arabic texts were passed on orally and at one point in time (a different point in time for different Qur'ānic texts!) reduced to writing, albeit in a very defective script. As knowledge of this mixed language, or of the Syriac element of it, was gradually declining – a bit like French and Latin phrases such as "*quod erat demonstrandum; cherchez la femme*", which, in English, are dying out today – the written text of reference became more and more difficult to understand for later generations. As a consequence, the defective writing was re-interpreted by adding distinctive dots and vowels. The result of this "incompetent" re-interpretation is the numerous opaque verses of the Qur'ān. That this reinterpretation was not uniform can be seen in the many variant readings and the existence of recitation schools.

Something that remains to be done is a comparison of different parts of the Qur'ān as to their proportion of Syriac words. Christoph Luxenberg discussed mostly Meccan surahs, so it would not be surprising that later surahs would turn out to be purer Arabic. This would help to subdivide the history of the Qur'ān into phases or periods (independent of Islamic tradition).

The next task logically would be a text critical edition of the Qur'ān, which would have to consider all attested readings and variants, but *not* as "deviations" of the "standard", i.e., Cairene Qur'ān edition (of the 20th century), but as variants on an equal footing. The result text-critical reconstruction should aim at is a text which is *yet to be inferred* from what can be found in the manuscripts, after application of well-established philological methods. From this text-critical edition a "chronological" Qur'ān might later be extracted.

At this point another misuse of terms must be mentioned. Historically speaking, the terms *"Qur'ān"*, *"Qur'ānic manuscripts"* etc. as such are highly questionable. If an early manuscript is found, the text of which can be found in the Qur'ān, then it is not legitimate to talk about a "Qur'ānic" manuscript, but only about a manuscript with a text which was later adopted or canonized as part of the Qur'ān. One can only talk about "Qur'ānic" manuscripts *after the attestation* of the first *complete* Qur'ān manuscript. Which manuscript can claim to be this oldest *complete* Qur'ān manuscript is a question never answered. Not a single of the many "standard" books written on the Qur'ān even deign to discuss this topic.[273] The reason is primarily that the importance of the question and its answer is not seen as such. To demonstrate how unscientific the designation "Qur'ānic manuscript" for early fragments is, let us imagine the following situation:

> In a book from the 15th century a fragmentary version of the story of "Snow White" is found. Two days later we can read the headline: "Earliest Manuscript of Grimm's Fairy Tales" found.

A professor of German literature producing such a blunder[274] would be a laughing-stock of his colleagues. And yet professors of Qur'ānic studies, who commit such blunders *regularly*, are treated with respect and represent the mainstream of their discipline. They serve as peers who destroy careers of revisionists (like in the case of Lüling) and prevent funding for research projects of those who question traditional views!

So what was the original Qur'ān: certainly not *a book*! – What probably did exist were collections of (later to become Qur'ānic) texts, which might have been called lectionaries (collections of liturgical texts, in Syriac: *qəryāna*). The standardization which led to the Arabic *Qur'ān* took place much later, maybe even later than the 8th century.

As we have seen, even the term "Qur'ānic Arabic" might be misleading, as the language these aforementioned texts were written in was not a fixed standard, but rather – like in the case of German urban dialects – represented different steps of interference between Syriac and early Arabic (dialects).

It is not unimaginable that after a consequent "Syro-Aramaic reconstruction" of the Qur'ān, in some places even Aramaic meters might appear (as Lüling postulated), which might increase the aesthetic value of the text.

In the case of Homer's epics, the Rigveda and the Avesta the situation is different for a number of reasons:

1. The preservation of the texts was protected by their meter.
2. These texts were not written in a mixed language. In the case of Homer the language (Ionian Greek) had some admixture of Aeolian (for metrical reasons), but these dialects were mutually intelligible. The same applies to Old and Younger Avestan.

3. In the case of the Rigveda the magical effect of the text is closely linked to its exact pronunciation, which is a further motivation for its precise phonetic transmission.
4. In the case of Homeric epics, and to a much lesser degree in the case of at least parts of the Rigveda and Avesta, the text had a long plot, which facilitated its memorization and acted as a preservative for its transmission.

Moreover, a comparison with more recently recorded texts from cultures where writing was introduced only a few generations ago, i.e., texts that have undoubtedly been transmitted for a long time only orally, these texts demonstrate some interesting facts about oral transmission in general:

1. There are no *original versions* of these texts, but only *specific versions* recorded at a *specific point in time.*
2. The text is constantly adapted, transformed, shortened or increased, according to audience, occasion and aim of the reciter.
3. As the examples from Africa and Kazakhstan show, oral literature is first of all entertainment and show, the recitation normally being accompanied with instruments (string or percussion instruments).
4. A good reciter must be able to improvise.
5. There are preservatives to protect the text from too much improvisation, transformation etc. They are meter, rhyme, alliteration and a clear plot.

If these texts, the old ones like the Homeric epics and the modern ones like the praise poems of Tswana chiefs, are compared to the Qur'ān, we come to a disillusioning conclusion:

The Qur'ān lacks all typical characteristics of oral literature.

The final and maybe strongest piece of evidence against a primarily oral transmission of the Qur'ān, however, is the importance of the *rasm* (the undotted consonant skeleton) for Islamic scholarship, as it is a mere graphemic abstraction without minimal linkage to the phonemic structure of the text.[275]

That orthodox Muslim scholars abhor dropping the axioms of their tradition is nothing we can blame them for. To doubt these axioms might be interpreted as apostasy, the punishment for which is death in many Muslim countries, apart from eternal torture in hell, if the same tradition is right. But the fact that modern Western Islamologists, paid by democratic governments, having grown up in the Western university tradition, and under no threat from a faith as belligerent as Islam, that professors of Islamic studies in Germany, Britain and elsewhere in the West so vehemently defend – or worse: not even bother to question – the old orthodox Muslim axioms, one of them being the primarily oral transmission of the Qur'ān; this fact requires an explanation.[276]

It is a symptom of intellectual laziness if a view is rejected primarily because it challenges the basis of one's research (e.g. the chronology of the Traditional Account). A good scholar would rather test the view and, if necessary, look for a new basis of further research. What the essence of scholarship should be will be discussed below.

First another question must be answered: in how far is Christoph Luxenberg's s new approach scientifically sound? Many of the questions asked in the present study go back to assumptions and claims in his book. The basic view underlying his analysis of Qur'ānic texts is the idea that Qur'ānic texts were composed in a language strongly influenced by Syriac and written down in a highly defective script, which later ceased to be understood correctly. So what he did was to take the rasm text and out of all the theoretically possible readings pick the ones that fit the context, not only the context of the text he was working on, but also the religious milieu in the Middle East of Late Antiquity. The historical claims of the Traditional Account, i.e., the Sīra (prophet's biography) and the Sunna were mostly dismissed by him as written centuries later and secondary. The latter assumption did not come out of thin air, the doubts cast upon the Traditional Account have filled several monographs and anthologies[277] and are not the object of the present study. What we are concerned with is the linguistic probability of his findings. Summing up the evidence, we come to the conclusion that none of the elements of his theory contradict linguistic universals, i.e., what can be observed in languages all over the world. This also applies to his concept of a mixed language, even if what he means is not a mixed language *strictu sensu*. The phenomenon he described has got a number of parallels, the closest one being Buddhist Hybrid Sanskrit, a case not of *translation* of a text in a closely related language, but a literal *transposition of forms*.

This does, of course, not mean that every detail in Luxenberg's work and each of his explanations is flawless and should be accepted at face value. The basis of good scholarship should always be scepticism, not faith. If this should sound like a negative attitude, a quote by Peter Ustinov should be adduced:

> Beliefs are what divide people. ... Doubt unites them.

The basic result of Luxenberg's book, the underlying Syriac element of many Qur'ānic texts and thereby the secondary nature of the Traditional Account as well as of Qur'ānic Exegesis, seems well founded to me considering the impressive evidence.

The strong linkage between the Qur'ān and early Islam on the one hand and a non-Trinitarian Christianity on the other, the main topic of several publications of Karl-Heinz Ohlig,[278] fit the picture as sketched by Luxenberg's research well. The parts of the present study dedicated to the comparative study of religion – with the aim of answering the question of how religions emerge and how they reinterpret the elements of predecessor religions, furthermore corroborate both Luxenberg's as well as Ohlig's assumptions.

At the end of this contribution we want to come back to the quotation of the great German orientalist Nöldeke which stood at the beginning of our endeavor: The general task of scholarly work is not to *please* anybody or to accumulate data to get a degree, but to find the *truth*, even if this truth might not be what fits one's *weltanschauung*.

Of course, post-modernists would go as far as to claim that there is no such thing as *truth*. But whoever thinks that a clear (i.e., culturally unbiased and universally valid) answer to a simple question like "*is the earth flat?*" in fact *is* possible has already dismissed this view as nonsense. The earth is *not* flat, and that is the *truth*, and likewise there is a clear answer to the question "how did Islam emerge?" The problem is to find it or better: to get closer to it – truth is not so much comparable to a train station a scientist can *arrive* at, but rather a light in the distance he or she should *aspire* to! Newton's definition of gravity could explain many phenomena hitherto inexplicable. In this respect he had come *closer to* the truth, but he had not *reached* it! Albert Einstein's view of *curvature of space* (which replaced the older view of gravity) could explain more than the predecessor theory, so he had again come *closer to* the truth. To say that Einstein has reached the truth would be equally wrong, as it cannot be excluded that another theory will be able to explain even more than the theory of relativity.

This latter point is the ultimate test scholars must conduct if they have to decide which theory is closer to the truth: Only if a *theory A* can explain everything a *theory B* can explain – plus something more, then and only then can we say it is a better theory.

But that is not the only litmus test for a good theory. First of all, the evidence (experiments, excavations, collected data etc.) must meet the standard requirements, e.g. it must be possible to repeat experiments under identical conditions with the same results. In historical disciplines the hard facts (coins, inscriptions, excavations) must be documented according to certain procedures. The evaluation of sources is very important as to their credibility. Then the argumentation must be logical and stringent.

And finally there is one last requirement: *falsifiability*.[279] This criterion was popularized by the German philosopher Karl Popper, who demanded that if a theory is considered to be good, then it must *in principle* be possible to falsify it. Einstein claimed in his theory that the speed of light is a universal physical constant. If an experiment or an observation yields data which prove one example of the speed of light being either faster or slower than this constant, this would *falsify* the theory of relativity. This has never been done; on the contrary, all experiments so far have corroborated the theory of relativity. But still one cannot claim that it has been proven, because it might be that under certain circumstances, which have not yet been thought of, the speed of light will differ. If such a case can be documented in the future, then the theory will be (at least partially) *falsified*, so at least it will have to be modified. So any theory has only got *preliminary* validity.

This also means that *absolute truth* can hardly be claimed for a *positive* statement. To take the example of the flat earth mentioned at the beginning: we can definitely say that a sentence like "the earth is flat" is wrong, as you can travel around it. So that is (absolutely) true. But a positive statement like "the earth is a sphere" is not *absolutely* true. It is, of course, *closer to* the truth, but meanwhile we know that the earth is flattened at the poles, so it is not a perfect sphere!

What does all this mean for the revisionists and their theories? First of all it is a question whether the findings of the revisionists can be called *one theory*. Considering that the findings of Karl-Heinz Ohlig, Gerd-Rüdiger Puin, Volker Popp and Christoph Luxenberg and the other authors of the first Inârah anthology[280] match so well that the conclusions present an alternative view of the first two centuries of Islam, it would certainly not be wrong to call it *one* theory.[281] If this new *theory A* is set off against the traditional view[282] (*theory B*), one will arrive at a number of conclusions:

- The *new theory* has many gaps, which still remain to be researched and cannot yet answer all questions related to the era of early Islam. This is due to the very nature of its claim: that the Traditional Account is secondary, – i.e., it is legend, exegesis and political program, not history, and should be separated from the analysis of Qur'ānic texts. Their evidence (Qur'ānic manuscripts, coins, philological studies, comparative religion etc.) is highly significant. It has no internal contradictions and the hard facts fit into the general picture, even if that picture is still rather sketchy.
- The *traditional theory* is a view of the world with no white spots on the map and presents a huge number of details about the life of the prophet (including many personal defects) and the first two centuries of Islam. The different historians and traditionarians (transmitters of traditions), however, differ on many major points and the number of internal contradictions is considerable. Some of the latter can only be explained away with admirable mental gymnastics, e.g. with the help of the concept of *abrogation* for conflicting Qur'ānic verses. The claims of this theory have no basis of hard facts, the material evidence (coins, excavations, inscriptions) as well as the reports by non-Muslim sources (e.g. early Christian authors), on the contrary, suggest that the conquest of the orient would have had to take place *without leaving any traces*. The fact that the first Islamic inscription begins with a cross, is written in Greek and belongs to the era of the 5th caliph (Muʿāwiya), is hardly reconcilable with the basic claims of the Traditional Account. Moreover, the importance of

a *rasm* text clearly contradicts the alleged primarily oral transmission of the Qur'ān.

Scholars of Islamic studies following the traditional view – the mainstream of what is to be found at Western universities – usually do not analyze the Qur'ān as they would do with a normal text. The prophethood of Muḥammad is axiomatic – Western scholars will at least claim that Muḥammad was *convinced* the Qur'ānic verses came from God. These scholars do not even consider the possibility that a text like the Qur'ān, with parts as different as the short surahs of the last *ǧuz'* ("part"; one thirtieth of the Qur'ān) and the legal passages of the Medinan surahs, might perhaps have been composed at *different times* by *different people*, a thought that every investigator of a similar text collection written in a different language would automatically have.

A modern theologian who claimed that the book of Genesis had been written by one person in one go would make a fool of himself, but in the case of the Qur'ān – the parts of which are stylistically much more divergent than the *Yahwist* and *Elohist* parts of Genesis – such a naïve approach is standard and anybody not following it is at best considered a dissident.

How could this view ever be falsified? Some doubt has already been cast on nearly every claim of the traditional view. But the representatives of the mainstream of Islamic studies pursue their studies as if nothing had happened.

The falsifiability of the *new theory*, by contrast, can easily be summarized as follows:

- Archaeological findings in Mecca revealing organic material (e.g. parchment) datable with the radiocarbon method could falsify the theory that the origin of Islam is to be found outside the Arabian peninsula.
- In the case of Christoph Luxenberg's theory the falsification would be a bit more difficult. To prove that some of his case studies are wrong would not necessarily falsify the theory as a whole, as he never claimed that *all* reconstructions must be correct. He has even corrected himself on a few occasions. To falsify his theory, one of his *core* assumptions or *core* claims would have to be disproven, e.g. if a manuscript were found which can be proven to be older than anything found so far and which displays readings which resemble those of the Cairene Qur'ān more than Luxenberg's Syro-Aramaic reading.
- Another piece of evidence corroborating the traditional view and falsifying the new theory could be texts from outside the Islamic world with references about early Islam, e.g. a *contemporary* and *datable* Byzantine manuscript with a historical report containing details about an Arabic prophet named Muḥammad from Mecca.

Should such pieces of evidence ever be found, the *new theory* or at least parts of it would be falsified and its representatives would have to accept this.

In the case of the traditional view a falsification is downright impossible, as it rests upon the complete and unquestioned faith in the trustworthiness of Islamic tradition, irrespective of its late attestation – and faith cannot be falsified.

Another philosopher who might be adduced in this context is William of Occam and his famous razor, which can be summarized as follows: In case we have several competing theories, the one which requires the least amount of exotic assumptions is the correct one.

Apparently traditional Islamologists think that the assumptions of the revisionists are "hard to swallow" and exotic, but only because they have become accustomed so much to their own much bigger assumptions that they are not aware of their size.

The revisionists' approach to a world religion might be labeled ethnocentric, lacking in respect for religious feelings and "*Western*" (in the Islamic world meanwhile a swearword), but truth is too valuable a good to be diluted by ideological reasoning.

The quasi-ideological attitude based on cultural relativism, postmodernism and political correctness so fashionable today in Western universities might seem to be "humane" and "open-minded" at first glance, as it denies the validity of objective truth and universally valid moral standards, which automatically assigns equal value to all cultures, religions and ideologies (finally the end of ethnocentrism!). What adherents of such an approach forget, however, is firstly that "truth" has a lot to do with *factual evidence* and secondly that "value" (of a culture, religion or view) can also be defined with regard to its *consequences*, e.g. on infant mortality, longevity, the literacy rate and peace.

Relating to the first point, there is a German aphorism which sounds as if it had been written especially for the situation in Islamic Studies:

"Beim Sturz einer Ideologie werden auch die Fakten befreit[283]
(when an ideology falls, the facts are liberated as well)."

Relating to the second point, the consequences, the following can be stated: A general *denial of the existence of truth and universally valid moral standards* will have the consequence that human rights, personal freedom and the lives of individuals have no more claim to acceptance, value or validity than fascism, racism and Nazism.

But is it really so that an ideology of intellectual self-censorship - in German the metaphor of "a pair of scissors in your head" - is the prevailing attitude? Well it cannot be denied that Islam as an object of academic study is generally considered "sensitive", which normally means that Western scholars are asked to cave in to orthodox Muslim sensitivities. Consideration for the feelings of others is certainly agreeable when directly dealing with people from other cultures (of course including Muslims), especially if they have never had contact with Western values. The first encounter should, as a rule, be characterized by friendliness and respect, *provided this behavior is shown by both sides*. In such cases it might even be advisable not to reveal one's own opinion about every cultural institution of one's counterpart *at once*, e.g. if that person should live in a polygamous marriage[284].

To demand such restraint from *scholars* at *Western universities* is an outrage! For a true scholar, it has to be irrelevant[285] whether his or her findings serve the "Dialogue of Religions", the cooperation with a partner university in the Middle East, fundraising in Saudi-Arabia or whether some religious group demands more respect for their religious feelings.

Otherwise it would only be logical to abolish astrophysics or paleontology only because some creationists demand respect for their religious feelings on the ground that according to their conviction the earth was created only 6000 years ago and that the big bang – or the dating of dinosaur bones – was an insult to their convictions!

The freedom of research – as well as religious freedom, which includes the right to *criticize* or *leave* a religion – is a precious right many generations have fought for, with many casualties, many tears and - at least in the West - preliminary success. It is based on the accomplishments of the age of enlightenment, on rational thinking and on human rights. We should not allow it to be curtailed in order to get the applause of people who favor blind faith to doubt, submission to liberty and the wording of old texts to humane instincts.

8. Bibliography

8.1 General Linguistic Disciplines

Bloomfield, Leonard (1933). Language. London/ New York.

Bußmann, Hadumod (1990). Lexikon der Sprachwissenschaft, 2nd ed. Stuttgart.

Campbell, Lyle (1997). American Indian Languages: The Historical Linguistics of Native America. Oxford/ New York.

Campbell, Lyle (1999). Historical Linguistics: An Introduction. 2nd ed. Edinburgh University Press 1998. MIT Press 1999.

Comrie, B. (1989). Language Universals and Linguistic Typology. 2nd ed. Oxford.

Coulmas, Florian (1981). Über Schrift. Suhrkamp Taschenbuch (paperback series) Wissenschaft 378. Frankfurt a. M.

Daniels, P.T./ Bright, W. (ed.) (1996). The World's Writing Systems. New York/ Oxford.

Fodor, István (1969). The Problems in the Classification of the African Languages. Center for Afro-Asian Research of the Hungarian Academy of Sciences. Budapest.

Gelb, I.J. (1963). A Study of Writing. A Discussion of the General Principles Governing the Use and Evolution of Writing. revised (2nd) edition. Chicago & London.

Greenberg, J. H. (1987). Languages in the Americas. Stanford.

Greenberg, Joseph H. (1957). Essays in Linguistics. Chicago/ London.

Greenberg, Joseph H. (1963). The Languages of Africa. Den Haag.

Haarmann, H. (1992). Universalgeschichte der Schrift. 2nd ed. Frankfurt/ New York.

Haarmann, H. (2001). Kleines Lexikon der Sprachen - Von Albanisch bis Zulu. München.

Haarmann, Harald (2002). Lexikon der Untergegangenen Sprachen. München.

Handbook of the International Phonetic Association. (1999). A Guide to the Use of the International Phonetic Alphabet. Cambridge University Press.

Keiler, A. R. (ed.) (1972). A Reader in Historical and Comparative Linguistics. New York.

Lord, Robert (1974). Comparative Linguistics. Teach Yourself Books. 2nd ed. London.

Mangold, Max (1973 ?). Sprachwissenschaft. Darmstadt.

Mangold, Max (2005). Duden vol. 6 - Das Aussprache-Wörterbuch (German Pronouncing Dictionary). 6th, revised ed., Mannheim/ Leipzig/ Wien/ Zürich.

Mangold, Max o.J. (ca. 2000). Bibel-Aussprachewörterbuch. Saarbrücken.

Mithun, Marianne (1999). The Languages of Native North America.

Cambridge Language Surveys. Cambridge University Press.
Schmitt, Rüdiger (1967). Dichtung und Dichtersprache in Indogermanischer Zeit. Wiesbaden.
Schmitt, Rüdiger (1981). Grammatik des Klassisch-Armenischen, mit Sprachvergleichenden Erläuterungen. Innsbruck.
Schubiger, Maria (1977). Einführung in die Phonetik. 2nd ed. Berlin/ New York.
Szemerényi, Oswald (1990). Einführung in die Vergleichende Sprachwissenschaft. Darmstadt.
Wendt, F. (1987). Fischer Lexikon Sprachen. Durchgesehene und Korrigierte Neuausgabe. Frankfurt am Main.
Online publication: Groß, Markus (2007). Zu Universalien des Sprachwandels. Ein Beispiel aus der Verbalmorphologie. http://webdoc2.urz.uni-halle.de/dot2007/publikation.php.

8.2 Semitic studies/ Afro-Asiatic Languages

8.2.1 Arabic, Semitic and Afro-Asiatic Studies

Bergsträsser, G. (1928). Einführung in die Semitischen Sprachen. Sprachproben und Grammatische Skizzen. München (*reprint:* Darmstadt 1963).
Brockelmann, C. (1906). Semitische Sprachwissenschaft. Sammlung Göschen. Leipzig.
Brockelmann, C. (1908/ 1913). Grundriß der Vergleichenden Grammatik der Semitischen Sprachen. Berlin (reprint: Hildesheim 1961).
Busse, Heribert (1987). Arabische Historiographie und Geographie, in: *Gätje, Helmut (ed.) (1987).* Grundriss der Arabischen Philologie. vol. 2: Literaturwissenschaft. Wiesbaden, p. 264-297.
Denz, Adolf (1982). Die Struktur des Klassischen Arabisch, in: *Fischer, Wolfdietrich (ed.) (1982).* Grundriss der Arabischen Philologie. vol. 1: Sprachwissenschaft. Wiesbaden, p. 58-82.
Diakonoff, I.M. (1965). Semito-Hamitic Languages. An Essay in Classification. Languages of Asia and Africa. Moskau.
Die Burda. Ein Lobgedicht auf Muḥammad von Al-Buṣîrî. Neu herausgegeben im arabischen Text mit metrischer persischer und türkischer Übersetzung von C.A. Ralfs. Wien 1860.
Fischer, Wolfdietrich (1982). Das Altarabische in Islamischer Überlieferung: Das Klassische Arabisch, in: *Fischer, Wolfdietrich (ed.) (1982).* Grundriss der Arabischen Philologie. vol. 1: Sprachwissenschaft. Wiesbaden, p. 37-50.
Fischer, Wolfdietrich (1982). Frühe Zeugnisse des Neuarabischen, in: *Fischer, Wolfdietrich (ed.) (1982).* Grundriss der Arabischen Philologie.

vol. 1: Sprachwissenschaft. Wiesbaden, p. 83-95.
Fischer, Wolfdietrich (ed.) (1982). Grundriss der Arabischen Philologie. vol. 1: Sprachwissenschaft. Wiesbaden.
Fischer, Wolfdietrich (ed.) (1992). Grundriss der Arabischen Philologie. vol. 3: Supplement. Wiesbaden.
Fronzaroli, Pelio (1964). Studi sul Lessico Comune Semitico. In: Lincei - Rendiconti Morali - 1964 - Serie VIII, vol. XIX, fasc. 7-12.
Gairdner, W. H. T. (1925). The Phonetics of Arabic. London.
Gätje, Helmut (ed.) (1987). Grundriss der Arabischen Philologie. vol. 2: Literaturwissenschaft. Wiesbaden.
Hecker, Karl (1982). Das Arabische im Rahmen der Semitischen Sprachen. in: *Fischer, Wolfdietrich (ed.) (1982).* Grundriss der Arabischen Philologie. vol. 1: Sprachwissenschaft. Wiesbaden, p. 6-16.
Heinrichs, Wolfhart (1987). Poetik, Rhetorik, Literaturkritik, Metrik und Reimlehre, in: *Gätje, Helmut (ed.) (1987).* Grundriss der Arabischen Philologie. vol. 2: Literaturwissenschaft. Wiesbaden, p. 177-207.
Jacobi, Renate (1987). Dichtung, in: *Gätje, Helmut (ed.) (1987).* Grundriss der arabischen Philologie. Band 2: Literaturwissenschaft. Wiesbaden, S. 7-19.
Jacobi, Renate (1987). Die altarabische Dichtung, in: *Gätje, Helmut (ed.) (1987).* Grundriss der Arabischen Philologie. Band 2: Literaturwissenschaft. Wiesbaden, p. 20-31.
Jastrow, Otto (1982). Die Struktur des Neuarabischen, in: *Fischer, Wolfdietrich (ed.) (1982).* Grundriss der Arabischen Philologie. vol. 1: Sprachwissenschaft. Wiesbaden, p. 128-141.
Kästner, H. (1981). Phonetik und Phonologie des Modernen Hocharabisch. Leipzig.
Kienast, Burkhart (2001). Historische Semitische Sprachwissenschaft. Wiesbaden, p. 56 f.
La Bordah du Cheikh el Bouṣiri. Poème en l'Honneur de Moḥammed. traduite et commentée par René Basset. Paris 1894
Meeker, Michael E. (1979). Literature & Violence in North Arabia. Cambridge Studies in Cultural Systems. San Diego.
Moscati, Sabatino/ Spitaler, Anton/ Ullendorf, Edward/ von Soden, Wolfram (1964). An Introduction to the Comparative Grammar of the Semitic languages. Phonology and Morphology. edited by Sabatino Moscati. Porta Linguarum Orientalium. Wiesbaden.
Musil, Alois (1928). The Manners and Customs of the Rwala Bedouins. New York: American Geographical Society.
Nevo, Yehuda D./ Koren, Judith (2003). Crossroads to Islam, The Origins of the Arab Religion and the Arab State, Amherst (NY).
Sasse, H.-J. (1981). Die semitischen Sprachen. In: *Heine, E./ Schadeberg, Th.C./ Wolff, E. (ed.)(1981).* Die Sprachen Afrikas. Hamburg: p. 225-238.

Sasse, Hans-Jürgen (1981). Afroasiatisch. *In: Heine, E./ Schadeberg, Th.C./ Wolff, E. (ed.)(1981).* Die Sprachen Afrikas. Hamburg: p. 129-148.

Schimmel, Annemarie (1987). Sufismus, in: *Gätje, Helmut (ed.) (1987).* Grundriss der Arabischen Philologie. vol. 2: Literaturwissenschaft. Wiesbaden, p. 338-357.

Stempel, Reinhard (1999). Abriß einer Historischen Grammatik der Semitischen Sprachen. Nordostafrikanisch / Westasiatische Studien 3. Frankfurt.

see also the review of *Weninger, st.* in: Kratylos 47 (2002): p. 216 ff.

Thelwall, Robin/ Sa'adeddin, M. Akram: Arabic (Illustrations of the IPA), in: Handbook of the International Phonetic Association. A Guide to the Use of the International Phonetic Alphabet. Cambridge, U.K.

Солнцев, В.М. (главний редактор) (1991). Афразийские Языки: Кушитские языки. Ливийско-гуанчские Языки. Египетский Язык. Чадские Языки. Кн. 2. Языки Азии и Африки IV. Москва.

Старинин, В. П. (1967). Эфиопский Язык. Москва.

8.2.2 Akkadian

Labat, René (o.J.). Manuel d'Épigrahie Akkadienne (signes, syllabaire, idéogrammes). nouvelle édition, revue et corrigée par Florence Malbran-Labat. Paris.

Липин, Л.А. (1964). Аккадский Язык. Москва.

8.2.3 Arabic and Arabic Dialects (including Maltese)

Al-Munǧid (المنجد) fī l-luġati wa l-'a'lām. (1984) aṭ-ṭib'atu s-sābi'atu wa l-'išrūn (27th impression). Beirut.

Ambros, Arne A. (1979). Einführung in die Moderne Arabische Schriftsprache, 2nd ed. München (with a record illustrating the pronunciation).

vocabulary printed separately as: *Ambros, Edith/ Ambros, Arne A. (1976).* Arabischer Mindestwortschatz und Glossar zur "Einführung in die moderne arabische Schriftsprache". München.

Ambros, Arne A. (1998). Bonġornu, kif int? Einführung in die maltesische Sprache. Sprachenreihe Reichert. Wiesbaden.

Aquilina, Joseph (1965). Maltese. Teach Yourself Books. London.

Arabic Phonetics (1963). Ibn Sīnā's Risālah on the points of articulation of the speech-sounds translated from Medieval Arabic by Khalil I. Semaan, M.A., Ph.D. Arthur Jefferey Memorial Monographs No. 2. 2nd edition. Lahore.

Ambros, Arne A. (1981). Ẓur Entstehung der Emphase in Allah, Wiener Zeitschrift für die Kunde des Morgenlandes 73 (1981), p. 23-32.

Bauer, Leonhard (ed.) (1957). Deutsch-arabisches Wörterbuch der Umgangssprache in Palästina und im Libanon. unter Mitwirkung von Anton Spitaler. Wiesbaden.

Borg, A./ Azzopardi-Alexander, M. (1997). Maltese. London.

Cantineau, J. (1960). Cours de Phonétique Arabe. Paris.

Fischer, Wolfdietrich/ Jastrow, Otto (1982). Lehrgang für die Arabische Schriftsprache der Gegenwart. 3rd, revised edition. Wiesbaden.

Grotzfeld, H. (1965). Syrisch-Arabische Grammatik. Wiesbaden.

Guillaume, A. (Übersetzer/ ed.) (1955). The Life of Muhammad. A Translation of Isḥāq's Sīrat Rasūl Allāh. with an introduction and notes by A. Guillaume. first published 1955, reprinted Karachi 1967.

Harder, Ernst/ Paret, Rudi (newly edited with major changes) (1959). Kleine Arabische Sprachlehre. Methode Gaspey-Otto-Sauer, 7th ed. Heidelberg.

Harrell, R.p. (1962). A short Reference Grammar of Moroccan Arabic. Washington.

Harrell, Richard p. (1965). A Basic Course in Moroccan Arabic. Washington, D.C.

Harrell, Richard p. (ed.) (1966). A Dictionary of Moroccan Arabic. Washington, D.C.

Heyworth-Dunne, J./ Goma'a, M.M. (n.d.). Spoken Egyptian Arabic (Linguaphone Oriental Language Courses). n.p.

Holes, C. (1989). Gulf Arabic. London.

Jaschke, Richard (1990). English-Arabic Conversational Dictionary. with a grammar, phrases, an Arabic-English Vocabulary and s supplement of new words and new phrases. 2nd ed. New York.
(translation with major additions of an older phrase book written in German; it describes the dialects of Syria and Egypt)

Kaye, Alan p. (1997). Arabic Phonology. In: *Kaye, Alan p. (ed.) (1997).* Phonologies of Asia and Africa (Including the Caucasus), vol. I: Asia. Winona Lake, Ind.: p. 187-204.

Kuhnt, Eberhard (1958). Syrisch-Arabischer Sprachführer. Wiesbaden.

Langenscheidts Taschenwörterbuch Arabisch

1st part: *Krotkoff, Georg (1976).* Arabisch - Deutsch. Berlin/ München/ Wien/ Zürich. 7th ed. 1983.

2nd part: *Schukry, Kamil/ Humberdrotz, Rudolf (1967).* Deutsch - Arabisch. Berlin/ München/ Wien/ Zürich. 8th ed. 1983.

Mitchell, T. F. (1956). An Introduction to Egyptian Colloquial Arabic. Oxford.

Mitchell, T.F. (1962; 10th impression 1978). Colloquial Arabic. Teach yourself books. New York.

Mokhtar, A. (1983). Lehrbuch des Ägyptisch-Arabischen. 2nd ed. Wiesbaden.

Munzel, Kurt (1958). Ägyptisch-Arabischer Sprachführer. Wiesbaden.

Qafisheh, H.A. (1977). A Short Reference Grammar of Gulf Arabic. Tucson.

Reichert, Rolf (1968). Polyglott Sprachführer Marokkanisch-Arabisch. Berlin.

Sciriha, Lydia (1996). Beginning Maltese (with tapes). University of Malta.

Seidel, A. (1907). Marokkanische Sprachlehre. Praktische Grammatik des Vulgärarabischen in Marokko. Heidelberg/ Paris/ London/ Rom/ St. Petersburg.

Shehadeh, Saa'eed, J. (Bearbeiter) (1979/ 83). Langenscheidts Sprachführer Arabisch. Berlin/ München/ Wien/ Zürich. 3rd ed. 1983.

Stowasser, Karl/ Moukhtar, Ani (1964). A Dictionary of Syrian Arabic (Dialect of Damascus). English.

Tapiéro, Norbert (1978). Manuel d'Arabe Algérien Moderne. 2e édition. supplément de 15 dialogues entre Maghrébins, sur la vie des immigrés avec traduction. Paris.

Thelwall, Robin/ Sa'adeddin (1990). Illustrations of the IPA: Arabic. In: JIPA 20/2: p. 37-39.

Tritton, A. p. (1943). Arabic. A Complete Working Course. Teach Yourself Books. Sevenoaks, Kent/ London.

Vollers, K (1906). Volkssprache und Schriftsprache im alten Arabien. Strassburg.

Wahrmund Adolf (1869). Handwörterbuch der Neu-arabischen und Deutschen Sprache, 3 vol., reprint Beirut 1980 (Librairie du Liban).

Wehr, H. (1968). Arabisches Wörterbuch für die Schriftsprache der Gegenwart. 4th ed. Wiesbaden.

Wehr, Hans (1960 ?). A Dictionary of Modern Written Arabic; edited by Milton Cowan. New York (reprint 1980, Libanon).

Woodhead, D. R./ Beene, Wayne (ed.) (1967). A dictionary of Iraqi Arabic. Arabic-English. Washington, D.C.

Wright, W. (1962). A grammar of the Arabic Language. translated from the German of Caspari and edited with numerous additions and corrections. 3rd edition. 2 vls. Cambridge.

Завадовский, Ю. Н. (1962). Арабские Диалекти Магриба. Москва.

Завадовский, Ю. Н. (1979). Тунисский Диалект Арабского Языка. Москва.

Лебедев, В.В. (1977). Поздний Среднеарабский Язык (XIII-XVIII вв.) . Москва.

Шарбатов, Г. Ш. (1961). Современный Арабский Язык. Москва.

7.2.4 Aramaic

Arnold, Werner (1989). Lehrbuch des Neuwestaramäischen. Semitica Viva. Series Didactica ed. by Otto Jastrow. vol. 1. Wiesbaden.

Bauer, Hans/ Leander, Portus (1927). Grammatik des Biblisch-Aramäischen.

Halle (reprint 1995: Hildesheim/ Zürich/ New York/ Vaduz).
Beyer, Klaus (1986). The Aramaic Language. Göttingen.
Brockelmann, Carl (1960). Syrische Grammatik mit Paradigmen, Literatur, Chrestomathie und Glossar. Leipzig - 13th, unchanged ed. 1981.
Daniels, Peter T. (1997). Classical Syriac Phonology. In: *Kaye, Alan p. (ed.) (1997).* Phonologies of Asia and Africa (Including the Caucasus) vol I: Asia.Winona Lake, Ind.: p. 127-140.
Garbell, Irene (1965). The Jewish Neo-Aramaic Dialect of Persian Azerbaijan. Linguistic Analysis and Folkloristic Texts. London/ The Hague/ Paris.
Healey, John F. (1980). First Studies in Syriac. University Semitics Study Aids 6. Birmingham (with tapes).
Hoberman, Robert D. (1997). Modern Aramaic Phonology. In: Kaye, Alan p. (ed.) (1997). Phonologies of Asia and Africa (Including the Caucasus) vol. I: Asia.Winona Lake, Ind.: p. 313-336.
Jastrow, Otto (1992). Lehrbuch der Ṭuroyo-Sprache. Wiesbaden
Marcus, David (1981). A Manual of Babylonian Jewish Aramaic. Washington D.C.
Muraoka, Takamitsu (1987). Classical Syriac. A Basic Grammar with a Chrestomathy. Porta Linguarum Orientalium vol. 19. Harassowitz. Wiesbaden.
Rosenthal, Franz (1961). A Grammar of Biblical Aramaic. Wiesbaden
Schulthess, Friedrich (1965). Grammatik des Christlich-palästinischen Aramäisch. Hildesheim.
Tsereteli, Konstantin (1978). Grammatik der Modernen Assyrischen Sprache (Neuostaramäisch). Leipzig; Russian edition: Церетели, К. Г. (1964). Совремменный Ассирийский Яык. Москва.

8.2.5 Hebrew

Cowley, A.E. (1946). Gesenius' Hebrew Grammar as Edited and Enlarged by the Late E. Kautzsch. second English edition, revised in accordance with the twenty-eighth German edition (1909) by Cowley. A.E.. Oxford.
Gesenius, Wilhelm (1915/1962). Hebräisches und Aramäisches Handwörterbuch über das Alte Testament. bearbeitet von Frants Buhl. unchanged reprint of the 17th edition of 1915. Heidelberg 1962.
Grether, Oskar (1951). Hebräische Grammatik für den Akademischen Unterricht. München.
Rendburg, Gary A. (1997). Ancient Hebrew Phonology. In: Kaye, Alan p. (ed.) (1997). Phonologies of Asia and Africa (Including the Caucasus) Vol I: Asia.Winona Lake, Ind.: p. 65-84.
Siddur Schma Kolenu (1997). Ins Deutsche übersetzt von Raw Joseph Scheuer. 2nd ed. Basel/ Zürich.

8.2.6 Ugaritic

Gordon, Cyrus H. (1965). Ugaritic Textbook; Grammar, Texts and Transliteration, Cuneiform Selections, Glossary, Indices. n.p.

Gordon, Cyrus (1955). Ugaritic Manual, 3 vols. Analecta Orientalia 35. Rome: Pontificum Institutum Biblicum.

Segert, Stanislav (1984). A Basic Grammar of the Ugaritic language. with selected texts and glossary. Berkeley, California/ Los Angeles/ London.

8.2.7 Ethiopian Semitic and South Arabic

Gragg, Gene (1997). Geʿez Phonology. In: *Kaye, Alan p. (ed.) (1997).* Phonologies of Asia and Africa (Including the Caucasus) Vol I: Asia.Winona Lake, Ind.: p. 169-186.

Hayward, Katrina/ Hayward, Richard J. (1992). Illustrations of the IPA: Amharic. In: JIPA 22/1&2: p. 48-53.

Höfner, Maria (1943). Altsüdarabische Grammatik. Leipzig.

Jahn, Alfred (1905). Grammatik der Mehri-Sprache in Südarabien. Wien.

Praetorius, Franz (1886). Aethiopische Grammatik. mit Paradigmen, Litteratur, Chrestomathie und Glossar. Breslau - Nachdruck New York 1955.

Rubin, Aaron (2010). The Mehri Language of Oman. Leiden.

Richter, Renate (1987). Lehrbuch der Amharischen Sprache. Leipzig.

Sima, Alexander (2009). Mehri-Texte aus der jemenitischen Šarqīyah. Transkribiert unter Mitwirkung von ʿAskari Ḥugayrān Saʿd; bearbeitet und herausgegeben von Janet C. E. Watson und Werner Arnold. Wiesbaden, 2009.

Старинин, В. П. (1967). Эфиопский Язык. Москва.

8.2.8 Somali

Abraham, R. C. (1962). Somali-English Dictionary. London.

Abraham, R.C. (1967). English-Somali Dictionary. London.

Andrzejewski, B. W./ Lewis, I. M. (1964). Somali Poetry. An introduction. Oxford.

Armstrong, Lilias E. (1934/1964). The Phonetic Structure of Somali (*First publication*: Mitteilungen des Seminars für Orientalische Sprachen zu Berlin, Nr. 37; *New publication*: Gregg International Publishers Ltd.). Farnborough, Hants., England.

El-Solami-Mewes, Catherine (1987). Lehrbuch des Somali. Leipzig.

Farah, Mohammed Ali/ Heck, Dietmar (1990). Somali-Wörterbuch: Deutsch-Somali, Somali-Englisch-Deutsch. Hamburg.

Keenadiid, Yaasiin C. (1976). Qamuuska Af Soomaaliga ("Dictionary of

Somali" (a monolingual Somali dictionary)). Florence

Puglielli, Annarita (1997). Somali Phonology. In: *Kaye, Alan p. (ed.) (1997).* Phonologies of Asia and Africa (Including the Caucasus) Vol I: Asia.Winona Lake, Ind.: p. 521-536.

Stepanjenko, D.I./ Osman, Mohamed Haji (1969). Краткий сомали-русский и русско-сомали словарь/ (Abwan Urursan) af soomaali iyo rusha iyo rush iyo af soomaaliga. Moskau.

Дубнова, Е. З. (1990). Современный Сомалийский Язык. Москва.

8.2.8 Old Egyptian

Hannig, R. (1995). Großes Handwörterbuch Ägyptisch- Deutsch (2800-950 v. Chr.). Mainz.

Schenkel, Wolfgang (1990). Einführung in die Altägyptische Sprachwissenschaft. Darmstadt.

8.2.9 Hausa

Jungraithmayr, Herrmann/ Möhlig, W.J.G. (1976). Einführung in die Hausa-Sprache. (= Marburger Studien zur Afrika- und Asienkunde, Serie A: Afrika, vol. 7.) Berlin*: D. Reimer.*

Kraft, C. H./ Kirk-Greene, A. H. M. (1973). Hausa. Teach Yourself Books. Sevenoaks, Kent/ London; 9th impression 1985.

8.3 Indo-European Languages

8.3.1 Indo-European Linguistics

Meier-Brügger, Michael (2000). Indogermanische Sprachwissenschaft. 7., völlig neu bearbeitete Auflage unter Mitarbeit von Matthias Fritz und Manfred Mayrhofer (7th, revised edition). de Gruyter Studienbuch. Berlin, New York.

Schmitt-Brandt, Robert (1998). Einführung in die Indogermanistik. Tübingen/Basel.

Tichy, Eva (2000). Indogermanisches Grundwissen. Bremen.

8.3.2 Germanic Languages

Bjørnskau, Kjell (1980). Langenscheidts Praktisches Lehrbuch Norwegisch. 6. ed. Berlin/ München/ Wien/ Zürich.

Cambridge International Dictionary of English, Cambridge University Press 1995.

Gerdes, Udo/ Spellerberg, Gerhard ((1983). Althochdeutsch, Mittelhochdeutsch: Grammatischer Grundkurs zur Einführung und Textlektüre. Königstein/ Ts.

Hutterer, Claus Jürgen (1999). Die Germanischen Sprachen. 4th, revised ed. Wiesbaden.

Jones, Daniel / Gimson, A. C./ Ramsaran, Susan (1993). Everyman's English

Pronouncing Dictionary, 14th edition. Indian reprint 1993. Delhi.
Kluge, F. (1883/ 1989). Etymologisches Wörterbuch der Deutschen Sprache. 23th, enlarged ed. of Elmar Seebold. Berlin/ New York 1999.
König, W. (1998). Dtv-Attas zur Deutschen Sprache. 12th ed. München.
Krause, Wolfgang (1970). Runen. Sammlung Göschen. Berlin.
Lehnert, Martin (1973). Altenglisches Elementarbuch. 8th, revised edition, Sammlung Göschen vol. 5125. Berlin/ New York.
Ranke Friedrich/ Hofmann Dietrich (1979). Altnordisches Elementarbuch. 4th, revised ed. Berlin/New York.
Steitz, Lothar (1981). Grammatik der Mundart von Saarbrücken. Beiträge zur Sprache im Saarland 2. Saarbrücken.

8.3.3 Greek

Adrados, Francisco R. (2000). Geschichte der Griechischen Sprache. Aus dem Spanischen übersetzt von Hansbert Bertsch. Tübingen und Basel.
Title of the Spanish original: Historia de la lengua griega. De los orígenes a nuestros días. 1999.
Bornemann, Eduard (1980). Griechische Grammatik. unter Mitwirkung von Ernst Risch. 2th ed.. Frankfurt a. M./ Berlin/ München.
Meier-Brügger (1992). Griechische Sprachwissenschaft. vol. I Bibliographie, Einleitung, Syntax. vol. 2. Wortschatz, Formenlehre, Lautlehre, Indizes. Berlin/ New York.
Meillet, A. (1965). Aperçu d'une Histoire de la Langue Grecque, 7th ed., n.p.
Osborne, R. (1996). Greece in the Making 1200 - 479 BC. London/ New York.
Palmer, L.R. (1986). Die Griechische Sprache. Innsbruck.
Powell, Barry B. (1991). Homer and the Origin of the Greek alphabet. Cambridge.
Rix, H. (1976). Historische Grammatik des Griechischen. Laut- und Formenlehre. Darmstadt.
Schmitt, Rüdiger (1977). Einführung in die Griechischen Dialekte. Darmstadt.
Schwyzer, E. (1934-1939). Griechische Grammatik,
I. Allgemeiner Teil, Lautlehre, Wortbildung, Flexion. München
II. Syntax und syntaktische Stilistik, vervollständigt und hg. von *Debrunner, A. (1950).* München; III. Register von *Georgacas, D. (1953).* München; IV. Stellenregister von und *Radt, F./ Radt, st. (1971).* München.
Text edition of the Iliad: Homer Ilias, herausgegeben von Eduard Schwartz mit der Übersetzung von Johann Heinrich Voss; bearbeitet von Hans Rupé; Neuausgabe und Nachwort: Bruno Snell, Augsburg 1994.

Thumb, A. Handbuch der Griechischen Dialekte, 2th ed. part I. of *Kieckers, E. (1932).* Heidelberg; II. Teil (with a paragraph about Mycenian) of *Scherer, A. (1959).* Heidelberg.

8.3.4 Albanian

Armin Hetzer/ Zuzana Finger (1993). Lehrbuch der Vereinheitlichten Albanischen Schriftsprache. Hamburg

8.3.5 Indo-Aryan Languages (= daughter languages of Sanskrit)

8.3.5.1 General Overviews

Bechert, Heinz/ von Simson, Georg (ed.) (1993). Einführung in die Indologie: Stand - Methoden - Aufgaben. 2nd, revised and enlarged ed. / with the collaboration of Daw Khin Khin Su, Petra Kieffer-Pülz. Darmstadt.

Cardona, G. (1987). Indo-Aryan languages, in: *Comrie, B. (ed.) (1987).* The World's Major Languages. London/ New York: p. 440-447.

Masica, Colin P. (1991). The Indo-Aryan Languages. Cambridge University Press.

Zograph, Georgij A. (1960). Die Sprachen Südasiens. Leipzig (Translation of: Зограф, А. (1960). Языки Индии, Пакистана, Цейлона и Непала. Издательство восточной литературы. Москва).

8.3.5.2 Sanskrit

Apte, Vasudeo Govind (1933). The Concise Sanskrit-English Dictionary. 2nd, revised edition. Bombay (Reprint Delhi 1989).

Bucknell, Roderick p. (1994). Sanskrit Manual. Delhi.

Edgerton, F. (1953). Buddhist Hybrid Sanskrit. Grammar and Dictionary. Vol. I-II. New Haven.

Macdonell, A. A. (1910). Vedic Grammar. Strassburg .

MacDonell, Arthur A. (1917). A Vedic Reader for Students. Oxford (reprint 1970/ Delhi 1971) .

Macdonell, Arthur Anthony (1916). A Vedic Grammar for Students. Delhi (1st Indian edition 1993; reprint 1995).

Mayrhofer, M. (1953-1980). Kurzgefaßtes Etymologisches Wörterbuch des Altindischen I-IV. Heidelberg.

Mayrhofer, Manfred (1978). Sanskrit-Grammatik mit Sprachvergleichenden Erläuterungen. 3rd, revised ed., Sammlung Göschen. Berlin/ New York.

Mayrhofer, Manfred (1986-). Etymologisches Wörterbuch des Altindoarischen. n.p.

Monier-Williams (1899). A Sanskṛit-English Dictionary. Oxford (Reprint New Delhi 1981).

Mylius, Klaus (ed.) (1979). Die Bhagavadgītā. Aus dem Sanskrit. Übersetzung, Einleitung und Anmerkungen von Klaus Mylius. Wiesbaden.

Shukla, N.p. (1979). The Buddhist Hybrid Sanskrit Dharmapada. Patna.
Whitney, William Dwight (1885). The Roots, Verb-Forms and Primary Derivatives of the Sanskrit Language, repr. 1945. London.
Text edition: Abhijñāna-Śākuntalam of Kālidāsa; ed. C. R. Devadhar/ N.G. Suru, Delhi et al. 1991 (first edition 1934).

8.3.5.3 Pali

Buddhadatta Mahāthera, A. P. (1957). Concise Pali-English Dictionary. Colombo (Reprint Delhi 1994).
Dhammadāyāda Chanting Book (1989). Dhammakāya Foundation. Pathumthani.
Elizarenkova, T.Y./Toporov, V.N. (1976). The Pali Language. Moskau.
Mayrhofer, Manfred (1951). Handbuch des Pāli. Mit Texten und Glossar. Indogermanische Bibliothek. Herausgegeben von Hans Krahe. Erste Reihe: Lehr- und Handbücher. Heidelberg.
Pāli-Thai-English-Sanskrit Dictionary. compiled by his Royal Highness Prince Kitiyākara Krommaphra Chandaburinarünath. Bangkok 1969.
Schmidt, Kurt (1951). Pali - Buddhas Sprache. Anfänger-Lehrgang zum Selbstunterricht. Konstanz.
Warder, A.K. (1963). Introduction to Pali. Pali Text Society. London.

8.3.6 Iranian Languages

Bartholomae, C. (1895-1896). Grundriß der Iranischen Philologie, Erster Band, 1. Abteilung (vol. 1, part 1), I. Vorgeschichte der iranischen Sprachen, II. Awestasprache und Altpersisch. Strassburg.
Bartholomae, C. (1904/ 1979). Altiranisches Wörterbuch. Strassburg 1904; letzter Nachdruck, zusammen mit den "Nachträgen und Verbesserungen" (last reprint, together with emendations), Berlin 1979.
Beekes, R.p.P. (1988). A Grammar of Gatha-Avestan. Leiden.
Boyce, Mary (1975). A Reader in Manichaean Middle Persian and Parthian. Texts with Notes, n.p.
Brandenstein Wilhelm/ Mayrhofer Manfred (1964). Handbuch des Altpersischen. Wiesbaden.
Geiger, Wilhelm/ Kuhn, Ernst (1985-1904). Grundriss der Iranischen Philologie, 2 vol., reprint 1974. n.p.
Gippert, Jost (1986). Zur Metrik der Gathas. In: Die Sprache 32/2 1986 [1988]: p. 257-275.
Hoffmann, K. et al. (1958). Iranistik. Handbuch der Orientalistik. Teil 1, vol. 4-1. Leiden.
Humbach, Helmut (1991). The Gāthās of Zarathushtra. and other Old Avestan Texts. in collaboration with Josef Elfenbein & Prods. O. Skjærvø.

Part I: Introduction - Text and Translation; Part II: Commentary. Heidelberg.

Humbach, Helmut (1959). Die Gathas des Zarathustra (2 vol.). Heidelberg.

Kellens, Jean (1989). Avestique. in: *Schmitt, Rüdiger (ed.) (1989).* Compendium linguarum iranicarum. Wiesbaden.

Mayrhofer, Manfred (1989). Vorgeschichte der Iranischen Sprachen; Uriranisch. in: *Schmitt, Rüdiger (ed.) (1989).* Compendium Linguarum Iranicarum. Wiesbaden.

Nyborg, H.p. (1964-74). A Manual of Pahlavi. I-II. Wiesbaden.

Oranskij, Iosif M. (1977). Les langues Iraniennes. traduit par Joyce Blau. Paris.

Russian original: *Оранский, И. М. (1961).* Иранские Языки. Языки зарубежново востока и Африки. Москва.

Payne, J.R. (1987). Iranian Languages, in: *Comrie, B. (ed.) (1987).* The World's Major Languages. London/ New York: p. 514-522.

Reichelt, Hans (1909). Awestisches Elementarbuch. Heidelberg (reprint Darmstadt 1967).

Reichelt, Hans (1911). Avesta Reader. Texts, Notes, Glossary and Index. Strassburg (photocopied reprint Berlin 1968).

Schmitt, Rüdiger (1989). Die Altiranischen Sprachen im Überblick. in: *Schmitt, Rüdiger (ed.) (1989).* Compendium Linguarum Iranicarum. Wiesbaden.

Schmitt, Rüdiger (1989). Iranische Sprachen: Begriff und Name. in: *Schmitt, Rüdiger (ed.) (1989).* Compendium Linguarum Iranicarum. Wiesbaden.

Schmitt, Rüdiger (2000). Die iranischen Sprachen in Geschichte und Gegenwart. Wiesbaden.

Schmitt, Rüdiger (ed.) (1989). Compendium Linguarum Iranicarum. Wiesbaden.

Sokolov, p.N. (1967). The Avestan Language (translated from Russian). Moskau.

Sundermann, Werner (1989). Mittelpersisch. in: *Schmitt, Rüdiger (ed.) (1989).* Compendium Linguarum Iranicarum. Wiesbaden, p. 138-164.

Sundermann, Werner (1989). Parthisch. in: *Schmitt, Rüdiger (ed.) (1989).* Compendium Linguarum Iranicarum. Wiesbaden, p. 114-163.

7.3.7 Slavic Languages and Balkan Linguistics

Bieder, Hermann (2006). Das Weißrussische in: *Rehder, Peter (ed.) (2006).* Einführung in die Slavischen Sprachen. Mit einer Einführung in die Balkanphilologie. Darmstadt (1st edition 1986).

Fiedler, Wilfried: Einführung in die Balkanphilologie. in: *Rehder, Peter (ed.) (2006).* Einführung in die slavischen Sprachen. Mit einer Einführung in die Balkanphilologie. Darmstadt.

8.3.8 Tocharian

Krause, W/ Thomas, W. (1960-64). Tocharisches Elementarbuch, 2 vol. Heidelberg.

Krause, Wolfgang (1955). Tocharisch. Handbuch der Orientalistik, ed. by Bertold Spuler. 1. Abt., 4. Band, 3. Abschnitt. Leiden.

Schmidt, Klaus T. (1993). Tocharische Literatur, in: *Bechert, Heinz/ von Simson, Georg (ed.) (1993).* Einführung in die Indologie, see above.

8.4 Other Languages and Language Groups

8.4.1 Chinese

Choy, Rita Mei-Wah (1981). Read and Write Chinese. A Simplified Guide to the Chinese Characters. with Cantonese and Mandarin Pronunciations Yale and Pinyin Romanizations. revised fourth edition. San Francisco, Cal.

Feifel, P. Eugen (Bearb./ Übers.) (1959). Geschichte der Chinesischen Literatur. Mit Berücksichtigung ihres Geistesgeschichtlichen Hintergrundes, dargestellt nach *Kikuya, Nagasawa*: Shina Gakujutsu Bungeishi. 2nd, revised edition. Darmstadt.

Forrest, R.A.D. (n.d.). The Chinese Language. London.

Kaltenmark-Chéquier, O. (1960). Die chinesische Literatur. Reihe: "Was weiß ich?" Nr. 19. Enzyklopädie des XX. Jahrhunderts. Hamburg; *Title of the French Original:* "La littérature chinoise" (from the collection "Que sais-je" No. 296) by H.G. Penth.

Karlgren, Bernhard (1923). Analytic Dictionary of Chinese and Sino-Japanese. Paris.

Karlgren, Bernhard (1949). The Chinese Language. New York.

Karlgren, Bernhard (1966). Grammatica Serica. Script and Phonetics in Chinese and Sino-Japanese. Taipei.

Ladstätter/ Linhart (1983). China und Japan – Die Kulturen Ostasiens. Wien/ Heidelberg.

McNaughton, William (1979). Reading & Writing Chinese. A Guide to the Chinese Writing System. Rutland (Vermont)/ Tokyo.

Norman, Jerry (1988). Chinese. Cambridge Language Surveys. Cambridge. University Press.

Park, Chang-Hai (1972). An Intensive Course in Korean, 2 vls. Seoul.

Shen, Yongqian / Tong, Xiuying (1995). Taschenwörterbuch Deutsch – Chinesisch; Chinesisch – Deutsch. Peking.

8.4.1 Japanese

Jorden, Eleanor Harz (1962). Beginning Japanese, Part I/II. (= Yale Linguistic Ser. 5) New Haven/ London: *Yale Univ. Press.*

Ramming, Martin (1960). Bemerkungen zur Problematik der Schriftreform in Japan. Sitzungsberichte der Deutschen Akademie der Wissenschaften zu Berlin. Klasse für Sprachen, Literatur und Kunst. Jahrgang 1960 Nr. 4. Berlin.

Sakade, Florence et al. (General Editor) (1959; revised ed. 1961). A Guide to Reading and Writing Japanese (revised edition). Rutland, Vermont/ Tokyo, Japan.

Shibatani, M. (1990). The languages of Japan. Cambridge Language Surveys. Cambridge/New York.

Takahashi, Morio (ed.) (n.y.). Romanized Japanese-English Dictionary. Tokyo/ Kobe.

8.4.3 Finnish

Englund, Robert (1953). Finnische Sprachlehre. Heidelberg.

Katara, Pekka (1957). Finnisch-Deutsches Wörterbuch. Dritte, vermehrte und verbesserte Auflage (3rd, revised and enlarged ed.). Helsinki.

8.4.4 Quechua

Galicia Panica, Mario B. (1988). Gramática Funcional del Idioma Quechua – de la Región Sur del Perú. Perú *(sic).*

8.4.5 Thai

Brown, J. M. (1967-69). AUA Language Center Thai course: Vols. 1, 2 & 3. Bangkok: American University Alumni Language Center.

Brown, Marvin J. (1985). From Ancient Thai to Modern Dialects *(includes several articles written between 1966 and 1976).* Bangkok.

Campbell, p./ Shaweewongse, C. (1957). The Fundamentals of the Thai Language. Bangkok.

Haas, M. R. (1956). The Thai System of Writing. Washington, D.C. (reprint 1980, Ithaca, NY, Spoken Language Services).

Haas, M. R. (1964). Thai-English Student's Dictionary. Stanford (reprint 1992).

McFarland, G. B. (1944). Thai-English Dictionary. 2nd ed. Stanford.

Noss, Richard B. (1964). Thai Reference Grammar. Foreign Service Institute. Washington, D.C.

Noss, Richard B. (1972). Rhythm in Thai. In: *Harris, Jimmy G./ Noss, Richard B. (ed.) (1972).* Tai Phonetics and Phonology. Bangkok: p. 33-42.

Tingsabadh, Kalaya/ Abramson, Arthur p. (1993). Illustrations of the IPA: Thai. In: Journal of the International Phonetic Association (JIPA) 23/1: p. 25-27.

Tumtavitikul, Apiluck (2001). Thai Poetry: A Metrical Analysis. In: *Tingsabadh, Kalaya/ Abramson, Arthur p. (ed.) (2001).* Essays in Tai Linguistics. Chulalongkorn University Press. Bangkok: p. 29-40.

Wershoven, J.E. (o.J.). Siamesisch. Hartlebens Bibliothek der Sprachenkunde für den Selbstunterricht. Wien/ Leipzig.

Морев, Л.Н. (1991). Сопоставитлъная Грамматика Тайских Языков. Москва.

ทองหล่อ กำชัย [*thɔɔŋlɔ̂ɔ kamchaj*] (*2530=1987).* หลักภาษาไทย [làkphaasăăthaj] *(=Sketch of the Thai Language).* 7th ed. Bangkok.

8.4.6 Tswana and Kiswahili (Bantu)

Brown, Rev. J. Tom (1962). Secwana Dictionary. Secwana-English and English-Secwana. Lobatsi, Bechuanaland Protectorate, South Africa.

Sandilands, Alexander (1953). Introduction to Tswana. Tigerkloff, Cape Province, South Africa.

Schapera, I (ed.) (1965). Praise Poems of Tswana Chiefs. translated and edited by I. Schapera. Oxford.

Velten, C. (1913). Praktische Suaheli-Grammatik. Berlin.

8.4.7 Turkic Languages

Gabain, A. v. (1974). Alttürkische Grammatik. 3rd ed. Wiesbaden.

Gabain, A. v./ Winter, W. (1958). Türkische Turfantexte IX. Ein Hymnus an den Vater Mani auf Tocharisch B mit alttürkischer Übersetzung [SA Abh. d. Dtsch. Akad. d. W. Berlin, 1956, 2]. Berlin.

Höhmann, Thomas (1995). Kasachisch für Globetrotter (Kauderwelsch vol. 92). Bielefeld (with a tape cassette).

Łabenda, Michal (2000): Język kazachski. Języki Azji i Afriki. Warszawa.

Menges, K. H. (1995). The Turkic languages and peoples: An Introduction to Turkic studies. 2nd ed. Wiesbaden.

Shnitnikov, Boris N. (1966). Kazakh-English Dictionary. London/ The Hague/ Paris.

Баскаков, Н.А. /Хасенова, А.К./ Исенгалиева, В.А./ Кордабаев, Т.Р. (редакционния коллегиа) (1966). Сопоставительная грамматика русского и казахского языков. Алма Ата.

Әсет, Б./ Шамалған Д. (1999). Қазақ тілінің сөздігі. Алматы.

Камбар-Батыр (1959). под редакцией М.О. Ауэзова и Н.С. Смирновой. издательство академии наук казахской ССР. Алма-Ата.

Кыз Жибек (1963). под редакцией М.О. Ауэзова и Н.С. Смирновой. издательство академии наук казахской ССР. Алма-Ата.

Қыз Жібек (1985). Пікір жазғандар К. Жұмағалиев К. Сейдеханов. Алматы.

Махмудов, Х. / Мусабаев, Г. (2001). Казахско-русский словарь. Алматы.

Наделяев, В. М./ Насилов, Д. М./ Тенишев Э. Р./ Щербак, А.М. (1969). Древнетюркский Словарь. Ленинград.

Ярцева, В. Н. Солцев, В. М Толстой, Н. И. (ed.) (1997). Языки мира:

Тюрские языки (Институт языкознания РАН, Российская академия наук). М: Издателъство "Индрик". Москва.

8.4.8 Creole Languages

Cassidy, Frederic Gomes (1961). Jamaica talk; Three hundred Years of the English Language in Jamaica. London.

Holm, John A. (1988). Pidgins and Creoles Volume 1: Theory and structure. Cambridge; Volume 2 (1989). Reference Survey. Cambridge.

Kortmann, Bernd/ Upton, Clive (2008). Varieties of English, 4 vols., Berlin: Mouton de Gruyter.

8.5 Religions

8.5.1 Overviews / Comparative Religious Studies

Gajda, Iwona (2002). Monothéisme en Arabie du Sud Préislamique. chroniques yéménites n° 10., in: http://cy.revues.org/document 132.html?format=print.

Jockel, Rudolf (1967). Die lebenden Religionen. Texte und Einführungen. Berlin/ Darmstadt/ Wien.

Mensching, Gustav (o.J.). Die Weltreligionen. Berlin/ Darmstadt/ Wien.

Odelain, O./ Séguineau, R./ Schierse, F. J. (1981). Lexikon biblischer Namen. Düsseldorf.

Title of the French Original: Dictionnaire des noms propres de la Bible.

Schoeps, Hans-Joachim (n.d.). Religionen – Wesen und Geschichte. n.p. (Bertelsmann).

8.5.2 Islam and Qur'ānic Studies

"*Licht ins Dunkel*" - Der Koran als philologischer Steinbruch, ein Gespräch mit Christoph Luxenberg, in: *Burgmer, Christoph (ed.) (2005).* Streit um den Koran. Die Luxenberg-Debatte: Standpunkte und Hintergründe. Berlin, p. 14-34.

Aleem, Abdul (1933). I'jāz al Qur'ân, in: Islamic Culture 7/1933.

Ben-Shemesh, A.: Some Suggestions to Qur'an Translators, in: Ibn Warraq (ed.): What the Koran Really Says, Language, Text and Commentary. Amherst (N.Y.) 2002.

Brother Mark (2000). A 'Perfect' Qur'an or 'So it was made to appear to them?'. A response to Islamic allegations concerning the Gospel, the Qur'an and Islam. New York .

Burgmer, Christoph (ed.) (2005). Streit um den Koran. Die Luxenberg-Debatte: Standpunkte und Hintergründe. Berlin.

Conrad, I. Lawrence (1987): Abraha and Muhammad. Some Observations apropos of Chronology and Literary Topoi in the Early Arabic Historical Tradition, originally published in: Bulletin of the School of Oriental and African Studies 50 (1987), p. 225-40; reprinted in: Ibn Warraq (ed.). The

Quest for the Historical Muhammad, Amherst (N.Y.) 2000, p. 368-391.

Der Koran (1980). Das Heilige Buch des Islam - nach der Übertragung von Ludwig Ullmann neu bearbeitet und erläutert von L-W. Winter. 12th ed. (1st ed. 1959). München.

Die Korrumpierte Tradition? Zur religiösen Geschichtsbildung, ein Gespräch mit Gerd-Rüdiger Puin, in: *Burgmer, Christoph (ed.) (2005).* Streit um den Koran. Die Luxenberg-Debatte: Standpunkte und Hintergründe. Berlin, p. 51-63.

Die Orale Rezeption des Koran, ein Gespräch mit Manfred Kropp, in: *Burgmer, Christoph (ed.) (2005).* Streit um den Koran. Die Luxenberg-Debatte: Standpunkte und Hintergründe. Berlin, p. 42-50.

Gerhardson, Birger (1961). Memory and Manuscript; Oral Tradition and Written Transmission in Judaism and Early Christianity.

Geyer, R. (1908). Zur Strophik des Qurâns, in: WZKM 22 (1908) p. 265-86; (English translation: The Strophic Structure of the Koran, in: Ibn Warraq (ed.): What the Koran Really Says – Language, Text and Commentary, Amherst (N.Y.), p. 625-646.

Gilliot, Claude (2005). Zur Herkunft der Gewährsmänner des Propheten, in: Ohlig, Karl-Heinz/ Puin, Gerd-Rüdiger (ed.) (2005). Die Dunklen Anfänge. Neue Forschungen zur Entstehung und frühen Geschichte des Islam. 2nd edition. Berlin, p. 148-178.

Graf von Bothmer, Hans-Caspar (1987): Architekturbilder im Koran – Eine Prachthandschrift der Umayyadenzeit aus dem Yemen, Pantheon, 1987, Volume 45, pp. 4-20.

Guellouz, Azzedine (1998). Der Koran. Ausführungen zum Besseren Verständnis. Anregungen zum Nachdenken. Aus dem Französischen von Heike Buerschaper. Bergisch Gladbach.

Title of the French Original: Le Coran. 1996.

Haneef, Suzanne (1979). What Everybody Should Know about Islam and Muslims. Lahore.

Hawting, G.R. (1999). The Idea of Idolatry and the Emergence of Islam: From Polemic to History. Cambridge Studies in Islamic Civilisation. Cambridge.

Ibn Warraq: Historische Methodologie und die Forderung nach Wohlwollen gegenüber dem Islam (translation of " Historical Methodology and Dogmatic Islamophilia"), in: Groß, Markus / Ohlig, Karl-Heinz (2010). Die Entstehung einer Weltreligion I, p. 382-422.

Jeffery, Arthur (ed.) (1937). Materials for the History of the Text of the Qur'ān. The Old Codices, Leiden.

Kermani, N. (1999). Gott ist Schön. Das Ästhetische Erleben des Koran. München 1999; also see the review by: Schmitt, Axel: Ist der Koran

Poesie?, in: http://www.literaturkritik.de/public/rezension.php?rez_id=5428&ausgabe=20021.1

Khoury, Adel Theodor/ Hagemann, Ludwig/ Heine, Peter (1991). Islam-Lexikon. Geschichte - Ideen - Gestalten. 3 vols. Freiburg/ Basel/ Wien.

Lan Tabur (1993). Themenregister des Al-Qur'ān al-Karīm. aus dem Arabischen übertragen und katalogisiert von Abu-r-Riḍā' Muḥammad Ibn Aḥmad Ibn Rassoul. Islamische Bibliothek. Köln.

Lincoln, Bruce (1996): Theses on Method, in Method & Theory in the Study of Religion vol. 8 (1996): p. 225-27.

Lüling, Günter (1993). Über den Urkoran. Ansätze zur Rekonstruktion der Vorislamische-Christlichen Strophenlieder im Koran. korrigierte, jedoch im Haupttext (p.1-542) seitengleiche 2. Auflage (revised 2nd ed.). Erlangen.

Luxenberg, Christoph (2004). Die Syroaramäische Lesart des Koran. Ein Beitrag zur Entschlüsselung der Koransprache. 2nd, revised and enlarged ed. Berlin.

Luxenberg, Christoph (2005). Neudeutung der Arabischen Inschrift im Felsendom zu Jerusalem, in: Ohlig, Karl-Heinz/ Puin, Gerd-Rüdiger (ed.) (2005). Die Dunklen Anfänge. Neue Forschungen zur Entstehung und Frühen Geschichte des Islam. 3rd ed. 2007. Berlin, p. 124-147.

Luxenberg, Christoph (2005). Weihnachten im Koran, in: *Burgmer, Christoph (ed.) (2005).* Streit um den Koran. Die Luxenberg-Debatte: Standpunkte und Hintergründe. Berlin, p. 35-41.

Maulana, Muhammad Ali (1978). A Manual of Hadith. London/ Dublin (Reprint 1983).

Neuwirth Angelika (1981). Studien zur Komposition der Mekkanischen Suren. Studien zur Sprache, Geschichte und Kultur des islamischen Orients. Beihefte zur Zeitschrift "Der Islam". Neue Folge Band (= vol.) 10. Berlin/ New York.

Neuwirth, Angelika (1987). Koran, in: *Gätje, Helmut (ed.) (1987).* Grundriss der Arabischen Philologie. vol. 2: Literaturwissenschaft. Wiesbaden, p. 96-135.

Nöldeke, Theodor (1910). Zur Sprache des Korāns. in: Neue Beiträge zur Semitischen Sprachwissenschaft. Strassburg.

English Translation in: Ibn Warraq (2011): Which Koran? - Variants, Manuscripts and Linguistics, Amherst (N.Y.), p. 83 - 130.

Noseda, Sergio Noja (2005). From Syriac to Pahlavi: The Contribution of the Sassanian Iraq to the Beginning of the Arabic Writing, in: Ohlig, Karl-Heinz/ Puin, Gerd-Rüdiger (ed.) (2005). Die Dunklen Anfänge. Neue Forschungen zur Entstehung und Frühen Geschichte des Islam. 2nd ed. 2006. Berlin, p. 266-292.

Ohlig, Karl-Heinz (2000). Weltreligion Islam – Eine Einführung. Mit einem Beitrag von Ulrike Stölting. Mainz/ Luzern.

Ohlig, Karl-Heinz/ Puin, Gerd-R. (ed.) (2005). Die dunklen Anfänge. Neue

Forschungen zur Entstehung und frühen Geschichte des Islam. 2nd ed. 2006. Berlin; title of the English translation: The Hidden Origins of Islam: New Research into Its Early History; Prometheus Books, Amherst (N.Y.), 2009.

Paret, R. (1966). Der Koran. Übersetzung. 9th ed. 2004. Stuttgart.

Paret, R. (1971). Der Koran. Kommentar und Konkordanz. 7th, unchanged reprint (2005) of the hardcover edition of 1977. Stuttgart.

Penrice, John (1873). A Dictionary and Glossary of the Koran. Reprint Delhi 1990.

Popp, Volker (2005). Die Frühe Islamgeschichte nach Inschriftlichen und Numismatischen Zeugnissen, in: *Ohlig, Karl-Heinz/ Puin, Gerd-Rüdiger (ed.) (2005).* Die Dunklen Anfänge. Neue Forschungen zur Entstehung und Frühen Geschichte des Islam. 2nd ed. 2006. Berlin, p. 16-124.

Puin, Gerd-R. (1996). Observations on Early Qur'ān Manuscripts in Ṣan'ā'. In: *Wild, p. (ed.) (1996).* The Qur'ān as Text. Leiden: p. 107-111.

Puin, Gerd-R. (1999). Über die Bedeutung der Ältesten Koranfragmente aus Sanaa (Jemen) für die Orthographiegeschichte des Korans, in: *Graf von Bothmer, Hans-Casper/ Ohlig, Karl-Heinz/ Puin, Gerd-Rüdiger (1999).* Neue Wege der Koranforschung, Magazin Forschung (Universität des Saarlandes) 1, 1999, 37-40, 46.

Puin, Gerd-R. (2006). Variant Readings of the Koran due to the Ambiguity of the Early Arabic Script, Including Variants of Ibn Mas'ūd and a Survey of the Transcription of Koranic texts. (unpublished article draft).

Radscheit, Matthias (1996). Die Koranische Herausforderung. Die Taḥaddī-Verse im Rahmen der Polemikpassagen des Korans. Islamkundliche Untersuchungen Bd. 198. Berlin.

Jan Vansina (1965). Oral Tradition. A Study in Historical Methodology (translated from the French by H. M. Wright). London.

Wild, Stefan (1994). " Die Schauerliche Öde des Heiligen Buches". Westliche Wertungen des Koranischen Stils, in: *Giese, A./ Bürgel, C. (1994).* Gott ist Schön und er Liebt die Schönheit. Festschrift für Annemarie Schimmel. Bern, p. 429-444.

Zafrulla Khan, Muhammad (Übersetzer) (1981). The Quran. Arabic Text – English Translation. 3rd, revised edition. Chichester (Sussex) (Reprint 1985)

8.5.3 Christianity and Biblical Studies

Augstein, Rudolf (2001). Jesus – Menschensohn. München.

Botterweck G. Johannes/ Ringgren, Helmer (1980). Theological Dictionary of the Old Testament, vol 4. Stuttgart.

Kautzsch, E. (1922). Die heilige Schrift des Alten Testaments. 2 vol.

Tübingen.
Kittel, Rudolf et al. (1974). Das Alte Testament Hebräisch-Deutsch. Biblia Hebraica mit deutscher Übersetzung. 16., verbesserte Auflage (1971). revidierte Fassung der Übersetzung Martin Luthers (1964) (The Old Testament in Hebrew and German, 16th, revised edition). Stuttgart.
Mangold, Max (n.d.). Bibelnamen. Saarbrücken.
Metzger, Bruce M. (1994). A Textual Commentary on the Greek New Testament. 2nd edition. Stuttgart.
Novum Testamentum Tetraglotton (1858). ed. by R. Stier. reprint Zürich 1981.
Ohlig, Karl-Heinz (1986). Fundamentalchristologie. Im Spannungsfeld von Christentum und Kultur. München.
Ohlig, Karl-Heinz (2000). Ein Gott in Drei Personen? Vom Vater Jesu zum "Mysterium" der Trinität. Mainz/ Luzern.
Preuß, Horst Dietrich/ Berger, Klaus (1991). Bibelkunde des Alten und Neuen Testaments. Erster Teil: Altes Testament. 6th ed. Wiesbaden.
Preuß, Horst Dietrich/ Berger, Klaus (1997). Bibelkunde des Alten und Neuen Testaments. Zweiter Teil: Neues Testament. 5th ed. Wiesbaden.
Rienecker, Fritz (ed.) (1991). Lexikon zur Bibel. 3rd ed. 1960. Wuppertal (2nd special ed. 1991).
Syriac Bible (1996). United Bible Societies. n.p. (West Syriac in Serto script).
The Interlinear Greek-English New Testament. George Ricker Berry (1897). with lexicon and synonyms. 26th printing 1982. Grand Rapids, Michigan.
The New Covenant commonly called The New Testament (1986). Pshiṭta Aramaic Text with a Hebrew Translation. Edited by the Aramaic Scriptures Research Society in Israel. The Bible Society. Jerusalem *(the Aramaic text is East Syriac in Hebrew script).*

8.5.4 Buddhism

Anonymous (1993). Guide to the Tipiṭaka. Introduction to the Buddhist Canon. Bangkok.
Bapat, P.V. (ed.) (1956). 2500 Years of Buddhism. Delhi (Reprint: 1987).
Bechert, H. / Gombrich, R. (ed.) (1989/ Neuaufl. 2000). Der Buddhismus: Geschichte und Gegenwart. [Transl. from English by Michael Schmidt]. München.
Original English title: The World of Buddhism. London 1988.
Bloch, Jules (1950). Les Inscriptions d'Asoka. Paris.
Budsir/TTV.2 for Windows (2000). (Budsir = Buddhist Scriptures Information Retrieval; computer program with the Buddhist Tipitaka and commentaries in digital form). Mahidol University. Bangkok.
Dhammadāyāda Chanting Book (1989). Dhammakāya Foundation. Pathumthani (contains all ritually relevant Pali-chants with an English translation).

Hinüber, Oskar v. (2000). A Handbook of Pāli Literature. Berlin/ New York.

Khantipalo Bhikku (1992). Buddhism Explained. Bangkok.

Notz, Klaus-Josef (1998). Das Lexikon des Buddhismus A-Z. Grundbegriffe, Traditionen, Praxis. 2 vols. Freibug im Breisgau.

Oldenberg, Hermann (Übers)/ Bechert, Heinz (ed.) (1922/ 1993). Reden des Buddha - Lehre, Verse, Erzählungen. Mit einer Einführung herausgegeben von Heinz Bechert. Freiburg/ Basel/ Wien.

Schneider, Ulrich (1978). Die Großen Felsen-Edikte Aśokas. Kritische Ausgabe, Übersetzung und Analyse der Texte. Freiburger Beiträge zur Indologie Band 11. Wiesbaden.

Schumann, Hans Wolfgang (1995). Der Historische Buddha. Leben und Lehre des Gotama. 4th ed. of the new edition. Diederichs Gelbe Reihe. München.

8.5.5 Hinduism

Barth, Auguste (1882; reprint: 1992). The Religions of India. authorized translation by Rev. J. Wood. Delhi.

Desika Char, p.V. (1993). Caste, Religion and Country. A View of Ancient and Medieval India. New Delhi.

Nath Seth, Kailash (n.d.). Gods and Goddesses of India. New Delhi.

Prabupāda, Bhaktivedanta (1981). Bhagavad-Gītā Wie Sie Ist. 5th ed. Vaduz *Original English title:* Bhagavad-gītā As It Is.

Radhakrishnan, p. (1979). Indian Religions. New Delhi/ Bombay (Reprint: 1990).

Stutley, Margaret (1998). Hinduismus. Eine Einführung in die Große Weltreligion. aus dem Englischen von Klaus Dahme. München.
Original English title: Hinduism. The Eternal Law. London 1985
Title of the German hardcover edition: Was ist Hinduismus?

Swami Swarupananda (ed.) (1982). Shrimad Bhagavadgita (Śrīmad Bhagavad-Gītā). With Text, Word-for-Word Translation, English Rendering, Comments, and Index. 13th revised edition. Calcutta.

Vasu, Srisa Chandra (1991 - new edition?). The Daily Practice of the Hindus. New Delhi.

Vivekananda, Swami (1893; 1976). Hinduism (new edition of a speech held in 1893 in the "Parliament of Religions"). Madras.

8.5.6 Other publications about religions

Malvania, Dalsukh D. (1986). Jainism. Some Essays. translated by Gopani, A.p., Jaipur.

Sacred Nitnem. (1976). Containing the Divine Hymns of the Daily Prayers by the Sikhs. In Gurmukhi and Roman Scripts. by Harbans Singh Doabia.

Second Revised and Enlarged Edition. Amritsar.

8.6 Literature

8.6.1 Literary und Cultural Studies

Grotzfeld, Heinz (1989). articles: Arabische Literatur (vol. 1, p. 178 ff.); al-Muʿallaqāt (vol. 4, p. 2057); Qaṣīda (vol. 4, p. 2373). in: *Harenbergs Lexikon der Weltliteratur (1989).* Autoren - Werke - Begriffe. 5 vol. 2nd ed., board of curators: François Bondy, Ivo Frenzel, Joachim Kaiser, Lew Kopelew, Hilde Spiel. Idee/ Konzeption. Bodo Harenberg. Dortmund.

Haymes, E.R. (1977). Das Mündliche Epos. Sammlung Metzler. Stuttgart.

Jansen, K.H. (1981). Afrikanische Literatur. In: *Heine, E./ Schadeberg, Th.C./ Wolff, E. (ed.)(1981).* Die Sprachen Afrikas. Hamburg.

Jens, Walter (ed.) (1998). Kindlers Neues Literaturlexikon. Chefredaktion Rudolf Radler. München.

Lord, A.B. (1965). Der Sänger Erzählt. Wie ein Epos Entsteht. München. *Original English title:* The Singer of Tales. Cambridge, Mass. 1960

Parry, Milman (collector)/ Lord, Albert Bates (editor/ translator) (1954). Serbocroatian Heroic Songs. with musical transcriptions by Béla Bartók. 2 vol. Cambridge/ Belgrad.

Parry, Milman: Ćor Huso: A Study of Southslavic Song, in: *Parry, Adam (1971) (ed.).* The Making of Homeric Verse. The collected papers of Milman Parry. Oxford.

Richards, I.A. (1985). Prinzipien der Literaturkritik. Suhrkamp Taschenbuch Wissenschaft. übersetzt von Jürgen Schlaeger. Frankfurt am Main; *Original English title:* Principles of Literary Criticism.

8.6.1 Indo-European Poetic Language

Meillet, Antoine (1968). Die Ursprünge der Griechischen Metrik, in: *Schmitt, Rüdiger (ed.) (1968).* Indogermanische Dichtersprache. Darmstadt.

Pisani, Vittore (1968). Indisch-griechische Beziehungen aus dem Mahābhārata, in: *Schmitt, Rüdiger (ed.) (1968).* Indogermanische Dichtersprache. Darmstadt.

Schmitt, Rüdiger (1968). Indogermanische Dichtersprache. Eine Skizze, in: *Schmitt, Rüdiger (ed.) (1968).* Indogermanische Dichtersprache. Darmstadt

Schmitt, Rüdiger (ed.) (1968). Indogermanische Dichtersprache. Darmstadt.

Schulze, Wilhelm (1968). Tocharisch Tseke Peke, in: *Schmitt, Rüdiger (ed.) (1968).* Indogermanische Dichtersprache. Darmstadt.

Wackernagel, Jacob (1968). Indogermanische Dichtersprache, in: *Schmitt, Rüdiger (ed.) (1968).* Indogermanische Dichtersprache. Darmstadt.

8.6.3 Text from Fictional Literature and Journalism

Broder, Henryk M. (2006). Hurra, Wir Kapitulieren. Von der Lust am Einknicken. Berlin.

Hanke, Manfred (1967). Die Schüttelreimer. Bericht über eine Reimschmiedezunft. Stuttgart.

Kipling, Rudyard: The Man who would be King. edition quoted: The Best of Kipling. New York 1968.

Noy, Dov (1963). Jefet Schwili Erzählt. Hundertneunundsechzig jemenitische Volkserzählungen aufgezeichnet in Israel 1957-1960. Berlin.

Sayo, Masuda (1998). Geisha - Ein Lebensbericht. In: Geisha - Vom Leben jenseits der Weidenbrücke. Aus dem Japanischen übertragen und mit einem Nachwort versehen von Michael Stein. Japanische Bibliothek. Insel Verlag. Frankfurt am Main und Leipzig; *Title of the Japanese original:* Geisha, kutō no hanshōgari (1957). Heibonsha Library, Tōkyō 1995.

8.7 History, Politics, Philosophy

Goetz, Hermann (1962). Geschichte Indiens. Stuttgart.

Moscati, Sabatino (1955). Geschichte und Kultur der Semitischen Völker. 2nd, revised ed. (new edition of "Storia e civiltà dei Semiti" [Bari, 1949]), German translation by E. Kümmerer. Stuttgart.

Popper, Karl (1935). Logik der Forschung. Wien. (English title: The Logic of Scientific Discovery).

Popper, Karl (1964). Naturgesetze und theoretische Systeme, in: H. Albert (ed.)(1964). Theorie und Realität. Tübingen p. 87-102.

Richter, Michael (2007). Wortschatz. Halle/Saale.

Schulze, Reinhard (1994). Geschichte der Islamischen Welt im 20. Jahrhundert. München.

8.8 Internet Sources and other publications

8.8.1 Internet Sources (retrieved in August, 2006)

General Websites:

http://de.wikipedia.org - Online-Encyclopedia

http://hdr.undp.org/statistics/data/- Human Development Report of the UN

http://www.literature.de - literature

http://www.zitate-aphorismen.de/zitate/interpretation/Michael_Richter/3097

Linguistics

http://titus.fkidg1.uni-frankfurt.de – Titus project of the Goethe-Universität in Frankfurt a. M., chaired by Jost Gippert (Thesaurus Indogermanischer Text- und Sprachmaterialien); the website offers digitalized versions of many of the important texts of almost all ancient Indo-European languages, apart from other very useful materials like grammars and software; the font *Titus Cyberbit Basic* used in the present study was created by the Titus project.

http://www.perseus.tufts.edu – ancient Greek literature in digitalized form.

http://www.ethnologue.com –webpage of the SIL (Summer Institute of Linguistics) with current data about nearly all languages in the world; moreover it offers useful software; the waveforms in the present study were created with SIL software.

Text editions

http://unbound.biola.edu - the bible in dozens of languages with search functions

http://www.arabicbible.com/bible/doc_bible.htm.

http://www.friesian.com/gita.htm - information about the Bhagavadgita.

http://www.uky.edu/AS/Classics/retiarius/kalevala.html – information about the Kalevala.

http://www.islamicity.com/mosque/quran – Qur'ān online with translation and many search functions.

http:// www.deenislam.co.uk/burdah/burdah.htm – information about the "Burda".

http://www.bbc.co.uk/religion/religions/islam/features/al_burda/ - the Burda as a sound file.

http://www.geocities.com/mutmainaa1/dhikr/burda.html – the "Burda" as a PDF-file.

http://www.boloji.com/sikhism/japujisahib/js01.htm – information about the Sikh religion

http://www.biblegateway.com/passage/?search= (Arabic bible).

http://www.perseus.tufts.edu/hopper/text?doc=Perseus%3Atext%3A1999.01.0134 %3Abook%3D3%3Acard%3D146 (translation of the Iliad by A.T. Murray: The Iliad with an English Translation, in two vols.. Cambridge, MA./London 1924)

Muslim websites and websites about Islam

http://www.islamic-awareness.org/Quran/Text/Mss/vowel.html – criticism against Luxenberg's theory

Main article: *Saifullah, M S M/ Ghoniem, Mohammad/ Zaman, Shibli (2005).* From Alphonse Mingana To Christoph Luxenberg: Arabic Script & The Alleged Syriac Origins Of The Qur'an, © Islamic Awareness, All Rights Reserved, first Composed: 20th December 2004, last modified: 26th June 2005 as well as: 'Abdullah David & M S M Saifullah: Concise List Of Arabic Manuscripts Of The Qur'ān Attributable To The First Century Hijra, on: http://www.islamic-awareness.org/Quran/Text/Mss/hijazi.html.

http://debate.org.uk/topics/history/quran.htm - Qur'ān critical website

http://www.muslim-answers.org/Introducing-Islam/miscons.htm - apologetic Islamic website

*http://www.literaturkritik.de/*public/rezension.php?rez_id=5428&ausgabe=2002 11R (review of *Kermani, N. (1999).* Gott ist schön. Das ästhetische Erleben des Koran. München 1999).
*http://www.answering-islam.de/*Main/Quran/Sources/alaha2.html (Heger, Christoph: The origin of the name "Allah")
*http://www.answering-islam.de/*Main//Shamoun/ishmael-baal.htm
*http://www.studytoanswer.net/*myths_ch3.html#ch3-6.
http://al-quran.info/?x=y#&&sura=24&aya=1&trans=en-marmaduke_pickthall&show=both,transliteration-english&ver=2.00 *(Koran in many translations, among others with Pickthall's version)*

Other websites
http://www.sfu.ca/~rastinm/PDF/Lesson%2001.pdf
http://www.sfu.ca/~rastinm/about.html (Simon Fraser University, Canada).
http://cnes.cla.umn.edu/resources/IranianPages/pahlavi_fonts.htm (University of Minnesota, Classical and Near Eastern Studies) (Middle Persian Font).
http://titus.uni-frankfurt.de/didact/idg/iran/mpers/mpersbsx.htm (Middle Persian: Data entry by D.N. MacKenzie, Göttingen 1993). (Gāndhārī Dharmapada: edited with an introduction and commentary by John Brough, London 1962 [London Oriental Series, 7.]; prepared by Jost Gippert and Katharina Kupfer, Frankfurt a/M 1995-1999.
*http://www.homestead.com/*bibleorigins*net/YahwehYawUgarit.html.

8.8.2 Text editions on CD
Al-qur'ānu l-karīm. 6th version - 6.31 - Sakhr (software company).
HODA Holy Quran Treasury. Tolou Computer Co.

Endnotes

Karl-Heinz Ohlig: Shedding Light on the Beginnings of Islam (p. 10-13)

---

1 Cf. among others: Ignaz Goldziher, *Islam and Parsism* (in the present anthology).

2 Karl-Heinz Ohlig/Gerd-R. Puin, *Die Dunklen Anfänge.* Neue Forschungen zur Entstehung und frühen Geschichte des Islam, Berlin 1,22005, 32007; English version: *The Hidden Origins of Islam*: New Research into Its Early History, Amherst (N.Y.) 2009 (Prometheus Books).

3 See my article in the present anthology "*Evidence of a New religion in Christian Literature 'Under Islamic Rule'*?"

4 Cf. Volker Popp's article in the present anthology: "*From Ugarit to Sāmarrā' – An Archeological Journey on the Trail of Ernst Herzfeld.*"

5 Cf. my article "From muḥammad Jesus to prophet of the Arabs – the Personalization of a Christological Predicate" in the present anthology.

6 Cf. Christoph Luxenberg, The Syro-Aramaic Reading of the Koran: A Contribution to the Decoding of the Language of the Koran, Berlin 2007.

7 Cf.: Christoph Luxenberg's article: "*Relics of Syro-Aramaic Letters in the early Qur'ān Code Ḥiǧāzī and Kūfi Ductus*" in the present anthology.

8 Cf. I. Goldziher, see above.

9 Cf. Volker Popp, "*The Influence of Persian Religious Patterns on Notions in the Qur'ān*" in the present anthology.

10 Cf. Markus Gross "*New Ways of Qur'ānic Research from the Perspective of Comparative Linguistics and Cultural Studies*" in the present anthology.

Endnotes
Volker Popp: From Ugarit to Sāmarrāʾ (pp. 14-175)

1 Ernst Emil Herzfeld (1879–1948) was a well-known German Near Eastern archeologist, scholar of ancient Near Eastern languages and civilizations and specialized in epigraphics. He was one of the fathers of the Near Eastern and Islamic archeology. His international renown is mainly based on his research of numerous ruins and his excavations, esp. from 1911-13 in Samarra and 1931-34 in Persepolis. His major fields of studies comprise Orientalist, philological, historical, archeological and architectural investigations, above all about the stone, copper and bronze age in Iraq and Iran, the civilizations of the Hittites, Babylonians, Assyrians and Achaemenids. Moreover, he dealt intensively with Parthian and Sassanian archeology, the genesis of Islamic art and architecture, as well as epigraphic and numismatic research about the eras of the Achaemenid, Sassanian and Islamic eras.

2 Stanislav Segert, A Basic Grammar of the Ugaritic Language. Berkeley/Los Angeles/London 1984; p. 162, text 88.53 (1.4:V:12-19).

3 Cyrus H. Gordon, Ugaritic Manual, Rom 1955, p. 263, N° 639: "mḥmd –the best/choicest of". mḥmd.ḫrs ["the best/choicest of gold"].

4 Alois Sprenger, Das Leben und die Lehre des Mohammad, Berlin 1869, p. 160-161.

5 Cyrus H. Gordon, Ugaritic Manual, p. 316, Nos. 1630-32. In Ugaritic, the form "Ṣ(a)M(a)D" means "tie the grapevine up to the stake, to harness a horse; to yoke an ox"; in Syriac *ṣmad* still has the meaning "to bind together".

6 The migration of the "Sea Peoples", one of them being the Philistines, after whom Palestine was named, had had an earlier impact on Troy and Mycene (Der Kleine Pauly, Munich 1979, entry: "Seevölkerwanderung").

7 Der Kleine Pauly, entry: 'Hatra'.

8 Eduard von Zambaur, Die Münzprägungen des Islams, Wiesbaden 1968, p. 75.

9 Clive Foss, Anomalous Arab-Byzantine Coins. Some Problems and Suggestions. §.11; An Anomalous Inscription at Tiberias. ONS Newsletter 166, London 2001, p. 8.

10 Robert G. Hoyland, Arabia and the Arabs, London 2001, p. 2-3: "For Herodotus (d. c. 430 BC) Arabia chiefly designates parts of eastern Egypt, Sinai and the Negev (2.8, 11-12,75,158; 3.5,9), which accords with the note of Pliny the Elder (d. AD 79) that 'beyond the Pelusiac [easternmost] mouth of the Nile is Arabia, extending to the Red Sea' (3.65). In Persian administrative lists, mostly from the reign of Darius (521-486 BC), a district called Arabâya is usually included be <-tween Assyria and Egypt, which is probably Herodotus' Arabia plus parts of the Syrian desert. The latter corresponds to Pliny's Arabia of the nomads', lying to the east of the Dead Sea (5.72). In order to seize the Persian throne from his brother, the young Cyrus led his army of ten thousand Greeks on an epic journey from Sardis to Babylon in 401 BC. On the way 'he marched through Arabia, keeping the Euphrates on the right' (Xenophon, An.1.4.19), the reference here being to the province of Arabia in central [?] Mesopotamia. This is qualified by

Pliny as 'the district of Arabia called the country of the Orroei' to the east of the Euphrates and south of the Taurus mountains (5.85)'."

11 Manfred Kropp, Orientalism and Dialogue of Cultures: Orientalism and Arabs before Islam. Conference on Orientalism, Dialogue of Cultures. The University of Jordan, Amman, (no date), p. 250: "But when, why and how did these people – or was it in fact another one – get this Arabic language?"

12 Encylopaedia Iranica, entry: Sasanian dynasty; online version: http://www.iranicaonline.org/articles/sasanian-dynasty

13 Richard N. Frye, The Heritage of Persia, New York 1963, p.235: "The story of the founding of the Sasanian dynasty is not unlike the story of Cyrus or even Arsaces, both of which generally conform to epic norms."

14 About the later significance of Gundeshapūr under Ḵosrow I (531-579 CE) see: Gerrit J. Reinink, Theology and Medicine in Jundishapur. Cultural Change in the Nestorian School Tradition, in: Alasdair McDonald, Michael Twomey, Gerrit Reinink (eds.), Learned Antiquity, Scholarship and Society, Leuven 2003, pp. 163-174.

15 Richard N. Frye, The Heritage of Persia, p. 242: "Prisoners were settled in Fars, Parthia, Khuzistan and elsewhere and they probably provided the basis of the later Christian communities of Iran."

16 Michael G. Morony, Iraq after the Muslim Conquest, Princeton 1984, p. 266-7.

17 John Walker, A Catalogue of Muhammadan Coins in The British Museum. A Catalogue of the Arab-Sassanian Coins. London 1941, p.124, N° B.[erlin] 39 = Kaiser Friedrich Museum, Berlin (Nützel, N° 93, Pl. II). Today in the inventory of the Bode Museum, Museum Island, Berlin; see also: Ryka Gyselen, Arab-Sasanian Copper Coinage, Wien 2000, p. 70: "A second problem emerges concerning the names themselves, which has not previously been considered in numismatic literature. Some of these names may well have been used as an epithet as well as a name."

18 Gerrit J. Reinink, Die Entstehung der syrischen Alexanderlegende als politisch-religiöse Propagandaschrift für Heraclius' Kirchenpolitik; in: Syriac Christianity under Late Sasanian and Early Islamic Rule, Aldershot 2005, III, p. 278-279.

19 J. Reinink, Alexander the Great in 7th-century Syriac 'Apocaliptic' texts, in: Syriac Christianity, IV, p.158-160: "In the fifth book of the History, Theophylact Simocatta (floruit during the reign of Heraclius) transmits an apocalyptic prophecy said to have been pronounced by Khosraus II after his flight into Byzantine territory from the usurper Bahram (590/91). After being insulted by the Byzantine general John Mystacon, the Persian shah is supposed to have spoken the following words to the general (according to the translation of Michael and Mary Whitby): 'If we were not subject to the tyranny of the occasion, you would not have dared, general, to strike with insults the king who is great among mortals. But since you are proud in present circumstances, you shall hear what indeed the gods have provided for the future. Be assured that troubles will flow back in turn against you Romans. The Babylonian race will hold the Roman state in its power for a threefold cycle hebdomad of years. Thereafter you Romans will enslave Persians for a fifth hebdomad of years. When these very things have been accomplished, the day without evening will dwell among mortals and the expected fate will achieve power, when the forces of destruction will be handed over to dissolution and those of the better life hold sway.'

According to the Whitbys, 'this prediction refers to the events of the early seventh century, when the Persians defeated the Romans for approximately twenty-one years (a threefold cyclic hebdomad) and were then defeated by Heraclius in a campaign which lasted six years (until 628'. (...)
Another explanation has been proposed by P. J. Alexander. Taking the year 591 (Ḳosrow's flight into Byzantine territory) as the starting point for Ḳosrow's prediction, Alexander thinks that the fifth hebdomad relates to the period between 619 (591+28) and 626 (591+35). (...). It is generally assumed that Theophylact did not take this report from his written source (John of Ephiphania), but that he reproduces here a contemporary oral tradition. Alexander dates this tradition between the beginning of Heraclius' campaigns and the emperor's decisive victory over the Persians in 627/8. Thérèse Olajos proposes a date by the end of the war (628). According to Michael Whitby, however, the prophecy probably circulated after Heraclius' final victory, since the prophecy's prediction of Roman victory is accurate. I have suggested earlier, that Ḳosrow's prophecy may have served Byzantine propagandistic purposes, 'um Leute, die günstig gegen den Perserkönig gestimmt waren, für den byzantinischen Kaiser umzustimmen'. This hypothesis presupposes that the prophecy circulated during Heraclius' campaigns, and perhaps not long before Heraclius final victory over the Persians. However this may be, the Ḳosrow-prophecy testifies the strong apocalyptic spirit of the time."

20 Christoph Luxenberg, The Syro-Aramaic Reading of the Koran, Berlin 2007, p. 237.

21 Supplement to the Thesaurus Syriacus of R. Payne Smith, S.T.P.; collected and arranged by his daughter J. P. Margoliouth, Oxford 1927, p. 313.

22 R. Paret, Koran, p.282.

23 According to the scientific consensus, the *Strategikon* was composed at the end of the 6th or beginning of the 7th century; see Oxford Dictionary of Byzantium. III, pp. 1962-1963.

24 Georg Ostrogorsky, Geschichte des byzantinischen Staates. München 1959, p. 67. How little Maurice was inclined to renounce on possession of the West is shown in his testament, which he wrote in the year 597, after having fallen seriously ill. According to this last will, his eldest son Theodosios in Constantinople was to rule the eastern domains, while the second, Tiberius should rule in Rome over Italy and the western islands. Rome was to be the second capital of the empire and residence of the emperor. The notion of a universal empire was not given up; moreover, the old idea of distribution of power in the Imperium Romanum (tetrarchy) was still alive.

25 Gerrit J. Reinink, The New Alexander: Apocalyptic Prophecies, in: The Reign of Heraclius (610-642), op. cit., p.82-83: "The city, together with its victorious symbol of the Christian Roman empire had fallen into the hands of the pagan enemy. In these years, fears for the impending definite fall of the empire increased, and what this meant within the wider perspective of the course of history was perfectly clear: the end of the Roman empire would usher in the very last terrors of world history, in the form of the invasions of the eschatological

peoples of Gog and Magog and the advent of the Antichrist." See also footnote 15: "By 'imperial eschatology' we understand the already ancient Christian idea that the Roman empire is the fourth empire of the book of Daniel, which, as the 'withholding power' (2 Thess. 2:7), would last until the advent of the Antichrist; cf. Podskalsy, Byzantinische Reichseschatologie, p.55, note 332 (...)."

26 P. J. Alexander, Historiens Byzantins et Croyances Eschatologiques, in: P. J. Alexander, Religious and Political History and Thought in the Byzantine Empire, Collected Studies, London 1978, p.4-5: "On retiendra que dans la première moitié du septième siècle il avait à Byzance des milieux qui croyaient que l'état romain ou byzantin avait été suffisament affaibli pour faire place, suivant la tradition mentionée dans la seconde Epître aux Thessaloniciens, au règne de l'Antéchrist."

27 Lawrence I. Conrad, Heraclius in Early Islamic Kerygma, in: The Reign of Heraclius (610-641), op. cit., p. 120: "Moreover, when Heraclius formally assumed the title of basileus in 629, he was the first emperor to assert his right to rule in the name of Christ as a 'dominatus'." See also footnote 34: Shahid: "Heraclius, Pistos en Christo Basileus".

28 Jan Willem Drijvers, Heraclius and the Restitutio Crucis, in: The Reign of Heraclius (610-641), op. cit., p. 186-188: "The 'Restitutio Crucis' was an evident symbolical act meant to establish a new imperial ideology and to mark a new beginning. Heraclius wanted to evoke and associate with David through whose descendant, Christ (2 Samuel 7:13) Christianity came to the world, which was first officially recognised by Constantine, the founder of the Christian empire. Through his association with these three figures, Heraclius aspired to the renewal of his reign, a new beginning, and the start of a new age after a successfully concluded war. In this respect, the date of the restitution is of great importance. The 21st of March was a carefully chosen date. It corresponds with the day of creation of the luminaries of the sun and the moon, or, in other words, the beginning of time. The repositioning of the Cross on 21 March, therefore, marks a new era in the history of the Creation. This new era had important eschatological and apocalyptic overtones. In his poem on the restoration of the Cross, George of Pisidia associates the revelation of the Cross with the resurrection of the dead, thereby clearly referring to the Day of Judgement. In the 'Apocalypse of Ps. Methodius', composed at the end of the seventh century, there is a clear association between the restoration of the Cross and the Second Coming of Christ, and the restitution was seen as foreboding the final emperor. According to this 'Apocalypse', the ending of all sovereignty and power on earth would be announced when the emperor would go to Golgatha, reinstall the Cross there, and put his crown on the Cross. He would then hand over the kingdom to God the Father, the Cross would be raised to heaven and the crown with it, because the Cross on which Christ had died was a sign that would be seen prior to the coming of the Lord (in Jerusalem), and the last Greek emperor would die.
Heraclius' imperial ideology, the beginning of a new age inspired by biblical and messianic concepts, asked for a new official titulature. Probably already by 629 Heraclius adopted the title of 'pistos en Christo basileus', which very adequately expresses the emperor's political and religious programme."

29 Mary Whitby, George of Pisidia's Presentation of Heraclius, in: The Reign of Heraclius (610-641, op. cit., 162: "Emphasised throughout is the mystical power

of the Cross, which has paradoxically burned to ashes the fire of the magi (12-14; 64-68) and has been more effective than the biblical ark in not only defeating the enemies, but causing them to turn upon themselves in civil strife (73-81). Finally, the live-giving Cross is connected with the occasion on which news of its restoration reached the capital – the Feast of Lazarus, a dead man restored to life (104-110). This poem is unified by its reiterated references to the Cross, frequent biblical allusion, and its uniform tone of exultation."

30 Was ist das Neue an Heraklius? Gerd J. Reinink, Bernhard Stolte, Introduction, in: The Reign of Heraclius (610-641), Leuven 2002, p. xi.: "'New' was the fact that Heraclius, supported by the Church, personally lead his troops in a 'holy war' against pagan enemies who tried to wipe the Christian empire out of existence. Also 'new' were the emperor's definition and application of measures meant to restore the ideological unity of the empire."

31 Jan Willem Drijvers, Heraclius and the Restitutio Crucis, in: The Reign of Heraclius (610-641), op. cit. p. 185: "There are interesting parallels between David and Heraclius, of which the latter must have been aware. Both kings did not come to the throne by way of orderly succession; both were killers of tyrants; both fought wars against infidels, won them, and brought back the sacred objects – the ark and the Cross – which were of great importance for their respective religions; both had relationships with women that were not pleasing in the eyes of God, and functioned as an intermediary between his people and God. This biblical king was thus the ideal prototype for a monarch of a Christian empire, who was also to serve as a link between his subjects and God. Heraclius recognised this and also took David as his role model. Earlier in his reign, Theodore Synkellos, in one of his sermons, had already compared Heraclius with David. Another allusion to David is made by Heraclius himself in an address to his soldiers during the Persian campaign."

32 Georg Ostrogorsky, Geschichte, op. cit., p. 81.

33 Gerrit J. Reinink, Die Entstehung der Syrischen Alexanderlegende als Politisch-Religiöse Propagandaschrift für Heraclius Kirchenpolitik, in: Gerrit J. Reinink, Syriac Christianity, op. cit., III, p. 276.

34 John Haldon, The Reign of Heraclius: A Context for Change?, in: The Reign of Heraclius (610-641), op. cit., p. 3.

35 Frank R. Trombley, Military Cadres and battles during the Reign of Heraclius, in: The Reign of Heraclius (610-641), op. cit., p. 250: "but the operations in Armenia and upper Mesopotamia may have included a large element of ethnic fighters, as did the force that fought at the battle of al-Yarmuk. It is impossible to comment on the military effectiveness of these combined formations except to note their success against the Sasanids in the 620s (...)."

36 Georg Ostrogorsky, Geschichte, op. cit., p. 82.

37 Wilferd Madelung, Apocalyptic Prophecies in Hims in the Umayyad Age, in: Religious and Ethnic Movements in Medieval Islam. 1992, p. 175: "'Abd Allâh b. Dinâr quotes Ka'b, saying: The Turks will alight at Amid and will drink from the Tigris and the Euphrates. They will work havoc in al-Jazîra and the people of Islâm will be unable out of consternation to do anything against them."

38 Michael Morony, Iraq after the Muslim conquest, Princeton 1984, p. 358: "On the other hand, the agreement allowed the Nestorians to continue to think that their belief in two natures (diphysitism) made them just as orthodox as the church of the West. (...) The Nestorian identity emerging at the end of the seventh century was one which derived its distinction in contrast to Monophysitism without requiring any break (from the Nestorian point of view) with the Orthodox Christians in the West."

39 L. Gardet, article 'Dîn', EI^2,II/ 293: "Dîn henceforth is the corpus of obligatory prescriptions given by God, to which one must submit. Thus dîn signifies obligation, direction, submission, retribution. Whether referring to the Hebrew – Aramaic sense or the ancient Arabic root, there will remain the ideas of debt to be discharged (hence obligation) and of direction imposed or to be followed with a submissive heart. From the standpoint of him who imposes obligation or direction, dîn rejoins the judgement of the Hebrew root; but from the standpoint of him who has to discharge the obligation and receive the direction, *dîn* must be translated *religion* – the most general and frequent use." (my emphasis) Why the Iranian etymology of the term does not convince the author of this article, is not explained. Two renowned German islamologists, Nöldeke and Vollers, both point out the Iranian origin of the word Dīn. The author, Gaudefroy-Demombynes, is apparently not convinced. If two characters as different as Nöldeke and Vollers agreed upon the etymology of the term, then this etymology should not be so easily dismissed as is the case in the EI^2. Moreover, it should be noted that a scholar like D. B. Macdonald is quoted as late as 1941 (Handwörterbuch des Islam, Leiden 1941, p. 99) with reference to Vollers' opinion concerning the Iranian origin of the term. His mention does not reject Vollers' opinion.

40 Heinrich Speyer, Die biblischen Erzählungen im Qoran, Gräfenhainichen 1931, p. 162: "In any case, the concept of Abraham as the father of the pagans who become believers (Rom. 4:11 ff.) is Christian. In Mt. 3:9 Christ rejects the opinion of the Pharisees and Sadducees, who refer to Abraham as their father. In Romans 4:16 ff. the faith of Abraham is mentioned, who is the father of all of us and who was given appointed father of a multitude of nations (cf. Gen. 17:5), who did not become weak in faith (Gen. 17:17) and who believed in the promise of the angels in spite of his and Sarah's age (Rom. 4:19-20). Thus Christianity assigned more importance to Abraham than Judaism, (...)."

41 Gerrit J. Reinink, Alexander the Great in Seventh-Century Syriac 'Apocalyptic' texts, in: Syriac Christianity under Late Sasanian and Early Islamic rule. Aldershot 2005, VI, p. 167.

42 Gerrit J. Reinink, Alexander the Great in Seventh-Century Syriac 'Apocalyptic' texts, op. cit., p.153: "The prefectures recorded in both lists represent territories which since the opening phases of the Persian-Byzantine war in 604 were occupied by Khosraus II, and which after the peace treaty in 628 between the emperor Heraclius and Kavadh, Khosraus' son and successor, were restored to Byzantium. There is no period in the long history of the wars between Byzantium and the Sassanians to which these data apply better than to the time of Heraclius' victory over the Persians and the Byzantine recovery of the Eastern provinces in 628."

43 Gerrit J. Reinink, Syrische Alexanderlegende, op. cit., p. 273.

44 Text of the Syrian Legend of Alexander: "... I know in my mind, that you made me bigger than all kings, because you made horns grow on my head, so that I can crush the kingdoms of the earth... ."

45 This is mentioned in Hans Bauer/ Portus Leander, Grammatik des Biblisch-Aramäischen. Halle 1927 (reprint 1995: Hildesheim/ Zürich/ New York/ Vaduz), § 53 b, p. 200.

46 This unusual dual is mentioned in Franz Rosenthal, A Grammar of Biblical Aramaic, 2nd revised edition, Wiesbaden 1961; § 44, p. 24.

47 E. Kautzsch, Die heilige Schrift des Alten Testaments. 2 vol., Tübingen 1922, p. 477.

48 Gerrit J. Reinink, Syrische Alexanderlegende, op. cit., p. 280.

49 Gerrit J. Reinink, Syrische Alexanderlegende, op. cit., p. 267-9.

50 Der Koran, transl. by Max Henning, revised by Murad W. Hofmann, op. cit., p. 219.

51 Wilferd Madelung, Apocalyptic Prophecies in Hims in the Umayyad Age, op. cit., p. 146.

52 John W. Watt, The Portrayal of Heraclius in Syriac Historical Sources, in: The Reign of Heraclius (610-641), op. cit., p. 67: "The Chronicler's attitude to Khosrau emerges very clearly in his remark attached to an incident involving Nathaniel bishop of Siazur, who expelled from his region an official who had created trouble for Christians at the time of the Persian siege of Dara. The 'Rad' is said to have told the shah: You fight for Christians, [the author refers to the real or false Theodosius, son of Maurice] yet I am banished by Christians. Nathaniel was therefore imprisoned for six years and then crucified, on which the Chronicler comments: Even if Khosrau made an outward show of love to Christians because of Maurice, nevertheless he was an enemy of our people. However divided the loyalties of the East Syrians may have been in earlier years, the writer of the Khuzistan Chronicle is thus empathic that Khusrau II was an enemy of Christianity. His view may be compared with that of Sabeos, whose theme is 'the story of the destructive and ruinous Khosrau' cursed by God'."

53 Translation: Muhammad Ahmad Rassoul, Lan Tabur, Köln 1413/1993, p. 784.

54 Lan Tabur, op. cit. S. 628.; Handwörterbuch des Islam, op. cit. 365: "Luqman, a legendary figure stemming from Arabic paganism, also found its way into the Kur'an and into later legend and poetry. (...) – Concerning Luqman's admonition: Be modest in thy bearing and subdue thy voice. Lo! in harshest of all voices is the voice of the ass. (...) Rendel Harris has found the model for this in Akhiqar: Lower your head, speak softly and look downward! For if the house were built through your voice, then a donkey would build two of them in one day." B. Heller, article: "Luqman" EI^2 V/811-12: "Once the Kur'an had consecrated Luqman as the wise utterer of proverbs, everything that was thought pious or sensible could be attributed to him. (...) it may be that many of these proverbs that belong to the general treasury of Near Eastern wisdom literature had already begun to penetrate into the Arabian Peninsula (...) The Christian Arab poet 'Adi b. Zayd of al-Hîra knew of Ahiqar, whom he calls al-Hayqar (see Nöldeke, Untersuchungen zum Achiqar-Roman, 25)."

55 Irfan Shahid, The Arabs in the Peace Treaty of A.D. 561, Arabica (1956), pp. 181-213.

56 A. Pertusi, Georgio di Pisidia Poemi. I. Panegerici Epici. Edizione critica, traduzione e commento, Ettal, 1959.

57 About corresponding reports about the Nabateans see: Joseph Patrich, The Formation of Nabatean Art, Jerusalem 1990, pp. 31-33. There also the note about an Aramaic-Arabic bilingual text in Nabataean script, p. 32, footnote 29a: A. Negev, Obodas the God, Israel Exploration Journal 36 (1986), p. 56-60.

58 The historical stability of the circumstances of late antiquity is conspicuous: In the former settlement area of Monophysite minority Christians in Mesopotamia with the see in Takrīt we today find the center of the Sunnite minority in Iraq, in the settlement area of the Syrian Christians in Khūzistān and Ḥīra the Shiite majority. Nağrān is the center of an Ismailite tribe in southern Arabia.

59 Irfan Shahîd, article "Ghassân", EI^2, II/ p. 1020-21.

60 Judith Koren & Yehuda D. Nevo, Methodological Approaches to Islamic Studies. In: Der Islam 68 (1991), p. 100-102. see also the note by Jeremy Jones, JESHO 46,4, Leiden 2003, p. 411-412: "In 1991, Judith Koren and the late Yehuda Nevo issued a methodological challenge to historians of Early Islam. They were encouraged to do so by their reading of the so called 'revisionist' historians, including Patricia Crone, Michael Cook, Gerald Hawting, Moshe Sharon, and John Wansbrough, whose work, Koren and Nevo believed, had completely undermined the foundations upon which the traditional positivist account of the rise of Islam had been constructed. None of the written Islamic sources for the first two hundred years of the hijra could be used as evidence for what had actually happened. Archeology, which in any case consisted of objective facts that were always to be preferred over subjective written sources, was therefore almost the only evidence available, and should be used to compose a new account of the origins of Islam that would be radically different from the traditional historical narrative. The polemical style permitted historians to dismiss this article as not worth an answer, while Nevo's unorthodox interpretation of material evidence embarrassed archaeologists into silence. What, it was widely asked, could have persuaded 'Der Islam' to waste space in this manner?" History has meanwhile answered this question. About the Arabic inscriptions on buildings of the Ghassanids in Syria in the 6th century CE see: Irfan Shahîd, article "Ghassân" EI^2 II/1021, moreover about a bilingual Ḥarran inscription of the year 568 CE: Adolf Grohmann, Arabische Paläographie, II, Wien 1971, p. 14, N° 2. The trilingual inscription of Zebed (Arabic, Aramaic, Greek) of the year 512 CE can be found in Brussels. The architrave of the Saint Sergius Church has the following dimensions: 76x305x16 cm; it is in the Musées Royaux d'Art et d'Histoire, Inv. N° 1308. Grohmann, op. cit., p.14, N° 1; see also the catalogue of the exhibition "Ex oriente", Aachen 2003, Mainz 2003, p. 259: The architrave of the Saint Sergius Church bears the following inscription in Greek, Aramaic and Arabic: "This is a sacred place." According to newest research it is the oldest epigraphic attestation of Arabic, see: Chr. Robin, L'Ecriture Arabe et l'Arabie pour l'Assience, Dossier Orssery Oct.-Jan. 2002, p. 62-69.

61 Irfan Shahid, article "Ghassân", EI^2 II/1020.

62 Irfan Shahid, article "Ghassân', EI^2 II/1020. Furthermore: S.C. Munro-Hay, The Coinage of Aksum, Neu-Delhi 1984, p. 81: †HZA†HAC†BACI†LEYC† = Ezanas

Basileus; p. 84: †HZA†NAB†ACI†LEY. Ezanas ruled in appr. 540 CE as a Christian king in Southern Arabia and the modern Eritrea. His successors had coins struck in Greek with their Byzantine vassal title. About the situation on the Arabian Peninsula at that time see: Barbara Finster, Arabien in der Spätantike, in: Archäologischer Anzeiger (1996), p. 287-319. Renè Tardy, Najrân, Chretiens d'Arabie avant l'Islam, Beirut 1999, also mentions the publication of a Syrian chronicle from South Arabia: A. Moberg, Le Livre des Himyarites, Lund 1924. There the story of a merchant from Nağrān is told, who traveled to Ḥīra, where he came in contact with Christianity and became the founder of this religion in Nağrān. Later and in other places, Ḥīra is attested as place of proclamation of the new faith. Irfan Shahid, article "Al-Hîra", EI^2 III/ p. 462: "Muhammad is said to have been in the habit of spending a month each year in a cave on Ḥīra' [the spelling without hamza is also found] engaged in tahannuṭ, presumably some form of religious devotion, and to have been visited here by an angel (Ibn Hišām, 152; cf. Ṭabarī, i, pp. 1147, p. 1555); this experience is sometimes identified with the beginning of revelation." Thus, interesting connecting points can be found which link the process of historicization of the Christological predicate muḥammad in Ḥīra and Nağrān in South Arabia, a town herself connected to Ḥīra.

63 G. Widengren, Die Religionen Irans, Stuttgart 1965, p. 283: "It cannot be doubted that the Islamic occupation of Iran ended a development which might have led to the total Christianization of Iran. It is conspicuous that as a competitor, Zoroastrianism as a living religion was no match for Christianity."

64 Wolfram Brandes, Heraclius between Restoration and Reform, op. cit., p. 15: "His alliance with the Chazars and the attack they launched together against the Persians through the Caucasus reminded many contemporaries of the fate of Gog and Magog, who according to the legend were excluded from the oikumene and locked behind the Caucasian Gates by Alexander the Great." See also footnote 152: On Gog and Magog in the Middle Byzantine Apocalyptic Literature, see Alexander, The Byzantine Apocalyptic Tradition, pp. 185-192.

65 G. Ostrogorsky, Geschichte des Byzantinischen Staates, op. cit., 93: "Executing the regulations of the treaty which the patriarch Kyros of Alexandria, told to do so by Martina, had signed with the Arabs and which gave the Byzantines a deadline for their withdrawal from the land, Byzantine troops left Alexandria 12th September 642 on a boarded a ship heading to Rhodos, whereupon (...)." The treaty is mentioned in Byzantine registers. About this point see G. Ostrogorsky, op. cit., p. 92, footnote 1: Dölger, Reg. 220.

66 In his Table of Arab-Sassanian coinage, Heinz Gaube mentions six attestations of dirhems of the year 20 from different mints. See: Heinz Gaube, Arabosasanidische Münzprägung, op. cit. Fold-out with table. See also: J. Walker, Catalogue I., op. cit., p. 3-4 and xxxv.-xxxvi. There a discussion concerning the dating according to the traditional Islamological view. For coinage of the year 20 of the mint Sakastān see also: Stephen Album, Tony Goodwin, The Pre-Reform Coinage of the Early Islamic Period, Oxford 2002, Pl. 25, Nos. 353-357.

67 Receipts of the Arab commander Amīr ʿAbdallah ibn Ǧābir about confiscated sheep on his campaign in Upper Egypt. Record dated 25th April 643. Vienna, Österreichische Nationalbibliothek (Austrian National Library), Papyrus Collection; see Prophyläen Weltgeschichte, vol. V., Frankfurt 1963, p. 65-65, text and fig.

68 Henri Lavoix, Catalogue des Monnaies Musulmanes de la Bibliothèque Nationale, Khalifes Orientaux, Paris 1887, p. 1, N° 1.

69 See the conclusion of Patricia Crone about the historically late appearance of inscriptions assigned by her to the Prophet of the Arabs: P. Crone, God's Caliph, op. cit., p. 24 and footnote 1. The coin from Zaranj can be found in the Berlin Collection, Walker I. p. 124, N° B. 39. N°

70 J. Walker, Catalogue I., op. cit., p. xxviii: "The importance of the coins lies in their providing us with contemporary data for corroborating, supplementing, or at times correcting the historians. Even so there are numerous cases where the coin evidence cannot be reconciled with the historical tradition." The only apt solution here is to start from scratch again. Numbers on coins, which do not indicate the era, neither refer to the era of the Prophet of the Arabs nor to that of a late Sassanians. They stand for an era which begins with the victory of Heraclius, i.e., the era of Arab mint authority. They had coins struck in the name of their rule, not according to the traditional report of the 9th century CE, when for the first time details of the flight of the Prophet were known, a migration from a town called Mecca, hitherto unknown to the possessors of the Qur'ān, to Medina.

71 Cécile Morrison, Catalogue des Monnaies Byzantines, Bibliothèque Nationale, Paris 1970, p. 765 (Années de Règne et Indictions. Constant II.). For Gadara: Augustus Spijkermann, The Coins of the Decapolis and Provincia Arabia, Jerusalem 1978, p. 128-29, N° 1. Coinage of Gadara ends in the year of the city 304 = 240/41 n. Chr.

72 Personal communication by Johannes Thomas, 17 March, 2006.

73 Adolf Grohmann, Arabic Inscriptions, Part II. vol. I, Löwen 1962, no. 268.

74 Joshua Green and Yoram Tsafrir, Greek Inscriptions from Hammat Gader: A Poem by the Empress Eudocia and Two Building Inscriptions, Israel Exploration Journal, Vol. 32, Nos. 2-3, Jerusalem 1982, p. 94-95.

75 G. Ostrogorsky, Geschichte des Byzantinischen Reiches, op. cit., 96: "The Emperor Constans did not ignore the necessity of religious reconciliation. Trying to find a compromise, he issued the Type of Constans, which ordered the ekthesis to be removed from the narthex of the Hagia Sophia, but at the same time tried hard to circumvent the actual debate and the edict of Heraclius by banishing under threat of punishment any discussion not only about the problem of energeia [divine power], but also about the problem of [divine] will. Concerning these two problems he thus arrived at the same crucial point where more than a century and a half before, after the publication of the Henotikon of Zenon, the problem of [Christ's] nature had arrived."

76 G. Ostrogorsky, Geschichte des Byzantinischen Staates, op. cit., 95, footnote 1 (Dölger, Reg. 230).

77 J. Walker, Catalogue I., p. 25-27, Nos. 35-ANS. 9 (coinage of Darabjird in the name of Muʿāwiya).

78 G. Ostrogorsky, Geschichte des Byzantinischen Staates, op. cit., 98.

79 G. Ostrogorsky, Geschichte des Byzantinischen Staates, op. cit., p. 102, footnote 1 (Dölger, Reg. 239).

80 J. Walker, Catalogue I., p. 33-35, Nos. ANS.7- 47.

81 J. Walker, Catalogue I., p. 29, M.19- p. 32, N° M. 20.

82 J. Walker, Catalogue I., p. 29. N° C. 1.

83 There are striking biblical parallels to this image of "water of life, coming forth from a rock", e.g. Ezekiel 47:1-12: "Then he brought me back to the door of the house; and behold, water was flowing from under the threshold of the house toward the east, for the house faced east (...)." The topic will be treated in more detail in a later publication.

84 "It is impossible to tell whether this pattern has been influenced by some of the late Sasanian gold coinage on which the name of the king is followed by his title, Khusro (king of kings), Kavad (kay)." (Rika Gyselen, Arab-Sasanian Copper Coinage, op. cit., S. 70).

85 J. Walker, Catalogue I., p.40, N° 58.

86 A comprehensive compilation of the historiographical literature of the Arabs about the conquest of the Kaʿba by al-Ḥağğāğ can be found in: Gernot Rotter, Die Umayyaden und der Zweite Bürgerkrieg (680-692), Wiesbaden, 1982, p. 238-243. Here we hear about the abundance of food of the besiegers - groats, cookies (kaʿk) and fine flour - and the hunger of the besieged. At the end the anti-caliph ʿAbdallāh bn Zubayr was dead. The exact location and time of his death has been fixed by Rudolf Sellheim: Der Zweite Bürgerkrieg im Islam (680-692). Das Ende der Mekkanisch-Medinensischen Vorherrschaft. Sitzungsberichte der Wissenschaftlichen Gesellschaft an der Johann Wolfgang Goethe-Universität Frankfurt/M., vol.8, year 1969, N° 4, Wiesbaden 1970, p. 109.

87 Julius Wellhausen, Das Arabische Reich, Berlin 1902, p. 345, quotes Theophanes: "A.M. 6243 (755 A.D.) the new rulers killed most (Christians) as adherents of a former dynasty, by slaughtering them perfidiously at Antipatris in Palestine." Then he continues: "(...) One does not understand how the Umayyads can be called Christians; here there must be an error or an interpolation (*my translation from the German*)." It might have been known to Theophanes at his time that the Umayyads were (Christian) "Old Believers", i.e., heretical Syrian Christians.

88 J. Walker, Catalogue I., pp. 33-35, Nos. ANS. 7- 47 (sequence of the years 53-60 of the Arabs).

89 J. Walker, Catalogue I., pp. 29-30, Nos. M.19-B.4.

90 J. Walker, Catalogue I., pp. 30-32, Nos. 38-Th.5.

91 J. Walker, Catalogue I., pp. 36, Nos. 49-RB.6.

92 Heinz Gaube: Arabosasanidische Numismatik, Braunschweig 1972, p. 99.

93 "The settlements of the deported Christians apparently followed the road from Khûzistân via Fârs, Kirmân, Sakâstân to Herat and Marw. Nihâwand and Ray probably were destinations for the deportations, as they were mints with the ʿabdallâh-motto. Due to deportations of tens or even hundreds of thousands of Christians from Syria, Cilicia and Cappadocia under Shâpûr I, and the resulting mixed marriages and later missionary work, Christianity must have become the most numerous minority religion in Sassanian Iran (...). In Western church

history Iranian Christianity has not received the attention it deserves. At the time of the Arab invasion [*the author assumes the correctness of Arabic historiography*] there were up to ten sees of metropolitans and 96 dioceses." Cf. also footnote 264: Concerning deportations as a political instrument of the Sassanians cf. E. Kettenhofen, Deportations II. In the Parthian an Sasanian Periods: Eir 7 (1994) 287-309 and 265: Zum Christentum im sassanidischen Iran (...) (Michael Stausberg, Die Religion Zarathustras, vol. 1, Stuttgart 2002, p. 237).

94 J. Walker, Catalogue I., p. 29, Cam. 1.

95 C. Saleman, Über eine Pehlevi-Arabische Münze. ZDMG 1879, p. 511.

96 In the depiction of the events in Arabic historiography around the son-in-law of the Prophet of the Arabs this call is mentioned for the year 37 of the hiğra. On the occasion of the battle of Siffin the followers of ʿAlī, who opposed the acceptance of the arbitration, allegedly uttered it. Therefore, islamologists render this motto as: "Arbitration belongs to God alone." (Heinz Gaube, Arabosasanidische Numismatik, op. cit., p.35).

97 See also the dirham struck in Gharshistan of the year 137 of the Arabs, Baldwin Auctions, London, Islamic Coin Auction 10, 2005, N° 56. It is first mentioned in: Oliver Codrington, Numismatic Chronicle, London 1894, p. 88.

98 The findings can be found in the Archeological Museum, Istanbul. Their condition is described as (1952): „Bu değerli koleksiyon maalesef bugün Müze Idaresinin ihmali yüzünden toz haline gelmiş bulunmaktadir." The discovery is mentioned in: Aziz Ogan, Asar-i Atika Nizamnamesi ve 1874' den itibaren yapılan hafriyat, Istanbul 1938, p. 48. The lead sealing mentioned here can be seen in: Ibrahim Artuk, Emevilerden Halife Abdülmelik bin Mervan adına kesilmiş essiz bir kursun mühür, Belleten, (Ankara) 16. 1952. pp. 21-25. Reprint in: Numismatics of the Islamic World, vol. 42, Studies Collected and Reprinted by Fuat Sezgin, Frankfurt 2004. Oleg Grabar, The Formation of Islamic Art, New Haven 1973, Abb. 21 (Seal of ʿAbd al-Malik, Istanbul Archeological Museum). In the sequence of illustrations the obverse and reverse were confounded, which is a hint that the depiction was not understood.

99 Personal communication by Prof. Johannes Thomas, 17 March, 2006.

100 See also: "Clay lamp with a biblical scene. (...) round body. (...) Long snout with a channel, on the round body with two pouring holes depicting the two scouts returning from the Promised Land, on their shoulders wearing an overdimensioned grape as proof of the fertility of the country. On the shoulder: vines and grapes. (...) Roman, Africa Proconsularis, 5th century CE. According to the Old Testament Mos. 2:13-18. A very rare topic of Christian art" (F. Bejaoui, Céramiques et Religion Chrétienne (1997) pp. 114. An identical clay lamp can be found in Harvard University Art Museum, Inv. 1932.56.76.)

101 Moshe Sharon, An Arabic Inscription from the Time of the Caliph ʿAbd al-Malik, BSOAS 29 (1966), pp. 367-372.

102 See surah 112:2. Franz Rosenthal (1953) discusses this topic in detail and comes to the conclusion: In view of this material, the suggestion may be made that as-samad in the Qur'ân is a survival of an ancient Northwest Semitic religious term, (...)." Franz Rosenthal, Some Minor Problems in the Qur'ân, The Joshua Starr Memorial Volume, New York 1953, p. 83

103 Muhammad I. Moshiri, A Pahlavi-Forerunner of the Umayyad Reformed Coinage. Journal of the Royal Asiatic Society 113, London 1981, pp. 168-172.

104 R.C. Zaehner, Zurvan, Oxford 1955, p. 182.

105 J. Walker, Catalogue II., p. 65, N° 169; p. 71, N° 178.

106 Christoph Luxenberg, Neudeutung der Arabischen Inschrift im Felsendom zu Jerusalem. In: Die dunklen Anfänge, Berlin 2005, p. 126-127.

107 Rika Gyselen, Arab-Sasanian Copper Coinage, op. cit., S. 70: "A second problem emerges concerning the names themselves, which has not previously been considered in numismatic literature. Some of these names may well have been used as an epithet as well as a name. For example the word 'abdallâh can refer to the name of an individual or it can simply mean "the servant of God", and in this case may be considered as epithetic. But both J. Walker and H. Gaube considered such words as names of minting authorities."

108 J. Walker, Catalogue I., p. xlvii, where he makes the following restricting remark: "Most of these agree with known mints and dates of 'Abdallâh ibn 'Amîr, and it is most probable that all of these coins were struck under that governor (q.v.)."

109 Heinrich Nützel, Katalog der orientalischen Münzen. I, Berlin 1898, N° 93, Tfl.II.

110 H. Gaube: Arabosasanidische Numismatik, op. cit., 82-3. The coin can be found on table 14, 2.2.2.1.

111 H. Gaube, Arabosasanidische Numismatik, op. cit., p. 70.

112 H. Gaube, Arabosasanidische Numismatik, op. cit., p. 36.

113 Alexander, S. Kirkbridge, Coins of the Byzantine-Arab Transition Period, The Quarterly of the Department of Antiquities in Palestine, Jerusalem 1948, p. 62, N° 62, Pl. XXVI. John Walker, Catalogue II, p. 52 , ASK 6 (ohne Abb.).

114 "The issue was probably issued by a minor chief named Muhammad rather than in the name of the prophet." (Baldwin's Auction Ltd., Islamic Coin Auction in London, 2004, Nos. 3117, 3118).

115 Clive Foss, Anomalous Arab-Byzantine Coins - Some Problems and Suggestions. O.N.s. Newsletter 166, London 2001, p. 7, N° 9.

116 3.2.24. Muḥammad b. 'Abdallāh for the year 67 in Harat (Heinz Gaube, Arabo-Sassanianische Numismatik, op. cit., p. 71. SICA 308).

117 Baldwin Auctions Ltd., Islamic Coin Auction N° 10, 2004, N° 3172.

118 A. Shams Eshrag, An Interesting Arab-Sasanian Dirhem, ONS Newsletter 178, London 2004, p. 45-46, with fig.

119 Drachm of the year 56 of the Arabs from the mint NAR (Narmashîr) in Kirmân, SICA 343; J. Walker, Catalogue I., p. 86, ETN 17; Baldwin's Auction's, Auction Number 45, London 2006, N° 1866.

120 J. Walker, Catalogue I., p. 97, Sch[ulman] 5.

121 Concerning the term "rasūl" the rendering "apostle" in Christianity should be noted. Moreover, the corresponding Hebrew verb, šalāḥ, is used with the prophets of the Old Testament (שְׁלָחֵנִי; Ex. 3:13 ff.; 4:13; Is. 6:8; Jer. 1:7). The term *rasūl allāh* is found in its Syriac form (*šelīḥe ḏ-alāha*) in the apocryphal Acts of Thomas (Handwörterbuch des Islam, Leiden 1941, p. 611).

122 This reading can be found in Martin Hartmann 1895. See his article: Mittheilungen aus der Sammlung Hartmann. I. Kupfermünzen abbasidischer Statthalter. (Zeitschrift für Numismatik, N° 19. [Berlin] 1895, pp. 97-102): In the name

of God, the messenger (apostle) of God is the chosen one (German: Im Namen Gottes, erwählt ist der Gesandte [Apostel] Gottes).

123 H. Gaube, Arabosasanidische Numismatik, op. cit., S. 62. About this 'Abd al-Malik of the chronicles see also: Gernot Rotter, Die Umayyaden und der Zweite Bürgerkrieg (680-692), op. cit., 77, footnote 522.

124 See also the inscription on the rim of a coin from Bishapūr of the year 50 of the Arabs: *bi-sm(i)-Allāh al-malik* (In the name of Allah, the King), Walker, Catalogue I., p. 18, N° ANS. 3.

125 J. Walker, Catalogue I., p. 26, Zub. 1. About the interpretation of the inscription *ḫalfat Allāh*, see: Patricia Crone, Martin Hinds, God's Caliph, op. cit., p. 5: "Leaving aside the fact that there were exegetes who disagree with Paret and that the provenance of the title is unknown, the texts leave no doubt that khalifat Allah (...) was understood to mean 'deputy of God'."

126 About the meaning of the Aramaic ḥlipā see: Christoph Luxenberg, Die Syro-Aramäische Lesart des Koran, Berlin 2004, 57: "der an Stelle Gesetzte, Substitut, Stellvertreter, Nachfolger (*translated from the German:* the one put in place, substitute, representative, successor)." As was the case with the term rasūl (apostle), the form ḫalīfa/ḥlīpā is originally Aramaic. This makes us re-evaluate the whole terminology of early Islam. Can it be understood from the perspective of the 'Arabīya? MḤMT from Ugarit was understood as such a kind of Arabic and therefore misunderstood.

127 H.R.A. Gibb, Artikel 'Amîr al- Mu'minîn', EI²,I/445: "From this time ['Umar, A.H. 58, according to the tradition of the Muslims] until the end of the Caliphate as an institution, amīr al-mu'minīn was employed exclusively as the protocollary title of a caliph, and among the Sunnis its adoption by a ruler implied claim to the office of a caliph, (...)." No further comment is necessary about the term "caliph", as the notion of the caliph as ruler stems from the time of Marwān II (127 of the Arabs/ 748 CE). His illegitimate rule was covered as "caliphate", he himself was designated with the title "caliph" in the sense of "spokesman of a clan".

128 It can hardly be doubted that the Apocalypse was written in the last decade of the 7th century (around 691/2 CE). See: Gerrit J. Reinink, Pseudo Methodius und die Legende vom römischen Endkaiser, Aldershot 2005, VIII, p. 85, footnote 15).

129 John Walker, Catalogue I., p. 25, ANS. 5.

130 The coin depicting a fish in a square with the inscription around the rim mentioning the muḥammad was found during excavations of the Hebrew University in Beth Shean (Scythopolis; Inv. N° 1331). About the symbol of the fish the German encyclopedia "Der Große Brockhaus" (1984) has the following to say: "In many religions the f. was a symbol of death and fertility. This has to be distinguished from the Christian symbol of the fish, as it was known in Asia Minor, Egypt, Africa and Southern Gaul since the 2nd century CE: The Greek letters of the word ICHTHYS for f. stand for the initial letters of the formula 'Iesous Christos Theou Yios Soter' (Greek: Jesus Christ, son of God, savior). In connection with one or even both parts of the Eucharist, the f. was also symbol of the Eucharistic salvation food." In another place we read: "Christian symbols (...) The Christians appeared as "orantes" (those who pray), their creed is symbolized by the fish (...)." Further specimen of this coin with muḥammad and

the fish in public collections: British Museum, London: J. Walker, Catalogue II., p. 217, Nos. 686-688; Paris, Bibliothèque Nationale, Lavoix Nos. 1532-34; New York, American Numismatic Society, George C. Miles, Rare Islamic Coins, Pl. IV, N° 90. Excavations: Alfred R. Bellinger, Coins from Jerash, 1928-1934. A.N.S., Numismatic Notes and Monographs, N° 81, New York 1938, p.124, N° 521, Pl. IX.

131 About the Muslim tradition of the construction of the temple see: Amikam Elad, Why did 'Abd al-Malik build the Dome of the Rock? A Re-examination of the Muslim Sources, in: Bayt al-Maqdis, Jerusalem and early Islam, ed. by Jeremy Jons. Oxford 1999, pp. 33-52. In the same anthology: Josef van Ess, 'Abd al-Malik and the Dome of the Rock. An Analysis of some Texts, p. 95-96: "We are indeed close to Jewish ideas. Creation took place on Mount Zion, from the foundation-rock (*eben shetiyya*) which was, as we have seen, 'in front of the Holy of the Holies'. We are of course not dealing with a creatio ex nihilo here; God needed a solid base for shaping the world. According to Jewish belief, His most important act in this process was the creation of Adam, for He created him from the clay which He found on the Mountain, i.e., from the 'place of his atonement', where the altar of Ex. 20:24 was to be erected. Theological speculation concluded from this that Mount Zion was the Paradise where Adam had lived and where God stayed with him; God brought him 'into His palace', which was called Eden. Afterwards, that is, after Adam's fall, God returned to Heaven; this would have been the moment, where he left a footprint on the Rock. In spite of that, or because of it, Mount Zion still projects into Heaven. This was, of course, derived from the fact that Mount Zion was the place of the temple; the Temple, the 'Holy of Holies', had established the presence of God.

What we have to ask is to what extent these ideas were taken over by Syrian Muslims and how they were transformed in the process. In Muslim tradition, too, we find the statement that the Rock is closest to Heaven, it represents the 'lower throne' of God, under which the entire earth is spread out. Therefore it belongs to Paradise, God sat there after the creation, and from there He returned to Heaven, after forty years, leaving his footprint on the ground. The Rock is also the place where God will be present again for the Last Judgement.

p. 101: There is some reason for assuming that 'Abd al-Malik wanted to renew the Solomonic temple; Priscilla Soucek and Heribert Busse have collected material for such a hypothesis; footnote 73: Soucek (1976), 74-78. Busse stresses the fact that the imitation relates to the entire ensemble on the Haram al-Sharif, not the Dome alone; the Dome and Masjid al-Aqsa form the same axis as the different parts of the church of the Holy Sepulchre (...)." Cf. also: Moshe Sharon, The Birth of Islam in the Holy Land, in: The Holy Land in History and Thought. ed. by Moshe Sharon, Leiden 1988, pp. 228-229.

132 Christoph Luxenberg, Die Neudeutung der arabischen Inschrift im Felsendom zu Jerusalem, op. cit. pp. 126-128.

133 About this cross potent on three steps several interpretations can be found: Transformed Cross potent on three steps, in: Münzen und Medaillen AG, Islamic Coins, Basel 1982, Lot N° 3; Cross with transverse bar omitted, in: Spink

& Son Ltd, (Robert Darley-Doran) Islamic Coins, Zürich 1986, Nos. 55,56; Shaft, or staff, terminating in orb or knob, on four steps. in: George C. Miles, Earliest Arab Gold Coinage, A.N.S. Museum notes 13, New York 1967, p. 212.

134 Philip Grierson has the following to say about this: "The nature of this object is uncertain. It may indeed represent nothing at all, since the main function was negative, that of not being a Cross. Grabar argues that it is a sceptre" (Philip Grierson, The Monetary Reforms of 'Abd al-Malik. Journal of Economic and Social history of the Orient, N° 3, Leiden 1960, p. 194).

135 See the article 'Baitylia' in: Der Kleine Pauly, I., op. cit., pp. 806-807: "The rites of covering this cult object with a cloth are the beginning of its taking an anthropomorphic shape, a process executed via the mythological figures of XAABON (= Arabic ka'ba – cube), the virgin mother of Dusares and Baytulos, the son of Uranus, the brother of El-Kronos." Due to the limited number of known cases we cannot decide whether these clothing rites concerning the omphalos-shaped stone pillar of the sun god of Emesa have been preserved to this day as a fetishist case of litholatry. In former times the Ka'ba used to receive its new cloth, the so-called kiswa [the kiswa is made of black brocade] on the 10th day ('āšūrā') of the month Muḥarram. This is the tenth day of the first month of the year, the Yom Kippur, the day when Solomon's temple was inaugurated. (Heribert Busse, Jerusalem and Mecca, the Temple and the Kaaba. An account of their interrelation in Islamic times. In: The Holy Land in History and Thought, op. cit., p. 240).

136 Sacred stones called "bethel" appear in their Aramaic plural form *bty 'lhya'* in the 8th century BCE in the treaty between Barga'ya of KTB and Mati'el of Arpad (stele II of Sfire near Aleppo, C 1-3. 6 f., 5-10); they have to be regarded as representing the divine guarantors of the treaty, who are mentioned in the inscription on the three steles of Sfire, the *bty 'lhy'* (Carsten Colpe, article Bethel, Der Kleine Pauly, I, op. cit., p. 877).

137 The biblical story of Jacob's Treaty with Laban can be found in Gen 31:43-55: "43. Then Laban replied to Jacob, 'The daughters are my daughters, and the children are my children, and the flocks are my flocks, and all that you see is mine. But what can I do this day to these my daughters or to their children whom they have borne? 44. 'So now come, let us make a covenant, you and I, and let it be a witness between you and me.' 45. Then Jacob took a stone and set it up as a pillar. 46. Jacob said to his kinsmen, 'Gather stones.' So they took stones and made a heap, and they ate there by the heap. 47. Now Laban called it Jegar-sahadutha, but Jacob called it Galeed. 48. Laban said, 'This heap is a witness between you and me this day.' Therefore it was named Galeed, 49. and Mizpah, for he said, 'May the LORD watch between you and me when we are absent one from the other. 50. 'If you mistreat my daughters, or if you take wives besides my daughters, although no man is with us, see, God is witness between you and me.' 51. Laban said to Jacob, 'Behold this heap and behold the pillar which I have set between you and me. 52. 'This heap is a witness, and the pillar is a witness, that I will not pass by this heap to you for harm, and you will not pass by this heap and this pillar to me, for harm. 53. 'The God of Abraham and the God of Nahor, the God of their father, judge between us.' So Jacob swore by the fear of his father Isaac. 54. Then Jacob offered a sacrifice on the mountain, and called his kinsmen to the meal; and they ate the meal and spent the night on the

mountain. 55. Early in the morning Laban arose, and kissed his sons and his daughters and blessed them. Then Laban departed and returned to his place." Martin Buber's German translation is much closer to the Hebrew original. He translates the term *Yəǧar Saḥaḏūṯā* (Jacob's pillar stone of the covenant) as "Schütthauf-Urkund": "... und etwas sei da zu einem Zeugnis zwischen mir und dir. Jaakob nahm einen Stein und richtete ihn als Standmal auf. Und Jaakob sprach zu seinen Brüdern: Leset Steine auf! Sie nahmen Steine und machten einen Wall. Laban rief ihn [Aramäisch] Jegar Sahaduta; Schütthauf-Urkund, aber Jaakob rief ihn Galed: Wall-Zeuge. Laban sprach: Dieser Wall ist Zeuge zwischen mir und dir am heutigen Tag. Darum ruft man seinen Namen Galed. Und Mizpa auch: Wacht, weil er sprach: Wacht halte Er zwischen mir und dir, wenn wir einander verborgen sind: bedrückst du je meine Töchter, nimmst du noch Weiber zu meinen Töchtern...! Sei auch kein Mensch bei uns, sieh, ein Gott ist Zeuge zwischen mir und dir. Und weiter sprach Laban zu Jaakob: Da dieser Wall und da das Standmal, das ich eingesenkt habe zwischen mir und dir – Zeuge sei dieser Wall und Zeugin das Standmal: nicht überschreite ich je diesen Wall zu dir und nicht überschreitest du diesen Wall zu mir und dieses Standmal zum Bösen! Der Gott Abrahams und der Gott Nachors mögen richten zwischen uns, – der Gott ihres Vaters! Jaakob schwur bei dem Schrecken seines Vaters Jizschak. Dann schlachtete Jaakob ein Schlachtmahl auf dem Berg und rief seine Brüder, das Brot zu essen. Sie aßen das Brot und nächtigten auf dem Berg. Frühmorgens machte sich Laban auf, er küßte seine Enkel und seine Töchter und segnete sie, dann ging Laban und kehrte zu seinem Ort zurück."

138 Baldwin's Auction Ltd, Islamic Coin Auction in London, London 2004, N° 3002.

139 Rachel Milstein, A Hoard of Early Arab Figurative Coins, in: Israel Numismatic Journal 10, Jerusalem 1988-69, p. 24, N° 133, Plate 3.

140 J. Walker, Catalogue II., p. 52, N° 140.

141 John Walker, Catalogue II., p. 32, N° 104. This coin is important as it is the first time in the West that in connection with a coin struck for the muḥammad the mint authority is mentioned. It is: "'abdallāh [title of the ruler] 'abd al-malik al-mu'minīn." For stylistic reasons the coin is mostly assigned to the mint 'Ammān (Baldwin's Auction Ltd., Islamic Coin Auction in London N° 9, London 2004, Lot N° 3169: "The first coin has no mint name and has a capital M with the Shahada around. It is attributed to Amman on grounds of style").

142 John Walker, Is the Caliph Bare-Headed on Umaiyad Coins? The Numismatic Chronicle, (London) 1936, pp. 321-323. George C. Miles, Earliest Arab Gold Coinage, A.N.S. Museum Notes N° 13, New York 1967, pp. 217-229.

143 John Walker, Catalogue II., p. 28, N° 92 (Al-Ruhā); this depiction has other interesting details, which can be identified very easily due to the good quality of dye-cutting. The eyes are unnaturally big and circular, which is a hint that they are not supposed to be eyes, but coins lying on the eyelids. This might be an indication that the person depicted is the eschatological Jesus: "But his long hair and beard resemble those of Christ on the Byzantine coin": George C. Miles, Earliest Arab Gold Coinage, op. cit., p. 216, Fn. 36.

144 John Walker, Catalogue II., p.25-26, N° Vat.1, P.8, ANS. 7.

145 John Walker, Catalogue II., p. 25, N° 85: "Very roughly drawn figure of the Caliph in which the head-dress has assumed the appearance of a halo; und p. 25, N° I. 1: Similar halo-type; l. downwards [muhammad/un] (sic)."

146 This can be demonstrated with the help of re-minted coins. "AE Fulus (5), Dimashq (SICA 1: 1706-713). Two with traces of cursive M undertypes (...)" (Baldwin's Auction Ltd, Islamic Coin Auction N° 9, London 2004, Lot N° 3168).

147 J. Walker, Cat. II, pp. 22-25.

148 In the office of Shraga Qedar, Jerusalem, I saw a lead sealing among the purchased objects bearing the inscription: "Arḍ Filasṭīn". For understandable reasons it was not published in Israel. From its fabric it can be inferred that the lead sealing is from the era of 'Abd al-Malik. Again, it is conspicuous that the text follows Hebrew models: "Arḍ Filasṭīn –Ereṣ Yiśra'ēl". Cf. also the parallel forms "elohīm eḥad" and "Allāh aḥad" in Surah 112, instead of the correct Arabic form: *Allāh wāḥid.*

149 Josef van Ess, 'Abd al-Malik and the Dome of the Rock, op. cit., p. 102, footnote 11: "(...) F.E. Peters has launched the interesting hypothesis that Heraclius already thought about building an octagon on the Temple Mount (or even started building it) after the Jews had reappropriated the place for their ritual during the rule of the Persians between 614 and 617 (Peters [1986], 88 and 95)."

150 Enrico Leuthold Jr., Due Rare Testimonianze Della Prima Monetazione Musulmana A Carthagine, Rivista Italiana di Numismatica, Roma 1967, p. 97.

151 A recent overview of the known specimens of this coin from Damascus and its distribution was given by Ludger Ilisch in an auction catalog (Dr. Busso Peus Nachf., catalog 363, Frankfurt 2000, p. 54). The coin from Ḥims from the year 72 of the Arabs has been described in SICA, N° 305. The coin for Ḥims was only struck in the year 72 of the Arabs, the one for Damascus in the years 72, 73 and 74 of the Arabs. Why was the striking of this coin discontinued? For the year 75 we have only got the already mentioned coin from Merw (John Walker, Catalogue I., p. 29, Cam. 1). Why did 'Abd al-Malik have coins struck in Merw in the year 75 of the Arabs? Was he no longer perceived as the New Joshua? Was he "stabbed in the back" in the East, because his notion of an apocalypse for the year 77 of the Arabs was no longer accepted?

152 Cécile Morrison, Catalogue des monnaies byzantines, op. cit., p. 272.

153 Cécile Morrison, Catalogue des monnaies byzantines, op. cit., p. 458.

154 Una miliaresia die Leone III con Constantino V coniata su un dirham umayyade di Wasit del 93 H. / 712 A.D. (Enrico Leuthold Jr., Milaresie Bizantine e Dirham Arabi, Milano 2005, p.10.11).

155 "Instant sur les pratiques destinées à mettre en valeur le dogme de l'Incarnation, le concile interdit la représentation ancienne et symbolique de l'Agneau au profit de celle du Christ sous forme humaine ..." (Cécile Morrison, Catalogue des monnaies Byzantines, op. cit., p. 397.398, mentions the decisions of the synod about this matter; for further information: Mansi XI, 977-980, trad. P.-P. Johannou, Les canons des conciles oecuméniques (Fonti, IX), Grottaferrata 1962, p. 219-220).

156 Georg Ostrogorsky, Geschichte des Byzantinischen Staates, op. cit., 113: "At the end of the year 695 a rebellion started against the government of Justinian II, and the Blue [charioteers] faction appointed the strategos of the Helladic theme Leontios as the new emperor. While the two main supporters of Justinian, the

sakellarios Stephanos and the logothete Theodotos were lynched by an angry mob, Justinian's nose was cut off. The dethroned emperor was sent to Cherson, where Pope Martin had once been in exile until his death."

157 This is why all non-imperial coins of the Ostrogoths in Italy and those of the Franks and other successors in the West are just imitative of imperial coins of varying fineness.

158 George C. Miles, Earliest Arab Gold Coinage, op. cit., p. 212. Miles knew about a specimen of this kind (National Museum of Pakistan [NM 1957, 1036]).

159 SICA, N° 343.

160 Carl Salemann, Über eine Pehlevisch-Arabische Münze. ZDMG, Leipzig 1879, p. 511. We read: "Although first published by Thomas in 1850 and correctly transliterated by Saleman in 1879, Walker (1941) regarded the coin as unread. [This is obviously wrong. As this coin was inaccessible to Walker, he summarized the description of Andreas Mordtmann, published in an article (ZDMG, 1880, S.155). Apart from the coin N° M. 53 of the year 69 of the Arabs from Ardashir-Khurra, Walker adduces another specimen of the year 75 of the Arabs from the same mint (N° T.18). After publication, this coin is also quoted by Thomas in the Journal of the Royal Asiatic Society, London 1850, p. 320]. However, it was Gaube (1973) who first supplied the correct interpretation of the legend, namely a Persian translation of the Arabic marginal legend." (SICA, p. 30-31). Already Carl Salemann had understood that it was a bilingual coin. Heinz Gaube (Heinz Gaube, Arabosasanidische Numismatik, op. cit., p. 78-79) summarizes the scholarly performance ascribed to Salemann as follows: "Even if all this should be due to coincidence, it will still be next to impossible to find anyone who could assign a plausible Arabic-Islamic meaning to this name. Therefore Salemann's explanation (without Mordtmann's suggestions for improvement, Z.D.M.G. 1880, 155) seems to be the most perspicuous and paleographically soundest, as our material evidence proves. Salemann reads the inscription as follows (we will retain his transliteration, but for technical reasons will replace Hebrew letters by Latin equivalents): (...)." Salemann had read and transliterated the Middle Persian inscription as "Book Pehlevi", i.e., according to the Iranist usage of the 1920s and 30s in Germany he had transliterated the text with the help of Hebrew letters and transposed it into Modern Persian. The Middle Persian "DARWBR" was thus rendered as Modern Persian "dawar". It seems hardly possible to see a real progress in Heinz Gaube's treatment of the inscription. Replacing the Hebrew letters, which do not need diacritics and are next to perfect equivalents of the Aramaic-Middle Persian originals is hardly a value added.

161 Heinz Gaube, Arabosasanidische Numismatik, op. cit., p. 35

162 Heinz Gaube, Arabosasanidische Numismatik, op. cit., p. 79

163 "El, (...)West Semitic divine appellative (...) < Protosemit. 'ilu – deus', (...); unlike Baal not linked to local or gentile qualifications, therefore an apt term to adopt Universalist notions of a highest god. (...) There are no traces of a Protosemitic E.-monotheism in the Old Testament (...), but there are indications of a pre-Mosaic henotheist E.-religion of the Hebrew patriarchs, which developed on

Canaanite soil (...), which is reflected in perfection in the phrase "E. Elyon, God Most High" for the God of Melchizedek of Salem (Gen. 14:18; 2:1 f.) (...). As an individual god next to others E. appears on Aramaic inscriptions from Sam'al and Sushin (...). In Ugaritic mythology he is accordingly the father of the gods ('b bn 'l)" (Der Kleine Pauly, op. cit., p. 226-7).

164 See: "'Ali b. ibn Ṭālib", L. Veccia Vaglieri, Artikel "Alī b. Abī Ṭālib', EI², I/ 384: "The phrase implied that it was absolutely improper to apply to men for a decision since, for the case in dispute, there existed a divine ordinance in the Kur'anic verse xlix, 8/9: (...)."

165 see also: L. Veccia Vaglieri, article 'Harūrā", EI², III/ p. 235-6.

166 Julius Wellhausen, Die Religiös-Politischen Oppositionsparteien im alten Islam, Berlin 1901, p. 4.

167 Ernst Horst, Segensreiche Sonne unseres Seins. Nachahmung oder Vollzug? – Zwei Wege der Mohammed-Nachfolge. Frankfurter Allgemeine Zeitung, 11th May, 2006, N° 109, p. 44: "Even the source of ingenious thoughts was a son of practical constraints. In a public presentation of the "Historisches Kolleg", Tilman Nagel explains how Muslim memory helped to solve contradictions concerning the prophet. (...) He said that he was working on his 'opus magnum', a biography of the Prophet Mohammed (F.A.Z., 24 February, 2006). Last October Nagel complained in a talk at the Hans-Seidel foundation: 'For years I have been appalled and bitter because of the missing willingness to deal with Islamic thought and Islamic culture in a serious, i.e., laborious manner.' It remains unclear what he intends to say with this statement. Does he mean we in the West should investigate Islam because it is a fascinating topic, worthy of being researched, or do we have to study to save our skin? Maybe both interpretations might contain a grain of truth. (...) The main source used in Europe for the life of Muḥammad is the biography of Ibn Isḥāq (died 768), which, however, was later revised. Here it is concealed – in the spirit of 'imitators' – that there are many notions, e.g. monotheism that the Prophet developed only gradually and did not receive from Allāh, but from other people [the actual conflict was rather between Christians and Zurvanists in the Iran of the 9th century. The Old Iranian Prophet in a new Arabic guise took over monotheism from Iranian Christians; *author's note*] In the Islamic world the main source of information about the prophet is the 'Book of Healing via Declaration of Rights of the Chosen one (sic) of *Ijad al-Jahsubi* ['Iyāḍ al-Yahṣubī] (died 1148/9). Nagel calls it the 'most read book of reference of the widespread Muslim refusal to break free from their iron cage of purportedly eternal truths and to enter a dialogue with other civilizations of the world as between equals.' For al-Jahsubi any doubt that Mohammed is competent for everything is even more condemnable than apostasy and should be punished by death accordingly. In one place he writes: 'Do not consider what you find in the books of some ignorant historians or exegetes of the Koran!' It has to be feared that Tilman Nagel's book about the prophet will suffer exactly this fate."

168 EI, vol. 4, p. 752 f.

169 The coin can be seen on the internet:
http://www.islamic-awareness.org/History/Islam/Coins/drachm8.html
The interpretation there is as follows: Arab-Sassanian coin of the Kharijite rebel Qatarī ibn al-Fujā'a, frozen in the year 75 AH. Date: 75 AH / 694-695 CE.

Contents: Obverse field: Typical late Arab-Sassanian bust. Obverse margin: *lā ḥukm illā lillāh* ("Judgement belongs to God alone"). Reverse field: Typical Arab-Sassanian fire-altar with attendants with mint (Ardashir Khurra). Comments: Weight = 4.08 gms; Walker has shown that the earliest coin of Qatarī ibn al-Fujā'a bearing the typical Kharijite slogan *lā ḥukm illā lillāh* comes from the year 69 AH / 688-689 CE and is prefixed with bism Allāh.[J. Walker, A Catalogue Of The Muhammadan Coins In The British Museum, 1941, Volume I - Arab-Sassanian Coins, British Museum: London, pp. 112-113.] And written in Persian: "Servant of God, Ktri, commander of the faithful". Further, this slogan is clearly reminiscent of the Qur'anic phrase *ini'l (sic) ḥukmu illā lillāh* [Qur'an 12:40, 12:67 and 6:57].[L. Treadwell, "Qur'anic Inscriptions On The Coins Of The Ahl Al-Bayt From The Second To Fourth Century AH", Journal Of Qur'anic Studies, 2012, Volume 14, p. 49.] (access 13 June, 2013).

170 Spink Coin Auction in association with Christie's, London, 12 Oct., 1993, Lot N° 523. The text of the inscription in the field of the coin is revealing in many ways. The ruler is mentioned as: "*'Abdallāh 'abd al-malik amīr al-mu'minīn*". Like in the case of the inscription in Gadara/Hammat Gader, where Mu'āwiya is mentioned, this is an indication that "'abdallāh" is the title of the ruler. The title "amīr al-mu'minīn" only points to the function of the ruler. In the inscription, 'Abd al-Malik's son, al-Walīd, is called "al-amīr al-Walīd bn amīr al-mu'minīn". The words "caliph" or "caliphate" do not appear at all. To claim that the title "amīr al-mu'minīn" was the title of the caliph has no historical basis. In the text of the inscription al-Walīd is designated as the heir apparent/successor. It seems to be the first mention of an heir apparent since the autonomy of the Arabs was founded in the year 20 of the Arabs (641 CE, the year of Heraclius' death).

171 The person in charge of the catalog of the auction house Spink, London, 12 October, 1993, Lot 523, renders the inscription in transliteration as follows: obv. field: "Bismillah al-Rah/ man al-Rahim amr/ 'Abdallah 'Abd al-Malik A/ mir al-Mu'minin bi'l -/ wafa hadha Amir / saba, rev. field: ahda bihi a/ l-Amir al-Walid / bin Amir al-Mu'minin/ sanata ahda Wa / thamanin, (...)."

172 T. Goodwin, A remarkable Standing Caliph fals. ONS Newsletter N° 151, London 1997, p. 5.

173 Koran 2: 256.

174 Volkmar Enderlein, Islamische Kunst, Dresden 1990, 30. Art historians have no explanation for this, as they cannot infer from Islamic history that it was the Persian 'Arabī/Arabs who built the castles. They think a man called Marwān was the ancestor of the dynasty of the castle owners. This man is then said to have been a Meccan, an Islamic Qurayš and cousin of 'Uṯmān, caliph and alleged editor of the Qur'ān. He is said to have been born in the year 2 or 4 of the hijra of the Prophet of the Arabs. (In this system of religious history prime numbers were reserved for the life data of important personalities. To adduce an example: The caliph Abū Bakr assumed office in the year 11 of the hijra, the caliph 'Umar in the year 13 of the hijra. With 'Alī, the prophet's son-in-law, it is the year 35 – the prime numbers 5 and 7 multiplied.) He helped the caliph 'Uṯmān with the redaction of the Qur'ān, as traditional literature tells us. The life of a supporter of

the caliph 'Umar – a position not important enough – is of course not linked to a prime number. At the end of his life he became rich seizing spoils in North Africa. For further information see also: C.E. Bosworth, article 'Marwan', EI^2, VI, p. 621. As the "Meccan" Marwān, like the "Meccan" Mu'āwiya, only appears in Islamic traditional literature, it seems justified to assume that the notion of the traditional account that there was a Sufyanid and a Marwanid branch of the Umayyad dynasty is just a later construction, which tries to link every historical event to a sacred prehistoric eon in Mecca. This period ended with the death of the son-in-law of the Prophet of the Arabs, 'Alī, in the year 40 of the hijra. After this "sacred eon" in the desert of Mecca the historical period beginning with the appointment of Mu'āwiya as the "amīr al-mu'minīn" in Darabjird in the year 41 of the Arabs follows. Therefore, the "desert castles" are not a Meccan "mirage", but walled Persian Paradisiac little gardens in the desert.

175 The seemingly continuing use – or re-use of Middle Persian inscriptions on the coins of al-Ḥağğāğ in Iraq after the year 77 of the Arabs concerns the year 79 of the Arabs in Bishāpūr (J. Walker, Catalogue I, p. 119, Th.16). However, there are an Arabic and a Persian coin from this mint of this same year. The Middle Persian inscription provides the Persian name of al-Ḥağğāğ, which casts doubts on his origin from the Arabian Peninsula. In coin inscriptions he appears as "Haqqaq Josephson" (HAKAK-i YUSFA(N).

176 Jaakko-Hämeen-Antilla, John the Baptist and early Islamic polemics concerning Jesus. Acta Orientalia 60, 72-67, (Lund) 1999, pp.72-87.

177 Frankfurt Allgemeine Sonntagszeitung, 16 April, 2006, N° 15, p. V1.

178 "'Abd al-Malik and Hajjaj bulk less largely in the historical memory of the west than do Muhammad and Charlemagne, but the coinage reform which they carried out in the Islamic empire may well have been of decisive importance in the transition from the world of the Arabian prophet to that of the restorer of the empire in the west." (Philip Grierson, The Monetary Reforms of 'Abd al-Malik, op. cit., p. 264)

179 The treasure of Spilling on Gotland of the year 1999 contains one specimen. Four more specimens had been known before. The correspondent of the "Frankfurter Allgemeine Zeitung", v. Lucius, reported about the find on the 4th of September 2003 under the headline: "Persian Coins on Gotland".

180 R. Paret, Der Koran, op. cit., 38.

181 In general, the term "Dēn/Dīn" is rendered as "faith" or "religion", according to the interpretation of the translator. As it is generally assumed that the Qur'ān is the revelation of the Prophet of the Arabs, which originated in Mecca and Medina on the Arabian Peninsula, the term sometimes has to be translated as "religion". Thus, the New Testament concept of the "faith of Abraham" (Dēn/Dīn Ibrāhīm) becomes the "religion of Abraham". "The faith of Abraham is often praised in the New Testament (Rom. 4:9; 16; Hebr. 11:8; 17; Gal. 3:6; James 2:23)" (H. Speyer, Die biblischen Erzählungen im Qoran, op. cit., 174).

182 About this question also see bilingual inscriptions (Latin/Arabic) from North Africa dated the year 97 of the Arabs (698 CE) in: J. Walker, Catalogue II., p. 78, no. 184. About Sulaymān as the earliest candidate for the office of the Mahdī: "Among the Umayyad caliphs, Sulaymān (96-9/ 715-17) seems to have been the first one to have encouraged the belief that he was the Mahdī who would restore

justice after oppression had become widespread under his predecessors" (Wilferd Madelung, article: "Mahdī", EI², V/1231).

183 At the time of the rule of 'Abd al-Malik the concept of Jesus as the "muḥammad" was not mentioned in the inscriptions on coins from North Africa.

184 "Den is not only divine wisdom but also its emanation as innate human wisdom (asn-xrad), a principle with far-reaching implications, for all beneficial knowledge thus of necessity falls within the compass of den" (Enc. Ir. article "Dēn", p. 279).

185 John Walker, Catalogue II, op. cit., p. 280 and footnote N° 4.

186 About this question see also the lead sealing with his name and the designation of his rule as caliphate: Christie's, London, 16 Oct, 2001, Lot 263, N° 12.

187 Islam Ansiklopedisi, Istanbul 1966, vol. X, pp. 621-640; the Arabic word sikka, with the Italian form "secchino" as a mediator, was adopted into English as "sequin".

188 Dirham of Harūn al-Rašīd ("Aaron the guided one/guiding one") of the year 181 of the Arabs. Morton & Eden, London 2006, Catalogue N° 18, N° 31.

189 "Arian debate", the first important doctrinal debate, which agitates the whole Roman Empire for half a century. (...) The presbyter Arius, educated in Antioch, who had triggered the debate, opposed his bishop Alexander, who considered the son as begot by the father since eternity and thus equal to the father in every aspect, and taught since 313 that the son was created by the father after the creation of time, thus being similar to the father, but nevertheless changing, a creature of God, a kind of being between deity and mankind." (Meyers Konversations-Lexicon, 4th ed., Leipzig 1885, I., p. 805).

190 "Adoptianism, doctrine of Elipandus, archbishop of Toledo, and of Felix, bishop of Urgelles (died 818), according to which Christ was indeed the true son of God due to his divine nature, but according to his human nature was only adopted as the son of God. The originators of this doctrine had the purpose in mind to oppose Moorish arguments against their doctrine, which was immediately banned by the Frankish Church under Charlemagne and oppressed" (Meyers Konversations-Lexicon, 4th ed., Leipzig 1885, I., p. 130).

191 "And Sulaymân, what was Sulaymān?! His concern was his belly and his private parts" – utterances ascribed to the Kharijite rebels in the Ḥiǧāz, Abū Hamza (P. Crone, God's Caliph, op. cit., p. 130).

192 P. Crone, God's Caliph, op. cit., p. 130.

193 The type of probably fictitious Umayyad caliph 'Umar belongs to the personnel of religious history of the 9th century CE. The apocalyptic aspects of the concept of the coming of the Mahdī are underlined by quotations, according to which both Jewish rabbis and Christian priests had foretold the caliphate of the Mahdī (al-Farazdaq, Diwan, 327). "We do not know him to be anyone but 'Umar b. 'Abd al-'Aziz" (Ibn Sa'd, v. 245). (Wilferd Madelung, article "Mahdi", EI², V/p. 1241).

194 G. Rotter, Die Umayyaden und der zweite Bürgerkrieg (680-692), Wiesbaden 1982, p. 197.

195 See Wilferd Madelung, article "Mahdī", EI. V/1230: "Al-Mahdī(A.), 'the rightly guided one' is the name of the restorer of religion and justice who, according to a widely held Muslim belief, will rule before the end of the world." About 'Umar as the Mahdī see in the same article, EI. V/ p. 1231-1232. The notion that 'Umar is the Mahdī was not universally shared. A Chorasanian who died in 125 CE of the Hijra is said to have rejected 'Umar, as his behavior did not match that of the Mahdī: "...rejected the view that 'Umar II was the Mahdī, stating that the Mahdī would do something 'Umar II had not done: he would refuse money returned to the treasury by someone who, after requesting it, found that he had no need of it."

196 J. Walker, Catalogue II, p. 260-261, Nos. 880-882.

197 See Wilferd Madelung, article 'Mahdî', EI²V/1234: "Matters will only grow in hardship, the world will only increase in backward movement, and the people in greed. The Hour will raise in the worst of the people. There will be no Mahdī but 'Isā bn Maryam".

198 R. Ghyselen, Arab-Sasanian Copper Coinage, op. cit., p.73.

199 "It seems more appropriate to interpret the word *manṣūr* in terms of propaganda. (...) However one may ask why, if *manṣūr* is not a proper name, there was any need to transcribe the Arabic word in Pahlavi on the same coin on which the Arabic word was already mentioned when it was so easy to give the Iranian equivalent, *peroz*, in Pahlavi. (...) The fact remains that all the Arab-Sasanian copper coins with the word *manṣūr* were struck in Istakhr, which may have been the stronghold of 'Abd al-Rahman ibn Muḥammad in the first years of the 80's." (R. Ghyselen, Arab-Sasanian Copper Coinage, op. cit., p. 73-74). The explanation of this phenomenon is pretty easy. The term *manṣūr* is a word from the language of the 'Arabī/Arabs. They were adherents of a special kind of Christology, which designated Jesus as *manṣūr*. For the Iranian public this Christological term was written in Pehlevi script and appeared to the Persians as an ideogram which stands for the apocalyptic Jesus.

200 The predicate *manṣūr* on silver coins of Ḥağğāğ bn Yūsuf in Yāzd of the year 81 of the Arabs, SICA 493; and on silver coins of 'Abd al-Raḥmān bn Muḥammad from Istakhr (Persepolis). To be found with a picture in the catalog of Baldwin's Auctions "Islamic Coin Auction 10", London 2005, Lot N° 18. About the use of messianic names of rulers in the 2nd century of the Arabs it has to be noted that at that time the notion of a "last emperor" was still current – in this case a "last caliph" – who will hand over rule to 'Īsā bn Maryam.

201 Here, Christ appears in the role of a divine warrior. The killing of enemies is a widespread messianic motive deriving from Is. 11:4; see als Apoc. 19:15; 4 Esra 13:10-27. (M. Henze, Syrische Danielapokalypse, Jüdische Schriften aus hellenistisch-römischer Zeit, N.F. 1,4, Gütersloh 2006, p. 61-62 a. footnote).

202 SyrDan. 29, ed. M. Henze, p. 60.

203 A.R. Anderson, Alexander's Gate, Gog and Magog, and the Enclosed Nations, Cambridge 1932, p. 16. G.J. Reinink dealt with the dating of Pseudo-Ephrem and comes to the following conclusion: "Seen in the light of Syriac apocalypses, which originated towards the end of the century, the end of the reign of Mu'āwiya I (680) or possibly of his son Yazīd I (683) mark the *terminus ante quem* for the composition of Pseudo-Ephrem's *memra*. In any case it must be considered very likely that this work is one of the earliest known examples of a

text originating in a Jacobite milieu, in which the Arabic conquests are interpreted from an eschatological perspective. The *memra*, however, has a didactive objective and the author aims at informing his "listeners" about how to behave during the far-reaching changes of their time (G.J. Reinink, Pseudo-Ephraems "Rede über das Ende" und die Syrische Eschatologische Literatur des Siebten Jahrhunderts"(ARAM 5:1&2, Oxford 1993, p. 462).

204 "So we come to the conclusion that syrDan was not influenced by Pseudo-Methodius. In the light of the enormous popularity of Pseudo-Methodius and his influence on later apocalyptical literature this can best be explained by the fact that the text was written before the 7th century, i.e., before the emergence of Pseudo-Methodius and its author can thus not have been familiar with the legends and exegetical issues of that text. How much earlier syrDan had been composed can hardly be inferred, the more so as there are only very limited indications. Klaus Berg suggested the 4th century for the time when the 'Young Daniel' was written. Similarly, we can assume a time of origin for syrDan in the 4th or 5th century." (M. Henze, Syrische Danielapokalypse, op. cit., 20. see also p. 6, there an indication can be found for the effects of the apocalypse in later times: D.B. Cook, An Early Muslim Daniel Apokalypse, Arabica 49, 2000, pp. 55-96).

205 Spink Coin Auction in association with Christie's, London 12, October 1993, Lot 523.

206 R. Ghyselen, Arab-Sasanian Copper Coinage, p. 30: "Another series, typologically very close to the former, features the word Farroxzad without patronym (type 16). The word can be understood as an epithet 'Born bestowed with (divine) glory', but also as a proper name." Moreover, Rika Gyselen points out that the inscription can be found on different types of copper coins, which cannot be ascribed to one minting authority, among other reasons because of their dating.

207 See Wilferd Madelung, article "Mahdī", EI^2,V/1233: "...there will be from us the Saffāḥ, the Manṣūr and the Mahdī who will hand it (sc. the caliphate) over to 'Īsā b. Maryam". This view of the caliph as "last emperor" is evidence for the lasting effect of Syrian apocalyptic notions.

208 G. Ostrogorski, Geschichte des byzantinischen Staates, op. cit., p. 125.

209 G. Ostrogorski, Geschichte des byzantinischen Staates, op. cit., p. 126.

210 Not only the depictions of the two sieges of Constantinople by the "Arabs" are similar, but also the understanding of these sieges as part of the apocalyptic event. See also: G. R. Reinink, Heraclius, the New Alexander, Apocalyptic Prophecies during the reign of Heraclius. In: The reign of Heraclius (610-641), op. cit., p. 82, footnote 10: "For 'conclusive evidence' regarding the empire's inhabitants interpreting events in apocalyptic terms, see Kaegi, 'Variable Rates', p.194, who points to the Pseudo-Daniel vision published by Berger (Die griechische Daniel-Diegese), which was written directly before the siege of Constantinople by the Arabs in 717/718 (cf. Winkelmann and Brandes, Quellen, pp. 317-318)."

211 The activities of the mint in al-Bab (Derbend) in the years 93, 114, 115, 117, 118, 119, 120, 121, 122, 123, 124, 125, 126 and 128 of the Arabs might be connected to the attempt of the Arab Empire to fend off the Chazars. The attack on Constantinople of the year 717-718 CE takes place in the years 95-96 of the Arabs. (M. G. Klat, Catalogue of the Post-Reform Dirhams. The Ummayad Dynasty, London 2002, p. 74-78). About the wall between the Caspian Sea and the Caucasus we read: "Derbent, seaport in Dagestan. ASSR, Russian Fed., at the Caspian Sea, (...). – in the 5th century a wall of a length of appr. 3 km (some ruins extant) stretched from the citadel Naryn-Klae to the sea." (Der Grosse Brockhaus, Wiesbaden 1984, V, 61).

212 G. Ostrogorski, Die Geschichte des byzantinischen Staates, op. cit., p. 118: "The Late Roman Empire is then replaced by the Byzantine Empire in the actual sense, which gives it a mystical-ascetic trait. The emperors themselves are mystics, the "liberator of the Holy Land", Herakleios, the "Lustre of Orthodoxy" Constantine, the "Servant of Christ" Justinian. (...) It is an empire of warriors and monks."

213 G.J. Reinink, Heraclius, the New Alexander, Apocalyptic Prophecies during the reign of Heraclius., The Reign of Heraclius, op. cit., p. 83, footnote 15: "By 'imperial eschatology' we understand the already ancient Christian idea that the Roman empire is the fourth empire in the Book of Daniel, which, as the 'withholding power' (2 Thes. 2:7), would last until the advent of Antichrist; cf. Podskalsy, Byzantinische Reichseschatologie, p. 55, note 332."

214 J. Walker, Catalogue II, pp. 32-40.). 'Abd al-Malik behaves like the collector of sacred districts. In all of them the messianic messenge of his movement must be proclaimed. The function of coins as means of propaganda is old.

215 Amikam Elad, Why did 'Abd al-Malik build the Dome of the Rock? A Re-examination of the Muslim Sources, Bayt al-Maqdis, Jerusalem and early Islam, ed. by Jeremy Johns. Oxford 1999, p. 34: "According to al-Wāqidi, the reason for its construction was that ['Abd Allah] ibn al-Zubayr had then taken control (...) of Mecca and, during the season of the hajj, he used to catalogue the vices of the Marwanid family, and to summon (the people) to pay homage (...) to him (as caliph). He was eloquent, and so the people inclined towards him. 'Abd al-Malik, therefore, prevented the people from performing the (...) hajj. (...) This became known to 'Abd al-Malik and he therefore prevented the (...) people from performing the hajj. The people remained in the situation for a while, [and then] became agitated and raised a clamor. He therefore built for them the Dome over the Rock and the [Friday]Mosque of (...) al-Aqsa in order to divert their attention from the hajj. They used to stand by the Rock and circumambulate (...) it as they used to circumambulate the Ka'ba, and slaughter [beasts] on the day of the feast (...)." The circumambulation of churches is an old custom, like the sacrifice of a lamb, which is slaughtered by the pilgrims and eaten. This tradition of the old Syrian church is still alive in the Caucasus, in Georgia at the Kazbek.

216 P. Crone, The First-Century Concept of the Hijra, Arabica, (Leiden) 1994, p. 355: "The most striking characteristics of emigrants in the Qur'ān is their association with holy war. Rewards are held out to 'those who emigrated... and fought and were slain' (3:194), 'those who emigrated and were slain and died' (22:57), 'those who believe and have emigrated and struggled with their possessions and their selves in the way of God' (8:71/73, 9:19/20), 'those who believe and have emigrated and struggle in the way of God' (8: 73/75), 'those

who have believed afterwards and emigrated, and struggled with you' (8:74/76), 'those who emigrated after persecution, then struggled and endured' (16: 109/111) (...)."

217 J. Walker, Catalogue II, p. 253, N° P.130.

218 J. Walker, Catalogue II, p. xxix: "Besides the Khutba there was another of the prerogatives of sovereignty that the Caliphs were careful to maintain, namely the Sikka, or 'coinage', which implied the control of the minting of gold and silver coins, especially the former. " If we follow this concept of the execution of the *sikka* by the ruler, then we have any right to ask how it could be that anonymous gold and silver coins were struck. As we have seen, the title "caliph" was not yet in use at that time. In the year 127 of the Arabs the first mention of the "caliphate" (regency) is attested. The title "imām" is not found in inscriptions of the first century of the Arabs. For the time of the Umayyads it is only assumed in the traditional historiographical literature.

219 Christie's, London, Islamic Art and Manuscripts, 16 October, 2001, p. 134, Lot 263, N° 2.

220 His place in traditional historiography is probably based on the depiction of his life style, which is contrasted against that of his predecessors. The entire depiction of the era of the Umayyads in the traditional account displays a repertoire of literary topoi. Abū Hamza has the following to say about this "caliph": "Then there took charge after him Yazīd b 'Abd al-Malik, a sinner in whom right judgement was not perceived. (...). Then he sat Habāba on his right and Sallāma on his left and said, 'Sing to me, Habāba, give me to drink, Sallāma'. Then, when he had become drunk and the wine had taken a hold on him, (...). Then he turned to one [of the] girls and said, 'Surely I shall fly!' " (P. Crone, God's Caliph, op. cit. , p. 131).

221 J. Walker, Catalogue II, p. 262, B. 50.

222 Christie's London, Islamic Art and Manuscripts, 16 October 2001, p. 134, N° 263, Lot 12. In an inscription there 'Utmān bn al-Walīd is mentioned.

223 Christie's London, Islamic Art and Manuscripts, 16 October, 2001, p. 134, Lot 263, N° 11, N°12.

224 J. Wellhausen, Das Arabische Reich, Berlin 1902, p. 234-235 (*my translation from the German*): "He set the other captives free and gave them presents; but before, they had to pay hommage to the two sons of Valid, who were incarcerated in Damascus. Marwan was intelligent enough not to appear under his own name, but as advocate of the heirs of Valid II. This cost the lives of the latter, as they were in the hands of their enemies."

225 J. Walker, Catalogue II, p. 260-261, Nos. 880-882, concerns the years 101-116 of the Arabs. In Kufa the desire for "justice" is expressed in inscriptions of all of the years 100-126 of the Arabs. A "microscopic" reading of the epigraphic material might yield considerable information about the social history of the time, on condition that one is ready to read "what is really in the inscription", instead of squeezing it into the Bed of Procrustes of the traditional account.

226 J. Walker, Catalogue II, pp. 227 f; 230; 275.

227 Dēn (…) Modern Persian Dīn, theological and metaphysical term with a variety of meanings: "the sum of man's spiritual attributes and individuality, vision, inner self, conscience, religion." (...) Royalty (xwadāyīh) is founded on the religion, and the religion on royalty and the exaltation of Iranian royalty (ērīh xwadāyīh) cannot be separated from the submission to the Mazdean religion (Denkard, ed Madan, I, p. 47, de Menasce, 1973, p. 65) (Mansour Shaki, article "Daena" Eir, II, p. 279). Cf. also the Modern Persian meaning of "xwadāyīh": "Godship, divinity, divine, an object of worship; the honor due to God". (F. Steingass, Persian-Englisch Dictionary, London 1892, entry: "ḫudā'ī").

228 x^varənah (Avestan) – "glory, splendor"; light-like anthropological-cosmological principle; important for the legitimation of the ruler; Middle Persian xvarrah, Greek tychē, Latin fortuna, Syriac gada; about this question see: Michael Stausberg, die Religion Zarathushtras. Stuttgart 2002, I, p. 480.

229 S. Moscati, article Abū Muslim', EI^2 I/141, "Abu Muslim, leader of the revolutionary 'Abbasid movement in Khurasan. He was of obscure antecedents, probably a slave of Persian origin."

230 C. Wurtzel, The Coinage of the Revolutionaries in the Late Umayyad Period, ANS Museum Notes 23, New York 1878, p. 192, no. 36.

231 About the term "Āl" see EI^2/345, "ĀL".

232 " Muslim" (A.) – participle IV von *s-l-m*, designates an adherent of Islam; Handwörterbuch des Islam, op. cit., p. 550.

233 C. Wurtzel, The Coinage of the Revolutionaries in the Late Umayyad Age, op. cit., p. 192, N° 37.

234 C. Wurtzel, The coinage of the Revolutionaries in the Late Umayyad Age, op. cit., p. 153, N° 38.

235 B. Carra de Vaux [L. Gardet], article "Basmala", EI^2 I/1085: "whatever is said in the Kur'an about al-Rahman is said elsewhere about Allah (Jomier, 370)."

236 About the veneration of St. Sergius by Ḵosrow II see: G. Wiessner, Christlicher Heiligenkult im Umkreis eines Sassanianischen Großkönigs. In: Festgabe deutscher Iranisten zur 2500 Jahrfeier Irans, ed. by W. Eilers, Stuttgart 1971, pp. 141-156.

237 Cf. C.-P. Haase, article "Ruṣāfa", EI^2, VIII/ p. 630-631.

238 Y. Nevo und J. Koren, Crossroads to Islam, op. cit., p. 410.

239 G. Wiessner, Christlicher Heiligenkult im Umkreis eines Sassanianischen Großkönigs, op. cit., p. 149.

240 G. Wiessner, Christlicher Heiligenkult im Umkreis eines Sassanianischen Großkönigs. Op. cit., p. 149.

241 G. Wiessner, christlicher Heiligenkult im Umkreis eines Sassanianischen Großkönigs, op. cit., p. 150-154.

242 In "Operation of the mint at Jarash in the jund al-Urdunn", Alan Walmsley, who has excavated at both Jarash and Pella, gave a summary of recent work at Jarash. The prosperity of the region in late antiquity was firmly based on agriculture and it is now clear that this prosperity continued throughout the Umayyad period. The remains of 23 churches have now been uncovered by the site, many containing elaborate mosaic floors damaged by Christian iconoclasts in the eighth century" (ONS Newsletter N° 174, London 2003, p. 3).

243 G. Ostrogorski, op. cit., p. 123.

244 G. Ostrogorski, Die Geschichte des byzantinischen Staates, op. cit., p. 180. See also footnote N° 5: "Mansi 12, 975 (= Caspar, Zeitschr. F. Kirchengesch. 52, 85, line 382)."

245 E. Leuthold, Milaresie Bizantine e Dirham Arabi, Milano 2005, p. 11-12.

246 G. Ostrogorski, Geschichte des byzantinischen Staates, op. cit., p. 130.

247 G. Ostrogorski, Geschichte des byzantinischen Staates, op. cit., p. 170.

248 Wilferd Madelung, article "Al-Mahdī", EI², V/ p. 1235.

249 A dirham from Ifriqiya of the year 137 of the Arabs, see: Sotheby's London, Coins, Medals and Banknotes,2 &3 May 2001, Lot N° 912. The coin from Gharshistān was first described in 1894 (O. Codrington, Numismatic Chronicle, London 1894, p. 88). More recent findings are attested. Baldwin Auctions Ltd and Arabian Coins and Medals (LLC), Islamic Coin Auction 10, London 2005, Lot 56 (with pictures): "This is the only recorded issue from the mint of Gharshistan, a district in northwest Afghanistan, around the headwaters of the Murghab in the Harat division of Khurasan."

250 "Say (O Muhammad, unto mankind): I ask of you no fee therefor, save loving kindness among kinsfolk." (surah 42:23). This motto is also found on the copper coin of Ḫālid bn Ibrāhīm of the year 138 of the Arabs, see C. Wurtzel, The Coinage of the Revolutionaries in the Late Umayyad Period, op. cit., p. 196, N° 46. The use of the term "muslim" as a personal name can be found on inscriptions of the 2nd century of the Arabs. A man called Muslim (bn ʿArrāf) is attested on Egyptian weights and measures of the year 119 of the Arabs. (Paul Balog, Umayyad, ʿAbbasid and Tulunid Glass Weights and Vessel Stamps, The American Numismatic Society, New York, 1976, p. 319, 321).

251 The connection of the "family" of ʿAbd al-Malik and the distribution of the notion of Jesus as the *muḥammad* in Syria in the time after 681 CE has been re-interpreted by the traditional account as follows: "He [al-Muhallabī] ends his report by saying that no one in Syria had ever doubted that the Banū Umayya were the sole relatives of the Prophet. In this context it is worth noting the report that, immediately after the ʿAbbasids victory, a delegation of Syrian notables visited the first ʿAbbasid caliph, Abū l-ʿAbbās al- Saffāḥ, and swore that they had been unaware that the Prophet had any other relatives or family worthy of succeeding him except the Umayyads, until after the ʿAbbasids had seized power" (Amikam Elad, Why did ʿAbd al-Malik build the Dome of the Rock? op. cit., p. 45).

252 R.C. Zaehner, Zurvan, op. cit., p. 336.

253 C. Wurtzel, The Coinage of the Revolutionaries in the Late Umayyad Period, op. cit., p. 186, N° 30.

254 SICA, p.343-345.

255 Baldwin's Auction Ltd and Arabian Coins and Medals (LLC), Islamic Coin Auction in London N° 9, London 2004, Lot 3172: "Anonymous Drachm, GRM-KR-MAN (unidentified mint in Kirman province) 70h, obv. Pahlavi legend MHMT PGTAMI Y DAT (Muhammad is the messenger of God) in place of governor's name, bism allāh walī al-amr in margin, 3,93g (Walker-, SICA-, Gaube-) (...). See the article "An Interesting Arab-Sasanian Dirham" by A. Shams Eshragh in ONS

Newsletter 178, which describes a coin struck from the same dies as the present specimen. However, on the Shams Eshragh specimen the 'l-amr in the 3rd quarter of the obverse margin has been erased from the die and replaced with 'llah." This coin is also discussed by Clive Foss, A New and Unusual Kharijite Dirham, ONS Newsletter N° 182, London 2005, p.11-13. Here the coin is treated according to the information found in the traditional historiography.

256 A. Shams Eshragh, An interesting Arab-Sasanian Dirhem, ONS Newsletter N° 178, London 2004, p.45-46.

257 "Walī (A.). (..) As a religious term walī roughly corresponds to our 'saint'; but the notion behind the term led to the development of an entire doctrine with practical implications, so that the use of the word has to be explained in more detail. The doctrine is not yet known by the Qur'ān. There the term walī has a number of meanings: a close relative, whose murder requires revenge (surah 17:35), friend of God (surah 10:63) or ally of God; it is also used for God himself, like in surah 2:257: 'Allah is the Protecting Friend of those who believe'; the same title is given to the prophet and is one of the names of God in the Islamic rosary." (Handwörterbuch des Islam, op. cit., p. 793-794).

258 We are dealing with the inscription and writing on the rim of the coin found in Shams Eshragh in the Newsletter 178 of the ONS.

259 The character mentioned by the traditional account as 'Alī bn Abī Ṭālib corresponds to the requirements of the fundamentalist Iranian legalists: "He engaged in warfare against 'erring' Muslims as a matter of duty, in order to 'sustain the Faith and to make the right way (al-hudā) triumphant' [This corresponds to the procedure of Zoroastrian religious judges against Iranians who converted to Christianity; *author's note*] (...) when battles ended, he showed his grief, wept for the dead, and even prayed over his enemies. Even the apparent ambiguity of his attitude towards the Harurites can be explained by his fear of disobeying God; though persuaded by them that the arbitration was a sin, he recognised also that to infringe the convention of Siffin was equally a sin (...)." Here we can see why, from an Iranian perspective, the designation 'walī al-amr' (representative of the *amr*) had to be given up and replaced by the reduced formula 'walī allāh' (friend of God). For an Iranian mind, it was a 'sin' to intervene in the divine chain of command, as it would be tantamount to blending. To accept arbitration means to blend divine and human will, which is 'širk' ("blending"; Modern Islamic understanding: "idolatry"). God is defined as 'lā šārik la-hu' ("he has no partner"). That is why 'Alī bn Abī Ṭālib was missing, when he did not accept the final battle, as it proves that he was not 'fortunate'. According to an Iranian, legalist model a leader has to leave the final decision to God, though convinced of his being chosen. Whoever trusts his own 'xvarnah', will fight until the end. Only then it will show whether he could rely on his 'fortuna'. Should he be defeated, then will happen what happened to Ḵosrow after his defeat against Heraclius. He will be defamed and killed. The EI continues: "Obedience to the divine Law was the keynote to his conduct, but his ideas were governed by an excessive rigorism, (...)." (EI² I/ p. 385: "'Alī bn Abī Ṭālib").

260 C. Wurtzel, The Coinage of the Revolutionaries in the Late Umayyad Time, op. cit., p. 176-177 (Group 4-A). "The development of the so-called Kharijī movement(s) during the Umayyad period is a complex matter. However, a glimpse at the activities of many of the groups and individuals referred to by the literary

sources as Kharijīs or any of several synonyms (Harūrīs, Shurat, Azraqīs, and others) reveals that they do not have much, if anything, to do with 'judgement' of any sort. The slogan allegedly used by the original Kharijīs was maintained by some of the later Kharijīs to lend to their activities a religious and historical legitimacy and sense of continuity. Their motto might also be translated 'Authority (or 'Law') belongs to God alone', which would more appropriately characterize their activities during the Umayyad period."

261 P. Balog, Umayyad, 'Abbasid and Tulunid Glass Weights and Vessel Stamps, op. cit., p. 109-113 (The Family of Muḥammad (Āl-Muḥammad).

262 P. Balog, Umayyad, 'Abbasid and Tulunid Glass Weights and Vessel Stamps, op. cit., p. 116: "In the name of Allāh. Order/ from the son of Hāshim for ho/nesty. Among those things which ordered / the amir / Salih b. 'Alī. At the hands of al-/Luqā.[Lukas] One-quarter qist, / full measure."

263 M.G. Morony, Iraq after the Muslim Conquest, Princeton 1984, p. 357: "It should be clear that the distinctive position of the 'Nestorian' Church developed in the early seventh century in reaction to the threat of a compromise with the Monophysites."

264 About the development of this doctrine see M. Morony, Iraq after the Muslim Conquest, op. cit., p. 358 and Fn. 100.

265 M.G. Morony, Iraq after the Muslim Conquest, op. cit., p. 355: "They seem to have been recognised as 'Nestorians' by the seventh century, since at the disputation of 612 Khusraw Parvīz [Khosrau II.] called them 'those who proclaim the name of Nestorius'. Monks from Nasibin who went to North Africa in the middle of the seventh century are called Nestorians in a Monothelite source. Rabban Hurmīzd is called 'our Nestorius' because he combatted local Monophysites, and Nestorius was used occasionally as a proper name. Later Nestorians preferred to believe that name did not mean that they were followers of Nestorius but that he would have agreed with them."

266 Surahs 3:110; 5:82; 2:141; 5:17; 5:73; 2:135.

267 The emergence of a 'Nestorian' identity is due to the foundation of theological schools. These schools might have been the model for the later founding of Muslim Schools of Law (Arabic (sg.): *maḏhab*) in Bagdad. This might, however, goes back to Zoroastrian traditions as well: "The 'Nestorian' identity became permanent because its doctrine was institutionalized in the liturgy and in the teaching of the schools. The organization and spread of schools among the Nestorians in the sixth and seventh centuries was one of the most powerful forces shaping the separate group nature of the Eastern church. This was mainly because the schools themselves imparted the doctrine and exegesis of Theodore of Mopsuestia. This began in the fifth century, when the works of Theodore were translated into Syriac for use in the School of the Persians at Edessa. When the school was closed in 489 by the Byzantine emperor Zeno, its members in dispersion carried Theodore's exegesis across the border to Nasibin, where the school was reconstituted under the patronage of Bar Sawma.(...) The curriculum included church doctrine and Greek sciences and took three years to complete. The study of theology involved the transcription and explanation of scripture, the

liturgy, the hymns, responses, and the commentaries of Theodore. Science meant mainly the study of logic and medicine at the hospital (...)." (M. Morony, Iraq after the Muslim Conquest, op. cit., p. 359). Similar institutions were not available for the "Old Believers" among the Christians of Iran. Their early center Gundeshapūr in Khūzistān, where the bishop of Antioch had been deported under Shapur I in the 3rd century CE, had come under the influence of the Nestorians.

268 J. Lassner, article "Hāshimiyya", EI² III./ p. 265: "Van Vloten, followed by other scholars, showed that the name had in fact a different origin. From some passages in the chronicles, confirmed by the heresiological literature, it is clear that the term Hashimiyya was applied in Umayyad times to a religious-political faction (...)."

269 "Harrān is a very old town in Mesopotamia, close to the source of the Balikh between Edessa and Ras al-'Ain. It is known as the home of Abraham and Laban, and especially famous as head area of the Sabians and their religion." (Handwörterbuch des Islam, op. cit., p. 167). "The characteristics of the tired old man, the plotting ancestor, the cold and dark evildoer are ascribed to the planet called kimanu by the Chaldeans (West-Semitic: Kaiwan) (...) in the planet prayer of the Arabic Picatrix (H. Ritter, Vortr. Bibl. Warbg. 1921/22, p. 118 f.); usually this is ascribed to the Sabians of Harrān, who, according to the reliefs of Urfa (appr. 150/200 CE) venerated K.-Saturn, among other star deities (J.B: Segal, Anat. Stud. 3, 1953, p. 107 ff.). In these, like in other astrological traditions of the Middle Ages, which are linked to late antiquity, the god preserves the negative features of gloominess, slowness and unfriendliness." (J. Seznic The Survival of the pagan. Gods, 1953, p. 39 f., 53ff. R. Klibansky/F. Saxl/ E. Panofsky Saturn and Melancholy, 1964, 127ff. 159ff. [17], 170 f. 186f.)" (Der Kleine Pauly, op. cit., III, p. 365).

270 About this question see the article "Dīn" (Handwörterbuch des Islam, op. cit., p. 98-99.

271 See also Markus Gross' article "New Ways of Qur'ānic Research", chapter 2.4 in the present anthology.

272 "The absence of mint-names on most of the gold dinars issued by the Umayyad and early 'Abbasid Caliphs poses a challenging problem of attribution which has not heretofore received the attention it deserves. Where were these dinars struck?" (G.C. Miles, Some Early Arab Dinars, ANS Museum Notes III, New York 1948, p. 93). In this list, G.C. Miles also described the new type of dinar which was struck in 132 of the Arabs with the inscription quoting surah 9:33.

273 "Dualism becoming language" (Die Versprachlichung des Dualismus): Lexical Dichotomies. The authors of 'Young Avestan texts' endeavored to use a separate or corresponding vocabulary for certain components of the world of good and the world of evil. This 'lexical dichotomy' reproduces, marks and specifies, on the linguistic level, the distinction of a 'sphere' of evil and one of good." (M. Stausberg, Zarathushtra, I, op. cit., p. 134).

274 Baldwin's Auction Ltd and Arabian Coins and Medals (LLC Islamic Coin Auction N° 11, London 2006, N° 147 (Dirham, al-Hashimiya, 138h.). The Corpus of Abbasid coins of Nicholas Lowick was meant to be a standard work for coins of this time. This book of the curator of the British Museum, London, was

published posthumously. Unfortunately, it must be considered the victim of an editorial mess.

275 An explanation why the ghost town of al-Hāšimīya cannot be found is given by J. Lassner, article 'Hāshimiyya' EI² III/ p. 265-266: "Hāshimiyya, name of the administrative capital of the 'Abbasids before the building of Baghdād, referring not to a single place but to wherever the Caliph chose to establish his residence. (...) The proclivity of the 'Abbasid Caliphs for this constant moving is still unexplained; it does suggest, that they were searching for a site which could satisfy certain particular needs."

276 A. Duri, article 'Baghdād', EI² I/908: map belonging to the article "Baghdād" with a round city marked in red. The sketch shows four gates, one for each of the Sassanian parts of the empire. The palace and the central mosque are also indicated.

277 Baldwin's Auctions Ltd and Arabian Coins & Medals (LLC), Islamic Coin Auction N° 10, London 2005, N° 57.

278 Leu Numismatics Ltd, Auktion 62, Zürich 1995, S.31, N° 259.

279 Baldwin's Auction Ltd. and Arabian Coins & Medals (LLC), Islamic Coin Auction in London N° 9, London 2004, N° 3266.

280 Leu Numismatics Ltd, Auktion 62, Zürich 1995, S. 31, N° 262.

281 Baldwin's Auctions Ltd. and Arabian Coins & Medals, Islamic Coin Auction N° 2, Dubai 2000, N° 244.

282 Leu Numismatics Ltd, Auktion 62, Zürich 1995, S. 31, N° 261.

283 Baldwin's Auctions Ltd & Arabian Coins & Medals (LLC), Islamic Coin Auction in London N° 7, London 2003, N° 69.

284 Siehe Irfan Shahid, article 'Najrān', EI²VII/872.

285 Leu Numismatics Ltd., Auktion 62, Zürich 1995, S. 31, N° 268.

286 T. Nagel, Untersuchungen zur Entstehung des Abbasidischen Kalifats, Bonn 1972, p. 93.

287 M. Morony, Iraq after the Muslim Conquest, op. cit. p. 211: "By 657 a birdhawn market existed at Kufā, (...) and the ambling birdhawn was rated as one of the excellences of Basra."

288 M. Morony, Iraq after the Muslim Conquest, op. cit., p. 188; p. 259.

289 T. Nagel, Untersuchungen zur Entstehung des Abbasidischen Kalifates, op. cit. p. 94.

290 T. Nagel, Untersuchungen zur Entstehung des Abbasidischen Kalifats, ibid. 94-p. 95.

291 T. Nagel, Untersuchungen zur Entstehung des Abbasidischen Kalifats, ibid. 95-96 (Ahmad bn Hanbal).

292 Wilferd Madelung, article "Al-Mahdī", EI²V/12: "The first 'Abbasid caliph gave himself the Kufan messianic name al-Saffāḥ in his inaugural sermon in the mosque of Kūfa in 132/749.“ (...) As for the Saffāḥ, he will pour out money and blood in abundance." Cf. also the depiction of the Abbasid traditional historiography of the time of al-Saffāḥ, al-Manṣūr and of the Mahdī.

293 W. Madelung, Apocalyptic Prophecies in Hims in the Umayyad Age, op. cit., p. 146: "The caliphate of Mu'āwiya was remembered as a time when money was

flowing for everybody. (...) 'Say four. The fifth will be that money will overflow among you, such that a man may be given a hundred dinars and he will get angry about it (deeming it little)."

294 G.-R. Puin, Der Dīwān von 'Umar ibn al-Ḫattāb, Bonn 1970, p. 160.

295 G.-R. Puin, Der Diwan von 'Umar ibn al-Ḫattāb, ibid., p. 69.

296 See R. Zaehner, Zurvan, op. cit., p. 334.

297 H. Waldmann, Heilsgeschichtlich verfasste Theologie und Männerbünde. Die Grundlagen des gnostischen Weltbildes, Tübingen 1994, p. 69; about this question see also: Fn. 210: "About the excessive angelology, e.g. in Qumran, which in many respects – up to the terminology used – was influenced by Iranian notions, and which might be considered as an important mediator of this notion, see the impressive compilations in Haag, 1968, p. 390. About the already mentioned Iranian terms in writings found in Qumran see the lists compiled by Sukenik in Dupont-Sommer, 1955 on p. 222 of the edition of 1981."

298 R. Gyselen, Arab-Sasanian Copper Coinage, op. cit., p. 73, p.138 (Type 24).

299 Wilferd Madelung, article "Al-Mahdī", EI²V/ p. 1233-1234: "the thesis of the identity of names was evidently already well-established there, since his supporters did not try to identify him with the Mahdī but with the Manṣūr (al-Ṭabarī, ii, 1676), a messianic figure originating in Yemenite beliefs." (...)."As for the Manṣūr, no flag of his will be turned back." Here, Christological predicates are re-interpreted and become agents in an eschatological scenario.

300 Leu Numismatics Ltd, Zürich, Auktion 62, Zürich 1995, p.33, N° 292 (with pict.).

301 Leu Numismatics Ltd. Auction Leue 62, Zürich 1995, 33, N° 301.

302 Wilferd Madelung, article "Al-Mahdī", EI²V/ p. 1231: "The term mahdī as such does not occur in the Ḳur'ān; but the name is clearly derived from the Arabic root *h-d-y* commonly used in the meaning of divine guidance."

303 C.E. Bosworth, The New Islamic Dynasties, Edinburgh 1996, p. 6.

304 P. Balog, Umayyad, 'Abbasid and Tulunid Glass Weights and Vessel Stamps, op. cit., p. 168-169, N°s. 505-506. In this period clients of the governor (amīr al-mu'minīn) appear for the first time in inscriptions. See ibid., p. 176-177: "Matar, mawlā amīr al-mu'minīn" Nos. 528-30.

305 Wilferd Madelung, article "Al. Mahdī", EI²V/ p. 1234: "'Matters will only grow in hardship, the world will only increase in backward movement, and the people in greed. The Hour will rise only on the worst of people. There will be no Mahdī but 'Isā b. Maryam.' The hadith given added prestige by the fact that al-Šāfiᶜī (d.204/820) transmitted it from al-Djanadī. Included by Ibn Madjā in his Sunnan, it was later interpreted by supporters of the belief in the Mahdī as meaning that no-one spoke in the cradle (mahd) except Jesus or that the Mahdī would rule only in accordance with the instructions of Jesus since only the latter, as a prophet, was infallible (...)." Here the close connection between the person of the Mahdī and his *fravaši*, the eschatological Jesus, is still visible.

306 Leu Numismatics Ltd, Auction Leu 62, Zürich 1995, p. 34, N° 310.

307 H. Lavoix, Catalogue des Monnaies Musulmanes de la Bibliothèque Nationale, Khalifes Orientaux, Paris 1887, p. 161, N° 697.

308 "In Rivayat (...) it is said that the inhabitants of Paradise will live in love and friendship, while the inhabitants of hell will be isolated from one another and only think of themselves" (M. Stausberg, Die Religion Zarathushtras, op. cit., p.

304). Therefore it is only consequent that the disbeliever will have "no lover here this day" (Surah 69:35).

309 M. Morony, Iraq after the Muslim Conquest, op. cit., p. 534. EI²VIII/ p. 567-568, "Rizḳ". There the Middle Persian etymology of the term is indicated, see Jeffery, The foreign vocabulary of the Qur'ān, p. 142-3, "...the believer is promised this divine allocation both in this life and the Hereafter, prompting him to continuous praise of this 'Best of Providers')."

310 "And some men say, 'God created the sinner that he might sin and burn in Gehenna, and the righteous man that he might be proclaimed righteous and enjoy happiness in Paradise'. And the question 'Wherefore?' is not to be asked. Man hath not dominion over existence. And others affirm the existence of freedom (i.e., free will) like the Christians" (E. Wallis Budge, The Chronography of Gregory Abū l-Faraj 1225-1286 The Son of Aaron, the Hebrew Physician Commonly Known as Bar Hebraeus, London 1932, p. 92).

311 Attested by coins in Ifriqiya of the year 145 of the Arabs.

312 As evidence the silver coins of three years shall suffice at this point. They can easily be found in the auction catalogs cited. The advantage of attestation in modern auction catalogs is that – unlike older standard works – they do not only offer the reader a description, but usually a high quality picture as well, which enables the reader to check the reading of the description: Baldwin's Auctions Ltd and Arabian Coins & Medals (LLC), Islamic Coin Auction in London N° 6, London 2003, N° 67: "al-Mahdī" (158-169h), Dirham, al-Yamama 166h, 2.89g (Lowick 573): Islamic Coin Auction in London N° 7, London 2003, N° 80: "al-Mahdī, Dirham, al-Yamama 167h, 2.61g (Lowick 578)"; N° 81: "al-Mahdī, Dirham, al-Yamama 168h, with the name of the governor 'Abd Allah b. Sa'id, 2.74g (Lowick 582)."

313 The corresponding passages of the traditional account describing the presence of the Sassanians in Arabia are cited in: P. Crone, Meccan Trade and the rise of Islam, Oxford 1987, p. 48-49.

314 E. Budge, Bar Hebraeus, op. cit., p. 116.

315 J.B. Segal, article 'Ibn al-'Ibrī (Bar Hebraeus), EI², III/ p. 804.

316 Mūsā al-Hadī, s. C. Bosworth, The New Islamic Dynasties, op. cit., p. 6.

317 M. Al-'Ush, Arab Islamic Coins preserved in the National Museum of Qatar, op. cit., p. 343, N° 1011 (Basra, Jahr 164), N° 1013 (Basra, Jahr 168).

318 S. H. Wehr, A Dictionary of Modern Written Arabic, Wiesbaden 1961, p. 651: "'ahd: close observance, strict adherence (to); keeping, fulfillment; commitment; obligation, liability; responsibility, pledge, vow; promise (..)."

319 M. Al-'Ush, Arab Islamic Coins preserved in the National Museum of Qatar, op. cit., p. 357, N° 1559, Arrān, 169, mentioning Moses; p. 361, N° 1568, Al-'Abbāssiya, 170, mentioning al-Hādī.

320 M. Al-'Ush, Arab Islamic Coins preserved in the National Museum of Qatar, op. cit., p. 340, N° 1502.

321 Y. D. Nevo, Z. Cohen, D. Heftman, Ancient Arabic Inscriptions from the Negev, vol I, op. cit.,p. 136.

322 Dr. B. Peus Nachf. Katalog 363, 2500 Jahre Persische Münzprägung, unter Mit-

arbeit von Dr. Lutz Illisch, Frankfurt/M. 2000, p. 62, Nos. 5799, 5800.

323 I. & C. Artuk, Istanbul Arkeoloji Müzerleri Teşhirdeki Islāmī Sikkeler Katalogu, Istanbul 1970, S. 62, N° 221. It is a unique coin.

324 I. & C. Artuk, Istanbul, op. cit.,S. 24, N° 202 (al-Muhammadiya, year 172).

325 I. & C. Artuk, Istanbul, op. cit., S. 78, N° 270 (Dirham, Sijistān, 172); Leu Numismatics Ltd, Auction Leu 62, Zürich 1995, p. 38, N° 362, Dirham, Arrān, 189).

326 M. Al-'Ush, Arabic Islamic Coins preserved in the National Museum of Qatar, op. cit., p. 468, N° 1770.

327 Here a few examples shall suffice: The dirham of Madinat al-Salām, year 146 (Lowick 1162), does not mention Manṣūr. How can it be that the rule in the alleged capital is anonymous? How can it be explained that gold coins struck between the years 132 and 169 of the Arabs are totally anonymous? (G. C. Miles, Some Early Arab Dinars, Museum Notes III, The American Numismatic Society, New York 1948, pp.104-107).

328 Lowick 2061.

329 Lowick 642.

330 The Dirham of Misr of the year 182 of the Arabs could be considered as an example (Lowick 508).

331 Evidence for this are the silver coins from 'Umān of the years 81 and 90 of the Arabs. (M. G. Klat, Catalogue of the Post-Reform Dirhams, The Umayyad Dynasty, op. cit., p. 190, Nos. 499-500).

332 The minting activities of the mint in al-Yaman begins with an anonymous copper coin of the year 157 of the Arabs. Copper coins of this mint in the name of the representation of rule of the Mahdī – identical to the muḥammad (the eschatological Jesus) – are attested for the years 157 and 158 of the Arabs. A silver coin according to local standards of the year 172 is the first known silver coin of Arab rule in Ṣan'ā'. Earlier evidence of the Arab Empire or a post-Sassanian administration in Ṣan'ā' cannot be found; see R.J. Bikhazi, Coins of al-Yaman, Al-Abhath, Beirut 1970, p. 17 & 20, Nos. 1-5.

333 Baldwin's Auction Ltd & Arabian Coins and Medals (LLC), Islamic Coin Auction in London N° 9, London 2004, N° 3284 (al-Ma'mūn, Dirham, San'ā' 210h, 1,44 g).

334 Hijāz 185, Tüb. Coll. AL7 B4; a gold coin mentioning the Ḥiğāz of the year 105 of the Arabs can be found in the collection of the American Numismatic Society. Originally it was part of the collection of the Egyptian princess Isma'īl; cf. G.C. Miles, Some Early Arab Dinars, op. cit., p.102, N° 84. A second specimen can be found in the Israel Museum. It was only found a few years ago by A. Berman during excavations in Kapernaum. In a later article the question will be discussed whether *ḥiğāz* really refers to a geographical area or rather is the Arabic translation of the "katechon".

335 S. Album, Sylloge of Islamic Coins in the Ashmolean, vol. 10, Oxford 1999, Pl. 23, N° 488.

336 "The fact that imāmān means 'priests' comes out very clearly in three superadded words preceding a verse corresponding to Jn. 9:24 (...): mukhātaba kūhūnān u-imāmān. Kūhūnān is clearly a loan-word deriving in all probability from the Syriac kohānā (priest), and is used as an equivalent of imāman. In the Persian Diatesseron, cases of double translation of this kind are frequent. Accordingly the three words mean, "talk (addressed by) the priests" (S. Pines,

"Gospel Quotations and Cognate Topics in 'Abd al-Jabbār's Tathbīt in Relations to early Christian and Judaeo-Christian Readings and Traditions", Jerusalem Studies in Arabic and Islam 9 (1987), p. 213).

337 G.C. Miles, Some Early Arab Dinars, op. cit., p. 111, Nos. 125, 124.

338 W. Madelung, Apocalyptic Prophecies in Hims in the Umayyad Age, op. cit., p. 168. These traditions are relatively recent, in spite of their purported age. The caliph is seen as the representative of a religious community. In the concept of the 'millet' (communities) he is the spokesman of the Muslims. Other communities have their spokesman as well. The Patriarch has therefore the function of a caliph of the orthodoxy etc. The mention of the Muhāğirūn points to the emergence of the legend not before the 3rd century of the Arabs. Without the notion of the Islamic hiğra (exodus) the muhāğirūn (emigrants) cannot be conceived. Here the attempt to find a new approach to Qur'ānic materials can be observed, after the initiators of Qur'ānic notions, the Aramaic 'Arabī, have disappeared. Their "hiğra" had been their journey to Jerusalem, their exile the deportation at the time of the Sassanian rule. In the third century of the Arabs the old Qur'ānic texts had to be re-interpreted. An early highlight of this movement for a new understanding of Qur'ānic texts is al-Ṭabarī's "Tafsīr".

339 Handwörterbuch des Islam, op. cit., p. 206.

340 In the collection Baldasari = Auction Leu 62, Zürich 1995, a dirham can be found which has been ascribed to this enemy of the family for the year 201 of the hiğra in Baghdad. The coin (N° 537) is described with a picture: "Anonymous, with mintmark mīm below rev." How can the author of the catalog (Dr. Ludger Illisch, Tübingen) ascribe an anonymous coin to an enemy of al-Ma'mūn who is only known in the traditional historiographical literature? Moreover, we read: "Tiesenhausen 1716 (attributed to Ibrāhīm al-Mubārak with reference to Fraehn)." This reveals the misery of ascribing coins instead of describing them. Instead of admitting that the coin is anonymous, which does not allow such an interpretation, the numismatist intervenes with a correction "according to the traditional account". This is highly debatable. If Islamic Studies develop like this, it will lead to a situation where in a hundred years a never-attested ruler is replaced by another never-attested one and the results are published as new findings. In the traditional account the rule in Baghdad from the end of the year 201 hiğra until the year 203 was in the hands of a man called Ibrāhīm bn Mubarāk bn al-Mahdī. Of course, his alleged coins are anonymous, see Sammlung Baldasari N° 538. Here again, the anonymous coins are ascribed to a ruler possessing the minting authority, whose name is a series of pious notions, which insinuate a genealogy.

341 W. Madelung, New Documents Concerning Al-Ma'mūn, Al-Fadl b. Sahl and 'Ali Al-Rida, in: Religious and Ethnic Movements in Medieval Islam, Hampshire 1992, p. 333.

342 Bar Hebraeus, Chronography, op. cit., p. 141.

343 Sammlung Baldasari = Auction Leu 62, Leu Numismatics Ltd, Zürich 1995, p. 49, N° 521.

344 Sammlung Baldasari = Auction Leu 62, Leu Numismatics Ltd, Zürich 1995, p. 48, N° 516.

345 Sammlung Baldasari = Auction Leu 62, Leu Numismatics Ltd, Zürich 1965, p. 46, N° 484.)

346 W. Madelung, New Documents Concerning al-Ma'mūn, al-Fadl b. Sahl and 'Alī Ridā, op. cit., p. 343. Similarly ibid., p. 345: "The startling announcement of the letter that al-Mam'ūn appointed 'Alī al-Riḍā in the belief that the 'Abbasid caliphate was about to come to an end after him and would be followed by the apocalyptic age of tribulation and the coming of the Mahdī must be seen in the light of the evidence that such expectations were very strong and widespread at the time."

347 Leu Numismatics Ltd, Auction Leu 62, Zürich 1995, p. 48, N° 514 (Dirham, al-Muhammadīya, year 202 of the Arabs, or year 202 of the meanwhile assumed 'hiğra' des Propheten der Araber.

348 The fact that messianic hopes and the expectation of the second coming of Christ lived on led to a fierce antagonism between movements expecting the Mahdī and the so-called Abbasids. As an example we might adduce the movement of the Qarmatians in Baḥrayn: "Related instances of Mahdism in the Muslim East during the 4th/10th century may be pointed out briefly without great elaboration: In East Arabia, al-Bahrayn was the stronghold of the Old Believer Carmatians since the year 286/900. (...) There, the expectation of the mahdī was extraordinarily vivid. The ruling missionary Abū Sa'īd al-Jannābī proclaimed his coming from the direction of the mountains in the course of AH 300 (AD 912-13). Like Yahyā b. Zikrawayh before him, Abū Sa'īd was later falsely considered to have declared himself the mahdī. According to Nasīr-i Khusraw who visited al-Ahsā' in 442/1051, a bridled horse was kept ready for Abū Sa'īd in front of his grave because tradition had it that he had announced his return." Here we are reminded of the "pack horse" of al-Saffāḥ, as well as the alleged appearance of a white horse without horseman at the time of the Zand rebellion in Southern Iraq. "The year 300 went by without fulfillment of the promise, but the idea of imminent Parousia did not suffer a lasting blow. This becomes clear from the events of 312/924. Crowds of people, indeed whole families from al-'Irāq moved to the Carmathian state in al-Bahrayn expecting to witness the Mahdī's immediate appearance and the founding of his rule over the world. At that time, Abū Sa'īd's son and successor Abū Tāhir was considered to be the *walī* (plenipotentiary) and the hujja (argument) of the mahdī. When he menaced Baghdad the same year, it was said, that this would bring about the disclosure of religious truth and the rise of the mahdī and that it would put an end to the 'Abbāsides, to the jurist, those who recite the Qur'ān and traditionalists. Although this speculation disappointed, the immediate expectation of the mahdī continued. Poetry of Abū Tāhir underlines the role of Jesus in it." (K. Franz, Parousia, Political Rule and the Bedouins of the Tenth Century CE. Beiruter Blätter, Mitteilungen des Orient-Instituts Beirut 10-11, Beirut 2002-3, p. 62).

349 S. Pines, The Jewish Christians of the Early Centuries of Christianity according to a New Source, Proceedings of the Israel Academy of Sciences and Humanities II.10, Jerusalem 1966, p. 277.

350 J. Johns, Archaeology and the History of Early Islam, JESHO 46,4 (Leiden 2003), p. 429: "The invocation on the north-east side particularly attracts attention (fig.

8): 'Muhammad is the messenger of God, May God bless him and accept his intercession on the day of the resurrection on behalf of his [His?} community' (Muhammad rasūl Allāh sallā 'alayhi wa-taqabbala shaf[ā]'atahu yawm al-qiy[ā]ma fī ummatihi). It calls upon God to accept the intercession of Muhammad for the Muslims on the Day of Judgement.
The idea is not Qur'ānic, for nowhere in the Qur'ān does Muhammad appear as an intercessor. What is more, the idea of Muhammad as an intercessor does not fit comfortably with the Umayyad conception of the caliphate, according to which the most direct path to salvation led through the caliph (Crone and Hinds 1986: 27-42).
After this appearance in the Dome of the Rock, Muhammad does not again appear in the role of intercessor for some 150 years." Obviously J. Johns recognizes two different appearances of the term muḥammad as well: the "*muḥammad*" of the Dome of the Rock and the *Muḥammad* of later tradition. He does not manage, however, to keep these two figures – 'Isā bn Maryam as *muḥammad* und Muḥammad bn 'Abdallāh – apart.

351 This unconvincing explanation still is accepted as sufficient: Bakka, which cannot be localized, is simply equated with Mecca/Makka. See the translation by Paret: "Das erste (Gottes)haus, das den Menschen aufgestellt worden ist, ist dasjenige in Bakka (d.h. Mekka), (aufgestellt) zum Segen und der Rechtleitung der Menschen in aller Welt." At least he mentions the form Bakka. Pickthall translates (at least in a modern edition): "Lo! the first Sanctuary appointed for mankind was that at Mecca, a blessed place, a guidance to the peoples."

352 W. Madelung, The Sufyānī between Tradition and History, in: Religious and Ethnic Movements in Medieval Islam, op. cit., III, p. 36.

353 Leu Numismatics Ltd, Leu Auction 62, Zürich 1995, p. 47, N° 501 (Dirham, Samarqand, 210 h.) and Peus Nachf. 2500 Jahre Persische Münzprägung, Katalog 363, Frankfurt 2000, p. 67, N° 5898 (Dirham, Abarshahr, 210 h.); Baldwin's Auctions Ltd & Arabian Coins and Medals (LLC), Islamic Coin Auction N° 11, London 2006, N° 64 (Dirham, Samarqand, 217 h.); Baldwin's Auctions Ltd and Arabian Coins and Medals (LLC), Islamic Coin Auction N° 6, London 2003, N° 96 (Dirham, Marw, 217 h).

354 Baldwin's Auctions Ltd & Arabian Coins and Medals (LLC), Islamic Coin Auction N° 5, London 2002, N° 104 (Dirham, San'ā', 217h.).

355 Baldwin's Auctions Ltd & Arabian Coins and Medals (LLC), Islamic Coin Auction N° 6, London 2003, No 95.

356 Baldwin's Auctions Ltd & Arabian Coins and Medals (LLC), Islamic Coin Auction N° 6, London 2003, N° 97.

357 Leu Numismatics Ltd, Islamic Coins, Auction Leu 62, Zürich 1995, p. 51, 562.

358 Baldwin's Auctions Ltd & Arabian Coins and Medals (LLC), Islamic Coin Auction N° 4, London 2002, N° 173 (Dirham, Mekka, 253 h.); see about this question also the annotation according to the traditional account: "In this period the Holy City of Makka was subject to almost constant civil strife. Gold dinars are recorded for 249h and the early 250s; for example, in 252h the gold covering the Makam Ibrahim was stripped so that it could be converted into dinars to pay

the troops. While two excessively rare first period Abbasid dirhams are known to have been struck in the Holy City in 201h and 203h, this is the earliest Abbasid Second Period dirham recorded from this mint." Thus traditional Islamic numismatics distinguishes between a First and a Second period of Abbasid rule. Contrary to this conventional view I see the end of the first period, which is marked by the end of Ma'mūn, as a totally new beginning.

359 S. MGH, Auct. antiquissimorum tomus XI, Chronicorum minorum, vol. II, Th. Mommsen (Hrsg.), Berlin 1894, S. 347. Personal communication by J. Thomas.

Endnotes
Karl-Heinz Ohlig: Evidence of a New Religion in Christian Literature "Under Islamic Rule"?, pp. 176-250

---

1 Cf. my article: Das Syrische und Arabische Christentum und der Koran, in: K.-H. Ohlig, Gerd-Rüdiger Puin (eds.), Die dunklen Anfänge. Neue Forschungen zur Entstehung und frühen Geschichte des Islam, Berlin [1]2005, [2]2006, p. 376-378; with further bibliography.

2 Robert G. Hoyland, Seeing Islam as Others saw it. A Survey and Evaluation of Christian, Jewish and Zoroastrian Writings on Early Islam, Princeton, New Jersey 1997.

3 Yehuda D. Nevo and Judith Koren, Crossroads to Islam. The Origins of the Arab Religion and the Arab State, Amherst, New York 2003, p. 103-135; p. 207-245.

4 Cf. about this question V. Popp, From Ugarit to Samarrā', in the present volume.

5 Cf. about this question Robert G. Hoyland, Arabia and the Arabs, London 2001, 2.3.

6 Xenophon, Anabasis I, 5 (Ed. Books I-IV by M.W. Mather and J.W. Hewitt, Oklahoma [USA] 1962, 75).

7 Plinius Secundus, Naturalis Historia V, XX 85, in: Die geographischen Bücher (II, 242-VI Schluss) der Naturalis Historia des Plinius Secundus, ed. by D. Detlefsen, Berlin 1904, 107, or in: Pliny, Natural History (in Latin and English), Volume II: Libri III-VII, ed. by H. Rackham, London und Cambridge (Massachusetts) 1947, p. 284.

8 Cf. about this question the article in the present volume by V. Popp, From Ugarit to Sāmarrā'.

9 Cf. about this question A.C. Klugkist, Die beiden Homilien des Isaak von Antiocheia über die Eroberung von Bet Hur durch die Araber, in: H.J.W. Drijvers, R. Lavenant, C. Molenberg, G.J. Reinick (ed.), IV Symposium Syriacum 1984. Literary Genres in Syriac Literature (in the following cited as: IV Symposium Syriacum), Rom 1987, p. 237-256.

10 So e.g. Ephrem the Syrian (died 373) in a hymn *De ecclesia* 44:21-26, and in *De crucifixo* 3,3.12; cf. about this question R.A. Darling, The "Church from the Nations" in the Exegesis of Ephrem, in: IV Symposium Syriacum 1984, ibid. p. 115.

11 Cf. Plinius der Ältere, op. cit. V 65 (Arabia with the epithet "beata"), in: Ed. Detlefsen, op. cit. p. 101; cf. about Ptolemy, Geography, Lib. V., Chapter 17 (Arabia Petraea), § 3, in: Claudii Ptolemaei Geographia. Edidit Fridericus Augustus Nobbe. Editio stereotypa, Tomus II, Lipsiae 1845, p. 97-108 (ed. F.A. Nobbe); cf. also about Ptolemy: D. H. Müller, article "Agraioi 2", in: Paulys Realencyklopädie der Classischen Altertumswissenschaft, new edition, ed. by Georg Wissovar, vol.1, Stuttgart 1893, p. 889.

12 Franz Altheim and Ruth Stiehl, Die Araber in der Alten Welt, first volume: Bis zum Beginn der Kaiserzeit, Berlin 1964, p. 6.

13 Cf. about this question the paragraph "Structures ecclésiastiques et rites liturgiques des Arabes chrétiens", in: Samir Abache, Les moines chez les Arabes chrétiens avant l'Islam, in: Patrimoine Syriac. Actes du colloque V: Le

monarchianisme Syriaque. Aux premiers sciècles de l'Église IIe – début VIIe siècles, vol. 2, Antélias (Liban) 1998, p. 300-302.

14 Cf. about this question K.-H. Ohlig, Das Syrische und Arabische Christentum und der Koran, op. cit. p. 366-404.

15 Cf. about this question e.g. Irfan Shahîd, Byzantium and the Arabs in the Fifth Century, Washington, DC, 1989, p. 330; 557-560.

16 I. Shahîd, ibid., p. 560.

17 Irfan Shahîd, Kap. IX. The Term Saraceni and the Image of the Arabs, in: Irfan Shahîd (ed.), Rome and the Arabs. A Prolegomenon to the Study of Byzantium and the Arabs, Washington, DC, 1984, p. 123-131.

18 Sven Dörper, Zum Problem des Völkernamens Saraceni, in: Neue Romania. Veröffentlichungsreihe des Studienbereichs Neue Romania des Instituts für Romanische Philologie (Sonderheft, ed. by Chr. Foltys and Th. Kotschi), N° 14, Berlin 1993, p. 95.

19 Hieronymus, In Hiezechielem VIII, 25,17; cf. S. Dörper, ibid. p. 92.

20 Irfan Shahîd, Rome and the Arabs, op. cit., p. 131-138.

21 Ptolemaius, Geographia, 5,17, §3, in: ed. F.A. Nobbe, p. 97-108.

22 Ammianus Marcellinus, Res Gestae, e.g. XXIV 1,10, in: Ammiani Marcellini Rerum Gestarum capita selecta, ed. Joannes Baptista Pighi (Bibliotheca Neocomensis, 2), Neocomi Helvetiorum 1948, p. 31. I. Shahîd mentions two more passages: XXII, 15:2; XXIII, 6,13.

23 S. Dörper, Zum Problem des Völkernamens Saraceni, op. cit., p. 97.

24 Eusebius of Caesarea, Onomastikon, Chapter about the book Genesis (Greek text with the Latin translation of St. Jerome, in: Eusebius. Das Onomastikon der biblischen Ortsnamen, ed. by Erich Klostermann [Die griechischen christlichen Schriftsteller der ersten drei Jahrhunderte – GCS – 11,1], p. 166.

25 Hieronymus, Vita Malchi (MPL 23, 53-60); German: "Leben und Gefangenschaft des Mönchs Malchus" (Life and Captivity of the Monk Malchus), in: BKV 15, 1914, p. 73-83.

26 Hieronymus, Vita Malchi, chap. 4 (German: BKV 15, op. cit. 76.77).

27 Hieronymus, Vita Hilarionis (MPL 23, 29-54); German: BKV 15, 33-72.

28 Hieronymus, chap. 25 (BKV 15, 54).

29 Hieronymus, Commentariorum in Amos prophetam libri III (Corpus Christianorum, series Latina [CCL], LXXVI, Turnholti MCMLXIX, p. 213-348).

30 Hieronymus, In Amos 5, p. 25-27 (CCL 76, 296).

31 A.C. Klugkist, Die beiden Homilien des Isaak von Antiocheia über die Eroberung von Bet-Hur durch die Araber, op. cit., p. 246.

32 A.C. Klugkist, Die beiden Homilien des Isaak von Antiocheia ..., ibid. 245, A. 28.

33 "He settled in defiance of all his relatives (עַל־פְּנֵי כָל־אֶחָיו נָפָל)" could also be translated as: "he settled down to the east of all his brothers".

34 A connection with Havilah or Nimrod, sons of Cush and grandsons of Ham (Gen. 10:7-8), is speculative. The following is said about his residence: "The beginning of his kingdom was Babel and Erech and Accad and Calneh, in the land of Shinar." (Gen. 10,10) – thus Mesopotamian cities. The connection with Havilah, a great-grandson of Shem (Gen. 10:29), is as unconvincing as a link with Gen. 2:11: "The name of the first is Pishon; it flows around the whole land of Havilah, where there is gold."

35 Harald Suermann, Die Geschichtstheologische Reaktion auf die Einfallenden Muslime in der Edessenischen Apokalyptik des 7. Jahrhunderts (Europäische Hochschulschriften, Reihe XXIII Theologie, vol. 256), Frankfurt a. M., Bern, New York 1985, p. 144.

36 Hieronymus, Liber de situ, chap. about the book Genesis (GCS 11:1, p. 167).

37 A text of Ephrem the Syrian would even be earlier. In the second sermon (Sancti Ephraemi Syri. Hymni et Sermones ... edidit, latinitate donavit, variis lectionibus instruxit, notis et prolegomenis illustravit Thomas Josephus Lamy, Tomus III, Meclelinia MDCCCLXXXIV [ed. Lamy], 110) he writes: "... and their screaming will rise up to heaven and from the desert a people will emerge, the son of Hagar, the handmaid of Sarah, who received the covenant with Abraham ...". It is not explicitly said in the text, but what is meant is probably the Arabs. Because of the apocalyptical structure of the speech, however, a late redaction can be suspected.

38 Hieronymus (St. Jerome), In Hiezechielem VIII, 25, 1:7 (CCSL 75, 335). Cf. about this question C.A. Willemsen, Sarazenen, in: LThK2 9, 326: St. Jerome tried to "prove that the S.(aracens), as descendants of Abraham's concubine (sic!) Agar rather deserved to be called Agareni. So the designation Agareni was, for a certain time, synonymous with S.(aracens)."

39 Summary in I. Shahîd, op. cit., p. 167, and S. Dörper, op. cit., p. 100, A. 12.

40 Isidore of Seville, Etymologia IX, 2:6 (Isidori Hispalensis episcopi Etymologiarum sive Originum libri XX, ed. by W. M. Lindsay, Tomus I: libri I-X [Scriptorum classicorum bibliotheca Oxonensis], Oxonii 1911 [without pagination]).

41 One exception is St. Paul, who, struggling with Judaism, the religion of his upbringing, writes in the letter to the Galatians: "For it is written that Abraham had two sons, one by the bondwoman and one by the free woman." (Gal. 4:22). He asserts that this may not be understood literally: "This is allegorically speaking, for these women are two covenants: one proceeding from Mount Sinai bearing children who are to be slaves; she is Hagar." (Gal. 4:24). Paulus adds: "Now this Hagar ["cliff"] is Mount Sinai in Arabia and corresponds to the present Jerusalem, for she is in slavery with her children." (Gal. 4:25). Here Paul calls the Jews themselves "children of Hagar", the Christians "children of promise" (Gal. 4:28), i.e. of Isaac. This is a rather violent iconographic theology, which was discontinued by Christians in the East. There the children of Hagar are always the "Arabs".

42 Die Schatzhöhle (The Cave of Treasures). Syrisch und Deutsch herausgegeben von Carl Bezold (edited in Syriac and German by Carl Bezold). First part: Übersetzung (translation). Aus dem syrischen Texte dreier unedirter Handschriften in's Deutsche übersetzt und mit Anmerkungen versehen von Carl Bezold, Leipzig 1883.

43 Die Schatzhöhle, ibid., p. 71.

44 Die Schatzhöhle, ibid., p. 37.

45 Pseudo-Sebeos, Histoire d'Héraclius, chap. 34, in: ed. Macler, p. 130 (concerning bibliographical information cf. 3.2, Text 7, about Pseudo-Sebeos).

46 Manuscript tradition is not good here. There are two manuscripts in Greek (Munich, 15th century, and Paris, 10th century); they have been edited by H. Usener, Weihnachtspredigt des Sophronius, in: (Rheinisches) Museum für Philologie, ed. by O. Ribbeke and F. Buecheler, NF 41. vol., Frankfurt a. M. 1886, p. 500-516; a Latin translation, which contains a few additions if compared to the Greek version, is from Lyon 1677 (MPG 87/3, 3.201-3.212).

47 This year can be considered as rather certain. In the introduction it is adduced that Christmas (25 December) in this year fell on a Sunday.

48 So also in the Latin version: MPG 87/3, 3.205 D.

49 So also in the Latin version: MPG 87/3, 3.206 B.C.

50 Y.D. Nevo and J. Koren, Crossroads to Islam, op. cit., p. 119.

51 R.G. Hoyland, Seeing Islam as Others saw it, op. cit., p. 72-73.

52 Cf. Y.D. Nevo and J. Koren, Crossroads to Islam, op. cit., p. 121: isolated incidents cannot be excluded, but the overall assessment is that "churches were not burnt or pulled down nor monasteries destroyed".

53 Lexikon der antiken christlichen Literatur (LACL), ed. by Siegmar Döpp and Wilhelm Gerlings, Freiburg, Basel, Wien 1998.

54 G. Röwekamp, Sophronius von Jerusalem, in: LACL, 364.

55 Doctrina Jacobi nuper baptizati, Greek text and French translation by Vincent Déroche, in: Gilbert Dagron, Vincent Déroche (ed.), Juifs et chrétiens dans l'Orient du VIIe siècle (Travaux et Mémores 11, revised by Gilbert Dagron and Denis Feissel [Collège de France. Centre de Recherche d'histoire et civilisaton de Byzance]), Paris1991, p. 47-229; immediately following: Gilbert Dagron, Commentaire, ibid., p. 230-273.

56 Harald Suermann, Juden und Muslime gemäß christlichen Texten zur Zeit Muhammads und in der Frühzeit des Islams, in: Holger Preißler, Heidi Stein (ed.), Annäherung an das Fremde. XXVI. Deutscher Orientalistentag vom 25. bis 29.9. 1995 in Leipzig, Stuttgart 1998, p. 145.

57 Vincent Déroche, ibid., p. 64.

58 H. Suermann, Juden und Muslime gemäß christlichen Texten zur Zeit Muhammads und in der Frühzeit des Islams, ibid., p. 145.146.

59 Doctrina Jacobi V 16; ed. V. Déroche, op. cit., p. 209-211.

60 H. Suermann, Juden und Muslime gemäß christlichen Texten zur Zeit Muhammads und in der Frühzeit des Islams, op. cit., p. 145.

61 H. Suermann, Juden und Muslime gemäß christlichen Texten zur Zeit Muhammads und in der Frühzeit des Islams, ibid., p. 147-148.

62 H. Suermann, Juden und Muslime gemäß christlichen Texten zur Zeit Muhammads und in der Frühzeit des Islams, ibid., p.148.

63 Theophanes Confessor, Chronographia, ed. by C. De Boor, Hildesheim 1963 (reprint of Leipzig 1883-1885), p. 336.

64 Chronicum ad annum Christi 1234 pertinens (CSCO 81; Scriptores Syri 36).

65 Y.D. Nevo and J. Koren, Crossroads to Islam, op. cit., p. 210.

66 Cf. about this question and about the apocalypses 3-4.

67 Pope Martin denied in a letter that during his captivity he had had any contact with Saracens including money business (Epistula 14, MPL 87, 199A). As nothing else can be inferred as to the contents, this letter and the question of its authenticity will not be discussed here.

68 B.R. Suchla, Maximus Confessor, in: LACL, p. 433.

69 Maximus Confessor, Epistula 14 (MPG 91, p. 533-544).
70 Maximus Confessor, ibid. (MPG 91, p. 539-540).
71 Y.D. Nevo and J. Koren, Crossroads to Islam, op. cit., p. 122.
72 Epistula 8 (MPG 91, p. 439-446).
73 Cf. Y.D. Nevo and J. Koren, Crossroads to Islam, ibid., , p. 121-122.
74 M. F.(rançois) Nau, Un Colloque du Patriarche Jean avec l'Emir des Agaréens et Faits Divers des Années 712 à 716 d'après le MS. du British Museum Add. 17193 ..., in: Journal Asiatique, 11e série, Tome 5, 1915, p. 225-279; Syriac text ibid., p. 248-256, French translation ibid., p. 257-267.
75 Harald Suermann, Orientalische Christen und der Islam. Christliche Texte aus der Zeit von 632-750, in: Zeitschrift für Missionswissenschaft und Religionswissenschaft 52, 1993, p. 126. In the following text Suermann keeps speaking about the Muslim interrogator and Islamic doctrine.
76 Y.D. Nevo and J. Koren, Crossroads to Islam, op. cit., p. 223-227.
77 Khalil Samir, Qui est l'Interlocuteur du Patriarche Syrien Jean III (631-648?), in: IV Symposium Syriacum 1984, p. 387-400: Samir discusses all possible hypotheses concerning the dialog partners and calls for a debate between John III and 'Umayr ibn Sa'd (ibid. 400).
78 Y.D. Nevo and J. Koren, Crossroads to Islam, ibid., p. 227.
79 A German translation of the most important passages can be found in: H. Suermann, Orientalische Christen und der Islam, op. cit.; p. 122-125.
80 Y.D. Nevo and J. Koren, Crossroads to Islam, op. cit. 224.
81 M.F. Nau translates, op. cit., p. 262, "la loi musulmane (Muslim law)", but adds in brackets: Mahgrân; H. Suermann, op. cit. 124, speaks of the "muslimischen Gesetz (Muslim law)". A preferable transcription of Mahgrân would be "m-Haggrāye"; Syriac text thus is concerned with the Law of the Hagarenes/Hagarites, or – as Nevo/Koren correctly translated – with the Law of the Arabs. There is no hint in the text which would justify a translation as "Muslim Law".
82 Y.D. Nevo and J. Koren, Crossroads to Islam, ibid., p. 225.
83 Y.D. Nevo and J. Koren, Crossroads to Islam, op. cit. p. 227.
84 Y.D. Nevo and J. Koren, Crossroads to Islam, ibid., p. 228.
85 Cf. Sebastian Brock, VIII Syriac Views of Emergent Islam, in: id., Syriac Perspectives on Late Antiquity, London 1984, p. 16.
86 'Iso'yaw patriarchae III., Liber epistularum, hrsg. und ins Lateinische übers. von (edited and translated into Latin by) R. Duval (Corpus Scriptorum christianorum orientalium, vol. 12, Scriptores Syri II, tomus 12), Löwen 1904, p. 182; German translation according to H. Suermann, Orientalische Christen und der Islam, op. cit., p. 128.
87 'Iso'yaw, ibid., p.172.; German: H. Suermann, Orientalische Christen und der Islam, op. cit., p. 129.
88 Cf. K.-H. Ohlig, Das syrische und arabische Christentum und der Koran, op. cit., p. 378-394.
89 'Iso'yaw, op. cit., p. 73; German: H. Suermann, op. cit., p. 128.
90 H. Suermann, Orientalische Christen und der Islam, op. cit., p. 128.

91 'Iso'yaw patriarchae III., Liber epistularum, edited and translated into Latin by R. Duval (CSCO Vol. 12), op. cit., p. 73.

92 Iso'yahw Patriarchae III liber epistularum (Syriac text), ed. by R. Duval (CSCO Vol. 11; Scriptores Syri, Tomus II), p. 97.

93 H. Suermann, Orientalische Christen und der Islam, op. cit., p. 129.

94 Iso'yaw, Brief an Mar Simeon aus Rew Ardasir, in: Iso'yaw Patriachae III liber epistularum, Latin translation (CSCO Vol. 12), p. 185-188.

95 Johannes Moschus, Pratum spirituale, Greek with Latin translation in: MPG 87/3, 2.847-3.116 (another Latin translation in: MPL 74, 119-240).

96 J. Pauli OSB, Johannes Moschus, in: LACL, 253.

97 Johannes Moschus, Pratum spirituale, c. CXXIII (MPG 87/3, 2.996.2.998).

98 Johannes Moschus, Pratum spirituale, c. CXXXVI (MPG 87/3, 3.000).

99 Johannes Moschus, Pratum spirituale, c. CLV (MPG 87/3, 3.024).

100 Johannes Moschus, Pratum sprituale, quoted according to R.G. Hoyland, Seeing Islam as Others saw it, op. cit., p. 63. In the Greek and Latin version of the Pratum spirituale in the "Migne" this remark cannot be found. Hoyland quotes it according to a translation of an Armenian version of the Pratum spirituale, p. 100-102, by Garitte. This one, however, is missing in his bibliography of Johannes Moschus (726). As this addition is not very important, the bibliographical information concerning Hoyland shall suffice.

101 Text edition: Histoire d'Héraclius par l'évêque Sebéos, traduite de l'Arménien et annotèe par F. Macler, Paris 1904 (ed. F. Macler); Armenian edition: Parmut'iwn Sebeosi, ed. G.V. Abgarian, Yerevan 1979; The Armenian History attributed to Sebeos, translated, with notes, by R.W. Thomson. Historical Commentary by James Howard-Johnston, Part I. Translation and Notes, Liverpool 1999 (ed. R.W. Thomson), Part II. Historical Commentary, Liverpool 1999.

102 Cf. about this question R.G. Hoyland, Seeing Islam as Others saw it, op. cit. 124.125. Y.D. Nevo and J. Koren, Crossroads to Islam, op. cit., p. 230, A. 68, mention that the manuscript, on the basis of which the History of Heraclius was edited, is from the 10th/ 11th century and obviously contains two parts of later authors. According to them, only the third book can be considered a genuine book of Sebeos. But even that one has a long transmission history, so that changes and additions in the text have to be assumed.

103 Pseudo-Sebeos, Histoire d'Héraclius, ed. F. Macler, p. 104-105.

104 Pseudo-Sebeos, Histoire d'Héraclius, chap. 30.

105 In ed. R. W. Thomas the Chapter numbering is different; the present text is in Chapter 42 (ibid. p. 95-97); Suermann has it as Chapter 40.

106 Pseudo-Sebeos, Histoire d'Héraclius, chap. 30; ed. F. Macler, op. cit., p. 94-102.

107 Pseudo-Sebeos, Histoire d'Héraclius, chap. 30; ed. F. Macler, ibid., p. 102.

108 The brackets inserted by me indicate a later addition; cf. about this question the following text.

109 Pseudo-Sebeos, Histoire d'Héraclius, chap. 30; ed. F. Macler, ibid., p. 95-96; German according to: H. Suermann, Juden und Muslime gemäß christlichen Texten zur Zeit Muhammads und in der Frühzeit des Islams, op. cit., p. 150.

110 H. Suermann, Juden und Muslime gemäß christlichen Texten zur Zeit Muhammads und in der Frühzeit des Islams, ibid.

111 H. Suermann, Juden und Muslime gemäß christlichen Texten zur Zeit Muhammads und in der Frühzeit des Islams, ibid., p. 154.

112 H. Suermann, Juden und Muslime gemäß christlichen Texten zur Zeit Muhammads und in der Frühzeit des Islams, ibid., p. 152.

113 Cf. about this Jewish apocalypse and text 22.

114 Y.D. Nevo and J. Koren, Crossroads to Islam, op. cit., p. 127.

115 Pseudo-Sebeos, Histoire d'Héraclius, Chap. 37, in: ed. F. Macler, p. 149.

116 Cf. above the text in brackets.

117 Surah 16:67 speaks positively about wine, surah 4:43 forbids to come drunk to prayer, while surahs 5:91 and 2:219 completely prohibit wine as a sin.

118 See also Claude Cahen, Note sur l'Accueil des Chrétiens d'Orient à l'islam, in: Revue de l'Histoire des Religions 2, 1964, p. 55.

119 Because of the totally different theological context, an influence of Marcionite notions of Jesus as a "fighter and merchant", which Ephrem the Syrian intensively deals with, seems very unlikely. Cf. about this question Han J.W. Drijvers, Christ as Warrier and Merchant. Aspects of Marcion's Christology, in: Id., History and Religion in Late Antique Syria, Aldershot (Great Britain), Brookfield (USA) 1994, XIII, p. 73-85. However, the possibility of such influences cannot be entirely dismissed, if we assume that they just survived as notions and motives.

120 Chronik von Seert, chap. 73, in: Addai Scher (Arabic edition) and Pierre Dib (French translation), Histoire Nestorienne (Chronique de Séert), première partie (II) (Patrologia Orientalis, éd. R. Graffin/F. Nau, tome V, fasc. 2), Paris 1950, p. 330-331.

121 René Tardy, Najrân. Chrétiens d'Arabie avant l'islam, Beyrouth 1999, p. 97-98; so also Irfan Shahîd, Nadjjran, in: The Encyclopaedia of Islam. New Edition, Volume VII, Leiden 1992, p. 871-872. The Kitāb al-Himyar here adduced is only extant in fragmentary form; the activities of the Jewish kings in the Yemen against the Christians, however, which were adopted into the Chronicle of Seert, are well attested. One can only surmise that concerning the passage mentioned, the chronicle of Seert is also based on older texts; cf. about the Book of the Himyarites: Irfan Shahîd, The Book of the Himyarites: Authorship and Authenticity, in: id., Byzantium and the Semitic Orient before the Rise of Islam, London 1988, p. 349-362.

122 As Y.D. Nevo and J. Koren, Crossroads to Islam, op. cit., p. 228, opine, these statements presuppose an interpolator, who assigns a "Basic Monotheism" to the Ismaelites. This, however, does not suffice: The clear appropriation of Muḥammad for Jewish interests, above all the return of Israel, hints at a Jewish redactor.

123 Pseudo-Sebeos, Geschichte des Heraklius, chap. 43, in: ed. R.W. Thomson, p. 102-103.

124 Pseudo-Sebeos, L'histoire d'Héraclius, chap. 36; in: ed. F. Macler, p. 139-140 (chap. 50 in: ed. R.W. Thomson, p. 144).

125 Cf. Y. S. Nevo and J. Koren, Crossroads to Islam, op. cit., p. 229-230.

126 F. R. Gahbauer, Anastasius Sinaita, in: LACL 27.

127 Anastasii Sinaitae Viae dux, (critical edition of the Greek text) by Karl-Heinz Uthemann (Corpus Christianorum, series Graeca [CCG], vol. 8), Turnhout, Brepols 1981 (Hodegos, ibid., p. 7-320).

128 Cf. about this question K.-H. Uthemann, ibid. XXX-CCXLVII.

129 Anastasius Sinaita, Viae dux I 1; ibid., p. 9, lines 45-49.

130 Anastasius Sinaita, Viae dux X 2,4; ed. Uthemann, ibid. p. 169-170, lines 5-12.

131 About Severus, Anastasios says, Viae dux VII 2; ed. Uthemann, ibid., p. 113, line 117-120, that he had teachers among the Jews, Greeks and Arabs, who only accepted parts of the scripture. This remark is dark, as neither Severus himself, nor Jews, Greeks (or at that time not even Arabs) could be reproached with this.

132 Anastasius Sinaiticus, Quaestiones et responsiones, in: MPG 89, p. 311-824 (Greek and Latin).

133 Anastasius Sinaita, Quaestiones et responsiones, 126, in: MPG 89, 776 BCE.

134 Jan J. van Ginkel, Jakob von Edessa in der Chronographie des Michael Syrus, in: Martin Tamcke (ed.), Syriaca. Zur Geschichte, Theologie, Liturgie und Gegenwartslage der syrischen Kirchen. 2. Deutsches Syrologen-Symposium (Juli 2000, Wittenberg; Studien zur Orientalischen Kirchengeschichte, Vol. 17), Hamburg 2002, p. 115.

135 According to J. J. van Ginkel, ibid., he was bishop from 682-686 and again in 708.

136 P. Bruns, Jakobus von Edessa, in: LACL, p. 327-329.

137 J. J. van Ginkel, Jakob von Edessa, op. cit., p. 116.

138 Jacob of Edessa, Scholion on 1 Kings 14:21ff., in: George Phillips, Scholia on Passages on the Old Testament by Mar Jacob, Bishop of Edessa, London 1864 (text and English translation).

139 Cf. J.J. van Ginkel, Jakob von Edessa, op. cit., p. 119: "Unfortunately, this chronicle has only been transmitted to us in fragmentary form" (including sources of information). About the authenticity and (il)legibility of the text many questions remain unanswered.

140 English translation in: The Seventh Century in the West-Syrian Chronicles, introduced, translated and annotated by Andrew Palmer, including two seventh-century Syriac apocalyptic texts, introduced, translated and annotated by Sebastian Brock, with added annotations and historical introduction by Robert Hoyland, Liverpool 1993 (ed. A. Palmer), p. 39.

141 Engl. translation in: ed. A. Palmer, p. 37-38.

142 Engl. translation in: ed. A. Palmer, p. 37-39.

143 Cf. about this question the discussion in: Y.D. Nevo and J. Koren, Crossroads to Islam, op. cit., p. 129-131.

144 Synodicon Orientale, Canon 16, Canon 18, translat. and ed. by J.-B. Chabot, Paris 1902, vol. 2 (French translation), p. 488-489.

145 M.F. Nau, Littérature Canonique Syriaque Inédite (Syriac text and French translation), in: Revue de l'Orient Chrétien, Tome IV (XIV), 1909, p. 128-130.

146 Y.D. Nevo and J. Koren, Crossroads to Islam, op. cit., p. 218.

147 Y.D. Nevo and J. Koren, Crossroads to Islam, op. cit., p. 213.

148 Cf. A. Klugkist, Die beiden Homilien des Isaak von Antiocheia über die Eroberung von Bet Hur durch die Araber, op. cit., p. 238.

149 Cf. A.C. Klugkist, ibid., p. 243.

150 Cf. A.C. Klugkist, ibid.

151 Cf. about this question text 4.
152 Y.D. Nevo and J. Koren, Crossroads to Islam, op. cit., p. 107.
153 About the fragmentary Chronicle of Jacob of Edessa cf. text 9, about the anonymous (West) Syriac chronicle cf. text 32.
154 Latin version in: Chronica Minora, pars prior, ed. and transl. by Ignatius Guidi (SSCO, Scriptores Syri, series tertia, tomus IV), Paris 1903, p. 3-32.
155 Thus also the hypothesis of Cl. Cahen, Note sur l'Accueil des Chrétiens d'Orient à l'Islam, in: Revue de l'Histoire des Religions 2, 1964, p. 52.
156 Chronica Minora (SSCO, Scriptores Syri III,4), op. cit., p. 31; German according to: H. Suermann, Orientalische Christen und der Islam, op. cit., p. 130.
157 Thus also C. Cahen, Note sur l'Accueil des Chrétiens d'Orient à l'islam, op. cit., p. 54.
158 H. Suermann, Orientalische Christen und der Islam, op. cit., p. 130.
159 R.G. Hoyland, Seeing Islam as Others saw it, op. cit., p. 591.
160 John bar Penkaye, Chronicle, chap. 14, in: German translation from the Syriac by Rudolf Abramowski, Dionysius von Tellmahre. Zur Geschichte der Kirche unter dem Islam (including a translation of books 14 and 15 of Johannes bar Penkaye), Leipzig 1940, 5.6.
161 Bar Penkaye, Chronicle, chap. 15, ed. Abramowski, p. 8.
162 Harald Suermann, Das arabische Reich in der Weltgeschichte des Johannàn bar Penkàje, in: Nubia et Oriens Christianus. Festschrift (liber amicorum) für C. Detlef G. Müller zum 60. Geburtstag, ed. by Piotr O. Scholz and Reinhard Stempel, Köln 1988, p. 70.
163 A. Mingana, Sources Syriaques, Leipzig 1907, p. 135-138.
164 Cf. also R.G. Hoyland, Seeing Islam as Others saw it, op. cit., p. 197: "His reconstruction of events also follows remarkably closely the traditional Muslim account ... ." It is historically interesting that he tells us about the zeal of Zubaye against those from the West, because he considered them transgressors of the law (Hoyland, ibid., p. 197).
165 These are discussed in the above-mentioned article of H. Suermann, Das arabische Reich, op. cit.
166 Text in English translation in: ed. A. Palmer, p. 15-21.
167 Chronicle, in: ed. A. Palmer, p. 18-19.
168 Chronicle, in: ed. A. Palmer, p. 19.
169 In: ed. A. Palmer, p. 43-44.
170 A. Palmer, ibid.
171 In: ed. Palmer, p. 43.
172 A. Palmer, ibid.
173 A. Palmer, ibid. p. 49.
174 Engl. transl. in: ed. Palmer, p. 49-50.
175 A. Palmer, in: ed. A. Palmer, p. 29.
176 Thus A. Palmer, ibid.; English transl. ibid., p. 29-35.
177 Maronitische Chronik, in: ed. A. Palmer, p. 30.

178 Claude Cahen, Note sur l'Accueil des Chrétiens d'Orient à l'islam, op. cit., p. 54. C. Cahen discusses the different versions of this chronicle mentioned in a contribution by C. Dübler in al-Andalus, 1946.

179 The History of Heraclius of Pseudo-Sebeos, which was influenced by apocalyptic notions, was introduced under "text 7"; two Coptic apocalypses will be dealt with under "text 26 and 27".

180 M. Steinschneider, Apokalypsen mit Polemischer Tendenz, in: Zeitschrift der Deutschen Morgenländischen Gesellschaft, 28. Band, Leipzig 1874, p. 628.

181 Aphrahat, Homilien, in: G. Bert, Aphrahates des Persischen Weisen Homelien (TU III, 3/4), Leipzig 1888, p. 69-88.

182 Cf. about this question Ephrem, Second Sermon, in: ed. Lamy, p. 189-212.

183 Syriac Apocalypse of Daniel. German translation and introduction: Matthias Henze, Apokalypsen und Testamente. Syrische Danielapokalypse (Jüdische Schriften aus hellenistisch-römischer Zeit. Neue Folge, vol. 1, fasc. 4), Gütersloh 2006.

184 M. Henze, ibid., p. 20.

185 Bernard Lewis, An Apocalyptic Vision in Islamic History, in: Bulletin of School of Oriental and African Studies, Volume XIII, Part 1, London 1949, p. 308.

186 Harald Suermann, Die geschichtstheologische Reaktion auf die einfallenden Muslime in der edessenischen Apokalyptik des 7. Jahrhunderts (Europäische Hochschulschriften, Reihe XXIII Theologie, vol. 256), Frankfurt a. M., Bern, New York 1985, p. 117.

187 Cf. also text 18.

188 Ephrem der Syrian, Sermo 2, in: ed. Lamy, p. 111-112.

189 Syriac text: Des heiligen Ephraem des Syrers Sermones III, ed. by Edmund Beck (CSCO, Volume 320, Scriptores Syri, tomus 138), Löwen 1972, p. 60-71; German translation in: Des heiligen Ephraem des Syrers Sermones III, übersetzt von Edmund Beck (CSCO, Volume 321, Scriptores Syri, tomus 129), Löwen 1972, p. 79-94 (ed. E. Beck). The text is not subdivided into Chapters. Syriac text and German translation also in: H. Suermann, Die geschichtstheologische Reaktion, op. cit., p. 12-33.

190 G. J. Reinick, Pseudo-Ephräms "Rede über das Ende" und die syrische eschatologische Literatur des siebten Jahrhunderts, in: Aram 5: 1 u.2, Oxford 1993, p. 462. Contrary to Reinick's opinion, the ductus of the text does not hint at a Jacobite author.

191 W. Bousset, Beiträge zur Geschichte der Eschatologie I, in: ZKG 20, 1899, p. 116.

192 H. Suermann, Die geschichtstheologische Reaktion, op. cit., p. 111.

193 Pseudo-Ephrem, Sermo 5, lines 45-53 (ed. E. Beck, p. 80-81).

194 Pseudo-Ephrem, Sermo 5, lines 61-72 (ed. E. Beck, p. 81).

195 Thus e.g. H. Suermann, Die geschichtstheologische Reaktion, passim, e.g. p. 112.

196 Pseudo-Ephrem, Sermo 5, lines 73 (ed. E. Beck, p. 81).

197 Pseudo-Ephrem, Sermo 5, lines 73-78 (ed. E. Beck, 81). So also implicitly in Sermo 2 (ed. Lamy, p.110).

198 Pseudo-Ephrem, Sermo 5, lines 91-92 (ed. E. Beck, p. 82); "robbers" again in lines 93.

199 Pseudo-Ephrem, Sermo 5, lines 160-167 (ed. E. Beck, p. 84).

200 H. Suermann, Die geschichtstheologische Reaktion, op. cit. 116; cf. also p. 126.

201 Pseudo-Ephrem, Sermo 5, lines 349-354 (ed. E. Beck, p. 89).

202 Pseudo-Ephrem, Sermo 5, lines 356-468 (ed. E. Beck, p. 89-92).

203 Pseudo-Ephrem, Sermo 5, lines 555.556 (ed. E. Beck, p. 94).

204 H. Suermann, Die geschichtstheologische Reaktion, op. cit., p.118.

205 Thus Harald Suermann, Einige Bemerkungen zu syrischen Apokalypsen des 7 JHDS, in: IV Symposium Syriacum 1984, op. cit., p. 328.

206 Ephrem, Sermo 2, Text in: ed. Lamy, op. cit.

207 Cf. above chap. 3.4 Einführung.

208 Ephrem, Sermo 2 (ed. Lamy, p. 190).

209 Thus G. J. Reinick, Der edessenische "Pseudo-Methodius", in: Byzantinische Zeitschrift 83, 1990, p. 22.

210 Francisco Javier Martinez, The Apocalyptic Genre in Syriac: The World of Pseudo-Methodius, in: IV Symposium Syriacum 1984, op. cit., p. 340.

211 Die Syrische Apokalypse des Pseudo-Methodius, ed. by G.J. Reinick (CSCO, Scriptores Syri, Tomus 220), Löwen 1993. German translation: Die syrische Apokalypse des Pseudo-Methodius, übersetzt von G.J. Reinick (CSCO, Volumen 541, Scriptores Syri, Tomus 221), Löwen 1993 (ed. G.J. Reinick). The edition with translation published by H. Suermann (Die geschichtstheologische Reaktion, op. cit., p. 34-85) is considered by Reinick as "much too critical and full of mistakes" (Introduction to the Syriac version, op. cit., p. XVI). A French translation of the text of the Vaticanum can be found in: F.J. Martinez, Eastern Christian Apocalyptic in Early Muslim Period. Pseudo-Methodius and Pseudo-Athanasius, Volume 1, Washington D.C. 1985. Pseudo-Methodius: Part I, Chapter I: The Syriac Apocalypse of Pseudo-Methodius (MP), p. 2-205.

212 About these Greek and Latin translations cf.: Die Apokalypse des Pseudo-Methodius. Die ältesten griechischen und lateinischen Übersetzungen, ed. by W.J. Aerts und G.A.A. Kortekaas (CSCO, Vol. 570; Subsidia, tomus 98), Löwen 1998.

213 G. J. Reinick, in: CSCO, Tomus 220, VII.

214 G. J. Reinick, in: ibid.; p. VII-XIV.

215 The person after whom the apocalypse was named is the Syrian bishop and martyr Methodios of Olympos (died during the persecution of Decius, thus in the middle of the third century), who was erroneously thought to be the author.

216 A part of the sources are mentioned by H. Suermann, Die geschichtliche Reaktion, op. cit., p. 130-136. These sources are very interesting from the point of view of the history of religion, as some of the motives they contain have entered the Qur'ān (e.g. the tales of Gog and Magog or motives from the Alexander romance).

217 Cush is one of the sons of (C)ham, a son of Noah. He was the father of the hunter Nimrod, who founded a great empire in Mesopotamia (Gen. 10:6-12; similarly in 1 Chr. 1:8-10). This mythical genealogy is dealt with again in Pseudo-Methodios. At that time, C(h)ush was a designation for Ethiopia.

218 Pseudo-Methodius, chap. 9:8-9; German according to: ed. G. J. Reinick, p. 32.

219 The thesis of a Jacobite author is merely based on the great importance of Cush (כּוּשׁ Kūš; also: Ethiopia) for the salvation history as presented. At that time, Ethiopia had already become Monophysite.

220 Pseudo-Methodius, chap. 10.6; German: ed. G. J. Reinick, p. 39.
221 Pseudo-Methodius, chap. 12,3; German: ed. G. J. Reinick, p. 54-55.
222 Pseudo-Methodius, chap. 13,15; German: ed. G. J. Reinick, p. 65.
223 Pseudo-Methodius, chap. 13,19; German: ed. G. J. Reinick, p. 67.
224 Pseudo-Methodius, chap. 13,21; German: ed. G. J. Reinick, p. 69.
225 Pseudo-Methodius, chap. 14,13.14; German: ed. G. J. Reinick, p. 77-78.
226 G. J. Reinick, Der edessenische "Pseudo-Methodius", in: Byzantinische Zeitschrift 83, 1990, p. 39.
227 G. J. Reinick, ibid.
228 G. J. Reinick, ibid., p. 40.
229 G. J. Reinick, ibid., p. 42-43.
230 Pseudo-Methodius, final sentences of chap. 10.
231 Pseudo-Methodius, chap. 11,5; German: ed. G. J. Reinick, p. 43.
232 Pseudo-Methodius, chap. 11,3; German: ed. G. J. Reinick, p. 42.
233 Pseudo-Methodius, chap. 11,17; German: ed. G. J. Reinick, p. 50.
234 Because, like already in chap. 11, Sicily is mentioned, which was only conquered in 827, and the land of the Greeks and Romans, which were conquered even later, Suermann (ibid., p. 150) thinks that the author "simply expanded the boundaries of experienced history".
235 Pseudo-Methodius, Chap. 13,6; German: ed. G. J. Reinick, p. 60.
236 G. J. Reinick, in: ed. G. J. Reinick, p. 60, A.20.
237 Pseudo-Methodius 13,11; German: ed. G. J. Reinick, p. 62.
238 The number 60 is also important in the Islamic traditional literature.
239 Pseudo-Methodius, chap. 5,5; German: ed. G. J. Reinick, p. 13.
240 Pseudo-Methodius, chap. 5,6; German: ed. G. J. Reinick, p. 13-14.
241 Pseudo-Methodius, chap. 5,1.2; German: ed. G. J. Reinick, p. 11.
242 Pseudo-Methodius, chap. 5, p.3-4.
243 Pseudo-Methodius, chap. 5,7; German: ed. G. J. Reinick, p. 14.
244 Pseudo-Methodius, chap. 5,8; German: ed. G. J. Reinick, p. 14.15.
245 Pseudo-Methodius, chap.5,9; German: ed. G. J. Reinick, p. 15.
246 H. Suermann, Die geschichtstheologische Reaktion, op. cit., p. 159.
247 About Mecca cf. the following text.
248 Thus F.J. Martinez, The apocalyptic Genre in Syriac, op. cit., p. 341.
249 F.J. Martinez, ibid., p. 342.
250 Syriac text and German transl. in: H. Suermann, Die geschichtstheologische Reaktion, op. cit., p. 86-97.
251 H. Suermann, ibid., p. 162.
252 Cf. H. Suermann, ibid., p. 171-174.
253 Thus H. Suermann, ibid., p. 163.
254 The Gospel of the twelve Apostles, together with the apocalypses of each one of them, ed. from the Syriac Ms. with a Translation and Introduction by J. Rendel Harris (ed. J.R. Harris), Cambridge 1900.
255 H. Suermann, Die geschichtstheologische Reaktion, op. cit., p. 175.
256 Han J.W. Drijvers, The Gospel of the Twelve Apostles: A Syriac Apocalypse from the Early Islamic Period, in: Id., History and Religion in Late Antique Syria, Aldershot (Great Britain), Brookfield (USA) 1994, chap. VIII, 209; the sources of the script are discussed on p. 209-211.
257 H. Suermann, Die geschichtstheologische Reaktion, op. cit., p. 191.

258 J.R. Harris, in: ed. J.R. Harris, p. 20-23.
259 H.J.W. Drijvers, The Gospel of the Twelve Apostles, op. cit., p. 189.
260 H. Suermann, Die geschichtstheologische Reaktion, op. cit., p. 178-191.
261 H. Suermann, ibid., p. 189-190.
262 H. Suermann, ibid., p. 189-190.
263 Apokalypse des Johannes, in: ed. J.R. Harris, p. 34-36.
264 Ibid., in: ed. J.R. Harris, p. 36; German according to: H. Suermann, Die geschichtstheologische Reaktion, op. cit., p. 102.
265 Apokalypse des Johannes, in: ed. J.R. Harris, p.36; German acc. to H. Suermann, op. cit., p. 102.
266 H.J.W. Drijvers, The Gospel of the Twelve Apostles, op. cit., p. 203.
267 Apokalypse des Johannes, in: ed. J.R. Harris, p. 37; German acc. to H. Suermann, ibid.
268 H.J.W. Drijvers, The Gospel of the Twelve Apostles, op. cit., p. 201, considers the "Northern" emperor, who will "come in the end" to be Constantine.
269 Apokalypse des Johannes, in: ed. J.R. Harris, ibid., p. 38; German acc. to H. Suermann, ibid., p. 106.
270 Diglath "is the exact equivalent of the Arabic Dijla, the river Tigris" (H.J.W. Drijvers, The Gospel of the Twelve Apostles, op. cit., p. 208).
271 Apokalypse des Johannes, in: ed. J.R. Harris, ibid., p. 38-39; German acc. to H. Suermann, ibid., p. 108.
272 H.J.W. Drijvers, The Gospel of the Twelve Apostles, op. cit. 201.
273 Cf. H.J.W. Drijver, ibid. 206.
274 This opinion is shared by H.J.W. Drijvers, ibid. passim and H. Suermann, ibid. 179.
275 Cf. K.-H. Ohlig, From muḥammad Jesus to Prophet of the Arabs.
276 H.J.W. Drijvers, The Gospel of Twelve Apostles, op. cit., p. 213.
277 Cf. K.-H. Ohlig, From muḥammad Jesus to Prophet of the Arabs, and Volker Popp, From Ugarit to Samarrā', both in the present anthology.
278 For the first time published in 1743 in Saloniki, then again by A. Jellinek, Bet ha-Midrasch, Leipzig 1855, vol. IV, VIII, IX and printed again on p. 117-126.
279 Heinrich Graetz, Geschichte der Juden, vol. 5, Darmstadt 1998 [Reprint of Leipzig 1909], p. 465. About the sources of information cf. ibid., p. 464-471. Similarly Bernard Lewis, An Apocalyptic Vision of Islamic History, in: Bulletin of the School of Oriental and African Studies, Volume XIII: Part I, London 1949, p. 309-311.
280 An English translation based on the edition by A. Jellinek in: B. Lewis, An Apocalyptic Vision, ibid., p. 311-320.
281 Cf. B. Lewis, An Apocalyptic Vision, ibid., p. 331-335.
282 Secrets, quoted according to the English translation by B. Lewis, An Apocalyptic Vision, ibid., p. 321.
283 H. Graetz, Geschichte der Juden, op. cit., p. 465.
284 B. Lewis, An Apocalyptic Vision, op. cit., p. 327.
285 B. Lewis, ibid., p. 328.

286 Homily about the holy children of Babylon, as the first of three Coptic sermons printed about this subject; edited and translated by Henri de Vis: Panégyrique des Trois Saints Enfants de Babylone, 1. Premier Panégyrique. Acéphale, in: Homélies coptes de la Vaticane II, texte copte publié et traduit par Henri de Vis (Cahiers de la Bibliothèque copte, Strasbourg), Louvain, Paris 1990, p. 60-120.
287 H. de Vis in his introduction to Panegyricus, ibid., p. 60.
288 H. de Vis, ibid., p. 62.
289 H. de Vis, ibid.
290 R.G. Hoyland, Seeing Islam as Others saw it, op. cit., p. 120-121.
291 Sermon about the Holy Children of Babylon § 36, in: ed. de Vis, p. 100.
292 R.G. Hoyland, Seeing Islam as Others saw it, op. cit., p. 121.
293 P. Bruns, B. Windau, Benjamin von Alexandrien, in: LACL, p. 107-108.
294 R.G. Hoyland, Seeing Islam as Others saw it, op. cit., p. 134-135.
295 Harald Suermann, Die Apokalypse des Ps.-Athanasius. Ein Beispiel für die koptische Auseinandersetzung mit der islamischen Herrschaft im Ägypten der Ummayyadenzeit, in: Walter Beltz (ed.), Die koptische Kirche in den ersten drei islamischen Jahrhunderten (Beiträge zum gleichnamigen Leucorea-Kolloquium 2002, Hallesche Beiträge zur Orientwissenschaft), Halle 2003, p. 183-197. Id., Koptische Texte zur arabischen Eroberung Ägyptens und der Umayyadenherrschaft, in: Journal of Coptic Studies 4, 2002, p. 167-186.
296 H. Suermann, Die Apokalypse des Ps.-Athansius, op. cit., p. 183.
297 Geschichte der Patriarchen 17 (Patrologia Orientalis 5, p. 68).
298 H. Suermann, Die Apokalypse des Ps.-Athanasius, op. cit., p. 192, with references to F.J. Martinez, Apocalyptic, p. 264-267.
299 Chronicle of John of Nikiu, chap. 121, 10.11; in: The Lines of John (c. 690 CE) Coptic Bishop of Nikiu, ed. and transl. by Robert H. Church, London 1916, p. 201.
300 Y. D. Nevo and J. Koren, Crossroads to Islam, op. cit., p. 233-235.
301 Christoph Luxenberg, Neudeutung der arabischen Inschrift im Felsendom zu Jerusalem, op. cit.
302 H. Suermann, Die Apokalypse des Ps.-Athanasius, op. cit., p. 184-185.
303 R. G. Hoyland, Seeing Islam as Others saw it, op. cit., p. 279-282.
304 English translation of the interpolation in R.G. Hoyland, ibid., p. 280-281.
305 Cf. Huge G. Evelyn White, The Monasteries of the Wadi 'n Natrun, vol. 2, New York 1932, p. 171-175.
306 H. Suermann, Die Apokalypse des Ps.-Athanasius, op. cit., p. 185.
307 H. Suermann, Die Apokalypse des Ps.-Athanasius, op. cit., p. 185.
308 H. Suermann, ibid., p. 186.
309 Henricus Tattam, Prophetae majores in dialecto Aegytiacae seu coptica, II, Oxford 1852, p. 386-405; French translation: Frédéric Macler, Les Apocalypses Apocryphes de Daniel, (Suite) III, in: Revue de l'histoire des religions 33, 1896, p. 163-176 (F. Macler, Les Apocalypses Apocryphes).
310 Cf. F. Macler, Les Apocalypses Apocryphes, p. 163: "Exaspérée par le malheur, elle (l'église copte) se réfugia dans des espérances apocalyptiques".
311 H. Suermann, Die Apokalypse des Ps.-Athanasius, op. cit., p. 196.
312 F. Macler, Les apocalypses apocryphes, p. 165.
313 F. Macler, ibid. p. 165.

314 Edition of the Coptic text by Francisco Javier Martinez, Sahidic Apocalyse of Pseudo-Athanasius, in: id., Eastern Apocalyptic, op. cit., p. 247-590 (Coptic/-Arabic p. 285-411).
315 Cf. H. Suermann, Die Apokalypse des Ps.-Athanasius, op. cit., p. 188-189.
316 Pseudo-Athanasius IX, 8 (ed. Martinez, p. 529).
317 H. Suermann, Die Apokylypse des Ps.-Athanasius, op. cit., p. 191.
318 Pseudo-Athanasius IX, 7 (ed. Martinez, p. 528).
319 F.R. Gahbauer, Germanus von Konstantinopel, in: LACL, 253.
320 Sancti Germani Patriarchae Constantinopolitani Epistolae Dogmaticae, in: MPG 98, 147 A -222 B.
321 All this in one column of a page in the "Migne".
322 Germanus, Dogmatische Briefe, MPG 93, 168 C.D.
323 Robert Volk, Johannes von Damaskus, in: LACL 344.345; id., Johannes v. Damaskus, in: LThK3 5, p. 895-896.
324 Johannes Damascenus (John of Damascus), Über die Häresien, Kapitel 100, in: Die Schriften des Johannes von Damaskus, Vol. IV, Liber de haeresibus. Opera polemica, ed. by Bonifatius Kotter (PTS 22), Berlin, New York 1981, p. 60-67 (ed. B. Kotter).
325 Johannes Damascenus, Disputatio Christiani et Saraceni, in: Die Schriften des Johannes von Damaskus, Vol. IV (PTS 22), ibid., p. 427-438. Greek with a French translation in: Jean Damascène, Écrit sur l'islam, ed. by Raymond Le Coz (Sources chrétiennes, 383), p. 228-250; the French version "translates" the term "Saracen" with "musulman (Muslim)", which in this case might be an admissible interpretation, but not an appropriate translation.
326 Disputatio Christiani et Saraceni, ed. B. Kotter, p. 432.
327 Ibid.; ibid., p. 438.
328 R. Volk, Johannes v. Damaskus, in: LThK35, p. 897.
329 Cf. B. Kotter, in: ed. B. Kotter, p. 71-77.
330 R. Volk, Johannes v. Damaskus, in: LThK35, p. 896.
331 If we assume that the 100th chapter is an addition by a later redactor, – which is possible, albeit not probable, – then that would mean that the point in time when Islam became a truly separate religion would have to be shifted to an even later era.
332 Liber de haeresibus 100; ed. B. Kotter, p. 60, lines 1-6. cf. about this question S. Dörper, Zum Problem des Völkernamens Saraceni, op. cit., p. 100.
333 He obviously considers the Morning Star and Aphrodite as two separate deities.
334 In John's treatise, Chabar (Xabar) is the Greek transcription of Arabic *kabar*, "(to be) great". As he adds the meaning "great" himself, no other interpretation is possible (as e.g. Syriac chabar = child, Arabisch ẖabar = news).
335 About the name of the pseudo-prophet cf. K.-H. Ohlig, From muḥammad Jesus to Prophet of the Arabs, in the present anthology, (see also A. 11, about the spelling "Mamed").
336 The theology of early surahs is pre-Nicean-Syrian. John did not know this history of theology and interpreted within the context of Arianism, a doctrine he knew well and which admittedly possesses similar traits.

337 Johannes Damascenus, Liber de haeresibus 100; ed. B. Kotter, p. 60, lines 7-13.
338 Johannes Damascenus, Liber de haeresibus 100; ed. B. Kotter, p. 60, lines 14, -61, lines 2.
339 Johannes Damascenus, Liber de haeresibus 100, ed. B. Kotter, p. 61, lines 17-25.
340 Johannes Damascenus, Liber de haeresibus 100; ed. B. Kotter, p. 61, lines 25-31.
341 Johannes Damascenus, Liber de haeresibus 100; ed. B. Kotter, p. 61, lines 32, -62, lines 54.
342 Johannes Damascenus, Liber de haeresibus 100; ed. B. Kotter, p. 63, lines 61-68; Johannes distinguishes between *hó theós* for "God" und *theós* (divine) for Jesus Christ.
343 Johannes Damascenus, Liber de haeresibus 100; ed. B. Kotter, p. 63, lines 69-70.
344 Johannes Damascenus, Liber de haeresibus 100; ed. B. Kotter, p. 64, lines 78-93.
345 Johannes Damascenus, Liber de haeresibus 100; ed. B. Kotter, p. 64, lines 96.
346 Johannes Damascenus, ibid.; ed. B. Kotter, p. 64, lines 96, -65, lines 99; cf. about this question surah 4:3.
347 Johannes Damascenus, ibid.; ed. B. Kotter, p. 65, lines 99.100; cf. surah 4:20.
348 Johannes Damascenus, ibid.; ed. B. Kotter, p. 65, lines 100-107.
349 Johannes Damascenus, ibid.; ed. B. Kotter, p. 65, lines 108.
350 Johannes Damascenus, ibid.; ed. B. Kotter, p. 65, lines 108-110.
351 Johannes Damascenus, ibid.; ed. B. Kotter, p. 65, lines 114 - 66, lines 148.
352 Cf. e.g. surahs 26:155-159; 11:65; 17:59.
353 A. Sprenger. Das Leben und die Lehre des Mohammed nach bisher grösstentheils unbenutzten Quellen, 1st vol., Berlin 21869, p. 518-525.
354 Johannes Damascenus, ibid.; ed. B. Kotter, p. 67, lines 149-156.
355 Johannes Damascenus, ibid.; ed. B. Kotter, p. 67, lines 149.150; cf. surah 5:112-115.
356 Johannes Damascenus, ibid.; ed. Kotter, p. 67, lines 152-156.
357 Thus H. Suermann, Einige Bemerkungen zu syrischen Apokalypsen des 7. JHDS., op. cit., p. 332; with bibliographical references for his thesis.
358 Other texts would have to be mentioned here: A Frankish chronicle of Fredegar, the "Siegeszeichen von Damaskus", Notes of the Pilgrim Arculf, a Vision of Henochs the Just, a Greek interpolation of the Syrian pseudo-Methodios, a disputation of a monk from Beth Hale with an Arab, the introduction of a code of laws of Ishoboct of Fars and a tale of Stephen of Alexandria. The authenticity of all these text fragments is highly questionable, mostly they have to be dated as much later and/or they are irrelevant for our questions.
359 German translation in Theodor Nöldeke, Zur Geschichte der Araber im 1. Jahrhundert d.H. aus syrischen Quellen, in: Zeitschrift der Deutschen Morgenländischen Gesellschaft 1875, p. 76-82; English translation (with deviations if compared to Nöldeke) in: ed. A. Palmer, p. 2-4.
360 R.G. Hoyland, Seeing Islam as Others saw it, op. cit., p. 116.117
361 Y.D. Nevo and J. Koren, Crossroads to Islam, op. cit., p. 110-114.
362 Cf. about this question Chr. Luxenberg, Neudeutung der arabischen Inschrift im Felsendom zu Jerusalem, op. cit.
363 The biography was allegedly written in the year 774 and summarized together with the biographies of two other founders of monasteries as the Quartmin-trilogy.
364 R.G. Hoyland, Seeing Islam as Others saw it, op. cit., p. 123.124.

365 Chronicle of 819, in: ed. A. Palmer, p. 7.

366 Cf. about this question R.G. Hoyland, Seeing Islam as Others saw it, op. cit., p. 87-91.

367 Cf. about this question e.g. Samir K. Samir, The Prophet Muhammad as seen by Timothy I. and other Arab Christian Authors, in: David Thomas (ed.), Syrian Christians under Islam. The First Thousand Years, Leiden, Boston, Köln 2001, p. 75-106.

368 Cf. about this question above, p. 226 f.

369 Cf. about this question V. Popp, From Ugarit to Samarrā', op. cit., and K.-H. Ohlig, From muḥammad Jesus to Prophet of the Arabs.

370 Cf. about this question o. V. Popp, From Ugarit to Samarrā', op. cit.

371 Cf. K.-H. Ohlig, Fundamentalchristologie. Im Spannungsfeld von Christentum und Kultur, München 1986, p. 175.

372 Die Schatzhöhle, ed. Bezold, p. 70.

373 According to Latin theology the statement that the Syrians have no share of the blood of Christ would have led to the conclusion that they would not be saved by the blood, the only basis of justification (cf. e.g. Tertullian, De carne Christi [around 210-212] 5:3 (CCL 2, 881): the cross is "the only hope of the whole world". The function of the cross within the context of salvation is explicitly mentioned in St. Augustine (cf. K.-H. Ohlig, Fundamentalchristologie, op. cit. p. 343-359).

374 Cf. about this question K.-H. Ohlig, Das syrische und arabische Christentum und der Islam, op. cit., p. 395-396.

375 There was a thesis current in the area – which goes back to Monophysite motives – that the nature of the human Jesus was not influenced by desires and passions from his conception to his death, that he was not subject to suffering and indestructible. In the 7th and 8th century, it led to violent debates, e.g. in the Armenian Church. Cf. about this question Peter Cowe, Philoxenus of Mabbug and the Synod of Manazkert, in: ARAM. A Festschrift for Dr. Sebastian P. Brock, Volume 5, 1 and 2, Leuven 1993, p. 115-129.

376 S. Brock, Syriac Views of Emergent Islam, op. cit., p. 21.

377 Cf. o. A. 119.

378 Cf. text 7 above.

Endnotes
Karl-Heinz Ohlig: From muḥammad Jesus to Prophet of the Arabs, pp. 251-307

---

1 Cf. K.-H. Ohlig, Weltreligion Islam. Eine Einführung, Mainz, Luzern 2000, p. 60–67.
2 See R.C. Zaehner, Zurvan. A Zoroastrian Dilemma, Oxford 1955, Chapter I (English translation of the Persian Report, p. 7 (below), 8.9.
3 I base my view especially on the following publications: Yehuda D. Nevo, Judith Koren, Crossroads to Islam. The Origins of the Arab Religion and the Arab State, Amherst, New York 2003, as well as articles of Volker Popp in Inârah anthologies: Die frühe Islamgeschichte nach inschriftlichen und numismatischen Zeugnissen, in: Karl-Heinz Ohlig, Gerd-Rüdiger Puin (eds.), Die dunklen Anfänge. Neue Forschungen zur Entstehung und frühen Geschichte des Islam, Berlin [1]2005, [2]2006, p. 16-123; Christoph Luxenberg, Neudeutung der arabischen Inschrift im Felsendom zu Jerusalem, in: ibid. p. 124-147; in the present anthology (German version): Volker Popp, Von Ugarit nach Samarra. Eine archäologische Reise auf den Spuren Ernst Herzfelds. In the following, these articles will be quoted in endnotes only in those cases, where a specific passage is referred to.
4 About this matter cf. my article "Evidence of a New Religion in Christian Literature 'Under Islamic Rule'?" in the present anthology.
5 Cf. Volker Popp, Die frühe Islamgeschichte, op. cit. p. 63-64.
6 About the most important Sassanian deportations, beginning with the reign of Shapur I (240-270 CE), cf.: Erich Kettenhofen, Deportations II. In the Parthian and Sasanian Periods, in: Encyclopaedia Iranica (ed. by Eshan Yarshater), Volume VII, Fascile 3, Costa Mesa (California, USA) 1994, p. 298-308.
7 Cf. V. Popp, Von Ugarit nach Samarra.
8 "*Meḥmat* – the angry one", makes no sense.
9 Cf. V. Popp, Von Ugarit nach Samarra.
10 Cf. V. Popp, Die frühe Islamgeschichte ..., op. cit. p. 63-64; cf. e.g. p. 66, pic. 16.
11 Johannes Damascenus, Über die Häresien, Liber de haeresibus opera polemica, in: Die Schriften des Johannes von Damaskus, vol. IV, ed. by Bonifatius Kotter (PTS 22), Berlin, New York 1981, haer. 100, p. 60, line 11. The form *Mamed* without "ch" (H) could be the transcription of the Syriac term *mamed* meaning *baptist*; but the possibility that what is meant here is *Maḥmed* is much more probable. The reason could be that in West Syrian dialects the originally pharyngeal "ḥ – IPA: [ħ]" was weakened, or simply that this phoneme is not a speech sound in Greek: the Greek letter Chi (X) was originally pronounced as an aspirated [kʰ], later as a velar fricative [x]; the glottal [h] appears in Greek as the "spiritus asper" only at the beginning of words (cf. also the Greek transliteration of Aramaic *Yuḥannā* as Ἰωάννης (*Iōannēs*) vs. Latin *Johannes*).
12 A. Sprenger, Das Leben und die Lehre des Mohammad nach bisher grösstentheils unbenutzten Quellen, 1st vol., Berlin [2]1869, p. 161.
13 Cf. Christoph Luxenberg, Neudeutung der arabischen Inschrift im Felsendom zu Jerusalem, op. cit. p. 124-147.
14 Botterweck G. Johannes/ Ringgren, Helmer (1980). Theological Dictionary of the Old Testament, vol. 4. Stuttgart, pp. 452.

15 Cf. Segert, Stanislav (1984). A Basic Grammar of the Ugaritic Language. Berkeley/ Los Angeles/ London; p. 162, text 88.53 (1.4:V:12-19); see also: Markus Gross: "New Ways of Qur'ānic Research", chapter: 6.6 "Muḥammad" and the Semitic Root "ḥ-m-d", as well as Volker Popp: "From Ugarit to Sāmarrā'", both in the present anthology.

16 Cf. also Romans 11:28.

17 Cf. also 1 Thess. 1:4; Kol. 3:12; 2 Tim. 2:10; 2 Pet. 1:10.

18 A. Sprenger, Das Leben und die Lehre des Mohammad ..., op. cit. p. 159.160.

19 A. Sprenger, ibid. p. 159.

20 A. Sprenger, ibid. p. 160.

21 Already Paul von Samosata (died 272) had polemically opposed the Greek understanding of Jesus as God's son: Fragmente aus dem Synodalbrief (nach 268), Nr. 5 (Friedrich Loofs, Paulus von Samosata. Eine Untersuchung zur altkirchlichen Literatur- und Dogmengeschichte, Leipzig 1924, p. 331), Akten der Disputation mit dem Presbyter Malchion, Nr. 8 (268; Greek and German: F. Loofs, ibid. 337); Diodor von Tarsus (died before 394), Fragments 11, 13, 15, 18, 29 (Syriac and German: Rudolf Abramowski, Der theologische Nachlass des Diodor von Tarsus, in: ZNW 42, 1949, pp. 31, 33, 37, 47), Fragments (of Diodorus) in Leontius, Contra Nestorium et Eutychen 3 (Greek: MPG 86, 1, 1865, 1388 A); Theodorus of Mopsuestia (died 428), from the theses refuted by Cyrill (Mansi 4, 45 [219]; Aphrahat (died after 345), Unterweisungen (Demonstrations) 14, 39 (Aphrahat, Unterweisungen. Zweiter Teilband. Aus dem Syrischen übersetzt und eingeleitet von Peter Bruns [Fontes Christiaani, Bd. 5/2], Freiburg, Basel, Wien et al. 1991, 376).

22 Aphrahat, Demonstration 14:33. Aphrahat mentions Jesus as member of a chain of prophets (passim) and calls him „the Great Prophet" (cf. also Demonstration 2,6; 4,6; [17,11]).

23 Cf. my monograph: Fundamentalchristologie. Im Spannungsfeld von Christentum und Kultur, München 1986, p. 90-124; p. 198-244.

24 Cf. my article: Das syrische und arabische Christentum und der Koran, in: K.-H. Ohlig, G.-R. Puin (eds.), Die dunklen Anfänge, op. cit. p. 370-394 (whole article: p. 366-404).

25 Cf. Fundamentalchristologie, op. cit. 635-638.

26 About the text cf. Y. D. Nevo und J. Koren, Crossroads to Islam, op. cit. p. 412-413.

27 About the text cf. Y. D. Nevo, J. Koren, Crossroads to Islam, ibid. p. 410-411.

28 Cf. V. Popp, Die frühe Islamgeschichte ..., op. cit. p. 66, pic. 17 and 18.

29 About the importance of the Dome of the Rock cf. V. Popp, Die frühe Islamgeschichte ..., op. cit. p. 81-85; Ch. Luxenberg, Neudeutung der arabischen Inschrift im Felsendom zu Jerusalem, op. cit. p. 143-145.

30 Syrische Danielapokalypse (Syriac Apocalypse of Daniel). Deutsche Übersetzung und Einleitung (German translation and introduction): Matthias Henze, Apokalypsen und Testamente. Syrische Danielapokalypse (Jüdische Schriften aus helle-

nistisch-römischer Zeit, vol. 1, fasc. 4), Gütersloh 2006; there, 20, Ausführungen zur Abfassungszeit.

31 G.J. Reinink, Die syrische Apokalypse des Pseudo-Methodius, transl. by G.J. Reinink (Corpus Scriptorum Christianorum Orientalium, Vol. 541), Einleitung (introduction) XX. XXI. However, Reinink thinks that the Dome of the Rock is an Islamic building, „the first of its kind in Islamic history" (ibid. XXI).

32 Johannes Damascenus, Über die Häresien, Liber de haeresibus opera polemica, haer. 100, op. cit., p. 64, p. 87-94.

33 Thus for the first time: V. Popp, Die frühe Islamgeschichte ..., op. cit. p. 67-76.

34 Aphrahat, Unterweisungen (Demonstrations). Erster Teilband (first half of the first volume). Aus dem Syrischen übersetzt und eingeleitet von Peter Bruns (Fontes Christiani, vol. 5/1), Freiburg, Basel, Wien et al. 1991, 82; for the English version the translation by John Gwynn was used: John Gwynn. From Nicene and Post-Nicene Fathers, Second Series, Vol. 13. Edited by Philip Schaff and Henry Wace. (Buffalo, NY: Christian Literature Publishing Co., 1890.) Revised and edited for New Advent by Kevin Knight:
http://www.newadvent.org/fathers/3701.htm

35 Aphrahat, ibid. p. 84.

36 Aphrahat, ibid. p. 85.

37 Aphrahat, ibid.

38 Aphrahat, ibid. p. 86.

39 Aphrahat, ibid. p. 95.

40 V. Popp, Die frühe Islamgeschichte, ibid. p. 85.

41 Why there is no longer a cross depicted above the "stones", like in the case of the stairs on coins of Heraclius a few decades before, cannot be answered with certainty. It might be the adoption of an archaic, e.g. Nabataean, symbolism, which is reinterpreted from an Old Testament perspective (V. Popp's view); alternatively it could be due to the non-acknowledgement of the soteriological effect of Jesus' death on the cross (about this question cf. my article: Das syrische und arabische Christentum und der Koran, op. cit. p. 395-396).

42 Cf. V. Popp, Die frühe Islamgeschichte, op. cit. p. 98.

43 About the text cf. Y. D. Nevo, J. Koren, Crossroads to Islam, op. cit. 418-419.

44 About the text cf. Y. D. Nevo, J. Koren, Crossroads to Islam, op. cit. 420-421.

45 Cf. among others Ignaz Goldziher, Islam und Parsismus; V. Popp, Der Einfluss persischer religiöser Raster auf Vorstellungen im Koran.

46 About this question cf. V. Popp, Die frühe Islamgeschichte, op. cit. p. 105-107.

47 V. Popp, Die frühe Islamgeschichte …, ibid. p. 106.

48 Cf. my article: Das syrische und arabische Christentum und der Koran, op. cit. p. 378-384.

49 Cf. I. Goldziher, Islam and Parsism; V. Popp, The Influence of Persian Religious Patterns on Notions in the Qur'ān.

50 Arabic Edition, Karachi (Pakistan) 1967; Arabic (with German commentary): Ibn Saad. Biographien Muhammeds, seiner Gefährten und der späteren Träger des Islams bis zum Jahre 230 der Flucht, vol. 1, Theil I: Biographie Muhammeds bis zur Flucht, ed. by E. Mittwoch, Leiden 1905, und Theil II: Biographie

Muhammeds. Ereignisse seiner medinischen Zeit, Personalbeschreibung und Lebensgewohnheiten, ed. by E. Mittwoch and E. Sachau, Leiden 1917.

51 About this matter cf. also A. Sprenger, Das Leben und die Lehre des Mohammad, op. cit. p. 156-157.

52 A. Sprenger, Das Leben und die Lehre des Mohammad, op. cit. p. 157.

53 A. Sprenger, Das Leben und die Lehre des Mohammad, Vorrede, I.

54 The historicity of both the Buddha and Zarathustra, even of a historical kernel, is far from undisputed. What tradition tells of their lives is so contaminated with obvious legends, exaggerations and later interpolations, that it is very hard to filter out a historical person.

55 The only testimonies that come into question are Qur'ānic texts; about this matter cf. p. 350 ff..

56 Y.D. Nevo and J. Koren, Crossroads to Islam, op. cit. p. 131.

57 Cf. Chr. Luxenberg, Neudeutung der arabischen Inschrift im Felsendom zu Jerusalem, op. cit. pp. 124.

58 Also cf. my article: Evidence of a New Religion in Christian Literature "Under Islamic Rule"?; there the question of the "information" contained in historicizing material is discussed.

59 However, there are many problems attached to this matter that have not yet been discussed, as the manuscript attestation of traditional literature generally ascribed to the 9th and 10th century, only sets in about three or four centuries later.

60 All quotations from the Qur'ān, unless otherwise indicated, are from Marmaduke Pickthall's translation, which is also available on the internet; in some cases Rudi Paret's German translation and commentary were also used: Der Koran. Übersetzung von Rudi Paret, Stuttgart [9]2004.

61 Cf. Chr. Luxenberg, Neudeutung der arabischen Inschrift im Felsendom zu Jerusalem, op. cit.

62 Y.D. Nevo and J. Koren, Crossroads to Islam, op. cit. p. 265.

63 Cf. Alfred-Louis de Prémare, Les Fondations de l'Islam, éditions du seuil, 2002, p. 290: the author mentions the incident when 'Umar had a text from the Bible that he liked copied, and was later reprimanded by the Prophet, who stated that it "suffices to read the Qur'ān".

64 Cf. about this question: Christoph Luxenberg, Die syro-aramäische Lesart des Koran. Ein Beitrag zur Entschlüsselung der Koransprache, Berlin [2]2004, p. 81-86.

65 Der Koran. Aus dem Arabischen übertragen von Max Henning, Stuttgart 1973.

66 R. Paret translates "Verpflichtung (obligation)" instead of "Bund (covenant)", so that the biblical context is hidden.

67 Cf. Q 2:89: Paret: "And (now) when a scripture (i.e., the Qur'ān) came to him, which confirmed what was already there (as revelation) ..., as what they already knew (referring to the content of the message), (in a new revelation), then they did not believe it." According to R. Paret the verse is addressed to the Jews; but before, in v. 87, Moses and Jesus are spoken of, so that the statement is about the disbelief of both groups, Jews as well as Christians. Pickthall translates: "And when there cometh unto them a Scripture from Allah, confirming that in their possession

though, before that they were asking for a signal triumph over those who disbelieved and when there cometh unto them that which they know (to be the Truth) they disbelieve therein."

68 Cf. e.g. Q 2:136: „We believe in Allah and that which is revealed unto Us and that which was revealed unto Abraham, and Ishmael, and Isaac, and Jacob. and the tribes, and that which Moses and Jesus received, add that which the Prophets received from their Lord. We make no distinction between any of them, and unto Him we have surrendered. …".

69 Cf. Gen 12-25. V. Popp opines that the reference to Abraham goes back to the early days of the movement. This is valid for many aspects; in surah 87:18-19 for example it says: "Lo! This is in the former scrolls, The Book of Abraham and Moses." Paret interprets the "scrolls" as first manuscripts of the revelation. The salvation aspect of the reference to Abraham, however, seems to stem from a later phase, after Islam had established itself as a separate creed, so it would not be expected to appear in such an early surah.

70 Cf. Evidence of a New Religion in Christian Literature "Under Islamic Rule"?

71 Cf. about this question: Gerd-Rüdiger Puin, Über die Bedeutung der ältesten Koranfragmente aus Sanaa (Jemen) für die Orthographiegeschichte des Korans, in: Hans-Caspar Graf von Bothmer, Karl-Heinz Ohlig, Gerd-Rüdiger Puin, Neue Wege der Koranforschung, magazin forschung (Universität des Saarlandes)1, 1999, p. 39-40.

72 It must be borne in mind that the notion "*religion*" goes back to a Western concept from a rather modern age. In the following, it will only be used for the sake of categorization from the perspective of the science of religion. The term *religion* in our modern sense is not an appropriate translation of the Arabic word *dīn*.

73 In Max Henning's German translation, op. cit., p. 80, counted as verses 138-139.

74 In verse 145 we read: "No soul can ever die except by Allah's leave". One might add: "No soul (like Jesus or other prophets before him) ...", whose death is then mentioned in the following verse 146.

75 Adel Theodor Khoury, Muhammad, in: id., Ludwig Hagemann, Peter Heine, Islam-Lexikon. Geschichte – Ideen – Gestalten, vol. 3, Freiburg, Basel, Wien 1991, p. 544.

76 In his translation of the Qurʾān (Der Koran. Aus dem Arabischen übertragen von Max Henning, op. cit. p. 585), Max Henning explains what it meant that Muḥammad was "taken in" by God): "Muḥammad was tenderly brought up by his grandfather."

77 Cf. Rudi Paret, Mohammed und der Koran. Geschichte und Verkündigung des arabischen Propheten, Stuttgart, Berlin, Köln, Main 1957, p. 32-35.

78 W. Montgomery Watt, B. Ursprung und Werdendes Islam, in: id., Alford T. Welch, Der Islam. I Mohammed und die Frühzeit – Islamisches Recht – Religiöses Leben (translation from the English by Sylvia Höfer, Die Religionen der Menschheit, ed. by Christel Matthias Schröder, vol. 25,1), Stuttgart, Berlin, Köln, Mainz 1980, p. 48.

79 Cf. about this question: W.M. Watt, ibid. p. 49-50.

80 Similarly W. M. Watt, ibid. p. 50.

81 Cf. about this question: V. Popp, Von Ugarit nach Samarra.
82 Theodor Nöldeke, Geschichte des Qorāns, 2nd edition revised and edited by Friedrich Schwally, 1st part: Über den Ursprung des Qorāns, 2nd part: Die Sammlung des Qorāns, Leipzig 1909.
83 http://wikiislam.net/wiki/Chronological_Order_of_the_Qur'an
84 Cf. V. Popp, Von Ugarit nach Samarra.
85 Add.(itamenta) IV. V: Continuatio Byzantina Arabica a. DCCXLI, belonging to: Isidori iunioris episcopi Hispalensis historia Gothorum Wandalorum Sueborum ad a. DCXXIV, in: Monumenta Germaniae historica, tomus XI: Chronicorum minorum saec. IV, V, VI, VII, Vol. II: Chronica minora, edidit Theodorus Mommsen, Berlin 1844 (Add. IV and V, the whole article: p. 323-369). My attention was directed to this text by Johannes Thomas, Professor of Romance Studies at the University Paderborn.
86 Concerning transcriptions: personal communication of Volker Popp.
87 Cf. ibid. Evidence of a New Religion in Christian Literature "Under Islamic Rule"?
88 Chr. Luxenberg, Die syro-aramäische Lesart des Koran, op. cit. p. 336-337, A. 352 (quotation: 337); the quotation was translated anew from the German version.
89 Cf. my article "Evidence of a New Religion in Christian Literature 'Under Islamic Rule'?"
90 Cf. about this question: F. Zoepel, Ostung. II. Im Christentum, in: LThK ^{2}1992, Vol. 7, p. 1294.
91 Rudi Paret, Der Koran als Geschichtsquelle, in: Der Islam 37, 1961, p. 35.
92 Cf. Gerd-Rüdiger Puin, Leuke Kome / Layka, die Arser / Ashab al-Rass und andere vorislamische Namen im Koran, in: K.-H. Ohlig, G.-R. Puin (eds.), Die dunklen Anfänge, op. cit. p. 317-340.
93 Patricia Crone, What do we actually know about Mohammed?; www.openDemocracy.net (webpage was accessed 31 June, 06)
94 P. Crone, ibid. p. 4.
95 P. Crone, op. cit. p. 1-2.
96 Cf. my article "Evidence of a New Religion in Christian Literature 'Under Islamic Rule'?"

Endnotes
Christoph Luxenberg: Relics of Syro-Aramaic Letters in Early Qur'ān Codices in Ḥiğāzī and Kūfi Ductus, pp. 308-338

1 Puin, Gerd-R. / Ohlig, Karl-Heinz (ed.). Die dunklen Anfänge, 3rd edition. Berlin 2007; The Hidden Origins of Islam: New Research into Its Early History, Amherst (N.Y.) 2009 (Prometheus Books).

2 Paret, Rudi, Der Koran. translation, 2nd Ed., Stuttgart, Berlin, Köln, Mainz 1982; all German quotations in the present article have been translated into English.

3 Note 18.: La Mosquée [sacrée]. V. sourate IX, 17.

4 Note 19.: Le serviteur d'Allah = Mahomet. // Kādū yakūnūna 'alay-hi libadā (var. lubada et lubbāda) « les Infidèles etc. ». Le sujet est incertain. Les commt. disent que c'est djinns, mais c'est peu probable.

5 Bell, Richard, The Qur'ān, Translated, with a critical re-arrangement of the surahs, Vol. I, Edinburgh 1937, Vol. II, Edinburgh 1939.

6 Note 3: The meaning is uncertain. The "servant of Allah" is usually taken to be Muḥammad, and "they" to refer to *ğinn*, which is possible if angels now speak.

7 Christoph Luxenberg, Die syro-aramäische Lesart des Koran. Ein Beitrag zur Entschlüsselung der Koransprache. 1st ed. Berlin 2000, 2nd ed. Berlin 2004, 3rd ed. Berlin 2007; English translation: The Syro-Aramaic Reading of the Koran: A Contribution to the Decoding of the Language of the Koran, Berlin 2007.

8 It is well-known that the Arabic words خير / *ḫayr* (*well-being, good, better*) and شر / *šarr* (*evil / worse, worse things*) can be used both as nouns and as an elative. That the grammarians of Classical Arabic declared the latter case to be *diptotic*, which excludes a final *alif*, is a rule not applied in the Qur'ān. A similar case (surah 18:71), where the spelling امرا was wrongly read as *imran*, because Arabic readers could not interpret it as an elative because of the final *alif* – the correct reading being *amarra* – was already discussed in my study "*Die syro-aramäische Lesart des Qur'ān*" (1st Ed. 2000, p. 166 ff., footnote 211; 2nd ed. 2004, p. 199 ff., footnote 242, 3rd ed. 2007, p. 298 ff., footnote 248).

9 The Qur'ān uses another loan-translation from Syro-Aramaic: مد / *madda* (*stretch [out]; extend*) in the sense of "to give (< stretch out o's hand)", which in Modern Arabic is understood as "to provide, equip", based on the following passages of the Qur'ān: surahs 3:124, 125; 17:6, 20; 23:55; 26:132, 133; 27:36; 52:22. For the Qur'ānic expression from surah 74:12 مالا ممدودا / *mālan mamdūdā* (lit.: an *extended* fortune = a *considerable* fortune) would be rendered in Modern Arabic (in the plural): أموالا طائلة / *amwālan ṭā'ila* (lit.: *long extended* = *considerable* fortune), which reflects the Qur'ānic طول /*ṭūl* (lit.: *length* = *riches* = *to be abundant*).

10 The Arabic conjunction ف / *fa* (< Old Aramaic פ, פא / *pā* = *fa*), which normally expresses a sequence or consequence in declarative sentences, should in this case be understood as *adversative*.

11 See e.g. BNF 328a, Bl. 3a, Z. 14: ويعلم ما فى السموت وما فى الارض , where the first فى has the today current final ى , while the second فى was written with a retroflex ى (ڡے). Similarly, but in reverse order in Bl. 12b, Z. 2-3: الرجال قومون على النسا بما فضل الله بعضهم على بعض

12 This explains why the open and unstressed first syllable *yu* was dropped in Modern Christian Colloquial Arabic, so that the name حنا is pronounced *ḥannā* without the final *nūn*, due to the unstressed final syllable.

13 So e.g.: a) *man* (= Arab. مَن *man / who*), pronounced as: *mān*; b) *men* (= Arab. مِن *min / of*), pronounced as: *mēn*, etc. In his *Syrische Grammatik* (Leipzig ²1898, reprint Darmstadt 1977), Nöldeke does not explicitly discuss this special feature of West Syriac. Only when explaining ܟܠ (*kull / kūl* = Arab. كل *kull / entirety, whole, everything, all*) he mentions the pronunciation in West Syriac (§ 48, 3rd par.) lengthened vowel in *kōl.*

14 Theodor Nöldeke, *Mandäische Grammatik*, Halle an der Saale 1975 (reprint Darmstadt 1964). Nöldeke dates the Mandaic writings dealt with to the years 650 and 900 CE, some pieces might even go back to Sassanian times (see Einleitung, p. XXII).

15 Rudof Meyer, *Hebräische Grammatik*, I, Einleitung, Schrift- und Lautlehre, 3rd, revised ed., Berlin 1966.

16 What follows are examples from the Qumran roll 1 Q Jes.[a], a text in vulgar language written about 100 BCE.

17 A. Spitaler, *Die Schreibung des Typus* صلوة *im Qur'ān*, in: Wiener Zeitschrift für die Kunde des Morgenlandes, 56th vol., Vienna 1960, p. 215, footnote. 8: "The rendering of long *ā* in medial position by *alif* is a *purely Arabic development*, cf. J. Cantineau, *Le Nabatéen* I, 47, -10: 'Sa notation par א est un *fait arabe* – assez postérieur, car l'inscription de en-Nemâra l'ignore encore.' At the time when the Qur'ān was first written down this development was not finished yet, cf. GdK III 31 f. In some cased the defective spelling of *ā* is used up to this day."

18 See C. Luxenberg, *Die syro-aramäische Lesart des Qur'ān*, 1st ed. Berlin 2000, p. 16; 2nd + 3rd ed. pp. 31 ff.

19 See e.g. C. Luxenberg, op. cit., p. 288, 15.2.

20 Thus e.g. in Modern Arabic dialects of Syria before verbs expressing an emotion, be that enthusiasm, a challenge or annoyance, e.g.: لفرجيه (*la-[a]farǧīh*): *I'll show him!; He is asking for it!)*

21 This spelling might correspond to Syro-Aramaic usage. The *Thesaurus* (II, 1809) interprets the particle ܠܐ (*lā'*) in (rather rare) vows as a negation (*formula est negandi cum jurejurando*), although the examples adduced rather point in the direction of an *emphatic* particle: ܠܐ ܚܝ̈ܘܗܝ ܕܫܢܝܘܬܟ (*lā ḥayyē-h d-šanyūṯā-ḵ*) *per vitam tuam, O demens!* ܠܐ ܚܝ̈ܝܟܘܢ ܘܠܐ ܚܝ̈ܘܗܝ (*lā ḥayyay-kōn w-lā ḥayya-w[hī]*) *per vitam vestram, perque vitam ejus!* Contrary to what his parallel examples would suggest, *Mannā* (364b) also assumes a negative formula, probably influenced by the Arabic لا: (القسم المنفي). Of course, according to context, a negation is also conceivable.

22 Arabic (*našara*) renders Aramaic ܦܫܛ (*pšaṭ*); Mannā (618b) adduces under (3) Arabic قدّم . أعطى (*qaddama, a'ṭā* / give [as a gift]) angibt.

23 Ṭabarī (XV, 208 f.) interprets مرفق (*mirfaq/marfiq*) laconically as ما ترتفقون به من شيء (probably meaning " what helps man to receive divine clemency"). Paret translates: "für Abhilfe sorgen (find a remedy)" (probably following the Lisān, X, 118b: والرفق والمرفق : ما استعين به / *ar-rifq, al-mirfaq, al-marfiq, al-marfaq*: (is) what comes to someone's aid); Blachère translates: "un adoucissement" and Bell: "a kindly arrangement", which reflects the modern Arabic meaning of رفق (*rifq / clemency*). The corresponding Syro-Aramaic root ܪܦܩ (*rpaq*), from which the Arabic root might have been borrowed (with slight semantic changes), is rendered by Mannā (751a) as رفق. حلم. لطف. صبر (*rafaqa, ḥaluma, laṭafa, ṣabara / to be mild,*

benign, friendly, patient), the nominal form ܪܦܩܐ (*rpāqā*) (751b) even more clearly as احتمال. صبر عظيم (*iḥtimāl, ṣabr*[un] *ʿaẓīm / patience, bearing suffering*). The *Thesaurus* derives this noun from Rebecca (*Thes.*, II, 3966, under ܪܦܩܐ Rebecca, nom. uxoris Isaaci,... Ap. lexx. valet patientia magna, الصبر ܡܣܝܒܪܢܘܬܐ ܣܓܝܬܐ ⁘ (*m-saybrānūṯā saggīṯā*), صبر شديد (*ṣabr*[un] *šadīd*) *great patience*). It cannot be excluded that this term became current in East Syriac as a denominative form, a view corroborated by *Mannā's* explanation. In any case, the context of the Qur'ānic passage rather suggests this understanding than the normal Arabic interpretation. The nominal form found in the Qur'ān مرفقا (*mirfaq*[an]) corresponds to the Syro-Aramaic infinitive ܡܪܦܩ (*me-rpaq*) with the prefix *m-* (verbal noun, in Arabic called: مصدر ميمي / *maṣdar mīmī*; cf. Brockelmann, *Syrische Grammatik*, § 174; Nöldeke, *Syrische Grammatik*, § 126).

Endnotes
Ignaz Goldziher: Read Anew: Islam and Parsism (Islamisme et Parsisme), pp. 339-356

---

1 *Original title:* Ignaz Goldziher, *Islamisme et Parsisme*, in: *Actes du Premier Congrès international d'Histoire de Religions*, p. 119-147, reprint in: id., Gesammelte Schriften, vol. IV, ed. by Joseph Desomogyi, Hildesheim 1970, p. 232-260. The sparse bibliographical data in the original footnotes have been amended (in italics) wherever possible.

2 After the present translation had been finished I came across an older translation of the same article: I. Goldziher: Influence of Parsism on Islam (translated by Q.K. Nariman); in: The Religion of the Iranian Peoples, by C. P. Tiele, Part 1, (from the German), with Darmesteter's "Sketch of Persia" and. I. Goldziher's " Influence of Parsism on Islam" (from the French), Bombay 1912 (p. 163-182). To give the reader an impression of this translation, this is the beginning: *"For long we have been content with the convenient assertion: Islam has sprung up all of a sudden full into broad daylight. The more we proceed with critical examination of the oldest documents of Islam, the more we are convinced that the Musalman tradition, hadith, which chronologically is, after the Qoran, the most ancient source of our information, does not carry us up to the early infancy of Islam except in a very feeble way (1). It often rather presents us with conflicting tendencies."*

3 Snouck Hurgronje, *Die Ẓāhiriten, ihr Lehrsystem und ihre Geschichte* (The Ẓāhirites, their Doctrinal System and their History). Beitrag zur Geschichte der muhammedanischen Theologie von Dr. Ignaz Goldziher, Leipzig, 1884, in: (Litteraturblatt) Literatur-Blatt für orientalische Philologie 1, 1884, p. 417.

4 Cf. Ignaz Goldziher, *Muhammedanische Studien II* (Muslim Studies), Halle 1890, p. 382-400: Ḥadīṯ und Neues Testament (Ḥadīṯ and New Testament).

5 Ignaz Goldziher, *Usages juifs. la littérature religieuse des Musulmans* (Jewish customs – the Religious Literature of the Muslims), in: Revue des Études Juives, XXVIII, p. 75. f.

6 E. Blochet, in: *Revue de l'Histoire des Religions*, V, 1882 (title of the article could not be verified). XXXVI, 1897 (150: reference to an article by E. Blochet, de James Darmesteter et ses critiques, in: Revue archéologique) and XL, 1-25; p. 203-236: *Études sur l'Histoire Religieuse de l'Iran. II. au Ciel du Prophète Mohammed.*

7 E. Blochet, *Études sur l'Histoire Religieuse de l'Iran. II. au Ciel du prophète Mohammed* (suite), in: *Revue de l'Histoire des Religions, XL*, p. 213.

8 Brockelmann, *Geschichte der Arabischen Literatur* (History of Arabic Literature), I, Weimar 1898, p. 134.

9 The caliph 'Uṯmān invited the Christian Abū Zubayd Harmala b. Munḏir, "who (had) visited the Persian kings and knew their customs", to his court. (*min zuwwār al-mulūk waḫāṣṣatan mulūk al-'ağam wa kāna 'āliman bi siyarihim*) Aġānī, XI, 24.

10 Cf. Blochet, *Revue de l'Histoire des Religions*, XXXVIII, 447 (article could not be verified).

11 *Journal Asiatique*, 1895, I, p. 167 (article could not be verified); M.A. Levy, *Beiträge zur Aramäischen Münzkunde Eran's und zur Kunde der Älteren Pehlewi-Schrift*, in: Zeitschrift der Deutschen morgenländischen Gesellschaft, XXI, 1867, p.

429, 458; James Darmesteter, *Coup d'Oeil sur l'Histoire de la Perse*, Paris 1885, p. 40; Sacred Books of the East, XXIV, (?) p. 171.

12 Aġānī, IV, 158.

13 Cf. E. Bratke, *Religionsgespräch am Hofe der Sassaniden* (Conversation about Religion at the Sassanian Court), n.p., 1899, 193, A. 1. According to the opinion of the Arabs the *tāǧ* (cf. Nöldeke, Fünf Moʿallaqāt, I, 36 about ʿAmr b. Kulṯūm, v. 26) is a characteristic attribute of Persian royal dignity. Legends were composed about the *tāǧ* of Khosrau (Ibn Hišām, 42, 4). On the other hand a Syrian chronicler explicitly remarks that Muʿāwiya did not wear the kelīla (= *tāǧ*). But this does not prevent Muslim legend from considering the diadem to be an attribute of the power of an Arabic mock king (Ibn Hišām, 441, 12)

14 Justi, *Geschichte des Alten Persiens* (History of Ancient Persia), (Universalgeschichte von Oncken), Berlin 1879, 221. About Persian political doctrines cf. Wilhelm, *Königthum und Priesterthum im alten Eran,* in: ZDMG, 1886, p. 102-110.

15 I. Goldziher, *Muhammedanische Studien, II*, op. cit., p. 32.

16 Cf. *Actes du XIe Congrès des Orientalistes,* Paris 1897. Troisième section, 70, note 3.

17 *Transactions of the IXth Congress of Orientalists*, London 1892, II, p. 104-106.

18 *Wiener Zeitschrift für die Kunde des Morgenlandes,* XIII (1899), p. 325, footnote 3.

19 Friedrich von Spiegel, *Die Traditionelle Litteratur der Parsen* (The traditional literature of the Parsees), II) *Einleitung in die traditionellen Schriften der Parsen, Theil 2: Die traditionelle Literatur der Parsen in ihrem Zusammenhange mit den angrenzenden Literaturen,* Wien 1860, p. 78.

20 F. v. Spiegel, ibid. 74.

21 Usd al-ghaba, V, p. 320.

22 I. Goldziher, *Muhammedanische Studien, II*, op. cit., p. 156.

23 Spiegel, *Eranische Alterthumskunde*, III, p. 577.

24 Söderblom, in: *Revue de l'Histoire des Religions,* XXIX, p. 241 (article could not be verified).

25 Ignaz Goldziher, Le culte des morts et des ancêtres chez les Arabes, in: Revue de l'Histoire des Religions, X, p. 356 ff.

26 Söderblom, l.c., p. 254.

27 A.V. William Jackson, *Weighing the Soul in the Balance after Death, an Indian as well as Iranian Idea,* in: Actes du Xe Congrès des Orientalistes, Genf 1894, Deuxième partie, I, p. 67 f.

28 F. v. Spiegel, *Traditionelle Litteratur der Parsen, II*, op. cit. (cf. A. 20), p. 87.

29 Cf. E. Blochet, *Études sur l'Histoire Religieuse de l'Iran. II. L'ascension au Ciel du Prophète Mohammed*, in: *la Revue de l'Histoire des Religions*, XL, 232, footnote 2.

30 Al-Dārimi, Sunan, p. 440. – Al-Šaybānī, disciple of Abu Ḥanifa, reports (Āṯār, ed. Lahore, p. 93) that the recitation of each word of the Qur'ān corresponds to six good deeds; the formula ALM, of which each letter is counted as one word, thus is equivalent to thirty good deeds.

31 Usd al-ghâba, I, p. 172.

32 Ibid., V, p. 586.

33 *Ibn Ḫallikān*, ed. by Wüstenfeld, Nr. 92.

34 Al-Ġazālī, *Iḥǧā ʿulūm al-dīn*, I, p. 250.

35 *Al-Muǧīr al-dīn, al-Ins al-ǧalil*, p. 263.

36 ibid., p. 263.
37 Sad-der, XII, p. 8.
38 Ibid. chapter LXVIII.
39 Ibid., LXXXII, p. 2.
40 *Le Zendavesta, I,* 13, footnote 36.
41 *Muwaṭṭa'*, I, 81; al-Buḫārī, Faḍā'il al-aṣḥab, Nr. 10
42 Octave Dupont und Xavier Coppolani, *Les Confréries Religieuses Musulmanes,* Algier 1897, p. 323.
43 Ḳût al-ḳulûb, I, p. 83.
44 Al-Dāraḳuṭnī bei al-Balawi, Alif-Ba, I, p. 371.
45 James Darmesteter, *Chants Populaires des Afghans,* Paris 1888-1890, p. 261.
46 Cf. my observations in the review I wrote about M. Carra de Vaux, *Le Mahométisme,* in: ZDMG, LIII, p. 385.
47 About the wood used for making toothpicks, detailed information can be found in al-Ǧāḥiẓ, *Bajdn,* II, p. 82.
48 Al-Ja'kûbî, *Annales,* ed. Houtsma, II, p. 121.
49 Ibid., p. 121.)
50 Musnad Aḥmed, I, p. 339 (sa-yunzal 'alayya fîhi); ibid., III, p. 490 (an yuktaba 'alayya).
51 ibid., I, 3 (below).
52 Al-Mustaṭraf, I, 10; Al-Balawi, Alif-Bā, I, p. 137-38. According to a saying attributed to Al-Šafi'ī, the use of the miswāk also leads to higher intelligence; al-Ḍamīrī, II, 145, s. v. 'uṣfūr.
53 Buḫārī, *Maġāzī,* Nr. 85.
54 Al- (Al-Ġurar) wal-durar (lithography from Tehran), p. 179.
55 *Shājest la shājest,* X, 20; XII, 13, Dādist. dīnik, XL, 8.
56 One of Muḥammad's "companions", 'Abdallāh b. Mas'ūd, was given the surname *sāḥib al-siwāk*; the original meaning of this title, which in any case was an honorary epithet, seems to have been unknown (or fallen into oblivion) (al-Nawawî, Tahḏīb, 370, 13); instead of *al-siwāk* the variants *al-sawād* and *al-sirār* can be found, which proves that the true meaning of this surname had been forgotten.
57 There is a real collection of traditions about this topic in the *Alif-Bā* des al-Balawī, I, p. 378 ff.
58 In al-'Abbār, *Takmila* (ed. de Madrid, Bibl. arab. hisp.), p. 533.
59 Musnad Aḥmad, II, p. 71.
60 Bei al-Ḍamīrī, II, p. 334; other versions tell a comparable story about donkeys, ibid. I, p. 298.
61 *Bundāhisch,* XIV, p. 28; XIX, p.3; Sad-der, XXXI, p. 8.
62 al-Ḍamīrī, I, p. 528; also in the Babylonian Talmud, B. Kamm, leaf 60 b: here it says that the barking of dogs is a sign for the presence of the prophet Elijah or of the Angel of Death – depending on whether the bark is cheerful or sad; also cf. E. Stave, *Über den Einfluss des Parsismus auf das Judenthum* (About the Influence of Parsism on Judaism), Haarlem, 1898, p. 131.
63 al-Makkarī, éd. de Leyde, I, p. 393.
64 Chardin, *Voyages en Perse,* éd. Langlès, Paris 1811, IX, p. 205.
65 Vendidad, Farg. XIII, p. 44-48.

66 Cf. my materials about the historical development of Ṣufism, in: *Wiener Zeitschrift für die Kunde des Morgenlandes,* XIII, 1899, p. 46-48.

67 The Bulgarians on the banks of the Volga thought that the barking of dogs was a good omen (yatabarrakūna bi-ʾuwā al-kalb), predicting happiness and abundant harvests (Ibn Fadhlān in Jāḳūt, I, 769, p.13).

68 I am not the first to advance this view: cf. e.g. Jacob, *Altarabisches Beduinenleben* (Bedouin Life of the Ancient Arabs), Berlin, 2nd edition 1897, p. 84 (he refers to Abraham Geiger, *Ostiranische Cultur* (East Iranian Culture), (?) p. 370). Ed. Hahn, *Die Haust(h)iere und ihre Beziehung zur Wirt(h)schaft des Menschen* (Domestic Animals and their Relationship with Human Economy), Leipzig 1896, p. 65: "The enormous overestimation [of the dog] that it enjoyed in the Zend religion of the Persians certainly contributed to the fact that after the victory of Mohammedanism it was frowned upon so much, but to completely block it from its [formerly high] position was of course not achieved."

69 René Basset, *Les Apocryphes Éthiopiens*, Paris 1893-1900, IX, p. 12 and 22.

70 *Livre d'Hénoch*, I, p. 6, 8.

71 Ağānī, VI, 93, 12. Abū Ṣufyān sent his caravans with merchandise of the Qurayš (ilā arḍ al-Ağam) up to the lands of the Persians. Above all about war-like incursions into Persian areas cf. Ibn Hišām, p. 938, 2.

72 I. Goldziher, *Muhammedanische Studien, I,* Halle 1889, p. 102; G. Jacob, Altarabisches Beduinenleben, Berlin, 2nd ed. 1897, p. 237. I will plan to come back to Persian allusions with Ancient Pre-Islamic poets on a different occasion.

73 Éd. Geyer, No. 24, 2. About marriages between close relatives cf. H. Hübschmann, *Über die Persische Verwandtenheirath*, in: ZDMG, XLIII, p. 618. (*in the French original, Goldziher erroneously had E. Kuhn as the author, transl.*).

74 Cf. Eduard Glaser, *Skizze der Geschichte und Geographie Arabiens von den ältesten Zeiten bis zum Propheten Mohammed, nebst einem Anhange zur Beleuchtung der Geschichte Abessyniens im 3. und 4. Jahrhundert n. Chr., auf Grund der Inschriften, der alten Autoren und der Bibel, II*, Berlin 1890, p. 193.

75 Quoted passages from: I. Goldziher, *Muhammedanische Studien, I,* op. cit. p. 103, A. 4.

76 Masʿūdi, *Tanbīḥ*, éd. de Goeje, 281, 16 ff.

77 Müller-Mordtmann, *Südarabische Denkmäler*, Wien 1883, p. 87 (article could not be verified); M. Joseph Halévy, *Traductions des Inscriptions Sabéens,* in: Journal asiatique, 1872, I, p. 524.

78 Similarly the Persians have the true religion that goes back to a remote era in antiquity; they called it *paoiryó dkaésha* like the original religion that had existed a long time before Zarathustra and only had to be re-established later (Sacred Books, XXIV, 87). This view can also be found in Firdausī, *dīnikuhen.*

79 Vendidad, Farg. V, p. 37.

80 See the opinions of older exegetes, as quoted by al-Kaššāf.

81 For further information cf. Ignaz Goldziher: *Ẓāhiriten,* Leipzig 1884, p. 61-63.

82 Amédée Querry, *Droit Musulman*, Paris 1871-1872, I, 17, art. 267 ff.

83 ZDMG, LIII, 383 (?).

84 Ignaz Goldziher, *Die Sabbathinstitution im Islam*, in: *Les Mélanges Consacré à la Mémoire du feu Prof. D. Kaufmann.*

85 *Le Zend-Avesta,* translated by J. Darmesteter, I: *La Loi (Vendidad), (Yashts), Le Livre de Prière (Khorda Avesta),* Paris 1892, p. 37 ff; III: *Origines de la Littérature*

---

et de la Religion Zoroastriennes, Appendice à la Traduction de l'Avesta (fragments des nasks perdus et index), Paris 1893, p. 57.

86 J. Darmesteter, in: *Revue des Études Juives*, XVIII, 9, Nr. 102 (article could not be verified).

Endnotes

Volker Popp: The Influence of Persian Religious Patterns on Notions in the Qur'ān, pp. 357-368

---

1 The Arabic *dīn* probably goes back to two different roots, Semitic *d-y-n* (right, just[ice], judgment) and Iranian *dēn* (from Avestan *daēnā-* 'insight, conscience'). Originally, it might have meant "the right view" and only later "religion". The two separate roots merged into a new term, which bears both original meanings.

2 Christoph Luxenberg, *Die Syro-aramäische Lesart des Koran*, Berlin 1st ed. 2000, 2nd ed. 2004.

3 J. Narten, *Zum Vokalismus der Gatha-Überlieferung*, in: *Studia Grammatica Iranica*, ed. by R. Schmitt, München 1986, p. 257.

4 Chr. Luxenberg, *Die Syro-aramäische Lesart des Qur'ān*, op.cit. p. 259.

5 Chr. Luxenberg, ibid. p. 303.

6 M. Stausberg, *Die Religion Zarathushtras*, Stuttgart 2002, 296.

7 H. Waldmann, *Heilsgeschichtlich Verfasste Theologie und Männerbünde. Die Grundlage des Gnostischen Weltbildes*, Tübingen 1994, p. 69.

8 M.G. Morony, *Iraq after the Muslim Conquest*, Princeton 1984, p. 530.

9 M. Stausberg, *Die Religion Zarathushtras*, op.cit., p. 473.

10 "'Farwardîn', the nineteenth day of the month; the first month of the Persian year, corresponding with March; also the name of an angel supposed to preside over it" (F. Steingass, Persian-English Dictionary, London 1892, p. 924).

11 H. Waldmann, *Der Kommagenische Mazdaismus*, Deutsches Archäologisches Institut, Istanbuler Mitteilungen: Beiheft 37, Tübingen 1991, p. 174-177.

12 "In any case, the notion of 'religion' in question is by no means identical in Mazdaism and Islam" (L. Gardet, article "Dîn", EI², II/293). This is denied for early Islam. Only the Legal Schools and Ḥadīṯ collections narrow the meaning of the term *"Dēn/Dīn"* down to the Islamic *"dīn"* and consider *Islām* to be that very *Dīn*. This took place only around the middle of the 9th century CE.

13 Cf. also: Chr. Luxenberg, *Die Neudeutung der Arabischen Inschrift im Felsendom zu Jerusalem*. in: *Die Dunklen Anfänge*, ed. by K.-H. Ohlig & G.-R. Puin, Berlin 2004, p. 128.

14 M. Shaki, article "*Dên*", in: EIr II/279.

15 Chr. Luxenberg, *Die Neudeutung der Arabischen Inschrift im Felsendom zu Jerusalem*, op. cit.

16 "... mâzdêsn dên (...) is a brilliance from the nature of Ohrmazd; its principal is the mind/thought of Axw, Ahû (q.v.; 'the supreme lord'), and its manifestation is the recitation and practise of the holy words (mânsr), which itself is the mean (paymân; Dênkard, ed. Madan, I, p. 326; de Menasce, 1973, p. 313). The essence of the Mazdaen religion is the wisdom of Ohrmazd, with knowledge and action (kunischn) as its essential elements; its ... purpose or function is to purify (ms.: heal) the mixed (...) creation (...) by conquering and destroying the adversary (...)" (M. Shaki, Artikel "*Dên*", in: EIr. II/279).

Endnotes
Markus Gross: New Ways of Qur'ānic Research, pp. 369-555

1 Nöldeke, Theodor (1910). *Zur Sprache des Korāns* (On the language of the Koran). in: *Neue Beiträge zur semitischen Sprachwissenschaft*. Strassburg, p. 5 ff.; an English version of the article, from which the translation of this and later quotations has been taken, has meanwhile appeared in the anthology edited by Ibn Warraq (2011): *Which Koran? – Variants, Manuscripts and Linguistics*, Amherst (N.Y.), p. 83 - 130, here: p. 87.

2 Luxenberg, Christoph (2004). *Die Syroaramäische Lesart des Koran*. Ein Beitrag zur Entschlüsselung der Koransprache. 2nd, enlarged and corrected edition. Berlin.

3 http://www.islamic-awareness.org/Quran/Text/Mss/vowel.html – quoted from the article: Saifullah, M S M/ Ghoniem, Mohammad/ Zaman, Shibli (2005). *From Alphonse Mingana To Christoph Luxenberg: Arabic Script & The Alleged Syriac Origins Of The Qur'an,* © Islamic Awareness, All Rights Reserved; First Composed: 20th December 2004, Last Modified: 26th June 2005.

4 Healey, John F. (1980). *First Studies in Syriac*. University Semitics Study Aids 6. Birmingham (with tapes).

5 Muraoka, Takamitsu (1987). *Classical Syriac. A Basic Grammar with a Chrestomathy*. Porta Linguarum Orientalium Bd. 19. Harassowitz. Wiesbaden.

6 The first grammars in transliteration for these two languages only appeared a few years ago, for Armenian: Schmitt, Rüdiger (1981). *Grammatik des Klassisch-Armenischen*, mit sprachvergleichenden Erläuterungen. Innsbruck; for Old Ethiopean: Tropper, Josef (2002). *Altäthiopisch, Grammatik des Geʿez mit Übungstexten und Glossar*. Berlin.

7 In the year 1993 a man named Ṣādiq Māl Allāh (born 1970) was beheaded in Saudi Arabia for the crime of possessing a bible.

8 It is by no means clear that Arabic *ummī* means "illiterate"; a whole contribution of a later anthology is dedicated to this word: Gilliot, Claude: *Die Schreib- und/ oder Lesekundigkeit in Mekka und Yathrib/ Medina zur Zeit Mohammeds*, in: Markus Gross / Karl-Heinz Ohlig (Hg.; 2008). *Schlaglichter: Die beiden Ersten Islamischen Jahrhunderte*, p. 37-63.

9 The biographical data of the first Four "Righteous" Caliphs given in brackets simply reflect the traditional view, their historicity being highly doubtful.

10 Guillaume, A. (translator/ed.) (1955). *The Life of Muhammad*. A translation of Isḥāq's Sīrat Rasūl Allāh. with an introduction and notes by A. Guillaume. first published 1955, reprinted Karachi 1967, p. 156-7; about the prophet's biography in general cf. Busse, Heribert (1987). *Arabische Historiographie und Geographie*, in: Gätje, Helmut (ed.) (1987). *Grundriss der Arabischen Philologie*. vol. 2: *Literaturwissenschaft*. Wiesbaden, p. 266.

11 e.g. http://www.usingenglish.com/forum/english-idioms-sayings/17132-stupid-stupid-does.html

12 Daniel Jones' renowned pronouncing dictionary (edition used: Jones, Daniel / Gimson, A. C./ Ramsaran, Susan. *Everyman's English Pronouncing Dictionary*, 14th edition. Indian reprint 1993. Delhi) gives the pronunciation [lɔ:], i.e. the same as for "law", as the first option, adding in brackets the alternative (and distinct) variant:

[lɔə]. *The Cambridge International Dictionary of English,* Cambridge University Press 1995, only has the first alternative for British English.

13 Neuwirth, Angelika (1987). *Koran,* in: Gätje, Helmut (ed.) (1987). *Grundriss der Arabischen Philologie.* Vol. 2: *Literaturwissenschaft.* Wiesbaden, p. 101; all originally German quotations have been translated by myself.

14 ibid. p. 103

15 *Die Orale Rezeption des Koran, ein Gespräch mit Manfred Kropp* (interview with Manfred Kropp), in: Burgmer, Christoph (ed.) (2005). *Streit um den Koran. Die Luxenberg-Debatte: Standpunkte und Hintergründe.* Berlin, pp. 46.

16 A more detailed analysis of this example will soon appear in a Festschrift for Gerd-R. Puin under the title "*Homer, Rigveda, Avesta, Koran - Mündliche oder Schriftliche Tradition, was ist Primär?*".

17 The conversation took place in the year 2004.

18 Puin, Gerd-R. (2006). *Variant Readings of the Koran due to the Ambiguity of the Early Arabic Script, Including Variants of Ibn Masʿūd and a Survey of the Transcription of Koranic Texts* (at the time the German original of the article was written, a text still to be published).

19 The translations used are the English one of Pickthall (from: http://al-quran.info (see also the bibliography) and my literal rendering of the scholarly German translation of Rudi Paret, *Der Koran. Übersetzung,* Stuttgart 1st edition 1966, 9th edition 2004; moreover, his commentary, in which he often discusses Bell's and Blachère's opinions as well, has been translated literally into English: *Kommentar und Konkordanz.* Stuttgart 1st edition 1971, 7th reprint (of the hardcover version of 1977); moreover, these versions have been compared with the digital version of the "Digitalen Bibliothek (Directmedia Publishing, Berlin)"; the transliteration of Qur'ānic passages is from Hans Zirker's version, which is downloadable as a pdf-file:
http://www.eslam.de/begriffe/t/transliteration_des_quran.htm

20 Paret, R. (1966). *Der Koran. Übersetzung.* 9th ed. 2004. Stuttgart.

21 Jeffery, Arthur (ed.) (1937): *Materials for the History of the Text of the Qur'ān. The Old Codices.* Leiden.

22 Analyzed text samples from the Odyssey, the Avesta and the Rigveda will be published in the Festschrift for Gerd-R. Puin.

23 Translation by A.T. Murray: *The Iliad with an English Translation, in two volumes.* Cambridge, MA./London 1924; in digital form on the following website:
http://www.perseus.tufts.edu/hopper/text?doc=Perseus%3Atext%3A1999.01.0134%3Abook%3D3%3Acard%3D146

24 This root has survived in the word *dino*-saur (lit. terrible saurian).

25 Cf. Schwyzer, E. (1934-1939). *Griechische Grammatik, I. Allgemeiner Teil, Lautlehre, Wortbildung, Flexion.* München.

26 The Homeric style is characterized by the frequent use of poetic formulae like e.g. "rhododáctylos éos - rosy-fingered dawn".

27 Aryan here is not the term as wrongly employed by the Nazis (the Germans are not Aryans!), but it designates the Indo-Iranian subgroup of Indo-European languages, the speakers of which called themselves "Aryans". "Iran" is derived from the genitive plural of this word (āryānam), the word itself originally meaning "hospitable". In modern India, all languages derived from Sanskrit are called Indo-Aryan, but not e.g. the Dravidian languages like Tamil, Kannada, Malayalam or Telegu.

28 A French example would be a combination like *il n'y en a plus*, which is pronounced as if it were one word: [ilnjãnaply]. The analytic orthography makes the reading of a French text considerably easier as opposed to understanding spoken French.

29 "Dark L" is the velarized sound at the end of a syllable like in "dull" [d], "light L" the one in other positions like in "lift" [lɪft].

30 Most native speakers of English are not aware of the fact that the /t/ after /s/ is not aspirated. To hear the difference try to say "mistake" and "Miss Take" (a woman named 'Take') very slowly. As there is a morpheme boundary in the second case, the /t/ remains aspirated.

31 Probably a Prakrit which is as different from Sanskrit as Italian from Latin.

32 The text and interpretation follows: MacDonell, Arthur A. (1917). *A Vedic Reader for Students.* Oxford (repr. 1970/ Delhi 1971), p. 9.

33 One offshoot of the method became famous under the name *Superlearning.*

34 Cf. Noseda, Sergio Noja (2005). *From Syriac to Pahlavi: The Contribution of the Sassanian Iraq to the Beginning of the Arabic Writing*, in: Ohlig, Karl-Heinz/ Puin, Gerd-R. (ed.) (2005). *Die Dunklen Anfänge. Neue Forschungen zur Entstehung und frühen Geschichte des Islam.* 2nd edition 2006. Berlin, p. 279, 291.

35 The language often called *Book Pahlavi* should better be called *Zoroastrian Middle Persian* as opposed to *Manichean Middle Persian*, which was written in a different script, which is also derived from an Aramaic writing system.

36 Cf. section 3.13.

37 Cf. Humbach, Helmut (1991). *The Gāthās of Zarathushtra.* Heidelberg.
as well as: Reichelt, Hans (1911). *Avesta Reader. Texts, Notes, Glossary and Index.* Strassburg, reprint Berlin 1968; for more Avestan words see also section 8.4.

38 The alternative designation Hīnayāna (lesser/deficient vehicle) was originally a derogatory name coined by the adherents of the Mahāyāna (great vehicle; a later development). Moreover, the more original Theravāda (= Sanskrit Sthaviravāda = Teaching of the Elders) only designates one of the different schools of Hinayana, the others having died out.

39 The tapes from Thailand unfortunately do not contain any bibliographical data.

40 Text from: *Dhammadāyāda Chanting Book* (1989). Dhammakāya Foundation, Pathumthani (Thailand), p. 44.

41 Pinyin is the official transcription system for Mandarin Chinese in the People's Republic of today.

42 The transcription with IPA (International Phonetic Association) symbols was made by myself.

43 According to Karlgren's terminology this language is called "Ancient Chinese".

44 Karlgren, Bernhard (1949). *The Chinese language.* New York, p. 77.

45 Karlgren, Bernhard (1966). *Grammatica Serica. Script and Phonetics in Chinese and Sino-Japanese.* Taipei, p. 23.

46 from: Jacobi, Renate (1987). *Die altarabische Dichtung*, in: Gätje, Helmut (ed.) (1987). *Grundriss der Arabischen Philologie.* vol. 2: *Literaturwissenschaft.* Wiesbaden, p. 21; the quotation is originally in German and has been translated by myself; it refers to the following book: Lord, A.B. (1965). *Der Sänger Erzählt. Wie ein Epos Entsteht.* München; title of the English original: *The Singer of Tales.* Cambridge, Mass. 1960.

47 Parry, Milman (collector)/ Lord, Albert Bates (editor / translator) (1954). *Serbo-croatian Heroic Songs.* with musical transcriptions by Béla Bartók. 2 volumes. Cambridge/ Belgrade.

48 cf. Parry, Milman: Ćor Huso: *A Study of Southslavic Song*, in: Parry, Adam (1971) (ed.). *The Making of Homeric Verse. The collected papers of Milman Parry*. Oxford, p. 442.

49 Noy, Dov (1963). *Jefet Schwili Erzählt. Hundertneunundsechzig Jemenitische Volks-erzählungen Aufgezeichnet in Israel 1957-1960.* Berlin.

50 Musil, Alois (1928). *The Manners and Customs of the Rwala Bedouins.* New York: American Geographical Society.

51 Meeker, Michael E. (1979). *Literature & Violence in North Arabia.* Cambridge Studies in Cultural Systems. San Diego

52 cf. the introduction of: Schapera, I (ed.) (1965). *Praise Poems of Tswana Chiefs.* translated and edited by I. Schapera. Oxford.

53 Brown, Rev. J. Tom (1962). *Secwana Dictionary. Secwana-English and English-Secwana.* Lobatsi, Bechuanaland Protectorate, South Africa.

54 Source: *Кыз Жибек* (1963). под редакцией М.О. Ауэзова и Н.С. Смирновой. издательство академии наук казахской ССР. Алма-Ата.

55 so e.g.. in the epic Kambar-Batir, published in several versions as: *Камбар-Батыр* (1959). под редакцией М.О. Ауэзова и Н.С. Смирновой. издательство академии наук казахской ССР. Алма-Ата.

56 *Қыз Жібек* (1985). Пікір жаз андар К. Ж ма алиев К. Сейдеханов. Алматы.

57 Cf. the introduction of Schmitt, Rüdiger (ed.) (1968). *Indogermanische Dichter-sprache.* Darmstadt, p. 2; p. 7.

58 Cf. Meillet, Antoine (1968). *Die Ursprünge der griechischen Metrik*, in: Schmitt, Rüdiger (ed.) (1968). *Indogermanische Dichtersprache*. Darmstadt, p. 44.

59 Cf. Wackernagel, Jacob (1968). *Indogermanische Dichtersprache*, in: Schmitt, Rüdiger (ed.) (1968). *Indogermanische Dichtersprache*. Darmstadt, p. 98.

60 Cf. Pisani, Vittore (1968). *Indisch-griechische Beziehungen aus dem Mahābhārata*, in: Schmitt, Rüdiger (ed.) (1968). *Indogermanische Dichtersprache.* Darmstadt, p. 156ff.

61 cf. Schmitt, Rüdiger (1968). *Indogermanische Dichtersprache. Eine Skizze*, in: Schmitt, Rüdiger (ed.) (1968). *Indogermanische Dichtersprache*. Darmstadt, p. 334 f.

62 See section 3.9.

63 The problem of metre and strophes in the Qur'ān has been treated by several authors, above all: Geyer, R. (1908). *Zur Strophik des Qurâns*, in: WZKM 22 (1908) p. 265-86; (English translation: *The Strophic Structure of the Koran*, in: Ibn Warraq (ed.): *What the Koran Really Says – Language, Text and Commentary*, Amherst (N.Y.), p. 625-646; Lüling, Günter (1993). *Über den Ur-Qur'ān. Ansätze zur Rekonstruktion Vorislamischer Christlicher Strophenlieder im Qur'ān.* Erlangen; Neuwirth Angelika (1981). *Studien zur Komposition der Mekkanischen Suren.* Berlin/ New York.

64 Ibn Rawandi, *On Pre-Islamic Christian Strophic Poetical Texts in the Koran: A Critical Look at the Work of Günter Lüling*, in: Ibn Warraq (ed.), *What the Koran Really Says – Language, Text & Commentary*, Amherst (NY) 2002, p. 653-712.

65 Powell, Barry B. (1991). *Homer and the Origin of the Greek alphabet.* Cambridge, p. 189.

66 The chapter is entitled: "Forty" as a Topos of Multitude and Prediction, in: Conrad, I. Lawrence: *Abraha and Muhammad.* Some Observations apropos of Chronology and Literary Topoi in the Early Arabic Historical Tradition, originally published in:

Bulletin of the School of Oriental and African Studies 50 (1987), p. 225-40; reprinted in: Ibn Warraq (ed.). *The Quest for the Historical Muhammad*, Amherst (N.Y.) 2000, p. 368-391.

67 see section 3.5

68 Hanke, Manfred (1967). *Die Schüttelreimer.* Bericht über eine Reimschmiedzunft. Stuttgart.

69 Source of most examples: Hutterer, Claus Jürgen (1999). *Die Germanischen Sprachen – Ihre Geschichte in Grundzügen.* 4th, enlarged edition, Wiesbaden, p. 115 ff.

70 Gerdes, Udo / Spellerberg, Gerhard (1983). *Althochdeutsch, Mittelhochdeutsch: Grammatischer Grundkurs zur Einführung und Textlektüre.* Königstein/ Ts., p. 142.

71 Lehnert, Martin (1973). *Altenglisches Elementarbuch.* 8th, improved edition. Collection Göschen vol. 5125. Berlin / New York, p. 34.

72 ibid., p. 18.

73 Ranke, Friedrich / Hofmann Dietrich (1979). *Altnordisches Elementarbuch.* 4th, corrected edition, Berlin/New York, p. 122.

74 Schulze, Wilhelm (1968). *Tocharisch Tseke Peke*, in: Schmitt, Rüdiger (ed.) (1968). *Indogermanische Dichtersprache.* Darmstadt, p. 34.

75 quoted from: Wershoven, J.E. (n.d.). *Siamesisch.* Hartlebens Bibliothek der Sprachenkunde für den Selbstunterricht. Wien/ Leipzig.

76 Andrzejewski, B. W. / Lewis, I. M. (1964). *Somali Poetry. An introduction.* Oxford, p. 42.

77 Englund, Robert (1953). *Finnische Sprachlehre.* Heidelberg, p. 217 ff.

78 Example from: Velten, C. (1913). *Praktische Suaheli-Grammatik.* Berlin, p. 51.

79 "Phonotactics" is a branch of phonetics and phonology. It deals with the rules in the phonological system of a language which restrict the possible combinations and positions of phonemes. In English, there is a phoneme [ŋ] (the "ng" in "thing"), which never appears at the beginning of a word (unlike e.g. in Thai). In Chinese, on the other hand, only "n" and "ng" are possible at the end of a word, and consonant clusters (like "pl, st" etc.) do not appear at all.

80 Personal communication.

81 Luxenberg, Christoph (2004), p. 18, footnote 6.

82 "Loose rhyme" is also known in other works of Arabic literature, a good example being al-Harīrī, cf. Rückert's German translation: *al-Harīrī: Die Verwandlungen des Abu Seid von Serug.* Aus dem Arabischen von Friedrich Rückert. Leipzig 1989. Loose rhyme was especially typical of the sayings of a group of people called "kāhin - soothsayer, magician" (*kāhin* corresponds to Hebrew כֹּהֵן - *kōhēn* - priest).

83 See section 2.4.

84 Hawting, G.R. (1999). *The Idea of Idolatry and the Emergence of Islam: From Polemic to History.* Cambridge Studies in Islamic Civilisation. Cambridge.

85 A last interesting fact should be mentioned about this particular surah. Since the end of the 19th century until recently German young boys grew up with the books of Karl May (1842-1812), a popular writer of adventure novels set in the American Old West and in the Orient. He is the only author who has got a publishing house dedicated entirely to his books (which are also published by other publishers). Many orientalists claim that their fascination for the Middle East started when they read Karl May

books at the age of 15. In several of his novels set in the orient one of the characters recites this surah (then called "sūrat al-imtiḥān - exam surah") to prove that he is not drunk, as the verbal forms of the same root were supposed to be confusing. No Muslim informant could corroborate this use of the surah, but it cannot be excluded that Karl May found this phenomenon in the travelogues published in his era.

86 Personal communication by Gerd-R. Puin.

87 Jacobi, Renate (1987). Dichtung, in: Gätje, Helmut (ed.) (1987). *Grundriss der Arabischen Philologie.* Band 2: *Literaturwissenschaft.* Wiesbaden, p. 15.

88 See Ibn Warraq (ed.) (2013). Koranic Allusions – The Biblical, Qumranic, Pre-Islamic Background to the Koran, Amherst (N. Y.).

89 cf. Grotzfeld, Heinz (1989). contributions: *Arabische Literatur* (vol. 1, p. 178 ff.); *al-Mu'allaqāt* (Bd. 4, p. 2057); *Qaṣīda* (vol. 4, p. 2373). in: *Harenbergs Lexikon der Weltliteratur* (1989). Autoren – Werke – Begriffe. 5 vols. 2nd ed. curatory board: François Bondy, Ivo Frenzel, Joachim Kaiser, Lew Kopelew, Hilde Spiel. Idee/Konzeption. Bodo Harenberg. Dortmund; as well as: Jacobi, Renate (1987). *Die altarabische Dichtung,* in: Gätje, Helmut (ed.) (1987). *Grundriss der Arabischen Philologie.* vol. 2: *Literaturwissenschaft.* Wiesbaden, p. 20-31.

90 See also: Heinrichs, Wolfhart (1987). *Poetik, Rhetorik, Literaturkritik, Metrik und Reimlehre,* in: Gätje, Helmut (ed.) (1987). *Grundriss der Arabischen Philologie.* vol. 2: *Literaturwissenschaft.* Wiesbaden, p. 177-207.

91 Meanwhile there are many versions on the internet, the one used for the German edition was: http://www.bbc.co.uk/religion/religions/islam /features/al_burda/.

92 Schimmel, Annemarie (1987). *Sufismus,* in: Gätje, Helmut (ed.) (1987). *Grundriss der Arabischen Philologie.* vol. 2: *Literaturwissenschaft.* Wiesbaden, p. 349

93 *Die Burda. Ein Lobgedicht auf Muḥammad von Al-Buṣîrî.* Neu herausgegeben im arabischen Text mit metrischer persischer und türkischer Übersetzung von C.A. Ralfs. Wien 1860.

94 Cf. Kermani, Navid (1999). *Gott ist Schön. Das Ästhetische Erleben des Koran.* München, p. 171; Kermani mentions seven secure (mutawātir), three recognized (mašhūr) and four non-canonical (šāḏḏ) recitation styles of the Koran, which are split up into sub-traditions (ṭuruq), amounting to a total of 80 different readings.

95 Gerd-R. Puin explained this in detail in a public talk at the university of Saarbrücken.

96 About the inimitability of the Koran see Neuwirth, Angelika (1987). Koran, in: Gätje, Helmut (ed.) (1987). *Grundriss der Arabischen Philologie.* vol. 2: *Literaturwissenschaft.* Wiesbaden, p. 127; Radscheit, Matthias (1996). *Die Koranische Herausforderung. Die Taḥaddī-Verse im Rahmen der Polemikpassagen des Korans.* Islamkundliche Untersuchungen vol. 198. Berlin; Brother Mark (2000). *A 'Perfect' Qur'an or 'So it was made to appear to them'?. A response to Islamic allegations concerning the Gospel, the Qur'an and Islam.* New York.

97 http://www.muslim-answers.org/Introducing-Islam/miscons.htm
under the chapter: Misconception #5: Muhammad wrote the Qur'an

98 Cf. Gilliot, Claude (2005). *Zur Herkunft der Gewährsmänner des Propheten,* in: Ohlig, Karl-Heinz / Puin, Gerd-R. (ed.) (2005). *Die Dunklen Anfänge. Neue Forschungen zur Entstehung und Frühen Geschichte des Islam.* 2nd ed. Berlin, p. 167.

99 Kermani, N. (1999). *Gott ist Schön. Das Ästhetische Erleben des Koran.* München 1999; see also the review by Schmitt, Axel: *Ist der Koran Poesie? Navid Kermani Considers the Koran to be an Aesthetic Pheonomenon,* e.g. in:
http://www.literaturkritik.de/public/rezension.php? rez_id=5428&ausgabe=200211

100 Cf. ibid., p. 346: "... , hardly any argument is as vehemently countered in the Koran as the claim that he is a poet. In altogether fifteen places the Koran directly or indirectly answers to the imputation obviously again and again made by disbelievers, that Mohammed is a sāḥir (magician), kāhin (soothsayer), šāʿir (poet) or generally maǧnūn, i.e. obsessed with Jinn."

101 ibid. in the subchapter "*Die Offenheit des Koran* (the openness of the Koran)", p.121-149.

102 Friedrich Rückert (1788 - 1866) was a German Romantic poet and translator, especially famous for his translations from Sanskrit, Persian and Arabic.

103 ibid., p. 183

104 Neuwirth Angelika (1981). *Studien zur Komposition der Mekkanischen Suren. Studien zur Sprache, Geschichte und Kultur des Islamischen Orients.* Beihefte zur Zeitschrift "Der Islam". Neue Folge vol. 10. Berlin/ New York .

105 Lüling, Günter (1974). *Über den Urkoran.* Erlangen, e.g. p. 32, where he re-ordered the verses 1-5 of surah 96 into two "Dreierkomplexe" (complexes of three), so that they yielded a metre and a rhyme.

106 The explanation of orthodox Islamic scholars is that of "abrogation", i.e. if the contents of a verse is in conflict with that of another verse, then the one which was revealed later (e.g. if it is Medinan and the other Meccan) abrogates (nullifies) the one revealed first. God, according to this view, must have constantly made blunders, which he later had to correct.

107 Wild, Stefan (1994). "*Die Schauerliche Öde des Heiligen Buches. Westliche Wertungen des koranischen Stils*", in: Giese, A./ Bürgel, C. (1994). *Gott ist Schön und er Liebt die Schönheit.* Festschrift für (Liber amicorum for) Annemarie Schimmel. Bern, p. 429-444.

108 In the original version of this article a German translation of Richard's book was used: Richards, I.A. (1985). *Prinzipien der Literaturkritik.* Suhrkamp Taschenbuch Wissenschaft. translated by Jürgen Schlaeger. Frankfurt am Main, p. 176.

109 This issue is well debated on Islamic homepages, e.g. on: http://islamqa.info/en/ref/1377

110 Jewish Thorah recitations recorded in Damascus display almost identical characteristics (personal communication of Gerd-R. Puin).

111 Nöldeke, Theodor (1910). *Zur Sprache des Korāns.* in: *Neue Beiträge zur Semitischen Sprachwissenschaft.* Strassburg; English Translation in: Ibn Warraq (2011): *Which Koran? – Variants, Manuscripts and Linguistics*, Amherst (N.Y.), p. 83 - 130, here: p. 87.

112 Ibid., p. 87.

113 Ibid., p. 89.

114 Ibid., p. 92.

115 Ibid., p. 107

116 Ibid., p. 107.

117 "Dia-logue" comes from Greek "dia-légesthai – to hold a conversation", the preposition and prefix "dia" meaning "through". It has nothing to do with the number "two", which in Greek would be "dyo". In Platonic "dialogues" there are usually more than two people discussing a topic, so the word does not limit the

number of speakers to two. And even if someone tried to make up a Greek word meaning a "conversation among three people", then the prefix should rather be "tri" (like in Τρι-ήρης - trireme; "three-oarer") or "tris-" like in "tris-megistos – threefold great". And last but not least it should be mentioned that limiting the conversation to three (meaning the "Abrahamitic religions", in Arabic: *ahl-kitāb*) would automatically exclude Buddhists, Hinduists and numerous adherents of smaller religions, not to mention atheists and agnostics. This limitation would certainly not be politically correct, fair or humane, but be tantamount to the adoption of the orthodox Islamic tripartition of the human race into *Muslims, ahl-kitāb* and *kuffār* (infidels).

118 For these writing systems Gelb created a category which he called "West Semitic syllabary", as he did not consider them real alphabets due to the missing vowel signs, cf. Gelb, I. J. (1963). *A Study of Writing*. Chicago & London, p. 197.

119 Thus the written word "baba" can mean "báabáa - indigo" (vowel length being indicated by two vowel characters and the high tone with the acute), "báaba - mother, aunt", "baabá – father" or "baabáa – eunuch". Most textbooks indicate both vowel length and tones, however in different ways.

120 It does not appear alone, the noun "moon" receiving the prefix "พระ- phrá-" before it.

121 Based on Gordon, Cyrus H. (1965). *Ugaritic Textbook*; *Grammar, Texts and Transliteration*, Cuneiform Selections, Glossary, Indices. no place.

122 Segert, Stanislav (1984). *A Basic Grammar of the Ugaritic Language*. Berkeley/ Los Angeles/ London; p. 145 ff.

123 The identical spelling of the emphatic particle "la (cf. Ar. *la*-)" and the negation "lā (Ar. 'lā')" is a major hindrance in the understanding of Ugaritic texts.

124 In many older Hebrew dictionaries the form is erroneously interpreted as Hitp. of an imaginary verb 'š-ḥ-h'.

125 Brandenstein Wilhelm/ Mayrhofer Manfred (1964). *Handbuch des Altpersischen*. Wiesbaden.

126 See section 2.5.

127 The ruling dynasty of the Parthian Empire (247 BC – 224 CE).

128 Cf. Schmitt, Rüdiger (2000). *Die Iranischen Sprachen in Geschichte und Gegenwart*. Wiesbaden, p. 44 ff.

129 The present analysis is mainly based on the information on the excellent homepage of the Titus project (Kārnāmag ī Ardaxšīr ī Pābagān; data entry by D.N.MacKenzie, Göttingen 1993; additions by Elio Provasi, Pisa 2010; TITUS version by Jost Gippert); the text in the original script, transliteration, transcription and German translation can be found under "Didactica":
http://titus.uni-frankfurt.de/didact/idg/iran/mpers/mpersbsx.htm.
Moreover, the text, as well as the linguistic history of Old and Middle Iranian languages in general, was discussed in a seminar led by Carl-Martin Bunz (Universität des Saarlandes; Institut für Vergleichende Indogermanische Sprachwissenschaft und Indoiranistik). It must be mentioned that I have personally greatly benefitted from the many discussions about historical linguistics with him.

130 http://titus.uni-frankfurt.de/didact/idg/iran/mpers/mpersbsx.htm

131 H.P. Nyborg in his mostly hand-written book "*A Manual of Pahlavi. I-II*" (Wiesbaden, 1964-74) consistently interprets such cases as more archaic forms with unvoiced plosives: ētōn nipišt.

132 About Middle Persian cf. Sundermann, Werner (1989). *Mittelpersisch*. in: Schmitt, Rüdiger (ed.) (1989). *Compendium Linguarum Iranicarum*. Wiesbaden, p. 138-164.

133 Japanese, like many other East Asian languages, is a "high context language", i.e. a sentence can hardly be translated without knowledge about the context, as e.g. the subject is not an obligatory part of the sentence.

134 Sayo, Masuda (1998). *Geisha - Ein Lebensbericht*. In: *Geisha - Vom Leben Jenseits der Weidenbrücke*. Aus dem Japanischen übertragen und mit einem Nachwort versehen von Michael Stein (translated and annotated by Michael Stein). Japanische Bibliothek. Insel Verlag. Frankfurt am Main und Leipzig; original Japanese title: Geisha, kutō no hanshōgari (1957). Heibonsha Library, Tōkyō 1995.

135 cf. among others Ramming, Martin (1960). *Bemerkungen zur Problematik der Schriftreform in Japan*. Sitzungsberichte der Deutschen Akademie der Wissenschaften zu Berlin. Klasse für Sprachen, Literatur und Kunst. Jahrgang 1960 Nr. 4. Berlin.

136 Mainly based on: Krause, Wolfgang (1970). *Runen*. Sammlung Göschen. Berlin, p. 14-24.

137 quoted from: *The Best of Kipling*. New York 1968, p. 423.

138 http://www.ethnologue.com/show_family.asp?subid=103-16

139 Kluge, F. (1883/ 1989). *Etymologisches Wörterbuch der Deutschen Sprache*. 23rd, enlarged edition of Elmar Seebold. Berlin/ New York 1999.

140 Lord, Robert (1974). *Comparative Linguistics*. Teach Yourself Books. 2nd ed., London, p. 72

141 Examples from: Gerald Erichsen: *Spanglish: English's Assault on Spanish;* http://spanish.about.com/cs/historyofspanish/a/spanglish.htm

142 www.ethnologue.com; example of such mixed languages are "Wutunhua" = Chinese-Tibetan-Mongolian (China), Norwegian Romani = Romani- "Rotwelsch" (German thieves' argot) -Norwegian (Norway), Media Lengua = Spanish-Quechua (Ecuador).

143 Bieder, Hermann (2006). *Das Weißrussische*, in: Rehder, Peter (ed.) (2006). *Einführung in die Slavischen Sprachen. Mit einer Einführung in die Balkanphilologie*. Darmstadt (1st ed. 1986).

144 cf. the summary in Fiedler, Wilfried: *Einführung in die Balkanphilologie*. in: Rehder, Peter (ed.) (2006). *Einführung in die Slavischen Sprachen. Mit einer Einführung in die Balkanphilologie*. Darmstadt; 2nd ed. 1986, as well as Wendt, F. (1987). *Fischer Lexikon Sprachen*. Durchgesehene und korrigierte Neuausgabe. Frankfurt am Main, p. 140 ff.

145 ibid., p. 140

146 At least they were considered to be two variants until the last Balkan war. Most textbooks and dictionaries had the terms "Serbo-Croat" or "Serbo-Croatian" in their title. Meanwhile, this *language with variants* has been split up into the separate languages "Serbian", "Croatian" and "Bosnian".

147 Armin Hetzer/ Zuzana Finger (1993). *Lehrbuch der Vereinheitlichten Albanischen Schriftsprache*. Hamburg, p. 3.

148 Menges, K. H. (1995). *The Turkic Languages and Peoples: An Introduction to Turkic Studies*. 2nd ed. Wiesbaden, p. 60.

149 Banerjee, Nikunja Vihari (1989). *The Dhammapada.* Delhi, p. 87; as well as Schmidt, K. (1951). *Pali – Buddhas Sprache. Anfänger-Lehrgang zum Selbstunterricht.* Konstanz, p. 15; the English translation in the third line is from: http://www.tipitaka.net/tipitaka/dhp/verseload.php?verse=393

150 Shukla, N.p. (1979). *The Buddhist Hybrid Sanskrit Dharmapada.* Patna, p. 5 (Kapitel III. Brāhmaṇa [3 a 1.5], 2nd half of the verse: p. 30 (p. 30 XVI Vācā [15 a 1.6]): yamhi saccaṃ ca dhammo ca

151 cf. Titus-Homepage

152 cf. Mayrhofer, Manfred (1951). *Handbuch des Pāli.* Mit Texten und Glossar. Indogermanische Bibliothek. Herausgegeben von Hans Krahe. Erste Reihe: Lehr- und Handbücher. Heidelberg; p. 18; the synopsis was made by myself.

153 Masica, Colin P. (1991). *The Indo-Aryan Languages.* Cambridge University Press, p. 51.

154 The quotations in the following are from: *Abhijñāna-Śākuntalam of Kālidāsa*; ed. C. R. Devadhar/ N.G. Suru, Delhi et al. 1991 (first edition 1934); a good introduction to Prakrit is: Alfred C. Woolner (1928). Introduction to Prakrit, reprint: Delhi 1975.

155 After publication of the present anthology in German the Semitist Manfred Kropp kindly informed me that similar cases of transposition can be observed between Old Ethiopean (Geʿez) and Amharic.

156 from: Bjørnskau, Kjell (1980). *Langenscheidts Praktisches Lehrbuch Norwegisch.* 6th ed. Berlin/ München/ Wien/ Zürich.

157 Greenberg, Joseph H. (1963). *The Languages of Africa.* Den Haag.

158 Greenberg's method of mass comparison has been heavily criticized in a number of publications, their application to the languages of Africa e.g. in Fodor, István (1969). *The Problems in the Classification of the African languages.* Center for Afro-Asian Research of the Hungarian Academy of Sciences. Budapest. The results, however, could mostly be corroborated by later research, albeit not in all details. This cannot be said about a similar study concerning the languages of the Americas: Greenberg, J. H. (1987). *Languages in the Americas.* Stanford. The reactions from specialists of Native American languages have been tantamount to devastating, especially those concerning his postulated macrophylum "Amerindian". Apart from vehemently negative reviews his book has even led to a "counter-book" by a renowned historical linguist: Campbell, Lyle (1997). *American Indian Languages: The Historical Linguistics of Native America.* Oxford/ New York. The numerous shortcomings of Greenberg's later publication, written at an advanced age, do not mean that his general classification of African languages, especially the macrophylum "Afro-Asiatic" has been dismissed by specialists as well.

159 Greenberg, Joseph H. (1957). *Essays in Linguistics.* Chicago/ London, p. 40; the Thai and Chinese examples are not from his article.

160 In other cases, words from the so-called Teochew dialect (dialect of the Southern Chinese town Chaozhou) were borrowed, as speakers of this language make up around 56 % of (the older generation of) overseas Chinese in Thailand.

161 A list of 100 "culture-free" lexical items put together by the American linguist Morris Swadesh, mainly used for lexicostatistical investigation; several variants of the list are currently used.

162 Stempel, Reinhard (1999). *Abriß einer Historischen Grammatik der Semitischen Sprachen.* Nordostafrikanisch / Westasiatische Studien 3. Frankfurt, p. 21

163 Cf.: Sasse, Hans-Jürgen (1981). *Afroasiatisch.* In: Heine, E./ Schadeberg, Th.C./ Wolff, E. (ed.)(1981). *Die Sprachen Afrikas.* Hamburg; p. 138.

164 This topic was discussed in detail in my online publication: Groß, Markus (2007). *Zu Universalien des Sprachwandels. Ein Beispiel aus der Verbalmorphologie.* http://webdoc2.urz.uni-halle.de/dot2007/publikation.php.

165 A classic about the language of Jamaica is: Cassidy, Frederic Gomes (1961). *Jamaica Talk; Three Hundred Years of the English language in Jamaica.* London; numerous other examples of similar cases in the English speaking world can be found in the copious four volume survey: Kortmann, Bernd/ Upton, Clive (2008). *Varieties of English,* 4 vols., Berlin: Mouton de Gruyter. The standard work of reference for Creole languages is: Holm, John A. (1988). *Pidgins and Creoles,* Volume 1: *Theory and Structure.* Cambridge; Volume 2 (1989). Reference Survey. Cambridge.

166 Steitz, Lothar (1981). *Grammatik der Mundart von Saarbrücken.* Beiträge zur Sprache im Saarland 2. Saarbrücken.

167 Cf. Лебедев, В.В. (1977). *Поздний Среднеарабский Язык (XIII-XVIII вв.).* Москва

168 Hecker, Karl (1982). *Das Arabische im Rahmen der Semitischen Sprachen.* in: Fischer, Wolfdietrich (ed.) (1982). *Grundriss der Arabischen Philologie.* vol. 1: *Sprachwissenschaft.* Wiesbaden.

169 Examples and their translations from Segert, Stanislav (1984). *A Basic Grammar of the Ugaritic Language.* with selected texts and glossary. Berkeley, California/ Los Angeles/ London.

170 Just before the present anthology was prepared for printing, Michael Schub directed my attention to another example in Biblical Hebrew: סֹפֶרֶת "sōpʰärät – [major] scribe"; the word appears only twice in the Bible, in both cases in enumerations, i.e., without context. Gesenius considers it a personal name.

171 Cf. Rabin, Chaim (1951). Ancient West-Arabian. London, p. 110, where he discusses the idea already proposed by: Vollers, K (1906). Volkssprache und Schriftsprache im alten Arabien. Strassburg

172 Cf. Bauer, Hans/ Leander, Portus (1927). Grammatik des Biblisch-Aramäischen. Halle, p. Marcus, David (1981). *A Manual of Babylonian Jewish Aramaic.* Washington D.C., p. 2; Luxenberg assumes the same process for the Qur'ānic languages.

173 Cf. Jastrow, Otto (1992). *Lehrbuch der Ṭuroyo-Sprache.* Wiesbaden, p.20.

174 Fischer, Wolfdietrich (1982). *Frühe Zeugnisse des Neuarabischen,* in: Fischer, Wolfdietrich (ed.) (1982). *Grundriss der Arabischen Philologie.* Band 1: *Sprachwissenschaft.* Wiesbaden, p. 85.

175 Cf. Rabin, Chaim (1951). *Ancient West-Arabian.* London.

176 ibid., p. 143, as well as p. 153.

177 The forms have been checked with native speakers.

178 cf. Лебедев, В.В. (1977). *Поздний Среднеарабский Язык (XIII-XVIII вв.).* Москва.

179 Cf. Seidel, A. (1907). *Marokkanische Sprachlehre. Praktische Grammatik des Vulgärarabischen in Marokko.* Heidelberg et al.; as well as: Harrell, Richard p. (1965). *A Basic Course in Moroccan Arabic.* Washington, D.C.

180 Cf. Tapiéro, Norbert (1978). *Manuel d'Arabe Algérien Moderne.* Paris

181 Cf. Завадовский, Ю. Н. (1979). *Тунисский Диалект Арабского Языка.* Москва.

182 Cf. Jaschke, Richard (1990). *English-Arabic Conversational Dictionary.* New York (Syrian and Egyptian dialect).

183 Cf. Stowasser, Karl/ Moukhtar, Ani (1964). *A Dictionary of Syrian Arabic (Dialect of Damascus).* English.

184 Cf. Woodhead, D. R./ Beene, Wayne (ed.) (1967). *A Dictionary of Iraqi Arabic. Arabic-English.* Washington, D.C.

185 Sciriha, Lydia (1996). *Beginning Maltese* (with tapes). University of Malta.

186 Bauer, Leonhard (ed.) (1957). *Deutsch-arabisches Wörterbuch der Umgangssprache in Palästina und im Libanon.* Wiesbaden.

187 The tables are based primarily on Moscati, Sabatino/ Spitaler, Anton/ Ullendorf, Edward/ von Soden, Wolfram (1964). *An Introduction to the Comparative Grammar of the Semitic languages. Phonology and Morphology.* edited by Sabatino Moscati. Porta Linguarum Orientalium. Wiesbaden, p. 111 ff.

188 Kienast, Burkhart (2001). *Historische Semitische Sprachwissenschaft.* Wiesbaden, p. 56 f.; this excellent publication had not yet been used for the original German version, it was, however, often referred to in other Inârah anthologies. His chapter dedicated to deictic elements is much more detailed than the short list above.

189 Luxenberg, Christoph (2005). *Weihnachten im Koran,* in: Burgmer, Christoph (ed.) (2005). *Streit um den Koran. Die Luxenberg-Debatte: Standpunkte und Hintergründe.* Berlin, p. 35-41.

190 He equates the Arabic verb "iqtarab - to approach" with Syriac "eṯqarra ", which also means "to receive the eucharist".

191 All Bible quotations have been taken from: http://unbound.biola.edu.

192 This fact has been mentioned by several orientalists, in the preceding anthology also by Volker Popp: *Die Frühe Islamgeschichte nach Inschriftlichen und Numismatischen Zeugnissen,* in: Ohlig, Karl-Heinz/ Puin, Gerd-R. (ed.) (2005). *Die Dunklen Anfänge. Neue Forschungen zur Entstehung und Frühen Geschichte des Islam.* 2nd ed. 2006. Berlin, p. 69.

193 This famous speech has been published as a booklet entitled: "Hinduism", Mylapore/ Madras 1976.

194 These similarities are mentioned in a number of books on both Christianity and Judaism, but not explained in detail. I was not able to find out who was the first to notice them.

195 Source: *Siddur Schma Kolenu (1997).* Ins Deutsche übersetzt von (translated into German by) Raw Joseph Scheuer. 2nd ed. Basel/ Zürich, p. 430 f.

196 http://en.wikipedia.org/wiki/Kaddish

197 Source: Healey, John F. (1980). *First Studies in Syriac.* University Semitics Study Aids 6. Birmingham (with tape cassette).

198 Cf. Boyce, Mary (1975). *A Reader in Manichaean Middle Persian and Parthian.* Texts with Notes, no place indicated; p. 47 ff.

199 The following examples are from: Gabain, A.v. / Winter, W. (1958). *Türkische Turfantexte IX. Ein Hymnus an den Vater Mani auf Tocharisch B mit alttürkischer Übersetzung* [SA Abh. d. Dtsch. Akad. d. W. Berlin, 1956, 2]. Berlin.

200 A few educated Turks seem to be aware of this fact. On the Turkish Wikipedia page for "Burhan Haldun Dağı" (Burkhan Khaldun, a mountain in Mongolia; the alleged birth place of Genghis Khan), we can read: "Budist olan Moğollar ve Türki kavimler Buda'yı burhan olarak adlandırmaktaydı... – The Mongols and Turkish tribes, being Buddhists, used to call the Buddha Burhan."

(http://tr.wikipedia.org/wiki/Burhan_Haldun_Da%C4%9F%C4%B1).
What might have saved the name from being banned as a first name after Islamization is probably the fact that is was believed to be derived from Arabic "burhān – proof", a term also used in Ottoman Turkish. Of course, Arabic *burhān* cannot be the source of the name, as it is unknown as a normal first name in the Arabic speaking world. This erroneous view is confirmed by the EI, which does not mention the Buddhist etymology in its article on Burhān al-Dīn (born 1345), a poet of Turkish (Oghuz) descent and a few other poets with this name, which was probably re-interpreted as Islamic with the addition of "al-Dīn", thus purportedly meaning "proof of the religion". None of these poets is of Arab descent.

201 Tocharian is normally written in the phonetically very exact Brahmi script.

202 Cf. Humbach, Helmut (1959). *Die Gathas des Zarathustra* (2 vols.). Heidelberg, above all p. 20 ff.

203 Mahatma Gandhi himself had undertaken to translate it and write a commentary and even many Westerners are said to have been influenced by this philosophical poem. Robert Oppenheimer, often called the father of the atomic bomb, is said to have quoted it after the first nuclear test in the desert of New Mexico in 1945 ("I am become Death, the shatterer of worlds") after he witnessed the first nuclear explosion in New Mexico in 1945.

204 Mylius, Klaus (ed.) (1979). *Die Bhagavadgītā.* Aus dem Sanskrit. Übersetzung, Einleitung und Anmerkungen von Klaus Mylius. Wiesbaden.

205 Source: Swami Swarupananda (ed.) (1982). *Shrimad Bhagavadgita (Śrīmad Bhagavad-Gītā).* With Text, Word-for-Word Translation, English Rendering, Comments, and Index. 13th revised edition. Calcutta, p. 71.

206 The Sanskrit text in original script can be found on: http://susanskrit.org/gita-chapter-two/51-2010-05-24-09-18-01.html

207 s. Popp, Volker (2005). *Die Frühe Islamgeschichte nach Inschriftlichen und numismatischen Zeugnissen,* op. cit. p. 16-124, as well the contributions in the present volume: Popp, Volker: *From Ugarit to Sāmarrā' – An Archeological Journey on the Trail of Ernst Herzfeld*, as well as Ohlig, Karl-Heinz: *From muḥammad Jesus to the Prophet of the Arabs – The Historicization of a Christological Epithet.*

208 "Traditional Account" designates the mainstream Muslim view of the prophet's biography and the history of Early Islam.

209 This root is discussed in detail in Nevo, Yehuda D./ Koren, Judith (2003). *Crossroads to Islam, The Origins of the Arab Religion and the Arab State*, Amherst (NY), p. 261 ff.

210 Gordon, Cyrus (1955). *Ugaritic Manual*, 3 vols. Analecta Orientalia 35. Rome: Pontificum Institutum Biblicum, pp. 54, 33.

211 Luxenberg, Christoph. Die Neudeutung der arabischen Inschrift im Felsendom zu Jerusalem, in: Puin, Gerd-R. / Ohlig, Karl-Heinz (Hg.). Die dunklen Anfänge, 3rd edition 2007. Berlin; the anthology has been translated into English and appeared under the title "The Hidden Origins of Islam" in the year 2010.

212 Botterweck G. Johannes/ Ringgren, Helmer (1980). Theological Dictionary of the Old Testament, vol. 4. Stuttgart, pp. 452.

213 Gesenius, Wilhelm (1915/1962). *Hebräisches und Aramäisches Handwörterbuch über das Alte Testament.* bearbeitet von Frants Buhl. reprint of the original edition of 1915; 17th ed. Heidelberg 1962.

214 Segert, Stanislav (1984). *A Basic Grammar of the Ugaritic Language.* Berkeley/ Los Angeles/ London; p. 162, text 88.53 (1.4:V:12-19).

215 About the change of meaning of this name see section 6.7.

216 Cf. Puin, G.-R. (1996). *Observations on Early Qur'ān manuscripts in Ṣan'ā'.* In: Wild, p. (ed.) (1996). *The Qur'ān as Text.* Leiden: p. 107-111; as well as Puin, Gerd-R. (1999). *Über die Bedeutung der Ältesten Koranfragmente aus Sanaa (Jemen) für die Orthographiegeschichte des Korans,* in: Graf von Bothmer, Hans-Casper/ Ohlig, Karl-Heinz/ Puin, Gerd-R. (1999). Neue Wege der Koranforschung, Magazin Forschung (Universität des Saarlandes) 1, 1999, 37-40, 46, moreover: Heger, Christoph: *The Origin of the Name „Allah",*
in: http://www.answering-islam.de/Main/Quran/Sources/alaha2.html.

217 Kästner, H. (1981). *Phonetik und Phonologie des Modernen Hocharabisch.* Leipzig.

218 Thelwall, R., Sa'adeddin, M.A. (1999). *Arabic.* In: Handbook of the International Phonetic Association. Cambridge University Press.

219 Mitchell, T. F. 1993. *Pronouncing Arabic.* 2 vols. Oxford.

220 Denz, Adolf (1982). *Die Struktur des Klassischen Arabisch,* in: Fischer, Wolfdietrich (ed.) (1982). *Grundriss der Arabischen Philologie.* Band 1: *Sprachwissenschaft.* Wiesbaden, p. 60.

221 *Arabic Phonetics* (1963). Ibn Sīnā's Risālah on the points of articulation of the speech-sounds translated from Medieval Arabic by Khalil I. Semaan, M.A., Ph.D. Arthur Jefferey Memorial Monographs No. 2. 2nd edition. Lahore.

222 See Gairdner, W. H. T. (1925). *The Phonetics of Arabic.* London.

223 See Fischer, Wolfdietrich (1982). *Frühe Zeugnisse des Neuarabischen,* in: Fischer, Wolfdietrich (ed.) (1982). *Grundriss der Arabischen Philologie.* vol. 1: *Sprachwissenschaft.* Wiesbaden, p. 85.

224 Jastrow, Otto (1982). *Die Struktur des Neuarabischen,* in: Fischer, Wolfdietrich (ed.) (1982). *Grundriss der Arabischen Philologie.* vol. 1: *Sprachwissenschaft.* Wiesbaden, p. 129.

225 in Arabic: "*tufaḫḫamu l-lāmu ta'ẓīman* – "making the lām emphatic serves to pay homage".

226 Cf. Sasse, H.-J. (1981). *Die Semitischen Sprachen.* In: Heine, E./ Schadeberg, Th.C./ Wolff, E. (ed.)(1981). *Die Sprachen Afrikas.* Hamburg: p. 225-238 as well as Stempel, Reinhard (1999). *Abriß einer historischen Grammatik der Semitischen Sprachen.* Nordostafrikanisch / Westasiatische Studien 3. Frankfurt.

227 See e.g. Park, Chang-Hai (1972). *An Intensive Course in Korean,* 2 vls. Seoul. The textbook starts with a very detailed part on pronunciation. On p. 0.311, a class of "lax" plosives (transcribed as "p, t, c, s, k") is opposed to a class called "tense" counterparts (written "pp, tt, cc, ss, kk").

228 The following list of arguments is partially based on Stempel's list with many explanations and additions; some authors leave the phonetic realization of emphatic phonemes open with a tendency to rather assume an ejective pronunciation, e.g. Rendburg, Gary A. (1997). *Ancient Hebrew Phonology.* In: Kaye, Alan p. (ed.) (1997). *Phonologies of Asia and Africa* (Including the Caucasus) Vol I: Asia.Winona Lake, Ind.: p. 65-84.

229 Rabin, Chaim (1951). *Ancient West-Arabian*. London, p. 195: he mentions the dialects of Palmyra described by Cantineau.

230 Cf. Diakonoff, I.M. (1965). *Semito-Hamitic Languages. An Essay in Classification*. Languages of Asia and Africa. Moskau, p. 19; in the English version Diakonoff calls them phonemes "with a glottal stop".

231 Hannig, R. (1995). *Großes Handwörterbuch Ägyptisch-Deutsch (2800-950 v. Chr.)*. Mainz, p. LVI; he writes them with the IPA symbols for ejectives: [p' t' c' k' s' ' x'].

232 Cf. Armstrong, Lilias E. (1934/1964). *The Phonetic Structure of Somali* (first publication: Mitteilungen des Seminars für Orientalische Sprachen zu Berlin, Nr. 37; new edition: Gregg International Publishers Ltd.). Farnborough, Hants., England; with a different interpretation: Puglielli, Annarita (1997). *Somali Phonology*. In: Kaye, Alan p. (ed.) (1997). *Phonologies of Asia and Africa (Including the Caucasus)* Vol I: Asia.Winona Lake, Ind.: p. 521-536; the sound is described as "postalveolar, pharyngalized and voiced"; it cannot be excluded that the phoneme has divergent realizations in different dialects; the native speakers of Somali I had the opportunity to record myself, pronounced this sound with a clear ingressive phase, the place of articulation being alveolar as opposed to dental for orthographic "d", i.e. they were not ejective. It must, however, be mentioned that in his standard book on Egyptian linguistics (Schenkel, Wolfgang (1990). *Einführung in die Altägyptische Sprachwissenschaft*. Darmstadt) Schenkel discusses a dissenting opinion that the set of phonemes transcribed as "ṭ, (former transliteration ḏ), g (ḳ'), ḳ" designate voiced phonemes. Due to the scanty (undebatable) comparative material, i.e. inherited Proto-Afroasiatic words attested in both Egyptian and Semitic, a definite answer to this question must be postponed.

233 Mitchell, T. F. (1993). *Pronouncing Arabic*. 2 Bde. Oxford, Bd. 2, p. 34.

234 Cf. Rabin, Chaim (1951). *Ancient West-Arabian*. London, p. 55.

235 Ibid., p. 126.

236 The example was mentioned to me in a personal communication by Christoph Luxenberg, who discussed it also in his "Syro-Aramaic Reading of the Quran".

237 Cf. Rabin, Chaim (1951). *Ancient West-Arabian. London,* p. 209.

238 The phonetic description in the extant grammars is not very clear, but it seems that this group of sounds in Mehri is both ejective and pharyngealized or rather in the middle of a transition process; see: Jahn, Alfred (1905). *Grammatik der Mehri-Sprache in Südarabien*. Wien; Sima, Alexander (2009). Mehri-Texte aus der jemenitischen Šarqīyah. Frankfurt; Rubin, Aaron (2010). The Mehri Language of Oman. Leiden.

239 Cf. Hoberman, Robert D. (1997). *Modern Aramaic Phonology*. In: Kaye, Alan p. (ed.) (1997). *Phonologies of Asia and Africa (Including the Caucasus)* Vol I: Asia.Winona Lake, Ind.: p. 313-336; Garbell, Irene (1965). *The Jewish Neo-Aramaic Dialect of Persian Azerbaijian. Linguistic Analysis and Folkloristic Texts*. London/ The Hague/ Paris; Arnold, Werner (1989). *Lehrbuch des Neuwestaramäischen*. Semitica Viva. Series Didactica edited by Otto Jastrow. vol. 1. Wiesbaden; Jastrow, Otto (1992). *Lehrbuch der Ṭuroyo-Sprache*. Wiesbaden.

240 The term "emphatic" should correctly only be used to designate the graphemes, independent of their articulation.

241 A velarized/ pharyngealized "l" does, of course, appear in nearly all dialects, e.g. in a form like "ṭalab", and in some dialects it even must be considered a phoneme, as it appears in words without other emphatic consonants, e.g. Moroccan Arabic: "ḷanba – lamp".

242 Translated from: Gesenius, Wilhelm (1915/1962). *Hebräisches und Aramäisches Handwörterbuch über das Alte Testament.* bearbeitet von Frants Buhl. identical reprint of the 17th ed. 1915, published in Heidelberg 1962; epithets with a genitive like "(Jahwe/ Elohim) Sabaoth < Lord of Hosts/ armies" will not be discussed here.

243 Summary and information about locations from: Preuß, Horst Dietrich/ Berger, Klaus (1991). *Bibelkunde des Alten und Neuen Testaments. Erster Teil: Altes Testament.* 6th ed. Wiesbaden, p. 36.

244 In the following, Hebrew Bible quotations will be accompanied by the corresponding Greek forms from the Septuagint (LXX) in original script; the transliteration of Hebrew employed here is a compromise between transliteration (one Hebrew character corresponding to a transliteration letter) and a (likely) phonemic interpretation. Shwa-sounds are thus written as uppercase letters and no difference will be made between spelling with or without mater lectionis. In the case of the vowels "i", "o" and "u" length will not be indicated, following the unclear situation in the Hebrew script, even in cases when comparison with other Semitic languages would allow the assumption of a long vowel.

245 In a friendly discussion, Gerd-R. Puin mentioned this passage as a good example of the transition from polytheism to monotheism; note the singular form in the verb "he said" as opposed to the (older) plural of the imperativ 1st Pl.

246 Vocalizations of Syriac bible quotation are from: *Syriac Bible* (1996). United Bible Societies. (no place indicated; West Aramaic text in Serṭā-ductus) as well as for deviations in East Syriac: *The New Covenant commonly called The New Testament (1986). Pshiṭta Aramaic Text with a Hebrew Translation*. Edited by the Aramaic Scriptures Research Society in Israel. The Bible Society. Jerusalem (the Aramaic text here is East Syriac written in Hebrew script); the ductus was transferred from purely Western Serṭā into the more neutral Estrangela, which is rather unusual with added Western (i.e. Greek) vowel letters; uppercase consonants in the transliteration are silent, uppercase vowels are reduced; gemination is only indicated where it appears in the written text (of the Aramaic in Hebrew script), the same applies to vowel quantities.

247 In modern Judaism "'adonaj" is used when *addressing* God, for God in the 3rd person the term "ha-šem – the name" is used instead.

248 It must be noted that the uppercase "a" in Hebrew counts as a variant of Shwa and is thus written as a (default) Shwa: "ə"; therefore the pronunciation is "Jehovah", not "Jahovah".

249 Kautzsch, E. (1922). *Die heilige Schrift des Alten Testaments.* 2 vols. Tübingen, vol. 1, p. 103.

250 Hannig, R. (1995). *Großes Handwörterbuch Ägyptisch-Deutsch (2800-950 v. Chr.).* Mainz; the abbreviations have been typed in full form; for typographical reasons the hieroglyphs appear in one line (i.e. not one on top of the other); moreover, a dotted line should be added underneath the last character.

251 Translation from: http://www.kchanson.com/ANCDOCS/westsem/mesha.html.

252 http://www.homestead.com/bibleorigins*net/YahwehYawUgarit.html

253 Hadley, Judith M (2000). *The Cult of Asherah in Ancient Israel and Judah: the Evidence for a Hebrew Goddess.* Cambridge, pp. 122-136; Rudolf Augstein in his book on Jesus mentions that two inscriptions, one of them found in Hebron in 1967, the other on the Sinai in 1975/76 which show that Asherah was venerated as Yahwe's consort (Augstein, Rudolf (2001). *Jesus – Menschensohn.* München, p. 294).

254 Cf. section 7.2, notes to the text, as well as: Marcus, David (1981). *A Manual of Babylonian Jewish Aramaic.* Washington D.C., p. 2.

255 Interpretation based on: Marti, D. Karl (1896). *Kurzgefaßte Grammatik der Biblisch-aramäischen Sprache.* London/ New York.

256 Syriac text and transliteration from: Muraoka, Takamitsu (1987). *Classical Syriac. A Basic Grammar with a Chrestomathy.* Porta Linguarum Orientalium Bd. 19. Harassowitz. Wiesbaden, p. 90 ff.

257 Cf. *Die Aussprache des Hebräischen bei den Samaritanern.* nach den Aufzeichnungen von H. Ritter und A. Schaade in Nāblus 1917, herausgegeben von A. Murtonen, in: Kahle, Paul E. (1962). *Die Kairoer Geniza. Untersuchungen zur Geschichte des hebräischen Bibeltextes und seiner Übersetzungen.* Berlin, Anhang II, p. 338 ff.

258 Cf. Preuß, Horst Dietrich/ Berger, Klaus (1997). *Bibelkunde des Alten und Neuen Testaments.* Zweiter Teil: *Neues Testament.* 5th ed. Wiesbaden. p. 246.

259 Metzger, Bruce M. (1994). *A Textual Commentary on the Greek New Testament.* 2nd edition. Stuttgart, p. 58 f.

260 Beyer, Klaus (1986). *The Aramaic Language.* Göttingen, p. 38 f.

261 Wahrmund Adolf (1869). *Handwörterbuch der Neu-arabischen und Deutschen Sprache*, 3 vols., reprint Beirut 1980 (Librairie du Liban.)

262 http://www.studytoanswer.net/myths_ch3.html#ch3-6

263 cf. http://www.answering-islam.de/Main//Shamoun/ishmael-baal.htm

264 Personal communication by Gerd-R. Puin.

265 Ben-Shemesh, A.: *Some Suggestions to Qur'an Translators,* in: Ibn Warraq (ed.): *What the Koran Really Says, Language, Text and Commentary.* Amherst (N.Y.) 2002, p. 239.

266 Arne A. Ambros, Arne A. (1981). *Zur Entstehung der Emphase in Allah,* Wiener Zeitschrift für die Kunde des Morgenlandes 73 (1981), p. 23-32; the article is worth reading esp. because of the many quotations from primary sources.

267 The same could be said about /u:/ [u] vs. /u/ [ʊ] in English and German (e.g. in "pool" and "pull" or German "Mut" and "Mutter").

268 The designations of varieties of Classical Aramaic are a bit confusing, the branches being East Aramaic (Language of the Babylonian Talmud; Mandaic), Central Aramaic = Syriac (again subdivided into East and West Syriac) and West Aramaic (Jewish-Palestinian Aramaic, Samaritan). So East Syriac does not belong to the East Aramaic subgroup!

269 p. 304-311.

270 It should be mentioned that the latter phrase has a Christian Arabic equivalent: باسم الآب والابن والروح القدس – "*bi-smi -l-ʾābi wa -l-ʾibni wa -r-rūḥi -l-qudus* (in the name of the father, and the son, and the holy spirit", which goes back to a Syriac phrase.

---

271 Gerhardson, Birger (1961). *Memory and Manuscript; Oral Tradition and Written Transmission in Judaism and Early Christianity.* Uppsala.

272 Jan Vansina (1965). *Oral Tradition. A Study in Historical Methodology* (translated from the French by H. M. Wright). London, p. 195.

273 A survey of "Qur'ānic" manuscripts is given by: 'Abdullah David & M S M Saifullah: *Concise List Of Arabic Manuscripts Of The Qur'ān Attributable To The First Century Hijra,* on: http://www.islamic-awareness.org/Quran/Text/ Mss/hijazi.html.
He starts his article with the words "Accurately dating early Qur'anic manuscripts is a difficult task.(...) There is only one dated manuscript of the Qur'an from the 1st century of hijra (...) and two from the 2nd century, forcing specialists to look elsewhere for comparative material." In the following text it becomes clear that these manuscripts are only fragments of the Qur'ān. According to a personal communication by Gerd-R. Puin, one of the better candidates for a (originally) full manuscript is DAM 20-33.1, also mentioned in the article. This manuscript was well described by Hans-Caspar Graf von Bothmer ("*Architekturbilder im Koran – Eine Prachthandschrift der Umayyadenzeit aus dem Yemen*", Pantheon, 1987, vol. 45, pp. 4-20.) and is in so far remarkable, as it contains illustrations of datable buildings (e.g. the Dome of the Rock, the Great Mosques of Ṣan'ā' and Damascus). However, the description reveals that in this manuscript only the beginning and the end of the Qur'ān can be read, the main part is rotten, so it is not clear how much of the Qur'ān it contained and in which form. Graf Bothmer dates it around 710–715 CE (the reign of the Umayyad caliph al-Walīd). This dating might be well founded, but strictly speaking it refers to a fragmentary manuscript, not a complete Qur'ān.

274 Apart from having lived in the 18th and 19th century, the Brothers Grimm (Jacob (1785 –1863) and Wilhelm (1786 –1859) only collected and edited their Fairy Tales, in many cases with variant endings and/or settings.

275 A table and graph made by Gerd-R. Puin clearly demonstrates the blatantly illogical claims of the Muslim orthodoxy concerning the rasm. At the time when the original German version of the present study appeared this graph was supposed to be published in an article entitled: "Variant readings of the Koran due to the ambiguity of the early Arabic script, including variants of Ibn Mas'ūd and a survey of the transcription of Koranic texts". In the meantime, the contents of this article originally written in English have appeared in a number of German articles by the same author in subsequent Inârah anthologies.

276 Some reasons for this caving in are obvious: the boundaries of the *Zeitgeist* ("all cultures are equally good"), emotional conservatism ("that's what we can read in all textbooks"), political correctness ("we have no right to hurt religious feelings"), post-colonial bad conscience ("we have no right to criticize others considering our crimes of the past") and the erroneous view that you do Muslims a favor if you tell them that their legends are history. But there is also another, more hidden reason: laziness and the lack of understanding as to what science and scholarship are all about.

277 See the anthologies by Ibn Warraq, e.g. *The Quest for the Historical Muhammad,* Amherst (N.Y.) 2000.

278 For the first time discussed in: Ohlig, Karl-Heinz (1986). *Fundamentalchristologie. Im Spannungsfeld von Christentum und Kultur.* München.

279 Cf. Popper, Karl (1935). *Logik der Forschung* (English title: *The Logic of Scientific Discovery*). Wien; as well as its short exposition in: Popper, Karl (1964). *Natur-*

gesetze und theoretische Systeme, in: H. Albert (ed.)(1964). *Theorie und Realität.* Tübingen p. 87-102.

280 Ohlig, Karl-Heinz/ Puin, Gerd-R. (ed.) (2005). *Die Dunklen Anfänge. Neue Forschungen zur Entstehung und Frühen Geschichte des Islam.* 2nd ed. 2006. Berlin; title of the English translation: *The Hidden Origins of Islam: New Research into Its Early History*; Prometheus Books, Amherst (N.Y.), 2009.

281 In the following just referred to as "new theory".

282 The traditional view might shortly be summarized as follows: Islam is a religion founded in Mecca by a prophet called Muḥammad, who received (what he considered) a divine revelation in Arabic, which was transmitted orally and standardized as a written text only a few decades later. This religion was spread over the whole Middle East by the first three caliphs. The historical events from the biography of the prophet to the fatḥ (conquest) of the Islamic/ Arabic Empire was described in great detail in the Traditional Account (i.e. the Islamic Historians and the Sunna). Many opaque Qur'ānic verses refer to events described by this Traditional Account and should be interpreted within this framework.

283 See: Richter, Michael: *Wortschatz*, 2007, p. 26; quoted from: www.zitate-aphorismen.de/zitate/interpretation/Michael_Richter/3097.

284 This general rule, of course, only refers to the desired behavior of people (including Westerners, but also Muslims) in countries that belong to other civilizations than their own. In the West itself, this rule is not applicable! It is the host who makes the rules (e.g. "take off your shoes", "no smoking", "equal rights for women!"), not the guest!

285 Bruce Lincoln, Professor of the History of Religions in the University of Chicago's Divinity School, has laid out thirteen rules for historians of religion to follow in: Bruce Lincoln, *Theses on Method, in Method & Theory in the Study of Religion*, vol. 8 (1996): p. 225-27. These rules have been summarized by Ibn Warraq in his article "*Historical Methodology and Dogmatic Islamophilia*", which has appeared in German (under the title "*Historische Methodologie und die Forderung nach Wohlwollen gegenüber dem Islam*") in the fifth Inârah anthology: Gross, Markus / Ohlig, Karl-Heinz (2010). Die Entstehung einer Weltreligion I, p. 382-422. The English original of the article as well as my German translation from the anthology can be found on the Inârah website: www.inarah.de/cms/historical-methodology-and-dogmatic-islamophilia.html.

About the contributors

Karl-Heinz Ohlig

Professor emeritus of religious studies and the history of Christianity at the University of the Saarland, chairman of Inârah (Institute for Research on Early Islamic History and the Koran); author of many books, including "Weltreligion Islam: Eine Einführung" (Islam as World Religion: An Introduction). Co-editor (with Gerd-R. Puin) of "The Hidden Origins of Islam". For more information, visit www.inarah.de.

Volker Popp

Studied ethnology, African and Islamic Studies, Turcology and Iranian Studies in Mainz, Frankfurt, Ankara and Teheran. For many years resident in Turkey, Kuwait and the United Arab Emirates. Helped to build up collections in museums in Kuwait, Qatar and Riyadh.

Christoph Luxenberg

Studied Semitic Studies, Germanic Studies and History. Doctoral dissertation about a Syriac manuscript; for many years academic teacher of Arabic and Aramaic; author of "The Syro-Aramaic Reading of the Koran: A Contribution to the Decoding of the Language of the Koran, Berlin 2007" and many articles on the subject, both in German and French.

Ignaz Goldziher (1850-1921)

Hungarian-Jewish scholar of Islam. Together with with Theodor Nöldeke and Snouck Hurgronje one of the fathers of Western Islamic studies. Most of his publications were written in German, some in Hungarian and a few in French. "Muslim Studies" (Halle, 1889–1890, 2 vols.) is probably his best known book.

Markus Gross

Linguist (esp. Phonetics and Phonology, Romance Studies, Indo-European Comparative Linguistics, Historical Linguistics, Oriental Studies); from the third anthology on co-editor of the series (together with K.-H. Ohlig).